599310

Deliberating American Monetary Policy

Deliberating American Monetary Policy

A Textual Analysis

Cheryl Schonhardt-Bailey
with assistance and advice from Andrew Bailey

The MIT Press
Cambridge, Massachusetts
London, England

MIT Press books may be purchased at special quantity discounts for business or sales promotional use. For information, please email special_sales@mitpress.mit.edu or write to Special Sales Department, The MIT Press, 55 Hayward Street, Cambridge, MA 02142.

This book was set in Palatino by Toppan Best-set Premedia Limited, Hong Kong. Printed and bound in the United States of America.

Library of Congress Cataloging-in-Publication Data

Schonhardt-Bailey, Cheryl, 1961–
Deliberating American monetary policy : a textual analysis / Cheryl Schonhardt-Bailey.
    pages   cm
Includes bibliographical references and index.
ISBN 978-0-262-01957-6 (hardcover : alk. paper)
1. Monetary policy—United States—History.   2. United States—Economic policy.
I. Title.
HG540.S36   2013
339.5'30973—dc23
2013005452

10   9   8   7   6   5   4   3   2   1

to Samuel and Hannah,
for distracting us with laughter and playfulness,
since there is more to life than work

Contents

**Additional materials (available at http://mitpress.mit.edu/
damp)**

Chapter 3 Appendixes
           3.C: FOMC Meeting Structure
           3.D: FOMC Membership
           3.E: Thematic Scores for Individual Members of the
                FOMC in 1999

Acknowledgments

Various portions of this book (in its many stages) were presented at annual meetings of the American Political Science Association; the History of Congress Conference (Yale, 2006); the Département d'économie et de gestion École normale supérieure de Cachan (2008); the Domestic Preferences and Foreign Economic Policy Conference (Princeton, 2008); the annual meetings of the Midwest Political Science Association (2009) and Southern Economic Association (Atlanta 2010); the Macroeconomics and Econometrics Conference (Birmingham, 2010); the Text as Data Conference (Northwestern, 2011); the Inaugural General Conference of the ECPR Standing Group on Parliaments (Dublin, 2012); Politics in Times of Crisis Conference (LSE, 2012); and the ESRC Research Methods Festival (Oxford, 2012). I am very grateful to the many discussants as well as the audiences at these conferences for their suggestions. In addition an earlier version of the Volcker Revolution case study in chapter 3 was published in *Political Analysis.*

For assistance on the interviews for chapter 5, I am grateful to Allan Meltzer, Adam Posen, Phil Bradley, Ken Shepsle, Stephen Ansolabehere, Jim Snyder, Patrick Dunleavy, and Mark Peterson. Brookings Institution provided office space and further assistance. The interviewees (both named and anonymous, as noted in chapter 5) were very generous with their time and remarkably frank with their assessments of the deliberations in which they took part. Their fascinating analyses and anecdotes could have comprised a book of its own.

Others gave me insightful advice at various points in this project, including Sarah Binder, Henry (Chip) Chappell, Jeff Frieden, William (Bill) Bernhard, William (Bill) Roberts Clark, and Lawrence Broz. MIT Press Senior Editor John Covell handled the manuscript with his usual efficiency and care; I couldn't have asked for a better editor.

I am hugely grateful to Gordon Bannerman for assistance in preparing the text files for analysis. I also thank STICERD (Suntory and Toyota International Centres for Economics and Related Disciplines) for financial support for this project. Mina Moshkeri (LSE Design Unit) provided patient and diligent assistance in helping to prepare all the graphs. Paul Horsler and Clive Wilson (British Library of Political and Economic Science) worked to locate the congressional hearings transcripts in hard copy or microfiche (all of which the St. Louis Federal Reserve Bank now helpfully posts on its website). Doreen Bailey lent encouragement over the years.

While I take full responsibility for the contents of this book (and any errors or omissions occurring within it), I could not have completed it without the unfailing assistance of my husband (also Deputy Governor of the Bank of Englnd and CEO of the Prudential Regulation Authority) Andrew Bailey. From his nearly three decades as a central banker, Andrew's expertise in monetary policy provided me with enormously helpful advice and inspiration throughout this book project, and particularly with respect to chapter 3.

Last but certainly not least, I thank Kathy Zeine, Sandy Schiffman, and Barb Dixon—who shared with me their time, their friendship, and their love throughout this project.

I dedicate this book to our children, Samuel and Hannah, who put up with parents working far too many hours on computers. But away from esoteric topics like monetary policy and textual analysis (of little interest to teenagers), they made me smile and laugh.

1   Introduction: Why Deliberation?

1.1   Introduction

Over the ten to fifteen years preceding the 2007 to 2009 financial crisis, US monetary policy was generally regarded as a success and Alan Greenspan's Federal Reserve (or "Fed") as the exemplar of astute decision-making in monetary policy. In the immediate aftermath of the crisis, reassessments of this policy success abounded. In years to come, we may expect to see yet further reappraisals of US monetary policy under Greenspan's Fed, as well as differing assessments on whether Ben Bernanke's Fed has dealt effectively with the turmoil of the crisis and its subsequent recession in the United States. What is clear from these reversals and differences of opinion is that the success or failure of monetary policy is by no means self-evident in the short run, nor is it immune to entire reversals of assessments. Monetary policy is by its nature a technical area of economic policy-making with substantial inherent uncertainty created primarily by the need for policy makers to form views on the future. As such, how policy makers conceptualize the means by which their monetary policy decisions affect the wider economy (i.e., the "transmission mechanism") is of critical importance. By studying the thinking of policy makers, we can better understand the influences that shape their decisions—and ultimately the outcome of policy itself. Capturing the thinking of policy makers is not a simple task; however, if we assume that how they talk to one another about monetary policy in formal settings—such as institutional committees—reflects their thinking, then we can make a good start.

The aim of this book is to examine systematically deliberation on monetary policy in the United States in two different institutions—the Federal Reserve and Congress. Monetary policy is a prime example of decision-making in a committee setting by a group of appointed rather than elected officials. Deliberation by the Federal Open Market Committee (FOMC) of the Federal Reserve leading to a vote of members is the means by which decisions on the setting of monetary policy are reached in the United States. In this respect arrangements in the United States are quite typical of those now used in many other countries around the world.

There is another important, but very different, committee process for monetary policy in the United States —namely the one that holds appointed policy makers accountable for their decisions to elected representatives in Congress. Here we examine deliberation on the oversight of monetary policy in the congressional House and Senate banking committees, as well as the assessment by senators of the sitting Federal Reserve chairman in consideration of his re-appointment. We focus on the relationship between the Federal Reserve and Congress, and on the motivations of members of Congress as they oversee the policy-making decisions of the Fed. We recognize that a vast literature already exists to explain the *end product* of monetary policy—that is, the policy outcome itself. Our task is to take one step back from the policy outcome to explore the *means* by which policy makers and politicians think about monetary policy in order to arrive at judgments on the possible policy alternatives. We therefore seek to analyze the *process* of conceptualizing, arguing, discussing, and *deliberating* on monetary policy by central bankers and politicians.

Because this book offers an empirical analysis of deliberation by committees, its value extends beyond the remit of scholars who are focused exclusively on monetary policy. That is, nonmonetary economists, scholars of deliberation, quantitative textual analysis researchers, and congressional scholars should all find value in the pages that follow.

First, this book challenges economists more broadly by introducing a new way to analyze committee decisions on economic policy. Textual analysis software is increasingly lending insights into psychology, sociology, political science, cognitive science, and so on—but economists have been slower to acknowledge its contribution to the study of decision-making. One challenge for economists concerns the persuasiveness of new ideas or new arguments. If, for example, members of an economic policy committee are *persuaded* (within the committee setting) to change their positions on a policy decision, what does this mean for predicting committee decisions, and thus for quantitative models such as reaction functions and more broadly attempts to fit "rules" to economic policy decisions? This book offers an empirical foundation to account for how deliberation shapes these decisions.

Second, scholars of deliberation and deliberative democracy have accumulated a large theoretical literature over the past few decades. However, relatively less work has been done on the empirics of deliberation, particularly in actual policy venues (or across institutional venues). We address this literature—and our book's contribution to this literature—more fully in chapter 2. Here we note that one challenge we pose to deliberative scholars is the innovative use of advanced textual analysis software to analyze committee deliberations systematically. These scholars are often explicitly dismissive of textual analysis software, which they judge to be no more than "a mechanical exercise" of little value (Steiner, Bächtiger, et al. 2004: 60). Far from mechanical, we show that such methods (if used appropriately) can be tremendously insightful.

Third, quantitative textual analysis researchers can be found in many disciplines, but here we direct ourselves to those in political science.[1] There are a number of current challenges facing the empirical study of political texts, for example, understanding the underlying dimensionality of textual data—is it easily captured in a single ideological dimension (usually Left–Right), or are there multiple dimensions required? If the latter, how do we measure and understand text in N dimensions? (Our use of correspondence analysis in chapters 4 and 5 explores this directly, though here the dimensionality is not about political ideology but about technical policy-making.) Quantitative textual analyses are also challenged on the extent to which they produce robust results. One way to validate findings is to subject them to an entirely different methodology. For instance, one might employ interviews with the policy makers who produced the text under investigation, asking them to assess the validity of the findings from the textual analysis. (We do this in chapter 5, using nearly two dozen in-depth elite interviews with former committee members and committee staff.) A second way to produce robust, defensible results from textual analysis is to ask, do my data look different when I examine them from different perspectives or use different methodological toolkits? If so, one may well have less confidence in the initial approach. If not—if the same fundamental results emerge again and again—the researcher can be fairly certain that she is on solid footing. (We reproduce our core results, using two alternative textual analysis software packages, and report these results in full in an extensive analysis in our book appendix IV.) Finally, the ultimate challenge for textual analysis researchers (indeed, one might even call it the "Holy Grail" of textual analysis) is gauging persuasion. Who, ultimately, is persuaded by the words of policy makers, and with what effect? How and why do words and arguments matter? Although we do not pretend to have discovered the Holy Grail of textual analysis, we do contend that we have gone some way to establishing and measuring the persuasive arguments of committee members—particularly in chapter 4 where we examine closely both the Volcker Revolution of 1979 and Greenspan's FOMC in 1999.

Fourth, as we detail later in this introductory chapter as well as in chapter 4, much of the literature on the political economy of monetary policy by congressional scholars is fairly dated (i.e., from the 1980s and 1990s). This might not matter for other issue areas, but much has transpired in US monetary policy over the past couple of decades (indeed, over the past few years) that makes these studies less applicable in an era shaped by an embedded "low-inflation consensus" but also heavily affected by the stresses of recession in the wake of the recent financial crisis. For congressional scholars interested in political economy, our use of automated textual analysis provides a good deal of leverage for tackling questions of how and when important shifts in Federal Reserve policy took place, and for understanding how and why decisions were made.

1.2   Why Deliberation?

Our approach is to seek to measure where possible the process of deliberation, so that we can assess more systematically the roles both of ideas and argumentation in shaping decisions on monetary policy by the FOMC, and its accountability to Congress for those decisions. We can also assess the contribution of different members of the FOMC and different members of Congress (and in both cases not only the role of individuals but also that of the chairman), as well as gauge how this may have evolved over time. By analyzing the argumentation and discourse of policy makers and politicians—in two very different institutions (the Fed and Congress)—we seek better to understand why and how policy changed over a critical period in US monetary policy history.

Monetary policy is made through a process of deliberating in meetings of a committee to a point where a decision is taken (through a vote) on the stance of policy until the next meeting (about six weeks later for the FOMC). We are fortunate that verbatim transcripts of everything that was said at FOMC meetings exist for the period since the mid-1970s. We can therefore directly observe the discourse and argumentation of policy makers. Likewise, there are verbatim records of both the semi-annual hearings on the Fed's Monetary Policy Report in both houses of Congress and the more infrequent Senate re-confirmation hearings for the sitting Federal Reserve chairman. Assuming (as we do) that what policy makers and politicians say is indicative of their intentions and preferences, the transcripts should provide us with the opportunity to assess these systematically, as well as why and how they changed over time.

Within the House Financial Services Committee and the Senate Banking Committee, legislators use the hearings on the semi-annual Monetary Policy Report of the Federal Reserve to say many things. Our goal is to ascertain the extent to which they offer reasons for their views on the performance of the Fed and its chairman; that is, the extent to which they deliberate. While "deliberation" is a term that requires careful definition (the subject of our second chapter), we employ it more informally here to refer primarily to *reasoned argument,* and the *process* of deliberation to refer to *how views are reached and decisions taken.* Although deliberation is at the heart of decision-making within public policy, its contribution remains inherently hard to measure and assess within a systematic framework. For some observers, deliberation is no more than ritualistic hot air, while for others it appears to serve a real purpose in influencing the behavior and decisions of policy makers. The difficulty in reaching clear answers lies in finding where and how deliberation matters (or not)—and for this, we require the means to measure and evaluate deliberation empirically. In pursuing this end, we adopt both a multi-method and multi-institutional approach.

The challenge of the transcript data is that they are words (and indeed, a vast number of them), rather than numbers. Moreover, despite (or perhaps because of) the plethora of modern textual analysis software, there is no commonly agreed-upon software or method for analyzing textual data. With this in mind, we adopt a multi-method approach. Our predominant approach employs automated textual analysis software to study empirically the verbatim arguments and statements of FOMC members and legislators as they discuss and deliberate on monetary policy over a period of 33 years (1976 to 2008). The software that we use—Alceste—is described in detail in our book appendix I, and specific aspects of the software are explained in chapters 3 and 4, as we apply them to our data. In brief, our approach measures systematically (and statistically) the characteristic words, phrases, and in some cases, the dimensionality of the discourse of committee members. The software considers the text as a large matrix of co-occurrences between lexical forms, and processes it with multivariate techniques. A key feature is that it can be used to identify the speakers' tendency to articulate particular ideas and arguments—ideas and arguments that can then be correlated with characteristics of the speaker (the name of speaker, party affiliation, constituency characteristics, etc.) and assigned statistical significance.

We do not, however, take the results of our textual analysis at face value. Adapting our software to our subject matter, we look more closely at exactly the form of argumentation, how that evolved over time—and, most important, how the deliberative process ultimately affected the policy outcome. (A good example of this is our closer investigation of the Volcker Revolution, in chapter 3.) Moreover, just as a laboratory researcher might use different levels of magnification to examine a specimen, we use different sets of time frames to gauge the thematic content and discourse of committee members—for example, a macro-perspective of several decades as well as a series of cross sections for the same set of hearings (chapter 4). Finally, we extract from our textual analysis numerical information (i.e., coefficients) that we are able to use in standard quantitative analysis to test some strands of argument in the literature on preferences of members of Congress.

In stark contrast to this statistical approach, a second way to understand the thinking of policy makers and politicians is to simply ask them directly how and why they argued a certain way in committee, and more broadly, how they might characterize and judge the deliberative process on monetary policy. For this, we conduct nearly two dozen in-depth interviews (i.e., about an hour each) with former FOMC members and individuals involved in the congressional oversight of monetary policy (including congressional staff and members of Congress). The interviews also serve as a means to gauge the extent to which our empirical findings accord with the personal experiences of members of the FOMC, Fed staff, members of Congress, and congressional staff who have been active participants in the formulation and oversight of monetary policy from the mid-1970s until 2008.

Finally, in our book appendix IV, we use two further automated textual analysis software packages to conduct a robustness check on our findings. We find, in short, very little variation in these results relative to our initial findings.

To our knowledge, this is the first study that uses textual analysis together with in-depth interviews with the actual producers of the textual data itself in a single multi-method framework. Our approach is even more unique in that it studies deliberative discourse on a particular topic (monetary policy) by two very different sets of actors (unelected policy makers versus elected politicians) within two contrasting institutions (the Federal Reserve and Congress). That is, we have sought to bridge the analysis of deliberation on a policy issue by Congress with the deliberation of that same issue by an agency with delegated authority over that policy. Again, as far as we know, no other study has attempted to study the role of deliberation in the policy-making process alongside its role in the process of formal accountability to the legislature by the same policy-making body. There are many advantages in this multi-institutional approach. For example, we are able to gauge the extent to which the two sets of actors (unelected policy makers versus elected politicians) talk *to* one another as opposed to *across* one another; we can better understand the nature of uncertainty and how it affects the understanding and decisions of both monetary policy makers and legislators who conduct oversight on monetary policy; and we can gauge the extent to which the preferences of both sets of actors are shaped by their relative institutional roles and how this shapes their understanding of and decisions on monetary policy.

1.3 Deliberation and Monetary Policy

Monetary policy is often viewed as a specialist or niche subject, highly technical in nature and only fully understood by specialists. While there is some truth in this, it is overstated. We hope that this book will help to dispel some of the mystique surrounding monetary policy by shedding light on how experts (in the FOMC) and nonexperts (in the Congress) conceptualize, discuss, and debate with one another on monetary policy.

Part of the mystery behind monetary policy arises from—in our view—the scant attention given in the literature to *how* decisions are made. Typically what we find is a vast amount of commentary devoted to trying to understand and second guess the actual decisions of monetary policy makers, with nothing (or very little) said about the process of arriving at these decisions. For example, many commentators have tried to construct "reduced-form" explanations of the decisions of the FOMC and similar committees in other countries—which, in effect (through regression), simplify the policy decision to a prediction based on a small number of "regular" relationships. These regular relationships translate into a policy "rule" that is intended to predict the policy decision. But no study has been able to identify a consistent and predictable policy rule that works to the point where it is adopted to set policy (Taylor 1999). Rather than an ex ante prediction of policy decisions, such rules tend to be used more as an ex post means to understand the conclusions of policy makers and how far they have diverged from the rule. Such diagnostic tools are useful, but they serve to indicate that something more is going on in the policy-making process. A more meaningful description of monetary policy making is given by Allan Meltzer in his history of the Federal Reserve, in which he employs a term developed by Otmar Issing, latterly of the European Central Bank, namely "rule-like behavior" (Issing 2003; Meltzer 2009: 1216). This depicts monetary policy-making as operating somewhere between discretion and a rule, which in turn suggests a need to understand the process by which policy makers mix rule-like and discretionary behavior.

To be fair, some studies of US monetary policy have examined some of the same source material as we do, namely the verbatim transcripts of FOMC meetings. However, once again, they have done so in order to create models to explain the *outcome* using econometric reaction function models that do not enable the authors to capture the deliberative content of the verbatim record (e.g., Chappell, McGregor, et al. 2005). With respect to congressional deliberation, some studies have begun empirically to measure the quantity and quality of deliberation, yet very little has been done with textual analysis software to measure the full content of committee deliberations—and no study thus far has adopted the multi-method, multi-institutional approach used here.

In short, research on monetary policy-making has fallen short of explaining *why and how* central bankers and members of Congress differ among themselves and between each other in how they think about monetary policy-making. The judgments and rationale of politicians and central bankers are commonly assumed to differ according to the means by which they attain office (election versus appointment), and/or by the goals they seek in their respective roles, but rarely if ever are these assumptions tested empirically and systematically. It is worth noting that our objectives for studying discourse within congressional committee hearings and within the FOMC are shaped by the remit of each committee setting. The FOMC is a body of technically skilled policy makers charged with reaching decisions on a repeated basis that are consistent with a mandate given by statute. Their assessments take into account prevailing uncertainty in an environment where policy-making is necessarily forward looking. Above all, policy needs to be viewed as credible by the many agents in the economy and thus to be time consistent. In contrast, legislators do not deliberate to a decision when they conduct oversight hearings (though senators do when they conduct re-confirmation hearings). Rather, members of Congress are holding the Federal Reserve to account through open questioning. This is a different form of deliberation, with different objectives. Whereas the objective of deliberation in the FOMC is clear, a core question in our study of Congress is "why are they doing it"? We elaborate on that question by considering whether the reason(s) changed over time and were linked to the success of policy-making, and whether members of Congress have ulterior motives in conducting oversight hearings on monetary policy.

1.4 The Framework for Making of Monetary Policy in the United States

1.4.1 Committee Structure

Decisions on monetary policy in the United States are made around every six weeks[2] by the Federal Reserve's Federal Open Market Committee. The FOMC comprises the seven members of the Board of Governors (including the chairman) and the presidents of the twelve district Federal Reserve Banks.[3] Formally, FOMC decisions are made by a majority vote of the voting members of the committee on a proposal that constitutes a directive to guide the conduct of open market operations by the Fed (these operations being the primary means to implement the decision on monetary policy). Committee decision-making in the FOMC provides an institutional framework within which to aggregate the preferences of individual policy makers and thus produce a collective decision (Blinder 2004; Chappell, McGregor, et al. 2005).

Members of the Board of Governors are appointed by the US president and confirmed by the Senate to serve fourteen-year terms.[4] The reserve bank presidents serve five-year renewable terms. They are appointed by the boards of directors of their banks, subject to approval by the Board of Governors.[5] At any point in time, the voting members of the FOMC comprise the seven members of the Board of Governors, the president of the New York Federal Reserve Bank and four of the presidents of the other eleven district banks.[6] It is not uncommon for a board governor seat to be vacant (awaiting appointment and confirmation of a replacement).

1.4.2   Goals and Objectives

Turning to the substance of monetary policy, the last thirty years have seen the emergence of a consensus worldwide around establishing and maintaining persistent low inflation as the appropriate goal of monetary policy. In the United States the shift to a consistent low inflation policy started with the so-called Volcker Revolution in 1979, followed by the disinflation of the 1980s and the subsequent entrenchment of low inflation. (Chapter 3 includes an in-depth study of the role of deliberation in the FOMC during the Volcker Revolution, in recognition of the importance of that period for creating the sustained change in policy-making.)

There are two important components to the policy of sustained low inflation. The first involves the emergence of the idea that low inflation maximizes the utility of the representative economic agent, consistent with the view that sustained low inflation is a necessary condition for sustained economic growth. On its own, however, monetary policy does not influence the long-run rate of growth of the economy; rather, according to the notion of the long-run neutrality of money (i.e., on their own monetary policy actions do not influence the steady-state growth rate of the economy over the long run), it is a necessary condition to enable other economic policies to affect the growth rate. The second important component of the sustained low inflation policy concerns the role of the institutions of monetary policy, central banks, and in particular the structure of the independence of central banks as a necessary condition for a policy-making framework that can deliver persistent low inflation as the goal of monetary policy.

Viewed from the perspective of the success of the last thirty years in moving decisively away from the high inflation of the 1970s, it is easy to take for granted the orthodoxy of the framework built around the idea of monetary policy committed to sustained low inflation delivered by the institution of an independent central bank. But any quick read of history indicates that the orthodoxy is a product of relatively recent history. In his history of the Federal Reserve, Meltzer describes the failure of monetary policy in the 1970s (the period of the so-called Great Inflation) as the product of a regime where "producers and consumers had learned that anti-inflation policies did not persist once unemployment rose, so they were hesitant to change their beliefs about long-term inflation" (Meltzer 2009: 850). For its part the FOMC did not distinguish adequately between nominal and real interest rates such that it "did not increase the market interest rate enough in response to inflation to offset the negative effect of inflation on (ex post) real interest rates and on expected future interest rates" (Meltzer 2009: 857). Meltzer concludes that "(t)he Great Inflation resulted from policy choices that placed much more weight on maintaining high or full employment than on preventing or reducing inflation," primarily owing to political pressures and the force of public opinion. More weight was given to inflation control only when the American public became willing to bear the cost (Meltzer 2009: 864–65). This provides context to explain a repeated pattern of policy errors (after all, FOMC members could observe that inflation was persistently high and thus monetary policy was failing).

Much of the literature in monetary policy focuses on explaining what happened (the policy-setting, and the consequence of the policy process defined as the realized inflation rate and the rate of growth of the economy) and from that inferring why changes in the policy-setting happened when they did. As such, it has little to say about *how* the change happened. Policy-settings are thus often used in reduced-form econometric analysis that seeks to explain the policy makers' reactions to key economic data, and other variables. This has led to a small industry estimating reaction functions or policy rules of various types. Such approaches can be used as a means to explain the votes and thus the average inflation preferences over their time in the job of monetary policy makers. Reaction function approaches are common at the level of the committee as a whole, in the form of monetary policy rules (Taylor 1999) and for committee members in the form of individual reaction functions (Chappell, McGregor, et al. 2005). Many of the original applications of rules and reaction functions were backward looking—namely trying to provide a framework for explaining past decisions. But this led to using them as forecasting tools, and then to recommendations that the credibility of policy could be enhanced if a rule was adopted such that policy-making was in essence on autopilot. The problem with this type of approach is that it takes no account of how policy makers react to particular shocks to the economy, since every shock is different and has a different source. Put simply, policy makers will want to know why and how a particular shock has emerged and what impact it is likely to have before deciding on their reaction. In contrast, rules and reaction functions, because they are of necessity reduced-form, are based on an average response to past shocks that have very different characteristics. They are not an accurate description of how policy is actually made, even if they can capture over time the broad thrust of policy.

1.5 A Short History of US Monetary Policy

1.5.1 Early Beginnings of the Fed
The period we study begins in the mid-1970s at the point where the postwar consensus on economic policy-making was recognized to be seriously broken by high inflation, and ends with the establishment of the primacy of the goal of low inflation and of monetary policy as the tool of short-run economic stabilization.[7] Before we turn to that period, it is essential to outline the early history of the Fed, as key elements in this history help shape current ideas and institutional arrangements surrounding monetary policy. For much of this historical account and some of our interpretation, we rely on Allan Meltzer's authoritative *History of the Federal Reserve* (Meltzer 2003, 2009). Meltzer provides the most extensive and incisive account of the origins, operations and political backdrop for the Federal Reserve up to 1986.[8]

For a large industrialized economy, the United States was late to establish a central bank. The Federal Reserve was founded in 1913, formally by Congress delegating responsibilities to the Fed using the power over the US currency given to Congress in the Constitution. The Fed was created as a part private, part public institution, "a peculiar hybrid" (Meltzer 2003: 725). The Federal Reserve Act of 1913 "represented a compromise between many different groups that had different purposes in mind. At one extreme were the proponents of a single central bank, owned by the commercial banks and run by the bankers," who focused more narrowly on the services that central banks offer to banks (Meltzer 2003: 65). An opposing group was comprised of those who argued against any kind of central bank. The main thrust of their argument was that, as a monopoly, a central bank "would run for the benefit of the bankers, particularly J P Morgan and other New York bankers" (Meltzer 2003: 66).

In June 1913 President-elect Woodrow Wilson proposed to Congress the so-called hybrid, which combined private and public control. Wilson recommended that control "be vested in the Government itself, so that the banks may be the instruments not the masters of business and of individual enterprise and initiative" (quoted in Meltzer 2003: 67) In the end, Wilson's compromise became the framework for the new central bank, with board governors politically appointed and situated in Washington, DC, together with regional banks situated in politically and strategically important cities (Binder and Spindel 2011), that were run by bankers. Meltzer contends that between the two entities, there was "no clear division of responsibility" (Meltzer 2003: 67).

The modern FOMC was not part of the original design of the Federal Reserve. It was created by the Banking Act of 1935 as the monetary policy making body of the Fed to resolve the problem that the structure created in 1913 "did not concentrate decision-making authority and responsibility" and thus prompted "a struggle for power and control" (Meltzer 2003: 3). The Banking Act shifted the balance of power to the Federal Reserve Board in Washington and away from the regional reserve banks, with the latter losing their semi-autonomous status and much of the independence given to them in 1913. In doing so, the 1935 Act created the central role of the FOMC.

The private ownership of the regional Federal Reserve banks by local member commercial banks was designed to act as a bulwark against influence from the national government. But agricultural and commercial interests became concerned that the Federal Reserve would act for the benefit of large banks against the interests of the public. This concern was reflected in a long-run stream of opposition to the Fed from congressional Democrats with mainly agricultural districts. The 1935 Banking Act addressed some of these concerns but could not do so comprehensively as long as monetary policy was thought to follow an objective that could be used to favor one interest group or another. This required a re-specification of the objective of monetary policy— something that took place many decades later, as a consequence of the failure of policy to deal with the high inflation of the 1970s.

1.5.2 Monetary Policy's Evolving Objective and an "Independent" Fed

This change, or re-specification, of monetary policy in the more modern era was anchored by the idea that sustained low inflation is the best means to deliver stable growth of the economy, along with the important principle of the long-run neutrality of money. These principles of policy-making have clarified the objective of monetary policy, which in turn has helped to clarify both the institutional structure of policy-making and the process of accountability of policy makers. The end result has been a much better definition of the role of the "independent" central bank.

To be clear, no central bank has *absolute* independence, in the sense that it is independent of the will of the people and thus elected representatives. In the case of the United States, Congress delegated powers to the Federal Reserve by drawing in turn on powers given to the legislature by the US Constitution. The objective of monetary policy at a high level is laid down in statute and can only be changed by amending that legislation. The Fed is thus given independence in terms of operating monetary policy to meet the objective given by Congress and the president. Congress can however initiate and (with the administration of the day) approve change to the objective that is to be met by the Fed and can alter the terms of the Fed's independence to operate to that objective. Over time some legislators (more often Democrats) have sought to increase the obligations on the Fed to achieve transparency and accountability to Congress in monetary policy in ways that typically did not at first find favor with Fed officials who sought to protect their independence. The latter tended to interpret such moves by Congress as a threat to the independence of the central bank in respect of monetary policy. To reiterate, constitutionally, as with all national central banks, the delegation of an independent role can be revoked or more likely modified. Independence is therefore to some degree qualified by the threat of modification. Other things equal, the threat is more likely to be exercised, and thus more powerful, when monetary policy is perceived to be unsuccessful. The administration is also an important player in this process, not least because the modern public tends to hold the administration responsible for the state of the economy (Meltzer 2009: 1217).

The objective of the Federal Reserve has changed and evolved over its lifetime. In the early years of the Fed, stable growth of the economy was not part of its formal mandate, and most of the Fed's leadership "would have denied any responsibility for economic activity or employment" (Meltzer 2003: 9). Nor for that matter, did price stability feature in the Fed's early mandate. In the 1920s the economist Irving Fisher worked to get Congress to mandate price stability as the goal of the Federal Reserve, an unsuccessful initiative that was opposed by the Fed itself. The Fed's original mandate was very much viewed as preventing financial crises and panics, and thereby smoothing the business cycle. In the language of modern central banking, the mandate placed the stability of the financial system at the forefront of the central bank's contribution to ensuring macroeconomic stability.

There was nothing unusual in these early views of the role of the Fed. It is a relatively modern idea that, while monetary policy does not have long-run effects on employment, expenditure and output in the economy (the long-run neutrality of money), there is a short-run transmission from monetary policy to economic activity, which makes monetary policy the most potent tool of short-run economic stabilization.[9] A lack of clear understanding of the transmission of monetary policy to economic activity and the price level (i.e., the effectiveness of monetary policy) substantially compromised not only the clarity of the Fed's own objective and actions, but also the oversight of Congress. Lacking a clear understanding of monetary policy's objective, one could hardly expect focused deliberation by policy makers and politicians. Indeed we argue that *the absence of clarity of the objective of policy is likely to have clouded the process of deliberation within the policy-making body and had adverse effects on the process of accountability to Congress.*

An essential element of this confusion involves the roles of monetary and fiscal policy, and their relationship to one another. In the post–World War II period, most politicians viewed monetary policy as unimportant for economic stabilization; rather, it was fiscal policy that mattered more. This was a view held not just in successive administrations, but also in the Fed itself. This postwar consensus reflected a change of view on the role of fiscal policy, from one that argued for balanced budgets as the peacetime norm, to one where government spending (and hence deficits) should substitute for cyclical weakness in private spending as the means to stabilize output. Within this framework, monetary policy should seek to control high inflation, but not in a way that meant high interest rates confounded the stabilization goals of fiscal policy. Monetary policy was therefore at best subordinated. This was an approach that brought short-run stabilization to the fore (via the operation of fiscal policy) but without any clear anchor (in terms of a policy objective such as a target for output growth or inflation) or set of rules. Thus the 1946 Employment Act emphasized employment and production as goals of the Fed, but without establishing a clear objective. In terms of relations between the Fed and Congress, the emphasis on the use of fiscal policy as a discretionary tool for economic stabilization was important because Congress approved the budget. The Fed could thus find itself in conflict with Congress (and the administration) when it attempted to use the monetary policy tool to counteract the inflationary effects of fiscal policy approved by Congress itself. The tendency in postwar policy-making was therefore for Fed chairmen to gravitate toward joining the formal coordination of economic policy through interagency coordination with the administration in order to seek influence over the primary policy tool (fiscal policy).

As should be evident from this short historical summary, the modern convention that monetary policy is the primary tool of short-term economic stabilization, and is thus aimed at delivering low inflation as the means to deliver stable growth, does not have long-established underpinnings.[10]

1.5.3   From High Inflation to Price Stability: An Evolving Interpretation for Independence

As we move into the second half of the 1970s, the dominant theme was the pressure of high inflation during that decade. The pressure of high inflation eventually led to a broad consensus that fiscal policy was too inflexible as a policy tool to perform the role of short-run macroeconomic stabilization, and as a consequence attention shifted to monetary policy as the primary tool of stabilization.

We thus arrive at our time period of interest. Figure 1.1 illustrates US monetary policy from the 1970s to 2008 in terms of its outcome (defined as the rate of consumer price inflation). This time period begins with high inflation and weak real economic growth but progresses to stable low inflation and stronger and more stable growth (see figure 1.2). The period covers the tenure of five chairmen of the Fed, three of whom were undoubtedly "strong characters"—Burns, Volcker, and Greenspan—and a brief period (in 1978 to 1979) of weak leadership under Miller. We also cover the initial years of Bernanke's term as chairman, but we take the view that judgment on strength of character in the role should only be made ex post.

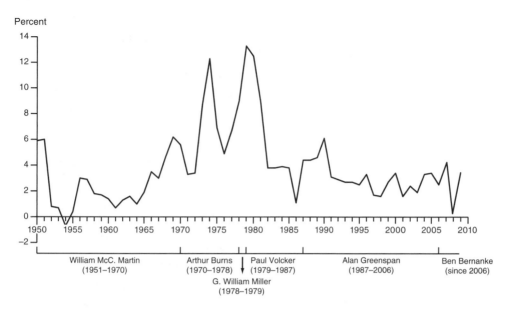

Figure 1.1
US consumer price inflation (percentage change YOY Dec/Dec)
Source: US Department of Labor, Bureau of Labor Statistics

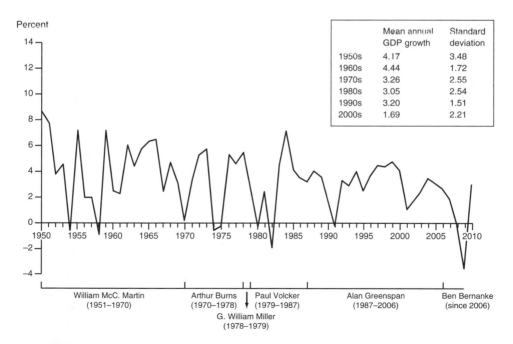

Figure 1.2
US gross domestic product (percentage change YOY based on chained 2005$)
Source: US Bureau of Economic Analysis

Within our period is the ascent to orthodoxy of the idea that an independent central bank responsible for monetary policy is the best institutional structure around which countries can achieve lasting low inflation and stable economic growth. The academic literature on independent central banks has been prolific over this period.[11] Its premise is that some of the mistakes in economic policy in the past resulted from a belief among politicians that it was possible to raise the level of output and employment permanently by accepting a higher rate of inflation—namely there was an assumed long-run trade-off between unemployment and inflation. Moreover, as politicians attempted to exploit this trade-off for electoral advantage (by boosting demand through higher government spending or seeking lower interest rates), permanently higher inflation generally resulted. The presumed trade-off therefore did not exist, at least not in the long run. Politicians seeking re-election nevertheless remained tempted to exploit any presumed short-run trade-off between unemployment and inflation, and thus were found repeatedly to prefer more inflationary monetary policies—which Kydland and Prescott termed the problem of "time inconsistency" (Kydland and Prescott 1977).

There are two important implications of time inconsistency for this context. First, an environment in which the goal of monetary policy is not well pinned-down (i.e., one where there is discretion to change the goal of policy) can lead to an average upward inflation bias (Svensson 2002). Second, a lot depends on whether the monetary policy institution can make binding, and hence credible, commitments about future policy-settings. An independent central bank with a clear goal to pursue low inflation provided the institutional framework to achieve lasting low inflation alongside the contribution from the ideas generated by economic theory that identified the problem of time inconsistency in the go–stop anti-inflationary policies of the 1960s and 1970s and the benefit of lasting low inflation in terms of stable economic growth.

A solution to the problem is for politicians to cede control of monetary policy to an independent central bank. Independent central bankers are thus empowered to pursue the objective given to them—for most countries, an explicit objective of achieving and maintaining price stability. By credibly delegating monetary policy authority to an "independent" central bank, a government demonstrates a commitment to alleviating the time inconsistency problem, and thereby demonstrating its commitment to price stability. What constitutes "independence" in this context is not, however, entirely self-evident. There are three potential levels at which independence can exist in respect of monetary policy: the goal or objective, the target, and policy-setting to meet the target.

Almost no central bank is independent in terms of setting the goal or objective of monetary policy; rather, this is a product of the political process, whether in legislation as in the United Sates, or more latterly Britain, or (as in the case of the European Central Bank) in the form of a treaty. The modern goal of monetary policy is typically price stability and, subject to that, supporting the policies of the government of the day for economic growth (or greater employment). The Federal Reserve is somewhat unusual in having an objective of growth, employment and stable prices, all of which are on an equal footing. Formally, the Employment Act of 1946 called for maximum employment and pur-chasing power, which was replaced in 1977 when Congress amended the Federal Reserve Act to incorporate the provisions of House Resolu-tion 133, namely maximum employment, stable prices and moderate long-term interest rates. The goal of monetary policy is therefore ulti-mately a product of the political process and the state itself; in this sense the central bank is not independent.

At the other two levels of operation of monetary policy—setting the target and setting the policy to meet the target—more often than not the central bank has independence to take its own actions, although subject to the conditions of the goal. For the Fed, in terms of pre-cision, setting the target has not extended beyond the language set out in the statutory objective of policy.[12] That said, for nearly all central banks, operational independence is accompanied by an impor-tant link to the political process that typically involves ex post account-ability by central banks to government and parliament in explaining their actions. Also independent central banks are typically connected to the political process in other ways—for example, senior appoint-ments (and re-appointments) to the central bank are in the hands of politicians.

Central bank independence in respect of monetary policy is thus more subtle than the simple headline would suggest. This matters for our study of the role of deliberation in policy-making and in the accountability process, for the simple reason that even though the legal framework for Fed independence has remained constant, how US policy makers and politicians think about independence has changed quite considerably. In other words, while the Fed has had a broadly unchanged degree of formal legal independence since it was founded,[13] the interpretation and operation of that independence has changed as the role of monetary policy within broader macroeconomic policy-making has changed.

1.6 Clarity and Confusion in Thinking about Monetary Policy: Dimensions and Uncertainty

1.6.1 Monetary Policy as a Single Dimension?

We contend that policy makers' reasoning and thinking on monetary policy-making is at least as important as the policy decision itself. But this is not the generally accepted view. Usually the focus is on the monetary policy outcome and commonly policy makers' views on this are depicted on a single dimension. That is, commentators tend to talk in dichotomous terms of "easy" or "tight" and of policy makers as "hawks" or "doves." These are convenient labels to cut through the complexity of policy-making, but they carry the great risk of oversimplification in ways that harm the interpretation of policy. Put simply, do policy makers think and talk in these terms, or is it an unnecessary (and perhaps unhelpful) oversimplification of reality? Few policy makers choose to pin on this sort of label; quite probably they recognize that the process of deliberating to reach a conclusion is more subtle than such a label implies.

The tendency to focus almost exclusively on the loose:tight or hawk:dove dimension amounts to using a simplistic categorization of the outcome to categorize the decision-making process. In that sense, it is reverse engineering; in other words, what policy makers think about policy and how they form their views is inferred from their eventual conclusion in the form of a vote. By focusing on the vote, monetary policy-making is envisaged as a relatively parsimonious exercise in terms of the decision frame. That is, in normal times[14] modern monetary policy involves a choice between raising or lowering the official interest rate (including how much in either direction)—or alternatively, leaving it the same. Complexity arises, however, in the analysis, assessment and deliberation that leads to the conclusion; by contrast, the choice of the conclusion itself is relatively simple.

The single dimensionality assumption that underlies much of the empirical analyses of FOMC voting behavior either implicitly or explicitly rests on the spatial voting model (e.g., Chang 2003). In this model, the single dimension is usually described in terms of ideology (conservative or liberal), and while other dimensions may be relevant, one dimension enables greater simplicity in terms of modeling and testing. Morris, for example, defends the simplicity associated with a single dimension and suggests that "it is not obvious what other aspects of monetary policy-making would be captured with additional dimensions" (Morris 2000: 38).

The problem revolves around the meaning of a "dimension." In spatial voting theory, dimensionality in an issue space refers to a mechanism that constrains actors' attitudes across a variety of issues (Poole 2005). Thus, when spatial theorists refer to dimensionality, they are usually thinking of a basic dimension that constrains voters' (or politicians') positions on a number of policy issues—being a conservative, for example, implies a preference for lower levels of taxation and lower levels of public spending. The key dimension is usually ideology and it is one's position on this dimension that allows a prediction of that person's position on government spending, taxation, social services, and so on.

The problem with this framework for analyzing FOMC voting is that monetary policy-making is a single issue (there is no bundling of other issues involved). Regardless of this difficulty, some researchers may nonetheless assume that the basic constraint mechanism is loose:tight. Not only does this not square well with the standard interpretation of dimensionality in spatial voting theory, but the conception of this basic dimension is itself vacuous—that is, loose:tight contains no broader ideology from which we might predict FOMC members' preferences on other policy dimensions. Divergent partisan preferences do not appear to explain the behavior of FOMC members (Falaschetti 2002), and so we cannot even infer party labels from the loose:tight continuum. This continuum is mere description—there is no basic constraint mechanism at work (i.e., no underlying substantive content).

We are therefore skeptical of the usefulness and viability of a single dimension with which to explain monetary policy-making by the Fed. Voting records oversimplify the decision-making process. It is almost self-evident that the preferences of FOMC members are captured only in part by their votes (Meade 2005). Moreover, in the FOMC, dissenting votes are infrequent—occurring in only 7.8 percent of all votes between 1966 and 1996 (Chappell, McGregor, et al. 2005).[15] Hence a focus on votes fails to reveal the arguments—and disagreements—that lie behind these votes. In essence we are less concerned with describing voting decisions per se and more concerned with understanding why members reached the conclusions they did. Our goal is to understand the motivations of FOMC members by focusing on what they said and the way they described their views, rather than just their votes. Above all, this explains why we think the transcripts are worthy of more intensive study.

1.6.2   The Uncertainty of Monetary Policy

Alan Greenspan has described uncertainty as the defining characteristic of the monetary policy landscape (Greenspan 2003). Monetary policy-making is a forward-looking exercise, and as a consequence uncertainty cannot be avoided. A policy maker cannot influence the rate of inflation in the immediate future (e.g., the next month) through an action taken now. Rather, making monetary policy involves taking a view on the evolution of the economy and inflation over a period to come that accords broadly with the period of time over which the impact of a decision on policy is likely to work its way through the economy (the period of the monetary transmission mechanism), which can be up to two years or more. The success, and thus credibility, of policy-making therefore depends on dealing with the inherent uncertainty of policy-making. This uncertainty surrounds not only how the economy and inflation will unfold but also the impact of a policy decision on that unfolding process, and the unknown future shocks to the economy. Central bankers reach their judgments under considerable uncertainty about the evolution of the economy, the public's behavior, financial innovation, errors in reported data, and judgments on separating persistent from temporary changes in the data (Meltzer 2009: 1237). A quote from Larry Meyer, a Fed governor, helps to illustrate the effect of uncertainty on decision-making. In 1997, FOMC members faced the puzzle of the combination of strong domestic demand growth in the United States, an unemployment rate that was widely assumed to be below the point at which the pressure on capacity would start to cause inflation to push up but persistently lower than expected inflation outturns. As Meyer commented at the time, "every time we [FOMC] got close to tightening rates, evidence came pouring in that inflation was not only well contained, but actually declining. Needless to say, we were surprised. We had never seen anything like this before" (Meyer 2004: 79).

In an uncertain world, the credibility of a policy-making process that depends on taking a view of the future can be enhanced by recognizing the limits of knowledge and the extent of ignorance. Decisions of all sorts involve both risk, which can be quantified, and uncertainty, which cannot (Knight 1921; King 2004). An older literature (Brainard 1967) focused on uncertainty about the impact of exogenous variables on the target variable of policy (either through uncertainty about the value of these variables or about their impact) and about the response of the target variable to policy action (the transmission mechanism of policy). Brainard (1967) made the point that if a policy maker is uncertain about the marginal impact of his policy instrument on the target variable, he should probably use the instrument in smaller measures. Blinder (1998) expands this characterization of the policy response by adding that using small doses of policy probably means that more doses will be required to get the job done. The key point here is that under conditions of uncertainty it is probably best for policy adjustments to be applied gradually (allowing some time to judge their early effects).

More recent research in the monetary policy field has emphasized other forms of uncertainty—for example, key structural parameters of the economy (Clarida, Gali, et al. 1999), or the accuracy of contemporary data measuring the performance of the economy (Orphanides 1998, 2001; Orphanides and Norden 1999).

Because monetary policy-making is inherently uncertain, policy makers have ample scope to question the economic data, the effectiveness of alternative policy actions, their own (and others') models of the economy—in short, uncertainty creates questions, and questions in turn create the opportunity for deliberation. Hence, uncertainty in a policy-making process involving a committee of decision makers should naturally lend itself to deliberation. How policy makers respond to uncertainty, however, depends on what they think is the optimal approach. In the spirit of the work of Brainard and others, one plausible policy response to uncertainty regarding the structure of the economy, is that of attenuation (Blinder 1998). A second response might place the emphasis more on protecting against worst-case scenarios by minimizing the maximum loss, which in some cases could imply a more aggressive policy response.

In sum, policy-making under conditions of uncertainty should naturally lend itself to deliberation among the members of the decision-making body. It also no doubt has an impact on the forms of accountability that policy makers face, and the ways in which policy makers are drawn out to give their views on how they reached decisions in the face of uncertainty. Put simply, the more uncertainty, the more likely it is that deliberation will matter in reaching a conclusion.

The FOMC is in many ways a classic deliberating body, charged with making public policy in an environment that must be forward looking, and in which there is substantial uncertainty around the facts of the time and the model(s) to be used to link those uncertain "facts" to the policy decision. In our view, it therefore represents prime territory to study the role of deliberation in a more comprehensive fashion. The period of the 1970s to the early 21st century is also particularly intriguing because it saw monetary policy begin as a failure and move to being perceived to be a great success. But deliberation within the FOMC is not the sole point of focus for monetary policy-making. As we have described, the ascendancy of the notion of the independent central bank has been accompanied (necessarily) by a greater emphasis on the accountability of the Fed to the body from which its power was delegated (Congress), to which we now turn.

1.7 Congressional Oversight of Monetary Policy

In many countries central banks are accountable for their monetary policy actions to the legislative branch of government. Typically a legislature has authority to require the central bank to explain its recent actions and how it sees those actions as consistent with the overall policy objective and goal of policy. Members of the legislature can praise or criticize the central bank for its actions, and they have a right to receive answers to their questions. All of this is done moreover in the public domain. The legislature does not have the power to mandate monetary policy actions (as this would breach the independence of the central bank), nor can it require the central bank to signal its forthcoming action (as this would remove the discretion of the independent agency). The legislature can, however, threaten to change the terms of central bank independence and the objective of policy through legislation, although the credibility of this threat depends on the constitutional system of the country.

We study the discourse and deliberation of members of Congress in the House and Senate banking committees during the oversight hearings on monetary policy for eight periods from 1976 to 2008 and the Senate reconfirmation hearings for Volcker, Greenspan and Bernanke over this same period.[16] By examining the evolution of congressional oversight of the Fed over this 33 year period, we aim better to understand the thinking of members of Congress in terms of how they interpret and carry out their role of holding the Fed accountable for its actions.

1.7.1 Congress, the Fed and the Great Inflation

Over the last quarter of the 20th century, there were two fundamental changes in the relationships among the Fed, Congress and the administration in respect of monetary policy. First, the role of Congress in US macroeconomic policy underwent a fundamental change: whereas in the early years Congress had a formal role in approving the primary short-term macroeconomic policy tool (fiscal policy), in the later years its role shifted to overseeing the agency responsible for the primary policy tool (the Fed in respect of monetary policy). A second change involved a strengthening of the views of Fed officials on independence. Whereas in the 1960s (under Chairman William McChesney Martin), the Fed sought to coordinate its operations with the administration's fiscal actions, by the later decades, such actions were perceived as counter to central bank independence. Indeed Meltzer argues that Fed officials realized that it was a mistake to forfeit the Fed's independence in order to engage in policy coordination with the administration, and moreover, it was this mistake that started the high inflation of the 1970s. Not only did policy coordination reduce independence, such coordination was a one-way street: "(t)he Federal Reserve supported administrative actions, but there was no reciprocity" (Meltzer 2009: 1224). These two changes are of course connected, since the impression that it was not in control of the principal macroeconomic policy tool led the Fed to seek greater influence via coordination with those who were seen to be in charge.

Martin's successor as chairman, Arthur Burns, described the root cause of the Great Inflation as being an embedded willingness in American society and politics to accommodate inflation, something that eventually infected the Fed itself (Burns 1979, 1987). There was, however, a strong degree of self-serving to Burns's commentary, given his own role in the failure of monetary policy in the 1970s to tackle high inflation, and the failure of the Fed to do its job in distinguishing one-time changes in the price level caused by (notably) oil prices, and a pattern of sustained higher inflation that set in (Meltzer 2009: 1227). Meltzer adds that in the 1960s and 1970s the Fed suffered from an excessive focus on short-term quarterly forecasts of the economy and inflation, and too little attention to the medium and long-term policy implications (consistent with failing to identify sustained higher inflation) (Meltzer 2009: 1232–33). It is plausible to conclude that the short-term focus of the Fed in this period was linked to its accommodation with politicians and their short-term horizons.

Within Congress, two features of the 1970s affected its relations with the Fed: (1) from an economic perspective, the experience of persistent high inflation had made evident to politicians and the wider public that policy had failed; (2) from a political perspective, the major changes in personnel and attitudes among the congressional leadership that followed the post-Watergate election of 1974 had swept away a number of the senior figures in Congress who had been entrenched in their positions and views on economic policy since the Great Depression of the 1930s.

Early in 1975 Congress used its constitutional power over the currency to adopt House Resolution 133, which instructed the Federal Reserve as its agent to pursue a particular broad setting of monetary policy.[17] HR 133 is a defining piece of congressional action for three reasons. First, as Meltzer notes, it was rare for Congress (as opposed to individual members) to call on the Fed to "do a better job" (Meltzer 2009: 986). Second, the Resolution appeared to strengthen the role of price stability in the Fed's mandate by leaning against the more common interpretation of the mandate in the 1946 Employment Act that emphasized full employment as the primary objective. Third, in the Resolution, Congress requested that the Fed avoid excessive long-term growth of the monetary aggregates, thus at least in part supporting the monetarist critique of the Fed (Meltzer 2009: 986).

The passage of the Humphrey–Hawkins Act in 1978 formalized semi-annual oversight hearings before the Senate and House banking committees.[18] The Act required the Federal Reserve Board to report in writing to Congress by February 20th each year on its and the FOMC's objectives for the money and credit aggregates for the year ahead, while in July of each year the Board had to provide a first report on its plans for the aggregates in the following year. Meltzer notes that this forced the Fed to pay more attention to medium-term objectives, "a potentially important change" (Meltzer 2009: 990). Also the Board's report had to explain how its monetary policy objectives would fit with the administration's economic program for the year and to congressional goals.[19] In fact the passage of the Act did nothing to improve the ability of the Fed to achieve announced monetary targets, and in 2001 Congress repealed the provision for monetary growth targets but retained semi-annual oversight hearings. Meltzer notes that the Act absolved the Fed from responsibility for achieving its announced money and credit ranges; rather, if conditions changed, the Fed had to explain to Congress the estimated impact of the change (Meltzer 2009: 991).

The immediate positive impact of the requirement for regular congressional hearings and the objective on policy established by Resolution 133 was hard to determine as inflation and unemployment remained high in the following years and the growth rates of the monetary aggregates failed to achieve the objectives set by the FOMC (and moreover there was no adjustment for so-called base drift—that is, the consequence of previously missing target growth rates, which made it much harder to judge the stance of policy at any moment in time).

1.7.2   In the Wake of the Great Inflation: The Effect of Stable Low Inflation on Congressional Oversight

One might think that the increased activism of Congress in the realm of monetary policy might have resulted in legislators who were better informed on, and more in tune with the Fed on monetary policy. Unfortunately, this rosy view ignores the simple fact that for the many decades preceding the 1970s, not only were the theoretical underpinnings for monetary policy weak, but also the role of monetary policy was either subjugated to fiscal policy and/or little understood. Hence it is hard to envisage that members of Congress had much vision of what they sought to achieve through oversight. One prime example of this lack of understanding involves the distributional consequences (for interest groups in the economy) of monetary policy. Such consequences are not at all straightforward, as they require a much clearer exposition of the transmission mechanism from monetary policy decisions to economic activity and the price level. Rather than exploring this transmission mechanism, legislators tended simply to interpret the consequences of monetary policy decisions within the older tradition of populist antipathy to the association of the Fed with private interests of large banks. Indeed Meltzer is relatively dismissive of legislators' willingness and ability to engage in active dialogue with the Fed on monetary policy: "(r)egrettably, few in Congress are informed enough to enter into a useful dialogue with the Board's chairman" (Meltzer 2009: 986).

There is, however, reason to think that members of Congress absorbed, if not the particulars, at least some of the core conceptual framework of monetary policy as it was evolving into a consensus around the stable low inflation objective, and the corollary role for central bank independence. In the words of a staff member of the House Financial Services Committee of the late 1970s, "preaching" from Fed officials to members of Congress certainly had an effect: "independence was so preached by the Fed and pushed upon other central banks around the world by the Fed, that . . . in a sense . . . the members of Congress just absorbed this idea: the Fed is an independent agency."[20] It seems plausible therefore to expect that a change in the nature of congressional oversight may have resulted from the Fed's success in achieving stable low inflation. Indeed it is reasonably uncontroversial to say that the form of oversight itself was conditional on the success of the central bank in achieving its objective of low inflation, and on whether there was a common acceptance among members of Congress that low inflation was the best way to achieve sustainable growth throughout the economy, and thus stable low unemployment. From our empirical analysis we find that the politics of oversight was shaped both by the policy outcome itself (the Fed's success or failure) and by the degree of consensus surrounding the objective of policy, namely the benefits of low inflation. Moreover these two shaping influences were closely interlinked, for the simple reason that it is easier to build a consensus around a successful policy.

But within this mix of policy success and congressional oversight lies a paradox. The rise of the emphasis on legislative accountability as part of the package of having an independent central bank came at a time when low inflation had been established for a longer period than at any time since the nineteenth century. In short, legislators came to play a larger role at a time when, arguably, there was in substance less for them to do. Certainly in an era of low inflation and stable growth, there was less need for legislators to signal their displeasure with the central bank. In particular, there was less need for Congress to use the threat of legislation to curb the Fed's powers. Havrilesky concluded that using a measure of the count of bills introduced, this form of threat from Congress was most common during periods of poor economic conditions, and that the president's influence over the Fed may in part at least emanate from the understanding of both sides that the president has the power to veto (or not) legislation emerging from Congress (Havrilesky 1993). In the United States (and elsewhere) the 1990s were the key period in which the new era of stable growth and low inflation came to be accepted as a more enduring part of the economic landscape. As low inflation became the norm, and as monetary policy became the primary tool to achieve and sustain macroeconomic stability, the role of congressional oversight likewise changed to fit the times.

1.8 Politics of Monetary Policy: Theoretical Underpinnings

1.8.1 Partisan Influence on Monetary Policy
Our focus on deliberation is quite distinct in the literature on the politics of monetary policy. The main thrust of that literature has been to gauge the influence of politicians on monetary policy-making (e.g., Alt 1991; Woolley 1994; Morris 2000; Chang 2003). With the growth of public choice theory in the 1970s, researchers began to investigate the extent to which elected officials—namely the president and Congress—might influence Fed officials, and thus seek to align monetary policy with their own political objectives. Over 35 years ago, Nordhaus identified the political business cycle (PBC), in which incumbent politicians seek high growth and employment, and low inflation in the lead-up to elections (Nordhaus 1975). As an extension to the PBC, it has been argued that partisanship further shapes macroeconomic policy, with Republican presidential administrations exhibiting tighter monetary policies than Democratic ones (Hibbs 1977; Chappell and Keech 1986; Hibbs 1986; Alesina and Sachs 1988; Chappell and Keech 1988; Williams 1990). But these conclusions were called into question by Woolley (1994), who notes that across the literature there is little empirical support for a partisan electoral cycle in postwar US monetary policy (Beck 1987; Nordhaus 1989; Beck 1990; Allen and McCrickard 1991). Franzese contends, moreover, that the empirical evidence for electoral cycles in macroeconomic outcomes is inconsistent and weak, although moderate evidence supports partisan distinctions in monetary policy, but even this was "only or primarily during 1973–1982" (Franzese 2002: 402). He and other authors have pointed to the effect of institutional and structural factors—in particular, central bank independence (and the conservative nature of central bankers) (Cusack 2001)—in mitigating electoral or partisan inflation cycles.

In short, the influence of politicians on US monetary policy making is dubious at best, and certainly even more so as the independence of the Fed became more clearly defined in the last quarter of the 20th century and as the perceived success of the Fed's monetary policy gave less cause for politicians to interfere. To be sure, politicians may seek influence over Fed policy—appointments and jaw-boning are two possibilities—but these are constrained by the checks and balances of the political process (in the case of the appointments) and the danger of establishing an unwanted reputation (for jaw-boning). Certainly central bankers tend to be quick to dismiss the idea of political influence (Meyer 2004: 85–86).

1.8.2   The Fed as the Agent of Congress

Agency theory offers a second perspective on the politics of monetary policy (Beck 1990; Alt 1991; Toma 1991). As with other principal-agent (PA) theories (Bendor 1988), the key insight is the existence of asymmetrical information between the principal and agent. Agents (in this case, the Fed) will attempt to pursue their own goals, which are in turn distinct from those of their principals (Congress and the president). In so doing, they will attempt to exploit their informational advantage over their principal(s). Questions have, however, been raised about how well the scenario of multiple principals (the president and Congress, but also the Senate and the House within Congress) can be encapsulated within the PA perspective (Morris 2000).

One key aspect of PA theory is, however, central to our analysis— namely the delegation of monetary policy authority by Congress to the Fed. This delegation of authority to an independent central bank is regarded as the means by which politicians circumvent the time inconsistency problem (Kydland and Prescott 1977). Delegation is also premised upon the belief that central bankers possess expertise that legislators lack. But expertise, coupled with the authority to formulate monetary policy, raises the issue of whether delegation translates into abdication "wherein the will of the people, as expressed by the people's elected representatives, neither constrains nor motivates the formulation of [monetary] policy" (Lupia and McCubbins 1994: 96). Lupia and McCubbins characterize the debate between scholars as one between those who equate delegation with abdication and those who contend that such practices as legislative oversight help to mitigate the ability of agencies to exploit their informational advantage in ways that would be harmful to legislators or the public more generally. At the center of this debate is a core disagreement about the ability of legislators to learn about the policy (monetary or otherwise). Those who view delegation as abdication dismiss the possibility that legislators are capable of learning about monetary policy, while those who view delegation in a more positive light, "assume, but do not demonstrate, that legislators learn from oversight . . ." (Lupia and McCubbins 1994: 97).

The fundamental question then is, to what extent do legislators learn about the intentions and activities of the Federal Reserve from the oversight hearings? Even if the actions of the Fed are easily observable by legislators, *and* the Fed chairman testifies truthfully in committee hearings, *and* he shares the preferences of members of Congress—congressional oversight of the Fed is still constrained by the fact that it is not a typical federal agency. For one, the technical nature of monetary policy (including complex models and extensive data) make the entry costs to understanding the subject quite high for most legislators. Second, delegation itself offers members of Congress a scapegoat (the Fed), should the economy take a downturn. Third, the Federal Reserve System is unique in that it does not rely on congressional appropriations for its financial support,[21] and thus it is absolved from the usual scrutiny of the appropriations process. Nonetheless, the Fed chairman does report twice a year to congressional banking committees on its monetary policy and the state of the economy more broadly. (Notably the chairman, governors, and other senior Fed staff give evidence frequently at other hearings of Congress, covering a range of subjects—that is, beyond monetary policy—for which the Fed has responsibility.) Given this testimony—and the dialogue and discourse between the Fed and legislators that results—how do we go about ascertaining empirically who influences whom; who learns what from whom; and in short, who benefits from whatever information, ideas, arguments that are conveyed, and understanding reached between the agency responsible for monetary policy and the institution responsible for overseeing that agency? To the extent that answers to these questions are possible, the likely means to achieve them lies in the investigation of the record of the oversight hearings.

As a final remark on the literature on congressional oversight, we recognize that committee hearings are one of a number of ways to conduct oversight (other techniques include audits, investigations, reports, etc.[22]). However, for monetary policy, hearings remain the most prominent and overt form of congressional oversight of the Fed. We also recognize that there is no a priori reason to believe that learning (through deliberation) is—or should be—a key objective of congressional hearings on monetary policy. Indeed we explore the possibility that members of Congress use these hearings for entirely different purposes, such as promoting favored policies; demonstrating support for key interest groups, and elevating their own political stature. We are agnostic on what legislators should or should not seek to accomplish in committee hearings on monetary policy; instead, our goal is to study empirically their words and arguments in order to measure with some degree of statistical precision their intentions in conducting oversight of the Fed's monetary policy. As such, we seek to contribute to the literature on congressional oversight an area of investigation that has been conspicuously overlooked—namely that of deliberation in oversight hearings.[23]

1.9   Our Data

As we have noted, our primary data consist of verbatim transcripts of the FOMC and congressional hearings, and to explore these, we employ computer-based textual analysis. In chapters 3 and 4, we supplement these data with other smaller datasets in order to conduct tests and analyses using more well-known quantitative approaches. And, in chapter 5, we challenge our findings with qualitative data from in-depth interviews of former members of the FOMC, as well as members of Congress and congressional staff from the House and Senate banking committees. Below we describe our primary datasets, leaving the descriptions of the additional data and methodologies to subsequent chapters.

For the FOMC, from 1936 until March 1976, the Fed published (after a five-year lag) a record of each of its meetings in the Minutes or Memoranda of Discussion. These were not verbatim transcripts; rather, they were extensive summaries of the contributions of each member to the meeting. In 1976 the Fed stopped publication of the Memoranda, apparently in response to pending legislation and a lawsuit that would, if successful, have required earlier publication (Chappell, McGregor, et al. 2005; Meltzer 2009). But the Fed continued to produce transcripts of meetings for use in producing its published record of policy actions, though most FOMC members were unaware of the practice of retaining transcripts. In 1993 Alan Greenspan acknowledged the existence of these transcripts and soon afterwards agreed to publish them (with some limited editing) after a five-year lag.

As of 2012 transcripts were published on-line from 1976 to 2006, Minutes from 1936 to 1967, and Memoranda from 1968 to 1976. We have used the full verbatim transcripts of the FOMC meetings for nine years, divided into three time frames: (1) 1979 (in two files, to differentiate the Miller and Volcker chairmanships), 1980 and 1981; (2) 1991, 1992, and 1993; and (3) 1997, 1998, and 1999. We have chosen nine years

covering broadly the beginning, middle, and end of the 20 years following the Volcker Revolution (1979–1981, 1991–1993, and 1997–1999).
This amounts to over 2.3 million spoken words. It covers three chairmen, starting with the brief period at the start of 1979 when William
Miller held the chair. We therefore cover the very last months of the
period up to late 1979 when policy lacked the resolve to stick at tackling
inflation, the beginning of the Volcker disinflation (starting with the
Volcker Revolution), and the subsequent entrenchment of low inflation
credibility under Greenspan.

We recognize that while the FOMC transcripts provide a verbatim
record of a policy-making body, this does not automatically make them
either an easy source to interpret or an inevitable gold mine of analytical insight. Indeed Alan Greenspan commented in an FOMC meeting
in October 1993: "People think reading the raw transcripts is a way of
learning things; I would suggest that if they spend six or eight months
reading through some of this stuff, they won't like it" (Greenspan 1993:
3). It has taken us considerably longer than six to eight months to do
what we hope is some justice to the value of the transcripts.

Why did Greenspan dismiss the likely value of the transcripts for
understanding the behavior of the FOMC? Apart from possibly thinking that reading such lengthy records would not be an exciting task,
there may be two other reasons: first, that the real debate takes place
outside the FOMC, hence limiting the value of the record; and second,
that the existence of the transcripts serves to stifle the quality and force
of the debate in the FOMC. These are themes that we consider in
chapter 3, which focuses on analysis of the FOMC transcripts, and in
chapter 5, which focuses on our set of interviews with former members
of the FOMC and Fed staff.

For Congress, our dataset consists of transcripts from hearings in the
House and Senate committees on the Fed's Monetary Policy Report
from the mid-1976 to 2008. There are 31 House hearings[24] and 30 Senate
hearings.[25] These hearings were part of the Full Employment and Balanced Growth Act of 1978 (named after its sponsors, Senator Hubert
Humphrey and Representative Augustus Hawkins). In these semi-
annual hearings, the Fed chairman presents and replies to questions on
the Fed's report on the economy and monetary policy. Although the
Federal Reports Elimination and Sunset Act of 1995 provided for the
termination of the legal requirements for the Humphrey–Hawkins
reports to Congress after 1999, the Fed and Congress agreed that the
reporting arrangements should continue unchanged. At the FOMC

meeting on 2nd and 3rd February 1999, the committee determined that the hearings had provided "an effective means to explain its policies and communicate its views on a variety of issues and had enhanced its accountability to the public and the Congress."[26]

In order to incorporate into our analysis congressional deliberation on monetary policy in a setting in which legislators were required to make a final decision, we have also used the text of Senate reconfirmation hearings for Volcker (1983), Greenspan (1992, 1996, 2000, 2004), and Bernanke (2009). Table 1.1 summarizes the timeline of our textual data.

1.10   Does Deliberation Matter in Monetary Policy? If So, Why and How?

The bottom line in our study is—as we title this concluding section— the question of whether deliberation matters in monetary policy. Our starting premise is that it *does* matter—why else would FOMC members and legislators in congressional hearings devote hundreds upon thousands of hours talking to one another in committees on monetary policy? We may, of course, be wrong, and if so, our analysis should reveal this. Even if we find that deliberation *matters*, it may be that it does not matter much, or that it matters only under certain circumstances.

We do not begin with a blind faith that deliberation matters. This chapter has, however, sought to establish reasons why we think it may matter in US monetary policy. In summary, even though the legal framework for the independence of the Fed has remained constant, (1) interpretations of this independence among policy makers and politicians have changed quite considerably—and so it may be important to gauge how their thinking and arguments on this have evolved; (2) policy makers do not generally envisage their decisions on monetary policy as falling along a single dimension, and so there are potential trade-offs to be made across dimensions, which may entail argued reasoning; (3) the uncertainty inherent to monetary policy decision-making (including the transmission mechanism) creates questions that in turn create the opportunity for deliberation; (4) studying the Fed and Congress together allows us insight into the ways in which each institutional setting shapes the ways that monetary policy is understood and discussed, as well as affording us the opportunity to gauge the dialogue (and level of understanding) on monetary policy between representatives of these two institutions; and (5) (which relates to point

Table 1.1
FOMC and Congressional Banking Committee transcripts analyzed

House and Senate oversight hearings

1976-1977 (Burns)	1979 (Miller)	1979-1981 (early Volcker)	1984-1986 (late Volcker)	1991-1993 (early Greenspan)	1997-1999 (mid-Greenspan)	2003-2005 (late Greenspan)	2006-08 (early Bernanke)

Senate re-confirmation hearings

			Volcker 1983	Greenspan 1992	Greenspan 1996 / Greenspan 2000	Greenspan 2004	Bernanke 2009/10

Federal Open Market Committee transcripts

		1979-1981		1991-1993	1997-1999		

4) we should also examine empirically the effects of changes in transparency and the chairman's leadership on the committees' discussions.

In the remaining chapters we first set out more clearly our understanding of "deliberation" as it pertains to monetary policy and our expected findings (chapter 2). Chapters 3 and 4 focus, respectively, on (1) monetary policy decision-making by the FOMC and (2) the oversight of this policy by congressional committees and the consideration of the reappointment of the Federal Reserve chairman by the Senate Banking Committee. Chapter 5 presents the findings of our in-depth interviews as a check on our empirical and statistical findings reported in the previous two chapters. Our final chapter returns to the question of whether and under what conditions deliberation matters for monetary policy making in the United States, and summarizes our key findings.

In thumbnail sketch, we identify several instances in which persuasion—as the product of deliberation—affected monetary policy outcomes during our sample of years drawn from the period from 1976 to 2008. In the case of the FOMC, our focus is on strategies of persuasion and how they were used by members. We identify Paul Volcker's emphasis on the need for monetary policy to be credible and thus influence the expectations of economic agents as the means by which he radically changed policy-setting in the FOMC and then persuaded members to stick to the approach in difficult times. Also we identify the use of different arguments used by FOMC members to achieve and sustain a change in the cycle of interest rates in 1999.

Turning to Congress, we identify that with respect to monetary policy oversight, constraints are created by the reactive nature of the participation by members of Congress and by specific institutional features that limit deliberation on monetary policy—including the electoral incentives of legislators (which affect both the ability and time available to learn from deliberation); the lack of technical expertise in monetary policy among members of Congress; the media showcase of the oversight hearings; and the membership size of the House and Senate banking committees. These constraints give rise to congressional passivity on the details of monetary policy. The important caveat to this assessment is that a small number of legislators consistently did offer a challenge to the Fed, but mostly on labor market issues, where their active participation helped demonstrate to constituents a concern for jobs.

2   Deliberation in Theoretical Perspective

2.1   Introduction

We note in the introduction that our analysis of monetary policy focuses on the process of decision-making—not the end product in terms of the policy outcome, but rather the means by which policy makers and politicians converse about monetary policy. Hence our primary concern lies with the deliberations among policy makers and politicians within a number of committee settings. We investigate empirically the discourse and deliberation among these actors as it pertains to one single theme—US monetary policy. Importantly, however, our study is unique in that it encompasses two different institutional committee settings, each with its own purpose and agenda. The first committee setting consists of the monetary policy decision body itself—the Federal Open Market Committee of the Federal Reserve. As we explain in the first chapter, members of this committee are appointed—not elected—officials of an "independent" central bank. Neither reserve bank presidents nor board governors represent any constituency per se.[1] The task confronting FOMC members is to assess and formulate monetary policy, bearing in mind that the collective decisions of the committee are subject to scrutiny by congressional oversight committees, as well as by financial markets and the public at large. Moreover the success of monetary policy is envisaged to depend in large part on the ability of policy makers to condition the expectations of these agents—the public, Congress, and markets—to be consistent with the goal of policy. The credibility of policy depends on the success of this conditioning.

Our second setting is the political body of Congress. This comprises two subsets of congressional committees, differentiated by their respective functions on monetary policy. The first is the congressional oversight committees—namely the House Financial Services Committee and the Senate Banking Committee, both of which conduct separate semi-annual oversight hearings on the Fed's Monetary Policy Report. These committees do not vote on any particular decision nor do they generate any formal report on the outcome of the hearings. Hence the product of deliberation in these committees is unclear. The second subset is the Senate Banking Committee as it evaluates the past performance of the sitting Federal Reserve chairman, with respect to his re-confirmation. Here the committee members are responsible for deciding whether or not to reappoint the Fed Chairman, and they vote accordingly. We do recognize, however, that the Senate is not acting independently in the appointment/reappointment process and that its role involves implicit or explicit bargaining with the administration.

While each of these settings is distinct, all involve actors who engage in repeated interaction with one another, thereby developing reputations for intellectual understanding of the subject matter, integrity and respect for other committee members, and general styles of interacting with one another. We expect that personalities can play a role (particularly for committee chairmen) in shaping deliberation within each setting; however, we expect to find that social and institutional norms (e.g., consensual decision-making and transparency) are critical in defining the nature and scope of deliberative activity for each committee. At this point we keep our expectations general; later in this chapter we are explicit in setting out specific hypotheses for our findings.

In this chapter we set out our conceptual framework. In particular, we (1) define deliberation as used in this study, (2) examine the normative merits of deliberation, (3) provide overviews of the empirical literature on motivations of committee members, and finally (4) offer more explicit expectations for our empirical findings.

2.2   Deliberation Defined

The academic literature on deliberative democracy offers a variety of definitions for deliberation (Page 1996; Elster 1998; Fishkin and Laslett 2003; Pettit 2003; Barabas 2004; Quirk 2005; Austen-Smith and Feddersen 2006; Crowley, Watson, et al. 2008), but most accounts agree on one fundamentally important characteristic—namely the *reason-giving requirement* (Gutmann and Thompson 2004; Thompson 2008). In policy-setting, actors are expected to engage in reasoned argument on the merits of public policy. For our purposes, deliberative discourse would entail members of the FOMC and legislators providing reasons for their claims and positions, and in turn, also responding to others' reasons and counter arguments. As Thompson notes (Thompson 2008: 505) reason-giving may extend beyond pure intellectual reasoning to include emotional appeals, rhetoric and personal experiences. Moreover, because the reasons pertain to what is deemed to be good public policy, the nature of the reasoning must be about a *public* good rather than a private good—that is, reasoning must be external to the committee members themselves (Bessette 1994: 48). (Put another way, the reasoning must not be self-serving.) A final component is that committee members must be willing to learn from one another—that is, they must be willing to be *persuaded* by the merits of their colleagues' reasoned argument.

If the core of deliberation is reason-giving, it is essential to stipulate both the content of these reasons and their purpose. The content of reasons may be said to exhibit at least two core features—information and arguments. Information may include empirical evidence, like facts, figures, scientific findings, and economic modeling. It may also extend to analyses of past, present and/or future policies and their consequences (Bessette 1994: 49). Arguments aim "to connect mere facts with desirable goals" (Bessette 1994: 52) and, as such, offer the potential for actors to employ ideas and ideology as roadmaps (Goldstein 1993; Goldstein and Keohane 1993) or as a means to present a particular interest as one that is beneficial to society in general (Schonhardt-Bailey 2001, 2006).

Reason-giving also serves a key purpose in a deliberative setting— namely to *persuade* other actors (both inside and outside the committee setting) to change their minds. However, persuasion need not entail a complete reversal of position, but rather may simply mean that a previously ambiguous understanding of an issue sharpens into a clear policy position (Bessette 1994: 55). Persuasion has typically been ignored by scholars concerned with preferences of political actors, and particularly the aggregation of these preferences within a rational choice framework. Recent work by Dietrich and List, however, has sought formally to model the means by which reason-based deliberation enables actors rationally to revise their preferences, as a result of changes in their set of motivating reasons (Dietrich and List 2012, 2013, forthcoming). The basic premise of this work is that actors' preferences are not unchangeable (as standard rational choice theory assumes); instead, reason-based deliberation is a fundamentally important means by which these preferences change.

2.3 The Normative Merits of Deliberation: The Good, the Bad and the Irrelevant

2.3.1 The Good and the Bad

The merits of deliberation are not unambiguous, although on balance most analysts consider it to be a desirable, if not ideal, component of democratic governance. As such, the literature on deliberative democracy generally assumes that deliberation among citizens, representatives and public officials has beneficial outcomes, such as enhancing political legitimacy and stability (Mutz 2008: 523). As an extension to these benefits, deliberation is said to improve the quality of public policy, partly through reducing the likelihood of errors of analysis and judgment but also by increasing public spirit attitudes among public officials (Lascher 1996: 504; Bächtiger, Spörndli, et al. 2005: 153)—the latter by forcing them to characterize their intentions in terms of a public rather than private good.

For some, however, deliberation is not altogether a good thing, as it may well help to further widen and solidify the differences between actors (Sunstein 2003; Sunstein 2009) by focusing their attention on the depth of disagreement between them. For example, "(a) participant may conclude that 'if *this* is what is at stake, then I really disagree!'" (Knight and Johnson 1994: 286). In this case, deliberation may well exacerbate rather than resolve conflict among actors. Another literature on policy decision-making in small groups moreover argues that poorly executed deliberation may result in "groupthink" that, among other detrimental outcomes, may lead to deeply flawed policy decisions (Janis 1972, 1982; t'Hart 1990). We contend, however, that these negative assessments usually confine themselves to particular circumstances that may ultimately be correctable, in order to deliver the more desirable outcomes for deliberation. In the context of monetary policy, our presumption is that real deliberation is indeed desirable for the reasons proffered above.

2.3.2 The Irrelevant

FOMC

A third assessment of deliberation is that it is neither good nor bad, but rather is irrelevant to understanding the policy process and policy decision-making. Notably, authors do not always explicitly say that deliberation is irrelevant; more often they simply ignore it in favor of other factors. Turning first to the literature on monetary policy committees such as the FOMC, we discuss in our introductory chapter the limitations of the reduced-form approach to estimating interest rate decisions. For these models, deliberation is regarded as unnecessary to understanding the policy decision, because the authors believe that they capture adequately the determinants of policy outcomes over time by reference to a small number of quantifiable variables. Thus the focus is on estimating the average policy response of each committee member over his or her tenure on the committee.

Policy-settings (e.g., the interest rate target set by the FOMC) are typically used in reduced-form econometric analysis that seeks to explain the policy makers' reactions to key economic data, and so on. This has led to an industry estimating reaction functions or policy rules of various types (and these can be applied either at the level of the collective policy decision or to the preferences for policy of individual members) (Taylor 1993; Clarida, Gali, et al. 2000; Chappell, McGregor, et al. 2005). The problem with the rules-based approach is that while it can helpfully summarize fluctuations in interest rates, it cannot explain the policy formulation process, namely how policy makers react to particular shocks—since every shock is different and has a different source.[2] Put simply, policy makers will want to know why and how a particular shock has emerged before deciding on their reaction. In contrast, rules and reaction functions, because they are of necessity reduced-form, will be based on an average response to past shocks that have very different characteristics. At the collective and individual decision making level they can reveal points of difference from an average rule of policy, but they cannot tell us much about why those points of difference emerge. An alternative literature analyses optimal monetary policy (Fuhrer and Moore 1995; Levin, Wieland, et al. 1999; Rudebusch and Svensson 1999; Taylor 1999). The attraction of optimal rules is that they make explicit the objective function of the policy maker. But they can often perform poorly as a tool to explain what actually happened precisely because they are parameterized without reference to the actual evidence.

While the literature on rules and reaction functions may offer some empirical analysis of the macroeconomic variables that appear to influence policy makers' decisions, it tells us nothing about the process by which policy is made and very little about how policy changes occur. To the extent that these approaches examine the actual words of policy makers, it is done selectively and usually just for the purpose of coding interest rate preferences (Meade and Thornton 2012). In a recent article by Chappell, McGregor, and Vermilyea on the FOMC, deliberation is said to "have little effect on the quality of the Committee's decisions, possibly because all useful information is shared prior to the policy decision" (Chappell, McGregor, et al. 2012: 840). We address this in detail in chapter 3.

Congress
A second—and quite varied—literature on legislative decision-making does not necessarily explicitly argue for the irrelevance of deliberation. Once again, authors often simply remove it from consideration altogether. One reason is that there exists a long-standing bias against the empirical investigation of political "talk," and particularly deliberation within committee settings (Bächtiger, Spörndli, et al. 2005: 225). For whatever reason, the trajectory of much of the empirical literature in legislative studies has been in the direction of roll call votes, thereby giving rise to estimations of dimensionality in voting behavior or the role of constituency and partisan influences more generally (to name but a few, Peltzman 1984; Poole and Rosenthal 1997; Snyder and Groseclose 2000; Poole 2005). Nonetheless, empirical studies of deliberation (including the present study) have recently begun to establish a foothold (Steiner, Bächtiger, et al. 2004; Bächtiger, Spörndli, et al. 2005). It is not our intent to survey the legislative behavior literature here but rather to suggest some reasons why deliberation has often been overlooked as an important feature of decision-making by legislative scholars.

At a basic level, it is useful to begin with the incentives of members of Congress—in particular, what do senators and representatives strive to achieve as committee members? Generally, members of Congress are assumed to seek key political goals through committee activity, and among these, three are most important: (1) re-election (Mayhew 1974, 2000), (2) good public policy, and (3) influence within Congress (Fenno 1973).

There is no reason, a priori, to assume that by pursuing any or all of these goals, that legislators do not employ deliberation as one tool among many. Deliberation may, for example, be used to enhance the rationale given by a legislator as he takes a value position on a political issue, just as it may be used in the process of arriving at a judgment as to what constitutes good public policy. However, it is important to acknowledge the constraints on time and energy that legislators face in pursuing re-election; it may be that deliberation becomes too costly a tool (in terms of time) and is thereby discarded (Bessette 1994: 107). Specifically, it may be that the electoral payoff that derives from serious discourse on public policy is heavily outweighed by the electoral payoff from other activities like constituency service, pork barrel politics, and raising monies to finance future election campaigns. As Bessette comments, "(e)lectoral considerations have generated massive disincentives for the members of Congress to spend their time reasoning together about broad national concerns. The more efficient Congress has become as an engine for the reelection of its members, the less it bears the character of a deliberative institution . . ." (Bessette 1994: 64).

Nonetheless, there are also strong motivations for legislators to acquire the expertise and expend the time and energy to deliberate on public policy (e.g., sense of achievement, respect from colleagues and others), and thereby to think that deliberation is *not* irrelevant. In an empirical study on campaign contributions and expertise in congressional committees, Esterling finds another motivation for legislators to engage in deliberative discourse in committee settings—namely the financial contributions accruing from political action committees that recognize the value of diligent ("workhorse") members as opposed to superficial ("show horse") members (Esterling 2007: 93). In sum, the irrelevancy of deliberation is generally *assumed* by many legislative scholars, but this assumption is unwarranted. In the end, the irrelevancy or relevancy of deliberation (both in policy committee and legislative committee settings) is an empirical question and, as such, is one that motivates this study.

2.4 The Empirics of Motivations of Members of the FOMC and Congressional Banking Committees

2.4.1 FOMC

As an unelected and (in legal structure) politically independent body of policy makers, the motivations of FOMC members are conspicuously distinct from those of elected officials, as will be seen below. First, regardless of their backgrounds and methods of appointment (i.e., whether they are governors or reserve bank presidents), FOMC members are required to follow the legislative mandate for monetary policy. The existence of the dual mandate—which was modified in the 1970s—introduces scope for uncertainty over how each FOMC member forms a single preference at each meeting. Hence what members say in meetings (their arguments and discourse) offers a means to understand how FOMC members form their preferences in view of the dual mandate.

A second area of motivation concerns the intellectual framework under which FOMC members operate. That is, at any given time FOMC members do not, as a whole, appear to have embraced a single model of the US economy and thus monetary policy. Indeed successive chairmen have disavowed adherence to a single model and expressed strong skepticism on such models.[3] So, again, we contend that the arguments and verbal exchanges within the FOMC offer a means to understanding the formation and aggregation of preferences of members.

Finally, the literature on the FOMC indicates that, notably in the years before the Volcker Revolution of 1979, the FOMC was conscious of the threat (explicit or implicit) of political pressure being brought to bear on the committee. This pressure was rarely described explicitly in FOMC meetings, but insofar as it was implicit, we may learn something by studying the verbal interaction within the FOMC.

Given uncertainty surrounding interpretations of the dual mandate, the lack of a single model of the US economy and monetary policy and the sometimes implicit but rarely explicit interpretation of political pressure on the FOMC, there are strong reasons to expect that deliberation mattered for policy decision-making in the FOMC. As we have already alluded, however, very little work exists on deliberation within monetary policy committees. The most extensive theoretical and empirical examination of the value of discussion (broadly defined) in monetary policy committees is by Blinder (Blinder 2004; Blinder and Morgan 2005). Blinder and Morgan find empirical evidence to suggest that monetary policy decisions made by groups are on average better than those made by individuals and in his book, Blinder offers four reasons for this. Monetary policy made by committee decision, rather than by an individual, is (1) less volatile, (2) less likely to veer toward extremes, (3) allows for the pooling of knowledge, and (4) encourages the application of different heuristics for solving difficult problems. At its core, individual committee members may have different preferences with respect to inflation, different ideas (or models) for how the economy works, different forecasts that shape their views, and different ways of processing information and making decisions (Blinder 2004: 38–54).

And yet, this assessment of the benefits of committee decision-making is not based on the deliberative process, but rather on the aggregation and balancing of knowledge. It is about a pooling of a wider spectrum of information inputs and decision-making processes. Blinder does not explicitly or implicitly suggest that arguments wielded by one member might change the views of other members, as in a deliberative forum where argued reasoning is essential. Rather, his depiction of the committee decision-making process is more one of aggregating the judgments and knowledge of individual members.

There are two recent papers that do, however, seek to measure empirically the quantity and quality of deliberation in the FOMC (Meade and Stasavage 2008; Woolley and Gardner 2009). We defer a fuller review and discussion of the empirical contribution of these papers to chapter 3, but in the context of our present focus on deliberation we highlight some of their key aspects. Both papers seek to gauge the effect on deliberation stemming from a 1993 decision to publish the verbatim transcripts of the FOMC meeting discussions.[4] In short, did FOMC members change the way that they deliberated once they knew that their words would be made public in five years' time? Meade and Stasavage find that publication of the meeting transcripts *did* change deliberation while Woolley and Gardner find that *it did not* (though they do find that a longer-run change—predating 1993—was taking place). Neither study uses full textual analysis to measure the entirety of the verbatim transcripts (as we do in this book). Moreover both studies use restricted (and quite different) definitions of deliberation: for Meade and Stasavage, deliberation refers predominantly to the likelihood of members offering dissenting views, with no scope for capturing their thinking on the dual mandate, models of the US economy or other issues; for Woolley and Gardner, deliberation requires within meeting interaction and exchanges among members. The latter thus excludes the more realistic and subtle forms of deliberative discourse in which what is said by one member at a given meeting is subsequently reflected upon by another member, thereby giving rise to changes of views in subsequent meetings. We acknowledge the difficulties in capturing this broader and more dynamic form of deliberation with the use of any form of empirical analysis. Indeed this is a challenge that we reserve for a later chapter that relies on qualitative data from in-depth interviews with former FOMC members.

2.4.2   Congress
Building on the previous section, we review briefly the empirical work on the preferences of members of the House and Senate banking committees. As noted above, the three goals of re-election, good public policy and influence in Congress may all be relevant for members of

these committees, but gauging their relative importance has been constrained by the data; that is, the most extensive data produced by
committees—namely textual data in the form of hearings, testimony
and deliberations—remain largely untouched by empirical researchers.[5] Rather, studies that have sought to gauge committee members'
preferences usually employ ideological measures from roll call data,
using NOMINATE or ADA scores (Grier 1989, 1991; Krehbiel 1991; Cox
and McCubbins 1993; Londregan and Snyder 1994; Poole and Rosenthal 1997; Maltzman 1998; Young and Heitshusen 2003), or measures
of constituency characteristics (Shepsle 1978; Adler and Lapinski 1997;
Adler 2000, 2002). Positing that banking committees seek to influence
Fed policy, some studies have observed a correlation between the
liberal/conservative ranking of the chair of the Senate Banking Committee and the subsequent ease/tightening bias in monetary policy
(Grier 1991; Chopin, Cole, et al. 1996; Grier 1996)—which might reflect
the veto power of the Senate over appointments to the Fed Board.
However, other studies have not found this correlation (Beck 1990).

More recently Chang argues that senators do influence monetary
policy through their "advice and consent" privilege[6] with respect to
Board of Governor appointments, which constitute seven of the twelve
members of the FOMC.[7] However, her coding scheme (on which she
does not elaborate) relies on her own manual reading and codification
of the hearings, and is moreover limited to just the Senate hearings
from 1974 to 1995 (Chang 2003: 45).

More broadly, scholars of legislative committees often examine the
extent to which legislators seek membership on committees with jurisdictions that provide district-specific benefits, and thus strive to distribute benefits to their constituents through committee activity (Adler
2002). For committees like banking, district-specific benefits are not
always self-evident—particularly given the weak theoretical underpinnings for the distributional consequences of monetary policy, as discussed in subsequent chapters.[8]

Monetary policy has a number of unusual characteristics that are
likely to have some effect on the nature of congressional oversight.
First, over time the idea of the long-run neutrality of money and monetary policy has become better understood (likely this improvement in
understanding is due in part to the perceived success of monetary
policy in achieving stable low inflation). Neutrality here means that
monetary policy does not itself influence the long-run rate of growth
of the economy; rather, it is a necessary condition to allow other eco-

nomic policies to effect the long-run growth rate. Those other economic policies are typically in the direct control of government and politicians. But monetary policy can have a short-run impact on particular sectors of the economy as a necessary condition for achieving and maintaining low inflation and stable growth. Some authors suggest that legislators may seek to "shift-the-responsibility" for implementing tight monetary policy to the Fed in order to escape the inevitable electoral harm from groups and industries that might suffer from such a policy (Kane 1980; Fiorina 1982; Beck 1990), and indeed this motivation may well have prompted support for the initial establishment of the Federal Reserve in 1913 (Binder and Spindel 2011).

The second characteristic of monetary policy is that the benefits of low inflation are comprehensive in the sense that they diffuse to all agents in the economy. Members of Congress cannot expect to enjoy constituency-specific electoral benefits from a low inflation outcome, since "no member of Congress can claim credit for bringing down inflation" (Beck 1990: 135). Indeed Beck concludes that members of Congress remain largely inactive in monetary policy because they cannot claim credit for lowering interest rates. He further maintains that risk-averse legislators do not attempt to reform the Fed (e.g., by repealing the Fed's current control over its own budget or by exerting pressure on the Fed to engage in credit allocation) because of the uncertain electoral payoff (Beck 1990: 143). In this view, Congress gives the Fed a relatively free rein in making monetary policy. Whereas, in principle, Congress could reverse decisions of the Fed, remove Fed governors, or even dismantle the Fed, members of Congress have never opted to do so.

We are thus left in a quandary as to the motivations of legislators who conduct oversight hearings on monetary policy. In the end, legislators may pursue any number of goals in congressional banking committees (and, as we note, employ deliberation as a tool at the same time), but the empirical research has thus far produced mixed findings. For instance, active participation in committee discussions might reflect electoral, good public policy, or influence in the chamber objectives; or, a more passive stance in these discussions might simply indicate an electoral motivation that is risk-averse and thus satisfied with shifting the responsibility for implementing unpopular policy to the Fed.

In order to unpack and measure more precisely the goals of committee members, we require a better way to gauge their participation in these hearings—and for this, we turn to the actual words and arguments used by members. We do not assume that the words spoken in the committee hearings are inherently deliberative in content (i.e., we do not assume that merely by speaking, they are exhibiting reasoned argument). Rather, by measuring empirically the textual data, we aim to gauge the motivations of members and given these motivations, the tendency for their discourse to approximate (or not) what we construe as deliberation. Specifically, we use automated content analysis first to capture the thematic structure of the committee deliberations and second to identify tendencies of particular members to speak to specific themes (and possibly to avoid others). We maintain that the words and arguments of politicians should reflect their distinct sets of aims and objectives; consequently what legislators say should provide an indirect measure for their motivations as members of the House and Senate banking committees. As far as we know, this is the first *systematic* study of the verbatim transcripts of the oversight hearings of the banking committees and the Senate re-confirmation hearings.[9]

2.5   Our Expectations and Hypotheses

We began this chapter by outlining the different institutional committee settings of our study: the FOMC, which assesses and formulates monetary policy; the two congressional oversight committees, whose members question the Fed chairman on the Fed's Monetary Policy Report but do not make any formal decision on this report; and the Senate Banking Committee as it evaluates the past performance of the sitting Fed chairman and whose members then vote on the decision whether or not to reappoint him. Members of both the FOMC and the Senate Banking Committee are thus tasked with making a judgment— the first on monetary policy and the second on whether to reappoint the Fed chairman. In their oversight of the Monetary Policy Report, members of the two congressional committees are not responsible for coming to any final judgment—either as individuals or as a committee. Hence, if the essence of deliberation relies on reasoned argument and persuasion, it would be inappropriate to expect the same standard of deliberation to apply in settings where a final decision is required as compared to settings where such a decision is not required. This is not to say that there is no expectation of deliberation in oversight committee hearings, but rather that the link between reasoned argument and persuasion is less direct. Reasoned argument in oversight hearings may serve to enhance intellectual understanding of monetary policy and help committee members arrive at their own informal assessments of the Fed's level of success in this capacity (which may in turn have repercussions for policy decisions elsewhere and at other times), but it is not intended to *persuade* any particular member or outside audience as to the merits of a pending judgment or decision on monetary policy. (Committee members may, however, seek to persuade their colleagues or outside audiences on some other policy stance, unrelated to monetary policy. Persuasion in this sense has no direct link to deliberative discourse on monetary policy per se.)

Our expectations for our findings are therefore conditioned by the nature of the institutional setting, but our common denominator for all three settings is the presumption that *deliberation matters for policy makers and politicians in monetary policy decision-making (broadly defined).* Yet it is one thing to say that deliberation matters and another to specify how it matters and why it is important. In order to achieve the latter, we argue that one must begin with a comprehensive grasp of the content of the discussions, arguments, exchanges, and ideas expressed by all the participants of the committee meetings. Once this content is measured empirically, it can be dissected into analytical sections (e.g., among other techniques, statistical analysis may be used to assign arguments to particular actors, or attributes of actors) for more detailed examination. At the heart of this process is an unpacking and assessment of the content of the positions taken by actors, the extent to which the content of these positions approximates reasoned argument, and some overall assessment as to whether the reason-giving by one or more actors is understood and responded to by other actors (and, in settings requiring a final judgment, whether some persuasion ultimately occurs).

Our empirical approach to deliberation is unique in that our point of departure involves understanding the *content* of reasons given by actors, and to achieve this, we rely on automated textual analysis software. Such an approach is not uncontroversial, as some authors have (wrongly) assumed that this implies a mechanistic and robotic approach to deliberation. For instance, Steiner et al. criticize such an approach for its inability to interpret "the culture of the political institution, the context of the debate, and the nature of the issue under debate" and because, quite simply, the understanding and measurement of deliberation "requires careful human judgment" (Steiner, Bächtiger, et al. 2004: 60). Such assessments are, in our view, inherently misplaced for three reasons. First, they assume that researchers who apply textual analysis software do not at the same time possess a thorough understanding of the subject matter of the textual data. We maintain that the use of such software precisely in cases where the subject matter under investigation is well understood by the researchers can afford an excellent opportunity for the deeper empirical understanding of large amounts of textual data. Second, where such approaches allow investigators to examine textual data using a variety of different analytical and statistical techniques, they can enrich the understanding of the deliberative discourse by, in effect, enabling its investigation under different analytical lenses. Third, ideally textual analysis should not be relied on exclusively; rather, an investigation that complements this approach with other methods (e.g., as we do with in-depth elite interviews) should afford the opportunity to conduct implicit and explicit robustness checks on the data and analysis. So, in short, we contend that there are a variety of ways to study deliberation empirically. And, in our view, the empirical contribution of this study to the literature on deliberation stems from (1) our novel application of textual analysis software to measure the substance of reasoned arguments; (2) the examination of deliberation within a given issue area—monetary policy— but by different sets of national actors (policy makers versus politicians) and in different institutional settings (the Federal Reserve and Congress); and (3) the multiple method approach, using textual analysis, further statistical analysis, and extensive in-depth interviews as a means to cross-check and challenge our conclusions. (Moreover our book appendix IV conducts a further robustness check on the textual analysis by checking our results against two other automated content analysis software packages.)

Thus, in our empirical analysis of the congressional banking committee hearings and the FOMC transcripts, we do not assume that by simply speaking, politicians and policy makers are deliberating; rather, we anticipate finding some elements of what we define as deliberation within their speeches. How much or how little deliberation is unknown a priori. Specifically,

We anticipate finding some evidence of reason-giving, using both information and arguments, and given these reasons, we expect to find that some members are subsequently persuaded by the arguments of their colleagues [hypothesis 1].

As noted above, this requires dissecting the data in a number of stages, and using a variety of analytical lenses through which to measure and understand the themes, arguments, conceptualization of theoretical and quantitative data, and ultimately the motivations of the participants of the various committees. Only once these tasks are completed can we begin to analyze the extent to which it might be said that politicians and policy makers actually deliberated on monetary policy.

We focus in particular on three issue areas: (1) the *quality of deliberations* in committee meetings; (2) the effect that *transparency* has had on deliberations; and (3) *institutional features* that enable or constrain deliberations in committees. For our purposes, quality pertains to the extent to which committee discussions consist of argued reasoning and a reasonably frank exchange of differing views, information and judgments. For the FOMC, this includes whether the speeches were mostly pre-prepared "canned" ones, or whether members felt at liberty to offer impromptu statements and assessments; and more broadly, whether committee discussions altered their views in any way in response to the arguments of their colleagues. For Congress, quality of deliberation is interpreted by the extent to which members of Congress actually sought to understand and/or discuss monetary policy. Evidence of other nonmonetary policy issues encroaching on their discourse would, in our view, constitute a lower quality of deliberation on monetary policy.

Transparency is a multi-faceted issue that, as we allude above, has been a particular focus for the FOMC. Among other aspects we examine whether the 1993–94 decision to release the transcripts for publication lessened deliberation within the meetings, and if so, how. For Congress, we attempt to gauge the more gradual trend over time to publicize hearings on monetary policy, and the effect that this may have had on the integral content of discussions on monetary policy.

For institutional features within the FOMC, *we contend that deliberative discourse can be influenced by*

1. *the **procedures and rules** of the institution (including the rules surrounding the transparency of its proceedings) [hypothesis 2];*

2. *the **membership** of the committee, which changes over time and particularly the personality and reputation of the chairman [hypothesis 3]; and*

3. *the **environment** in which the committee is operating at any given time (notably the clarity of understanding of the objective of policy and the perceived success of the operation of policy) [hypothesis 4].*

With respect to Congress, a number of hypotheses are suggested from the empirical literature on deliberation in legislatures. From their study of parliamentary deliberation in four countries (Germany, Switzerland, the United Kingdom, and the United States) (Steiner, Bächtiger, et al. 2004), Steiner and co-authors propose a number of test-able hypotheses for assessing if and when "political talk" influences political outcomes (Steiner, Bächtiger, et al. 2004). Their approach relies on a "theoretical" selection of key debates in particular issue categories. These debates are then manually coded according to pre-specified criteria.

Three of the hypotheses for which they find support are of particular relevance to our study of banking committee members. First, they hypothesize that the quality of deliberation in the second chamber (Senate) is higher than in first chamber (House) (Steiner, Bächtiger, et al. 2004: 87, 127–28)—a finding for which Mucciaroni and Quirk (2006) also find support, and for much the same reasons: second chambers are generally designed to give more thorough examination to policy proposals, their members typically have more extensive prior political experience, and are elected for longer terms (which reduces the elec-toral incentive). Moreover the number of members in second chambers is smaller, which lessens constraints on speaking time, enhances closer working relationships, and promotes stronger "civility" norms. Other reasons for higher quality deliberation by senators include lower party cohesion in the Senate relative to the House, which allows more scope for cross-party coalitions, and larger constituencies for senators, which creates crosscutting pressures (among groups, sectors, etc.) that appear to favor more open debate. With respect to monetary policy specifically, senators might be expected to deliberate more carefully since they— unlike their House colleagues—oversee Fed appointments to the Board of Governors. Adapted for this study,

We should expect the reasoning skills and judgments of senatorial banking com-mittee members to outweigh those of their House colleagues [hypothesis 5].

Second, Steiner et al. characterize legislative committees as non–public arenas and chamber debates as public, with the former expected to exhibit a higher quality of deliberation than the latter. This builds on the debate between the merits of secrecy in deliberation (i.e., behind closed doors) and the value of conducting "Government-in-the-Sunshine" (e.g., televised hearings) (Bessette 1994: 223–24). Secrecy is said to make for better deliberation by allowing legislators to engage in frank and honest discussion, away from the glare of publicity; yet, for others, transparent deliberation forces legislators to defend their positions in public, thereby making their arguments more considered and less self-centered (Chambers 2005: 257).

Steiner et al. contend that in committee settings, legislators are less exposed to external influences (thereby less pressured to adhere to the demands of constituents); and smaller "face-to-face" arenas also enable legislators better to reflect on issues and possibly change their opinions, to show respect for the views of colleagues, and to create working friendships. All these factors enhance mutual trust and thereby "lubricate the deliberative process" (Steiner, Bächtiger, et al. 2004: 88). Their findings suggest clear differences in deliberation between public and non–public arenas: legislators tend to employ discourse in public in order to "score points" with citizens, and in so doing, they tend to appeal to the common good with well-crafted arguments. In non–public settings, legislators craft their statements more toward their colleagues who, as policy experts, do not require elaborate explanatory arguments (Steiner, Bächtiger, et al. 2004: 131).

While on the whole, committees are no doubt less public than floor debates, the formal legality of monetary policy hearings in Congress (as prescribed by the 1978 legislation), alongside the frequent televised coverage of these hearings, makes them more public than other more mundane congressional hearings. One need only reflect on the media coverage of Alan Greenspan to accept that these committees are known to the American public and, as such, allow scope for legislators to "take stands" and at the extreme, even grandstand, as in the cases of Congressman (and subsequently, Senator) Bernie Sanders, Congressman Alan Grayson, or Congressman Ron Paul—all of whom enjoy YouTube celebrity status for their performances at banking committee hearings.

Our study does not provide us with a direct comparison between the deliberations of legislators on monetary policy in banking committees and equivalent deliberations in floor debates; however,

We suspect that committee hearings on monetary policy may exhibit a mixture of both public discourse and non–public discourse—that is, we expect to find both point-scoring on popular and high-profile issues, along with exchanges with experts on the details of monetary policy [hypothesis 6].

A third hypothesis from Steiner's work concerns political polarization and deliberation. While some authors have argued that deliberation may itself produce polarization, with members of the deliberative group moving to more extreme positions (Sunstein 2003, 2009), we do not explore this possibility. Like Steiner and his colleagues, we consider

polarization as exogenous to the discourse in monetary policy committee hearings. Steiner et al. posit that nonpolarized issues exhibit better
quality discourse among legislators than polarized issues (Steiner,
Bächtiger, et al. 2004: 89). Polarization is defined in terms of the ide-
ational, or ideological dimension (Poole and Rosenthal 1997; Fiorina,
Abrams, et al. 2005; McCarty, Poole, et al. 2006), but with a large degree
of variance among issues. Nonpolarized issues are those for which
elites agree on key values, while on polarized issues, elites display
sharp disagreements (Steiner, Bächtiger, et al. 2004: 89). As one might
expect, legislators interact more cooperatively on nonpolarized issues,
where they agree on core values.

Applied to monetary policy, the effect of polarization on deliberations in committee hearings is ambiguous. On the one hand, strong
evidence suggests that across the ideological spectrum, Congress has
become far more polarized in the past 30 years (Poole and Rosenthal
1997; McCarty, Poole, et al. 2006), and so we might expect more disagreement among committee members. On the other hand, the consensus among policy experts on the primacy of monetary policy for
economic stabilization and the focus on the end goal of low inflation
gained widespread and international acceptance during this same time
period (Bean 2007; Goodfriend 2007), and so we might expect to find
more agreement among legislators on the underlying objectives of
monetary policy. In short, we have two opposing influences on the
thinking of committee members: (1) the effect of ideological and partisan polarization within Congress as a whole and (2) pressure from the
Fed, underpinning the merits of stable low inflation (and central bank
independence) as the basis for economic stabilization. If there is one
fundamentally important test for the role of argued reasoning (deliberation) on policy decision-making, this is it. To what extent, then, were
members of Congress persuaded by the Fed's insistence on the primacy
of monetary policy, with the corollary role of an independent central
bank? This gives rise to our next hypothesis:

*On balance, we anticipate a greater influence for the new consensus surround-
ing monetary policy (and less of an influence for ideological or partisan polarization) and expect to find some evidence for the progression toward this
consensus among legislators over time [hypothesis 7].*

For convenience, we list a summary of our hypotheses[10] in table 2.1.

Table 2.1
Expected findings for empirical analysis

For the FOMC, House and Senate Oversight Hearings, and Senate Re-Confirmation Hearings	We anticipate finding some evidence of reason-giving, using both information and arguments, and given these reasons, we expect to find that some members are subsequently persuaded by the arguments of their colleagues [hypothesis 1].
For the FOMC, we contend that deliberative discourse can be influenced by	(1) the **procedures and rules** of the institution (including the rules surrounding the transparency of its proceedings) [hypothesis 2];
	(2) the **membership** of the committee, which changes over time and particularly the personality and reputation of the chairman [hypothesis 3]; and
	(3) the **environment** in which the committee is operating at any given time (notably the clarity of understanding of the objective of policy and the perceived success of the operation of policy) [hypothesis 4].
For Congress	We should expect the reasoning skills and judgments of senatorial banking committee members to outweigh those of their House colleagues [hypothesis 5].
	We suspect that committee hearings on monetary policy may exhibit a mixture of both public discourse and non–public discourse—that is, we expect to find both point-scoring on popular and high-profile issues, along with exchanges with experts on the details of monetary policy [hypothesis 6].
	On balance, we anticipate a greater influence for the new consensus surrounding monetary policy (and less of an influence for ideological or partisan polarization) and expect to find some evidence for the progression toward this consensus among legislators over time [hypothesis 7].

3   Deliberation in the FOMC

PART ONE—FROM 1979 TO 1999

3.1   Introduction

In this chapter we use the transcript records of the FOMC to assess the contribution of deliberation by individual members within the committee setting as a means to cast light on the fundamental transformation of monetary policy in the United States over the last 30 years. This period has seen the emergence of a strong consensus worldwide around establishing and maintaining persistent low inflation as the appropriate goal of monetary policy. The experience of the United States is quite typical in this respect, with the shift to a consistent pursuit of low inflation starting with the so-called Volcker Revolution in 1979, followed by the disinflation of the 1980s and the subsequent entrenchment of low inflation.

We seek to explain how monetary policy changed and likewise how the change was sustained and became a record of persistent low inflation. There are two parts to this chapter. The first part uses a sample of transcripts taken from a 20-year period starting in 1979 to identify changes over time in the form and content of deliberation in the FOMC. The second part of the chapter focuses in more detail on two events: First, the decisive break with high inflation made by Paul Volcker in 1979 and how he sustained the change through the difficulties of the next two years. Second, the reversal of earlier interest rate cuts during 1999 as an example of a change in the cycle of monetary policy in the low inflation era. We use these two case studies to explore in more detail the role of the deliberative process in the FOMC.

In both parts of this chapter, we find evidence that relates to hypotheses 1 through 4, as set out in our previous chapter. These include evidence of reason-giving and strategies of persuasion (hypothesis 1); and evidence that deliberative discourse was influenced by the procedures of the FOMC, particularly the rules surrounding transparency (hypothesis 2); membership of the committee, including the role of the chairman (hypothesis 3); and the environment in which the committee operated—particularly the clarity of its policy objective. We reserve our discussion of our findings as they pertain to these hypotheses to a final section, which follows both substantive portions of this chapter.

In sum, we seek to explain, drawing on the transcripts of its meetings, how the FOMC broke out of the failures of the 1970s. The challenge is how to undertake a systematic assessment of what is a body of text as opposed to a numerical dataset. We undertake this using full text analysis software.

3.2   Identifying the Preferences of Policy Makers toward Inflation

A large body of literature is devoted to observing and explaining the preferences of central banks toward setting monetary policy. Traditionally central banks did not state their goal(s) in explicit terms, and were not noted for the clarity of their communication, so the literature seeks to determine what preferences can be deduced from their actions. In contrast, more central banks now set out a quantitative goal, often a target for the rate of inflation. In this mode of operation, the literature devoted to revealing the preferences of policy makers tends to focus on assessing their behavior in returning the target measure to its stated goal (typically closing the inflation gap in an inflation targeting regime) and thereby determining their preference for stabilizing inflation versus stabilizing output. (Examples of this literature include (Sargent 1999; Taylor 1999; Clarida, Gali, et al. 2000; Cogley and Sargent 2001).

This choice of preference(s) can be summarized as a measure of inflation persistence.[1] Here we define inflation persistence to be the long-run effect of a shock to inflation—for a shock that raises inflation now by, say, 1 percent, by how much do we expect it to be higher at some future date and how long will it take to return to its previous level (Pivetta and Reis 2006). As a measurement tool it plays a useful role in explanations of the movement from an era of high inflation in the 1970s to one of low inflation in the 1990s. However, it is only a summary indicator, and the challenge for this literature has been that, particularly in a regime with no explicit quantitative target (e.g., the

United States, which instead has the unquantified mandate given to the Fed in legislation), there are multiple unstated variables at work. These can include the variation over time in the preference of the central bank for stabilizing inflation *and* output, changes over time in the target variable(s) at which the stabilization is aimed, and structural changes in the core parameters of the economy (e.g., the natural rate of unemployment).

The monetary history of the United States has provided fertile ground for explanations of the shift to low inflation for at least two reasons. First, the US record points to a high persistence of inflation in the later 1960s and 1970s, which is associated with a relatively strong preference among policy makers to stabilize output and thus accommodate the (upward) shocks to inflation. Preferences (as assessed by the change in the stance of policy) appeared to change very abruptly in 1979 when Paul Volcker assumed the chairmanship of the Federal Reserve and the period since then is characterized by a disinflation and then stabilization at a low level of inflation persistence.

But this apparent change in preferences begs a whole series of very important questions concerning why and how it happened. The fact that the modern consensus confirms the benefits of persistent low inflation does not alone explain why, how and when the Federal Reserve arrived at that conclusion (or at least it can only do so by assuming that at a particular moment in time "the light came on"). To answer these questions, we need better methods to assess the preferences of policy makers.

In particular, better methods are required to explain why and how the behavior of monetary policy makers changed over time (sometimes abruptly at one meeting as in 1979, sometimes over a number of meetings as in 1999). One school of thought seeks to explain such changes in terms of learning by policy makers, namely that learning from the mistakes of the past induces changes in preferences and thus the policy stance (Sargent, Williams, et al. 2004; Primiceri 2005). This has been fertile ground for modeling, but it still begs important questions around how it happened and why at a particular time. In particular, for an abrupt change such as 1979, was it a product of changes in leadership at the Fed? Was it due to the "technology" of analysis and policy implementation that changed the ability of the FOMC to determine and achieve a goal of low inflation persistence? Or, was there a role for deeper changes in social norms toward inflation and output/employment stabilization? Was there some change in political preferences that enabled a change in monetary policy? Any or all of these potential explanations may hold merit.

Prima facie, there is some support for all of these explanations. Studies have estimated inflation persistence under different chairmen of the Fed. Beechey and Österholm introduce dummy variables for chairmen into their analysis (Beechey and Österholm 2007). They find that during the Martin chairmanship (1955 to 1970) the Federal Reserve's implied target for headline CPI was slightly lower but not significantly different than under Greenspan. But it rose substantially (by four percentage points and more) during the Burns and Miller periods (1970 to August 1979). The subsequent Volcker era (1979 to 1987) saw a substantial decrease, to a level statistically indistinguishable from the Martin–Greenspan eras. But this alone does not prove that "it was the chairmen that did it," not least because monetary policy is the product of the deliberation of a committee (in this case the FOMC). The so-called Volcker Revolution of 1979 lends itself to a direct study of the "why and how" preferences changed because it appeared to be an abrupt and discrete change in policy. But it is likely to be harder to identify the contribution of a chairman to a change in preferences that takes place more gradually (e.g., insofar as these affect the degree of accommodation of supply shocks in the economy and the preference of policy makers for opportunistic disinflation; see Kuttner 2004; Kozicki and Tinsley 2005). Nonetheless, we attempt to identify the role played by Alan Greenspan in 1999 in the context of his well-known advocacy of the productivity shock in the US economy.

Evidence is available to support the view that changes in preferences toward monetary policy reflect changes in the technology of modeling, analysis and policy implementation. Monetary policy is now typically founded on New Keynesian models, which have improved the depiction of price- and wage-setting behavior in the economy and of the process by which economic agents form expectations about the future. But if better tools make better policy, exactly how does this process work and by how much does it make a difference? A complication here is that the history of the FOMC indicates an aversion among successive chairmen (and other, but not all, members of the FOMC) to viewing policy through the lens of a formal economic model. As such, formal models were viewed with skepticism, which was not unfounded. Skepticism of formal models fostered a more eclectic but judicious use of discretion at times when monetary policy was regarded as credible and well anchored in terms of the long-run goal of low inflation. But when policy was not viewed as credible and anchored to a long-run objective, the eclectic approach could be damaging insofar as it supported an inconsistent or "stop–go" approach (as in the 1970s).

It is sensible to relax the definition of a model used here to encompass a looser concept in which policy makers have an organizing framework(s)—"model(s)"—that they use to organize their thinking on how the pieces of the story on the economy and monetary policy fit together and that embody a small number of key principles and relationships given by economic theory. Moreover, since we are looking at a period in which monetary policy in the United States became better anchored to the long-run goal, and thus more credible, it is possible that policy makers reduced the level of their uncertainty over the "model" of the economy that they used to form policy and that this has enabled better policy-setting (not least because one important aspect of lower "model" uncertainty is a better understanding of the impact of the policy-setting itself on the expectations of agents in the economy). Thus, for instance, policy makers may have become less uncertain about the natural rate of unemployment in the economy. But, of course, if we accept the "better tools make better policy" approach, one is unable to account for the low level of inflation persistence in the 1950s and early 1960s, during which other forces must have been at work.

Did societal changes in attitudes toward inflation and output/ employment stabilization provide the backdrop to the successes and failures of policy? In a lecture delivered after leaving the office of Federal Reserve chairman, Arthur Burns set out "The Anguish of Central Banking" (Burns 1979, 1987). Burns acknowledged at the start of the lecture that despite their antipathy to inflation and "the powerful weapons they could wield against it" (p. 7), central bankers had failed utterly in their mission to control it. The analysis put forward by Burns of this failure rested on policy makers having overlooked the fundamental "persistent inflationary bias that has emerged from the philosophic and political currents that have been transforming economic life in the United States and elsewhere since the 1930s" (p. 9). Burns went on to argue that the New Deal and post–New Deal commitment to maximum or full employment and the expanding role of government regulation as a means to protect particular interest groups against competition (farm price supports, minimum wages, import quotas) fatally undermined the objective of maintaining stable low inflation. Burns characterized this as inducing "secular inflation" (p. 14). What, then, was the role of the central bankers?[2] The explanation that Burns proffered was that they too, despite having the power and tools to deal with the problem, were "caught up in the philosophic and political currents that were transforming American life and culture" (p. 15). More pointedly, he stated that "some members of the Federal Reserve family had themselves been touched by the allurements of the New Economics" (p. 15) and that to act otherwise would have meant that the Federal Reserve would have been "frustrating the will of Congress to which it was responsible" (p. 16). Burns went on to argue that while the FOMC did act to restrain inflation (in 1966, 1969, and 1974), it did not sustain that action for long enough because "it repeatedly evoked violent criticism from both the Executive establishment and the Congress and therefore had to devote much of its energy to warding off legislation that could destroy any hope of ending inflation. This testing process necessarily involved political judgments, and the Federal Reserve may at times have overestimated the risks attaching to additional monetary restraint" (p. 16).

Burns described monetary theory as a controversial area that did "not provide central bankers with decision rules that are at once firm and dependable" (p. 17). Central bankers could make errors at practically every stage of the process of making monetary policy, but "their capacity to err has become larger in our age of inflation" (p. 18) because agents no longer took it for granted that a higher level of inflation would be followed by a correction once a recession got under way. The conclusion for Burns was that the practical capacity for central bankers to curb "an inflation that is continually driven by political forces is very limited" (p. 21). Nonetheless, he saw signs of hope, that in the United States "a great majority of the public now regard inflation as the Number One problem facing the country and this judgment is accepted by both the Congress and the Executive establishment" (p. 23).

The Burns analysis had something for everyone in terms of arguments to support the various possible explanations for the behavior of preferences toward monetary policy. Meltzer comments that "[c]onsistency was not Burns's strength" (Meltzer 2009: 880). At the heart is an argument that broader societal and hence political pressures combined with the development of economic ideas to influence policy-setting in ways that could override the institutional structure (and thus the statutory independence of the central bank). Combined with this overarching assessment was an argument that the quality of the analytical toolkit of the monetary policy maker was inadequate to offset these pressures.

The continuing puzzle over how the shift in policy emerged survives even after allowing for the substantial literature on "How Alan Greenspan did it," in the sense of how he entrenched the shift to disinflationary policy established by Paul Volcker (e.g., Mankiw 2001; Blinder and Reis 2005). The 1990s were notable not just for a low average level of inflation but also for low volatility of inflation (substantially lower than the 1950s, the previous period of low inflation). Moreover the volatility of GDP growth in the US economy was substantially lower in the 1990s than in any other postwar decade. Studies of the period indicate that compared to the 1970s, the Federal Reserve responded more aggressively in terms of moving interest rates to a given move in inflation. And this response is consistent with the much lower volatility of interest rates in the 1990s, since it appears that economic agents started to adjust their expectations to assume a more aggressive response by the FOMC, which tended to damp future inflation and create a virtuous circle of policy (thus preemptive behavior worked).

A number of other theories have been put forward to support the success of the 1990s: that the Clinton administration made better appointments to the Fed Board (i.e., better economists were appointed)[3]; that it adopted a more prudent fiscal policy that finally established monetary policy as the tool of macroeconomic stabilization; that it refrained from commenting on monetary policy and more generally intervening in a way that bolstered the independence of the Federal Reserve, and thus its credibility in monetary policy; and that the FOMC, and Alan Greenspan in particular, became much more intense and thus better at reading the information and data on developments in the economy (Mankiw 2001).

This is the sort of list that would have made Arthur Burns forgo his anguish, but it begs a number of unanswered questions. What contribution and influence did these smarter governors of the Fed bring to the FOMC table? How did better fiscal policy feature in the monetary policy-making process? How did the decline of political comment bolster the credibility of the Fed? Did the FOMC shift gears in terms of its reading of the data on the economy and did this make a meaningful contribution to reducing uncertainty on the model of the economy?

A complication in describing the Greenspan era is the tendency to characterize policy making as discretionary in the sense that it reacted meeting by meeting to the news received during the intervening period.

Two quotations from Greenspan (in 2004 and 2003, respectively) aptly describe this approach (Blinder and Reis 2005: 7–8):

The economic world . . . is best described by a structure whose parameters are continuously changing. The channels of monetary policy, consequently, are changing in tandem. An ongoing challenge for the Federal Reserve . . . is to operate in a way that does not depend on a fixed economic structure based on historically average coefficients.

Some critics have argued that [the Fed's] approach to policy is too undisciplined—judgmental, seemingly discretionary, and difficult to explain. The Federal Reserve should, some conclude, attempt to be more formal in its operations by tying its actions solely to the prescriptions of a formal policy rule. That any approach along these lines would lead to an improvement in economic performance, however, is highly doubtful.

We return to the interpretation of discretion in the Greenspan period later in the chapter. In summary, we conclude that there is a lot more to understanding the shifts in monetary policy in the United States than can be revealed by statistical analysis and associated modeling (good though that can be) alone. At root, as with any policy-making function, we want to know what policy makers were doing, and why and how they were doing it.

3.3   The Limitations of Previous Empirical Studies of the FOMC

Commentators on monetary policy-making too easily lapse into talking in dichotomous terms of "easy" or "tight" and of policy makers as "hawks" or "doves." In contrast, policy makers do not tend to talk in these terms. The tendency to focus on the loose:tight dimension may be the product of a theoretical framework derived from spatial voting theory, overreliance on votes as the source of information on the preferences of policy makers, or some combination of the two.

The focus of our interest is on the "why" and "how" of the change in the preferences of FOMC members toward inflation persistence and the emergence of a credible commitment to low inflation. We are not of the view that a single dimension—namely a yes/no vote on a proposition for a monetary policy-setting—can provide the most useful framework in which to examine this change.

Voting records oversimplify the decision-making process. The preferences of FOMC members are likely to be captured only in part by the votes, as others have noted (Meade 2005). In the FOMC dissenting votes are infrequent. As Chappell et al. record, between 1966 and 1996 there were only 262 dissents in the FOMC out of 3339 voting observations (7.8 percent of votes were dissents). Of these dissents, 177 were for tighter policy and 85 were for easing (voting does not of course capture the preferences of the nonvoting members of the FOMC who nonetheless play a full part in the deliberation process in FOMC meetings and express their preferences). Meade and Stasavage note that the proportion of dissenting votes during the Greenspan period declined after 1993, as did the frequency of voiced disagreements in FOMC meetings by voting members but not nonvoting bank presidents (Meade and Stasavage 2008). They link these patterns of behavior to the decision by the FOMC to publish the transcripts of FOMC meetings. Prima facie, it seems odd to argue that publication of the transcripts leads to a change in behavior among voting but not nonvoting members of the FOMC, since the transcripts reveal the positions taken by all members whether they were voting or not. Also, viewed over time there is no such thing as a purely voting and nonvoting member when it comes to the reserve bank presidents since they rotate the voting roles (except for the New York president). So, in terms of a model of reputation that must be built up over the longer run given the delay in publishing the transcripts, it seems hard to argue that publication changed the behavior of voting but not nonvoting members.

Meade and Stasavage identify that a cause of the change in behavior of FOMC members toward dissenting could be the growing reputation of the chairman. They do not, however, consider whether the cause could also lie in changes to the broader environment of monetary policy (greater clarity on the objective of policy and greater apparent success in achieving that objective) (Meade and Stasavage 2008: 705–706).

We agree with Blinder et al., Chappell et al., and Meade that dissenting in the FOMC is too crude as a threshold for capturing preferences, and that dissents only record the preference of the member relative to the preference of the committee as a whole. Moreover we cannot be sure that the institutional framework did not act to regulate dissenting (a certain amount of dissenting is allowable under the rules of engagement, but not more). Nor can we be confident that changes in the framework of accountability and transparency (notably the publication of votes) have not affected the behavior of policy makers (Chappell, McGregor, et al. 2005). As Chappell and his co-authors note, "even when there are disagreements within the Committee, evidence of these disagreements may not show up in voting records." Meade shows that in the majority of instances revealed by the verbatim meeting records where members of the FOMC disagree with the chairman in the meeting, they do not dissent from the chairman's position in the vote (Meade 2005). Blinder et al. suggest strong internal pressure for votes to agree with the chairman's policy proposal, which likewise suggests that the voting records do not provide an accurate portrayal of the discourse of the FOMC (Blinder, Goodhart, et al. 2001).

A number of authors (Chappell, McGregor, et al. 2005; Meade and Sheets 2005; Meade and Stasavage 2008) examine FOMC transcripts in a limited fashion,[4] and with the risk of unavoidable subjectivity in the manual coding of transcript data (a problem that our methodology avoids). Systematic textual analysis ought to reveal more on the role of deliberation in the FOMC. As an example of the questions we ask, the FOMC comprises two groups of members—board governors appointed by the president and confirmed by the Senate Banking Committee, and reserve bank presidents appointed by their local boards subject to the agreement of the board chairman. An obvious question therefore, when examining how policy has been made by the FOMC, is to consider whether we can observe differences between the behavior of the two groups. Using textual analysis of what was said in FOMC meetings, we do this by incorporating a coding scheme that allows us to distinguish between the two groups of members. Our third hypothesis—which posits that deliberation can be influenced by the membership of the committee—is relevant here. We may expect to find some difference in the discourse of board governors versus that of bank presidents. One reason for this expectation is that in the late 1970s the reserve banks were typically ahead of the board governors in seeking to slow inflation (Meltzer 2009: 911). From their derivation of individual reaction functions for the period 1966 to 1996 (but excluding the Volcker period), Chappell et al. conclude that governors systematically on average favored more expansionary policy than bank presidents (Chappell, McGregor, et al. 2005: 184). Notably, these authors are unable to derive reaction functions for the Volcker period because they cannot compute a simple dependent variable, namely the policy preference expressed in a single numerical form.[5] The Volcker period was characterized by a more complex framework of operating target(s), but one that we can capture in our approach.

In sum, monetary policy made in a committee setting like the FOMC involves the aggregation of individual preferences of policy makers into a collective decision. Blinder has emphasized that this form of decision-making is distinctly different from a single individual maximizing a well-defined preference function. Moreover the greater emphasis placed over time on the accountability of policy makers for their actions, in pursuit of which the transparency of the policy-making process and outcome has been emphasized, indicates that we should give more attention to understanding how the process of aggregating individual preferences works. In other words, we should look more at the role of deliberation and how policy is made in order to understand the aggregation of preferences. This requires going beyond reduced form econometric estimation based on voting or some other summary indicator of the final preferences of policy makers.

3.3.1   A Closer Look at the Votes of Board Governors and Reserve Bank Presidents

Notwithstanding these reservations over voting records, we have used the Chappell et al. scores to compute simple statistics to demonstrate their result that reserve bank presidents were on average less likely to favor expansionary monetary policy. We have split their data into the Burns and Greenspan periods. We have also separated the two methods used by Chappell et al. in response to criticisms of voting records to compute the dependent variable in their reaction functions. The first uses voting records from FOMC meetings, specifically an aggregation of dissenting votes to compute a "net ease/tighten" measure for each member. The second is derived from their reading of the transcripts that they turn into a coding system.[6] This use of the transcripts is different to ours, since Chappell et al. use the narrative to derive a single measure of preference for each member rather than to explain how policy came to be formed. Their approach also differs from ours in that it uses an econometric approach (ordered probit) to derive preferences for "easing and tightening" based on a reading of the transcripts that uses control variables related to the state of the economy and the stance of monetary policy over time. Our approach has been agnostic to what constitutes "easy" and "tight."

In table 3.1 we compute the distribution of FOMC members according to Chappell et al.'s score of "Rank by net ease–dissent frequency" (defined as dissents for ease by a member minus dissents for tightness

Table 3.1
Distribution of FOMC members according to Chappell et al. (2005) "Rank by net ease-dissent frequency"

	Governors	Presidents	All
Burns period			
All: Voting (net ease scores), n = 50			
Median	19.50	31.00	19.50
Mean	19.98	29.18	25.50
All: Transcripts (reaction functions), n = 34			
Median	15.00	21.00	17.50
Mean	15.00	19.25	17.50
Greenspan period			
All: Voting (net ease scores), n = 33			
Median	13.50	13.50	13.50
Mean	13.85	19.05	17.00
All: Transcripts (reaction functions), n = 30			
Median	9.00	19.00	15.50
Mean	10.09	18.63	15.50

Note: Scores are rank orders. Scores for the Burns and Greenspan periods cannot be directly compared because of the different sample sizes.

divided by the total votes of that member) (Chappell, McGregor, et al. 2005: 42–45, 88–89). A sizable proportion of the rank scores is the same, reflecting those FOMC members who did not dissent. In the Burns period, the center comprises 28 percent of FOMC members, while in the Greenspan period this rises to 55 percent, since there were fewer dissents in the Greenspan era. In both the Burns and Greenspan periods a larger number of members have an average dissent on the net tightening than the net loosening side. In the Burns period, the distribution is 12 below the nondissenting center (which is 14 members) and 24 above it; in the Greenspan period the figures are 4 below, 18 in the center, and 11 above it. In the Burns period, 48 percent of FOMC members are on the dissenting to net tightening side, while, in the Greenspan period, it falls to 33 percent. The corresponding scores for the net loosening members are 24 percent in the Burns period and 12 percent in the Greenspan period. The picture is therefore similar in that in both periods the net tightening side was larger than the net loosening side, but the Greenspan period differs in having a much larger nondissenting center.

In both periods reserve bank presidents are distributed more on the net tightening side of the central tendency and board governors correspondingly on the net loosening side. In the Chappell et al. sample, governors account for 79 percent of ease dissents, while presidents account for 68 percent of tightness dissents. This conclusion is consistent with a largely older literature on voting behavior in the FOMC (Yohe 1966; Canterbery 1967; Puckett 1984; Woolley 1984; Beldon 1989; Havrilesky and Schweitzer 1990; Havrilesky and Gildea 1991; Chappell, Havrilesky, et al. 1993; McGregor 1996; Chang 2003). These studies typically went further in their analysis to identify the distribution of votes according to the party of the appointing president (for governors) and educational/career background (economists versus the rest). For instance, in their sample Chappell et al. identify that 74 percent of the dissents by governors appointed by a Democrat president were for ease compared with 48 percent of dissents being for ease by governors appointed by a Republican president (Chappell, McGregor, et al. 2005). We do not pursue these extensions in our work for a number of reasons. First, while the older literature had a strong presumption that administrations influenced the Fed, this literature pre-dated the emergence of a broadly based consensus around persistent low inflation as the objective of monetary policy. That consensus is not a matter of party politics in its foundations, and so in seeking to understand how this consensus emerged, we do not put an emphasis on a partisan explanation. On its own this assertion arguably would not be enough. But our second concern about the partisan approach is that the econometric results and evidence are not convincing. Chappell et al. point to the example of governors appointed by Reagan seeking to hold down interest rates in the election year of 1988 and the disagreements with reserve bank presidents in the FOMC during that year. They conclude that although they can produce statistically significant results for the party affiliation of governors, the Reagan period is a clear outlier. This contributes to our skepticism, as does the very limited statistical significance of Chappell et al.'s results, which test the outcomes of FOMC decisions according to the party of the administration (Chappell, McGregor, et al. 2005: 40–49).

We return to the analysis of governors versus presidents later to apply our own results to provide a breakdown of preferences according to Chappell et al.'s classification but using our thematic classes to illustrate differences in the subject matter emphasized by the two groups of members.

3.3.2   The Role of the Chairman

A further important influence on decision-making in the FOMC is the role of the chairman and how this has changed over time. In their study of the transcripts, Chappell et al. note that Alan Greenspan almost always set out his preference for the policy decision at the start of the policy go-around (i.e., ahead of the other members), whereas Arthur Burns did not have a fixed pattern of behavior. In their results the Greenspan and median policy positions of FOMC members are almost always identical (on only three occasions between 1987 and 1996, the period they study for Greenspan, did the recorded median position of the FOMC differ from Greenspan's own position and 76 percent of their reported preferences of members were identical to that of Greenspan). As a consequence Chappell et al. could not use econometric/statistical tools to analyze Greenspan's role as chairman (Chappell, McGregor, et al. 2005: 98), something that we do in the closer look at 1999. They also miss out the Volcker period because of the difficulty of identifying the measurable objective of policy, yet we start with the presumption that the abrupt change in policy in 1979 points to the importance of studying the role of the chairman in more depth. In sum, we think that it is important to look at the role of the chairman and how it may have changed over time because the process of deliberation in the committee setting to aggregate preferences requires leadership to set and pursue an agenda that can be used to deliver a majority outcome. Moreover we seek to understand better whether the process of forming a majority involved a simple aggregation of preferences or more strategic behavior, in which deliberation within the FOMC played a role.

3.4   Textual Analysis

3.4.1   Data and Methodology

We use full text analysis software (Alceste) to assess deliberation in FOMC meetings. By full text, we mean that the software literally analyzes every spoken word and through that maps a framework of argument and associates different elements of that framework with individual policy makers. In contrast with the partial coding of other analyses of these transcripts (Chappell, McGregor, et al. 2005; Meade 2005; Meade and Stasavage 2008), we use the full transcripts of meetings of the FOMC. Our approach enables us to weight numerically the relative importance of the main identified themes and the significance (using χ^2 values) of the association of individual policy makers with the themes.

Our premise is that the beliefs and arguments espoused by individual FOMC members should produce a distinct pattern of association between individuals and themes. We maintain that different themes of discourse that use different vocabulary will result in an observed word distribution that deviates systematically from one where the words are independent of each other. Hence we infer conditional independence of the structure of words and individuals for a given theme; patterns that deviate significantly and fit with our expectations for a particular theme are thereby evidence of the existence of that theme among FOMC members in a given time period.

As our focus is on the monetary policy decisions of the FOMC, we have edited the transcripts to exclude extraneous material[7] and included "tag lines" to identify each speaker's name and member type (chairman, board governor, bank president, or staff). We have also standardized key terms (the Fed, M1, M2, IMF, etc.) so as to impose control over the lemmatization process, and thus improving the robustness of our results over those obtained in earlier versions of this project.[8] Further details of this lemmatization are given in the Methods appendix (available online).

Our data cover the FOMC meetings for nine years, divided into three time frames: (1) 1979 (in two files, to differentiate the Miller and Volcker chairmanships), 1980 and 1981; (2) 1991, 1992 and 1993; and (3) 1997, 1998, and 1999. These comprise in total ten text files. Our sample thus includes transcripts from the Miller, Volcker, and Greenspan chairmanships. We do not include FOMC transcripts from Bernanke's chairmanship (i.e., from 2006 onward), as the first of these have only been made available by the Fed toward the conclusion of our study (January 2012).

3.4.2 The Economic Backdrop for FOMC Discussions

From 1936 until March 1976, the FOMC published (after a five-year lag) a record of each of its meetings in the *Memoranda of Discussion* (the Memoranda provide edited summaries of statements made by each member in the so-called policy go-around at FOMC meetings prior to the committee adopting a formal directive to guide the conduct of policy in the period up to the next meeting). The Fed then stopped publication of the *Memoranda*, apparently in response to pending legislation and a lawsuit that would if successful have required earlier publication. But the Fed continued to produce transcripts of meetings for use in producing its published record of policy actions. In 1993, Alan Greenspan acknowledged the existence of these transcripts and soon afterward agreed to publish them (with some editing) after a five-year lag.

Each annual set of transcripts (covering the regular FOMC meetings and any additional conference calls held between meetings) amounts to around a quarter of a million or so spoken words. We have chosen 9 years covering broadly the beginning, middle and end of the 20 years following the Volcker Revolution (1979–1981, 1991–1993, and 1997–1999). This amounts to over 2.3 million spoken words. It covers three chairmen, starting with the brief period at the beginning of 1979 when William Miller held the chair. We therefore cover the very last months prior to the Volcker Revolution, the beginning of the Volcker disinflation (starting with the Volcker revolution itself), and the subsequent entrenchment of low inflation under Alan Greenspan.

A closer look at the chosen years helps to explain the logic of the choice.[9] The year 1979 almost speaks for itself, as the year of decisive change (very much a year of two halves). It is therefore the only year that we break into two parts, to mark the change of chairman in the summer and the abrupt change of policy in October 1979. The next two years capture the difficult birth of the Volcker disinflation. The Federal Funds rate was allowed to rise sharply from around 11 percent in September 1979 to around 17 percent in April 1980. But evidence of a weakening economy caused a pause in the tightening of policy in the early months of 1980. At the same time there was a sharp rise in oil and gold prices and an increase in the nominal long bond rate pointed to rising inflation expectations notwithstanding a weakening of the economy. The FOMC responded and thereby allowed a 3 percent rise in the Funds rate in March 1980. This along with credit controls imposed in March contributed to a short recession in the first half of 1980. In response the FOMC acted in a way that allowed the Funds rate to fall by 8 percent between April and July. Economic growth recovered toward the end of 1980.

The story of 1981 is quite different. The FOMC acted to maintain the Federal Funds rate at a level that (using a contemporary measure of headline inflation) suggested very high short-term real interest rates of as much as 9 percent. There was a sharp recession toward the end of 1981 and into 1982. The FOMC did act in a way that brought the nominal Funds rate down in the second half of 1981, but only in line with the fall in headline inflation, thus preserving high short-term real rates. But throughout this period the long bond rate indicated that inflation expectations remained elevated and thus that the FOMC needed to maintain high short-term real rates in order to begin to acquire credibility. We assess the difficult start to the Volcker Revolution in more detail in the second half of this chapter.

In the late 1980s the FOMC raised the Federal Funds rate in order to reverse the rise in inflation and inflation expectations (action that had been delayed by the 1987 stock market crash). As a result of those actions, and the recession that accompanied the first Gulf War, inflation began to fall in 1991. But the unemployment rate rose throughout 1991 and into 1992 (the beginning of the "jobless recovery" that followed the recession of the early 1990s). Monetary policy in the early 1990s is quite typically described as being more restrictive than would have been the case if the inflationary pressures of 1987 and 1988 had been dealt with earlier. The FOMC was therefore cautious in lowering the Funds rate through 1992, but by the latter part of that year it was able to establish a nearly zero short-term real Funds rate (the nominal Funds rate was more or less equal to headline inflation), which it maintained until early 1994. During this period the unemployment rate fell to 6 percent without setting off a negative reaction from inflation expectations.

During 1994 and early 1995 the FOMC took preemptive action against evidence of a rise in inflation expectations as shown by the long bond rate. The action was successful in that the bond rate subsequently fell and the unemployment rate did not rise. It provided evidence that inflation and inflation expectations were more firmly anchored than before. It is the backdrop to our final three-year period at the end of the 1990s, during which low inflation was maintained even though the US economy grew in the 4 percent range on an annual basis between 1996 and 1999, and the unemployment rate fell below 4 percent for a while. The story of this period is associated with the Asian and wider emerging market crisis, alongside the rise in productivity growth in the US economy. Our study of the FOMC's actions in 1999 to raise the target interest rate and thereby reverse the cuts made in response to the Asian crisis provides a more detailed insight into decision-making in the era of more established low inflation.

3.4.3 The Value of the FOMC Transcripts

Our approach is to employ automated textual analysis software to assess qualitative data. We recognize that while the FOMC transcripts provide a verbatim record of discussions and deliberations, this does not automatically make them either an easy source to interpret or an inevitable gold mine of analytical insight.

A criticism of the value of the transcripts is that their publication since 1993 has served to stifle the quality and force of the debate in the FOMC. Meade and Stasavage set out the case for a deterioration in the quality of deliberation in a committee setting if the deliberation takes place more in the public domain (Meade and Stasavage 2008). They recognize that this contradicts the more conventional modern view that greater transparency in a policy-making process—particularly one like monetary policy that is inherently forward looking and relies on influencing the expectations of economic agents—produces better outcomes in terms of the policy objective and facilitates the accountability of policy makers (Goodfriend 1986; Faust and Svensson 2001; Geraats 2002; Chortareas, Stasavage, et al. 2003; Kohn and Sack 2003; Thornton 2003). Their model is heavily influenced by the assumption made on the motivations of members of the FOMC in terms both of reaching the correct decision and using the record of the meetings to create a reputation for members. A further important conditioning assumption for Meade and Stasavage is that all members of the FOMC bring private (to them) information that is relevant to the key variable(s) that influence the policy decision but on which the member is uncertain in terms of the accuracy or interpretation of the information (candidate variables are the output gap, growth in the monetary aggregates, etc.). Meade and Stasavage argue that when deliberation occurs in private there will be a greater incentive for members to reveal such private information. This is because when deliberation occurs in private, outsiders will establish inferences about the expertise of individual FOMC members based on the quality of the FOMC's collective decision rather than on the quality of individual contributions. A necessary condition here is that FOMC members care about their reputation in the eyes of these outsiders.

To support the Meade and Stasavage argument, it is necessary to believe that the five-year lag in publication of the FOMC transcripts does not undermine their case by creating too much elapsed time before the contribution of individual members can be assessed. Views differ on this point. Woolley and Gardner also use the transcripts to study changes in the pattern of deliberation in the FOMC over time (Woolley and Gardner 2009). They point out that in practice the five-year time delay before publication has meant that the transcripts have received little publicity and attention (indeed they calculate that since 1993 the only notable story involving the transcripts concerned the decision to release them rather than anything about the substance of their content). As such, Woolley and Gardner conclude that the transcripts have not been an effective device to create or strengthen the accountability of the FOMC.

Views from FOMC members on the effect of the decision to publish the transcripts suggest that there has been an impact on the discourse in meetings. At the time the issue of whether to release or not was live (1993), Alan Greenspan took the view that central banks should disclose all that they can up to the point where disclosure affects their effectiveness. His initial correspondence with Representative Henry Gonzalez (chair of the House Banking Committee at the time) demonstrated the concerns that Greenspan held, and in the FOMC discussion of publication of the transcripts he was against immediate release because ". . . (r)elease of videotape, audiotape, or a literal transcript would have a chilling effect on the free flow of ideas and the ability to bring confidential information to the deliberations" (FOMC Transcript, October 5, 1993).

And, in the House hearing on the subject, he explained that:

A considerable amount of free discussion and probing questioning by the participants of each other and of key FOMC staff members takes place. In the wide-ranging debate, new ideas are often tested, many of which are rejected. . . . The prevailing views of many participants change as evidence and insights emerge. This process has proven to be a very effective procedure for gaining a consensus. . . . It could not function effectively if participants had to be concerned that their half-thought-through, but nonetheless potentially valuable, notions would *soon* be made public [our emphasis]. I fear in such a situation the public record would be a sterile set of bland pronouncements scarcely capturing the necessary debates which are required of monetary policy-making. A tendency would arise for one-on-one pre-meeting discussions, with public meetings merely announcing already agreed-upon positions, and for each participant to enter the meeting with a final position not subject to the views of others. (quoted in Meade and Stasavage 2008: 704)

But, on the issue of *delayed* release of the transcripts (the eventual outcome in 1993) Greenspan said that "(p)eople think reading the raw transcripts is a way of learning things; I would suggest that if they spend six or eight months reading through some of this stuff, they won't like it" (Greenspan 1993: 3). The key difference here appears to be between immediate and delayed publication of the transcripts. That said, views on the impact of delayed release of the transcripts also differ.

Ed Boehne, President of the Philadelphia Federal Reserve Bank, commented in the FOMC conference call of October 5, 1993, that in the

1970s at the time of the publication of the Memoranda of Discussion, "meetings were much more formal, less give-and-take and there was a tendency for people to come in with prepared statements, which made it difficult for the subsequent give-and-take that I think has become a real strength of the Committee" (quoted in Meade and Stasavage 2008: 704).

In the June 1998 transcript, Boehne commented:

Quicker and more complete disclosure already has changed the nature of the Committee's deliberations. I am for the disclosure that we do, but we should not mislead ourselves about how it has changed the nature of these proceedings. I recall participating in routine, vigorous, and freewheeling debates in this room before we decided to release transcripts. Now, most of us read prepared remarks about our Districts and the national economy and even our comments on near-term policy sometimes are crafted in advance. Prepared statements were the rare exception rather than the rule until we started to release transcripts.

His comments reflect those made by Kansas City Reserve Bank President Thomas Hoenig in 1995: "the tape has had some chilling effects on our discussions. I see a lot more people reading their statements" (FOMC transcript January 1995, quoted in Meade and Stasavage 2008: 704–705). In response, Greenspan took a more moderate line: "there is very little evidence that the quality of our discussion has been reduced" (FOMC transcript January 1995, quoted in Meade and Stasavage 2008: 705).

Reflecting on meetings *after* 1993, Governor Larry Meyer commented:

FOMC meetings are more about structured presentations than discussions and exchanges. This surprised me. Each member spoke for about five minutes [in the review of the state of the economy], then gave way to the next speaker. Many read from a prepared text or spoke from a detailed outline, diverging only occasionally to include a comment on what was said earlier in the meeting. To my surprise, what evolved was not a spontaneous discussion, but a series of formal, self-contained presentations. (Meyer 2004: 39)

Meyer's initial assessment of the post-1993 FOMC meetings would seem to lead us to believe that these self-contained presentations offered no scope for real deliberation—that is, no opportunity for reasoned argument persuading members to change their views. Significantly, however, Meyer rejects this stance. His final analysis is that deliberation in the FOMC did matter—perhaps not within the space of a single meeting, but rather over time, from meeting to meeting. That is, in his view, persuasion occurred more subtly, with arguments asserted at one meeting taking root in the minds of other members so that changes in views (and votes) might emerge at a subsequent meeting:

So was the FOMC meeting merely a ritual dance? No. I came to see policy decisions as often evolving over at least a couple of meetings. The seeds were sown at one meeting and harvested at the next. So, I always listened to the discussion intently, because it could change my mind, even if it could not change my vote at that meeting. Similarly, while in my remarks to my colleagues it sounded as if I were addressing today's concerns and today's policy decisions, in reality I was often positioning myself, and my peers, for the next meeting. (Meyer 2004: 53)

An important change over the years that requires careful interpretation concerns the prevalence of open discussion of monetary policy in the Fed prior to the FOMC meeting. Meade and Stasavage construct their model on the presumption (for simplicity) that if deliberation moves from a private to a public venue, committee members do not resort to exchanging information before the actual meeting takes place (though they note that their model can still hold provided any pre-meetings does not involve all members of the committee). As described above, Alan Greenspan thought that immediate publication of a record of meetings would lead to pre-meetings and corridor conversations that reduce the actual meeting to more of a ritual. That said, there is a longer history of pre-meetings prior to the FOMC. Chappell et al. report a conversation with former Governor Jeffrey Bucher in which he described a "no-lobbying" before the FOMC rule that was in force in the Burns period, which meant that the chairman did not attempt to influence others' positions or mobilize support for his own position prior to FOMC meetings (Chappell, McGregor, et al. 2005: 115n.21). But we note later in this chapter that by the time of the Volcker Revolution in 1979, a meeting of the Board of Governors was held prior to the FOMC to discuss the proposed change to the operating procedure, and in that case a conference call of the FOMC was also held. Since then, discussions among the Board prior to FOMC meetings have become common, though these are presented as opportunities to receive briefing on the latest economic and financial data and exchange views, but not reach a conclusion. Governor Larry Meyer commented that governors regularly met shortly before FOMC meetings at which Alan Greenspan would share his views on the economic outlook and where he was leaning on the policy decision. Meyer describes these sessions as "a much truer give-and-take, a serious exchange of ideas" (Meyer 2004: 51). We conclude from this that while the history of pre-meetings of the Board of Governors pre-dates the decision to publish the transcripts, they have become more common and thus more a part of the overall FOMC process. And, as we find from our analysis, this has coincided with a more prominent role being played by governors in FOMC meetings.

What difference did publication of the transcripts make to FOMC deliberation? Later we provide evidence to support Boehne's depiction of the more "freewheeling debates" in the late 1970s/early 1980s and more "prepared statements" in the 1990s. But we start by being open-minded about the causes of the changes—they may be due to changes in the procedures around disclosure and transparency, or they may be due to changes in personnel and leadership in the FOMC, or they may be due to changes in the operating environment of monetary policy (as the objective of policy became better defined and its achievements more evident).

3.5   Results

3.5.1   Basic Statistics

Table 3.2 provides a summary of the basic statistics from Alceste for the ten sets of FOMC transcripts. For each full year of transcripts, the total word count varies between 206,064 (1993) and 344,401 (1981). We consider the possible meaning of this large variance in the length of FOMC discourse per year below. Likewise the number of unique words that were analyzed by the Alceste program ranges from 84,822 in 1993 to 132,087 in 1981.[10] The passive variables[11] (also referred to as tagged indicators) define characteristics of each speech or "case," and these include the speaker's name, whether they were a board governor or reserve bank president, and whether they were a voting member.

The initial context unit, or ICU, is the sampling unit. We divide the text so that ICUs are the individual speeches or comments made in the FOMC meetings. The elementary context unit, or ECU, is a sentence or group of sentences, which the Alceste program automatically constructs based on word length and punctuation in the text. As we explain in the Methodology appendix (book appendix I), the program uses the presence or absence of words in each ECU to calculate matrices on which to build the classification process. It then conducts two preliminary analyses, each using slightly different lengths for the contextual unit,[12] and so opts for the length that allows the greater proportion of ECUs to be successfully classified, relative to the total available. From table 3.2 we can see that the classification rates range from 66 percent in 1997 to 86 percent in 1993, averaging about 77 percent across the ten text files. This means that about 23 percent of each set of transcripts is residue or unexplained.

As described in the Methodology appendix, unlike cluster analysis software that employs ascending hierarchical classification, Alceste uses a recursive algorithm with a descending method in order to partition the corpus into classes using an iterative process in which the descending hierarchical classification method decomposes the classes until a predetermined number of iterations fail to result in further statistically significant divisions. This approach facilitates greater stability to the classes so that they are each as homogeneous as possible and as different as possible from one another.

The final two blocks in table 3.2 indicate the number of classes identified in each set of transcripts and the size of each class (as measured by the percentage of the total ECUs classified within each), the label we have chosen to identify the subject matter of the class, followed by a numeric classification of all the classes across the ten files into broader thematic groups (shown in parenthesis in bold). Table 3.3 provides the list of these broader groups. The most characteristic function words for each class, along with their χ^2 statistical significance (with the minimum chi-squared value for selection automatically set by the program, with one degree of freedom), provide an indication of the theme or frame of argument that unifies a class. The most characteristic words for each class are given in rank order (by χ^2 value). Similarly the most characteristic phrases are given for each class, again ranked by χ^2 value. The labels for each class (Fiscal Policy, etc.) are not automatically given by the Alceste program; rather, we have added the labels (State of the Economy in the Districts, Staff Assessment of the Monetary Policy Stance, etc.) based on an assessment of the most characteristic words for each class[13] and the most representative ECUs for each class. The labeling of the classes is derived from the top representative words and sentences (ECUs) given in the detailed reports generated by Alceste.[14]

The results presented in table 3.2 allow us to draw some simple summary conclusions on the evolution of deliberation in the FOMC. The length of FOMC meetings became shorter over time. The average annual word count in the early 1990s was 25 percent shorter than in the late 1970s/early 1980s, though the difference reduced to 11 percent in the late 1990s. Less was said in the earlier Greenspan period (early

Table 3.2
Basic statistics for FOMC transcripts

	1979 (Miller)	1979 (Volcker)	1980	1981
Total word count	99,592	183,361	257,941	344,401
Unique words analyzed	38,177	71,664	99,906	132,087
Passive variables (tagged indicators)	55	48	48	65
ICUs (= number of speeches/comments)	1,062	2,349	3,422	5899
Classified ECUs	2,132 (= 69% of the retained ECU)	4,802 (= 79% of the retained ECU)	6,799 (= 82% of the retained ECU)	7125 (= 78% of the retained ECU)
Lexical classes	6	5	4	4
Distribution of classes (%) and thematic content [thematic group, in bold]	1 (15) *Uncertainty on Setting the Target Range for Monetary Aggregates* **[8b]** 2 (15) *Uncertainty on the Interest Rate Decision* **[8a]** 3 (11) *US Economy Performance (Credit Conditions & Inflation)* **[1a]** 4 (12) *US Economy Performance and Staff Forecast (Demand and Output)* **[2a & 2b]** 5 (10) *Fed's Market Operations* **[4]** 6 (37) *Deliberation on Target Ranges for Monetary Aggregates & Interest Rates* **[7b & 7c]**	1 (32) *Staff Forecast for US Economy (Demand and Output, & Inflation)* **[1b & 2b]** 2 (20) *Deliberation on Target Ranges for Monetary Aggregates* **[7c]** 3 (20) *Effectiveness of Monetary Policy—Uncertainty over the Transmission Mechanism* **[8c]** 4 (16) *Reserves Levels and the Fed's Market Operations* **[4]** 5 (12) *Impact of the Volcker Revolution including Communication of the Policy Change* **[9b]**	1 (47) *Striving for Credibility* **[9b]** 2 (15) *Deliberation on the Target Ranges for Monetary Aggregates & Interest Rates* **[7b & 7c]** 3 (26) *US Economy Performance & Staff Forecast for Demand and Output (Evidence of Weakening)* **[2a & 2b]** 4 (11) *Performance of Non-borrowed Reserves Relative to Target* **[3]**	1 (32) *Choice of Monetary Policy Target/Framework* **[9a]** 2 (20) *Deliberation on Target Ranges for Monetary Aggregates & Non-borrowed Reserves* **[7c & 7d]** 3 (27) *Staff Forecast for US Economy (Demand and Output, & Inflation)* **[1b & 2b]** 4 (21) *Reserves Levels & the Fed's Market Operations* **[4]**

Table 3.2
(continued)

	1991	1992	1993
Total word count	224,962	225,627	206,064
Unique words analyzed	92,035	93,477	84,822
Passive variables (tagged indicators)	51	57	42
ICUs (= number of speeches/comments)	1,341	1,161	1,046
Classified ECUs	5,172 (= 83% of the retained ECU)	4,385 (= 72% of the retained ECU)	4,809 (= 86% of the retained ECU)
Lexical classes	6	5	5
Distribution of classes (%) and thematic content [thematic group, in bold]	1 (25) *State of the Economy in the Districts* **[1c & 2c]** 2 (12) *Financial Market Developments and Fed's Market Operations* **[4]** 3 (12) *Staff Assessment of the Monetary Policy Stance* **[7a]** 4 (10) *Credit Conditions, Banking System Stability* **[6]** 5 (9) *Deliberation on the Interest Rate Policy Decision* **[7b]** 6 (32) *Uncertainty around the Interest Rate Decision* **[8a]**	1 (18) *Staff Forecast for US Economy (Demand and Output, & Inflation* **[1b & 2b]** 2 (14) *Staff Assessment of the Monetary Policy Stance* **[7a]** 3 (22) *State of the Economy in the Districts* **[1c & 2c]** 4 (32) *Deliberation on the Interest Rate Policy Decision* **[7b]** 5 (14) *Financial Market Developments & Fed's Market Operations* **[4]**	1 (56) *Uncertainty on the Model of the Economy and Appropriate Monetary Policy Strategy* **[8c]** 2 (15) *State of the Economy in the Districts* **[1c & 2c]** 3 (12) *US Economy Demand and Output Performance, and Staff Forecast* **[2a & 2b]** 4 (9) *Deliberation on the Interest Rate Decision* **[7b]** 5 (8) *Fed's Market Operations* **[4]**

Table 3.2
(continued)

	1997	1998	1999
Total word count	258,552	268,772	262,514
Unique words analyzed	112,422	117,365	113,272
Passive variables (tagged indicators)	40	63	36
ICUs (= number of speeches/comments)	1,097	1,223	999
Classified ECUs	4,607 (= 66% of the retained ECU)	6,250 (= 82% of the retained ECU)	4,910 (= 71% of the retained ECU)
Lexical classes	5	7	8
Distribution of classes (%) and thematic content [**thematic group, in bold**]	1 (25) *Choice of Target to Achieve Monetary Stability; Role of Money Ranges* **[9a]** 2 (15) *Staff Assessment of the Monetary Policy Stance, and Deliberation on the Interest Rate Decision* **[7a & 7b]** 3 (24) *State of the Economy in the Districts* **[1c & 2c]** 4 (8) *Financial Market Developments* **[4]** 5 (27) *Staff Forecast for US Economy (Demand and Output, & Inflation)* **[1b & 2b]**	1 (17) *State of the Economy in the Districts* **[1c & 2c]** 2 (24) *Staff Forecast for US Economy (Demand and Output, & Inflation)* **[1b & 2b]** 3 (12) *Financial Market Developments* **[4]** 4 (10) *Outlook for the World Economy/Asia Crisis* **[5]** 5 (11) *Deliberation on the Interest Rate Decision* **[7b]** 6 (8) *Staff Forecast for the Rest of the World* **[5]** 7 (18) *Deliberation on Broader Issues on the Monetary Policy Stance and Strategy* **[9c]**	1 (23) *Deliberation on the Interest Rate Decision* **[7b]** 2 (11) *Productivity Growth in the US* **[2d]** 3 (12) *US Economy—Demand & Output (Strength of Domestic Demand)* **[2a]** 4 (12) *Financial Market Developments* **[4]** 5 (11) *Stance of Policy & How to Publish It / Transparency* **[9b]** 6 (11) *Staff Forecast for US Economy (Demand and Output, & Inflation)* **[1b & 2b]** 7 (12) *State of the Economy in the Districts (Output)* **[2c]** 8 (9) *State of the Economy in the Districts (Inflation)* **[1c]**

Table 3.3
Full list of major themes for FOMC transcripts, 1979 to 1999

---

1. US economy: Inflation
 1a. US inflation performance
 1b. Fed staff forecast for US inflation
 1c. State of the economy in the districts (evidence of inflation)

2. US Economy: Demand and output
 2a. US demand and output performance
 2b. Fed staff forecast for US demand and output
 2c. State of the economy in the districts (evidence on demand and output)
 2d. US productivity growth

3. Performance of the monetary aggregates and non-borrowed reserves

4. Financial market developments and the Fed's market operations

5. World economy (rest of the world)

6. Credit conditions, banking system stability/financial stability

7. Deliberation of the decision
 7a. Staff assessment of the stance of monetary policy
 7b. FOMC deliberation on the interest rate decision
 7c. FOMC deliberation on the target ranges for monetary aggregates
 7d. FOMC deliberation on the target for non-borrowed reserves

8. Uncertainty around the decision
 8a. Uncertainty around the interest rate decision
 8b. Uncertainty around the setting of target ranges for the monetary aggregates
 8c. Uncertainty around the model of the economy and the monetary transmission mechanism

9. Monetary policy stance, strategy, and communication
 9a. Choice of monetary policy target framework
 9b. Impact and credibility of monetary policy, including communication
 9c. Deliberation of monetary policy strategy

1990s) than in the Miller/early Volcker period or the later Greenspan period (late 1990s), which was in turn somewhat shorter than the Volcker period. Of course, this provides no conclusion on the content and quality of the deliberation.

A second simple result is that the average length of each speech/comment in the FOMC increased quite markedly over the period. In the first three years (Miller/early Volcker), the average length of a speech/comment was 83 words in 1979, 75 words in 1980, and 58 words in 1981. For the earlier Greenspan years the averages were 168 words in 1991, 194 words in 1992, and 197 words in 1993. Finally, for the middle Greenspan years the averages were 236 words in 1997, 220 words in 1998 and 263 words in 1999. In the late 1990s, the average speech/comment in an FOMC meeting was over three times as long as the average in the late 1970s/early 1980s. We conclude that the form of deliberation changed over the period we study. Whether, or to what extent, this change supports Ed Boehne's view that after 1993, when FOMC members knew that the transcripts would become public, the nature of deliberation changed toward speech-making depends on a more thorough assessment of the content of the deliberation, which we carry out below. However, one argument against the Boehne thesis is that our simple statistics indicate that the change in the form of deliberations had started before 1993. Woolley and Gardner produce a similar conclusion from their analysis of changes in the length and structure of the transcripts over time (Woolley and Gardner 2009). Their premise on deliberation is that a larger number of speeches of shorter length for a given total length of transcript indicate that members of the FOMC are engaging in exchanges with each other rather than making set-piece statements. They suggest three factors that will influence the degree of deliberation: first, the degree of disagreement among FOMC members, with more disagreement leading to more shorter exchanges; second, changes in the procedure of the FOMC (the "rules" of the meeting); and third, changes in the average experience of members, with the deliberative process reflecting the average level of inexperience/experience among members. Woolley and Gardner conclude that the Greenspan era is marked by a steady downward trend in deliberation. But, like us, they identify that this trend began before 1993, making it harder to draw the link to the decision on publication of the transcripts.

We agree with Woolley and Gardner that the level of disagreement among members of the FOMC should influence the form and content of deliberation. But, we think that understanding this relationship needs to be linked to changes in the substance of monetary policy, and particularly to the emergence of the low inflation consensus. This requires more focus on the substance of the exchanges. Specifically, we think that our results and those of Woolley and Gardner point more to the change of chairman as the most likely cause of changes in the form of deliberation. As for the third of Woolley and Gardner's factors influencing deliberation in the FOMC, the average experience of members, we are skeptical that this can be the driving force of what appears to be a longer term trend in the meetings. While the average experience of members has varied over time (and this could be a factor influencing shorter run changes in deliberation), there is no reason to believe that there has been a long-run trend in average tenure on the FOMC.

A third simple statistic that we examine is the number of lexical classes for each file that we study. Here the numbers are: 6, 5, 4, and 4 for the early period (treating 1979 as two files); 6, 5, and 5 for the middle period; and 5, 7, and 8 for the late 1990s. The distribution does not yield a strong finding, but it suggests that in the aftermath of the Volcker Revolution (1980 and 1981) deliberation in the FOMC was more tightly focused on a smaller number of thematic subjects, while it became more loosely focused in the late 1990s. As a final simple diagnostic test, we examine the distribution of lexical classes for each file. Two stand out as having a highly concentrated distribution around one class, 1980 (one class accounts for 47 percent of the total) and 1993 (56 percent of the total). We return to these findings when we examine the substance of the results below.

3.5.2 Main Findings

Assessing the structure of the transcripts and labeling the themes from our results is only the first step in our analysis. The meat of our results concerns how the presence of these themes in the discourse of the FOMC changed over time, and likewise the contributions of the FOMC and how they are associated with the themes we identify.

At the outset we also apply a simple plausibility check to our results, namely do they capture and classify particular major developments that we know from a quick inspection of the transcripts were discussed in the FOMC? We chose two "crises" that fell in the years we study to perform this plausibility check, namely the Savings and Loan crisis of the early 1990s and the Asia/emerging markets crisis of the late 1990s. Both of these were discussed by the FOMC in the context of US monetary policy.[15] Table 3.4 illustrates the attention given to financial stability and the banking system (group 6) in 1991 (attracting a weight of 10 percent of the total FOMC content based on the retained ECUs for that year). The height of the Savings and Loan crisis in the United States came in 1991, so this result is consistent with our prior. Table 3.4 also illustrates the large weight (18 percent) given to discussions of the world economy in 1998 (group 5). As the Asian financial crisis was at its height during 1998, the result is consistent with the known timeline of events.

Table 3.4

Distribution of major themes within each set of transcripts

Major themes in transcripts, grouped	1979 (Miller)	1979 (Volcker)	1980 (Volcker)	1981 (Volcker)	1991 (Greenspan)	1992 (Greenspan)	1993 (Greenspan)	1997 (Greenspan)	1998 (Greenspan)	1999 (Greenspan)
1 & 2: US Economy—performance & forecast (demand and output, and inflation)	23	32	26	28	25	40	28	52	42	56
3 & 4: Financial market developments, Fed's market operations, & growth of the monetary aggregates/non-borrowed reserves	10	16	11	21	12	14	8	8	12	12
5: World economy									18	
6: Financial stability/banking system					10					
7: Deliberation on the decision on the monetary policy stance	37	20	15	20	21	46	9	15	11	23
8: Uncertainty around the decision on the monetary policy stance	30	20			32		56			
9: Monetary policy stance & strategy		12	47	32				25	18	11
Total (=100 but for rounding)	(100)	(100)	(100)	(100)	(100)	(100)	(100)	(100)	(100)	(100)

Note: Distribution is defined as the share of retained ECUs that are classified into each theme.

In order to draw out the main conclusions, we extract from each thematic class the statistically significant tagged indicators. Significance is interpreted as the χ^2 value, with one degree of freedom, where:

Statistical significance (df = 1)	χ^2 value
NS	< 2.71
10%	< 3.84
5% (*)	< 6.63
1% (**)	< 10.80
< 1% (***)	≥ 10.80

χ^2 values below 10 are less robust but are nonetheless noteworthy. Very high values (e.g., over 50) are, on the other hand, highly robust. Our interpretation does not rely on or adhere rigidly to the specific intervals of these values (e.g., 200 as exactly ten times the significance of 20), but rather to a more relative standard in levels of categories, and particularly the designation of highly robust values (e.g., $\chi^2 \geq 50$).

Tables 3.4 to 3.7 set out a summary of the results on the substance of deliberation in the FOMC. Table 3.4 employs the categorizations of thematic groups from table 3.3 and presents the summary percentage distribution of these groups. Table 3.5 condenses those weights further, initially into two groups. The first contains themes 1 through 6, all of which seek to assess the economy and in particular, examine the relevant data and applicable models and forecasts. The second contains themes 7 through 9, which contain the discourse on the policy decision and the broader strategy of monetary policy (introducing issues, e.g., how to deal with uncertainty around the policy decision). In table 3.5 we then add a further division in the deliberative discourse between that focusing on the immediate decision on monetary policy (group 7) and that focusing on discussions of longer term monetary policy strategy (groups 8 and 9).

Table 3.6 is a summary of the highly significant member types (chairman, board governor, bank president, staff) for each of the thematic groups from table 3.3. Tables 3.A1 to 3.A10 of appendix 3.A at the end of this chapter list the levels of statistical significance of individual members of the FOMC for each thematic class in all the ten text files (i.e., statistical significance for a given member means that the

Table 3.5
Broad categorizations of major themes

Major themes in transcripts, grouped	1979 (Miller)	1979 (Volcker)	1980 (Volcker)	1981 (Volcker)	1991 (Greenspan)	1992 (Greenspan)	1993 (Greenspan)	1997 (Greenspan)	1998 (Greenspan)	1999 (Greenspan)
1 through 6: Assessment of Economy	33	48	37	49	47	54	36	60	72	68
7 through 9: Deliberation on Policy	67	52	62	52	53	46	65	40	29	34
Total (=100 but for rounding)	(100)	(100)	(100)	(100)	(100)	(100)	(100)	(100)	(100)	(100)
1 through 6: Assessment of economy	33	48	37	49	47	54	36	60	72	68
7: Deliberation on the immediate decision on monetary policy	37	20	15	20	21	46	9	15	11	23
8 & 9: Uncertainty and deliberation on monetary policy strategy	30	32	47	32	32	0	56	25	18	11
Total (=100 but for rounding)	(100)	(100)	(100)	(100)	(100)	(100)	(100)	(100)	(100)	(100)

Note: Distribution is defined as the share of retained ECUs that are classified into each theme.

Table 3.6
Summary of major themes and significant tags for FOMC member types

Major themes in transcripts, grouped	1979 (Miller)	1979 (Volcker)	1980 (Volcker)	1981 (Volcker)	1991 (Greenspan)	1992 (Greenspan)	1993 (Greenspan)	1997 (Greenspan)	1998 (Greenspan)	1999 (Greenspan)
1 & 2: US economy—Performance & forecast (demand and output, & inflation)	S (5) P (1)	S (5)	S (7) P (1)	S (5)	P (7) S (4)	P (10) S (5)	P (10) S (3)	P (10) G (3) S (3)	P (11) S (3) C (1) G (1)	P (11) S (5) G (3) C (1)
3 & 4: Financial market developments, Fed's market operations, & growth of the monetary aggregates/Non-borrowed reserves	S (4)	S (2)	S (2) C (1)	S (7) P (3)	S (7)	S (5)	S (7)	S (2)	S (1)	S (5)
5: World economy									G (4) S (4) P (3)	
6: Financial stability/banking system					G (2) S (3)					
7: Deliberation on decision on monetary policy stance	C (1) G (1) P (1)	P (3) G (2) C (1) S (1)	G (2) P (2) S (1)	P (2) C (1) G (1)	G (2) S (2) C (1)	G (5) P (4) S (2) C (1)	P (2) S (2) C (1) G (1)	S (3) G (2)	G (2) P (2) S (2)	P (4) G (3) C (1)
8: Uncertainty around decision on monetary policy stance	P (7) G (1)	P (8) G (2)			P (6) G (3) C (1)		G (4) C (1) S (1)			
9: Monetary policy stance & strategy	C (1) P (1)	C (1) P (1)	P (8) G (2) C (1)	P (6) G (3) C (1)				P (4) C (1) G (1)	G (3) P (2) C (1) S (1)	S (3) G (2)

Note: Tags for which χ^2 value is at least at the 1 percent significance level. C = chairman, G = board governor, P = bank president, and S = Fed staff. The number of members in each group that obtain statistically significant values for their tags is given in brackets, and member type is listed in each cell according to the number of statistically significant members.

Table 3.7
Broad categorizations of major themes: Total number of significant members across groupings of themes

Major themes in transcripts, grouped	1979 (Miller)	1979 (Volcker)	1980 (Volcker)	1981 (Volcker)	1991 (Greenspan)	1992 (Greenspan)	1993 (Greenspan)	1997 (Greenspan)	1998 (Greenspan)	1999 (Greenspan)
1 through 6: Assessment of economy	G (0) P (1)	G (0) P (0)	G (0) P (1)	G (0) P (3)	G (2) P (7)	G (0) P (10)	G (0) P (10)	G (3) P (10)	G (5) P (14)	G (3) P (11)
7 through 9: Deliberation on policy	G (2) P (8)	G (4) P (12)	G (4) P (10)	G (4) P (8)	G (5) P (6)	G (5) P (4)	G (5) P (2)	G (3) P (4)	G (5) P (4)	G (5) P (4)

Note: G = board governors; P = bank presidents (in italics).

discourse of that member is highly associated with the thematic content of the class). Table 3.7 narrows the nine categories from table 3.3 into two groups as in the first part of table 3.5.

Taking tables 3.4 to 3.7 together, we can highlight three main findings on the substance of deliberation in the FOMC. First, we find that over time there was a switch in the content of FOMC deliberation from a greater focus on deliberating on monetary policy itself toward more emphasis on the assessment of the state of the US economy and inflation. Our second main finding concerns the relative contributions of FOMC members, with a clear shift in the contributions of both board governors and reserve bank presidents. Our third finding involves using the net ease/tightness scores from Chappell et al. to determine whether we can detect a connection between the average preference of FOMC members and the subject matter on which they focus in their contributions to FOMC meetings (given the limited overlap of the time periods studied we can only make this assessment for 1991 to 1993). We conclude that significant contributions on the stance of monetary policy and the monetary aggregates/monetary conditions tend to be made by FOMC members who are more at the net tighten end of the Chappell et al. rank order, while there is no significant difference for other themes in FOMC meetings (e.g., the assessment of conditions in the US economy).

The Content of Deliberation

The upper panel of table 3.5 shows a shift in the weights of the two broad categories. The simple averages of the percentage weights for the assessment of the economy are 42 percent in the Miller/Volcker period, 46 percent in the early 1990s, and 67 percent in the late 1990s. The reverse is true for the weights on deliberation on policy, which are 58, 54, and 33 percent, respectively. The results suggest that the most marked shift in the content of FOMC meetings came between the early and late 1990s. The lower panel of table 3.5 indicates that the decline in the weight given to deliberation on policy was more pronounced for issues concerning the broader strategy of policy. Deliberation around the immediate policy decision shows a decline in the average contribution from 23 percent in the Miller/Volcker period to 16 percent in the late 1990s, while the broader issues show a decline from 35 percent to 18 percent.

Table 3.4 allows us to look more closely at the pattern of discussion of the themes across each year that we cover. Starting with the top half of the table, covering the themes on assessment of the economy, money and the monetary aggregates and financial markets, we can see that there is little trend in the weighting given to money and financial markets, though we think that (based on closer analysis of the ECUs) within this class there is a shift from discussing money and the aggregates toward spending more time on financial markets. The increase in the weight on assessment is evident in the top row of the table, covering the performance of the US economy, forecasting and inflation. A more detailed look at the bottom half of table 3.4 reveals some interesting findings. The weight on uncertainty around the decision on monetary policy by the FOMC appears in 1979 (for the Miller and Volcker periods in that year) and then again in 1991 and 1993 (in 1992 there is a heavy weight on deliberation on the immediate monetary policy decision). In contrast, the weight on broader discussions of monetary policy strategy is seen in 1980 and 1981, and again in the late 1990s. We examine the Volcker Revolution period of 1979 to 1981 and the reversal of policy in 1999 in more detail in the second half of this chapter.

To what extent did the change in the content of deliberation that we observe reflect the change in chairman? From table 3.6 we can see that unlike Volcker and Miller, Greenspan attracts significant scores in contributing to discussions on the US economy (groups 1 and 2) in the late 1990s. This fits Greenspan's well-known reputation for studying the data very hard and his conviction in the late 1990s that there was something important to be seen in the evidence on productivity growth in the United States. We return to this in our study of 1999.

A less well identified story concerns the pattern of findings in the early 1990s involving deliberation on the monetary policy stance (where 1992 shows a very large contribution) and uncertainty around the monetary policy stance (where 1991 and 1993 show large contributions). We use the most characteristic ECUs from our results to help with this part of the story. By looking at the most characteristic ECUs for group 7 (deliberation on the policy decision), we can detect a shift in the discourse over time. Below we reproduce the most characteristic ECU attributed to a member of the FOMC (not a member of the Fed staff) in group 7:

[1979 Miller Period]
. . . the third alternative would be to let the Fed Funds go up with the directive to 10½ percent and very quickly move the discount rate to, say, 10 or 10¼ percent to close the widening gap between the discount rate and the Fed Funds rate. (Chairman Miller)

This ECU illustrates Miller's essentially collegial style as described by Meltzer (Meltzer 2009: 941) and is phrased very much in terms of describing options to the FOMC.

[1979 Volcker Period]

. . . why do not we just see what the vote is, Mr. Chairman, on the bottom of alternative III and the top of alternative II, widening the range by a half percentage point. (Reserve Bank President Mayo)

The style remains essentially collegial in tone.

[1980]

. . . and if that constraint prevents our reaching our targets as we move toward September, then I would be prepared to lower that 9 percent at the right time. (Governor Rice)

[1981]

I think that is right. I would like to suggest that this time we observe the upper limits for the purpose of consultation and that at the time we crack through the 18 percent we have another telephone session. (Reserve Bank President Guffey)

In these two ECUs, Rice and Guffey are describing their thinking around the respective behavior of the monetary aggregates and the Fed Funds rate in the short term.

[1991]

I think your [Greenspan] recommendation of a 25 basis point cut in the Funds rate is appropriate, and in the context of more frequent discussions in the coming weeks, I would prefer the symmetric language. (Reserve Bank President McTeer)

I think staying where we are with alternative I is least likely to do that. We already have lowered the ranges one notch and by not going back up we send a signal that we have not given up on inflation. (Reserve Bank President Boehne)

There are two ECUs here because the results for 1991 separate out the discourse on interest rate setting and the setting of the path of monetary aggregates as required by the Humphrey–Hawkins Act. We can see here though a distinct shift in the language used toward greater clarity and agreement around a proposal from the chairman.

[1992]

. . . and it is also important to recognise that if we get into one of these situations, all institutions are going to be a lot more defensive. That may be good news in one sense. But it is bad news in another sense in that it makes it that much more difficult to deal with them. (Reserve Bank President Corrigan)

. . . we have had a very steep yield curve, very low short term interest rates relative to long rates, low recent inflation, extraordinary rapid growth in the narrow aggregates, which is disturbing, and almost no growth at all in the broad aggregates. (Reserve Bank President Jordan)

The results for 1992 are harder to interpret, though again there are two sets for group 7, separating the discourse on the monetary aggregates from the interest rate decision. The latter is harder to classify in the longer term development of FOMC discourse, a result we put down to the complication in that year of the overhang of the Savings and Loan crisis (which is identified separately in 1991 but appears to be more tied up in interest rate decisions in 1992).

[1993]

. . . [M]y preference would be for no change today but with an asymmetric directive toward tightening. I think having that on the record in the future is more likely to be in our favor than against us for reasons that Jerry Corrigan and Governor Mullins mentioned. (Reserve Bank President McTeer)

[1997]

In my view, there is almost a zero possibility that we would tighten between now and the next meeting. Therefore the best choice is to move to symmetry, largely to avoid an emotional or intellectual bias that might make us feel that we could not respond appropriately to any critical development. (Reserve Bank President McDonough)

Here the president of the New York Fed is setting out his view on the bias statement that would go with the decision on the target Funds rate. The bias statement was intended to provide a signal on the direction of likely future policy moves, although the precise interpretation of the statement was not always clear. It was replaced in 1999.

[1998]

Mr. Chairman, I support a ¼ point reduction in the Funds rate. I also think the current situation may require more than one 25 basis point cut in the funds rate in the future, and therefore I would prefer a directive with asymmetry toward ease. (Reserve Bank President Parry)

This is a clear statement of a forward-looking judgment on the direction of the target Funds rate in the short and more medium term.

[1999]

Mr. Chairman, I am happy to support your recommendation for sitting tight. I think Larry Meyer made a useful contribution yesterday. I have been thinking in my own mind about how to resuscitate the Taylor rule. I may not agree with everything he said, but I view it as a reasonable strategy. (Governor Gramlich)

Here Gramlich combines a view on the immediate policy decision with a broader comment on monetary strategy.

Overall, these ECUs point to the emergence over time of greater confidence over the direction of policy and greater clarity in the statements of FOMC members. In terms of the process of deliberation, the ECUs support our main finding that deliberation on the immediate policy decision declined over time as the FOMC became more confident of the framework of policy within which it was working.

The Relative Contributions of FOMC Members

Our second main finding concerns the relative contributions of FOMC members. Table 3.7 provides a summary using the same broad categorization of themes as above (Assessment of the Economy and Deliberation on Policy). The results suggest that the reserve bank presidents were much larger contributors to deliberation on policy in the Miller–Volcker period than they were in the Greenspan period. In contrast, the presidents played a larger role in the assessment of the economy in the Greenspan period. For their part, the board governors also made a larger contribution to the assessment of the state of the economy in the Greenspan period (for which they attract no significant scores in the Miller–Volcker periods).

We draw a number of conclusions from these results. First, we see some support for Larry Meyer's view that in the Greenspan period deliberation on monetary policy was more a matter for the chairman and board governors. There was relatively less deliberation on the policy decision in the Greenspan period, and it was more focused on the board members. Our results can also be used to provide some support for the suggestion from Blinder and Reis (2005) that the Clinton administration appointed better-qualified governors than its predecessors.

As for the reserve bank presidents, the finding that they played a larger role in the assessment of the economy in the Greenspan period is consistent with the view that Greenspan placed much more emphasis on drawing out information on the state of the economy that was not revealed in the official statistics. Thus the so-called go-round section of the FOMC, in which each member, and particularly the presidents, provide their assessment of developments in the economy since the last meeting (with the presidents providing first-hand accounts of what they see on the ground in their districts) appears to have grown in importance under Greenspan (this is evident in table 3.4, which shows the increased weight on the assessment of the US economy by the late

1990s, and in appendix 3.A to this chapter, which shows the distribution of significant tags for different FOMC members by theme).

The results can also be used to point to a deeper shift in the relative standing of the reserve banks and board governors over time. In the era of higher inflation there was more uncertainty around the strategy of monetary policy and more scope for disagreement within the FOMC. Some reserve banks took a quite different view on monetary theory and the right approach to tackling the inflation problem (the Federal Reserve Bank of St Louis was consistently in the monetarist camp), and more so in the period of high inflation.

Preferences of Members and the Subjects They Discussed
Our third main finding arises from using the net ease/tightness scores from Chappell et al. to determine whether we can detect a connection between the average preference of FOMC members and the subject matter on which they focused in their contributions to FOMC meetings. As described earlier, we compute the rank order of FOMC members according to Chappell et al.'s score of "Rank by net ease dissent frequency" (defined as dissents for ease by a member minus dissents for tightness divided by the total votes of that member) (Chappell, McGregor, et al. 2005). Given the limited overlap of the time periods studied we can only make this assessment for 1991 to 1993 (table 3.8).

The method used was to extract all the significant chi-squared scores for FOMC members from our results (see appendix 3.A to this chapter) and group those into four themes: the state of the US economy/forecasts of economic conditions ("real economy"); the stance of monetary policy, including monetary conditions; credit conditions and the stability of the banking system; and uncertainty around the policy decision and broader monetary policy strategy. We can label these four themes as real economy; money and the monetary policy decision; credit conditions and financial stability; and broader monetary strategy including uncertainty.

The next step was to apply the Chappell et al. rank order scores for FOMC members (on the ease/tightness distribution) to each of the significant chi-squared scores. Note that an FOMC member could score more than once under each theme (it is one score per chi-square not per member). We then computed mean and median scores for each theme for each of the two approaches used by Chappell et al. (votes and transcripts) and compared these scores to the mean and median rank order scores for all FOMC members. This allows us to see where

Table 3.8
Distribution of FOMC members for 1991 to 1993 by theme according to Chappell et al (2005): Rank by net ease tightness (scores are rank orders)

Mean	Voting	Transcripts
Mean score for all FOMC members	**17.00**	**15.50**
Mean rank score for themes		
Real economy	18.84	16.13
Stance of monetary policy/monetary conditions	21.00	23.75
Credit conditions and banking system stability	20.75	21.00
Monetary policy strategy	17.57	16.56

Median	Voting	Transcripts
Median score for all FOMC members	**13.50**	**15.50**
Median rank score for themes		
Real economy	13.50	16.00
Stance of monetary policy/monetary conditions	26.50	24.50
Credit conditions and banking system stability	20.75	21.00
Monetary policy strategy	13.50	16.50

in the distribution lays the average rank score for a member of the FOMC with a significant tag in each of the four thematic groups.

Care is required in interpreting these results because it is noticeable that the thematic scores are consistently distributed at or on the tightening side of the mean/median. That said, the summary scores for the real economy and monetary policy strategy themes are not much different from the aggregate mean and median scores, reflecting the larger number of FOMC members that attract significant chi-squares under these two themes. The monetary policy stance/monetary conditions and credit conditions/banking system stability scores show a clear distribution of members on the net tightening side. However, the sample sizes are very small (four/five members on the monetary policy stance and one/two for credit conditions and banking system stability).[16] One likely reason for this outcome is that, as calculated by Chappell et al., the distribution of dissents in the FOMC was roughly two to one in favor of dissents for a tighter stance of policy. It is possible that our analysis of the full text of FOMC meetings picks up larger contributions from a small number of dissenters than the (relatively) silent majority. In conclusion, on a small sample, we find that members of the FOMC attracting significant scores in our textual analysis for their contributions to meetings on the stance of monetary policy/

monetary conditions and credit conditions/banking system stability were on average more likely to favor a tightening of policy using the scores derives by Chappell et al.

3.5   Conclusions to Part One

Our analysis of the FOMC transcripts over twenty years from 1979 indicates three broad conclusions in terms of changes over time: (1) a shift in the substance of deliberation, from a greater focus on the strategy of monetary policy toward a focus on the state of the US economy; (2) a change in the form and style of deliberation toward shorter meetings, with longer interventions by members of the FOMC; and (3) a shift in the contributions of governors and reserve bank presidents toward the former talking more about monetary policy and the latter more about the US economy.

On the substance of deliberation, we find that the clear increase in the focus on assessing the state of the economy is associated with Alan Greenspan's time as chairman. But we think that this shift of focus may well more fundamentally reflect the deliberation on monetary policy changing with the establishment of a credible low inflation record. We see a pattern of development whereby during the Miller chairmanship and the initial period of Volcker's time in the office, deliberation in the FOMC conveys a sense of substantial uncertainty about policy and its effects, as we might expect. A change sets in from the middle period (the early 1990s) as the low inflation policy became much more clearly established. Interestingly, we observe some reappearance of deliberation around uncertainty in the setting of monetary policy in the later period (late 1990s) notwithstanding the greater clarity on the framework of low inflation. We put this down to uncertainty on the impact of the apparent productivity shock. The overall conclusion is perhaps rather obvious, namely that the substance of deliberation in the FOMC has changed over time as the apparent success of monetary policy, and perhaps more fundamentally the understanding of the framework and objectives of policy have improved.

On the process and nature of deliberation in the FOMC, our results provide support for a conclusion that over time a greater emphasis emerged on set-piece interventions by members. This could be a result of the publication of the transcripts after 1993, as the knowledge of the expected publication of the transcripts drove the real deliberation out of the FOMC meetings and into unrecorded "pre-meetings," with the

FOMC becoming the place for reading of prepared texts. If so, then we have evidence to support the negative impact of what we might call "extreme transparency" of policy-making. We do, however, observe that the timing of the shift in the nature of deliberation in the FOMC does not readily fit with the surprise decision in 1993 to publish the transcripts; rather, we can date the change from at least two years earlier. Our overall conclusion here is that while the decision on publication of the transcripts quite possibly contributed to a change in the style of deliberation, other causes also seem to have been at work. These other causes may reflect the contribution of a new chairman (Alan Greenspan) or may be a further reflection of the change in the environment of monetary policy-making (i.e., another reflection of the change in the substance of policy-making).

Our results suggest clearly that the deliberative form of policy-making is not invariant over time, and thus not invariant to changes in the success and understanding of monetary policy-making. At the least, we can say that changes in the form of policy-making, here represented by the form of deliberation, are part of the story of what was a fundamental change in economic policy-making. Next we turn to the more detailed examination of two points in time when a change of policy occurred, the Volcker Revolution of 1979 and the increases in the target rate in 1999.

PART TWO—THE VOLCKER REVOLUTION AND THE FOMC IN 1999: THE VOLCKER REVOLUTION

3.6 Introduction

Abrupt policy changes are fascinating to study but often awkward to explain. Traditional voting models and econometric tools are better suited to explaining more regular patterns in policy makers' behavior, not least because patterned behavior is more frequently observed. Although it is often easy to identify the causes of an abrupt change, it is much harder to explain why it happened at the particular moment in time.

Modern monetary policy has a strong focus on how policy decisions can effectively influence the expectations of agents in the economy (individual consumers and producers). It is crucially forward-looking in that it seeks to influence the behavior of agents over the coming period. This is inevitably a long-term and repeated process, and as such, the emphasis should be on avoiding sudden, dramatic, and unexpected changes to the direction of policy because agents will be more likely to form solid expectations if they believe they can "read" the behavior of policy makers. However, this line of reasoning depends crucially on agents regarding policy decisions as credible in the sense that they will deliver the stated goal of policy through consistent decision making. Because monetary policy is forward-looking and a repeated decision-making process over that forward period, agents need to attach credibility to the assertions of policy makers that they will stick at the task and their stated objective. The likelihood of policy being regarded as credible therefore depends on the context; if the stated objective (low inflation) has been consistently achieved, it is more likely that agents will believe it will be met in the future. On the contrary, if the objective of policy has not been met, agents are less likely to regard as credible assertions by policy makers that the future will be different. An abrupt change in policy is more likely to be needed in this context. The Volcker Revolution of 1979 is just such an example.

In October 1979, under Chairman Paul Volcker, the FOMC unanimously shifted its course in managing US monetary policy, which in turn eventually brought the era of high inflation to an end. His successor, Alan Greenspan, described the so-called Volcker Revolution as a "turning point" in the economic history of the United States that "rescued our nation's economy from a dangerous path of ever-escalating inflation and instability" (Greenspan 2005: 137). Moreover a unanimous decision was no small feat, particularly in the wake of the scale of division within the FOMC under Volcker's predecessor, G. William Miller, and this provides a further reason for studying in more depth the role of deliberation within the committee setting of the FOMC in order to understand better how this abrupt change was achieved.

There is no doubt that the change of chairman is an important part of the explanation. Meltzer summarizes the difference between Volcker and Arthur Burns as the former doing what the latter said was needed but could not be done, namely control money growth: "The different responses of the two men suggests a difference in their character that contributed to success in one case and failure in the other"(Meltzer 2009: 1024). Meltzer also notes that unlike Burns, Volcker did not adopt an approach of laying blame on groups in society for the problem of inflation (Meltzer 2009: 1097). But that is not the end of the story, and we seek to understand how Volcker *persuaded* other committee members

to endorse a policy that in the short run could be unpopular and eco-
nomically painful for the nation but in the long run would deliver
sustained lower inflation and in the process would lead Americans *to
expect* stable prices to persist. To understand the Volcker Revolution is
to understand the genesis of the Fed's *credible commitment* to lower
inflation.

We conclude that deliberation in the FOMC did matter. Volcker led
his colleagues in coming to understand and apply the idea of *credible
commitment* in US monetary policy-making. We are able to discern (1)
the arguments on which Volcker relied to gain the initial consensus for
the policy shift and differentiate these from (2) the core rationale that
he employed to sustain agreement in the midst of the turbulence during
the subsequent year. Our analysis allows us to identify and measure
Volcker's strategy in shaping the deliberations of the FOMC both over
the short and longer run. Our approach is novel in allowing us to
measure the development of this strategy within the committee setting.

We begin by reviewing the story of monetary policy between 1979
and 1981. Next we consider to what extent the more standard accounts
of the revolution explain the lines of argument used to achieve unanimity in the FOMC. We then apply our approach of automated content
analysis to the transcripts.

3.7 The Volcker Disinflation: The Story of the FOMC from 1979 to 1981

3.7.1 The Shift in 1979

During much of 1979 economic forecasts were pointing toward an
oncoming recession in the US economy and a rapid rise in the inflation
rate. There was a growing realization that past inaction by the FOMC
was contributing to deteriorating inflation expectations among the
public and instability in financial markets. Meltzer puts considerable
weight on a discernible shift in public opinion, with polls suggesting
that by 1979 a growing number of people considered inflation to be at
least as serious a problem as unemployment (Meltzer 2009: 1025). In
his view, this change in public opinion played an important part by
enabling the administration and Congress to accept a decisive approach
to achieving disinflation.

In Volcker's view, monetary policy was the only tool to address inflation, but the Fed lacked credibility in managing this tool and thus
that monetary restraint would be maintained. Volcker's conundrum

was how to provide such a demonstration. For this, he required firm support from his colleagues on the FOMC.

For the 18 months until July 1979, William Miller chaired the FOMC, while Paul Volcker was a permanent voting member as president of the Federal Reserve Bank of New York. Miller sought consensus in the FOMC but rarely achieved it. In June 1979, Miller achieved his desire of a unanimous vote. At that point he left the Fed to become Treasury Secretary in the Carter administration. During the first part of 1979, up to Miller's departure, policy was tightened three times, so that the target for the Fed Funds rate rose to 10½ to 10⅝ percent in July (in December 1978, the lower end of the Fed Funds target range had been 9¾ percent).

Volcker succeeded Miller as chairman at the end of July. At the August FOMC meeting, when the target range was raised by ¼ percent, there were two dissents, one for a larger move up and one for a smaller move. At the FOMC meeting on 18th September, Volcker successfully proposed an increase in the target range to 11¼ and 11¾ percent. The vote was eight to four. The Fed did not, as was customary, publish immediately the voting on the target, nor the target itself, leaving market participants and others to infer the movement in the target. But adjacent to the FOMC meeting, on 18th September, the Fed Board voted to raise the discount rate. The vote was split, with four in favor and three dissents for easier policy. The significance of the vote on the discount rate was that unlike the FOMC vote, it was published immediately, as was the rate. The publication of such a close vote gave an impression that the Fed might waver in its path of tightening policy. This created substantial disruption in financial markets, and the experience is often cited as the immediate reason for the subsequent abrupt change in policy.

The problem in Volcker's view was that the Fed's focus on interest rates (i.e., its targeting of the federal funds rate) created both a psychological and political barrier to tightening monetary policy significantly, inasmuch as fears of recession would raise the specter of political attacks against the Fed (Volcker and Gyohten 1992: 166). Hence Volcker envisaged a new operating target. Rather than targeting interest rates, an alternative strategy would entail targeting the money supply—in short, the new target would be the quantity of money in the system rather than its price. He became disillusioned with the presumed trade-off between unemployment and inflation (the Phillips curve), which in his words, "did not seem to be working well" and became willing to explore the monetarists' emphasis on controlling the money supply (Volcker and Gyohten 1992: 167).

The backdrop to Volcker's new plan was a divided FOMC, consisting of (broadly defined) three groups, those in favor of easier and tighter policy, and a third group of more orthodox monetarists whose stance was not one of ease or tightness per se but rather maintaining a closer link between policy and changes in the monetary aggregates. Those in favor of easier conditions—Governors Teeters, Rice, and Partee—focused on the presumed trade-off between inflation and unemployment. According to Partee, "a little inflation" was "a good thing" in that it "lubricated the economy and it was better to have low unemployment" (Greider 1987: 81). For those in favor of tighter policy, Governors Wallich and Coldwell (and less stridently, Volcker and Governor Schultz), the Fed's priority should be to stabilize prices (Greider 1987: 81). President Roos of the St. Louis Fed, and to a lesser degree other bank presidents—Black, Balles, and Kimbrel—formed a group of monetarists within the FOMC (Greider 1987: 98). Roos, the primary monetarist on the FOMC, criticized the Fed for failing to set and adhere to long-term goals in terms of growth in monetary aggregates and for its lack of transparency.

Prior to the unannounced FOMC meeting on Saturday, October 6, Volcker held a meeting of the Board of Governors and a conference call of the FOMC to canvass support for his proposed approach, that is, shifting from targeting the Fed Funds rate to targeting non-borrowed reserves by the member banks of the Federal Reserve system (but with no fixed monetary rule).[17] Among the governors, Coldwell and Wallich opposed the idea, fearing the inevitable volatility in interest rates that would result. Volcker viewed such volatility—and the uncertainty it would generate—in a more favorable light. With more uncertainty, banks would curtail their lending for speculative purposes—and even more so as Volcker proposed an added reserve requirement of 8 percent on lending by large banks (nonapplication of this to small banks was intended to head off criticism from Congress). For our purposes an important point was that the FOMC was not initially unanimous in its support for the new approach. The initial vote in the FOMC was twelve to five in favor among all members, and eight to three among the voting members. That it became a unanimous vote reflected the emphasis placed by Volcker on the need for a unanimous vote as a show of commitment (reflecting the experience of the reception of the announcement of the divided vote on the discount rate rise) though as Meltzer describes, some members of the FOMC felt able to support the change for reasons that were at variance to the view of the majority. (Thus Partee and Teeters favored a monetary target because it would permit the Funds Rate to fall, which was not consistent with Wallich's reservation; Meltzer 2009: 1031). This pattern of disagreement continued and later became a pattern of dissenting votes that lasted into 1981.

In Volcker's retrospective view, the message of 6th October was very simple: "We meant to slay the inflationary dragon" (Volcker and Gyohten 1992: 170). But Meltzer emphasizes that in the FOMC meeting Volcker emphasized that the change of policy target (to non-borrowed reserves) should be viewed as temporary. In doing so, he distinguished the need for a program that is "strong in fact" from a shift to a reserve target. The transcript contains the following exchange (quoted in Meltzer 2009: 1030):

Chairman Volcker: I am prepared, within the broad parameters, to go whichever way the consensus wants to go so long as the program is strong, and if we adopt the new approach so long as we are not locked into it indefinitely. (p. 10)

Mr. Eastburn [President, Federal Reserve Bank of Philadelphia]:   . . . There is a credibility problem if we launch this and stop and go with it. So I really think we are committed to this if we go forward.

Chairman Volcker: Well I don't want to accept that. (p. 15)

The significant point in this interchange is Volcker's unwillingness at the outset of the change in policy to accept that establishing the credibility of the new approach required it to be viewed as a longer term arrangement. The retrospective conclusion is that the Volcker Revolution achieved a lasting change in the weights given to unemployment and inflation in the monetary policy process toward controlling the latter, thereby establishing low inflation as the best way to increase employment in the long run. Achieving this outcome required the FOMC to stick to the anti-inflation policy until expectations of lower inflation became permanently embedded. There is no doubt that Volcker understood this point from the outset, but it did not translate into a commitment to stick to a single means of achieving the objective. In order to understand how this position was reconciled, we need to look at what happened next.

3.7.2   The Aftermath in 1980 and 1981

The record of the FOMC in 1980 is dominated by the rollercoaster pattern of interest rates and the growth of the narrow monetary aggregate (M1), which was the subject of most attention when deciding how to set the objective for non-borrowed reserves. The Federal Funds rate began the year at around 18 percent, fell to 8 percent in June, and was just under 20 percent in December. At the start of the year there were signs of some slowing in the rate of growth of credit extension, but with inflation remaining over 15 percent. In the middle of March, at the instigation of the Carter administration, the Fed announced a series of emergency credit controls designed to slow further the growth of bank lending. The package was delivered without enthusiasm by the Fed. While the controls were minimal in their extent, there was a sharp contraction in US economic activity in the second quarter, unemployment rose by 1.5 percentage points to 7.8 percent in July, and there was a contraction in the M1 money aggregate.

This sharp contraction in activity posed the fundamental challenge to the new monetary framework. In order better to enhance the credibility of monetary policy, the FOMC could either: (1) stick to its framework and respond to the contraction in the M1 aggregate, thereby loosening monetary policy and allowing interest rates to fall sharply, or; (2) stand against this interpretation of the framework on the view that it would take a stronger lead (and thus tighter policy) to establish persistent low inflation. Initially Volcker retained the view that credibility came from sticking with the announced framework even though that meant a sharp loosening of policy. Some FOMC members dissented, and in late May, Volcker agreed to compromise on the automatic nature of the monetary adjustment, and thus attenuate the easing of policy. But this move attracted dissent from opposite sides—President Roos who was the leading advocate of rigid monetary targeting, and Governor Partee, who opposed a narrow approach as a principle but found the easing created by the rigid policy framework attractive to his desire to see more stimulus.

Between May and July the credit controls were removed. The contraction in economic activity turned out to be brief, and by September the FOMC was faced with the need to tighten policy sharply, *and* to do so in the face of the upcoming presidential election. Policy was tightened, but with four dissents within the FOMC in favor of even sharper tightening. Nonetheless, at each FOMC meeting for the remainder of the year (before and after the election) policy was tightened further. By the end of 1980, with the clear outcome that the rate of money growth would exceed the annual targets set by the FOMC, members began to express concern at the loss of credibility for the policy framework, and the likely effect on inflation expectations. The problem was exacerbated by the growing difficulty of interpreting the monetary aggregates caused by changes in their definition (e.g., resulting from the passage of the Monetary Control Act). Support within the FOMC for monetary control was breaking down. The response from Volcker was more decisively to state the Fed's responsibility to lower inflation and more clearly to state the shorter term social costs involved in doing so (Meltzer 2009: 1072–74). Volcker later described the easing of policy in the spring of 1980 as perhaps his largest mistake as chairman. The volatility of policy during the year also led to extensive scepticism outside the Fed.[18] Meltzer asserts that while the Fed began its anti-inflation program in October 1979, it had to start over again in the fall of 1980 (Meltzer 2009: 1094). Volcker's account traces a more consistent strain of commitment to the goal of anti-inflationary policy even though there was intentionally a lack of commitment to a particular operating framework.

The interpretation of economic conditions in 1981 was complicated by the higher variability of output growth and complications in the interpretation of monetary conditions (changes in the regulations concerning deposit accounts—e.g., the growth of NOW accounts—made it difficult to separate portfolio shifts from policy induced changes in the growth of the aggregates). A further influence was the apparent commitment of the new administration to expand fiscal policy by reducing tax rates and increasing spending on defense. In 1981 the Reagan administration was also explicit in calling for "stable monetary policy, gradually slowing growth rates of money and credit along a pre-announced and predictable path" (quoted in Meltzer 2009: 1086).

Over 1981 as a whole, the Funds rate and the growth of the monetary base moved over wide ranges, though both showed a downward trend. In December 1981, the Funds rate averaged 12.4 percent, 6.5 percentage points below the December 1980 average, and 1.3 percentage points below October 1979. But there was far less evidence of any fall in ten year bond yields or real interest rates, indicating that confidence in the new regime was not yet high even though in early 1981 the twelve month average increase in consumer prices fell below 10 percent, more than seven percentage points below the peak (Meltzer 2009: 1084–86).

In the spring of 1981 the FOMC allowed the Funds rate to rise during a recession, such a significant change of practice that it began to enable a fall in measured expected inflation and thus increased credibility for the policy framework. It was reinforced later in the year when the FOMC did not ease policy with the unemployment rate rising and approaching 8 percent (it reached a postwar peak of 10.8 percent at the end of 1982). The FOMC was divided throughout 1981 in taking these actions (generally with Governors Partee and Teeters favoring less restraint and Governor Wallich more restraint). Nonetheless, the stance of policy in 1981 was a highly significant development because the cost of further reducing inflation would fall as the public became more convinced that these reductions would be permanent, and not a continuation of the stop-go fluctuations of the recent past. These developments were echoed in the increasingly strong advocacy by Volcker to Congress of what is now the orthodoxy that permanent low inflation is the best way to achieve high employment and stable growth, a point we develop further in the next chapter.

Next we set out a number of possible explanations for the Volcker Revolution and its timing.

3.8 Explanations for the Volcker Revolution

3.8.1 Politics and Tactics

Meltzer emphasizes that in contrast to the past, and as a consequence of a clear shift in public opinion toward regarding inflation as the primary economic problem (more so than unemployment), the Fed had the support of the administration and Congress for a robust anti-inflation policy (a support that straddled the Carter and Reagan administrations but began to decline later as the mid-term elections in 1982 approached,[19] though not before meaningful progress had been made toward establishing the credibility of the Fed) (Meltzer 2009: 1093, 1128).[20] This political support removed the prospect of Congress threatening or actually taking legislative action against the Fed as a disciplinary device to achieve a more accommodating monetary policy stance. On its own, the public opinion and political explanation appears to fall into the category of necessary but not sufficient. Why did Volcker change the operating procedure if there was such public and political support for decisive action on inflation?

The tactical explanation reinforces the political argument by asserting that Volcker chose to obscure the impact of the change in policy through the change in the operating procedure. Thus Volcker's approach of targeting non-borrowed reserves offered "a veil that cloaked the tough decisions" as well as a means to bridge the divisions within the FOMC: the FOMC could thus publicly claim "that it was no longer pegging its policy on interest rates, but on the level of M1" and this in turn "would obscure its hand and might deflect the public attacks when interest rates rose sharply. Fed members could explain, disingenuously, that the rising interest rates were attributable to 'market pressures'" (Greider 1987: 106–107). Or, as put in the more colorful words of the Chairman of the Council of Economic Advisors Charles Schultze:

In the mind of the Fed, this whole move was, in the broadest sense, a political move, not an economic move. In theory, the Fed could have kept on raising the bejesus out of the interest rates, but that's what it couldn't do politically. The beautiful thing about this new policy was that as interest rates kept going up, the Fed could say, "Hey, ain't nobody here but us chickens. We're not raising interest rates, we're only targeting the money supply." This way they could raise the rates and nobody could blame them. (Greider 1987: 120)

3.8.2 Economics

Previous studies have noted inherent difficulties in accounting for the Volcker Revolution using standard macroeconomic models (Primiceri 2005). Likewise the behavior of individual monetary policy makers in the Volcker Revolution cannot be explained using standard reaction function approaches (Chappell, McGregor, et al. 2005) because of the short lifetime of the regime established by the revolution (under three years) and the lack of precision in the announced operating target of policy (the dependent variable in a reaction function).

Much of the literature on the Volcker Revolution (summarized in Lindsey, Orphanides, et al. 2005) has focused on explaining the shifting beliefs of policy makers and how these could fit the observed stance of monetary policy. Yet these approaches are problematic in that they: (1) require an understanding of the beliefs of policy makers about variables that neither they (as contemporaries) nor later observers could directly observe—the output gap, the natural rate of unemployment, and the expected persistence of inflationary pressure incorporated by policy makers into whatever models of the economy they used. This leads to a deeper issue, namely; (2) how we can observe the macroeconomic model that each policy maker used to form his judgments on policy (here we use "model" broadly to mean the framework around which each policy maker organized his thinking and views). Subsequent literature tends naturally to impose a single model in order to provide a more tractable analytical framework, but at the risk of distancing the focus further away from the actual beliefs of policy makers. And to complicate matters; and (3) we need to understand the interaction of shocks (in this case to the US economy) and the beliefs (and hence the model) of policy makers (Sargent, Williams, et al. 2004).

Paul Volcker expressed on many occasions, inside and outside the FOMC, his skepticism at the rightness of any economic model to describe and capture the monetary policy task of the Fed. Moreover, as Meltzer notes, the FOMC did not discuss explicitly the analytical framework for thinking about inflation (a conclusion reinforced by our textual analysis results that provide no evidence to the contrary). Some members of the FOMC spoke in terms consistent with a Phillips curve model, while others put more weight on expectations and the credibility of monetary policy. The FOMC appears to have shifted its emphasis from unemployment to inflation without discussing the economic model to be used for doing so (Meltzer 2009: 1061). Here, for once at least, Volcker was consistent with his predecessors (and his successor). Fed staff had in the past relied on a simple Keynesian model with a nonvertical long-run Phillips curve. But neither William McChesney Martin nor Arthur Burns put any faith in economic models, and both were keen to say so in public. Meltzer cites Burns from the FOMC meeting in June 1977: "I have managed to get to my present age without paying much attention to what these equations have to say. . . . I see no reason for learning these things at the present time" (Meltzer 2009: 856–58, 914).

There is a clear link between the absence of reliance on economic models at the time and the difficulty of contemporary usage of models to explain the actions of policy makers at the time. One response to the limitation of standard macroeconomic models of the Volcker Revolution has been to use a learning approach that allows policy makers to adapt the parameters of their models over time. Some authors have suggested that rather than FOMC members making persistent mistakes during the so-called Great Inflation of the 1960s and 1970s, they displayed slow learning via adapting their expectations on, for instance, the natural rate of unemployment (Sims 1988; Cho, Williams, et al. 2002; Sargent, Williams, et al. 2004). This learning explanation suggests that policy makers updated their beliefs about the unobserved variables of their model of the economy in every period, and they implemented policy conditional on their current beliefs.[21] Unfortunately, as ex post analytical tools, learning approaches can become exercises in retrofitting to the data, that is, parameterizing to fit the change in the beliefs of policy makers as revealed by their decisions.

A second response has been to emphasize the role and impact of a new idea(s) on policy makers (Romer 2005). Here too there is a danger of retrofitting. Ex post, we can observe the development of an idea, and hence it is attractive to tie that idea in to the observed decisions of policy makers. Yet, without observing directly the beliefs of policy makers, we are unable to test whether the idea really influenced their beliefs. According to the ideas explanation for the Volcker Revolution, a new idea—namely that policy makers will stand a greater chance of achieving their desired outcomes if they are able to make credible commitments (in the sense that the public believes them) about the policies they will follow in the future—triumphed quite suddenly. This idea originated in the famous 1977 article by Finn Kydland and Edward Prescott (Kydland and Prescott 1977), one of whose examples was the effect of a credible commitment by monetary policy makers to future low inflation on the inflation expectations and hence wage and price increase demands of the public.[22] But it is much less clear to what extent, by 1979, Kydland and Prescott's idea had been absorbed and accepted by members of the FOMC.

3.9   Arguments for the Policy Change

We identify three prominent arguments that Volcker might have employed to convert his FOMC colleagues in October 1979.

3.9.1   Commitment and Credibility

Under the credible commitment argument Volcker would have appealed to the idea of time consistency (as developed by Kydland and Prescott 1977) to persuade colleagues that a change in policy would provide a future low inflation and thus influence the expectations of agents (Chari, Christiano, et al. 1998; Christiano and Gust 2000; Christiano and Fitzgerald 2003). If "commitment" had a bearing in the discussions, we should expect to see a greater weight on the importance of the credibility of the monetary policy framework, the expected impact of that credibility on inflation expectations, and possibly the inclusion of expectations in the models of FOMC members (the introduction of an expectational Phillips curve). FOMC members should be concerned about whether agents would believe their commitment to deliver lasting low inflation.

3.9.2   Change of Economic Model

Here Volcker would have persuaded policy makers that the long-run Phillips curve was vertical, with no scope for assuming a trade-off between inflation and employment (Romer and Romer 2002; Meltzer 2005). Support for this explanation would come from evidence that FOMC members both (1) discussed and (2) changed their position on the trade-off between inflation and employment. For those who changed, we might find evidence that they had come to accept the idea of a vertical slope on the Phillips curve. We should expect to see FOMC members devoting considerable attention to inflation and output/employment.

3.9.3   Money Matters

Under the monetary controls argument Volcker would have persuaded his colleagues that they had underweighted the role of money in their explanations of inflation (Meltzer 2005). Evidence of FOMC members merely describing their preferred target ranges for money would be necessary but insufficient as a demonstration of this causal argument. We should look for evidence that FOMC members had moved beyond recognizing the role of money in the inflationary process toward advocating the desirability of monetary control. Meltzer argues that from the mid-1970s most FOMC members had understood the role of money in causing changes in the rate of inflation, but they had not made the leap to wanting greater control over the growth of money (Meltzer 2009: 861). Alongside this leap we might also expect to see members of the FOMC distinguishing between one time changes in the price level (e.g., from oil price shocks) and changes in the persistent rate of inflation (Meltzer 2009: 857, 861, 915).[23]

In framing these arguments for the policy change, we should remember that since Volcker did not in October 1979 advocate anything beyond a temporary change to the operating procedure, he is unlikely to have expressed any lasting confidence in economic models per se, nor advocated adopting an orthodox monetarist position. There are therefore important doubts around how Volcker employed any of these arguments in the critical October 1979 meeting. And beyond that, how did he persuade the FOMC to stay the course throughout the next year?

It is conceivable that the deliberation in the October 1979 meeting lacked lasting substance such that the change in operating procedure was the lowest common denominator upon which FOMC members could all agree to confront the inflationary "dragon." But, if this was true, common sense would suggest that turbulent times would quickly strip away the flimsy veil of agreement to expose the underlying dissension and conflict among FOMC members. One would not expect the FOMC to have held steady to its new operating mechanism throughout the difficult conditions of 1980 and 1981. What, then, was the glue that held the committee together? Our findings suggest that Volcker's solution represented more than the lowest common denominator. Underpinning his new approach was a powerful idea that would in time break the back of the inflationary spiral.

3.10   Results of the Textual Analysis of FOMC Transcripts in the Volcker Revolution Period

Our aim is to discern which of the rationales appears to have support based on what was said by FOMC members over the period immediately before, during, and after the Volcker Revolution.

3.10.1   Identifying the Themes
We examine four text files covering the FOMC transcripts immediately before, during and immediately after the start of the Volcker Revolution—1979 (Miller), 1979 (Volcker), 1980, and 1981. Table 3.2 from the first section of this chapter provides a summary of the basic statistics for the four periods.

In the Miller period, 69 percent of the retained ECUs were classified as a representative pattern of text for each class. For the Volcker period, the retention rate rises to 79 percent for the remainder of 1979, 82 percent in 1980, and 78 percent in 1981. The lower rate of classification under Miller and consistently higher rate under Volcker suggests that the content and format of FOMC meetings were more focused under the latter chairman.

The final two blocks in each column of table 3.2 indicate the number of classes identified in each set of transcripts and the size of each class (based on an analysis of the most characteristic words for each class—those with high χ^2 values—and the most representative ECUs classified for each class), the label identifying the subject matter of the class, followed by a numeric classification of the classes into broader thematic groups (shown in parenthesis in bold).

While the Miller period contains six thematic classes, Volcker 1979 contains five, and 1980 and 1981 have only four thematic classes. As described in the earlier section of this chapter summarizing the results of all the FOMC sample, 1980 and 1981 are conspicuous in two ways:

they attain a higher rate of classification (the discourse is likely to have been more focused); and the range of themes discussed is narrower.

3.10.2   Schematic Overview of the Themes in the Volcker Revolution Period

Tree Diagrams
Figures 3.1 to 3.4 set out the *relative importance* of and the *relationships* between the classes. In figure 3.1 (the Miller period), classes 1 and 2—both of which relate to the monetary policy stance and FOMC members' uncertainty about changing this stance—are closely related, as are classes 3 and 4—both of which focus on the US economy. Classes 3 and 5 in the 1979 Volcker period (figure 3.2) are closely related, as both are concerned with the monetary policy stance and the impact of changing that stance. A key feature of figures 3.1 to 3.4 is the relative simplicity of the FOMC discussions under Volcker in 1980, and the distinct nature—in terms of size and content—of the "striving for credibility" class in that year, with that one class accounting for nearly half the classified ECUs. In other words, the FOMC dedicated the lion's share of its discussions in 1980 to the Fed's ability to demonstrate a credible commitment to lower inflation. The results for 1981 (figure 3.4) point to a change in the discourse away from a closer focus on striving for credibility toward the choices within the new operating framework,

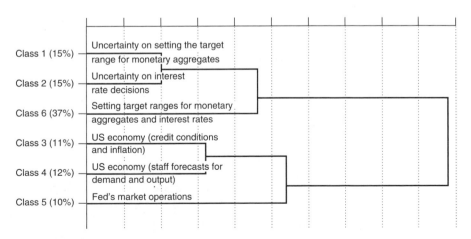

Figure 3.1
Tree graph of the classes for 1979 FOMC transcripts (Miller)

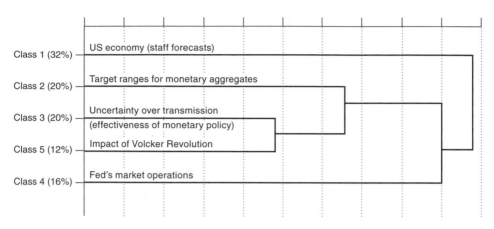

Figure 3.2
Tree graph of the classes for 1979 FOMC transcripts (Volcker)

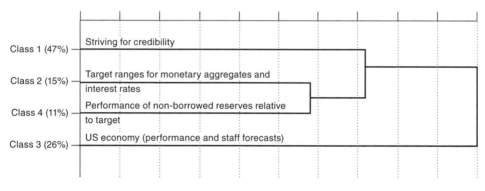

Figure 3.3
Tree graph of the classes for 1980 FOMC transcripts

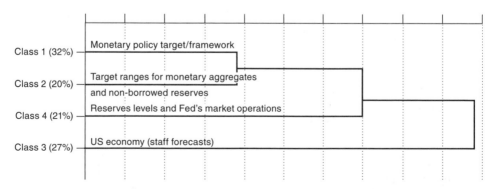

Figure 3.4
Tree graph of the classes for 1981 FOMC transcripts

suggesting less focus on whether the regime was sustainable and more on the choice of policy stance within that regime.

Correspondence Analysis
The tree diagrams provide a reasonably simple initial portrayal of the relationships between the themes (classes). Figures 3.5 to 3.8 extend this by placing the themes and the tags on a single correspondence graph—where distance between a class and a tag (or between two classes) reflects the degree of co-occurrence. As such, they provide a graphical presentation of the spatial relations between the classes.

For these graphs the program cross-tabulates classes and words in their root form in order to create a matrix that can then be subjected to factor correspondence analysis (Greenacre and Hastie 1987; Greenacre 1993).[24] In this way we obtain a spatial representation of the relations between the classes—in other words, we can observe *how* the classes are related to one another (and tags related to the classes), and not just that relationships exist. The positions of the points are contingent on correlations rather than coordinates, where distance reflects the degree of co-occurrence.[25] With respect to the axes, correspondence analysis aims to account for a maximum amount of association[26] along the first (horizontal) axis. The second (vertical) axis seeks to account for a maximum of the remaining association, and so on. Hence the total association is divided into components along principal axes.[27] The resulting map provides a means for transforming numerical information into pictorial form. It provides a framework for the user to formulate her own interpretations, rather than providing clear-cut conclusions. It is generally used to identify systematic relations between variables when a priori expectations of relationships are incomplete or absent (Nagpaul 1999).

Beneath the correspondence maps are the percentage associations for each factor. These describe the total variance in the corpus accounted for by a two-dimensional correspondence space. Dimensionality in this context requires careful dissection. Usually the dimensionality of the system is one less than the number of classes in the profile (Greenacre 1993).[28] The first two factors taken together account for 57 and 66 percent of the variance explained (measured by total inertia) for the Miller and Volcker periods of 1979, respectively. Again, the discourse in 1980 appears to be different: a two-dimensional spatial map captures 100 percent of the variance that is explained in the original correspondence tables. The circular appearance of this graph is a product of the

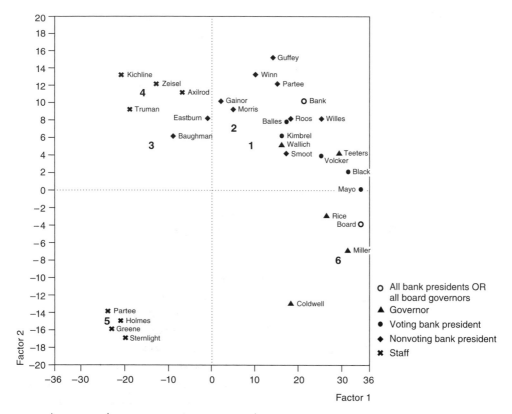

	Association	Cumulative
Factor 1	31.9%	31.9%
Factor 2	24.9%	56.8%

1 Uncertainty on setting target range for monetary aggregates
2 Uncertainty on interest rate decisions
3 US economy (credit conditions and inflation)
4 US economy (staff forecasts for demand and output)
5 Fed's market operations
6 Setting target ranges for monetary aggregates and interest rates

Figure 3.5
Correspondence analysis of classes for FOMC transcripts (Miller, 1979)

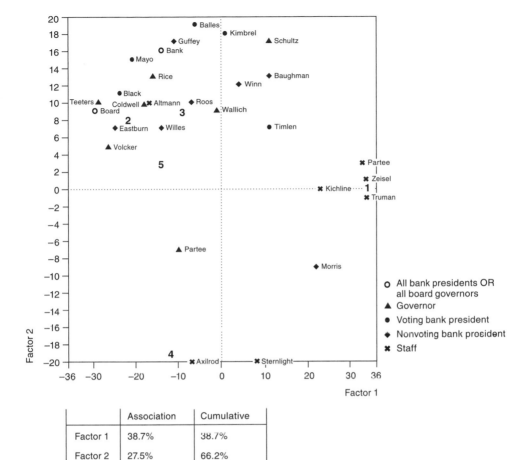

	Association	Cumulative
Factor 1	38.7%	38.7%
Factor 2	27.5%	66.2%

1 US economy (staff forecasts)
2 Target ranges for monetary aggregates
3 Uncertainty over transmission (effectiveness of monetary policy)
4 Fed's market operations
5 Impact of Volcker Revolution

Figure 3.6
Correspondence analysis of classes for FOMC transcripts (Volcker, 1979)

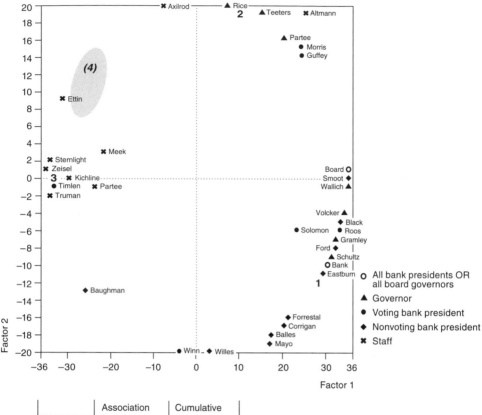

	Association	Cumulative
Factor 1	62.1%	62.1%
Factor 2	37.9%	100%

1 Striving for credibility
2 Target ranges for monetary aggregates and interest rates
3 US economy (performance and staff forecasts)
4 Performance of non-borrowed reserves relative to target

Figure 3.7
Correspondence analysis of classes for FOMC transcripts (1980)

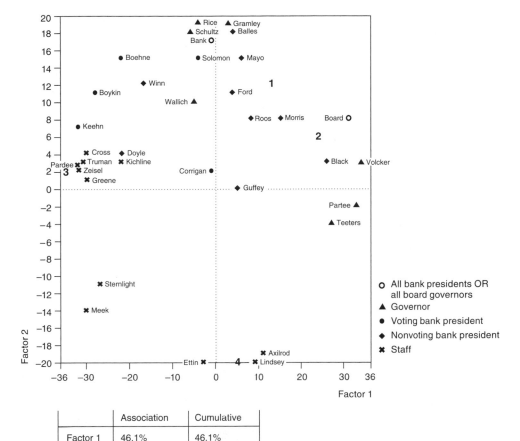

	Association	Cumulative
Factor 1	46.1%	46.1%
Factor 2	32.4%	78.5%

1 Monetary policy target/framework
2 Target ranges for monetary aggregates and non-borrowed reserves
3 US economy (staff forecasts)
4 Reserves levels and Fed's market operations

Figure 3.8
Correspondence analysis of classes for FOMC transcripts (1981)

space being two-dimensional,[29] and its peculiar appearance may indicate the so-called arch effect, which occurs when one variable has a
uni-modal distribution with respect to a second. De-trending may
remove the arch effect, but this method has been criticized for the
resulting loss of information and has been described as "taking a
sledge hammer to your data."[30] In 1981 the first two factors together
account for 79 percent of the variance. What is evident from figures 3.5
to 3.8 is that the deliberation of the FOMC in 1980 was more focused
in terms of thematic content than were meetings in the previous two
periods, and more so than in 1981 (and compared to the Greenspan
years that we have sampled). The low dimensionality observed in 1980
is indicative of discourse in the FOMC that was more thematically
concentrated.

In the correspondence graphs the thematic classes are indicated by
number and labeled below each graph, while tags for the names of
speakers (FOMC members and staff) are given by symbols. All four
graphs indicate a basic "dimensionality" in that discourse on the state
of the US economy and financial markets is generally separated from
discourse on the policy decision, the framework of monetary policy,
and uncertainty among FOMC members concerning policy. For the
Miller period of 1979 this division is evident along the first (horizontal)
dimension, suggesting a fairly simple structure to the discourse. The
second (vertical) dimension suggests a division between discourse
on monetary aggregates and the Fed's financial market operations
designed to influence those aggregates, and deliberation on the FOMC
decision and on the state of the US economy. The Volcker Revolution
period of 1979 shows a starker divide along the first dimension (horizontal), with the discourse on the US economy much further removed
from all the other classes. This suggests that while the FOMC discussed
the state of the economy, there was a much greater coherence among
the discourse on the policy decision and the money and reserves
targets. Again, this is not surprising. The correspondence graph for
1980 (figure 3.7) indicates a clear division between the discussion of the
credibility of policy and the other classes, which is evident in both the
first and second dimensions, once again illustrating that there was
something different about the structure of discourse in the FOMC in
1980. In contrast, the results for 1981 indicate that along the first (horizontal) dimension, the policy decisions of the FOMC were more closely
related to discussion of the state of the US economy. Instead, the first
dimension separates out discourse on the Fed's operations. That said,

the second (vertical) dimension indicates a division between discussion of the US economy and the policy decision/Fed operations. One conclusion we can draw from these results is that the Volcker Revolution period in late 1979 and 1980 involved a separation of the discourse on the economy from the discourse on monetary policy. This separation is less evident in the Miller period and in 1981. Our results therefore tend to support the view that the Volcker Revolution required a separation of discourse on the economy from discourse on monetary policy, no doubt as a means to break the cycle of monetary policy accommodating weak levels of economic activity and higher inflation.

Next we turn to the spatial positions of the classes and tags. These reveal that FOMC members (governors and presidents) and Fed staff tend to cluster around different themes, which in turn suggests that the themes covered by staff members (speaking in an advisory capacity at meetings) were often distinct from those of the actual FOMC members. In the Miller period (figure 3.5), Fed staff focused on the state of the US economy (classes 3 and 4) and on the Fed's financial markets operations (class 5) while FOMC members discussed policy-focused topics, notably the monetary policy stance (including the uncertainty surrounding changing it—classes 1 and 2) and target ranges (class 6). In the 1979 Volcker period (figure 3.6), Fed staff again focused on the US economy (class 1), with some attention also given to the implementation of the new policy stance (class 4). Meanwhile FOMC members were again more concerned with issues surrounding the monetary policy framework, such as the transmission mechanism and the impact of changing that policy framework (classes 3 and 5), and with monetary aggregate ranges (class 2).

In 1980 (figure 3.7), we again find a concentration of Fed staff clustered around the US economy theme (class 3) while FOMC members focus particularly on the issue of credibility (class 1), and the two groups overlap in discussing the monitoring of targets (class 2). Notably class 4 (i.e., the performance of non-borrowed reserves relative to the targets set by the FOMC) is drawn as an ellipse rather than a single point, which stems from its relatively small size in terms of classified ECUs. That is, when the weight of the classes is highly skewed (or when a large number of classes is identified), the program occasionally fails to locate the center point for the class with the fewest representative words, which for 1980 is class 4. Hence we have estimated the position of class 4 from the correspondence analysis of the representative words.[31]

In 1981 (figure 3.8), we see the typical clustering of Fed staff around the classes focused on the US economy (class 3) and the Fed's operations in financial markets (class 4), while FOMC members are clustered around the policy discourse classes (classes 1 and 2). We can also see that the summary tags for board governors and bank presidents are distributed such that the former are more focused on the choice of target ranges for money and reserves. Looking back to 1980, the bank presidents (as represented by their summary tag) were most closely aligned to the first class concerning the overall credibility of monetary policy, while the board governors were, as in 1981, nearer to the choice of target ranges within the policy framework. In the Volcker period of 1979, the two summary tags are most closely aligned, which points to the process of alignment among members of the FOMC achieved by Volcker at the outset of the Revolution. In the Miller period of 1979, the results suggest that the board governors were most aligned with deliberation on the immediate policy decision, while the bank presidents were more focused on uncertainty around policy. Overall, our results suggest that during this period the bank presidents devoted more time to discourse on the broader framework of monetary policy.

While the spatial graphs provide a visual representation of the data, we can obtain greater precision in measuring the relationships between tags and thematic classes from the levels of statistical significance assigned to each tag. In figure 3.9 we group all the classes into four categories: (1) US economy and the Fed's financial operations (including policy implementation); (2) monetary policy stance, uncertainty, and monitoring target ranges; (3) impact of the Volcker Revolution; and (4) striving for credibility. We present these as simple bar charts. As noted before, Fed staff are highly associated with discourse on the US economy and Fed operations, while FOMC members are associated with the monetary policy stance (and uncertainty surrounding it) and target ranges. The only significant member tag for the Impact of the Volcker Revolution in figure 3.9 (Volcker era) belongs to Volcker himself.

The more statistical output from Alceste helps guide an interpretation of the Volcker Revolution period, but it does not provide a conclusive assessment of the explanations for how Volcker achieved the decisive change within a committee process of decision making. Next we look in more detail at the text of FOMC members' discourse highlighted by Alceste and whether this supports or rejects each of the three rationales that Volcker might have used to gain the support of his colleagues, and to keep that support throughout 1980 and 1981.

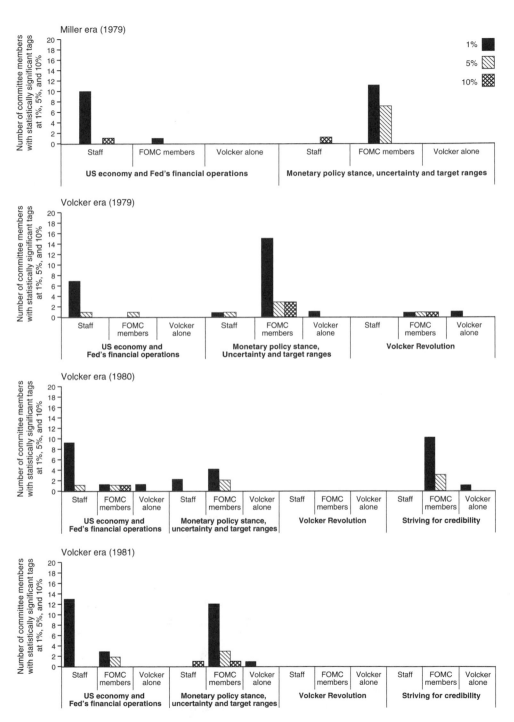

Figure 3.9
Grouped classes by committee member: Number of committee members with significant tags

3.11   Commitment and Credibility

For the Miller period, classes 1 and 2 relate to the uncertainty around the framework for monetary policy and the immediate decision facing the FOMC. Together, they account for 30 percent of the overall distribution of classes and they are closely linked in the tree diagram (meaning that the language used by members often overlapped). All of the significant tags for these two classes belong to members of the FOMC. The representative ECUs set out in appendix 3.B help illustrate the plight of a committee that was unsure of itself:

Let us not find ourselves locked into that same old situation as in the past. If we suspect at all that there is a danger of getting locked into that, there is some advantage in changing the numbers simply for technical reasons just to change the numbers. (Reserve Bank President Eastburn discussing setting the monetary aggregate targets)

Foolish consistency is the hobgoblin of a little mind, and everyone knows that you are a big mind! (Chairman Miller)

What we do not see is a clear commitment to gaining credibility for monetary policy through a consistent policy in the face of shocks to the economy that raised inflation. This is consistent with the widespread view that the Fed had severely damaged its credibility during the Great Inflation period of the 1960s and 1970s. It is also consistent with the view that in the face of uncertainty over the effectiveness of monetary policy, FOMC members would tend toward inaction (the risk-adjusted costs of doing something in the face of uncertainty seemed to outweigh the costs of doing nothing).

For the 1979 Volcker period, classes 3 and 5 ("effectiveness of monetary policy—uncertainty over the transmission mechanism" and "impact of the Volcker Revolution and communication of the policy change") relate to the framework for monetary policy. Together, they account for 32 percent of the overall distribution of classes and are more closely linked than other classes in the tree diagram. There are 13 significant tags for class 3, the effectiveness of monetary policy— all belonging to FOMC members—but *none* of these were Volcker's. Rather, Volcker's tag is highly significant ($\chi^2 = 226$) for class 5, the impact of the Volcker Revolution and communication of the policy change.

A closer look at the statements of committee members shows that to the extent that commitment was discussed, it was associated more with the effectiveness of monetary policy (class 3) rather than as part of a more narrow discussion on the impact of the Volcker Revolution (class 5). FOMC members' discussions of commitment within class 3 suggest that they viewed the credibility of the Fed as something to be gained, a change in tone from the uncertainty of the Miller period:

But I don't think that approach will be a very happy one unless people are pretty confident about our long term intentions. That's the credibility problem and the confidence we have to establish as I see it, and we haven't got a helluva lot of time as the recession comes along but particularly if it gets worse. (Chairman Volcker)

There is an immediate advantage in the publicity; there is a disadvantage not very far down the road if people read this as a commitment and in fact we are not going to be able to live up to that commitment. (Chairman Volcker)

These suggest that Paul Volcker envisaged the idea of a commitment in terms of the need for the Fed to establish credibility. To the extent that beliefs shifted, this was toward recognizing that the benefits of adopting a consistent anti-inflation policy outweighed the costs of doing nothing.

In 1980, FOMC members spoke clearly in terms of credibility, but in terms of minimizing risk and with a fair amount of uncertainty as to the means to achieving credibility. The single largest thematic class—"striving for credibility"—shows that as the committee grappled with targeting non-borrowed reserves, it was concerned with its ability to communicate the Fed's intentions to the public. For President Mayo, the determination to show commitment was clear:

That may make our success in controlling the aggregates seem a little better, but that could provide a false sense of security. I hope we handle it a bit better despite what I said about the basic adequacy of our record. We have to keep our eye on the ball and dig in. (Reserve Bank President Mayo)

Here we see a determination to stay the course and to renew public confidence in the Fed's commitment to managing inflation, which had not been evident in the preceding period. Of the 14 significant FOMC member tags for this class, Volcker's tag leads the rest by a fair margin, with Volcker's χ^2 value of 195.4, and the next nearest (belonging to President Corrigan) of 42.9.

By 1981, the dominance of credibility as a theme in the FOMC discourse had declined, with 32 percent of the identified thematic content being given over to the choice of the target/framework for policy.

Interestingly, Volcker attracted a larger χ^2 value (168.7) in 1981 for his association with the second class ("deliberation on the immediate decisions on targets for non-borrowed reserves and the monetary aggregates"), whereas in 1980 he attracted no significant χ^2 value for the equivalent class. This suggests that his contribution to the FOMC discourse shifted somewhat between the two years (in 1981 he does attract a significant χ^2 value in the class devoted to the broader policy framework, but the value is smaller (15.0 versus 195.4). The ECUs attracting the largest χ^2 values in the first class convey the sense that while there remained a clear understanding of the need for consistency in the policy framework, there was a greater prominence to admitting the limits of knowledge among FOMC members and a willingness to admit that there was a strong tactical element to the choice of the reserve target rather than a Fed Funds target, and to start to question the future of the framework put in place in 1979:

Mr. Chairman, I think you are right, and this is what we need to keep in mind, that there really is only one reason why we should have abandoned the Federal Funds target procedure to go to the reserve target. And that is because if we operate on Federal Funds, we explicitly take responsibility for what is happening to interest-rates and then this becomes a very, very difficult world to live in. (Governor Gramley)

The burden of my comment is not that we know any of these things empirically or logically. The burden is that we have all these uncertainties. . . . I am going a long distance in that direction but I do not think we can abandon M1 at this point, given all the emphasis on it. (Chairman Volcker)

The tone is different from the theme of "keep our eye on the ball and dig in" seen in 1980. Nonetheless, we do see evidence from the text of a clear shift in attitudes to commitment among FOMC members that followed from Volcker's abrupt change of policy.

3.12   Change of Model

A simple test of this explanation is whether FOMC members obtain statistically significant tags for classes devoted to inflation and output/employment. For the Miller period, there are two classes relating to inflation and activity in the United States, classes 3 and 4. Taken together, they account for 23 percent of the distribution of classes. But, in terms of statistically significant tags, those for Fed staff outnumber FOMC members by seven to one. The same is true for the 1979 Volcker period, where one class covers inflation and activity in the United States (class 1, accounting for 32 percent of the distribution of classes), but among the significant tags the staff outnumber FOMC members by six to none. In 1980 class 3, which focuses on the weakening of the US economy, shows a similar dominance of staff to FOMC members of seven to two. But in 1981 the equivalent score is eight to five, indicating that by then FOMC members were more concerned with developments in the economy. The tree maps also indicate that the classes devoted to inflation and activity in the US economy are separated from the classes devoted to the framework and stance of policy, most obviously in the Volcker periods. We appear to have a story that in both the Miller and Volcker periods there was a clear distinction between discussion of economic activity and inflation, and discussion of the monetary policy stance and framework. Staff, and not FOMC members, dominated the discussion of the US economy until 1981. On its own, this would not settle the argument on the case for a change of economic model since in the second study, of 1999, we do find explicit discussion of economic models in the ECUs on the monetary policy discussion. But for the Volcker period we find no such evidence. We therefore conclude that the FOMC did not justify the abrupt change in policy in terms of a change in their economic model used to determine monetary policy decisions.

3.13   Money Matters

If Volcker persuaded his colleagues of the importance of the role of money in the inflation process (i.e., that *money matters*), we should see evidence of a class(es) that emphasized not just the description of members' preferred target ranges for the monetary aggregates, but also that members were placing more emphasis on inflation as a monetary phenomenon. An absence of evidence of members focusing on the role of money in the inflation process would tend to confirm that the Volcker Revolution was not a triumph of strict monetarism.

For the Miller period, class 6 can be categorized as "target ranges for money and interest rates." This accounts for 37 percent of the overall distribution of classes. There are six significant tags for this class, five of which belong to members of the FOMC (with Miller himself attracting by far the largest level of statistical significance) and one belonging to a staff member. In the tree diagram this class is more closely linked to the classes on the stance of monetary policy and the uncertainty faced by the FOMC. But the representative ECUs for this class are entirely taken up by descriptions of the preferences of FOMC members for the target ranges for money, and not by analysis of the role of money in the inflationary process. The evidence appears to indicate that FOMC members devoted time to describing their preferences for the aggregates, but without a clear sense of a consistent link to an understanding of inflationary pressures in the context of monetary policy. There was a tendency to think of inflation as a problem somewhat divorced from the behavior of the aggregates.

Turning to the 1979 Volcker period, class 2 relates to deliberation on the target ranges for the monetary aggregates. This class accounts for 20 percent of the overall distribution of classes. There are 11 significant tags for this class, 9 of which belong to members of the FOMC and 2 belong to staff. The representative ECUs for this class are entirely taken up by descriptions of the preferences of FOMC members for the target ranges for money and reserves, and again not by analysis of the role of money in the inflationary process.

For 1980 and 1981, class 2 is again in both cases the class devoted to deliberation on the target ranges, accounting for 15 and 20 percent of the distribution of the classes, respectively, in the two years. In terms of significant tags, FOMC members outnumber staff by six to two in 1980 and four to one in 1981. As for 1979, the ECUs indicate that the discourse was entirely descriptive in terms of preferred ranges, rather than providing a focus on the role of money. It is also noteworthy that by 1981 more of the ECUs in this class are devoted to discussing the Federal Funds rate target.

We conclude that the *money matters* argument at best fits as an explanation of the Volcker revolution insofar as the targeting of non-borrowed reserves provided a vehicle to achieve greater restraint in policy-setting and for achieving consensus among the FOMC. But the evidence does not indicate that FOMC members set out to instigate a policy whose rationale lay in implementing strong monetarist principles.

3.14   Assessment of the Volcker Revolution

Abrupt policy changes such as the Volcker Revolution are by their nature difficult to explain using conventional analytical techniques. A good part of the literature on the Volcker Revolution seeks to explain the change in terms of shifts in the largely unobserved beliefs of policy makers. But the danger of this type of approach is that of retrofitting—

namely using the information ex post to fit a model that creates a story of shifts in unobserved beliefs. Such an approach is plausible only insofar as it fits the story as observed ex post. A study of how policy is made inevitably must try to answer the question from a contemporary perspective by studying the behavior of policy makers at the time.

A key finding from our analysis is the change in the form and substance of the discourse in the FOMC during this period. The more structured discourse of 1980 is conspicuous. The FOMC discourse appears to have been more focused, illustrated by the dominant "striving for credibility" class in that year. Thus the FOMC dedicated the larger share of its discussions in 1980 to the Fed's ability to demonstrate a credible commitment to lower inflation. Volcker's tag is the dominant one in the "striving for credibility" class in 1980. The discourse shifted again in 1981 toward a greater interest in alternative immediate policy targets to non-borrowed reserves, but our evidence suggests that this shift occurred only once the more decisive debate on credibility and commitment had taken place. Our evidence supports a view that in 1979, targeting of non-borrowed reserves provided a vehicle to achieve greater restraint in policy-setting and for achieving consensus among the FOMC. Although this fairly empirical debate on the role of money signified the decisive shift in policy, the general theme of "money matters" was quickly relegated in 1980 in favor of the theme of credible commitment to the new policy framework. Hence, while "money matters" appears to have been important in winning the initial argument, what sustained the evolution of policy through 1980 was the theme of credible commitment. Our analysis of the textual evidence suggests that FOMC members came to accept the importance of committing to an anti-inflationary policy. But, while members noted the role of inflation expectations, their commitment to an anti-inflationary policy was not set within a formal model of credibility and commitment. The tool for delivering the policy change was to adopt a monetary target (non-borrowed reserves), but again this was not done within a well-articulated framework of the role of money.

We can add further evidence to support our conclusions by using the interviews conducted in support of our work, where we were able to ask FOMC members and Fed staff of the time for their assessment of how the Volcker Revolution came about (chapter 5). We start with Paul Volcker's own view on the credibility issue:

I can understand that you have this big emphasis on credibility—first we had to stick to tight money and secondly we had to follow our own precept that if the money supply came down we had to ease. But that was a different kind of credibility. The first credibility was to convince the market that we were going to deal with inflation and the second was to maintain credibility with the whole approach of following the money supply—if that makes sense.

In the FOMC meeting of January 1982, Volcker set out the case for building credibility, not for its own sake, but to create flexibility later (i.e., the more credible the FOMC actions, the less constrained they would be in the future when they saw the need to diverge from a strict operating objective and/or the need to assert their independence from political pressure): "We do not build up credibility for the sake of building up more credibility. We build up credibility to get the flexibility to do what we think is necessary" (quoted in Meltzer 2009: 1100).

At the FOMC meeting in May 1982 the FOMC began to shift to an explicit interest rate target, and lowered the preferred range for the Fed Funds rate. Volcker later described this change in an interview (Mehrling 2007) as follows: "The Mexican crisis was brewing. The economic recovery had not appeared. I thought, aha, here's our chance to ease credibly. So we took the first small step."[32]

Volcker's comments over the years put the emphasis on the first of his two "credibilities," namely that the FOMC could convince people that it would deal with inflation and persist in that endeavor. But achieving the credible anti-inflation commitment relied on the demonstration by the FOMC of a clear shift in the operating framework, a point brought out in our interview with Steve Axilrod, the senior Fed staff economist of the time:

It was the credibility of the policy shift not the anti-inflation credibility. The latter was implicit in it but it was the credibility of the policy shift. We were making a policy shift, a paradigm shift. The market has to believe that we are going to continue with this policy.

The conclusion that what changed was the credibility of the anti-inflation commitment is not new or surprising. Our approach of using textual analysis allows us to draw out more explicitly a two-stage process in the FOMC deliberations, starting with an emphasis on the importance of money as the means to achieve the policy shift in 1979, but then changing decisively in 1980 to an emphasis on achieving credibility. We show that both stages were led by Volcker himself, and that in 1980, as the policy change came under intense pressure, the nature of the deliberation within the FOMC changed to one with a marked focus on one subject, namely achieving credibility for tackling inflation.

Finally, can we use textual analysis to make the link between the arguments used in the FOMC on the credibility of a consistent anti-inflation policy and the theoretical insight of Kydland and Prescott in their 1977 article on time consistency (Kydland and Prescott 1977)? In the article they developed the example of the inflation-unemployment problem, noting that standard policy prescriptions of the time led to the choice of monetary policy that is best in view of the current situation. They demonstrated that such a choice (which is discretionary in nature) would result in excessive rates of inflation without any reduction in unemployment, which was inferior to a consistent policy of maintaining price stability. It would be attractive to make the direct link to the emphasis on credibility in the Volcker Revolution, but, consistent with the atheoretical history of the FOMC, we can detect no sign that the FOMC discussed the work of Kydland and Prescott or more broadly talked in terms of "Rules Rather than Discretion" (the title of their article). And indeed this assessment of the role of Kydland and Prescott's article was confirmed by Volcker himself in our interview with him. Consistent with the conclusion of other studies (for instance, (Meltzer 2009)), we conclude that Volcker viewed commitment and credibility as a means to hang on to a more limited form of discretion in policy.

PART THREE—THE FOMC IN 1999

3.15   Introduction and Context

Studying the Volcker Revolution in more detail allowed us to take a closer look at how deliberation in a committee-based decision-making setting such as the FOMC worked at a time when there was not an inherited consensus around the objective and tools of monetary policy and the task of policy makers was to find a way out of a very difficult situation. We identified a crucial role for Volcker as chairman in laying out, and subsequently modifying, a major change in policy that enabled colleagues with quite disparate views on the objective and immediate setting of policy to coalesce around Volcker's position.

The legacy of the Volcker Revolution was not only the achievement of low inflation on a lasting basis but also a much greater credibility for the FOMC, which, we assume, would have affected the deliberation of the committee. Our second detailed study looks at a less dramatic change in the direction of monetary policy in 1999, twenty years after the Volcker Revolution. We are again interested in how decisions were reached and thus how arguments were used to support the conclusion. We start with the view that the process was more gradual than in the Volcker Revolution, consistent with the view of Larry Meyer in his account of his time on the FOMC. Meyer observed that he saw the FOMC process as one where arguments could be made to count if they were introduced and then allowed to develop over one or more subsequent meetings, something more akin to a process of germination (Meyer 2004: 53).

We use textual analysis to study the pattern of speech of individual members of the FOMC in order to isolate their lines of argument and seek to determine how these changed across meetings. Thus our approach is to use a more high frequency assessment than we did for the Volcker Revolution. In order to keep the output of the textual analysis manageable in scale, we combine pairs of meetings in 1999 and focus on the voting members of the FOMC (on the assumption that for this purpose the voting presidents were representative of the whole set). We therefore undertake an assessment of the arguments used by ten members of the committee over four pairs of meetings.[33]

The year 1999 is chosen because it features a clear turning point in the cycle of interest rates. The FOMC had cut its target for the Federal Funds rate by a quarter of a percentage point three times during 1998 in response largely to international developments in the Asia and Russian crises and the failure of Long-Term Capital Management. At the same time there was increasing evidence of an acceleration of productivity growth in the United States, something that Greenspan had identified at least two or three years earlier and that other FOMC members were now coming to believe (although it remained elusive in the official data until November 1999 when the Bureau of Labor Statistics revised up nonfarm productivity growth from 1990 onward). The issue for the FOMC was not so much whether productivity growth was accelerating but rather what was now the limit to such growth before it would generate higher inflation through, notably, labor shortages. Meyer comments that by May 1999 Greenspan's view on the fact of productivity acceleration was widely accepted among FOMC members, but there was a growing consensus among members and the Fed staff that the pool of available job seekers had fallen to a point at which it might ignite inflation; hence many members felt that a policy tightening was near (Meyer 2004: 151–54).

The FOMC raised the target Fed Funds rate by a quarter of a percentage point at its June meeting, noting that conditions had changed in ways that justified starting to withdraw the downward adjustment of rates introduced in 1998. Only one voting member, President McTeer of the Dallas Fed, dissented in June 1999 believing that the acceleration of productivity could sustain a lower rate of unemployment. The FOMC raised the target Fed Funds rate by a further quarter of a percentage point in both August and November of 1999 as the economy continued to demonstrate robust growth and a further tightening of the labor market, giving rise to concerns about future inflationary pressure. Meyer notes in his account that with the benefit of hindsight by the summer of 1999 the FOMC should have seen that the stock market was in an unsustainable asset price bubble. However, that was not part of the reasoning for raising the target interest rate because the committee had a natural caution when it came to second guessing financial markets (Meyer 2004: 143).

Finally in briefly reviewing the events of 1999, it is important to bear in mind that during the year the FOMC made two changes to its policy on issuing statements on its policy decision. In May, it decided to issue a statement not just when it changed the target rate but also when it changed its bias toward the future development of policy. In November, the committee moved again in order to play down the perceived undue significance attributed to a change in the bias statement as a result of the announcement made in May, so that in future it would be replaced by a published assessment of risks in each direction.

3.16 Analysis

We seek to understand whether the pattern of deliberation and the arguments made by FOMC members changed during the course of the three increases in the target rate and, if it did, the extent to which this appears to have influenced outcomes. In doing so, we aim to identify whether particular members, or groups of members, appear to have exercised a stronger influence. In particular, we study ten voting members of the FOMC, namely Chairman Greenspan, Governors Ferguson, Gramlich, Kelley, and Meyer, and Presidents McDonough, Boehne, McTeer, Moskow, and Stern. We use the cross data (*tri-croisé*) function within Alceste to identify those statements most associated with each member during each of the pairs of FOMC meetings during 1999 (February–March, May–June, August–October, November–December). This analysis crosses a tag (name of speaker, etc.) or a single word with the entire text and identifies the strongest statistical associations between the specified tag or word, and other words and phrases in the text.[34] Here we cross each of the FOMC members with the entire corpus for each pair of FOMC meetings. This allows us to identify those words and phrases that are most closely associated with each FOMC member. (As a conceptual shorthand, this analysis is akin to holding constant each of the name tags.)

For each name tag the program generates two classes (each with characteristic words and phrases, ordered by chi-squared significance). One class is unique to the vocabulary of the named member, and the other class consists of words and phrases that are *least* associated with that member. We focus here only on the first class, and from that, we examine the top ECUs (which automatically generated number 19).

The output from the cross data function includes the 19 statements (ECUs) most commonly associated with the individual in each pair of

Table 3.9
Distribution of ECUs by subject for ten voting FOMC members for pairs of FOMC meetings during 1999

	Feb–Mar	May–Jun	Aug–Oct	Nov–Dec
US economy	76.5	69	78	60.5
US inflation	26	24	26.5	21
Financial markets	4	4.5	4	4
World economy[a]	27.5	12.5	25	8
Money and credit	2	3.5	4	0
Policy decision[b]	50	72.5	50.5	94.5
Other	4	4	2	2
Total	190	190	190	190
US economy distribution of ECUs—for all ten voting FOMC members				
Demand and output	*46*	*35*	*35*	*29*
Productivity	*16.5*	*25.5*	*23.5*	*15.5*
Labor markets	*14*	*8.5*	*19.5*	*16*
US Economy distribution of ECUs—for nine voting FOMC members (excluding Alan Greenspan)				
Demand and output	*46*	*34*	*35*	*25*
Productivity	*2.5*	*13.5*	*9.5*	*8.5*
Labor markets	*13*	*4.5*	*16.5*	*13*

a. Includes oil prices and the US current account.
b. Includes strategy toward monetary policy decisions and announcements.

meetings. We categorize these statements according to their content as follows (giving a score of one where a statement is clearly attributable to one theme and allowing a split into two themes with a score of one-half each): *US Economy* (further split into demand and output, productivity and labor markets); *US Inflation; Financial Markets; World Economy, Oil and the US Current Account; Monetary Aggregates and Credit Conditions; the Monetary Policy Decision and Strategy*; and any *Other themes*. Table 3.9 sets out the scores for each theme and for each pair of meetings (and in our online appendix 3.E to this chapter, we provide the individual scores for members). Our focus is on using these statements to determine changes in the pattern of argument and contribution of individual members leading to the first rise in the target rate (the turning point in the cycle) and then the two subsequent increases.

First, we consider what changes are evident in the pattern of deliberation leading up to the turning point with the first rise in the target rate in June. Comparison of the first pair of meetings when no increase occurred (February–March) with the first increase (May–June) shows a shift from a focus on the state of the US and world economies to the policy decision itself. In contrast, there is little variance in the focus on inflation in the United States. In terms of individuals, we identify governors Gramlich and Meyer and presidents Boehne, McDonough, and Moskow as the major contributors to the shift in the content of the deliberation. Looking at their ECUs in more detail we can see the following themes. President Boehne focused on a data-based line of argument concerning the threat of inflation and the need to be more confident on productivity data to justify inaction. Governor Gramlich focused on a more theoretical and model-based approach highlighting the risk of a supply–demand imbalance and consequent inflation threat, adding to that the risk to inflation from delay arising from lags in the transmission of an interest rate change and thus the need for the FOMC to adopt a more forward-looking inflation targeting approach. President McDonough focused more on how to present a rise in the target rate. Governor Meyer focused on a model-based argument using an output-gap/NAIRU/Taylor rule approach to set out his less optimistic view on the risks to inflation. President Moskow concentrated more on reporting discussions with contacts in his district ("something profound is clearly happening in electronic commerce and its impact on firms"). What is also noteworthy is that Greenspan's ECUs do not focus explicitly on the monetary policy decision. We assess his contribution in more detail later. Our initial conclusion is that the deliberation around the first increase shows a coalescing of different arguments though there is a clear common framework justifying the action in the ECUs of governors Gramlich and Meyer supported by the evidence from Boehne and Moskow.

The second increase (in the August–October pair of meetings) shows a switch back to a focus on the world economy. Governor Gramlich accounts for the largest part of this change and the thrust of his argument was that the US economy, and thus inflationary pressure, had been previously restrained in terms of external demand by the Asian Crisis (a point also made by Fed staff in their assessment of the incoming news). Now there were signs of the crisis ending with recovery elsewhere in the world, and thus Gramlich introduced an argument for further tightening of monetary policy. Did other members of the FOMC pick up this line of argument? Three other members of the FOMC have ECUs with notable world economy contributions, Governor Ferguson and Presidents McDonough, and McTeer. This pattern is not unexpected, since Ferguson and McDonough in their roles as vice chairman of the Fed Board and president of the New York Fed, respectively, were (along with Greenspan) most engaged in international policy discussions, while McTeer's district (Dallas) had the strongest link to oil prices and the neighboring economy of Mexico (McTeer's ECUs show that he focused his interventions often on these two subjects). On the issue of the role of deliberation, we can detect a pattern here whereby Governor Gramlich introduced a new line of argument on the impact of the world economy and found allies in the more outwardly looking members of the FOMC (we also find support for this line from Governor Kelley, although not in as many of his ECUs). Alongside this new line of argument, Governor Meyer continued to make the case for a further raise in the target rate using the supply–demand/output gap/ NAIRU framework, and received explicit support from Governor Ferguson. A further new line of argument was the evidence produced on the increasing tightening of labor markets in districts, with President Moskow noting that "increasingly contacts are reporting that labor shortages are constraining business activity." We therefore conclude that the second increase in the target rate was supported by the introduction of a new line of argument alongside the continuing theme of the domestic supply–demand imbalance and new evidence on, particularly, labor market tightness.

Assessment of the third increase in the target rate is complicated by deliberation in the November–December pair of meetings that also included the decision to switch the FOMC's procedure on announcements from the bias to the balance of risks statement. This in part accounts for the large weight in the ECUs given to the policy decision and strategy (e.g., all of Ferguson's ECUs focus on this issue as he chaired the committee that examined the bias/risks statement). Nonetheless, we find some results from the ECUs that do not focus on the announcement issue among the other members for whom the ECUs are concentrated on the policy decision. Once again, Governor Gramlich switched his line of argument, away from the rest of the world and back toward the risk of domestic supply–demand imbalance but this time with a more explicit focus on the need to consider policy in a forward-looking inflation targeting framework. Governor Kelley's ECUs focus more on the risk of the economy overheating as portrayed in the incoming economic news. Governor Meyer continued with his focus on the supply–demand/output gap/NAIRU framework. President McDonough stuck to his focus on the presentation of policy, most likely because as president of the New York Fed he felt closest to the question of how financial markets would receive the news. From this, we conclude that once again a change in the target rate came about by combining a new line of argument (Gramlich on forward-looking inflation targeting) with a more continuous line (Meyer on imbalances), while other members married these arguments with their assessment of the incoming news and at least one member (McDonough) focused on the explanation and presentation of the decision.

A striking result is that Greenspan does not record an ECU that is attributed to the policy decision and monetary policy strategy. Instead, and consistent with the well-known story, his contributions are focused on acceleration of productivity growth in the US economy. But, in view of the change in policy, can we detect from analysis of the ECUs that his line of argument on productivity changed over the course of the year? Did Greenspan's contribution to the deliberation come from a different line of argument to that of other members? This does indeed seem to have been the case. In the February-March pair of meetings his focus was on the failure of economic models to capture productivity acceleration and thus the danger of placing too much weight on model outputs (which would point to increasing the target rate). He saw growing evidence in the economic data of the productivity story but had no way of judging how far down unemployment could go before the risk to inflation became too great. In the May–June pair of meetings Greenspan was unsure whether the acceleration of productivity had reached its peak, but he saw some evidence to think this may be so. By the August–October pair of meetings, his theme was that at some point the growth of labor compensation would exceed productivity growth leading to higher inflation, and "we may be getting to the bottom of the employment barrel." By the November–December pair of meetings, Greenspan's theme was that he could not argue that the economy was heating up were it not for the gradual decline in the pool of people willing to work and an increasing share of demand being met from imports. He also argued that it was not credible that the US economy could continuously attract investment to fund the current account deficit. From this we conclude that Greenspan pursued his own line of argument that was not inconsistent with the arguments of others but was done very much on his own terms. Nor do we see evidence of other members coalescing exactly around Greenspan's arguments; rather, they appear to have developed lines of argument on their own terms that were consistent in terms of the end result of policy.

The overall conclusion of this analysis of the FOMC decisions in 1999 may suggest that the deliberation was something of a melting pot of different arguments that somehow produced a consistent result. It suggests that the process of deliberation led to members advancing arguments that allowed them to justify an outcome on their own terms. Within this, we identify at least three different approaches to deliberation in the meeting. The first approach, represented by Greenspan and Governor Meyer, involved advancing over a series of meetings a line of argument that is developed as the evidence accumulates. Greenspan and Meyer did not share a common line of argument, but they do appear to have taken a similar approach to developing arguments (though Greenspan was much more given to infusing his line of argument with evidence of his own) and in doing so it was possible for them to reach the same conclusion on the policy decision. This is consistent with Meyer's own description (in his book) of arguments germinating over the course of several FOMC meetings. The second approach, represented by Governor Gramlich, involved a consistent underlying principle (like Greenspan and Meyer, a belief in the supply–demand imbalance approach to judging inflationary pressures) but a much greater willingness to introduce new lines of argument to support the policy decision meeting by meeting. The third approach, represented by reserve bank presidents, was much more evidence-based. Here data and evidence from contacts in the districts were used to develop a story on the economy and thus on the monetary policy decision at hand. As with the other approaches, the evidence-based one could emerge from a consistent underlying principle, but the singular feature of the contribution to deliberation is that the principle is more likely to be implicit compared to the first and second approaches. All three approaches are consistent with the view that persuasion can (and does) happen over time. However, our analysis allows us to discern different ways that individual members offer lines of argument that may attract others: (1) cumulative argumentation around a consistent theme; (2) emphasis on new argumentation to support a consistent theme (both approaches 1 and 2 can use evidence as support to greater or lesser extent); and (3) more explicit evidence-based argumentation where the consistent theme is thereby more implicit. We do not therefore find blinding flashes of conversion in the FOMC deliberation ("I believed X and because my colleague has said ABC, I now believe Y"), but we do find evidence of *strategies of persuasion* and a clear ability of the deliberative process to bring these different approaches to an agreed outcome.

We can compare our findings for 1999 and the Volcker Revolution. First, we observe that the roles of governors and reserve bank presidents changed from the pattern of the Volcker Revolution period when the presidents played a larger role in the deliberation on the strategy of monetary policy relative to the governors. This may, of course, lend support to the view that the Clinton administration appointed better governors at least than was the case in the late 1970s. A second finding is that in the more settled era of low inflation and enhanced credibility, monetary policy deliberation took place within a more explicit framework of models of the economy (the supply–demand/output gap/NAIRU framework) within which different views on policy could be expressed. Third, evidence and data on the economy was applied more intensively, in particular by the chairman and the reserve bank presidents. This appears to be the key to understanding the meaning of discretionary policy-making under Greenspan—that is, applying different insights and evidence within a broadly consistent model of the economy.

CONCLUSIONS ON DELIBERATION IN THE FOMC: FROM 1979 TO 1999

As a framework for our findings, we set out seven hypotheses in chapter 2, and of these, three are specific to the FOMC and one pertains both to the FOMC and Congress. Not all of our empirical results fit tidily into these hypotheses, but on the whole, our findings for the FOMC are consistent with our expectations. We list the hypotheses again below, for ease of discussion. Rather than taking each in turn, we summarize our findings from the textual analysis in light of these hypotheses, drawing upon each as they help to explain deliberation within the FOMC.

For the FOMC, House and Senate Oversight Hearings, and Senate Re-confirmation Hearings	*We anticipate finding some evidence of reason-giving, using both information and arguments, and given these reasons, we expect to find that some members are subsequently persuaded by the arguments of their colleagues* **[hypothesis 1]**.
For the FOMC, *we contend that deliberative discourse can be influenced by*	(1) *the* ***procedures and rules*** *of the institution (including the rules surrounding the transparency of its proceedings)* **[hypothesis 2]**; (2) *the* ***membership*** *of the committee, which changes over time and particularly the personality and reputation of the chairman* **[hypothesis 3]**; *and* (3) *the* ***environment*** *in which the committee is operating at any given time (notably the clarity of understanding of the objective of policy and the perceived success of the operation of policy)* **[hypothesis 4]**.

Our first hypothesis comprises two quite distinct expectations. The first is that FOMC members would employ information and arguments in reason-giving for their views on monetary policy. In a policy-making setting like the FOMC, this expectation is almost (but not entirely) self-evident. Certainly we find ample evidence of argued reasoning in the themes/classes from 1979 to 1999. We find evidence of a clear shift in the substance of these arguments over time. Members moved away from discussing the strategy and objective of monetary policy without a clear economic model to which evidence could be applied and began instead to discuss monetary policy in terms of the state of the US economy within the supply–demand/output gap/NAIRU framework. Consistent with our fourth hypothesis, the fundamental change in the economic environment, and thus the context of policy-making—that is, the Fed had established a record of credibility with respect to price stability—was reflected in changes in the nature of the process of deliberation in the FOMC.

The second part of hypothesis 1 concerns the key outcome of deliberation—evidence that members were *persuaded* by the arguments of their colleagues. The second part of this chapter offers two more in-depth assessments of deliberation separated by 20 years and therefore at very different points in terms of the credibility of monetary policy and the FOMC. We find quite different *strategies of persuasion* at work, but we conclude that in both cases the process of deliberation in the FOMC was used to bring about agreed outcomes. Thus deliberation did matter in our view.

Hypothesis 2 contends that the rules and procedures governing the proceedings of the FOMC will influence deliberation. In particular, we focus on the issue of transparency in the form of publication of the transcripts (after 1993). The key question is whether or not more transparency (in terms of the individual contributions of FOMC members) has resulted in less robust deliberative discourse. Our overall assessment is that while there is some evidence to suggest that publication of the transcripts made deliberation more formulaic (with less spontaneous exchanges and more set-piece interventions by members), this is by no means conclusive. We document different deliberative strategies in 1979 and 1999 as befitted the different circumstances, but we do not conclude that one clearly beat the other in terms of its efficacy. Moreover, because we date the change in deliberative discourse from at least two years prior to 1993, we suspect that other causes quite possibly were at work, including the evolving environment of monetary policy-making and/or the new chairman (Greenspan).

Our third hypothesis points to the makeup of the committee's members themselves on deliberation—including the roles of bank presidents and board governors, as well as the role of the chairman. Here we find a shift in the weight of contribution from bank presidents— from deliberation on the policy decision to the assessment of the economy—and an increase in the contribution of board governors on the policy decision. We cannot reject the possibility that this is the result of improvements in appointments of governors over time, though we suspect that presidents (whose appointments are not subject to the political process) may have served as a counterweight in the deliberation to the problematic political consensus that Arthur Burns identified as infecting the Fed. That is, in the 1970s, the presidents may have served as a counterweight against the compromised independence of the governors. As the consensus on low inflation became established, this counterweight became unnecessary.

On the role of the chairman, we are able to discern three very different characters at work. Miller strove for consensus in voting in an environment where there was no consensus on the objective of policy and how to achieve it. Volcker decisively changed the whole debate, and our more in-depth assessment of that period identifies the weight of his personal contribution. Greenspan transformed the mode of deliberation in a period where there was much greater consensus on the objective of policy and the model of the economy, and a record of real achievement by the FOMC.

In sum, this evidence of the changing mode of deliberation as the context of monetary policy changed leads us to conclude that in the FOMC, deliberation *did* matter, both for the policy process and its outcome.

Appendix 3.A   Thematic Classes for FOMC Transcripts

The following levels of statistical significance apply:

Statistical significance (df = 1)	χ^2 value
NS	< 2.71
10%	< 3.84
5% (*)	< 6.63
1% (**)	< 10.80
< 1% (***)	≥ 10.80

Table 3.A1
Thematic classes for 1979 (Miller) FOMC transcripts, with statistically significant tags for committee member types

Classes for 1979 Miller (thematic classification group in brackets)	Miller/Volcker tag (with χ^2)	Board governors (with χ^2)	Bank presidents (with χ^2)	Staff members (with χ^2)
Uncertainty on setting the target range for monetary aggregates [8b]		* (5.1) Partee	*** (49.5) Balles *** (14.5) Volcker ** (8.4) Eastburn * (4.7) Smoot (3.3) Winn	
Uncertainty on interest rate decision [8a]		*** (14.8) Wallich (2.8) Rice	*** (47.6) Morris *** (41.3) Roos *** (13.2) Willes *** (11.8) McIntosh * (6.6) Rankin * (5.4) Volcker * (5.1) Guffey (3.7) Eastburn	
US economy performance (credit conditions & inflation) [1a]			*** (67.0) Baughman	*** (37.6) Kichline *** (25.6) Axilrod ** (10.6) Pardee
US economy performance & staff forecast (demand and output) [2a & 2b]				*** (357.1) Kichline *** (130.9) Zeisel *** (67.9) Truman (2.8) Axilrod
Fed's market operations [4]				*** (256.9) Sternlight *** (251.6) Greene *** (231.3) Pardee *** (132.6) Holmes
Deliberation on target ranges for monetary aggregates & interest rates [7b & 7c]	*** (184.6)	** (10.0) Coldwell * (6.0) Rice	** (9.7) Mayo * (5.7) Black	* (5.2) Altmann

Table 3.A2
Thematic classes for 1979 (Volcker) FOMC transcripts, with statistically significant tags for committee member types

Classes for 1979 Volcker (thematic classification group in brackets)	Volcker tag (with χ^2)	Board governors (with χ^2)	Bank presidents (with χ^2)	Staff members (with χ^2)
Staff forecast for US economy (demand and output, & inflation) [1b & 2b]				*** (462.4) Kichline *** (140.4) Pardee *** (132.2) Zeisel *** (126.9) Truman *** (11.3) Sternlight * (5.5) Prell
Deliberation on target ranges for monetary aggregates [7c]	*** (34.0)	*** (22.9) Teeters ** (10.4) Partee * (6.0) Rice * (4.5) Coldwell	*** (46.9) Black *** (18.0) Guffey ** (7.1) Balles (2.72) Mayo	*** (25.8) Altmann * (4.0) Holmes
Effectiveness of monetary policy—uncertainty over transmission mechanism [8c]		*** (20.8) Wallich *** (15.0) Rice (3.6) Teeters (2.8) Schultz	*** (43.5) Roos *** (38.4) Eastburn *** (37.0) Winn ** (10.4) Baughman ** (9.1) Balles ** (8.2) Kimbrel ** (7.7) Willes ** (6.7) Mayo * (5.1) Black	
Reserves levels and Fed's market operations [4]		* (3.9) Partee		
Impact of Volcker Revolution, including communication of policy change [9b]	*** (230.1)		*** (42.6) Willes * (6.1) Timlen (3.2) Mayo	*** (621.1) Axilrod *** (149.2) Sternlight

Table 3.A3
Thematic classes for 1980 FOMC transcripts, with statistically significant tags for committee member types

Classes for 1980 (thematic classification group in brackets)	Volcker tag (with χ^2)	Board governors (with χ^2)	Bank presidents (with χ^2)	Staff members (with χ^2)
Striving for credibility [9b]	*** (195.4)	*** (31.1) Schultz *** (12.1) Gramley * (5.1) Wallich	*** (42.9) Corrigan *** (32.8) Roos *** (30.7) Mayo *** (22.1) Balles *** (20.6) Eastburn *** (17.8) Black *** (17.0) Solomon ** (10.0) Winn * (5.8) Ford * (5.8) Smoot	*** (60.5) Axilrod ** (9.5) Altmann
Deliberation on target ranges for monetary aggregates & interest rates [7b & 7c]		*** (31.3) Partee *** (20.8) Teeters * (6.0) Rice	*** (32.8) Guffey ** (8.1) Morris * (5.8) Czerwinski	
US economy performance and staff forecast for demand & output (evidence of weakening) [2a & 2b]			*** (16.8) Timlen * (5.7) Baughman	*** (669.6) Kichline *** (502.3) Pardee *** (229.3) Zeisel *** (89.4) Sternlight *** (73.4) Truman *** (29.9) Meek *** (12.7) Ettin
Performance of non-borrowed reserves relative to target [3]	** (8.0)		(3.5) Roos	*** (155.2) Sternlight *** (125.2) Axilrod * (3.9) Meek

Table 3.A4
Thematic classes for 1981 FOMC transcripts, with statistically significant tags for committee member types

Classes for 1981 (thematic classification group in brackets)	Volcker tag (with χ^2)	Board governors (with χ^2)	Bank presidents (with χ^2)	Staff members (with χ^2)
Choice of monetary policy target/framework [9a]	*** (15.0)	*** (33.1) Schultz *** (19.8) Gramley ** (9.1) Wallich * (4.1) Rice	*** (79.0) Roos *** (15.1) Ford *** (15.0) Winn *** (13.4) Morris *** (11.4) Mayo ** (9.2) Corrigan * (5.9) Black * (5.6) Balles (3.6) Forrestal	(3.5) Altmann
Deliberation on target ranges for monetary aggregates & non-borrowed reserves [7c & 7d]	*** (168.7)	*** (11.3) Teeters	*** (21.9) Guffey ** (8.6) Solomon	
Staff forecast for US economy (demand and output, & inflation) [1b & 2b]			*** (38.2) Keehn *** (34.8) Doyle *** (21.4) Boykin * (5.1) Boehne * (4.5) Winn	*** (475.2) Kichline *** (254.2) Zeisel *** (198.5) Cross *** (139.9) Truman *** (133.0) Pardee *** (86.7) Sternlight *** (52.9) Greene ** (7.8) Meek
Reserves levels and Fed's market operations [4]				*** (564.2) Axilrod *** (51.4) Lindsey *** (41.6) Sternlight *** (25.4) Ettin ** (9.9) Meek

Table 3.A5
Thematic classes for 1991 FOMC transcripts, with statistically significant tags for committee member types

Classes for 1991 (thematic classification group in brackets)	Greenspan tag (with χ^2)	Board governors (with χ^2)	Bank presidents (with χ^2)	Staff members (with χ^2)
State of economy in districts [1c & 2c]			*** (277.9) Keehn *** (86.7) Forrestal *** (70.8) Guffey *** (60.3) Parry *** (22.8) Hoenig *** (19.3) McTeer *** (12.6) Hendricks * (4.0) Stern	*** (87.7) Prell *** (41.5) Slifman *** (13.6) Promisel ** (8.2) Truman
Financial market developments & Fed's market operations [4]				*** (666.6) Sternlight *** (497.8) Greene *** (453.8) Cross *** (167.9) Lovett *** (135.1) Truman *** (121.1) Siegman *** (67.7) Promisel
Staff assessment of monetary policy stance [7a]		*** (14.1) Angell	*** (44.3) Hoskins ** (9.5) Black	*** (352.3) Kohn (3.1) Prell
Credit conditions & banking system stability [6]		*** (36.5) Mullins *** (30.4) LaWare		*** (78.6) Kohn *** (59.7) Prell ** (11.9) Stifman
Deliberation on interest rate policy decision [7b]	*** (43.2)	*** (11.0) LaWare * (5.7) Lindsey	(3.0) McTeer	*** (16.3) Sternlight
Uncertainty around interest rate decision [8a]	*** (97.4)	*** (101.2) Kelley *** (22.5) Angell *** (15.7) Phillips (3.7) Seger	*** (151.9) Corrigan *** (62.1) Melzer *** (27.8) Syron *** (15.3) Boehne *** (14.8) Black ** (8.6) Oltman * (5.0) Stern * (4.5) Hoskins	

Table 3.A6
Thematic classes for 1992 FOMC transcripts, with statistically significant tags for committee member types

Classes for 1992 (thematic classification group in brackets)	Greenspan tag (with χ^2)	Board governors (with χ^2)	Bank presidents (with χ^2)	Staff members (with χ^2)
Staff forecast for US economy (demand and output, & inflation) [1b & 2b]		* (4.4) Mullins	* (5.2) Parry * (4.9) Hendricks	*** (181.4) Prell *** (180.8) Truman *** (151.8) Stockton *** (25.9) Kohn ** (7.2) Simpson (2.8) Siegman
Staff assessment of monetary policy stance [7a]		** (7.5) Mullins		*** (307.1) Kohn *** (40.6) Prell
State of economy in districts [1c & 2c]			*** (42.6) Jordan * (4.5) Oltman *** (323.5) Keehn *** (109.0) Forrestal *** (77.6) Hoenig *** (75.1) Stern *** (48.3) McTeer *** (40.2) Parry *** (28.7) Syron *** (28.3) Boehne ** (10.1) Melzer ** (8.4) Black * (5.5) Hendricks * (4.7) Broaddus	
Deliberation on interest rate policy decision [7b]	*** (148.5)	*** (91.9) Lindsey *** (90.4) Kelley *** (35.4) Angell *** (28.2) Phillips *** (15.4) Mullins	*** (39.6) Corrigan *** (25.6) Syron ** (8.4) Melzer * (6.2) Black * (5.4) Boehne	
Financial market developments and Fed's market operations [4]				*** (1,287.0) McDonough *** (338.0) Sternlight *** (185.5) Lovett *** (106.9) Greene *** (22.4) Truman

Table 3.A7
Thematic classes for 1993 FOMC transcripts, with statistically significant tags for committee member types

Classes for 1993 (thematic classification group in brackets)	Greenspan tag (with χ^2)	Board governors (with χ^2)	Bank presidents (with χ^2)	Staff members (with χ^2)
Uncertainty on model of economy & appropriate monetary policy strategy [8c]	*** (31.8)	*** (78.0) Angell *** (69.3) Mullins *** (24.9) Lindsey *** (19.2) Kelley	* (3.9) Jordan (2.9) Corrigan	*** (67.1) Prell
State of economy in districts [1c & 2c]		** (10.5) Phillips	*** (169.2) Hoenig *** (151.2) Forrestal *** (83.8) Parry *** (44.9) Syron *** (44.3) Boehne *** (26.9) Keehn *** (17.0) McTeer *** (16.2) Broaddus *** (16.0) Melzer *** (12.9) Jordan * (4.7) Oltman	
US economy demand and output performance, & staff forecast [2a & 2b]			*** (107.1) Keehn	*** (549.9) Truman *** (48.4) Slifman *** (44.6) Prell * (5.5) Siegman * (4.7) Kohn
Deliberation on interest rate decision [7b]	*** (37.3)	*** (16.7) LaWare	*** (35.3) Corrigan *** (10.8) McTeer * (6.1) Stern	*** (44.5) Kohn *** (11.8) Bernard
Fed's market operations [4]				*** (678.5) Greene *** (419.6) Lovett *** (330.7) Fisher *** (234.9) McDonaugh *** (75.1) White *** (44.3) Siegman *** (18.9) Truman

Table 3.A8
Thematic classes for 1997 FOMC transcripts, with statistically significant tags for committee member types

Classes for 1997 (thematic classification group in brackets)	Greenspan tag (with χ^2)	Board governors (with χ^2)	Bank presidents (with χ^2)	Staff members (with χ^2)
Choice of target to achieve monetary stability; role of money ranges [9a]	*** (286.4)	*** (19.9) Rivlin	*** (30.3) Melzer *** (22.3) Boehne ** (8.8) Broaddus ** (8.5) McDonough (3.1) Jordan	
Staff assessment of monetary policy stance, & deliberation on interest rate decision [7a & 7b]		*** (31.2) Meyer *** (28.9) Gramlich * (6.4) Kelley		*** (221.0) Kohn *** (16.3) Truman ** (7.8) Bernard
State of economy in districts [1c & 2c]			*** (156.2) McTeer *** (140.9) Moskow *** (88.2) Guynn *** (79.4) Jordan *** (69.6) Hoenig *** (60.7) Minehan *** (15.7) Boehne *** (11.1) Broaddus ** (10.7) Stern (2.9) Parry	
Financial market developments [4]				*** (1,903.6) Fisher *** (260.2) Truman * (5.6) Stockton
Staff forecast for US economy (demand and output, & inflation) [1b & 2b]		*** (99.5) Meyer *** (39.0) Phillips ** (8.7) Kelley	*** (13.9) Parry	*** (208.9) Prell *** (37.6) Slifman *** (22.9) Stockton * (6.6) Kohn

Table 3.A9
Thematic classes for 1998 FOMC transcripts, with statistically significant tags for committee member types

Classes for 1998 (thematic classification group in brackets)	Greenspan tag (with χ²)	Board governors (with χ²)	Bank presidents (with χ²)	Staff members (with χ²)
State of economy in districts [1c & 2c]			*** (192.1) Guynn *** (179.7) Moskow *** (120.6) Jordan *** (71.9) Minehan *** (56.4) McTeer *** (55.8) Hoenig *** (34.5) Boehne *** (20.7) Rives *** (18.7) Stern *** (14.5) Broaddus * (5.9) Parry	*** (453.3) Prell *** (95.6) Stockton *** (28.7) Kohn
Staff forecast for US economy (demand and output, & inflation) [1b & 2b]	*** (14.1)	*** (56.1) Meyer * (4.6) Phillips	** (8.6) Parry	
Financial market developments [4]			* (4.9) McDonough	*** (2,379.4) Fisher
Outlook for world economy & Asia crisis [5]		*** (34.3) Kelley *** (32.9) Ferguson *** (28.9) Rivlin ** (6.7) Meyer	*** (64.4) McDonough	*** (29.3) Truman *** (18.7) Johnson * (4.9) Kohn * (4.6) Promisel
Deliberation on interest rate decision [7b]		*** (76.0) Gramlich *** (23.7) Kelley * (5.6) Ferguson * (5.2) Rivlin	*** (17.4) Boehne ** (8.7) Broaddus	*** (73.2) Bernard ** (10.0) Gillum
Staff forecast for rest of the world [5]		*** (11.0) Meyer	*** (16.8) McTeer ** (8.5) Parry	*** (340.8) Johnson *** (268.7) Hooper *** (56.7) Truman *** (33.3) Promisel * (3.0) Kohn
Deliberation on broader issues on monetary policy stance and strategy [9c]	*** (46.1)	*** (34.6) Gramlich *** (14.1) Kelley ** (7.2) Rivlin	** (8.9) Poole ** (8.3) Jordan	** (8.1) Truman

Table 3.A10
Thematic classes for 1999 FOMC transcripts, with statistically significant tags for committee member types

Classes for 1999 (thematic classification group in brackets)	Greenspan tag (with χ^2)	Board governors (with χ^2)	Bank presidents (with χ^2)	Staff members (with χ^2)
Deliberation on interest rate decision [7b]	*** (12.0)	*** (109.0) Gramlich *** (104.7) Ferguson *** (14.1) Kelley	*** (45.8) Poole *** (35.7) Broaddus *** (31.5) McDonough *** (20.3) Boehne	
Productivity growth in United States [2d]	*** (764.3)	(3.5) Rivlin		*** (134.9) Prell *** (20.9) Stockton
US economy—demand & output (strength of domestic demand) [2a]		*** (14.1) Kelley	(3.7) Minehan (3.1) McDonough	*** (57.5) Kohn *** (55.6) Johnson *** (24.3) Prell (3.1) Simpson
Financial market developments [4]				*** (2,145.8) Fisher *** (362.1) Alexander *** (72.0) Johnson *** (17.8) Simpson ** (6.9) Madigan
Stance of policy & how to publish it/ transparency [9b]		*** (58.4) Meyer *** (14.2) Kelley		*** (538.2) Kohn *** (24.6) Fox *** (12.5) Bernard

Table 3.A10
(continued)

Classes for 1999 (thematic classification group in brackets)	Greenspan tag (with χ^2)	Board governors (with χ^2)	Bank presidents (with χ^2)	Staff members (with χ^2)
Staff forecast for US economy (demand and output, & inflation) **[1b & 2b]**		*** (287.4) Meyer *** (21.5) Gramlich * (5.9) Rivlin	*** (64.5) Parry	*** (39.6) Stockton *** (15.2) Madigan ** (6.8) Prell
State of economy in districts (output) **[2c]**			*** (115.3) Moskow *** (85.5) Hoenig *** (82.3) McTeer *** (59.6) Parry *** (51.1) Guynn *** (15.0) Stern *** (13.3) Broaddus *** (12.1) Minehan ** (8.9) McDonough	
State of economy in districts (inflation) **[1c]**			*** (277.3) Jordan *** (71.3) Minehan *** (57.7) Poole *** (31.6) Moskow *** (11.1) Guynn (3.0) Broaddus	

Appendix 3.B: Characteristic Words and Phrases for FOMC Transcripts

Table 3.B1
Characteristic words and phrases for classes in 1979 (Miller) FOMC transcripts

Classes for 1979 Miller (thematic classification group in brackets)	Top ranking characteristic words	Top ranking characteristic phrases, or ECUs
Uncertainty on setting target range for monetary aggregates [8b]	know staff+ number+ look+ find ask+ happen+ trying error+ say	let us not #find ourselves #locked into that #same #old situation as in the past. if we #suspect at all that there is a danger of #getting #locked into that, there is some advantage in #changing the #numbers #simply for #technical #reasons just to #change the #numbers. [Eastburn] I wanted to #ask #Steve what his #reasons were for placing much #confidence on the existing #relationship, there is at least a #possibility that that #relationship has #changed. [Wallich] #foolish #consistency is the hobgoblin of a little #mind and #everyone #knows that you are a #big #mind! [Miller] we have,#looked at these #same #numbers, #Steve, and #frankly, we #come #out more on Dave's side than yours. We have here an array of the #different ms going up to M7. [Balles] we had slightly #different #figures in #mind. We #agree that we #ought to #adjust the #old #targets because of the revisions in the estimates on the ATS and NOW effect. [Black]
Uncertainty on interest rate decision [8a]	inflation+ recession+ polic+ econom+ think monetary- poli+ ease+ believe+ long+ easing	in my #view that would be counterproductive to the #long #run #anti #inflation #fight. If we have that big a #recession, the #hope of #keeping some #constraint on fiscal #policy is going to be #diminished, #inevitably. [Morris] in other #words, the saucer will be somewhat #deeper but not nearly as #deep as 1974–1975. I, too, would like to #see a #policy that is as #effective as #possible against #inflation. [Rice] I #thought it was the #best #way in which to wring #inflation out of the #economy and I still #think so. But the #deceleration that we have #experienced since September has not been #gradual. [Black] some #slowing of the #excessive growth that we #experienced in 1976, 1977, and a good part of 1978 was #clearly needed in an #effort to have an #effective #anti #inflationary #policy. [Black] I admit this is #likely to #exacerbate some of the #recessionary #tendencies in the #economy but I am not yet #convinced that we are #heading #toward the doom and gloom that some people are #portraying. [Coldwell]

Table 3.B1
(continued)

Classes for 1979 Miller (thematic classification group in brackets)	Top ranking characteristic words	Top ranking characteristic phrases, or ECUs
US economy performance (credit conditions & inflation) [1a]	price+ businesses factor+ ratio+ emerg+ gas expect+ energy mortgage+ institution+	Moreover, #financial #conditions in #mortgage markets have tightened further as indicated by #continued #increases in #interest-rates, declines in #mortgage #commitments, #reduced #deposit #flows to #thrift #institutions, [Kichline] to the #extent that it #represents inventory #accumulation, on the other #hand, it could be dangerous because it could #result in #excess #stocks, #leading later to #cutbacks in production, [Miller] on the other #hand, we have a #domestic economy where I think as a #result of the #energy #situation, with the revolution in Iran and the interruption of #oil #supplies it #appears that a very significant #increase in inflation is in #prospect for 1979 and 1980. [Miller] this #result #reflects the #maintenance of #fairly #strong #credit #demands relative to inflows of #traditional sources of funds. That is, #interest-rates remain well above fixed #interest-rate #ceilings and under those #conditions #institutions are not flooded with relatively low #cost funds. [Kichline] so the #supply picture is #tighter than it had been. Industrial #demand #appears to be quite good, even at these higher #prices And. of #course, #gold #reacts very #strongly in an #environment in which there is a sense of scarcity of #certain #important strategic #commodities. [Greene]
US economy performance & staff forecast (demand & output) [2a & 2b]	quarter+ decline+ annual housing construction forecast fourth+ March cent+ investment+	#industrial #production in May only #recovered #strike #related losses of the #previous #month, and #preliminary #information for June #suggests a #slight #decline in #output. #total #retail #sales in #real terms have #declined a #substantial 6½ percent from the #peak in #December. [Kichline] in the #construction and #business capital investment area the #forecast #incorporates a stronger #pattern of #spending in the #second #quarter than in the first. #Housing #starts #data for #March will be #available later today, but we have #assumed a strong #pickup from the #weather #depressed #February #pace. [Kichline] this #played a #key #role in the #recent #decline in #real #retail #sales. In regards to the future, we are #forecasting an #actual #drop in #real #income in the #second half of 1979 and only a #sluggish #recovery during 1980. [Zeisel] #final #sales in the first #quarter are #estimated to have #declined #following exceptional #growth in the #fourth #quarter. in #particular, #personal #consumption #expenditures have been #weak so far this #year. [Kichline] #Reports #available on the #residential #construction #sector #indicate a perceptible #slowdown of #activity is in process. #Housing #starts in #April were at a 1¾ million unit #annual rate, a shade below the #month #earlier #pace. Both #starts and permits in #April were 16 #percent below the #average level of the #fourth #quarter. [Kichline]

Table 3.B1
(continued)

Classes for 1979 Miller (thematic classification group in brackets)	Top ranking characteristic words	Top ranking characteristic phrases, or ECUs
Fed's market operations [4]	dollar+ bill+ treasury+ intervention+ currenc+ system+ mark+ sell Swiss Yen	this #brings our #intervention since Sunday #night to almost 1.2 #billion #dollars, which has been #equally #shared between the #system and the #Treasury. Since mid #June the #net #intervention by the #United #States has been 3.6 #billion #dollars. This #compares to the 4.1 #billion #dollars from our 3 partners in the #November 1 #package, for #Germany and, for #Switzerland. [Greene] as of 11:30 this #morning the #United #States #authorities had #sold #net something like 700 #million #dollars of #foreign #currency, #mostly #German #marks, since the #Carter #speech. [Greene] given the volatility of #market factors affecting #reserves, more than #usual reliance was #placed on adding or #absorbing #reserves on a #temporary #basis. #Outright #operations #included #purchases of 700 #million #dollars of #Treasury #coupon #issues early in the #period, sales of about 450 #million #dollars of #Treasury #bills to #foreign #accounts about #midway through the #period. [Sternlight] 7 #million #dollars #under the #Treasury's #swap line in #marks. As of this #morning the #Federal-Reserve's indebtedness in #marks #amounts to 556.9 #million #dollars #equivalent. In #addition, we #acquired enough #Swiss #francs to prepay the last 300 #million #dollars #equivalent of 1971 #debt by the #system and the #Treasury. [Holmes] sales and redemptions of #treasury #bills #amounted to 850 #million #dollars, #helping to #absorb #reserves during the #period. In the #latter part of the #interval the #system #bought 715 #million #dollars of #bills from #foreign #accounts in preparation for anticipated #reserve needs in coming #weeks. [Sternlight]
Deliberation on target ranges for monetary aggregates & interest rates [7b & 7c]	percent+ range+ direct+ fund+ move+ Fed-Funds-rate vote+ discount+ alternative+ prefer+	the third #alternative would be to #let the #Fed #Funds #go up with the #directive to 10½ #percent and very quickly #move the #discount #rate to, say, 10 or 10¼ #percent to #close the #widening gap between the #discount #rate and the #Fed-Funds-rate. [Miller] yes, one of us, #Nancy, had a 10½ #percent #top #limit but that was with a 9½ #percent #bottom. #Chuck had 9½ to 10¼, #Bob Black had 9¾ to 10¼, and #John Balles had 9¾ to 10¼. [Miller] and I would #treat the #range #asymmetrically; that is, I would #leave the #Funds #rate at 10 #percent or a tad above where it is now until the #aggregates begin to #move. [Partee] the M1 #range is 4 to 8 #percent and the M2 #range is 3½ to 7½ #percent; the #Funds #range is 9¾ to 10½ #percent, with the #initial #objective at the #prevailing #rate of 10 to 10⅛ #percent. [Altmann] #well, my reason for this, #Mr. Chairman, ultimately relates to what we do with the #discount #rate. If it were the #sentiment of the full #board to #go more than one half #percentage #point on the #discount #rate, then we are #stuck with a #Fed-Funds-rate below or equal to it. [Coldwell]

Note: The software highlights characteristic words within each ECU, thereby clarifying both characteristic words and phrases, in context. For all ECU tables, # indicates a characteristic word within the specific class. We have edited the ECUs slightly from the software-generated format, in order to make them more readable, and to indicate (with a hyphen) where words have been linked together in order to signify unique phrases or terms.

Table 3.B2
Characteristic words and phrases for classes in 1979 (Volcker) FOMC transcripts

Classes for 1979 Volcker (thematic classification group in brackets)	Top ranking characteristic words	Top ranking characteristic phrases, or ECUs
Staff forecast for US economy (demand and output, & inflation) [1b & 2b]	price+ quarter increase consumer+ sale+ fourth decline+ oil inventor+ forecast	we #continue to #forecast #comparatively #small #quarterly #declines in #real GNP #into #early 1980, #reflecting #weakness in #housing, #reduced #business #outlays for both #fixed #capital and #inventories and quite #sluggish #consumer demand. [Zeisel] much of this #weakness #represented the collapse of #large #car #sales in #response to uncertainties regarding #fuel #availability. But transitory #considerations aside, the #fundamentals #underlying #consumption have been #weak for some time, #particularly #real #personal #income growth, and the #principal #forces supporting #income #gains, #production and #employment, [Zeisel] of #course, the #outlook for #overall #activity depends #importantly on the #performance of #capital #spending. #Business #fixed #investment in #real terms #fell in the #second #quarter as shipments of equipment #dropped and truck #sales #continued the #decline that #began toward the end of #last #year. [Zeisel] one is the #continued #weakness #projected for #real #economic #activity #over the #balance of the #year. The #second is the view that the #recent #build #up in #cash #balances, both demand and #savings deposits, is in #part #temporary, #reflecting #economic uncertainties associated with the #energy #crisis, and will not #last. [Axilrod] #Germany. The #major #forces behind the #decline of the #dollar are of #course more #political than #economic. #Iran #continues to #hold the hostages. The #United #States freeze of #Iranian #assets #remains on. [Pardee (staff]]

Table 3.B2
(continued)

Classes for 1979 Volcker (thematic classification group in brackets)	Top ranking characteristic words	Top ranking characteristic phrases, or ECUs
Deliberation on target ranges for monetary aggregates [7c]	range+ alternative+ percent+ midpoint+ prefer+ point+ top+ upper M3 M2	why do not we just #see what the #vote is, Mr. Chairman, on the #bottom of #alternative III and the #top of #alternative II, #widening the #range by ½ #percentage #point. [Mayo] my #preference, which I could alter to some extent, would be an #aggregates #directive that would #trigger at an upward #move at #somewhere #around 6½ #percent on M1, which would be a #range of 3½ to 7½ #percent and at #around 9½ #percent on M2, [Black] on the #Fed-Funds-rate #specifically, I would #join those who think we #ought to #set the #range a #little higher, at 11¼ to 12 #percent. [Balles] with respect to a #specific target or a #range, my own #preference since we #started #setting targets has been to #set a #specific target, #recognizing that we will never #hit a #specific target but nevertheless having something #specific to #shoot at. [Baughman] if we #set a #range that would be my #midpoint with a 2 #percent #margin on either #side. But that would obviously #widen the #range from the 3 #percentage #points that we have had in the past. [Coldwell]
Effectiveness of monetary policy—uncertainty over transmission mechanism [8c]	think recession+ risk+ long+ interest rates problem+ inflation+ strateg+ term+ polic+	I was #tempted by the #position that you #took and the more I #thought about it, it #seemed #awfully #risky. The #recession has not #gone far enough to have any #restraining #influence. [Volcker] but I do not #think that that #approach will be a very #happy one #unless people are pretty #confident about our #long #term #intentions. That is the #credibility #problem and the #confidence we have to establish as I see it. And we have not got a helluva #lot of time as the #recession #comes along if #indeed it does #come along but particularly if it #gets #worse. [Volcker] I would want to #stand #pat. I would not #argue at this time for an #easing of #policy, but I would certainly #argue that any further #tightening would be a #dangerous #step to #take. [Rice] over recent #months, my #attention has been more #focused on #trying to moderate the #depth and the #length of any #recession that #seemed to be #clearly on its #way or perhaps already in #progress. [Guffey] there is an #immediate #advantage in the #publicity; there is a #disadvantage not very far #down the #road if people read this as a #commitment and in #fact we are not #going to be #able to #live up to that #commitment. [Volcker]

Table 3.B2
(continued)

Classes for 1979 Volcker (thematic classification group in brackets)	Top ranking characteristic words	Top ranking characteristic phrases, or ECUs
Reserves levels & Fed's market operations [4]	reserve+ borrow+ path+ total+ week+ December deposit+ require adjust+ excess	#December is the #base. It is #essentially the #growth #rates in #January and #February and #March #averaged. [Axilrod] #desk #operations since the #November 20 #meeting have been geared to #providing #reserves to support #growth #rates of 5 percent for M1 and 8 1/2 percent for M2 from #October through #December, with #similar #rates to continue into the early #January #period. [Sternlight] so it really is about 220 #million dollars #short of the #original #path; there was a #currency #shortfall involved. With #total #reserves #running #short, the #Manager #added roughly 150 #million dollars to the #original non #borrowed #path. [Axilrod] to obtain needed #reserves, #banks resorted to the #discount #window, so that #borrowing #averaged about 2.1 billion dollars or about 600 #million dollars above the #level #initially assumed in #constructing the non #borrowed #path. [Sternlight] so, early in the three #week #period, we did #add 150 #million dollars to non #borrowed when it appeared that the #gap between the #total #reserves #path and #total #reserves #demanded was something on the #order of 450 #million dollars. [Axilrod]
Impact of Volcker Revolution including communication of policy change [9b]	discuss+ comment+ procedure+ decide+ question+ inherent judgment+ want+ morning+ today+	#well, #let me #return to that. On the very general #question, #leaving aside modifications of the #kind you are #proposing, I just #want to be #explicit about whether we #want to continue this general #type of #procedure. [Volcker] in turning to this #matter, #let me just #mention a #couple of things. As #Mr. Roos #said #yesterday, #given the #new #technique we are #using and all the #complications of an annual and a short term #horizon, the Bluebook was #put #together admirably in my view. [Volcker] #well, if we have a #new #procedure, I will have a press #conference. Whether I have it #today or #Monday is an #open #question. [Volcker] I am just #putting this on the #table. #Let us #hear what #comments you have.[Volcker] I was #merely raising the #question of whether you #wanted to get the specifications of the #traditional as #well as the #new #procedure. [Coldwell]

Table 3.B3
Characteristic words and phrases for classes in 1980 FOMC transcripts

Classes for 1980 (thematic classification group in brackets)	Top ranking characteristic words	Top ranking characteristic phrases, or ECUs
Striving for credibility [9b]	think go say people+ problem+ let better cred+ thing+ ought	again, I #think we have to #put more #weight on #interest-rates than on the #aggregates. My preferred #aggregate is still M1b; it #conceptually #makes the most #sense. But it will be #looking #pretty #bad and its #interpretation will be #enormously #difficult. [Wallich] that may #make our #success in #controlling the #aggregates #seem a #little #better, but that could provide a false #sense of security. I #hope we #handle it a bit #better despite what I #said about the #basic adequacy of our #record. We have to #keep our #eye on the ball and dig in. [Mayo] #let us distribute this #draft. I #looked at it and the #language is not #perfect. I do not #know whether #people will even #agree with the #concept, but #let me #go over it and #tell you what I am #trying to #convey because the #language may not be adequate to #convey what I am #trying to communicate. [Volcker] we cannot #ignore the #fact that #regardless of what we #say and how we #interpret the #different #variables to the #public, they are #going to #make their own #reading on it. [Ford] A #lot of #people in the #real #world and I am sorry to belabor this but I #know we have them in the #real #world where I #live are hoping desperately that when this incompatibility #occurs we will do what we #said we were #going to do: [Roos]
Deliberation on the target ranges for monetary aggregates & interest rates [7b & 7c]	percent+ range+ upper lower+ growth fund+ rate+ alternative+ limit+ consult+	and if that #constraint prevents our #reaching our #targets as we #move #toward #September, then I would be prepared to #lower that 9 #percent at the #right time. [Rice] #right. Yes. I will ask another question later about the M2 #figure. I am #talking about citing a #figure that, as a #point of #departure, is the #midpoint of these #tentative #ranges and #implies that that is an #acceptable number but #shortfalls will be #accepted. [Volcker] I would #reluctantly #raise the #upper #limit to 18 #percent and I certainly would not #raise the #lower #limit at this #point. [Teeters] my #alternative would be to #raise the #point #targets for M1a, M1b, and M2 to make them essentially the #midpoints between #alternative a and #alternative b for the 2 month period and to #establish an 8 #percent #lower #end on the #Funds #rate rather than 9 #percent. [Partee] 5 #percent using our projection for #March that is, a #March projection with a #lower #growth than in #February. So M3 is #running 2 #points above the #committee's #target. [Axilrod]

Table 3.B3
(continued)

Classes for 1980 (thematic classification group in brackets)	Top ranking characteristic words	Top ranking characteristic phrases, or ECUs
US economy performance & staff forecast for demand and output (evidence of weakening) [2a & 2b]	dollar+ rise decline+ unit+ billion+ sale+ product+ price+ increase+ housing	real GNP is #expected to #show a #small #decline in the #current #quarter, be about #unchanged in the #fourth #quarter, and #recover #sluggishly next #year. The #recent #stronger #business #news we interpret as a #partial snapback from the #severe #drop in #activity during the #second #quarter, #particularly #evident in the #auto, #housing and #durable #home #goods #sectors. [Kichline] #new orders for ncn #defense #capital equipment #indicate the #developing #weakness in #commitments for longer #lead time #capital #outlays. In conjunction with the #decline since #early #last #year in #contracts for #commercial and #industrial #construction, these #data portend a #continued downtrend in #fixed #capital #spending #over the #balance of this #year. [Zeisel] #contracts for #commercial and #industrial #construction #indicate no #signs of #strength for at least the next #several #quarters. #Business #investment in #inventories also #declined in the #third #quarter as the #sharp #contraction in #industrial #output from the #second #quarter level #contrasted with a #strong upswing in real #final #demands. [Zeisel] in #addition, #expectations #began to #grow that our #price #performance would #improve, again because of the #domestic #slowdown. #Following #earlier glimmers in #individual #price #series #released in late #April, the #market waited with bated breath, and with few long #dollar #positions, for the #producer #price #index for #April to be #released on May 9. [Pardee {staff}] the #staff #forecast of #business #fixed #investment was not altered #significantly, and it #continues to portray #declines in real #outlays #over the #projection #period. #Activity in the near term is also #held down in the #forecast by the #projected #liquidation of #inventories. #Inventory #sales #ratios #remain high, #especially in #manufacturing, even with the #recent #increases in #sales. [Kichline]

Table 3.B3
(continued)

Classes for 1980 (thematic classification group in brackets)	Top ranking characteristic words	Top ranking characteristic phrases, or ECUs
Performance of non-borrowed reserves relative to target [3]	borrow+ reserve+ path+ discount+ level+ week+ total+ adjust+ fund+ rate+	more pressure was placed on the banking #system. #Discount #window #borrowing was #pushed #higher and #money rates #surged #upward. Restraint was reinforced about midway through the period when the non #borrowed #reserve #path was reduced by 170 #million dollars or by half of the then anticipated #bulge of #total #reserves above #path. [Sternlight] we would #technically #write down 750 #million dollars in the #path, but if #borrowing were #coming in #high, we would #adjust the non #borrowed #reserves down a bit and vice versa. [Axilrod] non #borrowed #reserves should #come out much #closer to their #path perhaps on the order of 100 #million dollars below for the five #week average. The #path for non #borrowed #reserves, moreover, was raised #explicitly by 150 #million dollars early in the period in #relation to the #path for #total #reserves, in recognition that the #initially assumed #borrowing #level of 2, [Sternlight] and #caused serious #questioning of the #system's resolve to #carry through its restraint program. #Accordingly, we have been #content in our #operations so far this #week to achieve a somewhat lower #level of non #borrowed #reserves that might be consistent with #borrowings in the 1. [Sternlight] as has happened after other recent #meetings, they did indeed #come in #high, and they #came in #high enough so that we did make an #adjustment in the non #borrowed #reserve #path as well as having the natural #consequence of the #higher #money #supply figures. [Volcker]

Note: Partee = Governor; Pardee = Fed staff.

Table 3.B4
Characteristic words and phrases for classes in 1981 FOMC transcripts

Classes for 1981 (thematic classification group in brackets)	Top ranking characteristic words	Top ranking characteristic phrases, or ECUs
Choice of monetary policy target/framework [9a]	think go ought thing+ target+ real+ problem+ people+ make interest-rate+	#Mr. Chairman, I #think you are right, and this is what we need to #keep in #mind, that there #really is only one #reason why we should have #abandoned the Federal Funds #target procedure to #go to the reserve #target. And that is because if we #operate on Federal Funds, we #explicitly take #responsibility for what is #happening to #interest-rates and then this #becomes a very, very #difficult #world to #live in. [Gramley] the burden of my #comment is not that we #know any of these #things empirically or #logically. The burden is that we have all these #uncertainties. I am basically #agreeing with #Frank Morris; I am #going a #long distance in that direction but I do not #think we can #abandon M1 because #people would #question our good faith if we #abandon M1 at this #point, #given all the #emphasis on it. [Volcker] then #maybe we have to #go to #Mr. Morris' #idea that we #look at some other #things, although my thrust in the #research would #probably be #different than his. I would say, if we are #going to re-examine what we shoot for, that we #ought to #pull out the #monetary-base and total reserves as #possibilities, along with whatever #measures he has in #mind, [Ford] well, I #think the primary #point, and what I will #try to #list in the testimony, is what #came #out of the #study. But in this #sense, it #seems to me the most #important #thing that #came #out of the #study is that the #present #technique was not that #bad. [Volcker] yes, but he #ignored the #fact that the #statistical #relationship between the #broader #aggregates and the #nominal GNP is much #closer than the #relationship between the #narrower #aggregates and the GNP it #seems to me [Morris]

Table 3.B4
(continued)

Classes for 1981 (thematic classification group in brackets)	Top ranking characteristic words	Top ranking characteristic phrases, or ECUs
Deliberation on target ranges for monetary aggregates & non-borrowed reserves [7c & 7d]	range+ language+ upper consult+ accept+ direct+ lower+ vote+ prefer+ say	I think that is #right. I would like to #suggest that this time we #observe the #upper #limits for the #purpose of #consultation and that at the time we crack through the 18 #percent we have another #telephone session.[Guffey] that might do it. I was just thinking of something similar; in #light of this #approach, the #committee #recognized that short term market interest-rates might #well #fluctuate #around levels #prevailing in recent days and that the #Fed-Funds-rate might #exceed the #range #specified. I hesitate at the #word #specified; I #guess #specified is all #right. [Volcker] I think we have two #choices. One is to #take what we think it probably would be, #let us #say 15 to 17 #percent, and then have a #symmetrical #range with enough room on either side, or we can #deliberately #put it off #center from that 15 to 17 #percent, #let us #say, John Balles, 11 to 17 #percent, because we #want to #trigger a #consultation at 17 #percent.[Solomon] I do not have any trouble with the #substance, but I find the #wording a little elliptical to my #literal mind. If, in effect, we are making inoperative the #upper #end of the #range between now and the next FOMC #meeting. I am not #sure that this #language #carries the #implication that at other times we would #want it to be #operative. [Solomon] in #summary, where I stand is a 7 to 7½ #percent target in M1b, #relaxing the M2 #constraint #language somewhat although I am not #sure that we should #put in a #numerical target if there is another way of doing it at 13 to 18 #percent #Fed-Funds-rate #range.[Solomon]

Table 3.B4
(continued)

Classes for 1981 (thematic classification group in brackets)	Top ranking characteristic words	Top ranking characteristic phrases, or ECUs
Staff forecast for US economy (demand and output, & inflation) [1b & 2b]	price+ sale+ unit+ tax cut treasury+ forecast industry+ business rise	#moreover, the #large #recent hike in #payroll #taxes will add #significantly to #compensation #costs #early this #year. By 1982, however, #increases in #compensation #costs should #moderate, reflecting the #extended period of #labor-market #slack, some #slowing of #inflation, and a #smaller Social #Security #tax #increase. It is not until 1982 that #productivity is #expected to #begin to contribute to alleviating the #impact of #rising #wages on #labor #costs. [Zeisel] homeownership has #remained a #key hedge against #inflation. #Moreover, the demand for #housing is #supported by #fundamental demographic #forces. Nevertheless, it is our view that #financial #considerations will #remain a #major #factor #damping #activity. We #expect that the #rise in the pre #tax #costs of servicing #standard #mortgage #contracts will #continue to outstrip #income growth, #increasingly dissuading or disqualifying #potential buyers. [Zeisel] but a number of #fundamental #factors #appear #likely to #continue to #damp #investment #outlays. The #cost of #debt #capital is #expected to #remain #high; after #tax #profit positions #relative to GNP are not #projected to #improve; and with #capacity #utilization #remaining low, we #expect #little demand for #expansion of #capital #stock, except in such fast #growing #sectors as #defense and the #energy #related #areas. [Zeisel] although #compensation is still #rising #rapidly, some #signs of moderation in #wages have #recently #emerged and we #expect this #trend to #continue, given the #environment of #sustained #high #unemployment #anticipated through the #projection period. Reduced #consumer #price #pressures should also contribute to #improved #wage #performance. We also #expect some #gains in #productivity. [Zeisel] but we #expect #costs and #price #increases #overall to #continue to decelerate in 1982 in an #environment of #increased #slack in #labor and #product #markets. There should also be #significant #benefits from the #substantial appreciation of the dollar. As a #result we are now #forecasting the gross #business #product #fixed weighted #price #index to #slow from an 8 percent rate in the #second half of this #year to about a 7¼ #pace in the #latter half of 1982. [Zeisel]

Table 3.B4
(continued)

Classes for 1981 (thematic classification group in brackets)	Top ranking characteristic words	Top ranking characteristic phrases, or ECUs
Reserves levels & Fed's market operations [4]	borrow+ reserve+ path+ week+ adjust+ million+ deposit+ December+ total+ average+	we addressed another question, which was: how #closely could #money have been controlled if we had had this graduated #discount #rate #structure that would #tend to #eliminate the #noise in the #amount of #discount #window #borrowing as a #function of the #Funds-rate - #Discount #rate #spread. [Lindsey] #instead, the #Desk aimed for, and achieved, non #borrowed #reserves in the #March 4 #week consistent with the 1 billion #dollars #borrowing #level that seemed to be emerging as the probable #level in the second four #week #sub-period. #Total #reserves #averaged about 380 #million #dollars below #path for the first four #week #sub-period. [Sternlight] was the seasonally adjusted total of demand deposits plus two-thirds or whatever fraction of other checkable deposits. [Axilrod] the shortfall was reflected in a #level of #borrowing that #averaged about 100 #million #dollars below the committee's #initial 850 #million #dollars #level while non #borrowed #reserves were just about on #path. In the second three #week #sub-period, ending #tomorrow, it looks as though #demand for #total #reserves will be about 150 #million #dollars below path. [Sternlight] for the first four #week #sub-period in the interval the four #weeks ended #April 29 #total #reserves were nearly equal to #path, a scant 22 #million #dollars below according to #latest #data. Reflecting the stronger aggregates, #required #reserves were 220 #million #dollars above their #path, but this was #offset by lower than expected #excess #reserves that #averaged only about 60 #million #dollars. [Sternlight]

Table 3.B5
Characteristic words and phrases for Classes in 1991 FOMC transcripts

Classes for 1991 (thematic classification group in brackets)	Top ranking characteristic words	Top ranking characteristic phrases, or ECUs
State of economy in districts [1c & 2c]	district+ sale+ quarter+ product+ manufacture+ inventor+ retail+ auto+ employ+ activit+	the #Dallas Federal-Reserve's #index of coincident #indicators has been #declining #fairly steadily but our leading #indicators have been #fairly #flat. I do not have an explanation for that. #Low #natural #gas #prices #continue to depress #drilling #activity in the #district. A #national #retail chain headquartered in #Dallas #expects a #weak #Christmas, following a #weak #Christmas #last #year. [McTeer] we are #seeing some #modest growth in #retail #sales along with some #indications of #increases in #orders in #major #industries. #Housing is #picking #up a #little at least #housing #starts are. But I must say that there is a #continuing sense of #pessimism among virtually all of the #business #people I #talk to, including #directors. [Forrestal] #nonresidential #construction is obviously quite #weak; #residential real estate #construction is #showing some #signs of recovery. #Sales #activity and #median #prices are above their #year ago #levels in #California ard in the #west in #general. #Permits for #new #construction are #up as are #housing #starts, at least for the #month of June. [Parry] #activity in our #district is moving #mostly sideways. #Agriculture is #showing some #weakness and #energy #continues to be quite #weak. There is some #activity still in the #residential #construction #area and some non #building #contracts for infrastructure #projects in the western part of the #district. [Hoenig] but because the #drought #conditions are #recent, #prices have not risen as much as one might #expect and, therefore, #farm income will be adversely affected. That is #beginning to #show #up in the #weakness of #sales of #agricultural #equipment, and the #main #manufacturers of #agricultural #equipment are #beginning to #pull back their #production #schedules for the #remainder of this #year. [Keehn]

Table 3.B5
(continued)

Classes for 1991 (thematic classification group in brackets)	Top ranking characteristic words	Top ranking characteristic phrases, or ECUs
Financial market developments & Fed's market operations [4]	dollar+ treasury+ German+ billion+ period+ market+ unit+ foreign+ Japan+ yield+	#typical late year #reserve needs dominated the #period, related to #currency outflows and increased #required #reserves, punctuated further at #times by some unexpectedly #high #treasury #balances. The #bulk of the need was #met with #outright #purchases, #including nearly 5 #billion #dollars of #bills and #notes #purchased from #foreign #accounts and 2. [Sternlight] in #yesterday's #auctions, the 3 and 6 month #issues #sold at #average discount rates of 5.50 and 5.63 #percent, #respectively, #compared with 5.86 and 5.84 #percent just before the last #meeting. The #Treasury paid down a #net of some 35 #billion #dollars in the #bill #market during the #period, #including the #maturity of 12 #billion #dollars in #cash #management #bills. [Sternlight] #Desk #operations were mainly of a #temporary nature, although near the #end of the #period the #desk began to #meet longer run #reserve needs through a 2 #billion #dollar #purchase of #bills in the #market and about 400 #million #dollars of #treasury #issues #bought from #foreign #accounts. [Sternlight] 4 #billion #dollars of #notes and 900 #million #dollars of #bills from #foreign #official #accounts. Except for a modest redemption of agency #issues, there was no #outright #transaction for the #system after #April 4. [Sternlight] the economic and #political turmoil in the #Soviet #Union and #elsewhere in #Eastern #Europe also weighed #heavily on the #mark throughout the #period. In the past two #weeks, the #dollar's rally has accelerated, and at #times the #dollar #mark #exchange-rate has #reached levels #over 15 #percent above the #February lows. [Cross]

Table 3.B5
(continued)

Classes for 1991 (thematic classification group in brackets)	Top ranking characteristic words	Top ranking characteristic phrases, or ECUs
Staff assessment of monetary policy stance [7a]	range+ inflation+ growth money stabil+ strateg+ cred+ object+ alternative+ committee+	the #easier #strategy is #accomplished by #raising #nominal GNP #growth to about 7 percent in 1992 and #keeping it there; the #baseline increases #nominal GNP #growth to 6 percent in 1992, then #gradually #reduces it #thereafter. [Kohn] the #path for #money that can #accommodate the #committee's #objectives for prices and #output #depends on an #assessment of the second and third #sets of #considerations the #underlying #forces working on spending and prices, [Kohn] I think #staying where we are with #alternative I is least #likely to do that. We already have #lowered the #ranges one #notch and by not going back up we #send a #signal that we have not #given up on #inflation. [Boehne] changing #interest-rates, in turn, by influencing opportunity costs and #velocity, would affect the #money #growth needed to #achieve the #committee's #objectives. In this regard, the #money #ranges should #give #sufficient #scope to deal with #potential #deviations from expectations; [Kohn] but as the #Bluebook points out on the bottom of #page 19, #long #run #alternative III, which #lowers all the #ranges ½ percentage point is more #consistent with the spirit and intent of our anti #inflationary #strategy. [Black]
Credit conditions & banking system stability [6]	credit+ bank+ loan+ household+ debt+ financial+ asset+ spend finance+ commercial	we have #corporate #profits that are very disappointing. We have a very heavy #debt #burden remaining for #consumers, for #businesses, and for #governments to the #extent that the #fiscal #problems of state and municipal #governments #really have taken away their #ability to have any stimulating #effect on the economy. [LaWare] but it is also in #banks, #insurance #companies, and #finance #companies, all with varying #degrees of exposure to these structurally #troubled areas of #commercial #real #estate, unleveraged #loans, and junk bonds. [Mullins] but the #extent of the #contractionary #effect on #spending of such #credit #restraint has been hard to assess. Similarly, #households no #doubt have reallocated #financial #portfolios from retail #deposits to #capital market #instruments. [Lindsey] the #banks and the #financial #sector generally are still quite #sluggish and the #overhang of #commercial #real #estate is still there and will be there for some time. [Boehne] and that is a very #large atypical #shift in the composition of #household #financial #assets out of #bank #deposits into various #securities #type #instruments, including #government #securities funds and so on. [Corrigan]

Table 3.B5
(continued)

Classes for 1991 (thematic classification group in brackets)	Top ranking characteristic words	Top ranking characteristic phrases, or ECUs
Deliberation on interest rate policy decision [7b]	asymmetr+ discount+ language symmetr+ fund+ prefer+ recommend+ direct+ version vote+	I think your #recommendation of a 25 #basis #point #cut in the #Funds #rate is #appropriate. And in the context of more #frequent #discussions in the coming weeks, I would #prefer the #symmetric #language. [McTeer] I would #favor the 25 #basis #point #reduction in the #Funds #rate #accompanied by a #discount #rate #change of ½ percentage #point, recognizing, of course, that the #timing decision for the #discount #rate itself is the #boards. [Corrigan] lacking that, then I would be in #favor of alternative A with a 50 #basis #point #cut in the #Fed #Funds #rate. but I could #live with 25 #basis #points now on the #Fed #Funds #rate if there were #asymmetric #language. [Keehn] #Mr. #Chairman, I certainly concur with your B #asymmetric #toward #ease #recommendation, but I would #prefer the #language in #version I—I do not want to quarrel about it; I am not going to #vote no over it. [Kelley] that is very #slightly in #favor of #version I, so I would #propose for a #vote alternative B #asymmetric #toward #ease and #version I with respect to the #language. [Greenspan]
Uncertainty around interest rate decision [8a]	think say go thing+ know make way+ risk+ try right+	if we #believe that, I #think we are #mistaken. I #think the #correction with #regard to household savings is #underway and is #going to #take #place and I #think the use of #monetary policy to #deal with that has to be very, very #carefully done so as not to #make it #worse rather than better. [Angell] I do subscribe to the #notion that the #economy is #going to pick up, but I #think we are playing with some #tender attitudes #out there. I would #say that the #risks are #probably even to #maybe marginally on the #down #side. But I #agree with those who are #concerned about the #outcome. [Boehne] the #worst #thing we can do is to #create more uncertainty. As to the #suggestion that we have to #make #dramatic moves my #view is that the market will #say the #Federal-Reserve has moved and #nothing will #happen. [Angell] I do not #want to #try to do any better at forecasting than the staff; I do not have any quarrel with #Mike's forecast at all. I do not #think we have ever been to this #place before, and I do not #know for #sure that that is the #way it is #going to #work, but it does #seem to me that this is a time for a little #patience. [Angell] but I do #think and this #goes back to what Bob Forrestal #said that one needs to #look at the #risks of the #outcome, if you will, not just the #risk of something #happening. [Syron]

Table 3.B6
Characteristic words and phrases for classes in 1992 FOMC transcripts

Classes for 1992 (thematic classification group in brackets)	Top ranking characteristic words	Top ranking characteristic phrases, or ECUs
Staff forecast for US economy (demand and output, & Inflation [1b & 2b]	quarter+ growth project+ forecast percent+ export+ year+ expect+ increase+ Greenbook+	our #forecast for the next two #years has #consumer #spending #rising #roughly in #line with disposable #income. Obviously, these two #variables can be #expected to be #highly correlated #over time. [Prell] but with #unemployment #remaining #relatively #high and #prices #decelerating, we #expect #compensation per #hour to #slow, much as it did in the mid-1980s #under #similar circumstances. [Stockton] #over the #past twelve #months, the #consumer #price inflation ex #food and #energy has #risen 3–3¾ #percent. With the considerable degree of #slack in #product markets and further #slowing in #underlying #labor #costs, we are #expecting this measure to drop below 3 #percent by the end of next #year. [Stockton] A #swing in #energy #prices is the main reason that the #overall #consumer-price-inflation is #projected to #rise #faster this #year than last. Our #oil-price #forecast implies that, after #declining #substantially on #net in 1991, retail #energy #prices will be #rising #moderately this #year and next. [Prell] even with this #moderate assumption about #oil-prices, the value of our #oil #imports is #projected to #increase because #rising #demand and #declining domestic #production #combine to #boost the quantity of #petroleum #imports. [Truman]

Table 3.B6
(continued)

Classes for 1992 (thematic classification group in brackets)	Top ranking characteristic words	Top ranking characteristic phrases, or ECUs
Staff assessment of monetary policy stance [7a]	fiscal stimulus term+ short+ rate+ long+ easing+ polic+ package+ yield+	unchanged, or even higher, #nominal #long #term #rates as a #result #probably would not undercut the #basic #stimulative #effect of an #easing, since #real #rates #likely still would be #lower, and if the #policy judgment were #correct, [Kohn] we have had a very #steep #yield #curve, very low #short #term interest-rates relative to #long #rates, low recent #inflation, #extraordinarily #rapid growth in the #narrow #aggregates, which is #disturbing, and almost no growth at all in the #broad #aggregates, [Jordan] both in #terms of what is #perceived in the #economics profession and #especially by the #incoming #administration and the new #Congress about what the role of #fiscal #policy has been and what the role of #monetary policy has been and, #therefore, [Jordan] #nominal #bond #yields #likely would fall in #response, since any increase in #inflation expectations in the current #circumstances #probably would be muted, and easier #monetary-policy should have an unambiguous, albeit small, #effect on #real #long #term #rates. [Kohn] #monetary policy in fact has been very #stimulative, and the #critical thing would be to back off from that #kind of #short #run #stimulus in the #narrow #measures before we do see the #future #inflation. [Jordan]

Table 3.B6
(continued)

Classes for 1992 (thematic classification group in brackets)	Top ranking characteristic words	Top ranking characteristic phrases, or ECUs
State of economy in districts [1c & 2c]	district+ sale+ retail+ manufacture area+ report+ housing construct+ business	we are #getting #pretty good #retail #sales #numbers not only in the #district but from all those #major #companies headquartered in the #district; the latter #reported very #strong #numbers in October as we now #see in the #national #statistics. They also #report #improving #optimism about #Christmas. [Jordan] when I try to elicit sympathy for how #tough things are in #southern #California where I am from, I get no sympathy at all. They think it is #well deserved! There have been #reports of a #pickup in #residential #activity throughout the #district: we are #seeing some #new #home #starts #pretty #well throughout the #whole #area. [Jordan] #retailers #continue to be very #cautious about their inventory levels. One #bright #spot in the #district that was #picked #up for the #nation in #Mike Prell's #report is the #sale of #single #family #homes. [Forrestal] we have #recently #seen #modest expansion in #orders, production, and #shipments by #producers of apparel, household #goods, and #construction #materials. And there is a parallel development of #improvement in the #retail #sector as #well, although #durable #goods #retailers are #reporting rather weak #sales. [Forrestal] but upscale #retailers are #reporting that #sales are #pretty #poor. #Auto #sales are #soft and that has gone on since the #last period. The one #sign of #strength that we have #seen is in the #housing #area for first time #home buyers, low price #houses are being built, but there has been a #slowdown again in #sales of upper price #houses. [Syron]

Table 3.B6
(continued)

Classes for 1992 (thematic classification group in brackets)	Top ranking characteristic words	Top ranking characteristic phrases, or ECUs
Deliberation on interest rate policy decision [7b]	I think go if risk+ we want+ not me say	and it is also important to #recognize that if we get #into one of these #situations, all #institutions are #going to be a #lot more defensive. That may be good news in one #sense. But it is #bad news in another #sense in that it #makes it that much more #difficult to #deal with them. [Corrigan] I could not #imagine a better time to experiment than #right now and to be #wrong. And thirdly, #standing tall might have another #advantage. It is amazing when I #go #out in #public that #everyone #thinks we #know something that #nobody #else does. #Given the #amount of disagreement #around this #table, it is unclear that we #know anything, but they all #think we #know something that #nobody #else does. [Lindsey] in my view this #financial #restructuring was #going to #happen and it could have been a #great #deal more traumatic than it is #given the #way #things have evolved so far. [Kelley] I #want to #ask #Ted a #question. I do not #mean to #try to #put too #fine a point on this, but it is just because I #find today's #discussions even more #difficult than #usual even though they are often very #difficult. [Syron] I do not #know that I #understand what is #going on with M2 either, but I will not #let that #stop me from #making a few #comments! [Stern]

Table 3.B6
(continued)

Classes for 1992 (thematic classification group in brackets)	Top ranking characteristic words	Top ranking characteristic phrases, or ECUs
Financial market developments & Fed's market operations [4]	dollar+ treasur+ reserve+ market+ mark+ currenc+ Deutsche intervention+ desk+ yen	again, we believed that the #market was #disorderly and the #American #authorities #intervened and #purchased 300 #million #dollars, #evenly divided between the #Treasury and the #Federal-Reserve. With #Europe #closed, only #Canada could #join in the #intervention and did so; the #Bank of #Canada #purchased. Both of us #sold #German #marks. [McDonough] #domestic #Desk #operations then #sought to #maintain this #degree of #pressure over the balance of the #intervening #period. The #borrowing #allowance was #initially #kept at 225 #million #dollars to reflect the #unchanged #spread between the #discount rate and the #Funds rate. [Sternlight] against this #background, the #Desk #purchased 3.7 #billion #dollars of #Treasury #coupon #issues in the #market on #September 1 and #purchased #additional #securities directly from #foreign accounts periodically #thereafter. [Lovett] the #Bank-of-Japan has #intervened on a number of #occasions to #support the #yen by #selling #dollars, #largely motivated by a view that a #weaker #yen both #contributes to and is #caused by #stock #market #weakness. [McDonough] the #United #States #Treasury #joined in the #intervention when on February 17th we #sold on their behalf 100 #million #dollars at 127.36 #yen to the #dollar. On February 20th, we #intervened again by #selling 50 #million #dollars at 128.13 #yen, with that #operation shared #equally by the #Federal-Reserve and the #Treasury. [McDonough]

Table 3.B7
Characteristic words and phrases for classes in 1993 FOMC transcripts

Classes for 1993 (thematic classification group in brackets)	Top ranking characteristic words	Top ranking characteristic phrases, or ECUs
Uncertainty on model of economy & appropriate monetary policy strategy [8c]	inflation+ think know long+ rate+ go term+ look+ model+ monetary-policy	I #really cannot #understand what is #going on; I #find it #hard to #believe that the #fundamentals do not have something to do with this in the #longer #run. [Syron] I #think #saying that this #model is nonsensical and totally at #odds with #reality #runs up against the #point that it does #contain some very #basic #notions that #people have talked about theoretically for a #long time, and it has #worked. [Prell] and it #puts us into a #way of being #perceived, and #maybe we #perceive #ourselves, that #says if we are anti #inflation, we are anti-growth. I have a-lot-of #trouble with the #slack #model, with the #Phillips curve #kind of #trade-off that calls for a forecast of #things like capacity and all #sorts of #things that I have #trouble with. [Jordan] so in that #sense I #think your #insight is a #correct one. The next #question you also #asked is: #okay, what other #intermediate #target #variable then do we use as a substitute for M2? If I #knew of one, I would supply it. [Lindsey] it is #clear that achieving the further #progress toward price #stability that #everyone is hoping for in 1993 #looks a bit remote at this #point. But the other #side of the #question is that while we may not be doing as #well as we #hoped, are we doing as badly as we #think? [Corrigan]

Table 3.B7
(continued)

Classes for 1993 (thematic classification group in brackets)	Top ranking characteristic words	Top ranking characteristic phrases, or ECUs
State of economy in districts [1c & 2c]	district+ area+ construct+ manufacture+ sector+ commercial business region+ report+ retail+	as far as the #regional #economy is #concerned, it #remains reasonably #healthy, which is the #report I have been providing for quite some time now. In #general, #construction is quite #strong; #retail #sales are #pretty good; #manufacturing is #mixed; #tourism, at least in the #western #part of the #district, has been #strong. [Stern] in the #single #family #sector we are #seeing more #building of spec #houses than we had earlier. The multifamily #sector #remains in the doldrums and #commercial #construction is still #soft, although we do #notice in many of the cities of the southeast, #particularly Atlanta, that there is some absorption of #space. [Forrestal] November #payroll #employment was #little changed from the recession low reached in October. #Moreover, #job #losses have #continued in such #areas as #construction and #manufacturing. On a more #positive note, #reports from #contacts in #California are no longer uniformly #negative. #Retail #sales are #improving some, and there certainly are good #conditions in some #sectors such as motion pictures, entertainment, and also #agriculture. [Parry] in #areas like Denver and Albuquerque we are #hearing more and more #comments about #boom like #conditions. We are #seeing more #speculation in #residential real #estate; and #loan growth is #fairly #strong, #especially in #areas such as Denver, #parts of Omaha, and Lincoln. [Hoenig] #retail #sales in the #district #continue to show #improvement; that #began in the #Christmas #season and there is some #continuation more recently. There has been a #fair bit of #improvement in consumer #durables #autos #particularly, though, were #affected by the #weather. [Syron]

Table 3.B7
(continued)

Classes for 1993 (thematic classification group in brackets)	Top ranking characteristic words	Top ranking characteristic phrases, or ECUs
US economy demand & output performance, and staff forecast [2a & 2b]	quarter+ export+ year+ product+ growth computer+ fourth+ increase+ goods ship+	however, #over the #second half of this #year these #exports are #projected to #rise by about 4½ #percent as #growth #increases #abroad. Their #growth is #expected to #slow somewhat next #year, despite the further #rise in foreign #demand, because of the #influence of the #higher dollar. [Truman] #turning to #imports, #growth #over the #past #year has #come #primarily in #imports from #Canada, the #United-Kingdom, Japan, #Mexico and Asia #increases in #imports from #China and Singapore have been particularly #large. [Truman] #meanwhile, the #expansion of the #domestic economy is #producing a #rapid #rise in non #oil #imports, #paced by record #increases in #computers and #substantial #increases in other #capital #goods and #industrial supplies. [Truman] the #forecast for #domestic #demand, calls for sizable #gains in #spending by both #consumers and businesses. #consumption #expenditures after sharply outpacing #income #gains last #year are #expected to #grow only a bit #faster than real #income #over the next two #years. [Slifman] given the weakness early this #year. However, this #implies a #gain of only two #percent #over the four #quarters of 1993, #shown at the right. We have 1994 #growth at 2.6 #percent #domestic #demand, the red #line, #paces the #advance, as #net #exports continue to decline. [Prell]
Deliberation on interest rate decision [7b]	symmetr+ asymmetr+ direct+ committee+ prefer+ support+ language alternative+ meet move+	my #preference would be for no #change #today but with an #asymmetric #directive #toward #tightening. I think having that on the #record in the future is more likely to be in our #favor than against us for #reasons that Jerry Corrigan and #Governor Mullins mentioned. [McTeer] it seems to me that as the #chairman you #ought to have the ability to #make a #move under #changing #circumstances as you see fit. #Asymmetry means to me that we would go into the #inter #meeting period ahead with a very strong #bias #toward #making a #change to #tighten, [Keehn] I #support your #recommendation, #Mr.-Chairman. Perhaps if we were starting from scratch, I would have some #preference for #symmetry but I do not think we #ought to #change from #asymmetry. [Oltman] this is an #operating #paragraph and it should #communicate what the #committee is thinking. I do not see any #inclination to #change in the #inter #meeting period. [Hoenig] I would #support no #change at this time. I would have a slight #preference for #symmetry; but having heard the #arguments for having already #made one #change, #changing back may be awkward now. [Hoenig]

Table 3.B7
(continued)

Classes for 1993 (thematic classification group in brackets)	Top ranking characteristic words	Top ranking characteristic phrases, or ECUs
Fed's market operations [4]	dollar+ yen Japan+ German+ operation+ reserve+ day+ treasury+ mark+ Bundesbank	the #desk #intervened on three #days since the #last meeting and #bought a #total of 1, 067, 500, 000 #dollars through sales of #Japanese #yen on behalf of the #United #States #monetary #authorities, #evenly divided between the #treasury and the Federal-Reserve. [McDonough] the #balance of the #reserve need was met #using #temporary #operations. The #Desk again made frequent #use of #fixed term multi #day #system RP's to #address the fairly certain and #evenly #distributed #reserve shortages that #occurred in the #early part of #each of the first two #maintenance #periods. [White] #Desk #operations continued to #seek #reserve conditions consistent with #Federal #Funds #trading #around three percent. The #borrowing #allowance was #cut by a #total of 150 #million #dollars in a #series of #steps that #reflected the #declines in the #seasonal component typical at this time of year. [Lovett] during the #following #week, the #Bank-of-Japan #purchased, #bringing the #total #purchased by the #Japanese #authorities over the #period to, the most pronounced #movement in major #exchange-rates, over the #period, has been the #appreciation of the #mark by 8. [Fisher] considering the #period since your #last meeting, there are three questions to be #addressed: first, why did we #intervene in #dollar #yen on #August 19th? Second, why has the #German #mark #appreciated #sharply against the #yen and also against the #dollar, even as the #Bundesbank has #lowered #interest-rates? [Fisher]

Table 3.B8
Characteristic words and phrases for classes in 1997 FOMC transcripts

Classes for 1997 (thematic classification group in brackets)	Top ranking characteristic Words	Top ranking characteristic phrases, or ECUs
Choice of target to achieve monetary stability & role of money ranges [9a]	think stability issue+ discuss+ want+ make question+ go target+ public+	yes, I #think the more #explicit we are #internally and the more we #discuss this #issue among #ourselves, the #better. I can honestly #say that if you #asked me to #go #around the #table and #make a #speech on this #subject for #everyone here that I could do it. [Greenspan] I #think the more #explicit we are in our #discussions, the #better, so that we all #understand #exactly where each one of us is. I am a little concerned about #going #public even in #Humphrey–Hawkins #testimony. I #think we can #address the #issue you #want #addressed, and I #agree that we #ought to, without getting too #explicit with #respect to a number. [Greenspan] the #legislation does not #require that we announce any particular #money #measure M1, M2, or anything #else. It #says something #broadly about #monetary-aggregates. I #think we could #try to #explain that #using something like #money growth to formulate policy to #achieve our #objective of price #stability is one #thing; [Jordan] I do not #mean to suggest that! All I am #saying is that I #think it would be #useful if we were more #explicit among #ourselves with #respect to what #measures we #ought to be #focusing on, where we #want to get to with those, and over what time frame. [Melzer] if I #decided to #use them as #targets with an assumed #velocity, I would #choose another. If we do get to the #point where we are #starting to #put #weight on these aggregates, I #think we will need a careful #discussion of how we #want to #use them. [Hoenig]

Table 3.B8
(continued)

Classes for 1997 (thematic classification group in brackets)	Top ranking characteristic Words	Top ranking characteristic phrases, or ECUs
Staff assessment of monetary policy stance, & deliberation on interest rate decision [7a & 7b]	polic+ action+ tighten+ inflation+ risk+ situation+ pre-empt+ committee+ uncertain+ scenario+	for this #exercise, I have #considered two #alternative #policy #responses, which illustrate some of the #trade-offs you would #face #under these #circumstances. In one #case, I #assume that #monetary policy #stabilizes the unemployment-rate at its #baseline #path, thus #allowing the effects of the higher productivity growth to show through into permanently lower #inflation. [Stockton] indeed, the need for #eventual #policy #tightening would still be a close #call in the #staff's #worst #case #scenario. If, in light of the #risk of increasing #inflation pressures, the #committee were #inclined to #tighten at an early date, #global #financial #developments might still suggest #reasons to postpone #action, at least for a short time, [Kohn] in my #view, there is almost a zero #possibility that we would #tighten between now and the next meeting. #Therefore, the #best #choice is to #move to #symmetry, largely to #avoid an emotional or intellectual bias that might make us #feel that we could not #respond #appropriately to any critical #development. [McDonough] the #reason is not only because of the #turmoil in #financial-markets but because of some #uncertainty about just how sharp the #economic #impact is going to be in #southeast #Asia and what the #spillover effects to other #developed #economies and [Meyer] second, if we #ultimately have to #play #catch up and #take strong #action, which #risks a #recession that #obviously could have doubly #adverse effects. It is this latter #possibility that #really frightens me. [Broaddus]

Table 3.B8
(continued)

Classes for 1997 (thematic classification group in brackets)	Top ranking characteristic Words	Top ranking characteristic phrases, or ECUs
State of economy in districts [1c & 2c]	district+ report+ industr+ retail+ region+ new+ manufactur+ area+ sale+ construct+	so, our #regional #labor-markets are very #tight. #Elsewhere, we are #hearing #reports of overbuilding in the #commercial real #estate #sector. These #reports are not universal across the #district, but we #hear that #especially in the southern #part of the #district there is overbuilding of #hotels and #office and #commercial #space for the first time in some time. [Broaddus] #orders for #new ship #construction are #booked #several years out. #Labor-markets in our #region also #remain #tight, an old and #familiar #story by now. Pockets of #special tightness #include #information #technology and #skilled crafts in #areas like marine and #oil related #work. [Guynn] that has now changed. Senior #city officials #told me #recently that #plans have been submitted for 40 #new #hotels in #Boston #proper. We also have #reports of 11.3 #million square feet of #speculative #office #space being #proposed for #construction in the greater #Boston #area within the next 12 to 18 #months. [Minehan] and in #several #areas in the #district #competition for #employers is so fierce that #employers are holding #job #fairs and #offering finder's fees and #signing #bonuses to #recruit #new #hires. [Parry] #commercial real #estate #activity, in #contrast, appears to #remain very #strong, #especially in the Washington #area but #generally around the #district as a #whole. #Elsewhere, #manufacturing #activity #moderated in November according to our #survey, but there is some #evidence of a #firming in this #sector so far in December. [Broaddus]

Table 3.B8
(continued)

Classes for 1997 (thematic classification group in brackets)	Top ranking characteristic Words	Top ranking characteristic phrases, or ECUs
Financial market developments [4]	panel+ Japan+ bond+ yen chart+ German+ page+ bottom+ red dollar+	the last #page of #charts relates to our open #market #operations in this #period. The #top #panel #covers #daily #Fed #Funds #trading; the #blue #lines #show the #daily ranges, the #vertical #red #lines #show the #standard #deviations, and the horizontal #red #lines indicate the effective #rates. [Fisher] the next #page of #charts contrasts the volatility of #federal #funds #trading and #operating #balances in #comparable #periods from last #summer and this #summer. The #daily range of #Federal #Funds #trading is #shown in #blue; the one #standard #deviation of #funds #trading around the #daily effective #rate and the effective #rate are #depicted in #red; [Fisher] on #page 3 of your #chart #package, #each of the three #panels #depicts the #Fed #Funds #daily #trading range and effective #rates for the four #maintenance #periods in #December and #January that surround #each of the last three year #ends: 1994 to 1995; [Fisher] not #shown are the dramatic declines in #spreads of stripped #yields of Brady #bonds #relative to #United #States #Treasuries from their #peaks #following the Mexican #crisis. #Shown at the #right is one result of the general decline in #bond #yields in #industrial #countries and optimism about #emerging #markets: [Truman] one could also #note that #relative to #United #States and #Japanese 10 year #rates, #German #rates have #backed #up by 25 #basis points since the #beginning of the #summer. [Fisher]

Table 3.B8
(continued)

Classes for 1997 (thematic classification group in brackets)	Top ranking characteristic Words	Top ranking characteristic phrases, or ECUs
Staff forecast for US economy (demand and output, & inflation) [1b & 2b]	quarter+ growth trend+ forecast invest+ slow+ fourth+ Greenbook+ project+ utiliz+	the #Greenbook #projects a nearly #unchanged #unemployment-rate, but a #declining #capacity #utilization rate even after taking #account of a #slowing in the #growth of #investment #spending in the manufacturing-sector and a #resulting #moderation in the rate of #increase in industrial #capacity. [Meyer] #third, the #upward #adjustment of #profits in the NIPA #revisions #suggests more of a cushion that might delay pass throughs of any #future #increases in compensation. While the #net #effect is still #likely to be #higher inflation #over the #forecast #horizon, any #increase will begin from a slightly #lower base, and at least #over the #forecast #horizon may be even more #modest than #previously #expected. [Meyer] #moreover, with #final #demand #exceptionally #robust, #prospects are good that the #expansion of #output will continue to #exceed the #growth of #potential, as #indeed it does for a while in the staff #forecast. [Kohn] in #addition, however, the #prospects of competitive #pressures #damping inflation #seem greater now because the #inventory #adjustment is #likely to #contribute to some slippage in the #level of #factory #capacity #utilization. [Prell] it may be hinted at in a #downward #revision to the #forecast for #net #exports and the less #favorable mix between #inventory #investment and #final sales now #projected for the #fourth #quarter. [Meyer]

Table 3.B9
Characteristic words and phrases for classes in 1998 FOMC transcripts

Classes for 1998 (thematic classification group in brackets)	Top ranking characteristic words	Top ranking characteristic phrases, or ECUs
State of economy in districts [1c & 2c]	district+ report+ manufactur construct+ sale+ industr+ retail+ region+ estate area+	#housing #activity #continues at a #strong #pace in the #district, with #single #family #home #construction and #sales being the #strongest. The only #area of softness is in Louisiana. One #sign of how #strongly the #tourism #industry in the #district is #affecting #housing markets is illustrated by a #report from one of our #directors at a #recent meeting. [Guynn] #housing #activity and non #residential #construction #activity in #general #remain #strong. #Auto #sales are #healthy. The weaknesses are in #agriculture, where I think the problems are #well recognized and are quite #severe in at least #parts of the #district, in #parts of the #manufacturing economy, and in mining #activity. [Stern] #Auto dealers in the #district are concerned about #shortages of #vehicles, as #well as #parts, that could #affect their #service #business. A #survey by our Detroit branch #found that spending by #business #firms in the Flint #area has been #particularly #affected. [Moskow] #manufacturing #activity #remains quite #strong in the #district. #Purchasing #managers #reports for January #indicated that #overall #activity #expanded at about the same #pace as in #December in Chicago and at a somewhat faster #pace in Detroit and Milwaukee. [Moskow] lower #financing costs have #added to the #construction #boom in #Texas. #Commercial #construction #remains #strong and #large #new projects are announced almost daily. At our #small #business #advisory #council meeting two #weeks ago, one of the members commented that #several of his law #firm's clients have decided in #recent months to become real #estate developers. probably a #sign of #trouble. [McTeer]

Table 3.B9
(continued)

Classes for 1998 (thematic classification group in brackets)	Top ranking characteristic words	Top ranking characteristic phrases, or ECUs
Staff forecast for US economy (demand and output, & inflation) [1b & 2b]	core+ growth inflation+ percent+ quarter+ trend+ forecast rise profit+ acceler+	I #expect both #slower #growth and #higher #inflation #over the next #year and a half. However, I #expect #faster #growth than in the #Greenbook #forecast, with the #rate of #expansion in GDP closer to #trend and a #slower #rate of #increase in #potential #output. [Meyer] #Mike has discussed the #key #elements in the #forecast. Most importantly, as he #noted, the #rise in the #level of #output has been about matched by an #increase in #estimated #potential, owing to #faster #trend #productivity, that #leaves the #output #gap about unchanged. [Kohn] with #inflation #subdued for now, most of these #increases are in #real #wages rather than in #nominal #wages. More #broadly, #real disposable #income #rose at an #annual #rate of almost 5 #percent in the #fourth #quarter. [Broaddus] the #Greenbook does not #project a further #increase in the #growth #rate of employment #cost #index #compensation for 1998 #over 1997. Unit #labor #costs in the #projection do #rise as a #result of the weak #productivity #growth. So, we do get a #projected 3 #percentage point #increase, on a #consistently #measured basis, in both the #core CPI and the #core #measures of #inflation. [Broaddus] first, it seems clear enough at this stage that #permanent #productivity #gains are a major force #driving this economic #expansion. The #staff has #revised #upward its #estimate of #productivity #growth. That #revision in #turn is #consistent with the #higher #level of #stock #prices in the current #Greenbook #forecast. [Broaddus]

Table 3.B9
(continued)

Classes for 1998 (thematic classification group in brackets)	Top ranking characteristic words	Top ranking characteristic phrases, or ECUs
Financial market developments [4]	treasur+ securit+ yield+ bond+ day+ trad+ indexe+ page+ chart+ bank+	on the next #page, there is a #chart that I #normally show you to illustrate conditions in the #Federal #Funds #market. In the #top #panel, the #green dashed #line is the committee's #target, the #blue vertical #lines #represent the #Federal #Funds #trading #range on #each #day, the #red horizontal tick is the #daily effective rate, [Fisher] and the #red vertical #line shows one #standard #deviation of the #Federal #Funds #trading #range. In the #bottom #panel, the #blue bars #depict on the left #hand #scale the #daily excess #reserves we in fact provided to the #banking #system, and the #red #dots indicate on the right #hand #scale the #deviation of the #daily effective Fed-Funds-rate from the #target. [Fisher] this is driving #Japanese #Treasury #bill rates toward and through #zero, not at the #auctions but in secondary #market #trading. Turning to the #top #panel of the next #page, you can #see #selected #credit #spreads in the American #markets #depicted in #various time slices: first, at the time of your #last meeting; [Fisher] focusing now on the #red #line in the #bottom #panel, which #depicts the benchmark #Japanese #government #bond #yield, in the #last few #days and since your #last meeting in fact there has been an #extraordinary #backup in this #yield. [Fisher] and simultaneously #enter forward #contracts to #sell dollars and #buy #yen. As the #Japanese #banks have swarmed into the #swap #market eager to #swap out of #yen and into dollars, #implicit costs of #yen #funding have fallen toward and through #zero for non #Japanese #banks, as you can #see in the #bottom #panel. [Fisher]

Table 3.B9
(continued)

Classes for 1998 (thematic classification group in brackets)	Top ranking characteristic words	Top ranking characteristic phrases, or ECUs
Outlook for world economy & Asia crisis [5]	risk+ downside Brazil+ scenario+ upside worse international+ Russia+ outcome+ world+	I see this #downside #risk of a #worse #case #outcome in Asia, should it #materialize, as #likely to spread to other #emerging market #economies and constituting the most #serious #threat to the United States and the #global #economies. [Meyer] Japan is more #deeply mired in #political paralysis. Other Asian #economies, especially #Indonesia, are in more desperate shape. #China, including #Hong #Kong, #Russia, and #possibly #Brazil, are more #fragile than we anticipated at that time. [Rivlin] turning to the nation, the #risks #clearly have #shifted to the #downside. #Global #financial stresses are closing in on the #American #economy and are #likely to continue to do so for some time. [Boehne] in fact, it #seems to me that the domestic #scenario is #distinctly one of #upside #risk, although we certainly should not ignore or forget the #possible #downside shocks that Governor-Rivlin #listed. [Kelley] for now, I think the #uncertainties in the #international #outlook #clearly justify waiting. However, I do think that, on #balance, the #risks remain definitely to the #upside and that we are #likely to have to #tighten this year. [Moskow]
Deliberation on interest rate decision [7b]	recommend+ symmetr+ direct+ asymmetr+ I support+ prefer+ sentence+ Fed-Funds-Rate agree+	#Mr.-Chairman, I #support a ¼ #point #reduction in the Funds rate. I also think the current situation may #require more than one 25 #basis #point #cut in the Funds rate in the #future, and #therefore I would #prefer a #directive with #asymmetry #toward #ease. [Parry] #Mr.-Chairman, I #came to this #meeting #prepared to #vote for an increase of 25 #basis #points in the #Fed-Funds-rate, and I also #came #prepared to dissent if we did not at least #move to #asymmetry. [Minehan] #Mr.-Chairman, I #support your #recommendation for no #change in the #Fed-Funds-rate and for an #asymmetric #posture. I have some considerable sympathy with the notion that, rather than just expanding the #policy #announcement, we have an #immediate #release of the #directive that would indicate [Meyer] #Mr.-Chairman, I #agree with the #proposed 25 #basis #point #easing #move and I would #prefer no #tilt for the #reasons that you articulated with #regard to that choice and that Gary-Stern reinforced in his comments. [Guynn] we have succeeded in #staying on schedule, if I may #use that term, and hopefully we will continue to do so. accordingly, I am putting on the table a #proposal to reduce the #Fed-Funds-rate #immediately by 25 #basis #points and a #recommendation that we #move to #asymmetry #toward #ease. [Greenspan]

Table 3.B9
(continued)

Classes for 1998 (thematic classification group in brackets)	Top ranking characteristic words	Top ranking characteristic phrases, or ECUs
Staff forecast for rest of world [5]	export+ net unit+ state+ dollar+ Asian drag+ Asia+ foreign+ countries	one #piece, but only a #piece, of the puzzle of the further #strengthening in #private #demand may be the same #Asian #turmoil that was reflected in the #sharper than anticipated #decline in #net #exports. [Meyer] however, whereas #phase one was accompanied by #offsetting #positive shocks in the form of #lower #United #States #interest-rates #stemming from safe haven capital #flows and #lower #oil-prices, [Meyer] our models decompose the #contributions of #United #States GDP, the black #bars, and #relative prices, the red #bars. Through part of 1998, the #stimulative #effect of the recent #dollar #appreciation increasingly boosts #import #demand, partly #offsetting the #restraining #effect of slower #United #States GDP growth. [Johnson] in #contrast, Canadian #net #exports benefited from strong #demand in the #United #States. The #net #export #drag incontinental #Europe was #offset by #robust growth in #domestic #demand, supported by low or declining #interest-rates, shown at the right. [Hooper] as reported in the middle left panel, the #Asian #developing #countries #account for nearly 20 percent of #United #States #exports. Our reading of #developments to date is that output growth in Korea and in several #southeast #Asian #countries will be #pushed into #negative numbers as #domestic #demand is severely #reduced by the financial-market #turmoil, higher #domestic #interest-rates, [Johnson]
Deliberation on broader issues of monetary policy stance & strategy [9c]	think I thing+ question+ way+ go long+ polic+ people+ stability	I do not pretend, obviously, to #know the #best #way to #address all of the very #difficult #questions we face on this #subject as we #go forward. [Broaddus] it is a bit puzzling that #people seemingly have not #given more #attention to that #question, but there is, I #think, plenty of time for them to undertake that #kind of stockpiling. [Prell] but #taking a #step back, all this #reminds me of something that I #think we have #known for a while, and that is that our economy is #fundamentally very resilient. [Stern] that does not #mean it will be from now on, but if we look at it in retrospect I #think it would have been. I would like to #take the #opportunity to #talk a bit about #monetary policy #strategy and in particular about a memo that we all get #called #monetary policy #rules, which I hardly ever hear referred to. [Gramlich] I do #think that the crucial #decision we have to make and have been making for a while is the recognition that the #longer we #wait, if our #analysis of this #process is #wrong, the more we will have to do to #stabilize the economic system. [Greenspan]

Table 3.B10

Characteristic words and phrases for classes in 1999 FOMC transcripts

Classes for 1999 (thematic classification group in brackets)	Top ranking characteristic words	Top ranking characteristic phrases, or ECUs
Deliberation on interest rate decision [7b]	think recommend+ issue+ want+ language go way+ make let symmetr+	#Mr.-Chairman, I am #happy to #support your #recommendation for #sitting tight. I #think #Larry-Meyer #made a #useful #contribution #yesterday. I have been #thinking in my own #mind about how to resuscitate the Taylor-rule. I may not #agree with everything he #said, but I view it as a #reasonable strategy. [Gramlich] I #think your advice and #recommendation are right on #target. I #think we #ought to keep this off the #table. We have enough difficulties explaining where we are and what we are #trying to do with #monetary policy; it would #serve no #purpose to confuse #matters with this unimportant #issue now. [Boehne] #Mr.-Chairman, I #agree #completely. I do not #think it #serves any #useful #purpose to #open this up to a wide range of #discussion at this #point. [Moskow] as #Ed-Boehne #said and I #believe Bob-Parry #said, we can still #use #words to #communicate anything we #want. But if we could #use the opportunity to get #out of the #box we are in on announcing the directive, it would be a very good #thing. [McTeer] Well, I am not #worried about any comparison with my speeches. Does anyone #else #want to #comment before I #make this great #recommendation? I #think there is a legitimate #question about the third #paragraph because it is a substantive #issue. [Greenspan]

Table 3.B10
(continued)

Classes for 1999 (thematic classification group in brackets)	Top ranking characteristic words	Top ranking characteristic phrases, or ECUs
Productivity growth in United States [2d]	hour+ earning+ product+ data number+ cost compens+ quarter+ profit+ measure+	7 #percent; it is 4 #percent. Now, 4 #percent is not of great consequence when #productivity is as strong as it is. When we #look at #total #compensation per #hour, the #figures are closer to 5 #percent, but unit #labor #costs are not #accelerating; #indeed, they are #declining, [Greenspan] but even if the ECI is #biased in that #regard, #compensation per #hour is not. #Preliminary #data for #compensation per #hour in the #fourth #quarter, at least for the non-financial corporate sector that I believe #probably mirrors the #total, #indicate an #average #annual growth rate of 3. [Greenspan] I might add that the #difference between the 3½ #percent and the 4.3 #percent in #compensation per #hour is #indeed a unit #labor #cost #increase of three #quarter of a #percent. [Greenspan] the #evidence of this in the underlying #data is #fairly clear-cut. That is, the speed #up of #productivity growth can #explain to a large #extent both the #significant #acceleration in GDP from the supply side, as a #number of you have #indicated, and the suppression of unit #labor #costs and #total unit #costs more generally, [Greenspan] if that is #indeed the case and if operating domestic #profit #margins #rose in the #second #quarter we do not have #official #data on that as yet but the #evidence points to an #increase, [Greenspan]
US economy— demand & output (strength of domestic demand) [2a]	demand+ saving+ domestic financ+ econom+ condition+ wealth+ world+ credit+ imbalance+	as I have noted, this is #not an #economy in need of more #positive #wealth #effects on #demand. This #brings me to a #final observation. There has also been a lot of discussion recently about the #internal and #external #saving #imbalances in the #economy. [Prell] at least the #downside risks in those #economies #appear to have #greatly #diminished. Under these circumstances it #becomes increasingly #important to trim the #strength of #domestic #demand here if we are to avoid putting #additional #pressures on United States #resources. [Kohn] all told, then, there's no reason to #doubt that #domestic #demand has retained #substantial #positive #momentum #into the #fall. #Moreover, as #Karen will be discussing, #improving foreign #economies are giving an increasing lift to our #export sales. [Prell] but the #upside risks of increased #pressure on #capacity from worldwide growth and the #potential for #growing #financial #imbalances now #seem both #greater and more pressing, [Minehan] I would like to talk first about the #international #side and then go back to the #domestic #side. I continue to be concerned about the possible #negative #effects, even #greater than those #reflected in the Greenbook, on our #economy from #events #abroad. [McDonough]

Table 3.B10
(continued)

Classes for 1999 (thematic classification group in brackets)	Top ranking characteristic words	Top ranking characteristic phrases, or ECUs
Financial market developments [4]	panel+ Euro+ dollar+ yen chart+ spread top red yield+ bond+	the first #page, #covering the #period from June 1 through August 20, presents a slightly #different configuration of #charts than I usually #show you. The #top #panel #depicts #United #States #deposit #rates, current and forward; the #middle #panel #shows #yields on #United #States #Treasury #securities; [Fisher] in the #third #page of #charts, the #top #panel presents a view of G3 #exchange-rates from the #dollar's perspective, #depicting the #value since #January of 1997 of one #dollar in #terms of the #euro in #red and the #value of one #dollar in #terms of the #yen divided by one hundred in green. [Fisher] #turning to the second #page, let me go over some #yield and #spread #relationships.In the #top #panel you can #see #yields on #selected 10 year #government #Bonds for the #United #States, the #United Kingdom, Italy, and #Germany and for the 10 year #United #States inflation indexed #security.[Fisher] #turning to the next #page, the fourth #chart #depicts #spreads on #selected longer #term #instruments to #comparable #United #States #Treasuries. I #included this #chart to emphasize the #noticeable #impact on #September 8th when we announced our special year #end #operations and again on #September 14th when we had a meeting with the primary #dealers to discuss the details of our #operation [Fisher] #turning to the second #page, the #top #panel #shows 10 year #yields in the #United #States, the #United-Kingdom, and #Germany. On the #left side the little numbers there are #basis points are the 2 to 10 year #spreads on #July 1 and on the #right side are the 2 to 10 year #spreads as of last #Friday. [Fisher]

Table 3.B10
(continued)

Classes for 1999 (thematic classification group in brackets)	Top ranking characteristic words	Top ranking characteristic phrases, or ECUs
Stance of policy & how to publish it / transparency [9b]	asymmetr+ committee+ direct+ announce+ action+ polic+ tighten+ tilt+ market+ adopt+	#announcing the #committee's #heightened #concern about inflation is #likely to raise rates; omitting such an #announcement is #likely to lower them. If in fact the #committee is now more #concerned about inflation and #hence more #likely to #give #serious #consideration to #tightening at the next few #meetings, it might #consider #adopting and #publishing an #asymmetric #directive. [Kohn] in addition to its #decision about the #stance of #policy #immediately after the #meeting, the #committee also needs to #consider its posture going forward. Such deliberations have always played a role at your #meetings, but their importance has been #heightened by the #committee's #policy of #giving a #public #rationale for its #action and by the option to #announce #changes in the #tilt of the #directive [Kohn] we had #explicitly told the #market that we would disclose the #tilt when the #committee wished to communicate to the #public a major #shift in its #views about the #balance of #risks or the #likely #direction of #future #policy [Poole] A #tilt would be #taken as indicating that the #committee might be #especially sensitive to #information suggesting that price pressures were #likely to #build. With the #markets on notice that #policy #action was #under #consideration, #responses to #incoming data are #likely to be relatively #intense and #markets volatile [Kohn] if this were the #committee's #view, then #publishing a #tilted #directive and encouraging the #market to #build in expectations of #tightening could ultimately be #misleading and could lessen the power of #asymmetry to #convey #information over time. [Kohn]

Table 3.B10
(continued)

Classes for 1999 (thematic classification group in brackets)	Top ranking characteristic words	Top ranking characteristic phrases, or ECUs
Staff forecast for US economy (demand and output, & inflation) [1b & 2b]	forecast Greenbook+ inflation+ growth staff+ baseline trend+ core favor+ project+	the further #upward #revision of the estimate of #trend productivity does #translate, as reflected in the #Greenbook, into a #slightly more #favorable #inflation #forecast #over the next #couple of #years. [Meyer] the #staff's revised #forecast features once again an #upward #revision to #growth and a #downward #revision to #inflation and hence a more #favorable #outcome for 1999 than was #projected in the last #Greenbook. [Meyer] #real interest-rates are #lower than their #natural levels and fall further #over the next two #years as the #nominal interest-rate is #held #constant while #inflation and, by #assumption, #inflation #expectations rise. [Kohn] 5 percent for the #core #inflation-rate #over the #year 2000. So the #staff #forecast says that we have not #lowered the #underlying #inflation-rate at all. We get the #same conclusion if we use the GDP #chain measure of #inflation. [Meyer] will #allow the effects of #prevailing #tightness in the labor-market to show through. We will maintain #growth at near #trend #over the #forecast #horizon with #gradual #upward pressure on #inflation. [Meyer]

Table 3.B10
(continued)

Classes for 1999 (thematic classification group in brackets)	Top ranking characteristic words	Top ranking characteristic phrases, or ECUs
State of economy in districts (output) [2c]	district+ sale+ manufacture+ activit+ retail+ housing construct+ sector+ remain+ region+	the rate in the #services #sector was 5¼ percent. #District #manufacturing #payrolls have #declined #slowly in 1999, although #employment has stabilized in #recent #months. Increased demand for #computers, #consumer #electronics, and telecommunication products, as #well as the resurgence of many economies in Asia, are #boosting #sales and #orders throughout the #high #tech #manufacturing-sector. [Parry] our #district's #housing market showed more #signs of strength in #December as indicated by rising #home #construction, #brisk #home #sales, and sturdy #price appreciation. A benevolently warm, delightful #December might have had something to do with that. #Surveys of #purchasing #managers indicate #continued #weakness in the #region's #manufacturing #sector. [McDonough] until quite #recently, #Boston enjoyed the #lowest class A #office #space #vacancy rate in the #country and very #low rates for class B #space as #well. #Rents for #commercial #space #continue to rise and now #exceed those in both #New #York and San Francisco. While #high rates obviously mean profits for #Boston building #owners, they could also deter #new or #expanding businesses from locating in #Boston. [Minehan] #elsewhere, #consumer #sentiment and #spending #remain very #strong essentially across the #board. We had a good #holiday #selling #season, according to the anecdotal information anyway. There is a-lot-of #speculative building in the #Washington #region, especially around Dulles airport, and in #several other #cities in our #district, notably Charlotte. [Broaddus] growth has been somewhat #slower #elsewhere and #residential #construction #activity has been flat or #down in #several urban #areas. #Slower appreciation in #sales #prices for #existing #homes is #evident in some #areas as #well. On the upside, we are seeing renewed demand for #district #electronic products. [Parry]

Table 3.B10
(continued)

Classes for 1999 (thematic classification group in brackets)	Top ranking characteristic words	Top ranking characteristic phrases, or ECUs
State of economy in districts (inflation) [1c]	contract+ report+ hear employee+ work+ skill+ director+ business firm+ company+	I was particularly #interested in #talking with #contacts and #others about the #labor-market #situation. I #heard from these #people the same #stories we have been #hearing about #problems in #recruiting #entry level #employees and #problems with increased turnover. [Poole] the general sense is that, as far as #health #care costs are concerned, it has been #bad in 1999 and it will be #worse next year. #People #mention #severe #shortages of nurses, aides, and other #health #care #workers. Those in the #health #care industry #talk about the #packages they have to #pay to #attract #people or to retain #workers. [Jordan] we also #hear from #temporary #firms that they are doing some retraining of #workers themselves. The tourism industry has been particularly #hard hit by labor #shortages. #Members of the #bank's #small #business New England #advisory #council #reported that restaurants and other tourist related #businesses in southern Maine were forced to close a couple of days during the week over this past #summer because there [Minehan] the stress in the #health #care industry is becoming #widespread. #Hospitals and #medical #schools are #increasingly squeezed financially. Physicians are more amenable to #unionization or dropping out of government #insurance #programs. Patients are turning to politicians more and more to #seek #relief from the deny and delay tactics of insurers. [Boehne] #anecdotal information on regional price pressures is quite similar to what I have been #reporting, as have #others. #Labor-markets are clearly #tight. #Business #people are #complaining about #finding #workers. [Guynn]

4   Congressional Committees and Monetary Policy

PART ONE—A BIRD'S-EYE VIEW OF THE MONETARY OVERSIGHT HEARINGS, 1976 TO 2008

4.1 Background

I don't suppose that anyone would still argue that the central banking system should be independent of the Government of the country. The control which such a system exercises, over the volume and value of money is a right of Government and is exercised on behalf of Government, with powers delegated by the Government. But there is a distinction between independence from Government and independence from political influence in a narrower sense. The powers of the central banking system should not be a pawn of any group or faction or party, or even any particular administration, subject to political pressures and its own passing fiscal necessities. (Allan Sproul, president of the New York Federal Reserve Bank letter to Robert R. Bowie, September 1, 1948; Meltzer 2003: 738)

To me, public accountability is a moral corollary of central bank independence. In a democratic society, the central bank's freedom to act implies an obligation to explain itself to the public. Thus independence and accountability are symbiotic, not in conflict. . . . While central banks are not in the public relations business, public education ought to be part of their brief. (Alan Blinder, Princeton University professor and former vice chairman, Federal Reserve Board; Blinder 1998: 69)

There are people who think the Fed should be above democracy. . . . We can debate the most fundamental questions in human existence, but God forbid anybody in elected office should talk about whether or not we need a 25 basis-point increase from the Fed. (Representative Barney Frank, incoming Democratic chairman of the House Financial Services Committee, January 2007; Guha and Kirchgaessner 2007)

Independence in respect of monetary policy and the accompanying obligations of transparency and accountability are typically regarded now as the cornerstones of "modern" central banks (Blinder 2004). The first two quotes above illustrate a shift in the priorities expressed by central bankers and academics from the mid- to the late 20th century. For Sproul, conflict between the Treasury and the Fed in the 1950s led him to resent the intrusion of political control by governments over the independence of the Fed (Hetzel and Leach 2001), whereas in the modern era, Blinder stresses that independence obliges central bankers to explain their policy decisions to the public, ex post.[1]

The views of American politicians can be rather different, as they tend to stress the inherent limitation of independence, given the legal and political context in which the central bank operates. In the 1950s, for instance, Representative Wright Patman (TX) challenged former Fed Chairman Marriner Eccles, "Who is master, the Federal Reserve or the Treasury? You know, the Treasury came here first" (Hetzel and Leach 2001: 44). And with respect to the Fed's relationship to Congress, Congressman Frank's quote above reflects a frustration toward a perceived deference to the Federal Reserve by the outgoing Republican Congress, a deference that he believed was undermining the obligation of the Fed to account for its use of the powers delegated to it by government.

Whereas in 1951, Rep. Patman perceived the Fed as clearly subservient to the Treasury, by 2007, Rep. Frank expressed frustration that perhaps the Fed had become *too* independent and autonomous. During that half-century much had changed in American monetary policy. How did these changes shape the perceptions and motivations of members of Congress vis-à-vis the Fed? The period of the 1970s to the end of the twentieth century was one in which monetary policy came to the forefront as the tool of macroeconomic stabilization. Hence, as low inflation became the norm, and as monetary policy became the primary tool to achieve and sustain macroeconomic stability, it is reasonable to think that the role of congressional oversight likewise changed to fit the times.

The focus of this chapter is on the relationship of the Federal Reserve vis-à-vis Congress, starting in the mid-1970s—the period of sustained high inflation—and ending in early 2008, thereby capturing the early days of the financial crisis.[2] The chapter contains four distinct parts, each defined by its own methodological contribution to our study: (1) a bird's-eye view of the discourse in the House and Senate banking committees as they conducted oversight hearings on monetary policy from 1976 to 2008, (2) a closer look at this same discourse but in eight periods (or cross sections), (3) an exploration of the effect of constituency characteristics on the thematic discourse of banking committee members, and (4) an investigation of both the words *and* votes of senators as they voted to reconfirm the Federal Reserve chairman.

The first two parts of this chapter use automated textual analysis software to explore the transcripts of the banking committees as they conducted oversight hearings, as described in our first chapter. The difference between the two parts is the level of analysis, with the first part focusing on the whole of the three decades in order to capture broader themes at a "meta" level, while the second part divides the transcripts into several different time periods in order to explore the discourse at a finer level of detail. In part one, we examine 61 hearings over a 33-year period in two composite corpora, one for the House and one for the Senate. In part two, we divide these 61 hearings into sixteen distinct corpora—eight each for the House and Senate. (Our book appendix II provides further details on the hearings selected, including background information on the partisan context and whether in the House, the hearing was conducted at the committee or subcommittee level. Our book appendix III lists the titles and sources for the hearings.) Together, parts one and two provide extensive empirical evidence on (1) the themes that do (and do not) interest legislators when they question the Fed chairman, (2) how these themes have evolved over three decades, and (3) differences in foci between both the Fed chairman and legislators, and between Democrats and Republicans.

Part three then extracts information from the textual analysis of the congressional transcripts in order to address directly the possibility that variations in the tendencies for committee members to focus on particular topics or themes may be partly the product of characteristics of their constituencies. In this part of the chapter we merge key statistics from our textual analysis with quantitative data in order to conduct exploratory analysis. Finally, in part four of this chapter, we use our textual analysis software to explore not only the words but also the decisions—in terms of votes—of senators in the Senate Banking Committee as they considered the merits of the sitting Federal Reserve chairman, with respect to his reappointment. For this we analyze the reconfirmation hearings for Volcker (1983), Greenspan (1992, 1996, 2000, 2004), and Bernanke (2009).

Throughout the chapter, we consider our findings in light of four of the hypotheses from chapter 2. Specifically, we expect to find evidence of reason-giving by legislators, and in part as the result of this deliberation, we expect to find that at least some of these committee members were persuaded by what they heard in the hearings (hypothesis 1). Finding evidence of persuasion is no easy task, as others have noted (Mutz, Sniderman, et al. 1996; Cobb and Kuklinski 1997; Finlayson 2007). Linking such persuasion to what committee members heard in committee is even harder. We do not pretend that our textual analysis offers the perfect means to capture such persuasion. We do, however, think that our analysis offers a way to explore the effect of one particularly important idea on which legislators may have been subject to persuasion by the Federal Reserve chairman—the idea that sustained low inflation is the best means to deliver stable economic growth (hypothesis 7). We expect that this objective for monetary policy became clearer to members of Congress over the period of our study—in part, the result of arguments from Fed officials, but also solidified by the success of the Fed's monetary policy itself. So our textual analysis should show a clearer definition of this idea of the low inflation consensus as spoken by members within the House and Senate Banking Committees. We do not, however, pin all on our textual analysis. If there is any evidence of the persuasiveness of this idea among members of Congress, we should also find it in our interviews. So, we return to this in chapter 5, where we interview congressional staff and members of the banking committees. More broadly, to the extent that we find a growing acceptance of the low inflation consensus among committee members in Congress, we expect to find a behavioral change in the ways and means by which they conducted oversight on monetary policy.

With respect to gauging deliberation on monetary policy by congressmen versus that of senators (hypothesis 5), and the balance of point-scoring discourse against that of monetary policy specifics (hypothesis 6), we examine evidence for each of these from the different methodological approaches adopted in all four parts of this chapter.

4.2 Textual Analysis of Congressional Oversight Hearings on Monetary Policy: A Bird's-Eye View from 1976 to 2008

We follow the same general approach for analyzing the congressional transcripts as we adopted for analyzing the FOMC transcripts in the previous chapter. Here we begin with two meta-text files, consisting of the entirety of the oversight hearings (1976 to 2008) for the House Financial Services Committee in one and the Senate Banking Committee in another.

4.2.1   The Themes

Table 4.1 provides summaries of the basic statistics from Alceste for the two sets of hearing transcripts. For each set of hearings, the total word count is about three-quarters of a million words, while the number of unique words that were analyzed by the program is about 300,000. The passive variables (tagged indicators) for the congressional transcripts include the date of the hearing, the speaker's name, the role of the speaker (committee chair or member; Fed chairman), and the party affiliation (for the legislators, but not the Fed chair).

The summary of the number of initial context units (ICU) per hearing is given in row four of table 4.1. Overall, it is not surprising to find that

Table 4.1
Basic statistics for aggregate House and Senate hearings on monetary policy, 1976 to 2008

	House hearings, 1976–2008	Senate hearings, 1976–2008
Total word count	758,092	700,368
Unique words analyzed	312,071	297,108
Passive variables (tagged indicators)	237	129
ICUs (= number of speeches/comments)	6,237	5,744
Classified ECUs	7,506 (= 92% of the retained ECU)	6,984 (= 91% of the retained ECU)
Lexical classes	9	9
Distribution of classes (%) and thematic content	1 (14) *Populist attack on Fed/ Greenspan (B. Sanders)* 2 (13) *Volcker defending anti-anflation stance (give & take; speculative)* 3 (13) *Fiscal policy* 4 (12) *Fed's regulatory activity* 5 (12) *Q&A format (process); mixed substance* 6 (11) *Monetary aggregates* 7 (10) *US real economy* 8 (9) *MCs prompting Fed chair on nonmonetary issues* 9 (6) *Capital inflows, exchange rate, current account deficit*	1 (14) *World economy & US external balance (trade & current account)* 2 (13) *Bank regulation & banking industry structure* 3 (12) *Q&A format (Volcker trying to define limits of Fed's knowledge / role)* 4 (12) *Fed appointments & relationship between Fed, Congress, & administration* 5 (9) *Education, training, & US competitiveness (labor market)* 6 (9) *Fiscal policy* 7 (9) *Monetary aggregates & objectives of monetary policy* 8 (9) *US real economy* 9 (14) *Criticism of Fed for failing to support growth (D. Riegle)*

more speeches appear in the House hearings (i.e., even though the length of each speech is more time-constrained, there are after all, about three times the number of members in the House Financial Services Committee than in the Senate Banking Committee).

We can see that for both the House and Senate hearings, over 90 percent of the ECUs are successfully classified, which is a remarkably high classification rate. The inverse of this is that just 10 percent of each set of hearings data is residue, or unexplained.

The bottom two blocks indicate the number of classes identified in each text file and the size of each class (as measured by the percentage of the total ECUs classified within each). Tables 4.A1 and 4.A2 in the appendix to this chapter provide the characteristic words and phrases for each class, and for the phrases, we identify each by the name of the speaker.

4.2.2 Schematic Overview of the Themes in the House and Senate Hearings

Figures 4.1 and 4.2 present tree diagrams of the clustering of the classes, where the nearer the proximity of the tree "limbs," the more overlapping is the vocabulary or terms (e.g., in figure 4.1 the greatest overlap in vocabulary is between classes 2 and 5).

A good starting point for our analysis is to understand the basic fault line that separates the themes in both the House and Senate hearings. Figure 4.1 illustrates a cleavage in the discourse between members of Congress and the chairman of the Federal Reserve. In figures 4.1 and 4.2 the classes in bold font are those for which the tags of members of Congress (name, party affiliation, role) are predominantly significant, whereas the italicized classes are those for which the chairman of the Fed is predominantly significant. The one class for which statistical significance is shared between Congress and the Fed (the Fed's regulatory activity, class 4, in figure 4.1) is indicated in regular font.

Over the period of the mid-1970s to 2008, representatives in the House hearings (figure 4.1) devoted their attention to (a) *criticizing the Fed* as out of touch with "real America" (a populist critique stemming mostly from Representative Bernie Sanders), (b) highlighting aspects of *fiscal policy*, and (c) predominantly from 2006 onward, the Fed's *regulatory activities*. Within this congressional discourse we also find a distinct presence for rhetoric that reflects the more formal process of hearings (e.g., "Let me ask a question . . .")—a class that we label *Q and A format*. For the House hearings there is little substantive content in

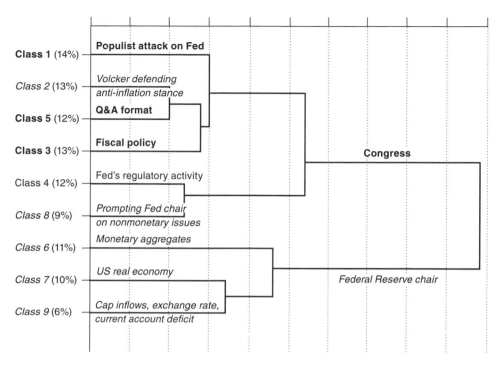

Figure 4.1
Tree diagram of relative associations between classes for House hearings, 1976 to 2008

this class, except to say that it is closely linked to another class (class 2), in which Chairman Paul Volcker and committee members interacted quite closely in conflict regarding the Fed's new monetary policy target and its determination credibly to commit to price stability.

It is conspicuous that members of Congress are largely silent on themes relating to the "guts" of monetary policy—namely discussion of *money growth*, the *real economy* and external issues such as *capital flows, the exchange rate, and the current account deficit*. On these issues, it is the Fed chair who dominates the discussion.

Bridging the divide between areas of concern to members of Congress and those of concern to the Fed chair are class 4, the *Fed's regulatory activity*, and class 8. The latter class is unusual in that committee members are seen to draw the chair (most notably Greenspan) into commenting on what might be described as "nonmonetary policy" issues such as Government Sponsored Enterprises (Fannie Mae and Freddie Mac), education policy, and Social Security. A plausible interpretation of this behavior is that members of Congress are seeking to

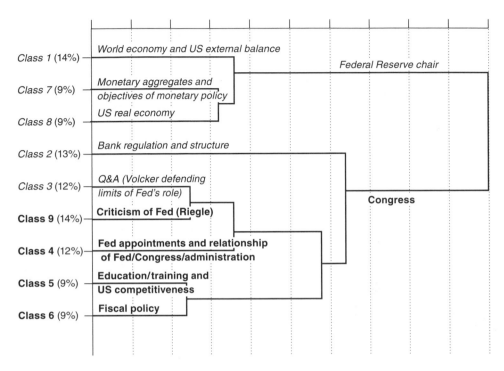

Figure 4.2
Tree diagram of relative associations between classes for Senate hearings, 1976 to 2008

draw the Fed chairman into lending his authority to support their position in a policy debate largely unrelated to monetary policy. We are not surprised that this behavior becomes more pronounced as the Fed's own reputation and credibility grows in terms of the successful pursuit of monetary policy. As such, members of Congress exploit a spin-off from successful monetary policy.

In the Senate hearings (figure 4.2), we observe the same cleavage in areas of focus between the Fed chair and senators, with core monetary policy areas of the world economy, monetary aggregates and the real economy the exclusive domain of the Fed chairman. Senators, like representatives, offer *critiques of the Fed's operations and priorities* (in the Senate, led by Donald Riegle) and devote some attention to *fiscal policy* issues. In contrast to the House, however, senators are seen to be more concerned with the *quality of American workers in the context of US international competitiveness*. Moreover, given the Senate's role in confirming appointments to the Board of Governors, it is perhaps not surprising to find more discussion concerning these appointments, and more broadly, the *institutional relationship between the Federal Reserve, Congress, and the administration.*

There is some overlap in—or shared statistical significance between—committee members and the Fed chair in discussions concerning *banking regulation* (class 2), but the bulk of the chi-squared significance is given to Bernanke during the financial crisis, so we present this in italics.

At this meta level the tree diagrams provide no information on changes in discourse over time, so we cannot yet comment on whether legislators became increasingly persuaded by the low inflation consensus. We can, however, observe a difference in focus by congressmen versus senators, with the latter more likely to discuss institutional issues—such as appointments to the Fed and intergovernmental relations between Congress, the administration, and the Fed—as well as issues relating to foreign economic policy—such as US competitiveness in the world economy.

Overall, the tree diagrams provide a reasonably simple initial portrayal of the relationships between the themes. Figures 4.3 and 4.4 extend this by placing the themes (or classes) and the tags on a single correspondence graph—where distance between a class and a tag (or between two classes) reflects the degree of co-occurrence.

Beneath the correspondence map for the House hearings (figure 4.3) are the percentage associations for each factor, with the first accounting for about 30 percent and the second accounting for an additional 21 percent. Hence a two-dimensional correspondence space accounts for about half of the total variation in the corpus. In total, seven factors are identified in the correspondence analysis.[3] For the Senate hearings (figure 4.4) the percentages are quite similar, and again the number of factorial dimensions is seven.[4] Dimensionality in this context, however, requires careful dissection.

From figure 4.3 we can observe first that the horizontal axis captures the same cleavage we saw in the tree diagram between the themes discussed by the Fed chairmen and those of interest to committee members—that is, Greenspan, Burns, Miller, Bernanke, and Volcker appear in the left hand quadrants, while the party tags and committee chair tag appear in the right hand quadrants. This same basic cleavage also appears in the Senate hearings (figure 4.4), but with the Fed classes and tags on the right side and those associated with senators on the left side (here it is the relative positions that matter, not the absolute). Hence it is quite apparent that the Fed chairmen and members of

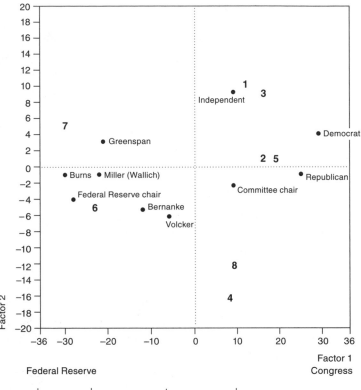

	Association	Cumulative
Factor 1	29.8%	29.8%
Factor 2	20.5%	50.3%

1 Populist attack on Fed/Greenspan
2 Volcker defending anti-inflation stance
3 Fiscal policy
4 Fed's regulatory activity
5 Q&A format
6 Monetary aggregates
7 US real economy
8 Representatives prompting Fed chair on nonmonetary issues

Figure 4.3
Correspondence analysis of House hearings—Composite (1976 to 2008)

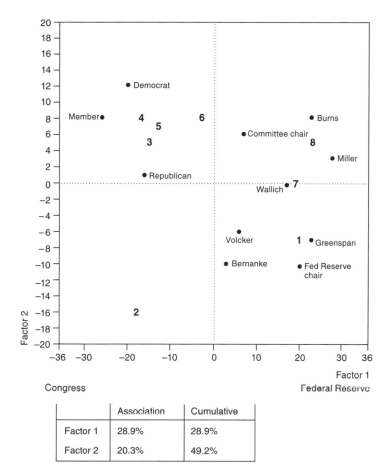

	Association	Cumulative
Factor 1	28.9%	28.9%
Factor 2	20.3%	49.2%

1 World economy and US external balance (trade and current account)
2 Bank regulation
3 Q&A format
4 Fed appointments and relationship between Fed, Congress, and administration
5 Education, training, and US competitiveness
6 Fiscal policy
7 Monetary aggregates
8 US real economy

Figure 4.4
Correspondence analysis of Senate hearings—Composite (1976 to 2008)

Congress tend to focus on different issues and themes in the oversight hearings. Moreover, because these differences in foci are so stark, we are able to take our interpretation of the dimensionality of the correspondence graphs a step further than we were able to do with the correspondence graphs for the FOMC.

First, for each graph, seven factors are required to account for the total variation, with six factors accounting for 95 percent of the variation for the House and 93 percent for the Senate. Inasmuch as the dimensionality of the system is usually determined to be one less than the number of classes in the profile (Greenacre 1993: 14), this means that for both graphs, further classes beyond eight are not plotted (i.e., the ninth class does not appear in either graph). In a more substantive vein, the high dimensionality of both sets of hearings is indicative of discourse that is thematically diverse—or in other words, the vocabulary is not particularly cohesive. A second, but related feature is that while the two-dimensional correspondence graphs are useful, their value is limited by the very fact that in these two cases they are, after all, attempting to capture a large number of dimensions in just a two-dimensional space. The program does allow us to investigate one further dimension with three-dimensional graphics. In these graphs (not presented here) we find, for example, that the third dimension for the House effectively distinguishes the unique vocabulary of anti–Fed populism (class 1) from that of fiscal policy (class 3), while for the Senate, the third dimension appears to untangle an association between classes 4 and 5—namely the institutional relationships between Congress, the Fed, and the administration on one side, and the issue of educating and training American workers to compete more effectively globally on the other. Given the difficulties in unpacking and interpreting the large number of dimensions, we will confine our discussion to just the first dimension, where, together with the tree diagrams, the picture is clearer.

A third feature of the two graphs is that two thematic classes—*US real economy* and *Monetary aggregates*—are consistently the remit of the Federal Reserve chairman; that is, members of Congress appear to steer well clear of discussion on these issues. Fourth, the tag for the committee chair appears with the Congress discourse for the House, but is more associated with the Fed discourse for the Senate—a feature that may suggest that in the Senate, the committee chair tended to delve more into the "guts" of monetary policy discussions than in the House (we return to clarify this point below). Finally, for both the House and

Senate, the issue of bank regulation is something of a discourse "outlier" in that it is positioned at a distance from the remaining classes. This is not surprising since bank regulation is not the stated focus of the Humphrey–Hawkins hearings.

An interim conclusion is therefore that taken at face value members of Congress and Fed chairmen talk across each other in oversight hearings. The content of their remarks is quite distinct. But further analysis suggests that the picture is not so simple. At the least members of Congress are seeking to "recruit" a successful Fed chair to support their view on a range of associated policy issues. Thus, while monetary policy is the stated focus of the hearings, there is a lot more going on in the actual discourse.

4.2.3   Significance of Themes over Time, by Political Party, and by Fed Chairman

As with our analysis of the FOMC transcripts in chapter 3, labeling the themes within the hearings is only the first step in our analysis. Figures 4.5 through 4.7 provide graphical presentations for how these themes varied (1) from 1976 to 2008, (2) by political party affiliation and role (committee chair or member), and (3) by Fed chairman.

Also as with the FOMC transcripts, we extract from each thematic class the statistically significant tagged indicators. The legend to the right of each graph depicts two groupings of significance—the first (smaller) from 2 to 50, and the second (larger) from 51 to 300. To distinguish the two groups, we size the boxes into small and large, and within each group, the darker the shading, the higher the χ^2 value. In short, the smaller and less shaded boxes indicate lower levels of significance, while the larger, more darkly shaded ones indicate higher significance.

In figures 4.5, 4.6, and 4.7, the top panel lists the thematic classes identified in the House banking hearings from 1976 to 2008, while the bottom panel lists the same for the Senate. Figure 4.5 maps out the varying levels of significance for each theme over time. The advantage of this graph is that we can observe for any year or collection of years, the themes that obtain some level of prominence *relative* to others that do not receive particular prominence. Hence the graph allows us insight as to the dynamics of discourse in monetary policy hearings over time. (Notably, for some years the *no* date tag acquires *any* significance, which suggests that for that particular hearing, none of the themes is unusually distinctive. In these cases other tags—e.g., the Fed

Chi-squared significance

- 251–300
- 201–250
- 151–200
- 101–150
- 51–100
- 41–50
- 31–40
- 21–30
- 11–20
- 2–10

a. House—all years

		1976 (Feb)	1976 (Jul)	1977 (Feb)	1977 (Jul)	1979 (Feb)	1979 (Jul)	1979 (Nov)	1980 (Feb)
Class 1	Populist attack on Fed/Greenspan (mostly by Bernie Sanders)								
Class 2	Volcker defending anti-inflation stance						☐	▨	■
Class 3	Fiscal policy			☐					
Class 4	Fed's regulatory activity		☐						
Class 5	Q&A format (process)	☐	☐	▨	☐	☐	☐	▨	☐
Class 6	Monetary aggregates	▨	☐				☐		
Class 7	US real economy		☐		☐		☐		
Class 8	Representatives prompting Fed chair on nonmonetary issues		☐					☐	
Class 9	Capital inflows, exchange rate, current account deficit					☐			

b. Senate—all years

		1976 (Nov)	1976 (May)	1977 (Nov)	1977 (May)	1979 (Feb)	1979 (Jul)	1979 (Nov)	1980 (Feb)
Class 1	World economy and US external balance (trade and current account)								
Class 2	Bank regulation and banking industry structure								
Class 3	Q&A format (Volcker trying to define limits of Fed's knowledge/role)								☐
Class 4	Fed appointments and relationship between Fed, Congress, and administration	▨	▨	▨	▨		▨		
Class 5	Education, training, and US competitiveness (labor market)								
Class 6	Fiscal policy								
Class 7	Monetary aggregates and objectives of monetary policy		▨	☐	☐	☐	▨		
Class 8	US real economy	▨	▨	▨	▨	▨			
Class 9	Criticism of Fed—for failing to support growth (by Don Riegle)	☐			☐				

Figure 4.5
Distribution of statistical significance for each thematic class, by congressional hearing. (a) House—all years; (b) Senate—all years.

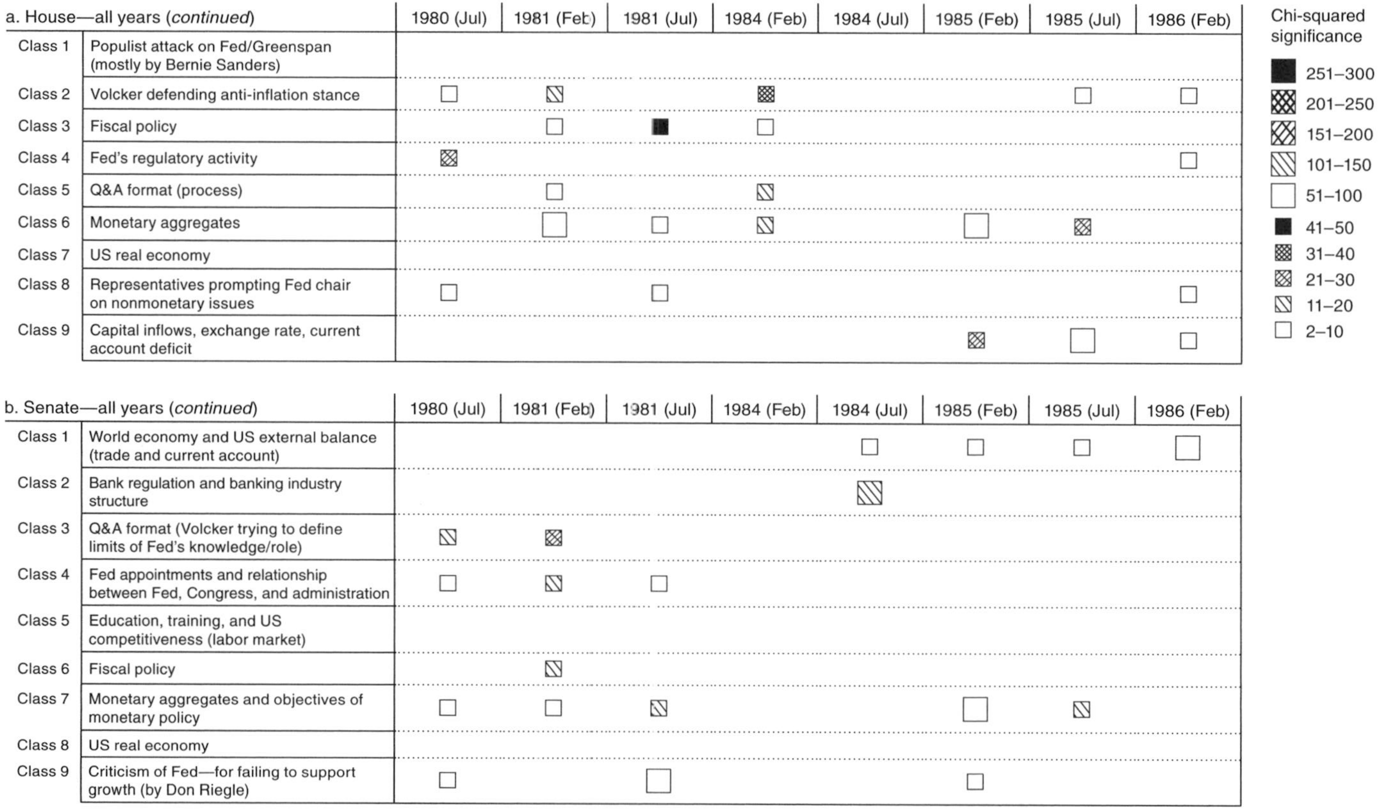

Chi-squared significance:
- 251–300
- 201–250
- 151–200
- 101–150
- 51–100
- 41–50
- 31–40
- 21–30
- 11–20
- 2–10

a. House—all years (*continued*)

Columns: 1980 (Jul) | 1981 (Feb) | 1981 (Jul) | 1984 (Feb) | 1984 (Jul) | 1985 (Feb) | 1985 (Jul) | 1986 (Feb)

- Class 1 — Populist attack on Fed/Greenspan (mostly by Bernie Sanders)
- Class 2 — Volcker defending anti-inflation stance
- Class 3 — Fiscal policy
- Class 4 — Fed's regulatory activity
- Class 5 — Q&A format (process)
- Class 6 — Monetary aggregates
- Class 7 — US real economy
- Class 8 — Representatives prompting Fed chair on nonmonetary issues
- Class 9 — Capital inflows, exchange rate, current account deficit

b. Senate—all years (*continued*)

Columns: 1980 (Jul) | 1981 (Feb) | 1981 (Jul) | 1984 (Feb) | 1984 (Jul) | 1985 (Feb) | 1985 (Jul) | 1986 (Feb)

- Class 1 — World economy and US external balance (trade and current account)
- Class 2 — Bank regulation and banking industry structure
- Class 3 — Q&A format (Volcker trying to define limits of Fed's knowledge/role)
- Class 4 — Fed appointments and relationship between Fed, Congress, and administration
- Class 5 — Education, training, and US competitiveness (labor market)
- Class 6 — Fiscal policy
- Class 7 — Monetary aggregates and objectives of monetary policy
- Class 8 — US real economy
- Class 9 — Criticism of Fed—for failing to support growth (by Don Riegle)

Figure 4.5
(continued)

Chi-squared significance

■ (solid black)	251–300
▩	201–250
▨	151–200
▤	101–150
☐	51–100
■ (solid black)	41–50
▩	31–40
▨	21–30
▨	11–20
☐	2–10

a. House—all years (continued)

	1986 (Jul)	1991 (Feb)	1991 (Jul)	1992 (Feb)	1992 (Jul)	1993 (Feb)	1993 (Jul)	1997 (Feb)
Class 1	Populist attack on Fed/Greenspan (mostly by Bernie Sanders)							
Class 2	Volcker defending anti-inflation stance					■		
Class 3	Fiscal policy				☐			
Class 4	Fed's regulatory activity							
Class 5	Q&A format (process)			☐		☐		
Class 6	Monetary aggregates							
Class 7	US real economy			☐		☐	☐	
Class 8	Representatives prompting Fed chair on nonmonetary issues			☐	▨		☐	
Class 9	Capital inflows, exchange rate, current account deficit							

b. Senate—all years (continued)

	1986 (Jul)	1991 (Feb)	1991 (Jul)	1992 (Feb)	1992 (Jul)	1993 (Feb)	1993 (Jul)	1997 (Feb)
Class 1	World economy and US external balance (trade and current account)	☐						
Class 2	Bank regulation and banking industry structure	▨						
Class 3	Q&A format (Volcker trying to define limits of Fed's knowledge/role)	☐						
Class 4	Fed appointments and relationship between Fed, Congress, and administration				☐	☐		
Class 5	Education, training, and US competitiveness (labor market)			▨				
Class 6	Fiscal policy					☐		
Class 7	Monetary aggregates and objectives of monetary policy				☐			
Class 8	US real economy				☐			
Class 9	Criticism of Fed—for failing to support growth (by Don Riegle)			▩		▨		

Figure 4.5
(continued)

Chi-squared significance

■	251–300
▨	201–250
⊠	151–200
▨	101–150
☐	51–100
■	41–50
▨	31–40
▨	21–30
▨	11–20
☐	2–10

a. House—all years (*continued*)

		1997 (Jul)	1998 (Feb)	1998 (Jul)	1999 (Feb)	1999 (Jul)	2003 (Feb)	2003 (Jul)	2004 (Feb)
Class 1	Populist attack on Fed/Greenspan (mostly by Bernie Sanders)	▨						☐	☐
Class 2	Volcker defending anti-inflation stance								
Class 3	Fiscal policy							▨	
Class 4	Fed's regulatory activity								
Class 5	Q&A format (process)								
Class 6	Monetary aggregates								
Class 7	US real economy	☐	▨	▨				▨	
Class 8	Representatives prompting Fed chair on nonmonetary issues				☐			☐	
Class 9	Capital inflows, exchange rate, current account deficit		▨	▨	☐				

b. Senate—all years (*continued*)

		1997 (Jul)	1998 (Feb)	1998 (Jul)	1999 (Feb)	1999 (Jul)	2003 (Feb)	2003 (Jul)	2004 (Feb)
Class 1	World economy and US external balance (trade and current account)	☐		⊠				☐	
Class 2	Bank regulation and banking industry structure				☐				
Class 3	Q&A format (Volcker trying to define limits of Fed's knowledge/role)								
Class 4	Fed appointments and relationship between Fed, Congress, and administration								
Class 5	Education, training, and US competitiveness (labor market)		☐	▨	☐			☐	▨
Class 6	Fiscal policy			☐				☐	⊠
Class 7	Monetary aggregates and objectives of monetary policy			▨					
Class 8	US real economy	☐	☐						
Class 9	Criticism of Fed—for failing to support growth (by Don Riegle)								

Figure 4.5
(continued)

Chi-squared significance

▨	251–300
▨	201–250
▨	151–200
▨	101–150
□	51–100
■	41–50
▨	31–40
▨	21–30
▨	11–20
□	2–10

a. House—all years (*continued*)

		2004 (Jul)	2005 (Feb)	2005 (Jul)	2006 (Feb)	2006 (Jul)	2007 (Feb)	2007 (Jul)	2008 (Feb)
Class 1	Populist attack on Fed/Greenspan (mostly by Bernie Sanders)	▨				■	□	▨	
Class 2	Volcker defending anti-inflation stance		□						
Class 3	Fiscal policy								
Class 4	Fed's regulatory activity		□			□	■	▨	▨
Class 5	Q&A format (process)		□						
Class 6	Monetary aggregates								
Class 7	US real economy	□				▨		□	
Class 8	Representatives prompting Fed chair on nonmonetary issues		□						
Class 9	Capital inflows, exchange rate, current account deficit								

b. Senate—all years (*continued*)

		2004 (Jul)	2005 (Feb)	2005 (Jul)	2006 (Feb)	2006 (Jul)	2007 (Feb)	2007 (Jul)	2008 (Feb)
Class 1	World economy and US external balance (trade and current account)	□						▨	▨
Class 2	Bank regulation and banking industry structure								
Class 3	Q&A format (Volcker trying to define limits of Fed's knowledge/role)								
Class 4	Fed appointments and relationship between Fed, Congress, and administration								
Class 5	Education, training, and US competitiveness (labor market)	▨	□			▨	▨	▨	
Class 6	Fiscal policy		■						
Class 7	Monetary aggregates and objectives of monetary policy								
Class 8	US real economy	▨				■	□		▨
Class 9	Criticism of Fed—for failing to support growth (by Don Riegle)								

Figure 4.5
(continued)

Chi-squared significance

- 251–300
- 201–250
- 151–200
- 101–150
- 51–100
- 41–50
- 31–40
- 21–30
- 11–20
- 2–10

a. House—all years

	Democrat	Republican	Independent	Committee chair	Committee member
Class 1	Populist attack on Fed/Greenspan (mostly by Bernie Sanders)				
Class 2	Volcker defending anti-inflation stance				
Class 3	Fiscal policy				
Class 4	Fed's regulatory activity				
Class 5	Q&A format (process)				
Class 6	Monetary aggregates				
Class 7	US real economy				
Class 8	Representatives prompting Fed chair on nonmonetary issues				
Class 9	Capital inflows, exchange rate, current account deficit				

b. Senate—all years

	Democrat	Republican	Independent	Committee chair	Committee member
Class 1	World economy and US external balance (trade and current account)				
Class 2	Bank regulation and banking industry structure				
Class 3	Q&A format (Volcker trying to define limits of Fed's knowledge/role)				
Class 4	Fed appointments and relationship between Fed, Congress, and administration				
Class 5	Education, training, and US competitiveness (labor market)				
Class 6	Fiscal policy				
Class 7	Monetary aggregates and objectives of monetary policy				
Class 8	US real economy				
Class 9	Criticism of Fed—for failing to support growth (by Don Riegle)				

Figure 4.6
Distribution of statistical significance for each thematic class, by party and role of committee members. (a) House—all years; (b) Senate—all years.

a. House—all years

Chi-squared significance	
■	251–300
▨	201–250
▧	151–200
▨	101–150
☐	51–100
■	41–50
▨	31–40
▨	21–30
▨	11–20
☐	2–10

	Burns	Miller (Wallich)	Volcker	Greenspan	Bernanke
Class 1	Populist attack on Fed/Greenspan (mostly by Bernie Sanders)				
Class 2	Volcker defending anti-inflation stance		▨		
Class 3	Fiscal policy				
Class 4	Fed's regulatory activity				▨
Class 5	Q&A format (process)				
Class 6	Monetary aggregates	▨		▨	
Class 7	US real economy	▨			■	☐
Class 8	Representatives prompting Fed chair on nonmonetary issues			▨	▨	
Class 9	Capital inflows, exchange rate, current account deficit			▨	☐	☐

b. Senate—all years

	Burns	Miller (Wallich)	Volcker	Greenspan	Bernanke
Class 1	World economy and US external balance (trade and current account)			▨	▨	
Class 2	Bank regulation and banking industry structure					☐
Class 3	Q&A format (Volcker trying to define limits of Fed's knowledge/role)			▨	▨	
Class 4	Fed appointments and relationship between Fed, Congress, and administration					
Class 5	Education, training, and US competitiveness (labor market)	☐				☐
Class 6	Fiscal policy			☐		
Class 7	Monetary aggregates and objectives of monetary policy	▨	▨			
Class 8	US real economy		☐		☐	☐
Class 9	Criticism of Fed—for failing to support growth (by Don Riegle)					

Figure 4.7
Distribution of statistical significance for each thematic class, by Fed chairman. (a) House—all years; (b) Senate—all years.

chairman or party affiliation—are the prominent ones.) The disadvantage of figure 4.5 is that it is more difficult to convey the varying levels of significance for *all* the classes, across *all* the years, since this creates numerous columns that span many pages. To address this difficulty, we present an alternative set of bar charts in our appendix to this chapter (figures 4.A1 to 4.A18), with each theme in a separate graph, thereby allowing the observer to view the whole period at a glance.

Significance over Time
Taking figure 4.5 and figures 4.A1 to 4.A18 together, we can highlight six findings. Below we present most of these fairly briefly, but in part two of this chapter, we again examine thematic changes in the discourse over time, but from the perspective of cross-sectional analysis.

First, discussion of monetary aggregates (classes 6 [House] and 7 [Senate]) is prominent from the mid-1970s until about 1984, but disappears thereafter. This provides a clear empirical basis for the more casual observation that by the mid-1980s, the focus on money growth had dissipated in the minds of monetary policy makers. The reasons for this are not hard to find. The Volcker approach of targeting a quantity measure was shock therapy without precision and without transparency. As the immediate need for this approach diminished, so the approach of focusing on the price of money (the target interest rate) re-appeared.

Second, in the wake of the Fed's shift to a determined anti-inflation stance in 1979, it is clear that Paul Volcker devoted considerable attention to explaining and defending this stance to members of Congress until nearly the end of his term in 1987 (class 2 [House] and part of class 3 [Senate]).

Third, to the extent that members of Congress directly challenged the decisions and institutional independence of the Fed, this is seen mostly during the period of the Great Inflation and is more evident in the Senate than the House, where its ability to approve appointments to the Board of Governors perhaps lent it greater authority (class 4 [Senate]). As the relationship between Congress and the Fed is core to our research, it is useful to examine more closely the actual words of senators on this topic during the 1970s as compared to later decades. In our appendix to this chapter, table 4.A2 lists the top ECUs for all the classes, including that of the *relationship between the Fed, Congress, and the administration*. Senator Proxmire, chairing the committee in 1977, paints the relationship between Congress, the Carter administration and the Fed as confrontational and hierarchical—with the Fed chairman (Burns) and the president as "the two most powerful men in our country" who then see their task as lecturing to members of Congress to "hold down federal spending." The top ECU from this class (as given in table 4.A2) is the launch of Proxmire's questions to Burns in May 1977, and the subsequent exchange between them helps to illustrate (a) the overt challenges from senators on the very fundamentals of monetary policy, and (b) something of the "anguish" felt by Burns (to which we referred in our earlier chapters) with respect to the Fed's ability to control inflation:

Proxmire: . . . Well, I have an article here from the reasonably reliable paper, the *Wall Street Journal*, which says the specifically revised forecast calls for a 4.9 percent increase in 1977 in real GNP, total output of goods and services and so forth, provides for 4.5 percent estimate in February, but you say 6 percent. Now inflation for 1977. What's your estimate of that?

Burns: I'm not good at estimating inflation, I'm sorry to say. All I can tell you is that it's going to be too high.

Proxmire: Well, I'm serious about pursuing that, Dr. Burns, because it's very hard for us to determine the wisdom or unwisdom of monetary policy unless we know what your fundamental assumptions are and certainly one is your expectation of what's going to happen to prices in the coming year. Isn't that correct? Shouldn't we have that information?

Burns: I wish I could give you a figure that I had great confidence in. My best guess is that the rate of inflation this year will be close to 6 percent.

Proxmire: And how about unemployment by the end of the year?

Burns: You're going to have me guessing all over the lot. What you will do with my guesses, I don't know, but I will give them to you provided you don't take them too seriously.

Proxmire: Anything you say I take very seriously, Dr. Burns.

In contrast, the complaint of Senator Bunning in 2006 to Ben Bernanke (from which the second ranking ECU from this class derives) does not offer any challenge on the *substance* of policy, but rather on the *process* of decision making in the FOMC. Bunning focuses on the perceived lack of transparency in FOMC minutes of the internal debate of the committee members. Taking the dialogue before and after the ECU (in bold) captured by the analysis helps to illustrate this further:

Bunning: . . . The Federal Reserve minutes say that there is a discussion of a range of options. But it turns out that the vote is almost always unanimous. . . . I cannot remember when the last dissenting vote in the FOMC occurred. Leading up to the June meeting, public statements by some of the Federal Reserve members indicated there might be a pause. But once again the vote was unanimous to raise rates. How much serious debate is there really if the Federal Reserve keeps coming up with unanimous decisions?

Bernanke: Senator, different committees have different approaches to decision-making. The Monetary Policy Committee in the United Kingdom, for example, like the Senate, is where everybody votes directly. And on a recent occasion, the Governor of the Bank of England was voted down in his recommendation.

Bunning: Gee, that would be a very pleasant surprise at times.

Bernanke: In the Federal Reserve, we are more of a consensus-based organization. We do try to come to an agreement among ourselves, the same way other organizations like the ECB do. But I assure you that we have lengthy and spirited discussions within the meetings, and outside the meetings with staff. And each person is contributing a perspective and a point of view to the policy.

Bunning: **Mr. Bernanke, they never show up in the minutes of the FOMC meetings. All this discussion, all this debate, never shows up in the minutes when we get them.**

Bernanke: Perhaps the minutes could be more detailed.

Bunning: Transparent?

Bernanke: Possibly. Another possibility, sir, is to look at some of the transcripts, which are of course only available with five-year lags. But they give a full verbatim description of the meeting. You will see there, if you look, quite a bit of debate and discussion. That is the tradition we continue today.

Bunning: It took me years of practice, but before Mr. Greenspan left, I was actually able to understand what he was talking about. There is still a problem with understanding what the Federal Reserve is thinking though totally. You have thought about bringing back the balance of risk statements or doing something else so people can understand what is going through all of your heads. Is that a fact? Is that going to happen?

Bernanke: In the short run, Senator, we are trying to maintain some continuity with previous practice so as not to confuse people who are paying attention to the Federal Reserve too much. But what we are doing, as was revealed in the minutes, we have set up a small committee which is going to help the entire FOMC think through our entire range of communications, all aspects, including the minutes, including the statements, and try to develop a better, more explicit, and more useful form of communication. And I will certainly keep congressional leaders apprised of this. And if anything happens that is a departure from past practice, I will certainly let you know about it and get your input.

Bunning: Last but not least, one thing different in your time as Federal Reserve chairman than when Mr. Greenspan, is the amount of attention the public is paying to statements from other Federal Reserve members. There was even a Bloomberg article yesterday about that. Do you have any problem with other Federal Reserve members speaking out with different points of view? Do you think that is good for the markets and the economy?

Bernanke: Senator, you were asking about differences of opinion and getting around group think, and this is one way in which members of the FOMC can express different shades of their views. We do not restrict, we do not coordinate, the speeches of FOMC members. They are going out on their own in their own districts and talking about whatever issues are important to them. And sometimes they make comments on monetary policy.

As this exchange between Bunning and Bernanke illustrates, challenges to the Fed in the early 2000s were less on the substance of monetary policy and more on the mechanisms of transparency. This less confrontational atmosphere (at least on the fundamentals of policy) is indicative of the changing nature of congressional oversight on monetary policy over this period.

This is not to say that heated remarks by committee members have become obsolete. Challenges to the Fed chair by individual members are not necessarily uncommon; indeed some are so prominent as to become well-known clips on YouTube (at least in recent years, as seen with Bernie Sanders, Ron Paul, and Alan Grayson). The oversight hearings thus offer individual members of Congress the opportunity to capture the media limelight (and speak to constituents in their districts) with their critiques against the Fed. YouTube is one thing, but statistically significant discourse over a long period is another thing. Our textual analysis reveals two such statistical anomalies in two classes, one in the House (class 1) and one in the Senate (class 9). In both cases the discourse is almost exclusively that of just one individual—in the House, Rep. Bernie Sanders (the only Democrat "Socialist" in Congress, an Independent from Vermont who has gone on to become senator for that state) and in the Senate, Senator Don Riegle (Democratic Senator for Michigan from 1977, and chair of the Senate Banking committee from 1989 to 95). Here we find clear evidence that both congressmen and senators engage in point-scoring, in support of hypothesis 6. This finding should not, however, come as a surprise to even the casual observer of these hearings. What is intriguing is that, in the aggregate, a single committee member (e.g., Sanders or Riegle) can influence the content of the larger discourse so prominently. Our further sections in this chapter shed more light on the empirics of point-scoring discourse in these committee hearings.

Fourth, it is not surprising that in the midst of the financial crisis, banking regulation rises to prominence in 2007–08 (classes 4 [House] and class 2 [Senate]). Interestingly, prior to the crisis, the Fed's regulatory activities received almost no significant discussion in the oversight hearings—except for two notable instances in the Senate hearings. These appear in 1984, with the failure of Continental Illinois National

Bank, and in 1999, following the Long-Term Capital Management problem of 1998. This lack of sustained attention to banking regulation is noteworthy (though here again we note that this subject matter is not the stated purpose of the Humphrey–Hawkins hearings), in view of accusations from both Democrats and Republicans on the failures of the other party to effectively challenge the Fed's regulatory activities in the decade preceding the financial crisis. We explore this point further in our next chapter, where we ask our interviewees for their views on the degree of attention paid by members of Congress (of both parties) to such matters in the Humphrey–Hawkins hearings.

In the late 1990s and continuing up to the financial crisis, senators become increasingly more focused on declining US international competitiveness and its link to deficiencies (particularly education and training) in the labor market (class 5). The intriguing element of this fifth finding is that there is no equivalent discourse in the House hearings—except for occasional references within the more populist critique of (then) Congressman Sanders.

Finally, fiscal policy receives regular, though not overwhelming, attention in the House hearings, and almost no significant attention in the Senate hearings—with the exceptional year of 2005, when discussions of spending on the Iraq war captured their attention (classes 3 [House] and 6 [Senate]). Discussions of fiscal policy, and particularly, the mix between fiscal and monetary policy, require closer examination, which we provide in section 4.2.4 below.

Our hypothesis 5 posits that deliberation by senators should be of better quality than that of congressmen. Our findings indicate that there is more of a contrast in the actual *content* of deliberation by the two sets of committee members from each house rather than in the quality of what was said. Thus, if the nature of the deliberative discourse is focused on one issue area—such as oversight of monetary policy—a given committee's interpretation of its role in conducting oversight may be understood more effectively by the substantive content of its discourse than by reference to any generic index of quality.[5] In short, "better" deliberation may be less revealing than "substantively different" deliberation.

Significance by Party and Chairman

Turning to figures 4.6 and 4.7, we can begin to isolate more clearly where committee members of different partisan orientation tended to focus their concerns, and the areas of focus for each successive Fed chairman.

First, both figures 4.6 and 4.7 illustrate the same thematic cleavage we observed in the tree diagrams and correspondence analysis. In particular, members of Congress acquire no statistical significance whatsoever for discourse on core issues in monetary policy—the battle against inflation, the US real economy, monetary aggregates, and so on—nor on issues of the US external balance or the world economy. For these issues the Fed chairmen repeatedly dominate the discussion. We do, however, observe one notable exception—namely that of Senator Riegle—whose discourse (both as committee chair and member) comprises the bulk of class 9 in the Senate. We have labeled this class "criticism of the Fed" but we note that a large share of Riegle's attacks focused on the Fed's perceived inattention to, or failure to support economic growth. (As an example from the second ECU in table 4.A2 of our chapter appendix, Riegle asserts: "I think you're too passive, quite frankly. I don't say that just to you, but I think the response of the Federal Reserve Board has been very modest, very guarded, very slow, and I think not adequate to the problem.") While the critical and less technical vocabulary in the class distinguishes it from the vocabulary of the Fed chairmen on the US real economy (class 8), it is important to note that Riegle's comments were relevant to the real economy. This feature of Riegle's discourse also helps account for the anomalous placement of the Committee Chair tag in the Senate correspondence graph (figure 4.4), where it is positioned nearer to the Federal Reserve classes on the right of the graph.

A second and related observation is that our two "limelight" members of Congress—Riegle and Sanders—are evident from their large chi square significance values in figures 4.6a and 4.6b. We also note that to capture the limelight, a member of Congress need not also hold the committee chairmanship. Riegle's critiques are significant even when he was not chairing the Senate Banking Committee, and Sanders' populist anti-Fed remarks (along with other such sentiments by some Democrats and Republicans) are not contingent on sitting in the role of committee chairman.

Following on from this, we also note that—perhaps contrary to conventional wisdom, and committee practice, which allows the chair to speak first—the committee chair does not appear to consistently outweigh the rhetorical significance of the members. This is particularly evident for fiscal policy, where the chair scores no statistical significance in either the House or the Senate hearings.

Finally, as anticipated from our earlier overview of Fed–Congress relations, challenges to the policies and priorities of the Fed tend to come more from the Democrats than the Republicans—as seen in class 1 (House), noting that Sanders caucuses with the Democrats, and in class 4 (Senate). Meanwhile Republicans are slightly more inclined to discuss banking regulation, but as this theme receives very little attention before the recent financial crisis, it should not be overstated.

Turning to figure 4.7, we can see that Fed chairmen are closely associated with particular themes: monetary aggregates for Burns, Miller, and Volcker; the fight against inflation for Volcker; the US real economy, the world economy (including trade and current account) and the willingness to explore nonmonetary policy issues for Greenspan; and regulation of financial institutions, along with the real economy for Bernanke. Figure 4.7 provides a concise summary of the priorities of each Fed chairman, but it also encapsulates the changing context of US monetary policy from the mid-1970s to 2008. It depicts the shift from commentary on monetary quantities to the US real economy, with the transition most obviously between the Volcker and Greenspan years.

4.2.4   A Closer Look at the Thinking of Fed Chairmen (using *Tri croisé*)

Our examination of the distribution of attention to the themes across time, party and Fed chairmen provides a good initial overview of the core ideas and areas of focus in the congressional hearings, but we can delve deeper by employing again the *tri-croisé* or cross-data analysis (as we did in the previous chapter). Here we cross each of the Fed chairmen and each of the two major party affiliations with the entire set of House hearings, and again, with the entire set of Senate hearings. This allows us to identify those words and phrases that are most closely associated with Burns, Miller, Volcker, Greenspan, and Bernanke, as well as those most closely associated with Republicans and Democrats in the House and Senate hearings.

For each relevant tag (Fed chairman, party label), the program generates two classes (each with characteristic words and phrases, ordered by chi-squared significance). One class is unique to the vocabulary of the Fed chairman or party label, and the other class consists of words and phrases that are *least* associated with the tag. We focus here only on the first class, and from that we examine the top ECUs (which automatically generated number 19).

Table 4.2 presents a simple list of the top phrases for each Fed chairman and party label. From a close reading of each set of 19 ECUs, we tally and group them into common categories. While there is of course some overlap between these categories and our thematic classes

Table 4.2
Distribution of major themes, by Fed chairmen and political party (count of top 19 ECUs)

House

Top themes, condensed	Burns	Miller	Wallich	Volcker	Greenspan	Bernanke	Republican committee members	Democrat committee members
Real economy (labor markets, US economy)	9	6	0	0	10	11	2	7½
Money, inflation, credit, & financial markets	10	8	10	16	7	0	0	3
External (world economy for Miller, Volcker, Greenspan; US competitiveness for Republicans)	0	3	0	1	1	0	7½	0
Fiscal policy	0	2	9*	2	1	0	5½	4½
Regulation of financial institutions	0	0	0	0	0	8	1	0
Other (process, relations between Congress, Fed, & administration; one War on Terror for Republicans)	0	0	0	0	0	0	3	4

Senate

Top themes, condensed	Burns	Miller	Wallich	Volcker	Greenspan	Bernanke	Republican committee members	Democrat committee members
Real economy (labor market, US economy, productivity)	7½	7½		0	6	6½	3	11
Money, monetary policy, inflation	10	9½		15½	½	5½	0	3
External (LDC debt for Volcker; current account for Greenspan; US competitiveness for Republicans)	½	0		2	1	0	1	0
Fiscal policy	0	2		1½	0	0	12	3
Regulation of financial institutions	0	0		0	1½	4	1	0
Bank lending	1	0		0	6	3	0	0
Financial markets/assets	0	0		0	4	0	0	0
Other (criticism of Fed & Homeland Security for Democrats; education & process for Republicans)	0	0		0	0	0	2	2

Note: Miller made only one appearance in the Senate in 1979; the other was made by Henry Wallich (vice chairman of the Board of Governors of the Federal Reserve). As a former economist at Yale, Wallich's expertise in fiscal policy prompted committee members to ask his advice on fiscal policy.

reported in the first part of this chapter, our cut into the data at this point is different, as we are not attempting to use the program to identify themes across the whole corpus but rather simply to identify vocabulary that is statistically associated with a particular Fed chairman or group of political party members. Moreover, for simplicity, we do not weight or list the ECUs in terms of their χ^2 ranking in the *tri-croisé* reporting, but rather treat all the reported ECUs equally. We are therefore applying a structured approach to capturing the meaning of the text. To aid in the interpretation, we convey the same distribution from table 4.2 in two graphs—figures 4.8 and 4.9.

From table 4.2 and figures 4.8 and 4.9, we observe that (1) the distribution in topics between Burns and Miller (in both the House and Senate) is quite similar, which is perhaps not surprising, given Miller's brief tenure following on directly from Burns's; (2) indicative of his revolutionary shift in monetary policy, Volcker is almost exclusively associated with discourse on money and inflation; (3) both Greenspan and Bernanke devote considerably more attention to the US real economy (including labor markets) in the House hearings than the Senate hearings; (4) as one would expect with the financial crisis, Bernanke devotes considerable attention to discussing the regulation of financial institutions—but notably, far more so in the House than in the Senate; and (5) the political party divide is far more distinct in the Senate than in the House, with Republicans focusing predominantly on fiscal policy and Democrats on the US real economy (particularly labor markets). This divide still appears in the House hearings, but overall, the discourse is spread across more areas.

Once again, we find clear contrasts between the House and Senate hearings in the *content* of deliberation. Exchanges between the Fed chair and House committee members have focused relatively more on labor market issues (US real economy) and more recently, the regulation of financial institutions. Meanwhile, partisan discourse appears to be more prominently defined by topics in the Senate than in the House—with Democratic senators relatively more concerned about labor market issues and Republican senators similarly more focused on fiscal policy. Of course, at this point we have not accounted for partisan majorities in Congress or the partisanship of the administration—though we do so in our next section. Nonetheless, even at this aggregate level it is evident that senators and congressmen tend to hone in on somewhat different areas of focus in their discourse with the Fed chairman.

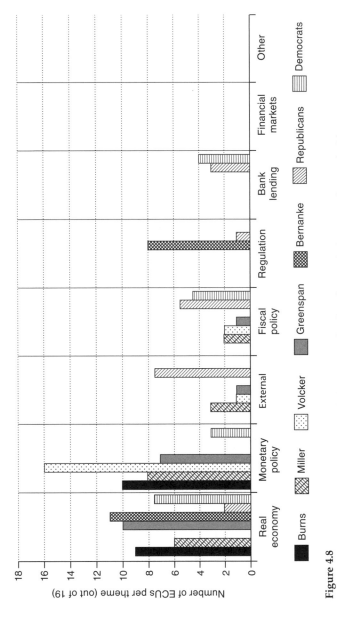

Figure 4.8
Major themes in House hearings, by Fed chairman and political party (using cross-data analysis)

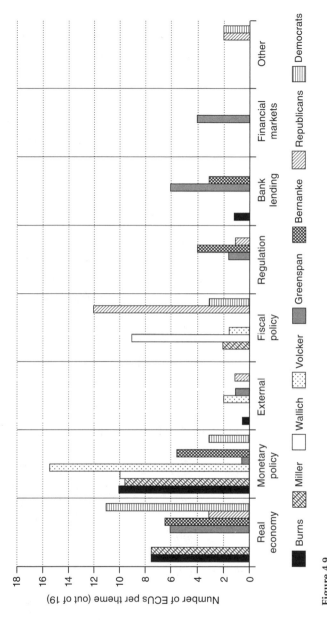

Figure 4.9
Major themes in Senate hearings, by Fed chairman and political party (using cross-data analysis)

The variations in the distributions tell part of the story of the differences among the Fed chairmen, but one aim of our project is to illustrate more fully the thinking of each chairman on monetary policy per se. To achieve this, we extract from the ECUs for each Fed chairman, those in which he describes his approach to monetary policy to the congressional committees. (These are listed in the third part of our appendix to this chapter.) From these descriptions we are able to extract the key points and differences in the comments of the chairmen, taking each in turn. We do not seek to distinguish between comments made to the House and Senate committees, though in the third part of our chapter appendix the comments are shown separately.

Arthur Burns

Arthur Burns placed an emphasis on describing monetary policy in the context of the business cycle, as befits his background in economics (his academic career had been associated with business cycle analysis). In terms of the direction of monetary policy he placed emphasis on *"the course of moderation,"* thus:

The principal contribution that the Federal Reserve can now make to the achievement of our nation's basic economic objectives is to adhere to a course of moderation in monetary policy.

What did he mean by a *"course of moderation"*? The ECUs reveal that Burns interpreted his role as one of *"formulating public policy,"* which appears to bear out an interpretation of the Fed being prepared to subordinate its independence in monetary policy to a broader objective of public policy alongside other objectives that were the responsibility of Congress and the administration. Thus Burns recognized inflation as *"a major consideration in formulating public policy."* An important part of this focus on public policy by Burns is his willingness to place regaining *"satisfactory levels of production and employment ahead of the **eventual** return to stability of the general price level"* (our emphasis on "eventual"). In a second quote, Burns describes the Fed as:

seeking to foster financial conditions that would facilitate a good expansion in economic activity without aggravating in any way the troublesome problem of inflation.

This can be interpreted as a willingness to foster growth without making a bad inflation problem worse. Finally, Burns also describes in familiar terms (Burns 1979, 1987) the origin of the inflation problem in the loose fiscal policies of the 1960s, which he associated with the Great Society initiatives of the Johnson administration.

This encapsulates the paradox of Arthur Burns, namely placing blame on other dimensions of public policy for creating the inflation problem while being prepared to harness and even subordinate monetary policy to those other dimensions of public policy.

William Miller

William Miller used stronger language in describing *"the war against inflation"* and he did not repeat the phrase *"course of moderation"* in the way that Burns did to Congress. Rather, Miller talked in similar terms of gradual adjustment in policy:

I have been a proponent of adjusting our economy to a slower growth mode, on a gradual basis, so we don't shock it, don't create dislocations, and don't interrupt the process of investment in a way that would trigger a serious recession.

Miller was clear that a *"recession is not going to cure inflation."* Moreover he used similar language to Burns in describing the mix of public policies that would tackle inflation:

It had been our report to this committee that with the strategic policies being put into place involving fiscal discipline, involving incomes policy, involving dollar and international account policies, involving energy policies, and involving monetary policies we would wring out inflation over 5, 6, or 7 years.

It is notable that monetary policy does not come first in this list, indeed it comes last. And Miller's ambition was to tackle inflation over a period of five to seven years (albeit that he was clear in describing the effects of the second oil price shock in setting back the timetable).

Miller used somewhat stronger headline rhetoric than Burns (*"war against inflation"*), but he operated in a similar framework in thinking of monetary policy as one among a number of public policies tackling inflation, and of a gradual adjustment downward of inflation.

Paul Volcker

As we would expect, the arrival of **Paul Volcker** as chairman marked a distinct break in the language used by the chairman to Congress. Volcker's language is clear and direct, talking of *"the need for greater monetary and price stability for its own sake."* Volcker's language did not include the moderation or gradualism of Burns and Miller:

Against the background of the strong inflationary momentum in the economy, the targets are frankly designed to be restrictive. They do imply restraint on the potential growth of the nominal GNP. The heart of the problem is that if inflation continues unabated or rises, real activity is likely to be squeezed. But, as inflation begins noticeably to abate, the stage will be set for stronger real growth. Monetary policy is designed to encourage that disinflationary process.

Moreover Volcker introduced a clear hierarchy of public policy objectives:

The experience of the seventies strongly suggests that the inflationary process undercuts efforts to achieve and maintain other goals, expressed in the Humphrey–Hawkins Act, of growth and employment.

Here we see the shift to the modern idea that low inflation is the necessary condition for stable economic growth. While he recognized that *"indefinitely continued high levels of unemployment and poor economic performance"* were not a satisfactory remedy, *"ratifying strong price pressures by increases in the money supply offers no solution."* This was different language to that of Burns when he described unemployment as *"deplorably high."* But Volcker recognized though that the success of anti-inflationary monetary policy was dependent on *"other public policies and private attitudes and behavior"*:

Monetary policy is only one part of an economic program. It is an essential part, but success is dependent on a coherent whole.

Volcker's language to Congress also introduced for the first time the notion of the importance of public attitudes and expectations toward future inflation:

The legacy of the seventies was deeply ingrained patterns of behavior in pricing, in wage bargaining, in interest rates, and in financial practices generally built on the assumption of continuing, and accelerating inflation.

Another noticeable shift in the language used by Volcker to Congress was to describe the Fed as being *"guided by the need to maintain financial discipline"*:

I think the markets reflect and it is apparent in other contexts that for the time being there is a particularly heavy burden on monetary policy in dealing with the inflationary situation.

The role and position of financial markets did not feature in the language of Burns and Miller. Volcker's change of language in addressing Congress was just as abrupt as his change in policy, recognizing the primacy of anti-inflationary policy, the role of public expectations of inflation, and the importance of financial markets.

Alan Greenspan

The language of **Alan Greenspan** has to be interpreted against the marked change in inflationary conditions. Unlike Burns, Miller and Volcker, Greenspan talked from a position of well-established low inflation. As we have noted elsewhere, this changed the whole dialogue with Congress in terms of substance and the language used. Greenspan talked about benign economic conditions resulting from the achievement of low inflation:

The essential precondition for the emergence, and persistence, of this virtuous cycle is arguably the decline in the rate of inflation to near price stability. In recent years, continued low product price inflation and expectations that it will persist have promoted stability in financial markets and fostered perceptions that the degree of risk in the financial outlook has been moving ever lower.

Greenspan's focus was therefore on the forward-looking outlook for inflation, but in terms of what it might be rather than what it ought to be:

Whether inflation actually rises in the wake of slowing productivity growth, however, will depend on the rate of growth of labor compensation and the ability and willingness of firms to pass on higher costs to their customers. That, in turn, will depend on the degree of utilization of resources and how monetary policy makers respond.

It is worth noting that Greenspan's language was cast in terms of a conditional outlook (continuing low inflation is conditional on the growth of labor compensation, etc.) rather than a more formal statement of risks on either side of the outlook.

Ben Bernanke

The contemporary orthodox statement of monetary policy that recognizes both the uncertainty in the outlook and the normal presence of risks on either side of the central case outlook is given by **Ben Bernanke**:

As always, in determining the appropriate stance of policy, we will be alert to the possibility that the economy is not evolving in the way we currently judge to be the most likely. One risk to the outlook is that the ongoing housing correction might prove larger than anticipated, with possible spillovers onto consumer spending. Alternatively consumer spending, which has advanced relatively vigorously on balance in recent quarters, might expand more quickly than expected. In that case, economic growth could rebound to a pace above its trend. With the level of resource utilization already elevated, the resulting pressures in labor and product markets could lead to increased inflation over time. Yet another risk is that energy and commodity prices could continue to rise sharply, leading to further increases in headline inflation and, if those costs pass through to the prices of non-energy goods and services, to higher core inflation as well.

There is no debate with Congress on the role of monetary policy (a feature also of Greenspan's language) and the low inflation consensus. Bernanke is explicit in setting out the lagged transmission mechanism of monetary policy:

Monetary policy works with a lag. Therefore our policy stance must be determined in light of the medium term forecast of real activity and inflation as well as the risks to that forecast.

Monetary policy is appropriately cast as forward-looking, and the exchanges with Congress should be on the outlook for the economy and inflation. It is, however, quite possible that members of Congress feel less confident debating what will happen with an expert who is armed with a forecasting machinery and a successful policy record than they were in the past arguing about a past record of policy that could not be regarded as a success.

PART TWO—A CROSS-SECTIONAL APPROACH TO THE MONETARY POLICY OVERSIGHT HEARINGS

4.3   Introduction

Our "bird's-eye" view of the 61 hearings is our first cut into the textual data, and as such our findings are preliminary. In this section we further our analysis in order to obtain more robust findings. We divide the hearings into 16 distinct corpora—8 each for the House and Senate banking committees. We follow our previous approach by identifying the themes of the hearings and how these themes evolved from 1976 to 2008. We also analyze differences in discourse between legislators and the Fed chairman, and between Democrats and Republicans.

The evolution of the discourse from the 1970s to 2008 is particularly important to our analysis as it provides some insight into the extent to which members of Congress became persuaded of the low inflation consensus (our hypothesis 7). As we have noted, we expect that this objective for monetary policy became clearer to members of Congress over time, partly from the arguments from Fed officials, and then solidified by the success of the Fed's monetary policy itself. So our textual analysis should show a clearer definition of the idea of the low inflation consensus as spoken by members within the House and Senate Banking Committees. We contend that as the expectations of economic actors changed alongside the long period of sustained low inflation, so too did the perceptions of members of Congress toward the Fed and with this, their conduct of monetary policy oversight. The nature of congressional oversight is thus seen to be dependent in part on the state of the economy, and in particular, on the Fed's success in achieving its objectives of low inflation and stable growth (high employment). While this dynamic in congressional oversight is not a particularly novel idea, it does strengthen the case for understanding better the deliberative discourse on monetary policy, because it raises questions as to whether legislators who conduct oversight of the Fed are willing and able to do so as effectively in the (seemingly) good times as well as they do during the bad times of high inflation or financial crises.

Aside from our general aim better to understand what members of Congress were seeking to achieve in the monetary policy oversight hearings, we also weigh the evidence with respect to the deliberative discourse of senators versus congressmen (hypothesis 5), and the balance of point-scoring discourse against that of monetary policy specifics (hypothesis 6).

4.4 The Monetary Policy Oversight Hearings, in Cross Section

4.4.1 An Initial Overview

Tables 4.3 and 4.4 report the basic statistics for each of the sixteen corpora—one for each chamber in each of the eight time periods.[6] These eight were chosen to reflect distinct periods in US monetary policy history, as broadly defined by the incumbent Federal Reserve chairman: Burns (1976–1977); Miller (1979); early Volcker (1979–1981); late Volcker (1984–1986); early Greenspan (1991–1993); mid-Greenspan (1997–1999); late Greenspan (2003–2005); and early Bernanke (2006–2008).[7]

Similar to our data in part one of this chapter, each speech, question or interjection in the hearings constitutes a case. Each case is then

Table 4.3
Basic statistics for House and Senate hearings on monetary policy, 1976 to 1986

	House hearings, 1976–1977	Senate hearings, 1976–1977	House hearings, 1979	Senate hearings, 1979
Total word count	85,623	64,515	35,013	28,320
Unique words analyzed	36,898	27,485	14,126	11,314
Passive variables (tagged indicators)	58	23	30	23
ICUs (= number of speeches /comments)	670	606	272	296
Classified ECUs	1,849 (= 74% of the retained ECU)	1,404 (= 71% of the retained ECU)	571 (= 57% of the retained ECU)	611 (= 68% of the retained ECU)
Lexical classes	5	5	5	4
Distribution of classes (%) and thematic content	1 (40) *Labor market/ employment & inflation* 2 (16) *Growth of monetary aggregates* 3 (13) *Capacity utilization & investment by firms* 4 (9) *Innovation in bank accounts w/ links to monetary aggregates* 5 (23) *Independence & structure of the FOMC*	1 (10) *Exchange rate, monetary policy, & world economy* 2 (37) *Transparency of the Fed; relations between Fed & Congress* 3 (19) *Monetary aggregates* 4 (10) *Labor markets/ employment* 5 (24) *Business investment & its financing*	1 (18) *Describing economic growth data* 2 (13) *Fiscal policy/ tax measures* 3 (38) *Inflation/ monetary policy* 4 (20) *Credit creation/ money growth* 5 (11) *Exchange rate/ cost of foreign currency debt*	1 (34) *Fed independence* 2 (29) *Monetary & credit aggregates, and innovation in bank accounts* 3 (21) *Labor markets, unemployment, & inflation* 4 (15) *Stance of monetary policy & objectives*

Table 4.3
(continued)

	House hearings, 1979–1981	Senate hearings, 1980–1981[a]	House hearings, 1984–1986	Senate hearings, 1984–1986
Total word count	130,888	93,607	116,992	113,866
Unique words analyzed	52,483	37,246	46,676	48,061
Passive variables (tagged indicators)	63	35	50	27
ICUs (= number of speeches /comments)	1,215	965	1,296	1,113
Classified ECUs	2,780 (= 71% of the retained ECU)	2,200 (= 75% of the retained ECU)	2,875 (= 76% of the retained ECU)	2,888 (= 81% of the retained ECU)
Lexical classes	7	5	6	6
Distribution of classes (%) and thematic content	1 (13) *Bank credit/structure of deposit banking/account types* 2 (11) *Fiscal policy (spending & deficits)* 3 (12) *Inflation problems* 4 (12) *Fiscal policy (tax)* 5 (10) *Productivity, inflation and the labor market* 6 (19) *Monetary aggregates* 7 (22) *Investment in housing & by small businesses*	1 (32) *Credit restraint (signals from monetary policy)* 2 (18) *Interest rates & credit conditions* 3 (16) *Monetary aggregates* 4 (9) *Fiscal policy* 5 (26) *Volcker Revolution/ anti-inflation policies*	1 (14) *Transparency of the FOMC (demands for more)* 2 (11) *Regulation of the banking system* 3 (10) *Fiscal policy* 4 (23) *US imbalances/ exchange rate/world economy* 5 (25) *Monetary aggregates* 6 (17) *Uncertainty & risks around forecasts of interest rates*	1 (18) *Capital flows/external imbalances/exchange rate/ world economy* 2 (16) *Bank failures (esp. Continental Illinois)* 3 (7) *Fiscal policy* 4 (7) *Structure of banking system/creation of "non-bank" banks* 5 (30) *Uncertainty around course of, and target of monetary policy* 6 (22) *Economic activity/ monetary aggregates & inflation*

a. The Senate did not hold its usual November hearing in 1979.

Table 4.4
Basic statistics for House and Senate hearings on monetary policy, 1990s to 2008

	House hearings, 1991–1993	Senate hearings, 1991–1993	House hearings, 1997–1999	Senate hearings, 1997–1999
Total word count	71,553	123,922	105,805	79,077
Unique words analyzed	30,949	52,456	43,153	36,796
Passive variables (tagged indicators)	34	37	47	33
ICUs (= number of speeches/comments)	510	815	670	398
Classified ECUs	1,517 (= 74% of the retained ECU)	3,084 (= 86% of the retained ECU)	2,374 (= 82% of the retained ECU)	1,905 (= 88% of the retained ECU)
Lexical classes	5	5	5	5
Distribution of classes (%) and thematic content	1 (14) *Fiscal policy* 2 (16) *Interaction of Fed with presidency & elections* 3 (18) *Credit flows/asset prices* 4 (24) *Economic outlook/inflation/money supply* 5 (27) *Bank lending—especially small businesses*	1 (15) *Health of banking system* 2 (38) *Role of Congress in economic policy/fiscal policy* 3 (7) *Fiscal policy* 4 (21) *Monetary aggregates* 5 (18) *Labor markets/unemployment*	1 (42) *Role of government in the economy (domestic & international)* 2 (24) *Economic activity & growth in the United States* 3 (14) *Labor markets/unemployment* 4 (10) *Asian & Russian crises* 5 (10) *Fiscal policy*	1 (15) *Structure of banking system/regulation* 2 (12) *Praising Greenspan & seeking his advice* 3 (10) *Fiscal policy* 4 (23) *World economy/Y2K conversion of IT system* 5 (40) *Economic outlook & growth*

Table 4.4
(continued)

	House hearings, 2003–2005	Senate hearings, 2003–2005	House hearings, 2006–2008	Senate hearings, 2006–2008
Total word count	98,507	97,601	113,723	99,451
Unique words analyzed	40,427	39,878	47,099	40,496
Passive variables (tagged indicators)	64	34	67	34
ICUs (= number of speeches/comments)	761	760	843	791
Classified ECUs	1,141 (= 61% of the retained ECU)	1,566 (= 56% of the retained ECU)	2,458 (= 72% of the retained ECU)	2,304 (= 76% of the retained ECU)
Lexical classes	6	5	5	6
Distribution of classes (%) and thematic content	1 (18) Labor markets, wages, employment 2 (19) Productivity, economic growth & investment by businesses 3 (26) Education & equality 4 (14) Social Security reform 5 (11) Fiscal policy 6 (12) Banking system/bank regulation/punishing foreign banks for misdemeanors	1 (22) Fiscal policy 2 (33) Praising Greenspan & seeking his advice 3 (20) Economic activity/ Role of monetary policy in sustaining growth 4 (10) Energy policy 5 (15) Labor markets/ earnings	1 (26) Education & income inequality 2 (17) Investment in corporates/role of hedge funds 3 (17) Inflation & economic activity 4 (17) Mortgage lending/ conduct of business 5 (23) Wages & productivity	1 (20) Challenging the Fed & Bernanke with introduction of legislation 2 (34) Economic activity & inflation 3 (17) Controls on the conduct of mortgage lending 4 (9) Foreign ownership of US firms/sovereign wealth funds/China 5 (9) Education & raising skills of labor force 6 (11) Wage inequality & employment

tagged with identifying characteristics (date, name of speaker, and for members of Congress, party affiliation and role—chair or member). In our chapter appendix (tables 4.A3 to 4.A10), we provide detailed information on the statistically significant tags for each thematic class within each of the sixteen corpora. We first outline the results, as presented in the relevant tables and figures. In the section that follows, we provide interpretations of these findings.

Taken together, tables 4.3 and 4.4 are informative but cumbersome, as they are difficult to digest in their entirety. We therefore summarize the findings from these tables into 10 thematic groups across the three decades. To do this, we assign each of the classes from the 16 sets of results to one of our thematic groups. The brackets after each class label in tables 4.A3 to 4.A10 indicate the thematic group to which the class was assigned. Combining themes from each period invariably runs the risk of joining themes that have the same subject matter (e.g., fiscal policy) but very different slants on the issue. Nonetheless, these thematic groups allow us to trace broad patterns over time within the discourse of oversight hearings. Figure 4.10 provides for each thematic group a timeline of the party and Fed chairman tags that are significant at the 1 percent level or greater (as indicated by the appropriate symbols for each party and for the Fed chairman). Figure 4.10 also identifies a subset of thematic groups for which more than one party attracts a significant tag (e.g., Democrat and Republican)—in these cases we conclude either that the theme attracts bipartisan support or that the parties disagree, but in doing so, each party tag acquires statistical significance.

From tables 4.3 and 4.4 (row 7) we obtain the percentage weight of discourse classified into each of the classes.[8] The shares are then summed and presented in table 4.5, where each column sums to 100. Table 4.5 thus provides a summary of the distribution of each thematic group, according to its share of retained ECUs. (Note that unlike figure 4.10, table 4.5 includes themes even when none of the party or Fed tags were significant at 1 percent, and so is a complete portrayal of the overall distribution across the thematic groups.) The added value of table 4.5 is that it allows the observer to scan the changes in the weights given to thematic groups over time. Visually, however, table 4.5 is less intuitive, so we present the table graphically in figures 4.11a to 4.11k.

Major themes in hearings, summarized	1976–1977 (Burns)		1979 (Miller)		1979–1981 (Volcker)		1984–86 (Volcker)		1991–1993 (Greenspan)		1997–1999 (Greenspan)		2003–2005 (Greenspan)		2006–2008 (Bernanke)	
House and Senate majority party	*H* Donkey	*S* Donkey	*H* Donkey	*S* Donkey	*H* Donkey	*S* Elephant Donkey	*H* Donkey	*S* Elephant	*H* Donkey	*S* Donkey	*H* Elephant	*S* Elephant	*H* Elephant	*S* Elephant	*H* Elephant Donkey	*S* Elephant Donkey
1. Inflation (US)					$	$	$	Donkey	$						$	$
2. US economy–output	$	$	$		Donkey						$	$	$	$		
3. Labor market/ unemployment	Elephant	Donkey								Donkey	Donkey *i*		Elephant Donkey *i*	Donkey	Elephant Donkey	Donkey
4. Money growth/ aggregates/credit	Donkey	$		$	$	Elephant Donkey $	$	$	$	$						
5. Financial stability/ banking system	$							$		$			Elephant		$	$
6. Fiscal policy (including Social Security)					Elephant Donkey $	Elephant Donkey	Donkey	Elephant Donkey	Elephant Donkey	Elephant		Elephant	Donkey	Donkey		
7. Independence of the Fed —relations between Fed, Congress, administration	Donkey	Donkey		Donkey												
8. Appraising the Fed a. Challenging the Fed							Elephant Donkey		Elephant Donkey	Elephant Donkey	Elephant Donkey					Elephant Donkey
b. Praising the Fed												Elephant Donkey		Donkey		
9. World economy (impact on US, exchange rate implications of monetary policy)			Elephant				$	$			$	$				Donkey
10. Other (education & inequality with links to labor market theme, and energy)													$		Elephant Donkey	$

Figure 4.10

Summary of major themes and significant party and Federal Reserve chairman tags (1976 to 2008). Significance here means that the χ^2 value is at least at the 1 percent significance level. Donkey symbol = Democrat; elephant symbol = Republican; ***i*** = Independent (Bernie Sanders), and \$ = Federal Reserve chairman. Classes in italics (classes 1, 2, 3, and 4) are linked by word and sentence overlap, as are classes in bold (7 and 8). In the Senate, Democrats held the majority in 1980, but Republicans held it in 1981. In 2006, Republicans held the majority in both the House and Senate, but in 2007 and 2008, Democrats were the majority in the House, while in the Senate Republicans and Democrats tied with two Independents

Table 4.5
Distribution of major themes within each set of congressional hearings

Major themes in hearings, summarized	1976–1977 (Burns)		1979 (Miller)		1979–1981 (Volcker)		1984–1986 (Volcker)		1991–1993 (Greenspan)		1997–1999 (Greenspan)		2003–2005 (Greenspan)		2006–2008 (Bernanke)	
	H	S	H	S	H	S	H	S	H	S	H	S	H	S	H	S
1. Inflation (US)	13	24	38	15	22	26	17	30	24						17	34
2. US economy output	40	10	18	21	22					18	24	40	19	20	23	11
3. Labor market/unemployment											14		18	15		
4. Money growth/aggregates/credit	16	19	20	29	19	66	25	22	45	21						
5. Financial stability/banking system	9		13		13		11	23	14	15		15	12		34	17
6. Fiscal policy (including Social Security)					23	9	10	7		7	10	10	25	22		
7. Independence of the Fed—relations between Fed/Congress/administration	23	37	34													

Table 4.5
(continued)

Major themes in hearings, summarized	1976–1977 (Burns)	1979 (Miller)	1979–1981 (Volcker)	1984–1986 (Volcker)	1991–1993 (Greenspan)	1997–1999 (Greenspan)	2003–2005 (Greenspan)	2006–2008 (Bernanke)
8. Appraising the Fed—challenging the Fed/praising the Fed				14	16 38	42 12	33	20
9. World economy (impact on US exchange rate/ implications of monetary policy)	10	11		23		23 10		9
10. Other (education & inequality—w/ links to Labor market theme— and energy)						26	26 10	9
Total (=100 but for rounding)	101	100	99	100	99	100	100	100
Total (=100 but for rounding)	*101*	*100*	*99*	*101*	*100*	*99*	*100*	*100*

Note: Defined as the share of retained ECUs that are classified into each theme (links with the percentage distribution classes in the last row of tables 4.3 and 4.4). Note also that the cell entries for this table do not always parallel the significant party and Fed tags given in figure 4.10, as the entries here include the weights of all themes—including those for which no important tags were statistically significant (e.g., where individual members might register significance, but not the party tag). Classes in italics (classes 1, 2, 3, and 4) are linked in terms of word and sentence overlap, as are classes in bold (7 and 8).

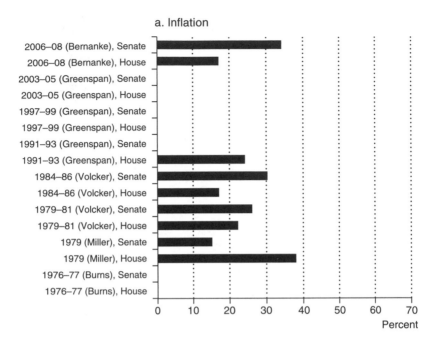

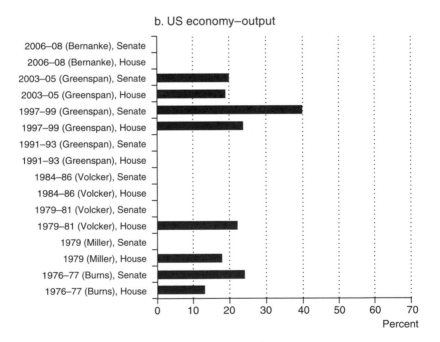

Figure 4.11
Distribution of major themes, by year, Fed chairman and congressional chamber (percent).
(a) *Inflation*; (b) *US economy–output*; (c) *Labor market*; (d) *Money growth, aggregates*; (e) *Financial stability*; (f) *Fiscal policy*; (g) *Independence of Fed*; (h) *Challenging the Fed*; (i) *Praising the Fed*; (j) *World economy*; (k) *Other (education and inequality).*

c. Labor market

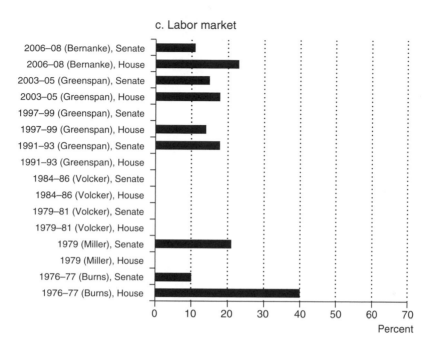

d. Money growth, aggregates

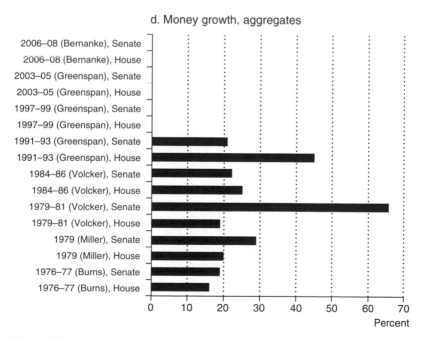

Figure 4.11
(continued)

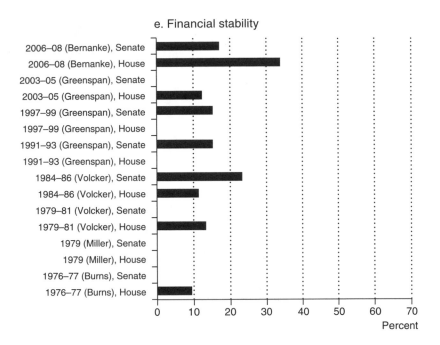

e. Financial stability

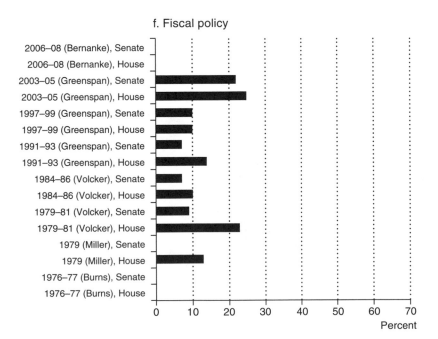

f. Fiscal policy

Figure 4.11
(continued)

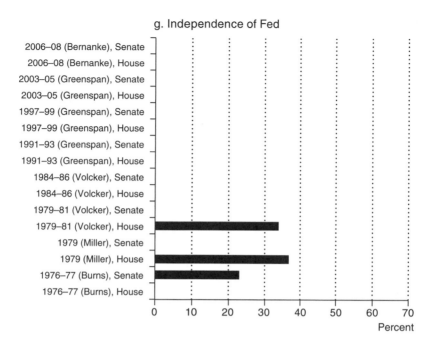

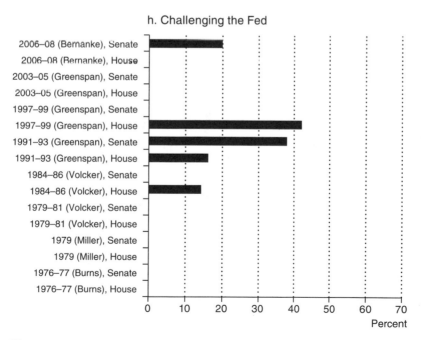

Figure 4.11
(continued)

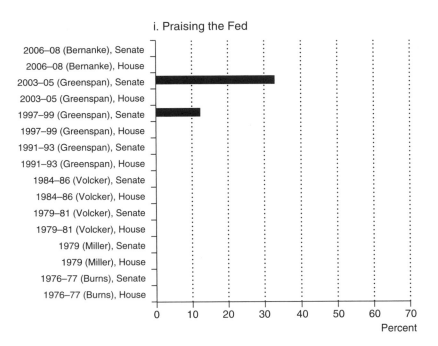

i. Praising the Fed

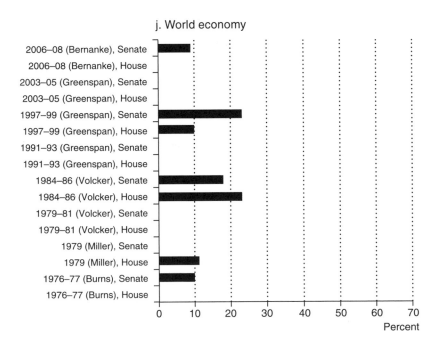

j. World economy

Figure 4.11
(continued)

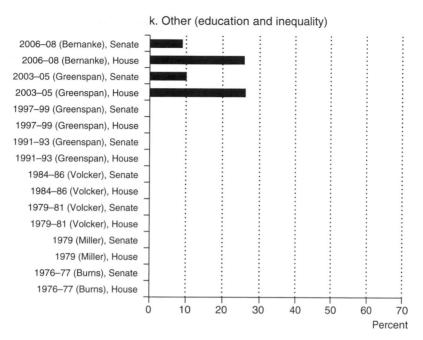

Figure 4.11
(continued)

4.4.2 Interpretation of the Results

We observe five main findings from the textual analysis.

Monetary Policy

In both figure 4.10 and table 4.5, we indicate in italics the four thematic groups that represent the "guts" of monetary policy—(1) *Inflation*, (2) *US economy and output*, (3) *Labor markets*, and (4) *Money growth* and the supply of credit. In gauging the goals and intentions of members of Congress, our first finding concerns what they apparently did *not* seek to do—that is, they did not seek to establish a prolonged discussion with the Fed chairman on the framework of monetary policy (a finding that accords with the results in the first section of this chapter). Of the 38 significant tags for these themes in figure 4.10, 21 (or 55 percent) are associated with the Fed chairman. However, the Fed chairman is never statistically significant for the labor markets theme; for this theme the Democrats clearly dominate. This is not particularly surprising, given the ideological orientation of Democrats and more generally, the sensitivity of members of Congress to jobs and employment. If we set aside this group from our definition of the "guts" of monetary policy, we find even greater dominance by the Fed chair: of the 24 significant tags, 21 belong to the Fed chair. In short, to the extent that members of Congress were engaged in discussions regarding the framework of monetary policy, their focus was almost exclusively on concerns about unemployment and labor markets, and it was Democrats more than Republicans who tended to express these concerns.

Our first conclusion is that members of Congress demonstrated very limited interest in debating the more technical details of monetary policy with successive Fed chairmen. The evidence indicates that this interest declined further over time (i.e., for the Greenspan and Bernanke periods, no party was significant for a monetary policy thematic group aside from labor markets). Thus, at least with respect to the details of monetary policy, members of Congress appear more passive than active (i.e., more willing to listen than to speak). Apart from where monetary policy might affect jobs, members of Congress appear uninterested in the details of monetary policy-making. Reasons for this passivity may well vary from member to member, but there are likely to be some commonalities. We return to this in our interviews chapter, where we ask our respondents to comment specifically on this finding.

Challenges to the Fed
Our second finding concerns the areas in which members of Congress were more likely to challenge the Fed chairman—namely the structure and governance of the arrangements for monetary policy-making, and in particular the transparency of the Fed and thus the quality of accountability to Congress. Themes seven and eight, which appear in bold in figure 4.10 and table 4.5 ("Independence of the Fed —Relations between the Fed and Congress/the administration" and "Appraising the Fed") are relevant here. The pattern of significant tags (figure 4.10) and sizes of thematic groups (table 4.5 and figures 4.11a to 4.11k) indicate a trend from (1) direct questioning of Fed independence in the Burns and Miller periods, moving to (2) more moderate questioning of the Fed's actions during the Volcker and early Greenspan years, to (3) outright praise for Greenspan and the Fed in the middle and later Greenspan years, to (4) finally, a reversion to moderate challenges to Fed operations in the initial Bernanke period.

From this evidence we glean some support for our contention that the intensity of challenge from Congress is conditional on the success of the Fed in pursuing its objective with respect to monetary policy. Figure 4.10 also indicates that in the early period the Democrats were more likely to challenge the Fed than the Republicans, again consistent with the tradition of populist criticism of the Fed. The emergence of a bipartisan consensus toward praising the Fed chairman (at least in the Senate) could of course be consistent with Barney Frank's criticism that Congress had gone soft on the Fed.

Thus the degree of challenge from Congress to the Fed does appear to be negatively related to the success of the Fed in pursuing low inflation and stable economic growth. In a period in which poor economic performance was current or within recent memory (marked by a higher rate of inflation, weaker growth and a higher level of unemployment), there appears to have been more contention between members of Congress and the Fed chairman, but this was more focused on the governance of the Fed, in terms of its transparency and accountability to Congress. This challenge came more from Democrats than Republicans (consistent with the tradition of populist criticism of the Fed). Later, as the Fed's success became more apparent, commentary by members of Congress on the Fed's performance became more positive and bipartisan.

Our first two findings (on monetary policy and challenges to the Fed) help us understand better the motivations of members of Congress in oversight hearings. With respect to the details of monetary policy, they appear content to adopt a passive stance—except where issues of jobs and unemployment may be at stake, and here Democrats have been more vocal than Republicans. However, with respect to the governance, accountability, and transparency of the Fed, members of Congress (and again, more so with Democrats) take a far more active stance in their questioning of the Fed chairman—but only in "bad" economic times, when challenging the Fed offers politicians the opportunity to shift the blame for the economy away from them and onto the shoulders of the Federal Reserve. Conversely, when the economy appears to be doing well, senators in particular are generally more likely to express their praise and gratitude to the Fed chair and/or solicit his advice on nonmonetary policy issues.

The shift in discourse is of particular relevance to this study, as it is indicative of an attitudinal change in both the way that legislators perceived their role as overseers of the Fed's monetary policy, and their motivation to use the hearings as a means to pursue other objectives. For instance, in the corpus from the 2003 to 2005 Senate hearings (table 4.4), about a third of the classified text was devoted to praise for Greenspan and efforts to obtain his advice on other matters. A characteristic phrase from this class (the second ranked ECU) is from Sen. Schumer: "... and that is why, when he comes here, we all want to ask him

*a whole lot of questions because we respect his judgment. . . . I think the way
you have handled monetary policy in the last few years has been excellent."*

Diverting Greenspan's attention to nonmonetary policy issues was
a commonly used tactic in this period. Some committee members, for
example, sought his advice on ways to finance Social Security or on
how to deal with derivatives. The latter is intriguing since it goes to
the heart of the issue of congressional oversight in the years preceding the financial crisis. In the third highest ranking ECU for this class
in the 2003 to 2005 corpus, Senator Crapo asked Chairman Greenspan
about efforts to create a new regulatory regime for derivatives. The tone
of the question is tentative and cautious, and is prefaced with a general
sentiment of gratitude (hence the classification of this ECU, which is
indicated in bold):

... we have for the last 2 years faced, on two or three occasions, efforts to
change the manner in which we regulate derivatives. Under the Commodities
Futures Modernization Act of 2000, the President's Working Group and others
recommended a structure by which we approach the management of commodities in a number of contexts, **and derivatives were handled in a particular
way under that approach. By the way, let me interject. I want to thank you,
the Secretary of the Treasury, the chairman of the Securities and Exchange
Commission,** and the chairman of the Commodities Futures Trading Commission for being so prompt in responding to our letter in inquiring about this yet
once again this year when the amendment came forward on the energy bill
once again to try to make this change in a way that we regulate derivatives.

Placing the ECU in context, Crapo then went on to note his concern
that any effort to create a new regulatory regime for derivatives would
"create some confusion with regard to the regulator," and he asked
Greenspan: "Is there a reason that we should change our approach to
the regulation of derivatives or does the Commodities Futures Modernization Act still represent a very solid approach to managing this
issue?" Greenspan replied that the 2000 Act was "excellent" and
required no change, whereby Crapo then queried, "I know you have
done this before, but could you give us your understanding of why
derivatives are helpful in our markets?" Not surprisingly, the reply
from Greenspan was a lengthy one, to which Crapo responded: "Well,
thank you very much for that extended explanation. Each time we face
this issue we pick up a little support and our strength grows, and I
think it is because we are better able to explain to the members of the
Senate the issues as you have just done. So thank you very much." And
so ended the questioning from that senator.

While Crapo's questioning did raise the issue of derivatives, its failure effectively to challenge Greenspan on the merits of derivatives regulation illustrates the deferential attitude shown to the Fed chairman in what could be construed as reasonably "good" economic times.

Inflation

Given our contention that the Fed's success in achieving low inflation shaped the nature of oversight, we should expect to see the debate on monetary policy evolve to match the evolution of thinking on the role and content of monetary policy. Specifically, we should expect to see a sharpening of the focus on inflation as the objective of monetary policy. Figure 4.10 indicates that from around the time of the Volcker Revolution in 1979 to the early 1990s, the chairman of the Fed attracts a significant tag for the inflation theme. This disappears for the mid- and late Greenspan periods (when neither Greenspan nor the committee members are statistically significant for an inflation theme) but resumes in 2006 to 2008 when Bernanke acquires significance for his discussion of inflation in both chambers. Table 4.5 and figure 4.11a show the same pattern. In the Burns hearings, we observe no class on inflation per se, which illustrates a lack of clear focus on inflation as a monetary policy objective. This is also the case for the later Greenspan periods, which similarly receive no significant tags. This begs the question, if not inflation, what *did* concern Greenspan? With respect to monetary policy in the two later Greenspan periods, we can see that the Fed chairman shifted attention to discussions on the US economy and output (figure 4.10, row 2, and figure 4.11b). From our previous chapter on the FOMC, we know that a key area of focus for Greenspan during this period was on explaining the "new economy"—that is, the persistence of low inflation during an era of relatively strong growth. Hence the focus was not on inflation per se, but rather more on explaining the causes of both the new economy and productivity, and on speculating on its persistence. It would seem that with the success of the Fed in tackling inflation, inflation itself was relegated to almost a non-issue—at least until the early Bernanke period. This last observation—namely the reappearance of inflation as an identified thematic class cannot be related to the re-emergence of inflation but may reflect Bernanke's greater disposition to targeting inflation as the explicit target of monetary policy. (The ECUs for the inflation classes in 2006 to 2008 capture an emphasis on Bernanke reporting actual and expected levels of inflation rather than the objective of an inflation target, but this should not be surprising since to advocate an inflation target to Congress would amount to requesting a change of the statutory mandate of monetary policy.)

Overall, the pattern of significance for the inflation classes indicates a period in the 1970s when inflation was clearly a problem in the United States, but it was given little attention in the congressional oversight hearings in terms of identifying solutions. The classic period of attention to inflation as a problem was during the 1980s up to the early 1990s, and this was a time when inflation did feature in the congressional discourse—but was dominated by the Fed chairman. With the waning of the threat to monetary stability from high inflation, the discourse on monetary policy, and in particular on inflation, was much reduced until its recent re-emergence in the Bernanke period. Hence we do not find a simple linear pattern to the discourse—that is, there is no linear progression toward a more focused discussion of inflation as an objective of monetary policy across the entire three decade period. What we find is a progression toward the more focused discussion of the monetary policy objective (low inflation) —but only up to a period of sustained low inflation. Once inflation appears to have been "tackled," it disappears as a significant theme for both Greenspan and the committee members, and other topics of interest rise to the forefront of the hearings' discourse. The interesting feature here is that in the early Bernanke period, inflation remained low (in the range of 2 percent), but Bernanke (and not the committee members) chose to highlight the theme nonetheless.

With respect to the discourse on monetary aggregates, the picture is quite clear. Figure 4.10 (row 4), table 4.5 and figure 4.11d all indicate a decline over time in the presence of a significant tag for the money growth/money aggregates theme. This supports the view that the debate on monetary policy became focused on the final objective of achieving and maintaining low inflation rather than the intermediate objective of money growth. This may not seem like a very radical conclusion, but it indicates that congressional hearings developed in line with the consensus of thinking on monetary policy.

While the empirical results paint a clear picture of shift in discourse on inflation in the congressional banking committees, they are less clear in showing the actual *deliberation* (or lack thereof) in the form of words used within the hearings. For this, we turn to the representative phrases (or ECUs) for the thematic classes, and then put these in context of the exchanges that took place between legislators and the Fed chairman. What we find in comparing the early Volcker years (1979 to 1981) with those of Greenspan nearly two decades later (1997 to 1999) is a striking difference in the use of persuasion by the Fed chairman. In the wake of the Volcker Revolution of 1979, Volcker was besieged by committee members for the high and volatile interest rates of that period, and he in turn persistently sought to persuade them of the need to remain firmly committed to reigning in inflation. Failure to do so would only exacerbate the problems to which they alluded. For instance, from the 1979 to 1981 House hearings, we obtain the class *Inflation Problems*, which constitutes 12 percent of the classified ECUs (table 4.3). The highest ranked ECU from this class comes from an exchange between Volcker and Congressman Jim Mattox (D). We indicate the ECU in bold, and present its context both preceding and following the ECU by Volcker:

Mattox: Mr. Volcker, . . . if I were to be classed, I would probably be classed as a hostile questioner; and I say that without much hesitation, in a polite sense. You see, I don't agree with many of your actions. I don't agree with many of the actions that the Federal Reserve is carrying out, and I think we have a chicken-and-egg type process taking place. The Federal Reserve, somehow, doesn't seem to understand that these really high interest rates are actually causing inflation. . . . Frankly, if I were your boss, I would fire you. I would try to start over. I am not sure I would do any better, but you know, when things are as bad as in this economy today, I would try to make some changes. I am just being very honest about it. . . .

Volcker: I would like to convince you, if I could, that firing me and firing the Federal Reserve Board isn't going to eliminate the real problems that we have, and you wouldn't get any better result. **But be that as it may, I think we are very aware of the kinds of problems that you suggest. I think there are elements of the chicken and the egg in this situation as you describe it.** I don't think high interest rates cause the inflation. I think they actually get into the price indexes. Let me put it to you this way. I don't know how to get interest rates down, quite literally, without dealing with inflation and the fiscal situation. I don't know what other tools we have, because if we simply try to get them down by increasing the supply of money and credit, then the result, I believe, will be more inflation and not less. All the forces in an inflationary economy that produce high interest rates will be acting full speed. I am sure as I am sitting here, that if we exploded the money supply, in a very short period of time you would be facing higher interest rates rather than lower. The real enemy in that sense, of the homebuilder in particular, who is producing a long-range asset that is financed over a long period of time and is heavily dependent upon interest rates, is inflation. I think many homebuilders understand that.

A second example of Volcker's efforts to persuade members of Congress of the importance of prioritizing inflation as the root of the problem is from the same class in the 1979 to 1981 House hearings, and is from an exchange with Congressman Gladys Spellman (D) (the fourth ranked ECU for this class):

Spellman: Mr. Volcker, since your program apparently means little relief, if any, on interest rates this year, and since the lack of affordable housing is becoming a very serious problem. . . . What would you suggest to head off a worse crisis in housing?

Volcker: **I am going to give you an answer that I think goes to the fundamentals of this, Mrs. Spellman. Housing is going to be in a difficult situation unless we can come to grips with this inflationary problem.** That has been the lesson of history: Housing does well in stable economic conditions; . . . I think we are all deluding ourselves if we think that that industry is going to be healthy and prosperous in a context of continued or accelerating inflation. I think the fundamental point we have to keep in front of us is that the housing industry is the sufferer; they are the point men, so to speak, when we get into this kind of a problem we have now.

Volcker's persuasive efforts were similarly directed toward senators. In the Senate hearings in 1980–81 is a class that comprises 26 percent of the classified ECUs and for which Volcker alone is significant. We label this *Volcker Revolution /anti-inflation policies* and the following representative sentences, or ECUs, (ranked fourth and fifth, respectively) further illustrate his efforts to impress upon legislators the importance of dealing with inflation, and particularly in getting people to expect low inflation (and thereby adjust their actions accordingly):

Volcker: There are risks in the present situation, without question, in terms of the pressures on the money markets. A much greater risk, in my mind, **would be in failing to carry through on the effective anti-inflationary policies because we would just be prolonging this agony and see inflation recur again and again over the years ahead with a decreasingly satisfactory economic performance.** I would urge us to face up to the problem now, as I think we are doing, and to carry through on that effort.

Volcker: **These policies can and will be effective. But if they are to work, they must be sustained with conviction. Then, the apparent reluctance of many to bet on reduced inflation—in financial markets, in wage bargaining, in pricing, and in other economic decisions—will change.** As they do, the unwinding of the inflationary process should be much easier.

During these early Volcker years the dialogue between committee members and the Fed chair was often direct, blunt and sometimes heated. The contrast between that period and the late 1990s could hardly be more striking. The tone of the hearings in 1997 to1999 was set by Greenspan, for which the following overview of the economy was typical (and is from his opening statement in the July 1997 House hearing, rather than derived from a particular thematic class):

Greenspan: The recent performance of the economy, characterized by strong growth and low inflation, has been exceptional—and better than most anticipated. During the first quarter of 1997, real gross domestic product expanded at nearly a 6 percent annual rate, after posting a 3 percent increase over 1996. Activity apparently continued to expand in the second quarter, albeit at a more moderate pace. The economy is now in the seventh consecutive year of expansion, making it the third longest post–World War cyclical upswing to date. Moreover our Federal Reserve Banks indicate that economic activity is on the rise, and at a relatively high level, in virtually every geographic region and community of the nation. The expansion has been balanced, in that inventories, as well as stocks of business capital and other durable assets, have been kept closely in line with spending, so overhangs have been small and readily conceded. This strong expansion has produced a remarkable increase in work opportunities for Americans. A net of more than 13 million jobs has been created since the current period of growth began in the spring of 1991. As a consequence the unemployment rate has fallen to 5 percent—its lowest level in almost a quarter century.

Such remarks on the robust health of the US economy were understandably welcome news to committee members, but all this good news had two conspicuous effects on the discourse. First, it left legislators with little to criticize or challenge. Second, in view of this, it afforded them the opportunity to re-direct Greenspan toward other topics. In the House hearings of 1997 to 1999, we find a large class (42 percent of the classified ECUs) that we label *role of government in the economy (domestic and international)* (table 4.4). Both political parties are statistically significant for this class (figure 4.10, row 8a, and figure 4.11h). For this class, the ECUs show Greenspan replying to members' concerns about relations between the US Treasury and the IMF, with an aerospace merger between Boeing and McDonnell Douglas, and financial modernization. Hence, once inflation appears to have been tackled, there is no dialogue between congressmen and the Fed chair about monetary policy, but rather a diffuse dialogue on other subjects—all of which begs the question as to what members sought to do in the monetary policy oversight hearings. In the Senate hearings of 1997 to 1999, about one-third of the classified ECUs were given to a class that we label *praising Greenspan and seeking his advice* (table 4.4, table 4.5) and for this class, both parties are again statistically significant (figure 4.10, row 8b). The following ECU (ranked third), is by Senator Alfonse D'Amato (R) in July 1997 and is representative of this class. (We again indicate the ECU in bold, and provide the surrounding context.)

D'Amato: Mr. Greenspan, as many have noted on countless occasions, the Federal Reserve has done a remarkable job under your tenure. Our economic expansion is in its 7th year, making it the third longest in the post–World War II period. . . . With the economic boom continuing, I believe now is a good time for us to look more carefully at those areas and those people who may have been left behind. I am increasingly concerned about local communities who face economic disruptions because of businesses or Government facilities closing shop. Also, as you will note in your remarks, workers continue to worry about their job security despite one of the lowest unemployment rates since the 1970s. I would appreciate your insights as to whether this means enough is being done to educate our workers to use new technologies. Finally, I am also concerned about whether some consumers may have too easy access to credit and are being taken advantage of by financial institutions. . . . Mr. Greenspan, under your stewardship, I believe that you have brought equanimity to the marketplace, as it relates to the policies and the programs that you have implemented. There have been those who over the years have been rather critical and have been ready to assail you and the Federal Reserve's policy whenever they disagreed with respect to interest rates thinking that that was the panacea for everything. **You have had a steady hand at the tiller, you have navigated some very difficult seas and we are deeply appreciative. And I think all of my colleagues share that opinion of your continued leadership.**

The form of questioning by D'Amato is typical—gentle nudging of Greenspan on issues of concern (e.g., educating workers in new technologies, easy credit access by financial institutions)—but amid a general tone of praise and deference. Once again, the brief attention given to "easy credit" may be seen (in hindsight) as something of a challenge to the Fed on practices that contributed to the financial crisis, but the limited focus and overall light touch of committee members meant that such "challenges" were of little effect—and certainly not weighty enough to merit an actual thematic class in our textual analysis.

Fiscal Policy and Monetary Policy

Our fourth finding concerns the coverage of fiscal policy in the oversight hearings. Of the fourteen significant tags for this thematic class, seven belong to Democrats, six to Republicans and just one to the Fed chairman. Clearly, members of Congress were more attentive to fiscal policy concerns in oversight hearings than were Fed chairmen. From figure 4.10 we see that during the Volcker and early Greenspan periods, both parties tended to discuss fiscal policy concerns in the oversight hearings, regardless of the party of the president. In the late 1990s and early 2000s, however, the party in opposition to the president's party tended to dominate the fiscal policy discussions (particularly during 2003 to 2005, when the Democrats were also the minority party in

Congress). These discussions during the later period constituted swipes at President G. W. Bush's economic policies, employing the credibility of Greenspan and the Fed to gain leverage (e.g., "Don't you think, Mr Greenspan, that the budgetary implications of this spending plan . . ."). The following is illustrative of this partisan strategy. (The ECU, in bold, is ranked second in the fiscal policy class in the Senate hearings of 2003 to 2005, where the class size is 22 percent of the classified ECUs):

Senator (Tom) Carper (D): There is a recurring theme, . . . particularly from our side of the aisle, and I just want to pick up where Senator Bayh has left off. **When we run a deficit in Federal operations in our budget, we have the ability to borrow from trust funds, and we borrow from the Social Security Trust Fund, we borrow from Medicare trust funds and other trust funds that exist.** I think we have pretty well exhausted all of those. When that is not enough, we look around the country to see if there are investors in the United States who are willing to loan the Federal Government some money and buy our securities, and there are plenty of people and institutions who are willing to do that. When we have pretty well brought in those dollars from potential investors with the interest rates they can yield, then we turn around and look around the world to see who outside of our borders will lend this money. . . . And so far, so good. My fear—and I think you touched on it right at the end—is that we reach a point, almost like on a seesaw, where you start going in the other direction, and potential investors, whether they are banks or individuals around the world, look at the United States, and they look at our securities, and they look at our inability to balance our Federal deficit or to even come close to managing our fiscal matters in a responsible way.

Democratic senators like Carper thus sought to draw Greenspan into a partisan debate about fiscal management, particularly on Social Security. During a period of increased ideological polarization (Poole and Rosenthal 1997; Fiorina, Abrams, et al. 2005) one might expect oversight hearings to offer an opportunity for members of Congress to gain political traction in areas of fiscal policy where credit-claiming (and blaming) is easier to link to policy outcomes than with monetary policy. With continuing ideological polarization during the 2006 to 2008 period (McCarty, Poole, et al. 2006), the absence of party tags for fiscal policy seems puzzling. However, this may be in part the product of a new focus on the world economy[9] by Democrats (figure 4.10, row 9), but more strikingly, the emergence of new issues that concerned both Democrats and Republicans (figures 4.10, row 10, and 4.11k)—particularly education, raising skills in the workforce (thereby lessening wage inequality) and energy. Indeed figure 4.11k shows a broader growth in the importance of these new issues in both the later Greenspan and early Bernanke periods, as they captured a little over a quarter of the classified discourse in the oversight discussions in the House and about ten percent in the Senate.

The results therefore indicate that fiscal policy was always an issue on which members of Congress sought to engage the Fed chairman during the monetary policy oversight hearings. There may be more than one possible explanation for this interest. First, the post–World War II consensus on economic policy gave a larger position to fiscal policy over monetary policy as the tool of stabilization, but this eroded with the inflation problem of the 1970s and a realization that the room for maneuver in adjusting fiscal policy-settings was too limited. A second possible explanation for the interest in fiscal policy is that this is an area where by *taking positions,* members of Congress can attract more direct electoral benefit from their constituents (in contrast, monetary policy does not have such visible distributional benefits and hence electoral advantage).

These two explanations would suggest more debate (and greater tension) around the mix between monetary and fiscal policy in the early part of the period than later. Our results indicate that before the 1990s the discourse in congressional hearings was more focused around the combination of fiscal and monetary measures—the policy mix. A good example[10] of this is from the fiscal policy class from the House hearings, 1979 to 1981, where the class size is 11 percent of the classified ECUs (table 4.3):

Delegate (Walter) Fauntroy (D):[11]   In preparation for assuming the role of chairman for the Domestic Monetary Policy Subcommittee, I quite frankly became convinced of the wisdom that you have been giving us for several years; namely that in order to really regulate inflation you need, not only to regulate monetary policy, but cooperation from the Congress and the president in fiscal restraint that balances the budget and that reduces deficit spending. Therefore, as a function of my role as chairman of the Congressional Black Caucus I was able to convince my colleagues in fashioning a constructive alternative to the Reagan administration's proposals to come in with a proposal that was balanced indeed, gave 7 billion dollars in surplus. A budget that eliminated altogether deficit spending in an effort to cooperate. What puzzles me, as puzzles the Chair of our JEC, is that as an independent agency, while you have praised the action thus far by the Congress and the president, in spending, **you have not exercised the authority of the independence that you have in judging administration and congressional actions that are pending that will substantially increase the deficit over the long run**. Why can't we have that independent voice raised as a caution to a policy that is going to substantially increase military spending and at the same time reduce the revenues available to the country?

By the late 1990s, the discourse on fiscal policy had changed. In the wake of a sustained period of successful monetary policy, members of Congress recognized that the reputation and credibility of the Fed chairman could be used to further their personal/party position on fiscal policy. Hence they sought Greenspan's explicit or implicit support on fiscal policy issues with increasing regularity. With stable low inflation more embedded, and monetary policy more accepted as the primary tool for short-term macroeconomic stabilization, the discourse on fiscal policy shifted from a focus on the policy mix to an emphasis on more "micro" fiscal policy issues. This could take two forms: first, members of Congress seeking to enlist the Fed chairman (and thus his credibility derived from success in monetary policy) to support or attack the fiscal policy of the administration of the day;[12] and second, debating individual fiscal measures, and particularly large ones like Social Security, enhancing the skills of the labor force, education, and energy. The rise of issues like education and energy are seen in our "other" category (group 10) in figures 4.10 and 4.11k. With respect to committee members shifting their attention to such "micro" fiscal issues as investment-oriented tax policy and Social Security, the following two ECUs (each ranked second) from the House and Senate hearings in 1997 to 1999 are indicative:

Congresswoman (Marge) Roukema (R):   I expect that you will give some advice to Congress on maintaining (1) fiscal restraint; (2) genuine deficit reduction; and (3) investment-oriented tax policy. . . . I would respectfully request if you would give some time in your statement to advice that you might give the Congress with respect to our responsibility here in terms of maintaining the fiscal restraint, **how we balance that fiscal restraint with what is genuine deficit reduction, not only short term, but longer term. Particularly, I would appreciate any comments you would want to make about an investment oriented tax policy.** I think all three of these issues are extremely relevant to the work that you are doing and to our overall question as to, not only employment rates, but the rate of inflation in the economy.

Senator (Rod) Grams (R):   What if Congress, instead of trying to move to more of a personalized retirement account, would decide to look at the old system and tinker around the edges and maybe raise payroll taxes to fix the Social Security problem instead of pursuing reform? **Would these taxes absolve the problems of Social Security in the long run? How would that tax again affect national savings and investment interest rates, et cetera?**

The common feature throughout the period under review is that fiscal policy issues were always present in some form or other. But we conclude that there was a change in the focus of the debate on fiscal policy. Up to the later 1990s, there was more debate around the policy mix (i.e., the combination of monetary and fiscal policy measures), and thereby more discussion by both parties on this issue. By the late 1990s, with low inflation and stable economic growth more established, and with monetary policy accepted as the tool for short-term stabilization, there was a change in the focus on fiscal policy toward what might be described as "micro" issues. Members of Congress were also more inclined to seek to use the Fed's reputation for success in monetary policy to support or attack the administration's fiscal policy.

Banking Regulation and Financial Stability

Turning our attention to discussions on financial stability and the banking system, it is important to recall our caveat from chapter 1—namely that the monetary policy oversight hearings are not the only occasions during which members of the congressional banking committees discuss issues of concern with Fed officials. Both banking committees held (and continue to hold) other hearings that may be directed toward matters of banking regulation and financial stability. These hearings may be held at the request of a committee member or events of the day may give rise to them. However, while the Humphrey–Hawkins legislation required a semi-annual report on monetary policy and appearances by the Fed chairman, as our results indicate when issues within the Fed's remit beyond monetary policy (notably the stability of the financial system and banking regulation) were prominent at the time these would be covered in the questioning at the Humphrey–Hawkins hearings.

While table 4.5 and figure 4.11e show that a reasonably consistent portion of the discussions was devoted to financial stability, figure 4.10 indicates that it was the Fed chairman who appeared to dominate these discussions. The overall picture here is more complicated and must be unpacked by referring to tables 4.A3 through 4.A10 in our chapter appendix. In the 1970s and early 1980s only the House hearings featured financial stability as a thematic class. In the 1976 to 1977 period, Burns dominated the discussions, whereas during the early Volcker years (1979 to 1981), a mixture of Democrats and Republicans, *individually*, obtained statistical significance for this class (neither party tag obtained significance, thereby indicating more variance within the parties). During the mid-1980s (table 4.A6) we see in the Senate committee Volcker dominating the discussion on the banking system, but individual senators (both Democratic and Republican) obtaining significance for the theme of bank *failures* (i.e., Continental Illinois). Similarly in the House hearings, we find a mixture of members—again, individually rather than as party groups—obtaining significance. From these findings it appears that to the extent that financial stability and regulation were topics on which committee members sought to engage the Fed chairman, they did so as individual members rather than in a conspicuous partisan fashion.

In light of the recent financial crisis of 2007 to 2009, discussions on financial stability in the three Greenspan periods are particularly intriguing. In the early Greenspan period (1991 to 1993), Greenspan alone dominated discussion of financial stability in the Senate by speaking to the overall health of the banking system, but no equivalent theme appears for the House. In the mid-Greenspan period (1997 to 1999), we again see no theme of this nature in the House hearings, but in the Senate 15 percent of the discussion was devoted to the banking system and regulation (table 4.4), with Greenspan obtaining only weak statistical significance and Senators Reed and D'Amato (the latter committee chairman) obtaining relatively more significance as individuals. In the late Greenspan period (2003 to 2005), only the House hearings reveal a class on financial stability—namely the concern for bank regulation and attempts to punish foreign banks (e.g., UBS and Crédit Lyonnais) for alleged violations of banking laws. For this class, the Republican tag obtains significance—in part, the result of discussions led by Representative Kelly (committee vice chairman), who queried Greenspan on issues such as anti–money laundering legislation (e.g., Title III of the Patriot Act).

What might we glean from these findings with respect to the attention given by members of Congress to the banking system and financial stability in the lead-up to the crisis? The simple—albeit cautious—response is that judged by the content of the Humphrey–Hawkins hearings, neither party sought seriously to challenge the Fed on financial stability and banking regulation during the 1990s. In the early 1990s, with Democrats as the majority party in Congress, members appeared content to defer these issues to Greenspan and in the late 1990s, with Republicans as the majority party, the engagement with Greenspan tended to focus more on financial modernization but was nonetheless less than robust.

Some examples of the ECUs help to illustrate this general attitude of deference to Greenspan on banking issues. The first ECU (ranked first, from the 1991 to 1993 Senate hearings) is from an exchange between Senator (Terry) Sanford (D) and Greenspan:

Sanford: As a general proposition, do you believe we need more capital in the banking system?

Greenspan: **An adequate capital cushion is critical to maintaining the safety and soundness of individual banks and protecting the deposit insurance fund from excessive losses. A significant commitment of capital from owner-shareholders also ensures that these individuals will have strong incentives to oversee and control the risk-taking activities of bank managers.** The Federal Reserve is in the process of phasing-in risk-based capital standards and, in fact, the overwhelming majority of United States banking organizations already meet the end of 1992 minimum ratios. We believe that in the long-run banking organizations should maintain capital ratios well above these minimum standards and that, in particular, the authorization of new powers should be limited to strong, highly capitalized banking institutions. We recognize at the present time that the earnings and asset quality problems facing some of our banking organizations will complicate their ability to raise capital. Thus it seems reasonable that for some institutions increasing capital ratios will require a transition period and reasonable phase-in arrangements before higher levels of capital can be attained. During the phase-in period, organizations with capital deficiencies or asset quality problems will be monitored closely to assure that they do not embark on aggressive expansion activities or engage in other imprudent activities. Whether higher capital ratios will lead to an increase in the dollar volume of capital in the industry is a difficult question. In some situations, mergers and acquisitions involving highly capitalized banks, as well as other types of balance sheet restructurings, will produce institutions with higher capital ratios without bringing more capital into the industry as a whole. In other cases, raising capital ratios will bring additional capital into the industry. The net effect will depend on the future size and structure of the United States banking system. In any event, our principal objective is to ensure that individual institutions have sufficient capital in relation to their risk assets in order to promote the safety of the United States banking system and to protect the interests of United States taxpayers.

Sanford followed up the question with another:

Sanford: You have talked about the credit crunch and the reluctance of banks to continue lending. A number of items are being discussed to encourage additional lending focus on accounting changes or in the lowering of interest rates. Do you believe these items are sufficient to encourage banks to begin lending again? If not, what else should we be doing?

Greenspan answered with another extended response, to which Sanford offered no further comment or challenge. The impression is that members such as Sanford were content to receive Greenspan's answers as given, with no engagement in dialogue or exchange.

By the late 1990s, discussion had shifted more to issues of financial modernization and in some cases reflected more engagement with Greenspan, as the following exchange from the 1997 to 1999 Senate hearings (highest ranking ECU) illustrates:

(Paul) Sarbanes (D):   Merchant Banking HR 10, as reported out of the Senate Banking Committee last year, authorized merchant banking as one of the new powers permitted. However, HR 10 specifically provided that ownership interests in companies pursuant to the merchant banking authority could be held "only for such period of time as will permit the sale or disposition thereof on a reasonable basis," and that during the period such ownership interests are held "the bank holding company does not actively participate in the day-to-day management or operation of such company or entity.". . . It appears that eliminating [some] restrictions would permit a bank holding company to own an unlimited number of commercial companies of any size for any period of time and manage them on a day-to-day basis. Is this correct? What implications does this have for breaking down the separation of banking and commerce?

Greenspan: Merchant banking, in its simplest terms, involves making temporary investments in the equity or debt securities of a company for the purpose of achieving a profit on the eventual sale or disposition of the investment. These investments may involve the acquisition of a controlling interest in, or even 100 percent of the equity of, a company. Merchant banking is a volatile activity and, unless constrained, could lead to a significant breach in the walls separating banking and commerce. . . . The Board believes merchant banking activities should be permitted through the holding company structure, which provides a more effective shield against the dangers of mixing banking and commerce. **In addition the holding company structure best protects insured depository institutions and the Federal safety net from the volatility of merchant banking activities, prevents the spread of the Federal safety net, and its related subsidy,** to companies engaged in these newly authorized activities, and ensures a fair and level competitive playing field for all entities engaged in merchant banking activities. The bill passed by the Senate Banking Committee in 1998 placed certain limits on the merchant banking activities of the bank holding companies to mitigate the potential that these activities would allow the blending of banking and commerce. . . . The bill passed earlier this month by the Senate Banking Committee, however, did not contain similar restrictions on the merchant banking activities of the banking organizations. We presume that this change was made to permit the banking agencies added flexibility in defining the time periods and permissible management relationships for various types of merchant banking investments. We believe that language to carry out this intent should be included in the legislation.

By the late Greenspan period (2003 to 2005), the Republicans took the lead in discussing bank regulation, but only in the House; no equivalent theme emerges in the Senate. Of course, by 2006 to 2008 (table 4.A10), as we enter the early stages of the financial crisis, more attention is given to banking issues by Bernanke and individual members of Congress (mostly Democrats). In sum, our conclusion here is that members of Congress *of both parties* failed to probe very deeply or consistently the issue of financial stability in the years leading up to the crisis. Where questions were asked of Greenspan, generally the answers were lengthy and the questioner usually accepted the response with no further dialogue or follow-up.

4.5   Assessment of Hypotheses

In chapter 2 we set out three expectations of our findings from our textual analysis of the monetary policy oversight hearings. We pause at this point to assess the evidence thus far in respect of these hypotheses.

Drawing on the work of Steiner et al., and Mucciaroni and Quirk (Steiner, Bächtiger, et al. 2004; Mucciaroni and Quirk 2006), we expected to find the reasoning skills and judgments of senatorial banking committee members to outweigh those of their House colleagues (hypothesis 5). Whereas both sets of authors employ empirical methods for assessing "good" and "poor" styles of legislative debate (levels of participation, informative value, respect for other participants, etc.), our approach is quite different. Our methodology aims to capture more the *content and substance* of the discourse rather than the style or mode by which it was expressed. Hence our assessment of the reasoning skills and judgments of banking committee members is concerned with their ability to engage with the Fed chairman on the substance and merits of monetary policy. Ultimately we would like to gauge the extent to which committee members understood (1) the underlying objectives of monetary policy, (2) the ways in which the Fed could be judged to be meeting these objectives, and (3) the implications of the Fed's conduct of monetary policy for other critical issues areas—like the labor market and wider economy. And, to the extent that members can be seen to be exhibiting this understanding, were there differences between senators and congressmen?

Our first observation is that *neither* set of committee members sought to engage with the Fed chairman on the particulars (the guts) of monetary policy. From our composite results in part one, we saw a clear cleavage between the areas of focus of the Fed chairman and members of either the House or Senate banking committee. In this sense, there was no real difference between the House and Senate committees. We did, however, find that senators were more likely to question the Fed chairman on institutional issues (e.g., appointments to the Fed and intergovernmental relations between Congress, the administration and the Fed) and on issues relating to foreign economic policy, like US competitiveness in the world economy. In the aggregate, moreover, fiscal policy received more attention in the House hearings relative to the Senate hearings (with the exceptional year of 2005, when spending on the Iraq war captured the attention of the Senate committee). In the later Greenspan years we found another intriguing difference between the two committees: senators were more inclined to offer explicit praise for the Fed chairman and then seek to use Greenspan's and the Fed's reputation in their pursuit of their other policy objectives. While these differences of substance are noteworthy, the key point here is that with respect to monetary policy per se, committee members of both chambers were about equally willing to leave the details to the Fed chairman. This finding appears to be quite robust (with one exception, which we address below) and is one that we take up further in our interviews, in our next chapter.

We also draw upon work of Steiner et al. and Mucciaroni and Quirk for our sixth hypothesis, where we expected to find members engaging in point-scoring on popular and high-profile issues, and in addition we expected them to engage with the Fed chairman on the details of monetary policy. The second part of this hypothesis was not borne out by our findings (as just discussed), but with one important exception that pertains to both hypotheses 5 and 6. That is, we find that committee members—and particularly Democratic members—*did* tend to focus on the implication of monetary policy for labor markets. In this respect, committee members were able to hone in on one aspect of monetary policy for which they could score points with their constituents: jobs and employment. The Fed chairman is never statistically significant for the labor markets theme; rather, it is the Democratic members who dominate this theme.

We do find ample evidence for the first part of hypothesis 6, namely that committee members engaged in scoring points with their questions and statements, perhaps with the intention of, in Mayhew's words, *taking stands*. Such discourse would characterize the hearings more as public arenas—somewhat akin to debates on the chamber floor. Aside from the conspicuous cases of Bernie Sanders and Don Riegle, other examples of high profiles of individual members can be found in tables 4.A3 through 4.A10, where one or a few members dominate a particular thematic class. For example, in table 4.A3, we observe a very high (over 100) chi-squared value for Chairman Reuss in discussions of monetary aggregates, which indicates that he tended to dominate this discussion during the 1976 to 1977 House hearings. Across the 85 classes listed for all the time periods (tables 4.A3 to

4.A10), we find ten cases in which an individual member receives a very high (over 100) chi-squared value, with four of these belonging to the committee chairman. Beyond the very high chi-squared values, many members obtain statistical significance of at least 1 percent. In sum, we can conclude that a tendency exists for committee members to speak to particular themes, and by so doing, perhaps *take stands* on these issues for the folks back home. (In part three of this chapter, we investigate these anomalous cases in further detail.)

Viewed from a constituency interest perspective, Chairman Reuss's focus on monetary aggregates is an unusual issue on which to take a stand, but it most probably reflects his interpretation of his role as committee chairman (i.e., as a remit to provide more challenge to the Fed chairman on issues of monetary policy than came from other committee members). The more common areas for which committee members sought to score points with their constituents were institutional challenges to the independence of the Fed (in the era of high inflation) or acquiring advice/recommendations from Greenspan on politically sensitive topics like Social Security reform, education, income inequality, and energy (in the era of low inflation). Hence in bad economic times the tendency is to score points by shifting blame to the Fed, while in good economic times, legislators seek not only to praise the Fed chairman but also to seek his support for specific (nonmonetary) policy stances. For the most part the tendency is for them to focus on areas of greater familiarity and greater potential for electoral gain—namely fiscal policy and populist antipathy toward the Fed. Based on these findings, we conclude that for members of Congress, oversight hearings on monetary policy provide a more public arena for taking stands for electoral gain.

Our final hypothesis (hypothesis 7) for the congressional oversight hearings anticipated some evidence of greater acceptance of the low inflation consensus among committee members—a consensus that should be bipartisan (and more broadly, non-ideological). This consensus should thus buck the many-decades trend toward increasingly ideological polarization among members of Congress. The inherent difficulties in gauging the evidence for this hypothesis are (1) finding tangible evidence of persuasion among legislators and (2) linking these changed views to the arguments and actions of the Federal Reserve. Our findings in this regard are piecemeal, but they are supportive.

In a broad sense, we find negative rather than positive evidence for the persuasive effects of the low inflation consensus—that is, neither the committee members nor Greenspan bothered to talk about inflation after the early 1990s, as seen most clearly in figure 4.11a. Instead, Greenspan preferred to discuss the real economy and productivity growth (as he did in the FOMC meetings). While Greenspan focused on these issues, committee members sought other topics on which to engage the Fed chairman—topics that were more politically rewarding and on which they could be seen to be taking stands or scoring political points with their constituents.

What about evidence of legislators actually being *persuaded* of the importance of committing to low inflation as the objective of monetary policy (and the corollary independence of the central bank to pursue this objective)? Here we have strong evidence of active, persistent and extensively *reasoned arguments* on the part of Chairman Volcker. Both from the perspective of three decades of hearings, and in our closer look at the actual arguments made by Volcker (particularly the new emphasis on public attitudes and expectations, and the idea that low inflation is the necessary condition for stable economic growth) we find a clear campaign by the Volcker Fed to *persuade* members of Congress of the importance of delivering on low inflation. His language to Congress (as compared to his predecessors) changed the nature of the discourse in the oversight hearings and allowed the Fed to withstand the political heat resulting from high and volatile interest rates. If the evidence of persuasion is clear, what about those who were meant to be persuaded? How did they respond? For them, the evidence is that inflation—as a topic—became a non-issue during much of the Greenspan period. In this sense, our finding is of what they did *not* discuss, rather than what they did. With Bernanke, this changed, as we have noted. The reason for its re-emergence in the early Bernanke period is not because inflation itself had become problematic, nor because committee members suddenly changed their minds about the low inflation consensus. Rather, during the 2006 to 2008 hearings, it was Bernanke himself who chose to focus on the topic of inflation, which we surmise may reflect his greater disposition to targeting inflation, as the explicit target of monetary policy.

Ideally we would like to have a control case (or theme) that was not subject to a parallel form of argued reasoning, by which our findings on inflation and monetary policy discourse might be compared. We have something of a natural control in the form of the discourse on fiscal policy. On fiscal policy there is no consensus equivalent to that on monetary policy, and as a consequence we find that (1) in all but one case, only committee members (and not the Fed chairman) are

statistically significant; (2) the theme itself is fairly consistently discussed across the whole of the time period (i.e., we see no period in
which it becomes a non-issue); and (3) members of both political parties
quite frequently resort to drawing the Fed chairman into talking about
fiscal policy as a way to score political points. By comparison, (1) the
Fed chairman dominates the discussion on the core monetary policy
topics (excepting labor markets); (2) discourse on the theme of inflation
fell away, as one would expect as the low inflation consensus (and price
stability itself) became embedded; and (3) to the extent that committee
members could score political points on monetary policy, it was only
with respect to jobs—otherwise, they sought to divert the attention of
the Fed chairman to other (micro) fiscal policy objectives.

**PART THREE—DO CONSTITUENCY CHARACTERISTICS
INFLUENCE THE DISCOURSE OF BANKING COMMITTEE
MEMBERS?**

4.6   Introduction

The first two parts of this chapter have employed textual analysis software to (1) capture the broader overview of the discourse in the House
and Senate banking committees as they conduct oversight of the Federal
Reserve's monetary policy and (2) examine in closer detail the motivations of members of Congress as they conduct this oversight. In part
one, we examined 61 hearings over a 33-year period (1976 to 2008) in
two composite corpora, one for the House and one for the Senate. In
part two, we divided these 61 hearings into 16 distinct corpora—eight
each for the House and Senate. Together, parts one and two provide
extensive empirical evidence on (1) the themes that do (and do not)
interest members of Congress when they question the Fed chairman,
(2) how these themes have evolved over three decades, and (3) differences in foci between both the Fed chairman and members of Congress,
and between Democrats and Republicans. We have not, as yet, directly
addressed the possibility that variations in the tendencies for committee members to focus on particular topics or themes may be partly the
product of characteristics of their constituencies. Here we explore this
possibility by merging key statistics from our textual analysis with
quantitative data in order to conduct exploratory analysis.

   Throughout this chapter we have sought to understand better how
legislators think about and discuss monetary policy in congressional

committees, and at the same time, to link these considerations to their underlying motivations as elected officials. From our overview of the goals of members of Congress in chapter 2, we believe that electoral considerations are foremost in their minds. Mayhew's "electoral connection" thesis (Mayhew 1974) has shaped many decades of literature on Congress, giving rise to demand-side models of congressional organization, procedures and policy (Shepsle and Weingast 1995; Adler and Lapinski 1997; Adler 2000, 2002). The basic premise of these models is that members of Congress are re-election maximizers, and as such, they seek legislative committee assignments that are most likely to secure benefits for their districts. More broadly, the committee system in Congress allows members to engage in distributive policy-making by conferring more control over those policies of particular relevance to representatives from certain types of constituencies, in exchange for less control over policies with little or no relevance to these constituencies. With this overall division of labor, legislators then engage in logrolling behavior—namely the exchange of favors through reciprocal voting in order to acquire a majority for legislation. In a committee system, instead of trading votes, legislators exchange rights of influence over policy jurisdictions (Weingast and Marshall 1988).

The composition of membership on any given committee is thus said to reflect the constituency characteristics of representatives who expect to gain from benefits over which that committee has jurisdiction. Predictably, then, members of the House and Senate banking committees should represent districts that might have the most to gain from policies over which these committees have influence. On the one hand, we have noted that oversight of monetary policy confers no direct electoral benefit to committee members, and so it is unclear the extent to which constituency characteristics play any role in either the membership of these committees or the tendencies of members to focus on particular topics within monetary policy hearings. Yet, on the other hand, congressional hearings that purport to discuss the Fed's actions on monetary policy are not confined solely to the topic of monetary policy—many other related (and unrelated) topics are discussed (Social Security, education, energy, etc.). Hence it is plausible that these topics outside monetary policy do indeed reflect the particular concerns of the constituencies that committee members represent.

From a broader interests-based perspective, some authors have attempted to apply a pressure group policy perspective to show how the preferences of legislators affect Fed policy-making (Woolley 1984;

Kettl 1986; Morris 2000: 23; Romer and Romer 2003: 9, 14; Chang 2003). Havrilesky summarizes its underlying logic:

Politicians who find it difficult to make their redistributive programs palatable may subsequently attempt to mask the adverse consequences by influencing monetary policy. Variations in government expenditures and taxation invariably affect interest and exchange rates. Disincentives for productive effort that arise from government tax and transfer programs may also have adverse effects on growth and unemployment rates. When interest groups affected by these adverse consequences of redistributive policy generate sufficient flak, there is pressure on the Federal Reserve to "do something." Pressure can flow either directly, from interest groups, or indirectly, from interest groups through politicians. (Havrilesky 1993: 13–14)

And, in a variant of the pressure group approach, Stratmann finds some evidence to suggest that campaign contributions affected the roll call voting behavior of legislators on financial services regulation in 1991 and 1998, but more so for junior legislators than for senior ones (Stratmann 2002). Taken together, this research suggests that members of the congressional banking committees may well deliberate on the basis of constituency interests—that is, what they say may be a product of who they represent. We explore this possibility.

Below we first describe our data and discuss its representativeness (section 4.7), and then move on to our statistical analysis (section 4.8). We summarize our key findings in our conclusion.

4.7   Data

To test the possible link between constituency characteristics of committee members and their particular thematic foci in monetary policy committee hearings, we use E. Scott Adler's constituency data on demand-side measures for committee types (Adler 2002, 2011).[13] Adler contends that certain congressional committees are "constituency oriented," meaning that they confer benefits to various types of constituencies—to farming districts, inner cities, financial centers, and so on. Because legislators often benefit electorally from the government benefits accruing to their districts, they seek assignments on those committees with jurisdictions over policies that benefit their particular constituency (legislators from agricultural districts seek memberships on agricultural committees; those from coastal districts seek assignments on, say, the Merchant Marine and Fisheries Committee, etc.) (Adler 2002: 54). With this in mind, Adler assesses each House committee's policy jurisdiction to compile a demand-side profile of district characteristics for each committee. For the House Financial Services Committee,[14] Adler predicts that members tend to come from districts with "destitute urban districts or those with large numbers of constituents employed in banking/finance" (Adler 2002: 56). That is, committee members tend to represent their districts' concerns regarding inner city issues[15] or issues relating to banking and finance. As Humphrey–Hawkins hearings fall into the latter category, we select Adler's variables that capture legislators' concerns over inflation, unemployment, banking and finance. A simple demand-side model would predict that, all else held constant, committee members from districts with high unemployment or relatively large banking sectors would be more likely to focus on themes relating to jobs or finance and banking, respectively. For the theme of inflation, we contend that such a model should have no explicit expectations for constituency characteristics, given our exposition earlier of the low inflation consensus as benefiting all.

In sum, our variables from Adler's dataset are: *bank assets* in state[16] (in million$); *blue-collar workers* in district; *unemployed* persons in district; and persons (14+) in district *employed in finance, insurance, and real estate* (each of these three employment measures are expressed as a percentage of the district labor force). For blue-collar workers, unemployment and financial employment, we next calculate the quintiles[17] for both the district and the state. As bank asset data are available only at the state level, these data are calculated in state-level quintiles only. Quintiles data are based on *all* members of Congress—for each chamber, and for each time period—thereby allowing us to compare our banking committee members with the larger membership for each chamber. To these constituency data, we add the following individual and institutional variables: *Chamber* (House, Senate); *Party affiliation* (Independent, Democrat, Republican); *Status* on committee (chairman, member); and the *Date*[18] of the hearing.

Our second set of variables derive from the same groupings of thematic classes that we have used earlier in this chapter. To recap, we collapse 85 specific classes identified in our textual analysis of the sixteen corpora across the three decades of hearings (tables 4.A3 through 4.A10) into the following thematic groups: *US inflation; US economy output; Labor market and unemployment; Money growth, aggregates and credit; Financial stability and the banking system; Fiscal policy (including Social Security); Fed independence and relations between the Fed, Congress, and the Administration; Challenging the Fed; Praising the Fed; World economy;* and *Other issues (education, inequality, energy)*. For each group, we identify committee members whose name tag acquires at least the minimum chi square statistical significance[19] for any of the specific classes that fall into that thematic group.[20] Hence each committee member receives a measure of statistical significance for each thematic group, and for each of the eight time periods across the three decades. In many cases, members may obtain significance in only one thematic group and for one time period; hence all other entries are zero.

A final note concerns representativeness of the dataset. In the first half of this chapter, we have used the complete verbatim transcripts from the 61 hearings over the 33-year period—so, for these particular years, there is no sample since the textual data reflect all that was said during these hearings. Yet these 61 hearings are nonetheless a sample of all the Humphrey–Hawkins hearings held by the congressional banking committees over that same period, and so we have made inferences to the overall time period based upon this sample of hearings.

In this part of the chapter, the notion of representativeness is somewhat trickier. To begin, we have a subset of our original set of hearings—that is, those hearings for which Adler's data are available, which amounts to 45 hearings from 1976 to 1999. From the results of our textual analysis on these hearings, only those committee members whose name obtains the minimum level of significance[21] are included in the dataset—hence members whose overall contribution to the discourse is (statistically) minimal or nonexistent are not included. Who is this (statistically) silent contingent of the hearings? On the one hand, this contingent of members is of little concern to our study, as their verbal participation—and therefore their contribution to the deliberative process—is negligible. On the other hand, insofar as our data for this section are definitely a sample of some larger population, it is useful to convey some notion of the representativeness and the size of the sample, relative to that larger population.

To say that the larger population is simply all the members who sit on these committees is not good enough, since our study is not about their mere presence but rather what they contributed to the discourse in the monetary policy oversight hearings. Minimal and incomplete records of attendance prevent us from knowing who all were present at any point during (or for the duration of) the hearings. We can, however, begin with the committee membership itself, which we detail fully in our book appendix II. If we simply tally the numbers of members for our 45 hearings—*and* allow for repeats among members whose tenures span multiple hearings—we obtain 774 member-cases for the House and 366 member-cases for the Senate, for a total of 1,140 member-cases. It is important that we describe these as *cases* rather than *members* inasmuch as a single member may obtain multiple measures of significance from our textual analysis (i.e., from multiple time periods) and thereby have more than one entry. This holds especially for committee chairmen (or those who become chairmen). For instance, Congressman Barney Frank is entered as three cases in our dataset, as his name tag obtains significance for fiscal policy in 1979 to 1981, both fiscal policy and challenging the Fed in 1984 to 1986, and the labor market in 1997 to 1999. So, by using *member-cases* to describe our population, we are allowing for the possibility that *all* committee members for *all* 45 hearings could—in theory—have obtained statistical significance for one (and only one) of the thematic classes (regardless of whether they actually attended all or any of the hearings). This is certainly an overestimate of the population because it assumes that *all* members attend (not all do, in fact) and *all* contribute to the committee discourse in such a way as to make their presence known in a statistical analysis of the hearing transcript. Nonetheless a member-case estimate of the population as 1,140 is probably as near as we can approximate.

4.8   Analysis

4.8.1   Descriptive Statistics

Using simple descriptive statistics and frequencies, in tables 4.6 and 4.7 we provide a first glance at our data. From table 4.6 we see that our dataset includes 275 cases of significance for committee members. Using our *overestimated* population figure of 1,140 for all the member-cases, this means that our sample is about 24 percent of all member-cases for our set of hearings. Put another way, about 76 percent of potential member-cases (specifically, opportunities for members to offer a (statistically) distinct contribution to the discussion) are absent—though not because they were not selected but because they do not exist.

Three further features are of particular relevance from table 4.6. First, the median value for all but one of our thematic classes ("praising the Fed") is zero, which suggests that most members do not contribute significantly to many of the topics. Bearing in mind from our previous footnotes that all of our member-cases must have $\chi^2 \geq 2$ for at least one

Table 4.6
Descriptive statistics of variables

Variable	N	Min.	Max.	Mean (median)	Skewness (SE)	Std. deviation
χ2 Values for thematic classes						
Inflation (US) (theme 1)	123	0	65	1.9 (0)	6.7 (0.22)	7.2
US economy output (theme 2)	165	0	158	2.5 (0)	9.3 (0.19)	14.1
Labor market/unemployment (theme 3)	105	0	312	9.5 (0)	6.7 (0.24)	36.4
Money growth, aggregates, credit (theme 4)	197	0	135	3.4 (0)	8.2 (0.17)	14.3
Financial stability/banking system (theme 5)	174	0	115	3.5 (0)	5.9 (0.18)	12.1
Fiscal policy (including Social Security) (theme 6)	226	0	209	10.6 (0)	4.4 (0.16)	22.4
Independence of the Fed/relations between Fed, Congress, and administration (theme 7)	49	0	52	6.3 (0)	2.4 (0.34)	12.3
Appraising the Fed—challenging (theme 8a)	111	0	243	9.4 (0)	6.6 (0.23)	27.2
Appraising the Fed—praising (theme 8b)	22	0	130	15.2 (3.8)	3.2 (0.49)	29.2
World economy (impact on US, exchange rate, implications for monetary policy) (theme 9)	133	0	58	1.8 (0)	6.0 (0.21)	6.5
Other (education, inequality, energy) (theme 10)	0					
Values for constituency, institutional, & individual variables						
Party (1 Independent; 2 Democratic; 3 Republican)	275	1.0	3.0	2.4 (2)	0.29 (0.15)	0.5
Unemployment (in quintiles)	275	1.0	5.0	2.9 (3)	0.13 (0.15)	1.4
Bank assets (in quintiles)	275	1.0	5.0	3.9 (4)	-0.87 (0.15)	1.3
Blue-collar labor (in quintiles)	275	1.0	5.0	3.1 (3)	-0.80 (0.15)	1.3
Financial employment (in quintiles)	275	1.0	5.0	3.3 (4)	-0.26 (0.15)	1.3
Chamber (1 House; 2 Senate)	275	1.0	2.0	1.3 (1)	0.78 (0.15)	0.5
Status (1 member; 2 chairman)	275	1.0	2.0	1.1 (1)	3.66 (0.15)	0.2
Date (1 1976–77; 2 1979; 3 1979–81; 4 1980–81; 5 1984–86; 6 1991–93; 7 1997–99)	275	1.0	7.0	4.3 (5)	-0.23 (0.15)	2.1

Table 4.7
Frequencies of constituency, institutional, and individual variables

Variable	Value	Frequency	Percent	Cumulative percent
Party	Independent	1	0.4	0.4
	Democrat	161	58.5	58.9
	Republican	113	41.1	100.0
Unemployment	1st quintile	55	20.0	20.0
	2nd quintile	60	21.8	41.8
	3rd quintile	66	24.0	65.8
	4th quintile	46	16.7	82.5
	5th quintile	48	17.5	100.0
Bank assets	1st quintile	21	7.6	7.6
	2nd quintile	26	9.5	17.1
	3rd quintile	47	17.1	34.2
	4th quintile	53	19.3	53.5
	5th quintile	128	46.5	100.0
Blue-collar	1st quintile	37	13.5	13.5
	2nd quintile	63	22.9	36.4
	3rd quintile	57	20.7	57.1
	4th quintile	66	24.0	81.1
	5th quintile	52	18.9	100.0
Financial employment	1st quintile	27	9.8	9.8
	2nd quintile	62	22.5	32.4
	3rd quintile	45	16.4	48.7
	4th quintile	74	26.9	75.6
	5th quintile	67	24.4	100.0
Chamber	House	187	68.0	68.0
	Senate	88	32.0	100.0
Status	Committee member	258	93.8	93.8
	Committee chairman	17	6.2	100.0
Date	1976–77 hearings	46	16.7	16.7
	1979 hearings	23	8.4	25.1
	1979–81 hearings	45	16.4	41.5
	1980–81 hearings	13	4.7	46.2
	1984–86 hearings	48	17.5	63.6
	1991–93 hearings	46	16.7	80.4
	1997–99 hearings	54	19.6	100.0

thematic class, this suggests that most members who do actively contribute to the discussion tend to gravitate to one or two topics, and thereby obtain statistical significance for only these topics. Second, for all the thematic classes the distribution is positively skewed, meaning that extreme values for member-cases may influence our analysis (a point on which we elaborate below). Third, as we saw earlier in this chapter, topics from our "other" category (i.e., education, inequality, and energy policy) become relevant only during the more recent hearings (2003 to 2008) and as the limited time frame of Adler's data does not allow us to include these hearings, this thematic class falls out of this part of our analysis.

With respect to the distribution of our independent variables, we can see from table 4.6 that three constituency variables—*Bank assets, Blue-collar labor,* and *Financial employment* are negatively skewed. Our categorization into quintiles in table 4.7 allows us to examine these demand-side variables more clearly. One variable in particular—*Bank assets*—is quite unusual in its distribution among the quintiles. A demand-side model would likely predict greater involvement by members from districts in which banks have a strong presence, and for the *bank assets* variable, we find that nearly half the cases (47 percent) do indeed fall into the 5th quintile. Disaggregated by chamber, the finding is only slightly less for Senate committee members—namely 48 percent of House member-cases fall into the 5th quintile, compared to 44 percent of Senate member-cases in this same category. This suggests that the overall contribution to the hearings' discourse is skewed toward members who represent districts and states in which there is a sizable banking sector. Interestingly, the *financial employment* variable shows only a slight skew to the 5th quintile, with about 24 percent of member-cases. However, if we divide this into House and Senate committees, we find a much more prominent skew toward the 5th quintile for the Senate (33 percent) than for the House (20 percent), which lends some support to a demand-side model. At least for the Senate, the hearings' discourse is slightly skewed toward members who represent states with relatively larger financial employment sectors.

For *blue-collar labor*, although the measure of skewedness (table 4.6) is negative, the quintile distribution (both in aggregate and separated into chambers) is not conspicuously skewed toward the higher quintiles. Together with *unemployment*—which exhibits a fairly even distribution—neither of these two variables supports a demand-side model. Both *bank assets* and *financial employment* are, on the other hand, more consistent with a demand-side model. That is, those members who represent states in which there are relatively larger banking sectors and have more people employed in financial services tend to contribute more to the discussions in the oversight hearings. For House members, this appears to hold only for districts that are situated in states with larger banking sectors.

4.8.2 Further Analysis

In order to test the extent to which variations in the tendencies for committee members to focus on particular topics may be the function of the characteristics of their constituencies, ideally we would regress each of our thematic discourse variables on the set of constituency and control variables described above. However, we confront the problem that most members do not talk about most topics. From a data perspective, this creates a large number of zeros in the dataset. Hence regression (even on the log transformed data) is not appropriate. One might instead use a logit model on, say, whether a member scored above a threshold score on a particular topic. However, such a model would obviously create a blunt and arbitrary threshold for the data. To avoid applying such a "sledgehammer," we instead adopt an approach that seeks to retain the underlying distribution of members' scores (albeit at the cost of statistical elegance).

In figures 4.12 through 4.30 we use boxplots in order to unpack the distribution of our variables. These plots enable a visualization both of the median values and the variation around the ranges and interquartile ranges. Originally devised by Tukey (1977), boxplots divide the data into quartiles. Around 25 percent of the values fall below the lower quartile, around 50 percent fall below the median, and around 75 percent fall below the upper quartile. The distance between the upper and lower quartiles comprises the interquartile range, which is drawn as a "box." The highest and lowest values may be drawn as lines (called "whiskers") extending from the box to each end point, in which case extreme values are subsumed within these whiskers. Alternatively, if the researcher wishes clearly to identify extreme values (as we do here), extreme values may be identified as distinct symbols, and the whiskers thereby shortened (Tufte 1983: 123–25; Wallgren, Wallgren, et al. 1996: 51).

Distribution of Scores on Themes, by Party

Figures 4.12 through 4.21 are boxplots for all of our relevant thematic classes. Each plot shows the distribution of χ^2 values for each thematic

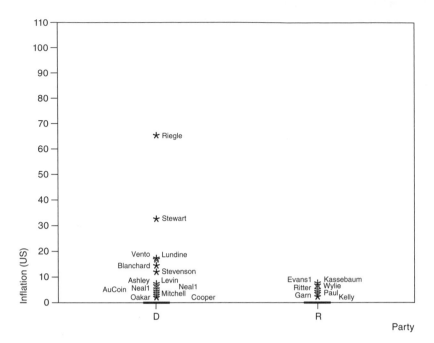

Figure 4.12
Distribution of committee members' chi-squared values for *Inflation* thematic class, by party affiliation

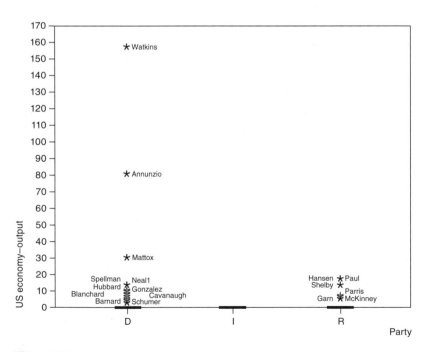

Figure 4.13
Distribution of committee members' chi-squared values for *US economy–output* thematic class, by party affiliation

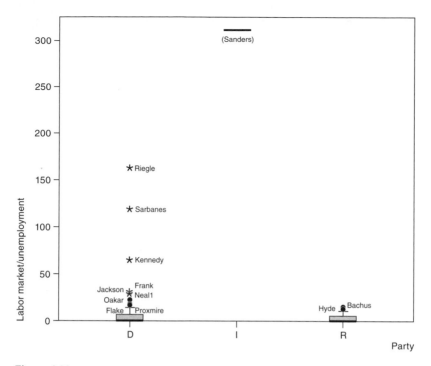

Figure 4.14
Distribution of committee members' chi-squared values for *Labor market/unemployment* thematic class, by party affiliation

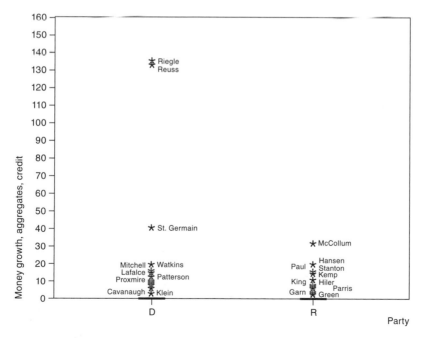

Figure 4.15
Distribution of committee members' chi-squared values for *Money growth, aggregates, credit* thematic class, by party affiliation

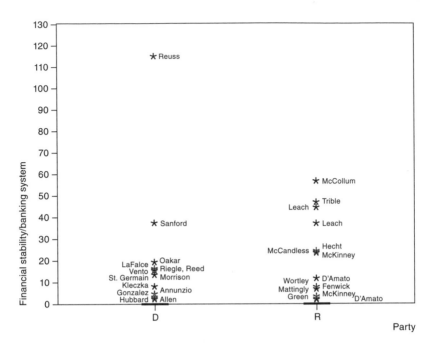

Figure 4.16
Distribution of committee members' chi-squared values for *Financial stability/banking system* thematic class, by party affiliation

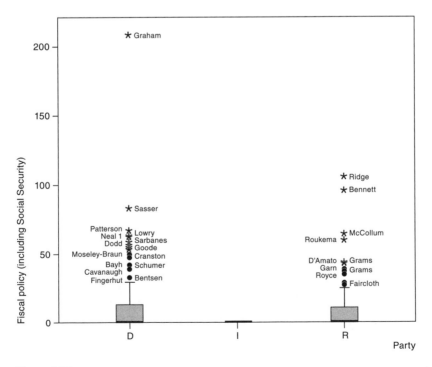

Figure 4.17
Distribution of committee members' chi-squared values for *Fiscal policy (including Social Security)* thematic class, by party affiliation

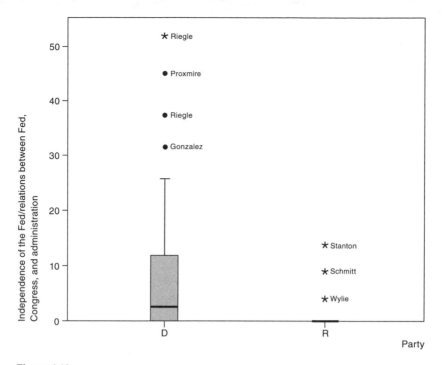

Figure 4.18
Distribution of committee members' chi-squared values for *Independence of the Fed/ relations between Fed, Congress, and administration* thematic class, by party affiliation

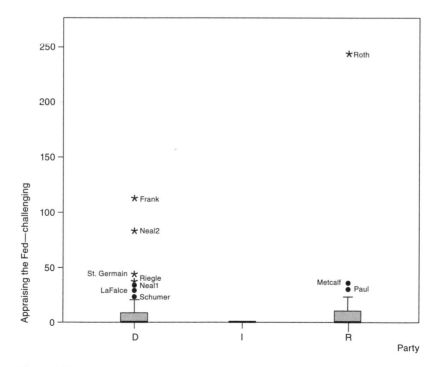

Figure 4.19
Distribution of committee members' chi-squared values for *Appraising the Fed (challenging)* thematic class, by party affiliation

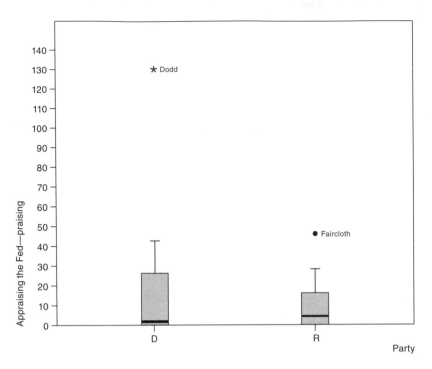

Figure 4.20
Distribution of committee members' chi-squared values for *Appraising the Fed (praising)* thematic class, by party affiliation

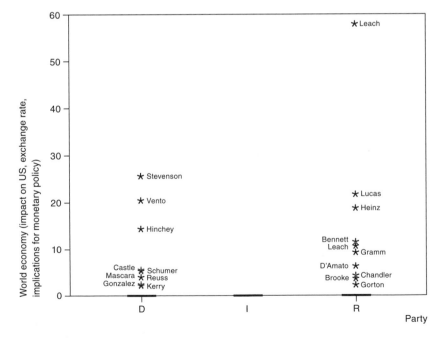

Figure 4.21
Distribution of committee members' chi-squared values for *World economy* thematic class, by party affiliation

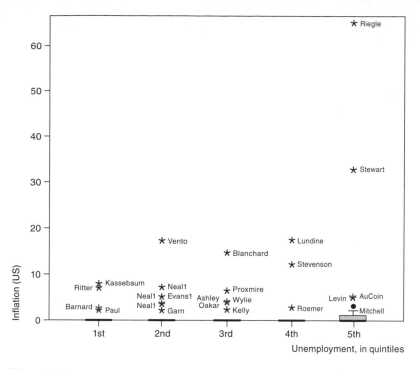

Figure 4.22
Distribution of committee members' chi-squared values for *Inflation* class, by unemployment in district

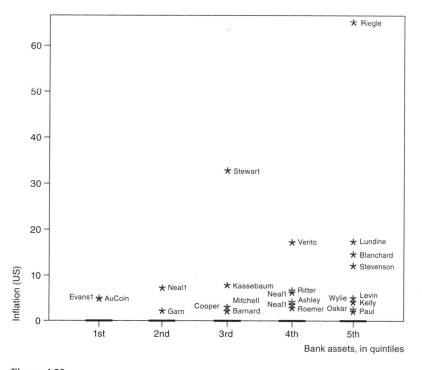

Figure 4.23
Distribution of committee members' chi-squared values for *Inflation* class, by bank assets in district

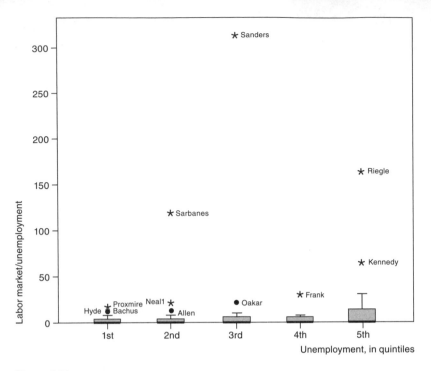

Figure 4.24
Distribution of committee members' chi-squared values for *Unemployment* class, by unemployment in district

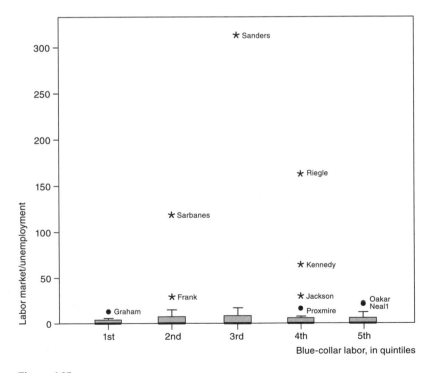

Figure 4.25
Distribution of committee members' chi-squared values for *Unemployment* class, by blue-collar labor in district

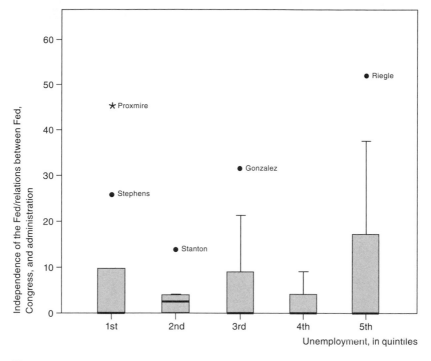

Figure 4.26
Distribution of committee members' chi-squared values for *Independence of Fed* class, by
unemployment in district

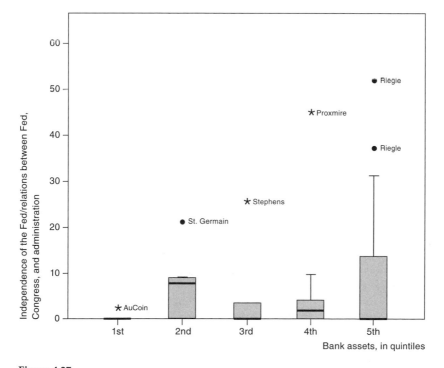

Figure 4.27
Distribution of committee members' chi-squared values for *Independence of Fed* class, by
bank assets in state

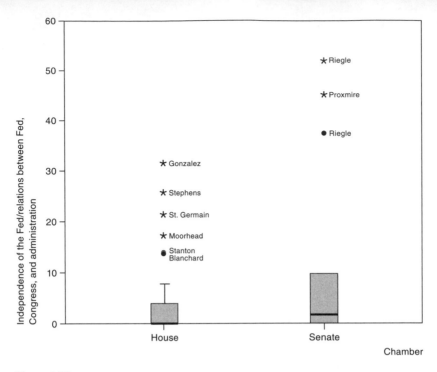

Figure 4.28
Distribution of committee members' chi-squared values for *Independence of the Fed* class in the House and Senate

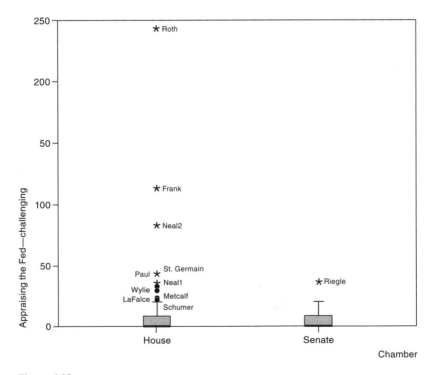

Figure 4.29
Distribution of committee members' chi-squared values for *Challenging (appraising) the Fed* class in the House and Senate

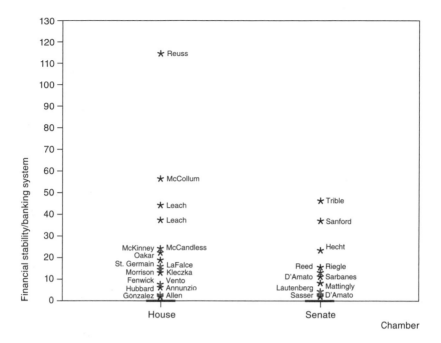

Figure 4.30
Distribution of committee members' chi-squared values for *Financial stability* class in the House and Senate

variable, by the party affiliation of the member (and for two key themes—inflation and financial stability—also by date). (Bear in mind that—given our description of member-cases and the example of multiple entries for Barney Frank—the name of an individual member may appear twice in a box plot, as seen in figure 4.12 for Neal1.[22]) In only two figures do we have a significant variation in the values to draw an actual "box" (figures 4.18 and 4.20). In all other figures both the box and the whiskers are collapsed at about zero—which is what we would expect from our median values in table 4.6. Of greater interest, however, are the extreme values for the member-cases that we identify by name. Bearing in mind that differences in the distributions across the thematic classes do not warrant a rigid adherence to a common *y* axis for all figures, we can nonetheless observe an overall story of extreme values. That is, in most—but not all—cases, a small number of committee members exhibit a dominant role in the discourse of topics.

For purposes of discussion, it is helpful to divide the figures into themes in which (1) the committee chair and/or one or two prominent members dominate the discussions, (2) a small collection of members play a significant role, and (3) no individual member is distinct. In the first category are *Inflation, Labor market, Money growth, Financial stability, Fiscal policy,* and *Challenging the Fed* (figures 4.12, 4.14, 4.15, 4.16, 4.17, and 4.19). For the theme of inflation (figure 4.12), Senator Riegle (chairman), and Senator Stewart (member) are the two prominent member-cases. Moreover in a separate boxplot, where we segregate the inflation class by hearing date instead of party (not shown here), we find that most of the member-cases for inflation appear in the late 1970s and early to mid-1980s, with virtually no significant attention given to this theme in the 1990s (as one would expect, with price stability becoming embedded in the 1990s, and discussions of inflation lessening in the oversight hearings).

Congressman Bernie Sanders[23] (member) features as the dominant member-case for labor market issues (figure 4.14), although Riegle and Senator Sarbanes (ranking member) are noticeable second and third players. Once again, Riegle is a key outlier for money growth (figure 4.15), as is Congressman Reuss (chairman), who is also a dominant member-case for financial stability (figure 4.16). Senator (Bob) Graham is the single dominant outlier for fiscal policy (figure 4.17)—although, notably, we see small "boxes" for both party members, indicating at least a bit more involvement across the committee memberships on this topic. Congressman Roth (Republican Subcommittee Ranking Member) features as the single top member-case in discussions that challenge the Federal Reserve (figure 4.19), although Congressman Frank (a subsequent chairman) and Congressman (Richard) Neal (member) are distant second and third Democratic member-cases.

All in all, in six of our relevant thematic classes, only nine individual legislators dominate the discussions, and of these, six are committee leaders (ranking member, chairman, or subsequent chairman). This is not to say that other members play *no* role in the discourse, but rather that their contributions are not as significantly focused on a particular theme.

In our second category are the themes *US economy output, independence of the Fed,* and *world economy* (figures 4.13, 4.18, and 4.21). For US economy output and world economy, we see a bunching up of member-cases along the lower (though still statistically significant at 1 percent) χ^2 values, that is, in single or double digits, and there is a mixture of chairmen and members. For Fed independence (figure 4.18), there is a clear partisan difference, with Democrats exhibiting enough member-cases to enable a classic box and whisker distribution, while for Republicans, all but three members obtain a χ^2 score of zero. This reinforces our finding earlier in this chapter, where we saw that Democrats tend to challenge the governance of the Fed more than Republicans.

In our final category is just one theme—*praising the Fed* (figure 4.20). Here we find typical box and whisker plots for both parties. While the χ^2 values are nearly all in the single or double digits, we do nonetheless observe a grouping of committee members, with no extreme cases. This reinforces our contention from earlier in the chapter that *both* parties (Republicans slightly more so, noting the higher median value) tended to congratulate Greenspan and the Fed for delivering what appeared to be a highly successful monetary policy in the 1990s. Unlike other themes where individual members (usually chairmen) dominate the discussions, a significant group of committee members from both parties jump onto the bandwagon to praise Greenspan and the Fed.

Distribution of Scores on Selected Themes, by Constituency Variables
Figures 4.22 through 4.25 present the distributions of χ^2 values for two key monetary policy themes—inflation and unemployment—by quintiles for district or state unemployment, bank assets or blue-collar workers. In figure 4.22 are the same top two individuals that we saw for inflation in figure 4.12, namely Senators Riegle and Stewart. What is striking about figure 4.22 is that if we exclude these two extreme member-cases, the distribution of the remaining cases spans across all the district quintiles for unemployment, thereby reinforcing the importance of price stability regardless of a representative's electoral sensitivity to unemployment in his district. With respect to the distribution of members according to the size of the banking sector in their districts (figure 4.23), we observe a bunching of members in the fifth quintile (also reported in table 4.7), with Riegle the extreme outlier in this category. One might be tempted to interpret the large banking sectors in the states of these members as swaying their attention more toward the theme of inflation—but a visual inspection of figure 4.23 does not lend support to such an interpretation.

Turning to the labor market theme (figures 4.24 and 4.25), we find once again that Congressman Sanders is a highly unique member-case. As Congressman (At Large) of Vermont, Sanders' constituency falls right in the middle of the quintile distribution for both unemployment and blue-collar labor—and yet, his χ^2 value on the theme of labor markets dwarfs all other members, regardless of the economic conditions in their districts. Clearly, his status as an ideological Independent is well-earned, as his famous diatribes against Greenspan in the House Financial Services Committee (HFSC) do not appear to be the product of heightened unemployment or a large contingent of lesser skilled workers in his state of Vermont.

In sum, members from districts/states with *relatively* high unemployment, large numbers of blue-collar workers, or large banking sectors do not appear to focus exclusively (or predominantly) on either inflation or unemployment. Rather, as the descriptive statistics suggest, members from states with relatively large banking sectors (and to a lesser extent with more employed in the financial sector) appear to be just more active in the overall committee discussion (that is, obtaining χ^2 significance for at least one of the topics, and thereby obtaining the status of a "member-case"[24]). While this is not a jaw-dropping conclusion, it does help to show the limitations of extrapolating too far from a demand-side approach.

Figures 4.26 and 4.27 present distributions of χ^2 values for the *Fed Independence* discourse theme—that is, where committee members were most strident in their opposition to the Fed and its policies (during the period of high inflation)—with reference to unemployment and bank assets in the state/district of the committee member. There appears to be slightly more scope for members from districts/states with relatively higher unemployment or relatively larger banking sectors to challenge the Fed more in the hearings, but the evidence is not overwhelming. Once again, it is the conspicuous outliers—most of whom were (or were to become) committee chairmen (Riegle, Proxmire, Gonzalez, St. Germain)—that tell the story. Demand-side measures are thus not particularly promising in their contribution to our understanding of the areas of discourse on which members chose to focus.

Distribution of Scores on Selected Themes, by Chamber

What about differences between the Senate and House committees? We know from our earlier sections that members of the Senate Banking Committee exhibited more of a tendency to praise the Fed chairman in good economic times, and in so doing, to elicit his (and the Fed's) support for nonmonetary policy objectives. Because this thematic class appears *only* in the Senate, we cannot display a comparison across the chambers—but what about related classes that sought to evaluate and appraise the performance of the Fed chairman or challenged the independence of the Fed? We examine the boxplots for these differences between the House and Senate committees in figures 4.28 and 4.29.

Earlier in this chapter we characterized *Fed independence, challenging the Fed,* and *praising the Fed* as following something of a continuum, from fundamentally challenging the Fed (in the 1970s and 1980s) to effusively praising it (in the 1990s). In its discourse on "independence of the Fed" in the 1970s and 1980s (figure 4.28), committee members questioned core issues of Fed governance (e.g., transparency) and the Fed's stature vis-à-vis Congress and the Administration. Because it is the Senate Banking Committee (and not the HFSC) that confirms appointments to the Board of Governors of the Federal Reserve, one might expect more involvement across all the Senate committee members on this topic—and indeed that is what we find. For the Senate, the box is larger, and the median χ^2 value for the Senate is 1.8, while for the House it is zero. In figure 4.29, where the theme of "challenging the Fed" is less confrontational than questioning its governance, there is just one extreme outlier from the HFSC—Congressman Roth (Subcommittee Ranking Member). Overall, the upward tail of outliers is certainly greater for House than for Senate committee members, which may support the notion that at least in the HFSC, members were more prone to criticize the Fed. And, as noted previously, the theme of "praising the Fed" emerges only in the Senate hearings—no such discourse is evident in the HFSC. Moreover we found earlier that there appeared to be a committee-wide (bipartisan) outpouring of praise for the Fed and Greenspan himself from senators. Members of the HFSC were apparently not as impressed (or, at least, chose not to express it verbally). In sum, we find a story of greater swing in sentiment among members of the Senate Banking Committee than among members of the HFSC. In the 1970s and 1980s, when the Fed was still battling high inflation, senators appear to have been harsher in their oversight than were their counterparts in the House. By the 1990s, inflation had fallen and monetary policy seemed to be running smoothly and successfully—hence Senate committee members duly expressed their praise. Across the period, *members* (excluding chairmen) of the HFSC appear to be relatively less prone to either censure or praise of the Fed. Put another way, in hard times, House committee members—as a whole—appear to have expressed somewhat less overt criticism; and as monetary policy improved, their sentiments did not seem to shift quite as positively as did senatorial committee members.

In our final graph (figure 4.30) we return to one of the economic themes—financial stability[25]—which cements the finding from figure 4.16, namely that Congressman (and Chairman) Reuss is the one member-case who contributed in an extraordinary fashion to discussing financial stability and the banking system. With respect to chamber, one is hard-pressed to find much difference in the attention given to this topic by members of the HFSC versus that of their colleagues in the Senate Banking Committee (at least, during the Humphrey–Hawkins hearings).

4.9   Summary

Our goal in this section of the chapter has been to examine more closely the link between constituency characteristics of committee members and their particular thematic foci in monetary policy committee hearings. We have posited that a simple demand-side model would predict that committee members from districts with high unemployment or relatively large banking sectors should focus more on themes relating to jobs or finance and banking, respectively. For the theme of inflation, we had no explicit expectations for constituency characteristics.

In short, our findings are *not* supportive of a simple demand-side model, except in a very limited way. Rather, our findings illustrate the importance of a small number of (verbally) dominant individuals in the committee discourse. Most, though not all, of these are committee chairmen, ranking members or future committee chairmen. These individuals are seen to be highly unique in their language and their tendency to focus on particular themes. Their uniqueness stems from their very high χ^2 values for key themes that are identified in the textual analysis of the hearings. This is not, however, to dismiss the *overall* contribution of the larger contingent of committee members who, together, help to comprise and shape the committee deliberations as a whole. As we have seen in the first two parts of this chapter, the entirety of the committee discourse is the product of many individuals—both committee leaders and ordinary members, not to mention the Federal Reserve chairman himself. The contribution in this part of the chapter has been not only to assess the merits of a demand-side model for understanding the committee discourse, but also to isolate and identify more clearly the nature of unique players in the hearings.

In summary, we obtain three key results. First, we find that the overall distribution of member-cases with respect to the scale of bank assets in the state of the senator's or congressman's district is skewed toward states with large values of assets and greater employment in the financial sector.

Our second result is that from visual inspection of the distribution of the data using boxplots, it is striking that a small number of committee members exhibit a predominant role in the discourse of topics. For example, in six of our relevant thematic classes (*Inflation, Labor market, Money growth, Financial stability, Fiscal policy,* and *Challenging the Fed*), only nine individual members of Congress dominate the discussions, and of these, six are committee leaders (ranking member, chairman, or subsequent chairman). Even so, for two themes—*independence of the Fed* and *praising the Fed*—committee members in general become more engaged in the discussions (though for the latter topic, only in the Senate).

Our third result is that comparing the HFSC with the Senate Banking Committee, senators appear to react more to the perceived success or failure of the Fed's monetary policy (at least in their discourse), while *members* (excluding chairmen) of the HFSC appear to be relatively less prone to either censure or praise of the Fed. While the findings here are not definitive by any means, they do point to an intriguing difference in the way that senators and congressmen react to the Federal Reserve and its policy outcomes.

PART FOUR—THE BEST MAN TO KEEP THE JOB? MERGING WORDS WITH VOTES IN THE PROCESS TO RECONFIRM THE FED CHAIRMAN

4.10 Introduction

The focus of this book is on the arguments and reasoning that central bankers and members of Congress employ to understand monetary policy, and as such we have not sought to explain policy outcomes per se. But to say that we are interested in the deliberations of congressional banking committee members is not to say that we are uninterested in their more overt expressions of preferences. However, as the committees do not produce votes on the outcome of the Humphrey–Hawkins hearings, there is no direct measure or tangible expression of members' final stance with respect to these hearings. There is, however, one occasion during which committee members have the chance to express, with votes, their acceptance or rejection of the Fed's recent performance in managing monetary policy—namely the decision by the Senate on whether or not to re-appoint the existing Federal Reserve chairman.

In this final part of the chapter, we seek to bridge the gap between what congressional committee members *say* and what they *do* with respect to monetary policy by examining what is (arguably) their most conspicuous vote in this area. We do not include in our analysis the initial appointments hearings and votes, as these are not in any way indicative of their satisfaction (or lack thereof) of the Fed under his leadership. Our concern here is not with the perceptions or expectations of an untested nominee; rather, we seek to gauge the arguments and reasons that legislators use to evaluate the past performance of Federal Reserve chairmen. As such, it is worth bearing in mind that a key difference between the Humphrey–Hawkins and the reconfirmation hearings is that while the former is concerned with the exercise of monetary policy (and specifically with the chairman as the embodiment of that policy), the latter is concerned more with the performance of the chairman himself across all the Fed's responsibilities (of which monetary policy is one). A second contextual difference between the two sets of hearings is that whereas the oversight hearings are held twice a year, the decision to reconfirm is far less frequent (once every four years) and so it involves an evaluation of several years' of chairmanship, rather than what transpired in the previous six months.

As far as we know, there are no previous studies that seek to bridge what senators say during the Fed chairman reconfirmation hearings, and how they ultimately vote. For that matter, empirical studies of deliberation in Congress do not usually include roll call votes, although there are some exceptions (Schonhardt-Bailey 2008). By merging discourse with votes, we are effectively bringing together the multidimensionality of deliberation with the single, or low dimensionality of congressional roll call votes (Poole and Rosenthal 1997; Poole 2005).[26] That is, we are able to observe spatially both the complexity of senators' deliberations in the committee hearings *and* their final votes[27] on whether or not to reconfirm the Federal Reserve chairman.

Previous studies have generally concluded that members of Congress seek to use the appointments process to the Federal Reserve to exert political (particularly partisan) influence over monetary policy. Perhaps the most extensive recent study is by Chang, who models and empirically tests how politicians' policy preferences are translated into monetary policy outcomes (Chang 2003). She contends that "independence does not imply total freedom from political authority. . . . By appointing the appropriate members, the president and Senate basically keep the Fed in line with their preferences while still allowing for the Fed's freedom on a day-to-day basis" (Chang 2003: 5). Our approach differs from hers in two important respects. First, she (like others) explicitly adopts a single dimension to capture preferences of senators and FOMC members. As we have noted earlier, this is (in our view) an overly stylized interpretation of preferences that our approach avoids. Instead, we recognize that the reasons and arguments that congressional committee members employ are just as fundamentally important to understanding their preferences as are their final votes. Hence our bridging of their discourse and votes should enable a richer understanding of their preferences with respect to monetary policy. Second, whereas she examines the appointments of board governors over the 20 years from 1975 to 1994, we focus only on the Fed chairman, but over three decades (1979 to 2010).

Notably, any study of the Fed appointments process must investigate the role of the Senate in this process. While Chang argues that the Senate has veto power over who the president nominates, this is of course limited by the fact that the Senate has never formally rejected a nominee to the Board of Governors. Even so, the reconfirmation hearings allow senators to express their independent judgments of the Fed chair, based upon their impressions of his record in office. It is important to recognize that for some senators, these judgments may not be as blunt as whether to reappoint or not, but rather may be something more subtle. Since there is no precedent for the Senate rejecting the incumbent chairman, members may instead use the hearings as an opportunity to express their dissatisfaction rhetorically—namely the hearings become a device for seeking to influence the chairman. While the Senate has not rejected the re-nomination of a Fed chairman outright, failure to reappoint is not unusual. For instance, in 1978 and 1979, although Chairman Burns wanted to be reappointed, President Carter chose not to re-nominate him. And, in 1987, Volcker stood down from the chairmanship, arguably to avoid the risk that he would not be re-nominated by the Republican administration of Ronald Reagan. (Volcker, a known Democrat, had experienced difficulty with his 1983 reconfirmation—as we describe below—and possibly did not want to incur the same risk again.) In these cases, the non-reappointment of the Fed chairman thus occurs *before* the hearings.

In short, we recognize that by precedent the formal decision by the Senate does not allow outright rejection of the incumbent Fed chair. While the outcome of the vote itself may not be in question, the process nonetheless offers senators the opportunity to express various shades of dissatisfaction for the public record and therefore to seek to influence the future actions of the chairman. What some senators *say* in the hearings thereby allows more insight into their reservations and doubts. We note also that while the Senate does not have a history of rejecting nominees, dissenting votes are cast, and on occasions in more than a merely nominal number, thus there appears to be some information in the scale of dissenting votes.

4.11 Data

One might assume that the reconfirmation hearings and subsequent floor votes are reasonably straightforward as data. To some extent this is true, but there are some important contextual factors that require mention. First, although Volcker was initially appointed in August 1979 by a vote of 98–0, by 1983 the effects of the Volcker Revolution had raised the ire of many groups who lodged documentary evidence with the Senate Banking Committee in opposition to his re-nomination.[28] The re-nomination vote in July 1983 was 84–16, which according to Senate records, was the most "no" votes recorded against a Fed chairman to date. Second, two of Greenspan's four reconfirmations are difficult from a methodological perspective: in February 1992, he was reconfirmed by unanimous consent, and in June 2004, the Senate recorded just a voice vote. Only in June 1996 and February 2000 do we have variation in the roll call votes, with the former recorded as 91–7 and the latter 89–4. With no variation across members for the 1992 and 2004 votes we are unable to bridge the discourse with the vote, and so instead we merge all four reconfirmations for Greenspan into a single corpus for our analysis. Admittedly, this means that both the size and the time horizon of the corpus for Greenspan make it distinct from the single sets of hearings and votes for Volcker and Bernanke. As a result we might expect to see relatively more variation in the number of themes for the Greenspan corpus, given the longer time frame—but even so, there is no reason to expect an inherent bias relative to that of Volcker or Bernanke. Finally, the pattern for Bernanke's appointment and initial reconfirmation in late 2009/early 2010 echoes that of Volcker: in February 2006 he was confirmed by a simple voice vote, but having faced the turmoil of the financial crisis, he experienced a larger dissent for his reconfirmation than did Volcker, with a final Senate vote in January 2010 of 70–30.

4.12   Analysis

4.12.1   Volcker Reconfirmation (1983)

We present the results of our analyses of the three corpora in the now-familiar format, with the basic statistics described in table 4.8, the graphical representation of the relationships between the classes in the tree diagrams (figures 4.31 through 4.33), and the two-dimensional correspondence analyses in figures 4.34 through 4.36. To avoid redundancy, we assume familiarity with these representations and move directly to the interpretation of each reconfirmation hearing.

As we have noted above, Volcker faced unprecedented opposition in his 1983 reconfirmation hearing, and the textual analysis results capture essential elements of this opposition. For instance, the largest thematic class by far (51 percent) is labeled *Questioning reappointment of Volcker (politics and the Fed)*. The discourse of this class broadly pertains to whether the Fed can or should stray from adhering to the preferred policy direction of the administration. Questions concern, for instance, the alignment of terms for both the Fed chairman and the US president, the extent to which Volcker perceived the Reagan administration to have opposed his policies, and the budgetary independence of the Federal Reserve. Senator Sarbanes (D) is the one member who is robustly statistically significant for this class (χ^2 value of 37). In his exchange with Volcker, Sarbanes questioned Volcker both on the issue of aligning the terms of the Fed chair and US president (in order to allow the president to choose his favored candidate, instead of inheriting a previous appointee) and on the extent to which Volcker perceived his policies to have been at odds with the preferences of the Reagan administration. Both aspects of his questioning relate to the tension between the Republican administration and Volcker's management of the Fed—particularly with respect to Volcker's persistent emphasis on reining in inflation. The latter part of the exchange is indicative of this class (and again, the representative ECU is in bold):

Sarbanes: **Well, you do not have discussions at the Federal Reserve, do you, that you are pursuing a policy counter to or contrary to what the administration wishes you to follow?** Have you done that?

Volcker: We do not have discussion at the Federal Reserve—

Table 4.8
Basic statistics for Senate re-confirmation hearings (Volcker, Greenspan, Bernanke)

	Volcker (1983)	Greenspan (composite of 4: 1992, 1996, 2000, 2004)	Bernanke (2009)
Total word count	27,957	109,549	71,130
Unique words analyzed	10,403	44,078	32,583
Passive variables (tagged undicators)	28	57	32
ICUs (= number of speeches /comments)	307	917	547
Classified ECUs	465 (= 57% of the retained ECU)	2292 (= 72% of the retained ECU)	1472 (= 71% of the retained ECU)
Lexical classes	4	5	5
Distribution of classes (%) and thematic content	1 (20) Money growth, credit, and interest rates 2 (10) Problems in US real economy (especially LDC debt) 3 (19) Anti-inflation 4 (51) Questioning re-appointment of Volcker (politics and the Fed)	1 (17) Real economy & monetary policy 2 (18) Bank failures & resolution (1992) 3 (20) Deficits (fiscal, current account), plus consumer & corporate debt 4 (9) Bank regulation & restriction on the corporate structure of banks 5 (35) Re-appointment process (and praising Greenspan)	1 (50) Financial crisis (response by Congress: Dodd–Frank) 2 (16) Bernanke's/Fed's response to crisis (especially improving banking supervision) 3 (8) Monetary policy (focus on Fed's mandate) 4 (15) Fed's operations in the crisis (lending standards) 5 (11) Fed's rules and regulation, in response to the crisis

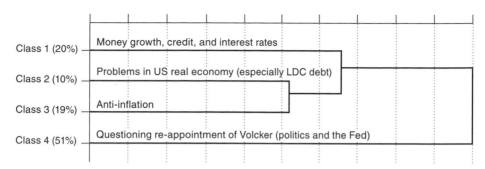

Figure 4.31
Tree graph of the classes for Volcker's Senate re-confirmation hearing (1983)

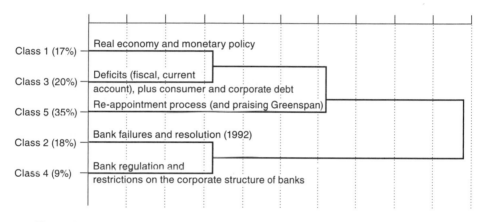

Figure 4.32
Tree graph of the classes for composite of Greenspan's Senate re-confirmation hearings
(1992, 1996, 2000, 2004)

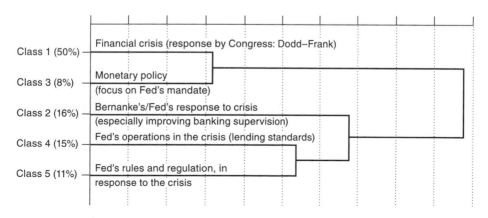

Figure 4.33
Tree graph of the classes for Bernanke's Senate re-confirmation hearing (2009)

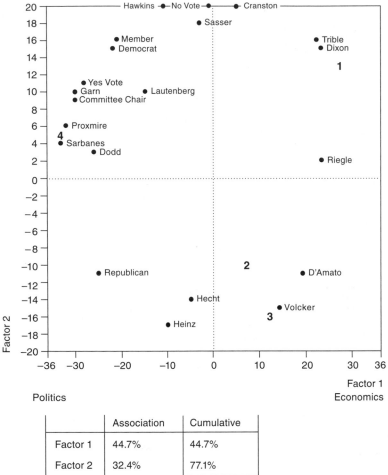

	Association	Cumulative
Factor 1	44.7%	44.7%
Factor 2	32.4%	77.1%

1 Money growth, credit, and interest rates

2 Problems in US real economy (especially LDC debt)

3 Anti-inflation

4 Questioning re-appointment of Volcker (politics and the Fed)

Figure 4.34
Correspondence analysis of classes for Volcker's Senate re-confirmation hearing (1983)

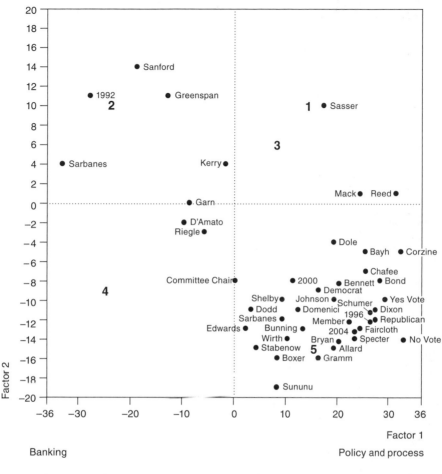

	Association	Cumulative
Factor 1	33.4%	33.4%
Factor 2	27.4%	60.8%

1 Real economy and monetary policy
2 Bank failures and resolution (1992)
3 Deficits (fiscal, current account), plus consumer and corporate debt
4 Bank regulation and restrictions on the corporate structure of banks
5 Re-appointment process (and praising Greenspan)

Figure 4.35
Correspondence analysis of classes for composite of Greenspan's Senate re-confirmation hearings (1992, 1996, 2000, 2004)

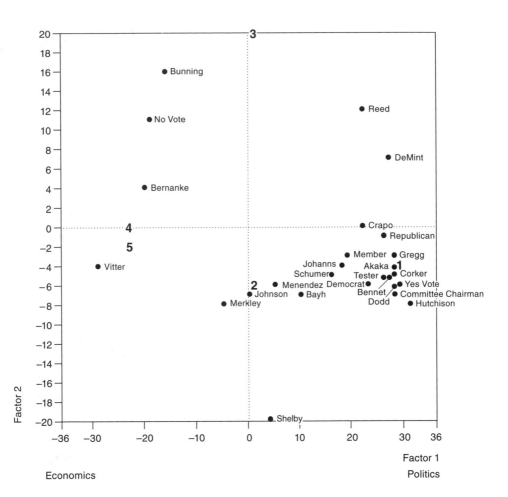

Figure 4.36
Correspondence analysis of classes for Bernanke's Senate re-confirmation hearings (2009)

Sarbanes: Do you feel that you have followed policies contrary to what the administration wishes you to pursue?

Volcker: Again, I would have to make the distinction I have just made. I think we are conscious at times that a particular decision we make may not be quite—

Sarbanes: If you have not followed such policies, why were you re-appointed?

Volcker: I presume in the broadest sense there is a consistency, just looking at monetary policy itself. I take it there is a broad sense of sympathy as to the basic objectives, the basic approach. I just do not think I can pin down that that means agreement on every particular policy decision. We have had many differences with the administration on particulars of monetary policy and other matters. We do not always take the same positions on legislative matters for instance.

Sarbanes (whose tag for this class was significant at $\chi^2 = 37$) voted in favor of Volcker's reappointment.

The next two classes in terms of size focused on *Money growth, Credit and interest rates* and *Anti-inflation*. Typical of the former class is the following ECU by Senator Dixon (D): ". . . are you or the folks at the Federal Reserve now contemplating any increases in the discount rate or any marked tightening of the money supply?" In this and other phrases from this class we see a more short-term focus on the connection between changes in the monetary aggregates and inflation, whereas in the *Anti-inflation* class (for which Volcker's tag is the only robustly significant one at $\chi^2 = 21$), the focus is very much on staying the course in order to get inflation under control. In this class Volcker faced criticism for allowing high interest rates, but in response he noted that interest rates would fall in time, if the progress against inflation continued. Volcker argued that only by maintaining control over inflation could the economy ultimately achieve sustainable growth and more favorable interest rates. In short, his focus was on maintaining a credible commitment to low inflation and by doing so, he argued that the public would expect low inflation in the future and behave accordingly. And, with lower inflation, interest rates would fall.

Both the tree graph (figure 4.31) and the correspondence analysis (figure 4.34) highlight the distinct discourse of class 4, *Questioning reappointment of Volcker (politics and the Fed)*, relative to the other three classes. In the correspondence analysis, class 4 falls to the far left while the other three classes are situated in the right hand quadrants, with class 1 (*Money growth, credit, and interest rates*) farthest to the right. Broadly speaking, the divide between the left and right quadrants is one of politics versus economics, so we label this first dimension accordingly on the horizontal axis. Not surprisingly, both the yes and no vote tags appear in the left quadrant, but with the no vote at the extreme top and the yes vote more toward the center. There is a considerably wider vertical divide between the Democrat tag at the top and the Republican tag in the lower quadrant. Taking on board the spatial positions of the voting and partisan tags, along with the name tags of senators who voted against Volcker (Cranston, Hawkins) and those who voted in favor (Hecht, Heinz), it is evident that the second (vertical) dimension suggests a clear partisan divide on the discourse, but one that narrows considerably when it comes to the vote. This seems to support our earlier contention that senators tend to use the reconfirmation hearing more as an influencing device, thus enabling some verbal partisan clashes but with the votes more closely aligned. The two dimensions (politics versus economics; Democrats versus Republicans) capture over three quarters (77 percent) of the total variation, with the first accounting for about 45 percent and the second 32 percent.

4.12.2   Greenspan Reconfirmations (1992, 1996, 2000, 2004)

For the Greenspan reconfirmation hearings, there are five main themes (*Real economy and monetary policy; Bank failures and resolution (1992); Deficits (fiscal, current account), plus consumer and corporate debt; Bank regulation and restriction on the corporate structure of banks;* and *Reappointment process (including praising Greenspan)*), but of these the single largest concerns the reappointment process. While this class comprises 35 percent of the classified ECUs, it is nowhere near as large (relative to the other classes) as the parallel class for Volcker. The critical difference is, however, in the content of this class compared with the reappointment class for Volcker. For Greenspan, the overriding sentiment of this class is bipartisan praise for Greenspan personally, and for the Federal Reserve more generally. Within this bipartisan (or cross-party)[29] context, the top ECUs nonetheless illustrate the tendency for senators to exploit the reappointment hearing for political point-scoring. For instance, senators occasionally attempt to inflict mild partisan jabs at one another, as seen in this exchange between Senators Bennett (R) and Sarbanes (D), after President Clinton had re-nominated Greenspan in January 2000:

Bennett: When I sat as a very junior member of the minority on the far end of the table, I remember the first time you came here. **If I may, Senator Sarbanes, the kind of grilling you gave the chairman would have left me with** the impression that, had you had the opportunity, you would have recommended to the new president that he appoint somebody else besides Alan Greenspan. Now, after these years of experience, we are all here saying what a great decision it was for President Clinton to have appointed Alan Greenspan. There may have been some value in his being somewhat protected from a presidential action as he took the steps that I believe were significant in helping us to get this recovery underway.

Sarbanes: Well, I do not deny for a moment that we are now at the lowest unemployment in 30 years and the lowest inflation in 30 years. I believe that is a tremendous achievement. I particularly thank Chairman Greenspan because I think he resisted those, some within the Federal Reserve System, who were arguing that if the unemployment rate went below 6.7 percent, the inflation rate would start going up almost automatically and that, therefore, as the economy moved down toward that level—we were then up at about 7.5 percent unemployment—as it moved toward that level, the Federal Reserve should move to restrain the economy by raising interest rates. That advice was firmly resisted and the economy was allowed to continue to grow and bring the unemployment rate now down to 4 percent. It is hard to get much below that without serious problems. Although it has encouraged a lot of training, which I think is . . . very important in drawing people into the workforce, we have not had an inflation problem. It is a very good economy. I am prepared to salute those who have helped to contribute to it, including, I might observe, the Congress. . . .

In the third ranked ECU from this class, Senator Connie Mack (R) not only expressed his support for Greenspan in March of 1996, but then went on to explain why, in his view (which clearly reflects the low inflation consensus), low inflation is the key to stable growth. Following on from this, he criticized the (Democratic) Clinton administration for its fiscal policy and concluded by advertising his own bill, which proposed abolishing the Fed's dual mandate of maintaining low inflation and high employment and replacing it with a single monetary policy goal of price stability:

Mack: **Certainly I intend to support the nomination of Alan Greenspan for this position. I do have a few comments I would like to make at this point.** In my opinion, the Federal Reserve has an important role to play in our economy, and I am confident that the nominee coming in front of this committee today will take that role seriously. The Federal Reserve can only accomplish one long-term objective, protecting the value of our money. The Federal Reserve has the power to do a great deal of damage, however, and if the Federal Reserve adds too much money to the economy inflation is the result and our currency falls in value. In the late 1970s when monetary authorities attempted to boost growth, my constituents in Florida, and I know everyone throughout the country, saw one third of their savings eroded by inflation in three years. . . . One third of it was gone in three years, and I do not think that should happen again. In recent years the Federal Reserve has managed its duties well. . . . In my view the reason gold prices and bond yields are down is because inflationary expectations are down. For the past 5 years, a well-conducted monetary policy has kept inflation below 3 per cent. This is an extraordinary record given our experience during the two decades before then. . . . Americans are benefiting from a Federal Reserve concerned about inflation. This record must stay intact. Nonetheless, in recent months with signs of weakness in the economy it has become commonplace to blame the Federal Reserve for slow growth. The president and other critics of the Federal Reserve Board refuse to look at the impact of fiscal policy on economic growth. Increases in taxes, regulation in government burdens during President Clinton's Administration have slowed the potential growth in the economy. . . . I will stand second to no one in my support of policies which enhance economic growth. Economic growth does not come from appointing easy money advocates to the Federal Reserve. If it did, counterfeiting would be legal. Real growth comes from entrepreneurial activities, savings, and investment. The way to increase these activities is to free the economy from the handcuffs of government. We must cut taxes, reduce spending, and slash regulation. For these reasons I have introduced the Economic Growth and Price Stability Act. This bill is designed to minimize inflation and thereby maximize economic growth. The Federal Reserve can best maximize economic growth by keeping prices stable. Any attempt to use the Federal Reserve to boost growth always results in higher interest rates, more inflation, less employment, and slower growth over the long run. I hope the nominee understands this.

The proposed legislation did not pass, nor did Mack's second attempt at it in 1999. Mack's persistence in pursuit of changing the mandate of the Fed to better reflect the spirit of the low inflation consensus does illustrate, however, that the consensus had acquired some firm believers within Congress, but was by no means endorsed by all.

And finally, in one further ECU for this class (ranked tenth), Senator Phil Gramm (R) succinctly exemplifies the tendency to wage partisan battles (here, against the Democratic Clinton administration), but within a broader sentiment of bipartisan support for Greenspan:

Gramm: **Let me say that I think in the past some may have challenged the presidential nominees for various positions. I have voted against relatively few, feeling that within broad limits the president has the right to appoint his own people and that elections have consequences.** But I would say that the president has certainly strengthened his record. Alan Greenspan deserves to be confirmed. In an era when we often do not have very much good to say about the president for a very good reason, there is not very much good to say about the president, I think it is important to note that this is an excellent nomination. I intend to vote for Alan Greenspan, and I think the president has shown good judgment in his nomination.

Turning to the tree graph and correspondence analysis for the Greenspan reconfirmation hearings (figures 4.32 and 4.35), the findings are markedly different from those of Volcker. First, classes 2 and 4 are both concerned with banking and for both classes, Greenspan is the most significant tag. *Bank Failures and Resolution (1992)* is specifically focused on the troubles that arose in 1991 concerning the Bank Insurance Fund for the Federal Deposit Insurance Corporation, which saw a deficit of $7 billion. By the end of 1992, this deficit had reduced to about $100 million, owing to better economic conditions and a more favorable interest rate environment for banks. While Greenspan's tag obtains a χ^2 value of 36 for this class, several senators also obtain some significance (χ^2 values for Graham, Riegle, D'Amato are 30, 12, and 5, respectively). On *Bank regulation* (class 4), Greenspan's tag is more dominant at $\chi^2 = 50$, with only one other senator obtaining statistical significance (Graham, $\chi^2 = 7$). The distinct discourse of these two banking classes (with top words such as *bank+, loan+, asset+, commercial* for class 2, and *board+, supervis+, regul+, supervisor+* for class 4) situates these two classes to the left of the plot. Finally, the only year tag that is relevant for either of these two classes is 1992, meaning that issues of banking were statistically insignificant for the 1996, 2000, and 2004 hearings.

Turning to the right-hand quadrants of the correspondence graph, we find classes 1, 3, and 5, but with the latter falling well toward the bottom. For class 3—*Fiscal and Current Account Deficits, and Consumer/Corporate Debt*—Greenspan is highly significant ($\chi^2 = 197$). No senator obtains statistical significance for this class. All the top ECUs for this class are from the 1992 hearing, where senators extract comments and appraisals from Greenspan on both deficits, on the decline in real estate values, on consumer credit card debt, and so on.

The *Reappointments process* class (5) is conspicuous in its political process vocabulary (with characteristic words such as *chairman+, president+, nominat+, want+*), while the remaining two classes (*Monetary policy* and *deficits*) are concerned with economic policy (with *rate+, growth+, inflation+* characteristic words for the former, and *problem+, create+, real estate, saving+* for the latter). The most visually apparent aspect of the graph is, of course, the clustering of tags in the lower right quadrant, around the theme of reappointing and praising Greenspan. Here we find not only a plethora of significant senators' tags but also the close clustering of the yes/no votes, the Republican/Democrat tags, and the year tags of 1996, 2000, and 2004. Indeed it is this tight cluster that illustrates most clearly the bipartisan sentiment in favor of Chairman Greenspan from 1996 onward. Importantly, we do *not* find the sort of spatial divide between the party tags that we found in the Volcker graph.

Finally, broadly speaking, the horizontal axis divides the two banking classes (2 and 4) on one side and themes relating to economic policy and political process (classes 1, 3, and 5) on the other. These latter three classes account for 72 percent of the distribution of ECUs, along with the vast majority of the significant tags (figure 4.32). Clearly, senators focused the bulk of their attention on economic policy and political process. As described above, to the extent that banking issues were addressed in Greenspan's reconfirmation hearings, the discussion occurred mainly in 1992, and even then, it was Greenspan who dominated the discussion.

4.12.3   Bernanke Reconfirmation (2009)

Bernanke's reconfirmation hearing is distinct from both Volcker's and Greenspan's for the obvious reason that it fell in the midst of the financial crisis, and so the discourse is predominantly focused on assessing the reasons for the crisis, the Fed's (and Bernanke's) response to the crisis, and the congressional effort to enact legislation (the Dodd–Frank Wall Street Reform and Consumer Protection Act) that sought to construct safeguards against a similar crisis in the future.

Before we begin our analysis, it is worth surveying briefly what the press reported as the key arguments and main themes, since news coverage of the hearing was extensive, partly owing to heightened criticism of the Federal Reserve and of the tumultuous events of the financial crisis in the preceding months and years. Press reports of the hearing[30] highlighted four broad topics: (1) Committee Chairman Christopher Dodd's argument that the Fed should give up a large share of its financial regulation authority (with powers transferred to a new agency), thus allowing the Fed to focus on monetary policy; (2) harsh criticism of Bernanke from some Republicans (particularly Senator Jim Bunning, who promised to block the nomination and labeled Bernanke's tenure as a "failure"[31]); (3) accusations that lax regulatory oversight by the Fed contributed to the crisis, that it failed to anticipate the housing crisis, and that it should not have bailed out such institutions as American International Group (AIG) and Citigroup; and (4) Bernanke's defense of the actions of the Fed, with acknowledgments that mistakes had been made and corrections were being put in place to avoid these in the future. With this overview, one might ask, what need is there for full textual analysis of the hearing? What more can we learn about the arguments of the hearing and positions of the speakers that we could not learn from reading every available press report—or even reading the actual hearing transcript ourselves? These same questions might apply to all our previous corpora, but as this hearing is quite recent and more contained, the questions are particularly relevant here. We return to address this in our conclusion to this section.

Table 4.8 shows five thematic classes for the Bernanke reconfirmation hearing: *Legislative response by Congress to the financial crisis (Dodd–Frank)*, *Bernanke's / the Fed's response to the crisis (especially measures to improve banking supervision)*, *Monetary policy in the context of the Fed's mandate*, *Fed's operations in the crisis (especially lending standards)*, and the *Fed's rules and regulation, in response to the crisis*. Of these, the largest class by far (i.e., 50 percent of the classified ECUs) is the *Legislative response to the crisis*, which focuses on the Dodd–Frank Act. This legislation[32] had been introduced in the House of Representatives on December 2, 2009, just one day before the Senate reconfirmation hearing for Bernanke, so it is not surprising that it takes up much of their attention in the hearing. For this first class, 12 senators are statistically significant,[33] as are both party tags (for Democrats and Republicans, with χ^2 values of 142 and 35, respectively). The single largest tag is the Yes vote tag, with a χ^2 value of 302. The significance of both party tags and the yes vote suggest a bipartisan (or cross-party) convergence around this theme among those who voted in favor of Bernanke's reappointment.

The glue that holds this class together is that senators were eager to discuss elements of the Dodd–Frank legislation (e.g., the proposal to strip away the Fed's regulatory authority, in the face of opposition from the Fed), but were also seeking to grapple with ways to assign blame (where appropriate) and claim political credit (where possible). Senator Corker (R) is the top-ranking senator for this class, and the following excerpt contains the fourth and second top-ranking ECUs for this class. In it, Corker offered his support for Bernanke's nomination, but then went on to chastise him for failing to recognize that by lobbying Congress for the Fed to keep regulation (in opposition to Dodd's proposal), he was undermining the credibility of the Fed:

I think you know that I was happy that the administration decided to re-nominate you. And I think you knew coming into these confirmations, unless something really strange happened, that I was going to support you, and I am. OK? I am becoming slightly frustrated, though, and I know that you are probably going to be confirmed, and I do not know when that is going to happen. . . . But I have worked very closely with you over the last . . . year and a half. And **we have talked about a lot of things important to our country. And what I have appreciated about you is I absolutely do not believe you have a political cell in your body, as I have said publicly many times, and I really believe you wake up every day trying to do what you think is best for our country**. But I am concerned . . . I mean, you have worked very closely with both administrations. This is not partisan. I think much of that has hurt your credibility some. And just as you mentioned, . . . on the fiscal side I do think that you end up getting used as a tool for administrations to advance policies that they think is good, it is outside the monetary policy issue. And I just would caution you, I think that hurts you. OK? The Bush, the stimulus was ridiculous. I mean, it was silly. It was sophomoric, and it had no effect, and you supported it. And . . . what happens on the Senate floor when Ben Bernanke says that he supports something, because of the respect not only of you but the position, that has an effect. Same thing with the Obama stimulus. . . . I think the same thing is happening right now in financial regulation. And as I said . . . 6 to 8 months ago, at maybe the last Humphrey–Hawkins meeting, I think to the extent that the Federal Reserve continues to thrust itself in the middle of things . . . being the systemic regulator, which, again, we are going to have another systemic risk, we are going to have another failure, we are going to have—I do not care who the Federal Reserve chairman is. **I do not care what kind of reg bill we pass. It is going to happen. And it just seems to me that the more you thrust yourself in the middle of those things that are outside of monetary policy and outside of being lender of last resort, the more you do things to damage the institution.** . . . I know you are lobbying us heavily right now as far as what the Federal Reserve role should be in regulation. And on a private basis, I want to hear that.

Further ECUs from the top ten in this class illustrate senators' difficulty in assigning blame for the causes of the crisis and claiming political credit for legislative responses to the crisis:

Schumer (D):   First, I want to say to you that I sat in the room with many others, Senator Dodd and Senator Shelby, I believe, and some others in this room, when we were told about the imminent collapse of the financial system and panic was in the air. We have lots of problems. This economy is not moving well enough from my purposes, or, I think, from anybody here, but we are not in the Great Depression which we might have been. And in a sense, you are a victim in this society when you solve a problem, you are better off than you avoid a problem, even though society is better off that the problem was avoided, and I think people forget how important that is. **It is easy to criticize. It is easy to say it could have been done a different way. But at that moment, action was needed and needed quickly or we would have had financial collapse, and you did act quickly and I think, you know, that—well, I talked to Warren Buffet.** He said the government deserves a high grade for its efforts to prevent the collapse of the financial system and rescue the economy from imminent free fall, and you played a major role there, and I hope my colleagues will remember that. . . .

Menendez (D): And to give us a sense, when we say we avoided—because, you know, I think Senator Bayh mentioned that, or maybe Senator Schumer or both, mentioned that sometimes when you avoid harm from happening, you get no credit for it. But give us a sense of what would have happened had we just said, you know, let the markets do it on their own. Let them figure it out.

These ECUs nicely illustrate an underlying difficulty for legislators who seek to claim political credit for averting crises, as opposed to solving a tangible and existing present problem. As Barney Frank had noted in the immediate aftermath of the House of Representative's initial rejection of the 2008 Emergency Economic Stabilization Act (dubbed the "$700 billion bailout package"): "It is hard to get political credit for avoiding something that hasn't yet happened" (2008; October 2).

As can be seen clearly in the tree graph (figure 4.33), the class most closely associated with this *Financial crisis–Legislative response* class is *Monetary policy, Focus on the Fed's mandate* (class 3). With Bernanke and Senator Bunning (R) as the only two significant tags for this class (with χ^2 values of 17 and 19, respectively), this class captures a distinct aspect of the hearing that was also highlighted in press accounts—namely Bunning's targeted and critical questioning of Bernanke. Bunning's critique focused on various elements related to the Fed's monetary policy—for instance, implications for inflation from the falling value of the dollar and rising prices of gold and oil; the limits of pursuing quantitative easing—and in particular, the Fed's perceived failure to deliver on the employment half of its dual mandate. Bunning essentially argued that the Fed should abandon the pursuit of maximum employment in favor of a single pursuit of price stability (echoing Senator Mack's legislation of the 1990s). The following exchange is illustrative of this class (with Bernanke's ECU ranked second and Bunning's ranked 15th):

Bunning: The Federal Reserve has a dual mandate: maximum employment and price stability. But unemployment is at its highest level in decades. And in early and mid-2008, with oil at 150 dollars a barrel and prices of basic staples skyrocketing, opinion polls showed that inflation was the public's highest concern, even more so than jobs or the housing market. Why has the Federal Reserve failed so badly in its mandate? Is employment an appropriate objective for monetary policy? Should the Federal Reserve have a single mandate of price stability?

Bernanke: The Federal Reserve's performance should be judged in terms of the extent to which its policies have fostered satisfactory outcomes for economic activity and inflation given the unanticipated shocks that have occurred. . . . I support the Federal Reserve's dual mandate of maximum employment and price stability. These congressionally mandated goals are appropriate and generally complementary, because price stability helps moderate the short-term variability of employment and contributes to the economic employment prospects over the longer run. Under some circumstances, however, there may indeed be a temporary trade-off between the elements of the dual mandate. For example, an adverse supply shock might cause inflation to be temporarily elevated at the same time that employment falls below its maximum sustainable level. In such a situation, a central bank that focused exclusively on bringing inflation down as quickly as possible might well exacerbate the economic weakness, whereas a monetary policy strategy consistent with the Federal Reserve's dual mandate would aim to foster a return to price stability at a lower cost in terms of lost employment.

In contrast to classes 1 and 3, both of which contain (to varying degrees) a dialogue between senators and the Fed chairman either on the legislative response to the crisis or on possible legislation in the future to change the Fed's mandate, the remaining classes (2, 4, and 5) are all concerned with specific operations of the Federal Reserve (*Banking supervision, Lending standards,* and *Fed's rules and regulation*). Similar to the groupings of Fed-specific and Congress-specific classes that we saw in our bird's eye analysis of the Humphrey–Hawkins hearings, classes 2, 4, and 5 are more closely aligned in the tree graph, relative to classes 1 and 3. For all the former classes Bernanke is the most statistically significant tag—specifically, for *Banking supervision* (class 2), Bernanke is the only significant name tag (χ^2 value of 63), but for *Lending standards* and *Fed's rules and regulation,* a small number of senators also acquire significance.[34]

The correspondence graph (figure 4.36) lends a further clarity to the overall picture, by enabling us to see two dimensions in the relationship between the classes and tags. As with the Greenspan hearings, there is a clustering of senators around one theme—in this case, the legislative response to the crisis (class 1). At the other extreme of the horizontal graph are two of the classes for which Bernanke is significant (classes 4 and 5, *Lending standards* and *Fed's rules and regulation*), while *Banking supervision* (class 2) falls midway between the extremes. Broadly speaking, this horizontal axis divides the more political discourse among senators on the right and more economic and regulatory discourse (for which Bernanke is highly significant) on the left. A further divide is apparent on the vertical axis, where monetary policy falls at the extreme top (situated in close proximity to both Bunning's tag and the no vote tag), and the remaining classes fall in the lower quadrants. This vertical divide is perhaps less a dimension and more a singling out of the distinct language used by Senator Bunning and his focus on the Fed's monetary policy and its dual mandate (as opposed to the remaining classes, which dealt with congressional responses to and interpretations of the crisis, and the Fed's responses to the crisis).

If we compare the analyses of the reconfirmations of all three Fed chairmen, we find intriguing differences on the role of partisanship and senators' final votes. For Greenspan's reconfirmation hearings, neither party affiliation nor the senator's final votes vary enough to provide any insight—but this is because over much of the period of Greenspan's tenure, the Fed was perceived as delivering a successful monetary policy and so there was little for legislators to criticize. Rather, they sought to capture some of the glow surrounding Greenspan's and the Fed's prestige by linking that to specific (nonmonetary) policy objectives and stances. For both the Volcker and Bernanke hearings, the story is quite different. For Volcker, senators' discourse reflects a partisan cleavage, but this narrows considerably when it comes to the vote. That is, senators appear to have used the hearing as an influencing mechanism to express their displeasure with Volcker's anti-inflationary policies, but in the end, that partisan difference narrows considerably (and in the Senate vote, the 16 opposing senators were evenly divided—eight Democrat and eight Republican). For Bernanke, with the financial crisis the overwhelming feature of the hearing and the Dodd–Frank Bill a focal point for senators' attention, there is little partisan divide in the discourse of senators—that is, most of them sought to discuss the legislative response to the crisis, along with interpretations for how to assign blame and credit. On the vote itself, of the 30 opposing senators, 12 were Democrat/Independent and 18 were Republican. The defining discourse on the No Vote came from Senator Bunning's critique of Bernanke, as can be seen by the positions of the tags for Bunning and the no vote in figure 4.36. Both Bunning (Republican) and Senator Sanders (Independent) had threatened to block Bernanke's confirmation with a filibuster. Representing "diametrically opposed views on most issues" the strength of the combined opposition was interpreted by some as reflecting "the breadth of anger faced by Bernanke [which had been] sparked by the Wall Street bailouts."[35] So, rather than any clear partisan story for the Bernanke reconfirmation hearing, we find an interesting alignment of opposition by (some) Republicans with Sanders' unique brand of Democratic Socialism. Indeed, this odd alignment reflects the broader anti–Federal Reserve "coalition" between Tea Party Republicans and Democratic Populists, which resonated in the immediate wake of the crisis.

A feature of the reconfirmation hearings is the proximate measures of "focused" discourse—namely the percentage of ECUs classified and the percentage variation captured in two dimensions in the correspondence analysis. From table 4.8, we see that 57 percent of the retained ECUs were classified for the Volcker hearing, compared with 72 percent for Greenspan and 71 percent for Bernanke. This means that the Greenspan and Bernanke hearings contained words and phrases for which there was greater cohesion in terms of co-occurrence, relative to that in Volcker's hearing—or simply put, there was more discernibly shared language among the participants in the Greenspan and Bernanke hearings than there was for Volcker. The dialogue between senators and the Fed chair had more common language. This is not to say, however, that the issues had become simpler or lines of argument had reduced. Rather, the reverse seems to be the case, as seen by the percentage variation accounted for in a two-dimensional representation of the discourse (figures 4.34, 4.35, and 4.36). The discourse for Volcker is reasonably well represented in a two-dimensional space, with the first dimension (politics versus economics) accounting for about 45 percent of the variation. For Greenspan, the first dimension (banking versus policy and process) had fallen to about 33 percent and for Bernanke, this first dimension (the Fed's "economic" response to the crisis versus Congress's "political" response to the crisis) had fallen further to about 30 percent. For both Greenspan and Bernanke, the reconfirmation hearings had become more multidimensional—and so less easily captured in a two-dimensional correspondence space. Whereas for Volcker, the primary issue was inflation, for Greenspan, the discourse evolved into other (often nonmonetary) topics, and for Bernanke, the discourse reflected underlying confusion as to where to lay the blame for the crisis, how to interpret the causes of the crisis, the ideological/partisan implications of the crisis, and ultimately how to obtain political credit for creating safeguards against future financial crises—not to mention the role of monetary policy as part of the larger picture.

So, in the end, what did we learn with our textual analysis of the Bernanke reconfirmation that we could not have gleaned from the press reports or a careful reading of the hearing transcript? First, with respect to Bunning's heated critique, we can see that—unlike the majority of other senators—he focused on the Fed's monetary policy and particularly its maximum employment and price stability dual mandate. Importantly, it is his arguments on monetary policy—rather than those of his colleagues who focused on the legislative response to the crisis—

that appear to have framed the nature of the opposition (no vote) to Bernanke's reappointment. Second, senators engaged in little direct dialogue with Bernanke with respect to the Fed's operations during the crisis, or its measures taken to correct its past mistakes on banking supervision. Instead, they sought to frame the way forward as one that required a major overhaul of the entire federal structure for overseeing financial stability, and not one that could be dealt with by the Fed enacting changes within its own set of procedures. Third, senators were keen to identify who and what to blame for the crisis and in a somewhat disgruntled fashion, they lamented that whatever political credit might be achieved for averting a full-fledged financial meltdown, this was illusory in the absence of tangible evidence that without such action, a meltdown would have been inevitable. Finally, without some form of textual analysis, it is difficult to acquire a systematic understanding of the historical evolution in US monetary policy, as reflected in the reconfirmation hearings of the Fed chairman. As we have seen, the partisan element dissipated after Volcker's period, with bipartisan (or cross-party) unity in support of the chairman and the Fed under Greenspan. With Bernanke, partisanship did *not* account for the cleavage in the discourse, but rather we saw an alignment of unusual ideological bedfellows in the opposition against Bernanke. Moreover the correspondence analysis helps to underpin that the reconfirmation hearings are more often used as an influencing device to allow senators to express their displeasure with the Fed chairman, even though they are unwilling to take that displeasure to its extreme by voting against his reappointment.

4.13   Chapter Conclusion

Any public institution that undertakes a policy function such as monetary policy under powers delegated by statute needs to carry out its decision making role consistent with the objective it has been given and will be subject to a system of accountability for its actions. In the third chapter we assessed the evolution of decision making in the FOMC from the late 1970s and by examining the verbatim transcripts we sought to assess not only how the objective of policy was pursued over time but also how the interpretation of the objective itself changed. We described how the process of deliberation in the policy-making setting changed over time, and how this change appeared to be related to the success of the FOMC in achieving the stated objective of the time.

In this chapter we have focused on the system of accountability of the FOMC to Congress, using the verbatim transcripts of the hearings created by the statutory requirement placed on the chairman by the Humphrey–Hawkins Act to report twice a year to both houses of Congress. Underpinning our analysis are two broad questions concerning such accountability, namely: Does it result in what could be described as a truly exacting form of examination of policy-making; and, second, what motivates members of Congress in their oversight role to put the effort into holding policy makers to account in an area of public policy-making that is highly specialized in its technical content and is their motivation state contingent in the sense that it varies with the perceived success of policy-making?

The literature on the role of congressional oversight vis-à-vis the Federal Reserve is thin. Moreover it is now quite dated, a limitation that is made more important by the changes seen both with respect to the understanding of the role of the Federal Reserve in monetary policy (the recognition that delivering low inflation is the best way to secure sustainable economic growth and low unemployment), and the success of the Fed in achieving this objective.

At the start of this chapter we identified a number of the hypotheses set out in chapter 2 that are relevant to the activity of congressional oversight, namely:

A: We anticipate finding some evidence of reason-giving, using both information and arguments, and given these reasons, we expect to find that some members of the congressional committees are subsequently persuaded by the arguments of the Fed chairman. (hypothesis 1)

B: We should expect the reasoning skills and judgments of senatorial banking committee members to outweigh those of their House colleagues. (hypothesis 5)

C: We suspect that committee hearings on monetary policy may exhibit a mixture of both public discourse and nonpublic discourse—that is, we expect to find both point-scoring on popular and high-profile issues, along with exchanges with experts on the details of monetary policy. (hypothesis 6)

D: On balance, we anticipate a greater influence for the new consensus surrounding monetary policy (and less of an influence for ideological or partisan polarization), and expect to find some evidence for the progression toward this consensus among legislators over time. (hypothesis 7)

Our main findings are summarized as follows:

• Few members of Congress have demonstrated interest in using the Humphrey–Hawkins hearings to challenge Fed chairmen on the more technical aspects of monetary policy-making. The exceptions to this pattern of behavior have been a number of the committee chairs in both houses and a very small number of members who have taken a strong stance in opposition to the Fed (notably Don Riegle and Bernie Sanders). For some, but not all, committee chairmen, the task appears to have carried an obligation to play the dominant role in providing the challenge to the Fed chairman on the intended subject matter of the hearings.

• Fed chairmen have used the hearings to convey a clear narrative on monetary policy, and over time we can see differences in the focus of chairmen (e.g., a clear break between Miller and Volcker, and differences between Volcker and Greenspan). As such, whatever the role and contribution of members of Congress, the accountability process appears to provide an opportunity for a clear description of policy from the chairman.

• Among members of Congress, Democrats have tended to challenge the Fed more than Republicans (Riegle was a Democrat, while Sanders is an Independent who participates in the Democrat caucus).

• In bad economic times, oversight hearings could be used by members of Congress to seek to shift blame to the Fed.

• At the other end of the spectrum, the growing success of monetary policy over our time period, and particularly in the Greenspan years, appears to have reduced the scale of challenge from Congress (though Sanders is the exception here). Oversight is therefore state contingent in its form and apparent degree. Moreover in their discourse senators appear to react more to the perceived success or failure of the Fed's conduct of monetary policy than House members. Senators are more likely to either praise or censure the chairman.

• Members of Congress appear to have accepted the low inflation consensus as the objective of monetary policy over time insofar as our evidence suggests that inflation became a non-issue in the oversight hearings. This is, of course, a form of negative acceptance—congressional oversight did not challenge dogs that failed to bark. (The exception to this finding comes at the end of our period of study when Bernanke sought to focus the oversight hearings on to the low inflation objective of monetary policy, though with little sign that members of Congress embraced it with enthusiasm as a subject of discussion.)

• Linked to the state contingent nature of oversight is the evidence that members of Congress sought to use the process to attach the name of a successful chairman (notably Greenspan) to their views on other aspects of public policy (fiscal policy, Social Security reform, education and training policy).

• Consistent with this, over the time period we study the discourse on fiscal policy became more focused on microeconomic issues of tax and spending policies and less so on macroeconomic issues concerning the use of fiscal and monetary policy as short-term stabilization tools (and thus the overall fiscal balance). This is consistent with a greater focus over time on members of Congress using the oversight hearings to exploit the electoral connection aspects of fiscal policy.

• Senators appear to have been more focused on institutional issues than House members (e.g., the relationship of the Fed to government), and they have been more focused on aspects of foreign economic policy (i.e., senators are somewhat more internationalist in their outlook).

• The reconfirmation hearings for Fed chairmen suggest that the talk was generally more partisan than the voting (Bernanke's reconfirmation is to some degree the exception here on the partisanship of the talk in that he attracted opposition from a Republican "right" (Senator Bunning) and Independent/Socialist (Senator Sanders) alignment). In large part this may well reflect the constrained nature of the reconfirmation voting—no Fed chairman has ever been rejected by the Senate, and the rules of the game indicate that were a chairman's support by the administration or Congress to be in substantial doubt, he would have stood down rather than face rejection. We conclude that the reconfirmation hearings have been more focused on the use of talk to influence the future behavior of chairmen once reconfirmed.

• Overall, hearings in Congress appear to have been more akin to a public debating arena on broad areas of economic policy than a process of closely focused challenge and accountability on monetary policy.

The process of accountability for monetary policy does not demonstrate anything like the same cohesion in terms of subject matter that we see in the policy discourse of the FOMC. Intuitively, this is hardly a surprising conclusion. A cynic could conclude that we have done no more than turned up evidence that congressional oversight of the Fed consists of two sets of people who tend to talk across each other. But this does not in itself devalue the purpose of congressional oversight, even if it cautions us that telling this story is not as easy as we might have thought.

A change in the nature of congressional oversight appears to have resulted from the Fed's success in achieving stable low inflation. Thus the form of oversight has been conditional on the success of the Fed in achieving its objective of low inflation, and on whether there is a common acceptance among members of Congress that low inflation is the best way to achieve sustainable growth throughout the economy, and thus stable low unemployment. We therefore argue that the politics of oversight were shaped both by the policy outcome itself (the Fed's success or failure) and by the degree of consensus surrounding the objective of policy, namely the benefits of low inflation. However, it is reasonable to conclude that these two features are interconnected; in other words, the apparent success of policy-making was a condition for acceptance by members of Congress of the objective of policy.

Studying the time period from the 1970s onward has enabled us to demonstrate that as a mechanism of accountability, congressional oversight of monetary policy has been more focused and robust during the bad times of high inflation and financial crisis than during the good times. Again, this is hardly a surprising finding, but it is striking that during the Greenspan years the process of accountability changed so that members of Congress were increasingly keen to use the hearings to recruit the chairman to their point of view on other areas of broad economic policy.

The literature on congressional oversight provides mixed findings for the motivations of members of Congress in the oversight process. These can include a desire for electoral advantage (which could include an electoral interest in shifting the responsibility for implementing unpopular policy), to contribute to achieving good public policy outcomes, or to seek influence in the chamber as a means of career advancement. Our results indicate, not surprisingly, that Democrat members of Congress tend to be more focused on issues of employment than Republicans. Also, as monetary policy became more successful, and the dominant tool of short-term macroeconomic stabilization, members of Congress focused more on microeconomic aspects of fiscal policy (tax and spend measures) rather than the overall balance of the budget, an area that is more naturally conducive to exploiting the electoral connection.

Finally, what do these conclusions suggest for the accuracy of the four hypotheses we think are relevant to the congressional hearings? Hypothesis 1 demands a process of reason-giving and argumentation that persuades members of Congress on the actions of the Fed. We see plenty of evidence of reason-giving by Fed chairmen over the period we examine, and we take an increasing lack of challenge from members of Congress as evidence of persuasion. But, we do not see evidence that such persuasion, and therefore the process of accountability, resulted from a two-sided process of deliberation on the subject matter of monetary policy. Very few members of Congress appear to have taken up this challenge. We do, however, see that on one key issue—the low inflation consensus—the Fed chairman (together with the Fed's delivery of price stability) persuaded some, if not most, members of Congress. Hypothesis 5 demands evidence that the deliberative skills of Senators outweighed those of House members. We do find evidence of differences in the subject matter covered in the two committees, but we do not find convincing evidence that deliberation, and thus accountability, was better in the Senate than in the House. Hypothesis 6 requires evidence that deliberation in the two committees of Congress covered both the technical subject matter of monetary policy and point scoring on issues of the day. Our findings are more nuanced than this hypothesis would suggest. The nature of the deliberation in the two committees changed as monetary policy became more successful, and in this important sense the effectiveness of accountability is state contingent. An important feature of this change is the way in which the challenge posed by members of Congress when policy was less successful gave way to a form of point scoring in which members sought to win over a successful Fed chairman to their point of view on other issues of broad economic policy. Our conclusion on hypothesis 7 backs up this finding, namely we think that the progressive absence of challenge on monetary policy as it became more successful supports a conclusion that legislators came to accept the new consensus surrounding monetary policy.

APPENDIX TO CHAPTER 4

Part One: Tables 4.A1 and 4.A2

Table 4.A1
Characteristic words and phrases for classes in House hearings, 1976 to 2008

Class	Top characteristic words	Examples from top four characteristic phrases, or ECUs
Populist attack on Fed/Greenspan (mostly B. Sanders)	people+ job+ wage+ work+ education+ skill+ American+ lose inequality+ society+	Mr. Greenspan, nice to see you again. I always #enjoy your presentations, as you #know, and I never cease to be astounded about how your observations about our economy are so far removed from the reality that I see every #day in my state, #middle #class #people and what I see all over the #country. It is like we #live in two different worlds. You #talk about optimism. I see in my state and around this #country that the #middle #class is shrinking, that ordinary #people are #working longer hours for lower #wages. I see that since 2001, three #million more #Americans have become #poor. I see more and more #Americans without any #health insurance. I see retirees now #losing the #benefits that corporate #America #promised to them. I see older #workers #worried about the #pensions that they were #promised but which they may never get. And that is what I see. That is the #bad news. But the good news, which I haven't #talked about enough, is that many of your friends, the wealthiest #people in this #country are doing phenomenally well. [Rep. B. Sanders, Feb 2004] Well, you —#tell you #now, maybe, Mr. Greenspan, one of the problems we have is you #talk to CEOs, I #talk to #working #people. And what #working #people #tell me is they are #losing good #paying #jobs, parents are #worried about the #fact they are sending their kids to #college now for information #technology #jobs; those #jobs are going to China. You are #telling me we are #creating good #paying #jobs with good #benefits? [Rep. B. Sanders, Feb 2005]

Table 4.A1
(continued)

Class	Top characteristic words	Examples from top four characteristic phrases, or ECUs
Volcker defending anti-inflation stance	go thing+ right+ sense+ trying problem+ happen+ can't say situation+	I think I would #agree with the #thrust of his statement. We have got to #come to grips with this #problem, and that is what we are #trying to do at the Federal-Reserve. But the process is #going to #go much more smoothly, much more rapidly, and we are #going to get #down to that unemployment-rate much more quickly, if the other arms of #policy are in tune with that objective. [Volcker Feb 1980] I have been fascinated, during the 10 years that I have been here, at Congress #lack of desire to have a fiscal #policy or a governmental #policy to control the economy of this country. We have always said, "let the Federal-Reserve do it." Now, when #things #go #wrong, and the inflation-rate #goes up, we always say it's the Federal-Reserve's fault. I think it is only fair to state for your #point, and the Federal-Reserve's #point, that although certainly monetary-policy has a great #deal to do with the #problem and unemployment, inflation and fiscal #policy are the #responsibility of the Congress, and fiscal damage is the #direct #responsibility of the Congress. It is governmental #policy, governmental spending, and governmental fiscal #policy that is clearly #responsible for the unemployment #figures that you show in your projection. It is very #comfortable and it is very convenient to #blame the Federal-Reserve. But the #blame rests #right here, in these three buildings and across the street, in the Capitol of the United States. I do have one concern, which I have always had, and I think it is a concern of yours. [Rep. McKinney (R), Feb 1981]

Table 4.A1
(continued)

Class	Top characteristic words	Examples from top four characteristic phrases, or ECUs
Fiscal policy	tax cut tax+ spend budget+ deficit+ revenue+ bill+ expenditure+ reduction+	If we #pass the #tax #cut #bill, and I am talking about the multiyear personal #tax #cuts, not the business and the targeted personal #tax #cuts if we #pass the whole #package now, then we will build into the system an additional 75 #billion dollars in personal #tax #cuts for 1983. That indicates to me that we will be facing this time next year a #budget-deficit of somewhere between 60 and 100 #billion dollars. And we are going to have to make some very difficult #choices. Now the #choices will be as follows. Either we will go into that basic #social safety net, #Social #Security retirement #program, disability #program, and there is some indication that the #Reagan #administration wants to do that. But I think that the #Congress will reject that approach. Or we will go into #defense #spending, and I think neither the #Congress nor the #president will want to do that. We can't go into the 100 #billion dollars of interest on the #national debt. So we will be looking at now 110 #billion dollars. [Rep. Neal (D) July 1981] So, Mr. #Greenspan, it is safe for me to say, #opposes making the #president's #proposed #tax #cuts #permanent unless they go along with increases in other #taxes and #cutting #expenditures that we now have in other #programs. [Rep. Ackerman (D) Feb 2005]

Table 4.A1
(continued)

Class	Top characteristic words	Examples from top four characteristic phrases, or ECUs
Fed's regulatory activity	regul+ bank+ disclosure+ mortgage+ loan+ lend legislat+ agencies+ regulator+ practice+	We continue to work with #organizations that #provide counseling about #mortgage products to current and potential #homeowners. We are also #meeting with market #participants #including #lenders, investors, servicers, and community #groups to discuss their #concerns and to gain #information about market developments. We are conducting a top to bottom #review of possible actions we might #take to help #prevent recurrence of these problems. First, we are committed to #providing more effective #disclosures to help consumers defend against improper #lending. Three years ago, the #Board began a #comprehensive #review of #regulation Z, which #implements the #Truth in #Lending Act. The #initial focus of our #review was on #disclosures #related to credit #cards and other revolving credit accounts. After conducting #extensive consumer #testing, we issued a proposal in may that would #require credit #card issuers to #provide clearer and easier to understand #disclosures to customers. In particular, the new #disclosures would highlight #applicable rates and fees, particularly penalties that might be #imposed. The proposed #rules would also #require #card issuers to #provide 45 days' advance notice of a rate increase or any other change in account terms so that consumers will not be surprised by unexpected #charges and will have time to explore alternatives. [Bernanke July 2007] We are certainly aware, however, that #disclosure alone may not be sufficient to #protect consumers. #Accordingly, we #plan to exercise our #authority #under the #home #ownership and equity #protection act to #address #specific #practices that are #unfair or deceptive. We held a #public hearing on June 14th to discuss #industry #practices, #including those pertaining to prepayment penalties, the use of escrow accounts for taxes and #insurance, stated income and low documentation #lending, and the evaluation of a borrower's ability to repay. The discussion and ideas we heard were extremely useful, and we look forward to receiving additional #public comments in coming weeks. Based on the #information we are gathering, I expect that the #Board will propose additional #rules #under the #Home #Ownership and Equity #Protection Act later this year. In #coordination with the other federal #supervisory #agencies, last year we issued principles based #guidance on nontraditional #mortgages, and in June of this year, we issued #supervisory #guidance on sub-prime-lending. These statements emphasize the fundamental consumer #protection principles of #sound underwriting and effective #disclosures. In addition, we #reviewed our policies #related to the #examination of non #bank subsidiaries of #bank and financial holding #companies for compliance with consumer #protection #laws and #guidance. [Bernanke July 2007]

Table 4.A1
(continued)

Class	Top characteristic words	Examples from top four characteristic phrases, or ECUs
Q&A format (process)	ask+ Mr. question+ Dr. answer+ comment+ hear say understand hope+	#Mr. Sanders, you have #asked a #question. Let's #let #Mr. Greenspan #answer that and then we'll have plenty of time for additional #questions when the other #members have had a #chance to #ask #questions. [Rep. Castle, Chair (D), July 1997] That is my #feeling. I #want to convey it to you and to the #members of this #committee, and now I #want to raise a #question with you unless you have some #comment to make on my feelings before I #ask the #question. [Rep. Mitchell (D) July 1979]

Table 4.A1
(continued)

Class	Top characteristic words	Examples from top four characteristic phrases, or ECUs
Monetary aggregates	range+ aggregate+ growth+ monetar+ velocit+ target+ rate+ money+ consistent+ quarter+	The #tentative #ranges for the #broader #aggregates in 1982 were left unchanged at 6 to 9 percent and 6½ to 9½ percent for M2 and M3 respectively. However, we would #anticipate actual #growth #closer to the midpoint in 1982, #consistent with the #desired reduction over time. #Setting precise #targets has inevitably involved us in consideration of the effects of technological and regulatory #change on #monetary measures. Those #technical considerations should not obscure the #basic thrust of our #intentions that is, to #lower progressively effective #money and #credit #growth to amounts #consistent with price #stability. We believe the #targets for both 1981 and 1982, and our #operations, are #fully #consistent with that #objective. I have often #emphasized that #money #supply data like many other financial and economic data have some inherent #instability in the #short run. The trend over time is what counts, both as a measure of #monetary-policy and in terms of economic effect. For some months in the latter part of 1980, as you will recall, the rise in M1 was relatively rapid. [Volker July 1981] However, the #operational guide from day to day in #conducting #open market #operations has typically been the so called #Fed-Funds-Rate the #rate #established in inter bank trading of #reserve balances. Translation of #money stock #objectives into day to day management of the #Fed-Funds-Rate is effective if the #relationship between the public's demand for cash balances and #short term market #interest-rates is relatively #stable and #predictable. But in an environment of high and relatively volatile inflation-rates, the #relationship between #interest-rates and #money or, for that matter, between #interest-rates and economic activity is more difficult to appraise. Moreover, the #operating #techniques over time may have contributed to #excessive #supplies of #credit by encouraging a #view by banks or others that they could count on access to liquidity at #interest-rates reasonably #close to whatever levels were currently #prevailing. #Consequently, we are now placing more #emphasis on controlling the provision of #reserves to the banking system which ultimately governs the #supply of #deposits and #money to keep #monetary #growth within our #established #targets. In changing that #emphasis, we #necessarily must be less concerned with day to day or week to week #fluctuations in #interest-rates, because those #interest-rates will respond to #shifts in demand for #money and #reserves. [Volcker Nov 1979]

Table 4.A1
(continued)

Class	Top characteristic words	Examples from top four characteristic phrases, or ECUs
US real economy	rise product+ price+ pace expansion+ increase+ output consumer+ firm+ household+	Since the closing #months of 1976, our #nation has #experienced a #vigorous and broadly based economic #expansion. The #gains in the #industrial #sector have been #especially #impressive; during the #past 8 #months, the #combined #output of #factories, mines, and #power #plants has #risen at an #annual rate of 9½ percent. #Activity in other #sectors of the economy also has #increased briskly. As a #result #total #employment in #June was almost 3 million #higher than #last October an #unprecedented #gain in so short a #period. The #unemployment-rate #remains #high; but it has #declined in #recent #months by nearly a full #percentage point, despite #rapid growth of the #labor #force. The rate of #utilization of our #industrial #plant #capacity also has #risen #significantly, and now #exceeds 83 per #cent in manufacturing. #Demand for #consumer #goods has #continued to propel the #expansion. With #confidence buoyed by #improving economic #conditions, #consumers have been spending freely from #current #income besides #adding #significantly to their #personal indebtedness. The #strong buying mood of #consumers is #reflected in the #personal #saving rate, which in the first half of this year #averaged less than at any time since the #early 1960s. [Burns July 1977]
		. . . and this #accelerated #increase in #output per #hour has #enabled #firms to #raise workers' #real wages while #holding the line on #price #increases. #Gains in #productivity #usually vary with the #strength of the economy, and the #favorable #results that we have #observed during the #past two years or so, when the economy has been #growing more #rapidly, almost certainly overstate the #degree of structural #improvement. But #evidence #continues to mount that the #trend of #productivity has #accelerated, even if the #extent of that #pickup is as yet unclear. #Signs of #major technological #improvements are all #around us, and the benefits are #evident not only in #high tech #industries but also in #production processes that have #long been #part of our #industrial economy. Those technological #innovations and the #rapidly declining #cost of #capital #equipment that embodies them in #turn #seem to be a #major #factor behind the #recent enlarged #gains in #productivity. #Evidently, #plant managers who were involved in planning #capital-investments #anticipated that a #significant #increase in the #real rates of #return on #facilities could be achieved by exploiting #emerging #new technologies. [Greenspan July 1998]

Table 4.A1
(continued)

Class	Top characteristic words	Examples from top four characteristic phrases, or ECUs
Representatives prompting Fed chair on nonmonetary policy issues	bank+ endeavor+ central+ system+ intervention+ treasur+ involve+ tool+ manner+ definit+	With #respect to the GSE regulator #issue (=Government Sponsored Enterprises), I have not commented, you know, nor have any of my colleagues on the specific #structure or the form of the regulator. In our testimony, I have #argued the necessity of increasing the share of home mortgages purchased by the GSEs which are securitized rather than kept in #portfolios at we at the Fed #perceive a significant subsidized rate. But we haven't thought through any of the #issues with #respect to where the regulator is located and what he does. With #respect to the so #called overdrafts that the Federal-Reserve #essentially has been #changing, what happened was that initially we #perceived that, as a #matter of convenience, it was quite #helpful to treat GSEs #differently from other private corporations in #various #different things, #specifically the payment #principal and interest to the banks. What occurred as a consequence of our varying from how we #handle other private corporations, was a huge increase in what we #call daylight overdrafts, which are very large, intraday lending. And what we #chose is that, as these drafts got very large and these institutions got very large and the amounts got very large, was to effectively #handle these #issues of payments exactly the way all private organizations do; [Greenspan July 2004] Let me just say that we are having #conversations, as we always do, on #issues of the #structure of international financial institutions with the #Treasury. We are the #relevant agencies in this regard, or the ones who are most directly #involved. The #Secretary is the senior member of our representation with the IMF—I am the alternate delegate. We are the two who are effectively interfacing with that. I don't think it is #appropriate for me to be discussing what it is we discuss or the like. I think it is #appropriate for us to be thinking about these #issues; and, #obviously, we are. [Greenspan Feb 1999]

Table 4.A1
(continued)

Class	Top characteristic words	Examples from top four characteristic phrases, or ECUs
Capital inflows, exchange rate, current account deficit	foreign+ unite+ abroad export+ trade+ countries+ dollar+ inflow+ domestic international+	If the budgetary deficit absorbs #amounts #equal to 5 percent or more of the GNP as the economy grows and that is the present #prospect for the "current services" or "base line" budget not much of our #domestic savings will be left over for the investment we need. Over the past year, our needs have been increasingly met by savings from #abroad in the form of a #net capital #inflow. That money has come #easily; amid #world economic and political uncertainty, the #United #States has been a highly #attractive #place to invest. But part of the #attraction for investment in #dollars has been #relatively high interest-rates. In #effect, the growing capital #inflow has, directly or #indirectly, #helped to #finance the #internal budget, by the #same token #helping to moderate the pressures of the budget-deficit on the #domestic #financial-markets. At the #same time, the #flow of funds into our capital and money #markets pushed the #dollar higher in the #exchange #markets even in the #face of a growing #trade and current #account deficit and the #dollar appreciation in turn undercut our worldwide #trading #position further. [Volcker Feb 1984]

By now, a substantial adjustment in #exchange-rates has been made, placing our #producers in a stronger #competitive #position. But we also know, from hard experience here and #abroad, that changes in actual #trade #flows necessarily lag changes in #exchange-rates by a period extending into years, that #currency adjustments can assume a momentum of their own, and that sharp #depreciation in the #external #value of a #currency #carries pervasive inflationary #threats. No doubt, some #depreciation in the #dollar, after the rapid run up, could be absorbed without a sharp or immediate impact on #domestic prices. But we cannot afford to be complacent. #Inevitably, #prospects for balance in our #internal capital #markets and therefore #prospects for interest-rates remain for the time being #heavily #dependent on the #willingness of #foreigners to #place huge #amounts of funds in #dollars and on the incentives for Americans to employ their money at home. In essence, the financing of both our current #account deficit and our #internal capital needs so long as the government deficit remains so high is #dependent on a historically high #net capital #inflow. [Volcker Feb 1986] |

Note: The software highlights characteristic words within each ECU, thereby clarifying both characteristic words and phrases, in context. For all ECU tables, # indicates a characteristic word within the specific class. We have edited the ECUs slightly from the software-generated format, in order to make them more readable, and to indicate (with a hyphen) where words have been linked together in order to signify unique phrases or terms.

Table 4.A2
Characteristic words and phrases for classes in Senate hearings, 1976 to 2008

Class	Top characteristic words	Examples from top four characteristic phrases, or ECUs
World economy & US external balance (trade & current account)	foreign+ domestic unit+ capital+ value+ moreover decline+ balance+ debt+ demand+	Although #financial contagion #elsewhere has been #limited to #date, more #significant knock on #effects in financial-markets and in the economies of #Brazil's #important #trading #partners, #including the #United #States, are still possible. #Moreover, the economies of #several of our #key #industrial #trading #partners have shown #evidence of weakness, which if it deepens could further depress #demands for our #exports. Another downside risk is that growth in #capital spending, #especially among manufacturers, could #weaken #appreciably if #pressures on #domestic #profit #margins mount and #capacity utilization drops further. And it #remains to be seen whether #corporate #earnings will disappoint #investors, even if the slowing of economic growth is only moderate. #Investors #appear to have incorporated into #current #equity #price #levels both #robust #profit expectations and #low compensation for risk. As the economy slows to a more #sustainable pace as expected, #profit forecasts could be pared back, which #together with a #greater sense of vulnerability in #business #prospects could damp appetites for #equities. A downward correction to #stock #prices, and an #associated #increase in the #cost of #equity #capital, could compound a slowdown in the growth of #capital spending. [Greenspan Feb 1999] The #contraction in #Asian economies, along with the rise in the #foreign #exchange #value of the dollar over 1997, #prompted a #sharp #deterioration in the #United #States #balance of trade in the first quarter. #Nonetheless, the American economy proved to be unexpectedly #robust in that period. The growth of real GDP not only failed to slow, it climbed even further, to about a 5½ percent annual rate in the first quarter, according to the #current national #income #accounts. #Domestic #private #demand for #goods and #services #including personal #consumption expenditures, #business #investment, and #residential expenditures was #exceptionally #strong. #Evidently, optimism about jobs, #incomes, and #profits, #high and rising wealth to #income #ratios, #low #financing #costs, and falling #prices for #high tech #goods fed the appetites of #households and #businesses for consumer durables and #capital #equipment. In #addition, inventory #investment #contributed #significantly to growth in the first quarter, #indeed, the growth of #stocks of #materials and #goods outpaced that of #overall output by a wide #margin during the first quarter, adding 1 3/4 percentage points to the annualized growth rate of GDP—although #accumulation of some #products #likely was unintended [Greenspan July 1998]

Table 4.A2
(continued)

Class	Top characteristic words	Examples from top four characteristic phrases, or ECUs
Bank regulation & banking industry structure	bank+ regul+ agencies+ regulatory loan+ safe+ institution+ compan+ author+ soundness	We #held a public hearing on June 14th to discuss #industry #practices including those pertaining to prepayment penalties, the #use of escrow accounts for taxes and #insurance, stated income and low documentation #lending, and the #evaluation of a borrower's #ability to repay. The discussion and ideas we heard were extremely useful and we look forward to receiving #additional public comments in coming weeks. Based on the #information we are gathering, I expect the #board will #propose #additional #rules #under HOEPA later this year. In coordination with the other #federal #supervisory #agencies, last year we #issued #principles based #guidance for nontraditional #mortgages, and in June of this year we #issued #supervisory #guidance on subprime-lending. These statements emphasized the fundamental consumer #protection #principles of #sound underwriting and effective #disclosures. In addition, we #reviewed our policies related to the #examination of non #bank subsidiaries of #bank and financial #holding #companies for compliance with consumer #protection #laws and #guidance. As a result of that #review and following discussions of the office of thrift #supervision, the FTC, and state #regulators as represented by the conference of state #bank #supervisors and the American Association of Residential #Mortgage #Regulators. [Bernanke July 2007] Recently, I think they perhaps tightened a bit, actually, because of some concerns that were initially prompted by the sub-prime-mortgage #lending #issues. Again from the Federal-Reserve's perspectives, our #principal concern is the #safety and #soundness of the #banking #system. What we have done recently is work with other #regulators such as the SEC and the OCC and, in some #cases also with foreign #regulators, the financial services #authority in the United-Kingdom for example and German and Swiss #regulators, to do what we #call horizontal #reviews which is that #collectively we look at the #practices of a large set of #institutions, both #commercial #banks and investment #banks, to see how they are managing certain #types of #activities. For example, the financing of leveraged buyouts, abridged equity and the like. And trying to make an #evaluation of what are best #practices, trying to give back #information back to the #companies and trying to #use those #reviews to #inform our own #supervision. And so we are very aware of these #issues from the perspective of the #risk taking by large financial #institutions and we are studying them, trying to #provide #information to the #institutions themselves, and using them in our own #supervisory #guidance. [Bernanke July 2007]

Table 4.A2
(continued)

Class	Top characteristic words	Examples from top four characteristic phrases, or ECUs
Q&A format (Volcker trying to define limits of Fed's knowledge/role)	answer+ question+ problem+ judgment+ different+ way+ say thing+ try precise+	In #concept, #obviously, something is #better than #nothing. And what you can get in practice, in some #sense, is what we have to settle for. I would hate to see getting something for the sake of getting something at the expense of giving up a more adequate program. But that's not a #judgment I can #make, whether you have that realistic #choice before you. The more, the #better, within #reason. And as I said before, there is no #danger that you are going to get too much. I would certainly feel the more you could get, the #better. But in the end, something is #better than #nothing, quite #obviously. I think there is inevitably it can't be completely identified some #kind of psychological threshold in terms of market response, and if you go under 50 billion dollars which, I think, has become #kind of a symbol I don't see any #way you're going to get any positive psychological impetus from it. You will #avoid some disappointment. I don't #know whether that adequately #answers the #question or not. [Volcker July 1985] So if you #deal with those three #areas, you would have gone a long #ways toward #dealing with this #situation. You have this #whole #series of insurance #questions that you touched upon, and I think there are very real serious #questions in my #mind partly because they are so #difficult. They are pressing, but maybe they do not have the same #degree of legislative priority, in my opinion, #simply because it is not quite so clear what #directions to go in. I would also say, and maybe less sweepingly, but quite important and a #matter of priority in the current environment and a #matter you are going to have to #deal with #anyway because the present law expires are the provisions in the Garn St. Germain Act for failed institutions to be taken over by an out of state institution. This has been very #useful in some #instances and still, I think, is too narrowly written to #deal with all the #problems that we have today. One #aspect of that is the #problem of #agricultural banks that are individually very small but are very important in terms of the local community. [Volcker February 1986]

Table 4.A2
(continued)

Class	Top characteristic words	Examples from top four characteristic phrases, or ECUs
Fed appointments & relationship between Fed, Congress, & administration	chairman+ appoint+ Federal-Reserve+ Congress+ Mr. Dr. president+ thank+ member+ Democrat+	#Thank you, #Dr. Burns, for another most #impressive statement. We are very grateful to you for your interesting analysis. I'm struck by the fact that both you and President-Carter, the two most powerful men in our country according to the judgment of many distinguished people #agree very largely on our economic outlook and #agree that the no. 1 enemy overwhelmingly is inflation. I understand that you #met #yesterday, along with other economic experts, with President-Carter at the White #House. The story in the paper this #morning said the following: Jimmy-Carter reiterated his gospel of fiscal restraint to #congressional #Democratic leaders and they didn't like it much. The #President had the #congressional #Democrats down to the White #House #yesterday #morning for a 2 hour #meeting with cabinet #members, his chief economic advisers and #Federal-Reserve-Board #chairman Arthur-Burns. According to the lawmakers, one #central theme dominated the pitch made by #President-Carter and his aides: hold down #federal-spending; "The only time we need to have strong government spending is if we have a weak private economy," one congressman #quoted the #President as stating. (Proxmire, Chair (D) May 1977) #Mr. Bernanke, they never show up in the #minutes of the FOMC #meetings. All this #discussion, all this #debate never shows up in the #minutes when we get them. (Bunning (R) July 2006)

Table 4.A2
(continued)

Class	Top characteristic words	Examples from top four characteristic phrases, or ECUs
Education, training, & US competitiveness (labor market)	job+ educat+ skill+ people+ class+ inequalit+ wealth+ trade+ American+ China+	The uncertainties that #middle #class #families face are not the uncertainties that the columnist that Senator-Bennett #mentioned and #others and economists #worry about as often perhaps as they should. I know and appreciate your acknowledging the widening #gap of income in our #society. I #commend you for adding your voice to that discussion. I agree with you that we should #look at ways to improve #education and #training of our #citizens, but I do not think that is nearly enough. #Globalization has had a #tremendous #impact on #workers in this #country, on #communities, on teachers, on firefighters, on cities' ability to deliver services to their constituents. There is no question that good paying #manufacturing #jobs have gone offshore. Fourteen years ago, the #trade deficit in this #country was 38 billion dollars. Today, announced just this week, it exceeds 760 billion dollars. George-Bush the first said that a 1 billion dollar #trade deficit translates #into 13,000 #lost #jobs. You do the math. Of course, we must #trade with the #world. The question is not if we will #trade with other countries; rather, it is how we will #trade with them and who will #benefit. [Brown (D) February 2007] . . . one says, #compete down to the lowest #wage, lowest #health #care, #lose a #pension. And the other says, which I espouse, which is race up, which means you level the #playing field on #trade and you #address the costs you can, #health #care, energy, protect #pensions, and then you race like crazy on #education and innovation. That is the #American way. My #concern right now is that in a state like mine, because we make things, grow things, and have been the #leaders in doing that, we now #find ourselves struggling in a #global economy because we do not have those elements in place. We have #lost another 19,000 #manufacturing #jobs just in the first half of this year. What I cannot seem to grasp in the graphs and #numbers that you have is really the #impact of this as it #relates to #middle #class #jobs, good paying #jobs in #manufacturing in #America. I do not believe we can have a strong economy unless we make things in this #country. That is what we do, make things and invent things, in #Michigan. [Stabenow (D) July 2006]

Table 4.A2
(continued)

Class	Top characteristic words	Examples from top four characteristic phrases, or ECUs
Fiscal policy	tax cut social+ taxe+ spend trillion securit+ budget+ medicare+ entitlement+	Four years ago, we found ourselves at a crossroads, and the #administration chose a #path that led from record #surpluses to record #deficits, both in our #fiscal accounts and our current accounts, our trade balance overseas, and much of that is being financed now by foreign central banks. And we have that opportunity, I would #suspect, the #obligation to try to change that course. The CBO has estimated that the federal budget-deficit for #fiscal year 2005 will be 368 #billion #dollars. That does not include an 80 #billion #dollar supplemental for iraq and more than likely another 50 #billion #dollar supplemental next year, given the troop #sizes we will have in Iraq. It does not include cost of #Social #Security privatization, whatever they may be, and it does not include other operations. We have record #deficits, stemming primarily from the #tax #cuts and from the steadily increasing #spending for needed #defense and homeland #security measures. Another aspect of the President's #budget for 2006 is the #cutting of numerous #entitlement and domestic discretionary #programs without effectively reining in the #deficit. [Reed (D) 2005] In fact, he has a total of 153 #billion #dollars, when you take out the #taxes like #Social #Security that are counted as #spending #cuts. But the problem is that he has 164 #billion #dollars of new #spending #programs. The #cuts he proposes are basically one time #cuts, #freezing salary increases, #eliminating 100, 000 jobs, which Ronald Reagan did in 1982, which Ronald Reagan did in 1983, which George Bush did once. Never, ever did they in fact happen. The problem is when you #add the new #spending the President proposes, that total #spending for non #defense purposes actually goes up 13 #billion #dollars above current services. The total level of #revenues is 313 #billion #dollars of new #taxes over a 5 year period. #Defense is #cut by 187 #billion #dollars. #Defense and new #taxes #add up to 102 percent of #deficit #reduction. It is going to be #virtually impossible to #cut #defense any further at the end of this 5-year period and, in fact, at the end of 3 years, you're going to have made the big #defense #cuts. [Gramm (R) February 1993]

Table 4.A2
(continued)

Class	Top characteristic words	Examples from top four characteristic phrases, or ECUs
Monetary aggregates & objectives of monetary policy	range+ monetar+ aggregate+ target+ money+ growth+ velocit+ supply+ consistent+ upper	#Assuming that further "structural" shifts into now account from non #transaction accounts are by that time minimal, "shift adjusted" #targets and data should not be necessary. The #tentative #range for M1 in 1982 was #set at 2½–5½ percent, the #midpoint of 4 percent is three quarters percent below the #midpoint of the #closely #comparable current #range for M1b "shift adjusted." The #tentative #ranges for the #broader #aggregates in 1982 were left unchanged at 6–9 percent and 6½–9½ percent for M2 and M3, respectively. However, we would anticipate #actual #growth #closer to the #midpoint in 1982, #consistent with the #desired reduction #over time. #Setting precise #targets has inevitably involved us in #consideration of the effects of technological and regulatory #change on #monetary #measures. Those #technical #considerations should not obscure the basic thrust of our #intentions that is, to #lower #progressively effective #money and #credit #growth to amounts #consistent with price #stability. We believe the #targets for both 1981 and 1982, and our operations, are #fully #consistent with that #objective. The #tentative #range for M1 in 1982 is substantially below the #range of 6–8½ percent specified for recorded M1b #growth for 1981. [Volcker July 1981] Lowering the #ranges during the 1980s, for instance, #served as an important signal of the anti #inflationary #commitment of the #Federal-Reserve. In some #circumstances, the #monetary #aggregates can also be of value by serving as #indicators of the thrust of #monetary-policy. Deviations of #money #growth from #expectations may well signal that #policy is not having its intended effect, and that adjustments should be #considered. #Over much of our nation's financial #history a number of #measures of the #money #supply had reasonably predictable #relationships with #aggregate income. The #period of #rapid financial #change had not yet begun, and measuring #money was more straightforward. Recognition of these predictable #money income #relationships was the #basis for the #Federal-Reserve's increased emphasis on #money in the 1970s and the #subsequent Humphrey–Hawkins legislation. And at the beginning of the 1980s, the Congress passed the #Monetary #Control #Act and the #Federal-Reserve #adopted procedures to provide greater assurance that #targets for M1 could be #achieved. But, even by the mid 1970s, the #relationship of the #monetary #aggregates to the economy was becoming more complex. Financial innovation and deregulation significantly altered the spectrum of available #transaction and saving #instruments. [Greenspan February 1993]

Table 4.A2
(continued)

Class	Top characteristic words	Examples from top four characteristic phrases, or ECUs
US *real economy*	percent+ quarter+ unemployment-rate+ average+ rise month+ labor+ annual+ rate+ pace+	The #fall in #housing demand in turn prompted a sharp #slowing in the #pace of #construction of new homes. Even so, the backlog of unsold homes #rose from about 4½ months' supply in 2005 to nearly 7 months' supply by the #third #quarter of #last #year. #Single #family #housing #starts have #dropped more than 30 #percent since the #beginning of #last #year, and #employment growth in the #construction sector has #slowed substantially. Some tentative #signs of #stabilization have recently appeared in the #housing market. New and existing home #sales have flattened out in recent #months. Mortgage applications have #picked up, and some #surveys find that homebuyers' sentiment has improved. However, even if #housing demand #falls no further, #weakness in residential investment is likely to #continue to weigh on economic growth over the next few #quarters as homebuilders #seek to reduce their #inventories of unsold homes to more comfortable levels. Despite the #ongoing adjustments in the #housing sector, overall economic prospects for households remain good. Household finances appear generally #solid and delinquency #rates on most types of #consumer loans and residential mortgages remain low. [Bernanke February 2007] Real activity in the United States expanded at a #solid #pace in 2006, although the #pattern of growth was uneven. After a first #quarter rebound from #weakness associated with the effects of the hurricanes that ravaged the gulf coast the #previous #summer, #output growth #moderated somewhat on #average over the remainder of 2006. Real GDP is currently #estimated to have increased at an #annual #rate of about 2.75 #percent in the #second half of the #year. As we #anticipated in our July #report, the United States economy appears to be making a transition from the rapid #rate of expansion experienced over the preceding several #years to a more sustainable #average #pace of growth. The principal source of the #ongoing #moderation has been a substantial cooling of the #housing market, which has led to a marked #slowdown in the #pace of residential #construction. However, the #weakness in #housing market activity and the #slower appreciation of house prices do not #seem to have spilled over to any significant extent to other sectors of the economy. #Consumer spending has continued to expand at a #solid #rate, and the demand for #labor has remained strong. On #average, about 165,000 jobs per #month have been added to non #farm #payrolls over the past 6 #months, and the #unemployment-rate, at 4. . . . [Bernanke February 2007]

Table 4.A2
(continued)

Class	Top characteristic words	Examples from top four characteristic phrases, or ECUs
Criticism of Fed for failing to support growth (D. Riegle)	that+ we've+ go you've out maybe say there+ else+ want+	In the meantime, people who have got to get from #today to next week to next month to 6 months #down the road are having a very, very difficult time doing it. People here in this town are #getting by all #right. They have health care. #They've got #pretty good salaries, for the most part, and so #forth. It's not true #out in the countryside. #That's why #you've got something of a political rebellion underway. I don't know how to get the message through to the Federal-Reserve. I don't think you're hearing it because I don't #see it #coming back #out of your testimony or your prepared statement #today. I don't detect the urgency about this problem that the people are #asking for. Now you may #say, #well, they don't #understand. #That's #sort of what the President has been #saying, that things are better than the people think they are. If he believes that, #somebody #really needs to #sit him #down and have a talk with him because people know #what's #going on in their lives, and the anxiety that they're reflecting in these polls and this consumer survey data from Michigan is #real. [Riegle, Chair (D) July 1992] I think you're too passive, quite #frankly. I don't #say that just to you, but I think the response of the Federal-Reserve board has been very modest, very guarded, very slow, and I think not adequate to the problem. The message you're #getting back from the public is that they #want more done because the sickness #out there is more pervasive and deeper than #we've #seen before. You yourself have #said it. #You've #said #you've not #seen economic conditions like these and confidence problems like these ever before in your professional lifetime. There has to be a link between that observation and what people are #reacting to and experiencing in their own lives when they #tell us that and we get that message. We're #going to have to do something that #goes beyond what we normally do to try to respond to it. I don't #understand how #there's a disconnection between the #signals we're #getting and the policy response that we're making in return to the #signals. #You've got to explain that here #today. #You've got to #tell us why we #can't do more when more is needed. [Riegle, Chair (D) February 1992]

Part Two: Figures 4.A1 through 4.A18

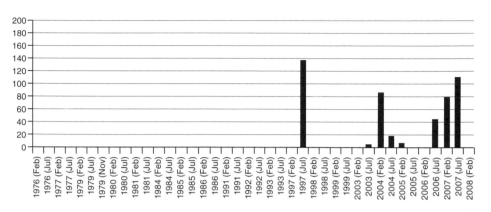

Figure 4.A1
House hearings, 1976 to 2008 (chi-squared values)—Class 1: Populist attack on Greenspan (mostly B. Sanders)

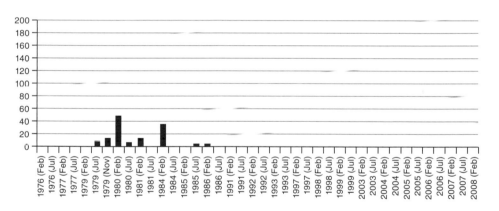

Figure 4.A2
House hearings 1976 to 2008 (chi-squared values)—Class 2: Volcker defending anti-inflation stance

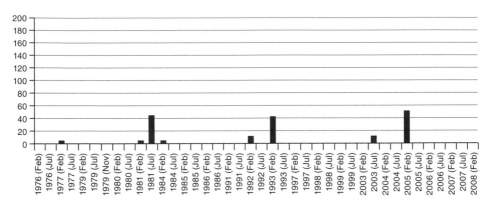

Figure 4.A3
House hearings 1976 to 2008 (chi-squared values)—Class 3: Fiscal policy

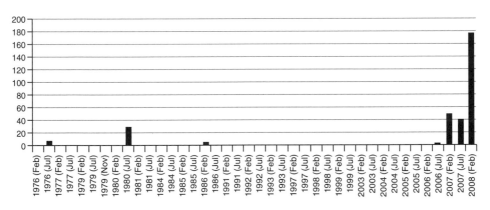

Figure 4.A4
House hearings 1976 to 2008 (chi-squared values)—Class 4: Fed's regulatory activity

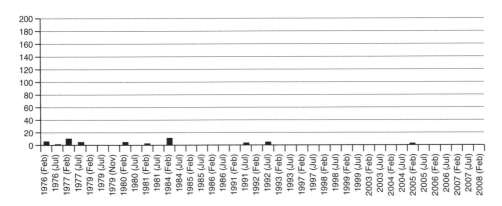

Figure 4.A5
House hearings 1976 to 2008 (chi-squared values)—Class: 5 Q&A format (process) mixed substance

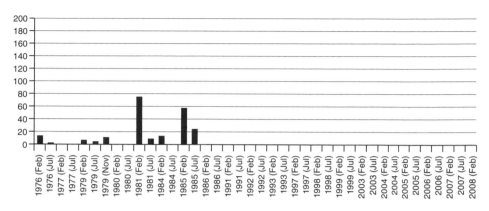

Figure 4.A6
House hearings 1976 to 2008 (chi-squared values)—Class 6: Monetary aggregates

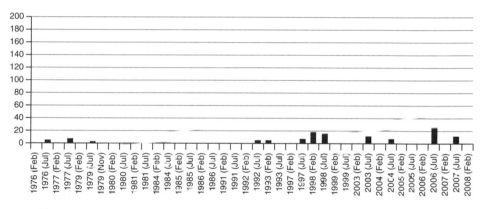

Figure 4.A7
House hearings 1976 to 2008 (chi-squared values)—Class 7: US real economy

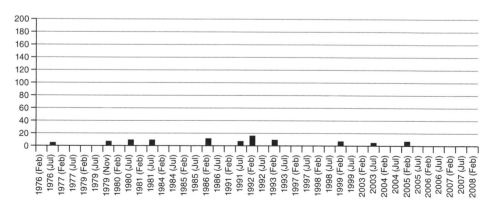

Figure 4.A8
House hearings 1976 to 2008 (chi-squared values)—Class 8: Members prompting the Fed chairman on nonmonetary policy issues

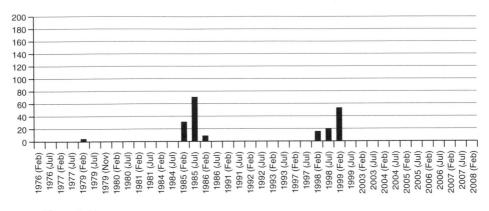

Figure 4.A9
House hearings 1976 to 2008 (chi-squared values)—Class 9: Capital inflows, exchange rate, current account deficit

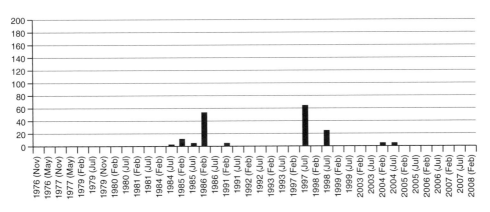

Figure 4.A10
Senate hearings 1976 to 2008 (chi-squared values)—Class 1: World economy and external balance (trade and current account)

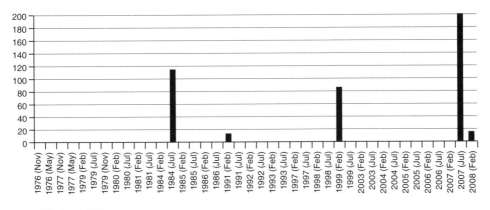

Figure 4.A11
Senate hearings 1976 to 2008 (chi-squared values)—Class 2: Bank regulation

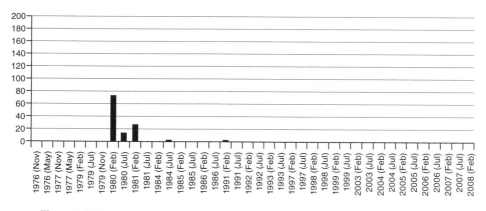

Figure 4.A12
Senate hearings 1976 to 2008 (chi-squared values)—Class 3 Q&A format (process)

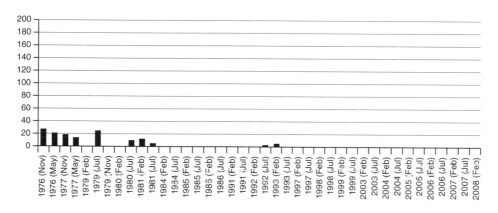

Figure 4.A13
Senate hearings 1976 to 2008 (chi-squared values)—Class 4: Fed appointments and relationship between Fed, Congress, and administration

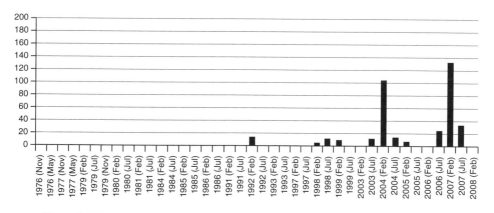

Figure 4.A14
Senate hearings 1976 to 2008 (chi-squared values)—Class 5: Education, training, and US competitiveness

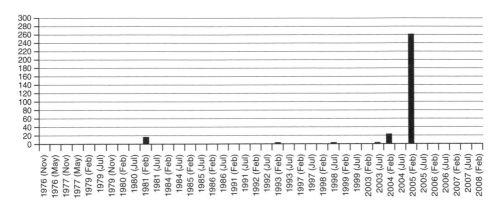

Figure 4.A15
Senate hearings 1976 to 2008 (chi-squared values)—Class 6: Fiscal policy

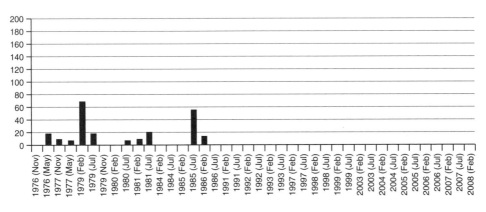

Figure 4.A16
Senate hearings 1976 to 2008 (chi-squared values)—Class 7: Monetary aggregates

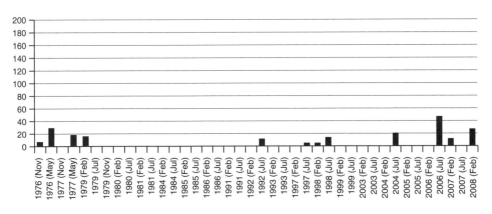

Figure 4.A17
Senate hearings 1976 to 2008 (chi-squared values)—Class 8: US real economy

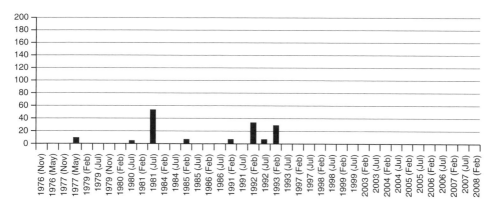

Figure 4.A18
Senate hearings 1976 to 2008 (chi-squared values)—Class 9: Criticism of Fed (for failing to support growth)

Part Three: Core Statements of Fed Chairmen on Monetary Policy (extracted from *Tri-croisé* ECUs)

Burns

House

We knew from a careful reading of history that the turnover of money balances tends to rise rapidly in the early stages of an economic upswing. Consequently we resisted the advice of those who wanted to open the tap and let money flow out in greater abundance. Subsequent events have borne out our judgment.

I believe that the course of moderation in monetary policy pursued by the Federal Reserve last year has contributed to economic recovery. The Board are pleased to learn that the Senate Banking Committee, in its recent report on the conduct of monetary policy agrees with this view.

The downward adjustments of those growth ranges served to reassure the business and financial community that we intend to stick to a course of moderation in monetary policy. Another indication of our firm resolve was the prompt action taken some weeks ago to ward off a threat of excessive growth of the monetary aggregates.

Unemployment is still deplorably high, and activity in not a few of our nation's industries remains depressed. Continuance of moderately rapid expansion is, therefore, essential to the restoration of our economic well-being as a nation.

I must report, moreover, that despite the gradual reduction of projected growth ranges for the aggregates during the past two years, no meaningful reduction has as yet occurred in actual growth rates. That unintended consequence is partly the result of data deficiencies that complicate the already formidable task of adjusting or approximating monetary growth objectives. Some of the data deficiencies we have experienced are being overcome. Even so, monetary measurement will continue to lack the precision of a science. So too will the Federal Reserve's actions aiming to influence developments in financial markets.

Senate

The underlying trend of costs and prices thus is still clearly upward, and inflation must remain a major consideration in formulating public policy. We at the Federal Reserve recognize our responsibility for sticking to a course of monetary policy that will promote further economic expansion, so that our nation may regain satisfactory levels of production and employment. We also recognize that monetary policy needs to be consistent with an eventual return to stability of the general price level.

Let me take this opportunity to state unequivocally once again that further reductions in the growth ranges of all the major monetary aggregates will continue to be needed if the United States is to succeed in unwinding the inflation that still plagues our economy.

The Federal Reserve has pursued a moderate monetary policy during the course of this recovery, seeking to foster financial conditions that would facilitate a good expansion in economic activity without aggravating in any way the troublesome problem of inflation.

I believe that the course of moderation in monetary policy pursued over the past year has significantly aided the process of recovery in economic activity. We at the Federal Reserve remain deeply concerned about the high level of unemployment that still exists in our country. We recognize the need to regain more prosperous economic conditions. We also recognize, as thoughtful Americans generally do, that lasting prosperity will not be achieved until our country solves its chronic problem of inflation. The inflation that is still damaging our economy and troubling our people began over a decade ago largely as a consequence of loose fiscal policies. During the early 1970s, the underlying inflationary trend was aggravated by a variety of special factors; poor crop harvests here and abroad, a worldwide boom in economic activity, devaluation of the dollar in international exchange markets, and an enormous run up in the prices of gasoline, fuel oil, and other energy items brought on by the OPEC cartel.

The principal contribution that the Federal Reserve can now make to the achievement of our nation's basic economic objectives is to adhere to a course of moderation in monetary policy.

Miller

House

The oil price shock, as I say, sets us back in our timetable for winning the war against inflation. It had been our report to this committee that with the strategic policies being put into place involving fiscal discipline, involving incomes policy, involving dollar and international account policies, involving energy policies, and involving monetary policies we would wring out inflation over 5, 6, or 7 years. We have been put back in that timetable, in my opinion, by 1 year or more. And we are now going to start downward in wringing out inflation from a higher plateau than we otherwise would have reached.

The inflation rate for 1979, measured on the GNP deflator, shows an 8.75 percent increase, a rather disturbing rate that is causing us difficulty in adjusting the economy to our long term objectives.

Monetary policy continues to be an important influence on the performance of the economy, and there are some exogenous forces whose effects it might well be able to offset. However, monetary policy cannot simultaneously offset the inflationary impulse of the rise in oil prices and the contractionary impact of the income transfer to foreign oil producers.

We do not anticipate pegging the Fed Funds rate at any particular level although avoiding sharp shifts in policy will allow us gradually to wind down inflation without a severe economic downturn.

I have been a proponent of adjusting our economy to a slower growth mode, on a gradual basis, so we don't shock it, don't create dislocations, and don't interrupt the process of investment in a way that would trigger a serious recession.

Senate

I would say we must rely upon our best judgment, and it seems to coincide with the outlook in the President's Economic Report for a growth rate in 1979 below the trend. Now if there are those who prefer a more restrictive policy and produce a recession, I would argue with them that they are wrong. A recession is not going to cure inflation.

Now the balance we are seeking is moderation, a slow growth philosophy for a period of time to get inflation down. We are not seeking a recession.

I think we ought to accommodate more through monetary policy and not have the tendency to become too stimulative in fiscal policy.

Volcker

House

As part of the process of restoring price stability, as I see it, this continuing effort reflects not simply a concern about the need for greater monetary and price stability for its own sake critical as that is. The experience of the Seventies strongly suggests that the inflationary process undercuts efforts to achieve and maintain other goals, expressed in the Humphrey–Hawkins Act, of growth and employment.

The legacy of the Seventies was deeply ingrained patterns of behavior in pricing, in wage bargaining, in interest rates, and in financial practices generally built on the assumption of continuing, and accelerating inflation. Starving an inflation of the money needed to sustain it is a difficult process in the best of circumstances; it was doubly so when the continuing inflationary momentum was so strong. Now, after a great deal of pain and dislocation, attitudes have changed, there is a sense of greater restraint in pricing and wage behavior.

Against the background of the strong inflationary momentum in the economy, the targets are frankly designed to be restrictive. They do imply restraint on the potential growth of the nominal GNP. The heart of the problem is that if inflation continues unabated or rises, real activity is likely to be squeezed. But, as inflation begins noticeably to abate, the stage will be set for stronger real growth. Monetary policy is designed to encourage that disinflationary process. But the success of that policy and the extent to which it can be achieved without great pressure on interest rates and stress on financial markets that have already been heavily strained will also depend upon other public policies and private attitudes and behavior.

In approaching our own operational decisions, the actual and prospective size of the budget deficit inevitably complicates the environment within which we work. By feeding consumer purchasing power, by heightening skepticism about our ability to control the money supply and contain inflation, by claiming a disproportionate share of available funds, and by increasing our dependence on foreign capital, monetary policy must carry more of the burden of maintaining stability and its flexibility, to some degree, is constrained. Monetary policy is only one part of an economic program. It is an essential part, but success is dependent on a coherent whole.

The experience of recent months demonstrates that monetary and fiscal policies alone cannot by themselves offset the present instability of our domestic and international economic affairs. We need urgently to develop comprehensive stabilization policies. As the chairman has emphasized, the direction of economic activity has changed swiftly in recent months. We have acute problems of recession and inflation. There have been unprecedented changes in interest rates and the imposition and removal of extraordinary measures of credit restraint. The fiscal position of the federal government is changing rapidly. In these circumstances, confusion and uncertainty can arise about goals and policies, not just those of the Federal Reserve, but of economic policy generally. That is why I particularly welcome the opportunity to be here to emphasize the underlying continuity in our approach at the Federal Reserve and its relationship to other economic policies, matters that are critical to public understanding and expectations. The Federal Reserve has been, and will continue to be, guided by the need to maintain financial discipline.

Let there be no doubt, the Federal Reserve is determined to make every reasonable effort to work toward reducing monetary growth from the levels of recent years, not just in 1980, but in the years ahead.

I think the whole weight of my remarks is that the one thing we can do really constructively, from this standpoint and from the domestic standpoint, is to reduce the demands on our credit markets. How do you do that constructively? You don't want to do it by reducing home building, by reducing business investment, and all the rest. The obvious way to do it is to reduce the budget deficit, take some of the pressure off our markets. To the extent that that is influencing the market artificially in a sense, a reduction in the deficit will be effective.

Obviously, a satisfactory answer cannot lie in the direction of indefinitely continued high levels of unemployment and poor economic performance. On the other hand, ratifying strong price pressures by increases in the money supply offers no solution; that approach could only prolong and intensify the inflationary process, and in the end to undermine the expansion.

Senate

Let there be no doubt, the Federal Reserve is determined to make every reasonable effort to work toward reducing monetary growth from the levels of recent years, not just in 1980, but in the years ahead. The policy actions taken on October 6th of last year, which entailed changes in our operating techniques to provide better assurance of containing the growth in the money supply, were one demonstration of that commitment.

The Federal Reserve has been, and will continue to be, guided by the need to maintain financial discipline a discipline concretely reflected in reduced growth over time of the monetary and credit aggregates as part of the process of restoring price stability.

I think the markets reflect and it is apparent in other contexts that for the time being there is a particularly heavy burden on monetary policy in dealing with the inflationary situation.

An effective program to restore price stability requires reducing growth in money and credit over time to rates consistent with the growth of output and employment at stable prices. That is the basic premise of our policies.

Greenspan

House

To a considerable extent, investors seem to be expecting that low inflation and stronger productivity growth will allow the extraordinary growth of profits to be extended into the distant future.

The essential precondition for the emergence, and persistence, of this virtuous cycle is arguably the decline in the rate of inflation to near price stability. In recent years, continued low product price inflation and expectations that it will persist have promoted stability in financial markets and fostered perceptions that the degree of risk in the financial outlook has been moving ever lower. These perceptions, in turn, have reduced the extra compensation that investors require for making loans to, or taking ownership positions in private firms. With risks in the domestic economy judged to be low, credit and equity capital have been readily available for many businesses, fostering strong investment. And low mortgage interest rates have allowed many households to purchase homes and to refinance outstanding debt.

A consequence of the rapid gains in productivity and slack in our labor and product markets has been sustained downward pressure on inflation.

Notwithstanding a reasonably optimistic interpretation of the recent productivity numbers, it would not be prudent to assume that even strongly rising productivity, by itself, can ensure a noninflationary future. Certainly wage increases, per se, are not inflationary, unless they exceed productivity growth, thereby creating pressure. Inflationary price increases can eventually undermine economic growth and employment. Because the level of productivity is tied to an important degree to the stock of capital, which turns over only gradually, increases in the trend growth of productivity probably also occur rather gradually. By contrast, the potential for abrupt acceleration of nominal hourly compensation is surely greater. As I have noted in previous appearances before Congress, economic growth at rates experienced on average over the past several years would eventually run into constraints as the reservoir of unemployed people available to work is drawn down.

Senate

In recent years, continued low product price inflation and expectations that it will persist have promoted stability in financial markets and fostered perceptions that the degree of risk in the financial outlook has been moving ever lower.

Investors seem to be expecting that low inflation and stronger productivity growth will allow the extraordinary growth of profits to be extended into the distant future.

Whether inflation actually rises in the wake of slowing productivity growth, however, will depend on the rate of growth of labor compensation and the ability and willingness of firms to pass on higher costs to their customers. That, in turn, will depend on the degree of utilization of resources and how monetary policymakers respond.

Bernanke

House

Monetary policy works with a lag. Therefore our policy stance must be determined in light of the medium term forecast of real activity and inflation as well as the risks to that forecast. Although the FOMC participants' economic projections envision an improving economic picture, it is important to recognize that downside risks to growth remain. The FOMC will be carefully evaluating incoming information bearing on the economic outlook and will act in a timely manner as needed to support growth and to provide adequate insurance against downside risks.

As always, in determining the appropriate stance of policy, we will be alert to the possibility that the economy is not evolving in the way we currently judge to be the most likely.

Senate

As always, in determining the appropriate stance of policy, we will be alert to the possibility that the economy is not evolving in the way we currently judge to be the most likely. One risk to the outlook is that the ongoing housing correction might prove larger than anticipated, with possible spillovers onto consumer spending. Alternatively consumer spending, which has advanced relatively vigorously on balance in recent quarters, might expand more quickly than expected. In that case, economic growth could rebound to a pace above its trend. With the level of resource utilization already elevated, the resulting pressures in labor and product markets could lead to increased inflation over time. Yet another risk is that energy and commodity prices could continue to rise sharply, leading to further increases in headline inflation and, if those costs pass through to the prices of non-energy goods and services, to higher core inflation as well.

The recent rise in inflation is of concern to the FOMC. The achievement of price stability is one of the objectives that make up the Congress's mandate to the Federal Reserve. Moreover, in the long run, price stability is critical to achieving maximum employment and moderate long term interest rates, the other parts of the congressional mandate.

We are trying to balance a number of different risks against each other. With respect to inflation, as I said, our anticipation is that inflation will come down this year and be close to price stability this year and next year. If it does not, then what we will be watching particularly carefully is whether or not inflation expectations or non-energy, non-food prices are beginning to show evidence of entrenchment, of higher inflation, as you point out. That would certainly be of significant concern to us and one that we are watching very carefully.

Part Four: Tables 4.A3 through 4.A10

Table 4.A3
Thematic classes for 1976 to 1977 congressional hearings, with statistically significant tags for party affiliation and Fed chairman

Classes for House hearings, 1976–1977 (with thematic classification group indicated in brackets)	Democratic tag (with χ^2 value)	Republican tag (with χ^2 value)	Burns tag (with χ^2 value)	Other tags (with χ^2 value)
Labor market/employment & inflation (3)		*** (49.9)		*** (82.5) Member
Growth of monetary aggregates (4)	* (4.1)			*** (133.1) Chairman Reuss-D
Capacity utilization & investment by firms (2)			*** (126.2)	
Innovation in bank accounts w/links to Monetary aggregates (5)			*** (31.6)	
Independence & structure of the FOMC (7)	*** (51.9)			*** (44.0) Member
Classes for Senate hearings, 1976–1777				
Exchange rate, monetary policy, & the world economy (9)			(3.0)	*** (25.8) Stevenson-D
Transparency of the Fed; relations between Fed & Congress (7)	*** (86.1)	* (6.4)		*** (45.1) Chairman Proxmire-D *** (34.4) Member
Monetary aggregates (4)		(3.3)	*** (46.2)	
Labor markets/employment (3)	*** (26.2)			*** (16.2) Chairman Proxmire-D ** (9.7) Member
Business investment & its financing (2)			*** (67.4)	

Statistical significance (df = 1)	χ^2 value
NS	< 2.71
10%	< 3.84
5% (*)	< 6.63
1% (**)	< 10.80
< 1% (***)	≥ 10.80

Note: Tags are given for individual members only for those classes in which neither party affiliation nor Fed chairman is a dominant tag, or where a tag (e.g., the committee chairman or member) is unusually significant (applies also for tables 4.A4–4.A10).

Table 4.A4
Thematic classes for 1979 congressional hearings, with statistically significant tags for party affiliation and Fed chairman

Classes for House hearings, 1979 (with thematic classification group indicated in brackets)	Democratic tag (with χ^2 value)	Republican tag (with χ^2 value)	Miller/Wallich tag (with χ^2 value)	Other tags (with χ^2 value)
Describing economic growth data (2)			*** (11.5) [Miller]	
Fiscal policy/tax measures (6)				* (5.7) Cavanaugh-D *** (11.9) Evans-D ** (8.0) Ritter-R
Inflation/monetary policy (1)	* (3.9)			*** (14.7) Blanchard-D *** (17.1) Vento-D
Credit creation/money growth (4)				*** (15.7) Patterson-D *** (15.1) Paul-R *** (40.4) St. Germain-D *** (15.1) Watkins-D
Exchange rate/cost of foreign currency debt (9)		*** (11.7)		*** (57.9) Leach-R
Classes for Senate hearings, 1979				
Fed independence (7)	*** (39.5)			** (9.7) Chairman Proxmire-D *** (52.0) Riegle-D *** (34.1) member
Monetary & credit aggregates, and innovation in bank accounts (4)			*** (12.8) [Miller] *** (26.9) [Wallich]	
Labor markets, unemployment, & inflation (3)				* (4.4) Chairman Proxmire-D
Stance of monetary policy & objectives (1)			(2.8) [Miller]	*** (32.8) Stewart-D

Table 4.A5
Thematic classes for 1979 to 1981 congressional hearings, with statistically significant tags for party affiliation and Fed chairman

Classes for House hearings, 1979–1981 (with thematic classification group indicated in brackets)	Democratic tag (with χ^2 value)	Republican tag (with χ^2 value)	Volcker tag (with χ^2 value)	Other tags (with χ^2 value)
Bank credit/structure of deposit banking/account types (5)				*** (115.0) Chairman Reuss-D *** (56.7) McCollum-R *** (37.6) Leach-R *** (16.9) LaFalce-D *** (13.7) Chairman St. Germain-D
Fiscal policy (spending & deficits) (6)	*** (105.8)	*** (11.8)		*** (130.2) Member
Inflation problems (1)			*** (77.4)	
Fiscal policy (tax) (6)			*** (30.2)	*** (26.2) Frank-D *** (21.1) Carman-R
Productivity, inflation and the labor market (1)			*** (50.9)	
Monetary aggregates (4)			*** (19.0)	*** (19.6) Hansen-R *** (19.4) Mitchell-D *** (16.1) Stanton-R
Investment in housing & by small businesses (2)	*** (93.4)	* (5.6)		*** (157.7) Watkins-D *** (139.3) Member *** (81.8) Annunzio-D
Classes for Senate hearings, 1980–1981				
Credit restraint (signals from monetary policy) (4)	*** (15.6)			*** (135.4) Riegle-D *** (53.6) Member
Interest rates & credit conditions (4)		** (8.9)		*** (11.0) Chairman Garn [in 1981]-R
Monetary aggregates (4)			*** (28.7)	
Fiscal policy (6)	*** (72.7)	** (10.4)		
Volcker Revolution/anti-inflation policies (1)			*** (28.2)	

Table 4.A6
Thematic classes for 1984 to 1986 congressional hearings, with statistically significant tags for party affiliation and Fed chairman

Classes for House hearings, 1984–1986 (with thematic classification group indicated in brackets)	Democratic tag (with χ^2 value)	Republican tag (with χ^2 value)	Volcker tag (with χ^2 value)	Other tags (with χ^2 value)
Transparency of FOMC (demands for more) (8a)	*** (113.8)	*** (88.1)		*** (204.2) Member *** (113.2) Frank-D
Regulation of the banking system (5)				*** (44.6) Leach-R *** (24.7) McCandless-R *** (23.1) McKinney—R *** (19.3) Oakar-D
Fiscal policy (6)	*** (126.4)			*** (74.7) Member
US imbalances/exchange rate/world economy (9)			*** (98.2)	
Monetary aggregates (4)			*** (41.3)	*** (31.8) McCollum-R
Uncertainty & risks around forecasts of interest rates (1)			*** (16.9)	
Classes for Senate hearings, 1984–1986				
Capital flows/external imbalances/exchange rate/world economy (9)			*** (17.2)	*** (18.9) Heinz-R
Bank failures (especially Continental Illinois) (5)				*** (46.9) Trible-R *** (23.8) Hecht-R *** (15.8) Riegle-D
Fiscal policy (6)	*** (107.2)	*** (10.8)		*** (129.7) member
Structure of banking system/creation of "non-bank" banks (5)			*** (17.7)	
Uncertainty around course of, and target of monetary policy (1)	*** (41.0)			
Economic activity/monetary aggregates & inflation (4)			*** (32.7)	*** (65.4) Riegle-D

Table 4.A7
Thematic classes for 1991 to 1993 congressional hearings, with statistically significant tags for party affiliation and Greenspan

Classes for House hearings, 1991–1993 (with thematic classification group indicated in brackets)	Democratic tag (with χ^2 value)	Republican tag (with χ^2 value)	Greenspan tag (with χ^2 value)	Other tags (with χ^2 value)
Fiscal policy (6)	*** (112.1)	*** (26.3)		*** (127.7) Member
Interaction of Fed with presidency & elections (8a)	*** (130.2)	*** (91.4)		*** (214.4) Member
Credit flows/asset prices (4)			*** (96.2)	
Economic outlook/inflation/money supply (1)			*** (89.9)	
Bank lending—especially small businesses (4)			*** (47.6)	
Classes for Senate hearings, 1991–1993				
Health of banking system (5)			*** (107.2)	
Role of Congress in economic policy/fiscal policy (8a)	*** (76.0)	*** (22.0)		*** (52.9) Member *** (36.3) Chairman Riegle-D
Fiscal policy (6)		*** (238.0)		*** (110.5) Member *** (208.7) Gramm-R
Monetary aggregates (4)			*** (547.5)	
Labor markets/unemployment (3)	*** (318.6)			*** (162.8) Chairman Riegle-D *** (118.40 Sarbanes-D

Table 4.A8
Thematic classes for 1997 to 1999 congressional hearings, with statistically significant tags for party affiliation and Greenspan

Classes for House hearings, 1997–1999 (with thematic classification group indicated in brackets)	Democratic tag (with χ^2 value)	Republican tag (with χ^2 value)	Independent tag (Bernie Sanders) (with χ^2 value)	Greenspan tag (with χ^2 value)	Other tags (with χ^2 value)
Role of government in the economy (domestic & international) (8a)	*** (28.8)	*** (62.8)			*** (46.2) Member
Economic activity & growth in United States (2)				*** (264.2)	
Labor markets/unemployment (3)	*** (22.4)		*** (312.0)	*** (19.6)	*** (21.7) Lucas-R *** (20.7) Vento-D
Asian & Russian crises (9)					*** (63.8) McCollum-R *** (54.5) Goode-D *** (38.8) Bentsen-D *** (38.0) Royce-R
Fiscal policy (6)	* (5.5)	* (5.2)			
Classes for Senate hearings, 1997–1999					
Structure of banking system/regulation (5)				* (4.6)	*** (13.6) Reed-D *** (11.8) Chairman D'Amato-R
Praising Greenspan & seeking his advice (8b)	*** (118.3)	*** (130.1)			*** (222.8) Member
Fiscal policy (6)	* (6.5)	*** (26.2)			*** (49.2) Moseley-Braun-D *** (47.3) Bayh-D *** (43.0) Grams-R *** (37.1) Allard-R *** (43.2) Member
World economy/Y2K conversion of IT system (9)				** (8.6)	*** (11.7) Bennett-R
Economic outlook & growth (2)				*** (128.1)	

Table 4.A9
Thematic classes for 2003 to 2005 congressional hearings, with statistically significant tags for party affiliation and Greenspan

Classes for House hearings, 2003–2005 (with thematic classification group indicated in brackets)	Democratic tag (with χ^2 value)	Republican tag (with χ^2 value)	Independent tag (Bernie Sanders) (with χ^2 value)	Greenspan tag (with χ^2 value)	Other tags (with χ^2 value)
Labor markets, wages, employment (3)	*** (87.3)	*** (20.9)	*** (119.9)		*** (204.9) Member
Productivity, economic growth & investment by businesses (2)				*** (89.3)	
Education & equality (10)				*** (174.4)	
Social Security reform (6)	*** (106.7)				*** (71.1) Member
Fiscal policy (6)	*** (54.5)				*** (17.2) Member
Banking system/bank regulation/punishing foreign banks for misdemeanors (5)		*** (27.0)			*** (128.8) Chairman Kelly-R
Classes for Senate hearings, 2003–2005					
Fiscal policy (6)	*** (11.8)				*** (46.7) Reed-D
Praising Greenspan & seeking his advice (8b)	*** (17.4)				*** (35.3) Member *** (28.3) Bunning-R *** (24.1) Dodd-D *** (19.0) Carper-D
Economic activity/role of monetary policy in sustaining growth (2)				*** (138.1)	
Energy policy (10)		(3.2)			*** (84.7) Dole-R *** (68.9) Enzi-R
Labor markets/earnings (3)	** (7.7)				*** (36.9) Sarbanes-D

Table 4.A10
Thematic classes for 2006 to 2008 hearings, with statistically significant tags for party affiliation and Bernanke

Classes for House hearings, 2006–2008 (with thematic classification group indicated in brackets)	Democratic tag (with χ^2 value)	Republican tag (with χ^2 value)	Bernanke tag (with χ^2 value)	Other tags (with χ^2 value)
Education & income inequality (10)	*** (44.6)	*** (20.7)		*** (44.7) Chairman Frank-D *** (40.3) Member
Investment in corporates/role of hedge funds (5)			*** (46.9)	
Inflation & economic activity (1)			*** (194.9)	
Mortgage lending/conduct of business (5)			*** (35.1)	*** (80.0) Watt-D
Wages & productivity (3)	*** (54.5)	*** (58.6)		*** (135.1) Member
Classes for Senate hearings, 2006–2008				
Challenging Fed & Bernanke; proposing new legislation (8a)	*** (80.3)	*** (23.0)		*** (52.0) Member
Economic activity & inflation (1)			*** (123.7)	
Controls on the conduct of mortgage lending (5)			*** (28.6)	*** (21.6) Brown-D
Foreign ownership of US firms/sovereign wealth funds/China (9)	*** (10.8)			
Education & raising skills of labor force (10)			*** (15.2)	*** (16.1) Dole-R
Wage inequality & employment (3)	*** (113.7)			*** (145.0) Menendez-D *** (91.9) member

5   In Their Own Words—Perspectives from the FOMC and Congressional Banking Committees

5.1 Introduction

This chapter extends the approach used in the previous two chapters to present politicians, FOMC members and Fed and congressional staff with the results of our textual analysis. Hence our purpose here is to "triangulate" along the lines suggested by Gaskell and Bauer (2000), by incorporating an independent method—namely elite interviews—to corroborate the results from our use of textual analysis to study deliberation. In the conclusion to this chapter we set out the main findings from the interviews in respect of the hypotheses from chapter 2. Since the interview approach is intended to encompass the whole scope of our work, all the hypotheses are potentially relevant here. To be clear, we describe the hypotheses as potentially relevant since the interviews may cast light on any of them, but not doing so does not on its own invalidate a hypothesis; rather, we may not have found the evidence to support or invalidate it through interviewing.

To our knowledge, this is the first time (at least in economics and political science) that researchers using textual analysis software have sought directly to question the actual policy makers and politicians who generated (or helped generate) the texts under investigation. Such interviews are not about "counting opinions or people but rather exploring the range of opinions, the different representations of the issue" (Gaskell 2000: 41). Aside from questioning our interviewees on the findings of our automated textual analysis, we also use the interviews to gain a better understanding of the motivations of the participants, and their perceptions of the motivations of other participants (in particular, the perceptions of FOMC members vis-à-vis those of members of Congress, and vice versa). Of course, just like any other data sample, the inferences that we can draw from our interviews are contingent on the quality of our sample of interviewees. In this regard we do not claim to have a fully representative sample of participants of the FOMC meetings and congressional hearings; rather, we have obtained a *reasonably good* sample of relevant and informed participants, who are listed in order of interview date in table 5.1.

From his "25 years of qualitative research," Gaskell argues that there is no fixed amount for the number of in-depth interviews as it depends on the nature of the research project. He remarks that "more interviews do not necessarily imply better quality or more detailed understanding" as "there are a limited number of interpretations" of reality and after a while, the research finds "that no new surprises or insights are forthcoming" (Gaskell 2000: 38, 43).We contend that we have obtained a *reasonably good* sample of relevant and informed participants in the FOMC meetings and congressional hearings of the Senate and House banking committees based on the composition of experience and backgrounds of our 22 interviewees. In short, we have in our sample, one *chairman of the Federal Reserve* (Volcker); three *vice chairs of the Board of Governors* (Blinder, 1994–1996; Rivlin, 1996–1999; Kohn, 2006–2010); two *members of the Board of Governors* (Lindsey, 1991–1997; Kohn, 2002–2006)[1]; five *bank presidents* of four different reserve banks (Hoskins and Jordan, both of Cleveland, covering years 1987–2003; Broaddus of Richmond, 1993–2004; Poole of St. Louis, 1998–2008; and Minehan of Boston, 1994–2007); three consecutive *Federal Reserve directors for monetary policy analysis* (whose job entailed accompanying the Fed chairman to congressional hearings)—and who were simultaneously *secretary to the FOMC* (thus in charge of administrative details attendant to the FOMC meeting, including writing up the minutes so as accurately to reflect the tenor and content of FOMC discussions), which together covers 27 years (Axilrod, 1980–1986; Kohn, 1986–2002; Reinhart, 2001–2007); two former *members of Congress* who served on either the House Financial Services Committee (Barrett, 2003–2011), or the Senate Banking Committee (Bayh, 1998–2010); two *key members of the staff* for the House Banking Committee during the years leading up to and including the passage of the Humphrey–Hawkins legislation (Galbraith, 1975–1980; D'Arista, 1976–1978); and two *current staff economists*—including the chief economist (Smith, 2006–)—for the House Financial Services Committee; three *current staff advisors to senators* on the Senate Banking Committee; and one *staff advisor* for another Senate committee. (As the current congressional staff interviewees requested anonymity, and Smith requested verification before using any quote attributed to him,

Table 5.1
Details of interviews

Name	Date of Interview	Place/mode	Background of Interviewee (relevant positions at Fed or in Congress; and education)
Paul Volcker	May 13, 2010	In person, London (LSE)	Chairman of Federal Reserve, 1979–1987; President of New York Federal Reserve Bank, 1975–1979 [Chairman of President Obama's Economic Recovery Advisory Board, 2009–2011] BA, Princeton; MA, Harvard (Political Economy); Rotary Fellow, LSE
Lee Hoskins	September 12, 2010	Email	President of Cleveland Federal Reserve Bank, 1987–1991; Economist, Research Officer at Philadelphia Federal Reserve Bank (1969–1972), becoming Vice President in 1973 BA, MA, PhD (Economics), UCLA
Jerry Jordan	September 21, 2010	Phone	President of Cleveland Federal Reserve Bank, 1992–2003; Senior Vice President of Director of Research at Federal Reserve Bank of St Louis; Member of President Reagan's Council of Economic Advisers, 1981–1982 PhD (Economics), UCLA
Steve Axilrod	September 30, 2010	In person, London (LSE)	Staff Director and Secretary of the FOMC, and Staff Director for monetary and financial policy for Federal Reserve Board of Governors, 1952–1986 AB, Harvard (Economics); MA (Planning), University of Chicago
Al Broaddus	October 11, 2010	Phone	President of Richmond Federal Reserve Bank, 1993–2004 (prior to 1993, he held a variety of posts with the bank over a 34-year career) BA (Political Science), Washington and Lee University, 1961 MA, PhD (Economics), Indiana University, 1970, 1972

Table 5.1
(continued)

Name	Date of Interview	Place/mode	Background of Interviewee (relevant positions at Fed or in Congress; and education)
Anonymous/ non-attributable	October 12, 2010	Phone	Staffer/Advisor to Member of Senate Banking Committee
Don Kohn	October 14, 2010	Phone	Vice Chairman of Federal Reserve Board of Governors, 2006–2010; Member, Federal Reserve Board, 2002–2010; before that, holding several positions at the Fed over a 40-year career, including Director of the Division of Monetary Affairs (1987–2001) and Secretary of the FOMC (1987–2002). BA (Economics), College of Wooster PhD (Economics), University of Michigan
William (Bill) Poole	October 25, 2010	Phone	President of St. Louis Federal Reserve Bank, 1998–2008; Member of the Council of Economic Advisers, 1982–1985; Senior Economist, Board of Governors of the Federal Reserve System, 1969–1974 PhD (Economics), University of Chicago
Alan Blinder	November 24, 2010	Phone	Vice Chairman of Federal Reserve Board of Governors, 1994–1996; Deputy Assistant Director of CBO, 1975 [Economic Advisor to Al Gore and John Kerry, during the 2000 and 2004 presidential campaigns] AB (Economics), Princeton University MSc (Economics), LSE PhD (Economics), MIT
David Smith* *Agreed to be recorded but his quotes non-attributable	November 30, 2010	Phone	Chief Economist, House Financial Services Committee, 2006– [previously positions include Senior Economist at the Joint Economic Committee; advisor to Senator Edward Kennedy] BA, Tufts MA (Education), Harvard

Table 5.1
(continued)

Name	Date of Interview	Place/mode	Background of Interviewee (relevant positions at Fed or in Congress; and education)
Lawrence (Larry) Lindsey	December 1, 2010	Phone	Member of Federal Reserve Board of Governors, 1991–1997; [Director of the National Economic Council, 2001–2002; Assistant to President George W. Bush on economic policy] AB, Bowdoin College AM (Economics), PhD (Economics), Harvard
James Galbraith	December 6, 2010	Phone	Executive Director of the Joint Economic Committee. US Congress, 1981–1982; Economist, Committee on Banking, Finance and Urban Affairs, U.S. House of Representatives,1975–1980 [Assisted in drafting the Humphrey–Hawkins Full Employment and Balanced Growth Act of 1978] AB, Harvard MA, Yale PhD (Economics), Yale Marshall Scholar, King's College, Cambridge
Anonymous/ non-attributable	December 7, 2010	Phone	Staffer, House Financial Services Committee

Table 5.1
(continued)

Name	Date of Interview	Place/mode	Background of Interviewee (relevant positions at Fed or in Congress; and education)
Cathy Minehan	January 6, 2011	Phone	President of Boston Federal Reserve Bank, 1994–July 2007 (first woman to be appointed CEO of any FRB Bank); First Vice President and Chief Operating Officer of Boston Federal Reserve Bank, 1991–1994 Joined the Federal Reserve in 1968 as a bank examiner of the FRB, New York BA, University of Rochester MBA, New York University
Jane D'Arista	January 13, 2011	Phone	Staff Economist for Banking and Commerce Committees of the US House of Representatives & Principal Analyst in the international division of the Congressional Budget Office, 1966–1978; Principal Analyst for International Affairs in the Fiscal Analysis division, Congressional Budget Office, 1981–1983; Chief Finance Economist, Subcommittee on Telecommunications, House of Representatives, 1983–1986 BA, Barnard College
Anonymous/ non-attributable	January 24, 2011	In person, Capitol, Washington, DC	Staffer/Advisor to Member of Senate Homeland Security Committee (speaking more generally to Senate Committee deliberations on technical issues)

Table 5.1
(continued)

Name	Date of Interview	Place/mode	Background of Interviewee (relevant positions at Fed or in Congress; and education)
Anonymous/ non-attributable	January 24, 2011	In person, Capitol, Washington, DC	Staffer / Advisor to Member of Senate Banking Committee
Alice Rivlin	January 25, 2011	In person, Brookings, Washington, DC	Vice-Chair, Federal Reserve Board of Governors, 1996–1999; First Director of newly established Congressional Budget Office, 1975–1983; Deputy Director, Office of Management and Budget, 1993–1994; Director of OMB, 1994–1996 (first woman to hold the Cabinet-level position) [Appointed to the National Commission on Fiscal Responsibility and Reform, 2010] BA, Bryn Mawr College PhD, Radcliffe College
Evan Bayh	January 26, 2011	Phone (from Brookings)	US Senator, Indiana (D) and Member of Senate Banking, Housing and Urban Affairs Committee (1998–2010); Chairman of the Subcommittee on Security and International Trade and Finance (1996–2010) Business Economics & Public Policy undergraduate degree, Indiana University, JD, University of Virginia School of Law
Anonymous/ non-attributable	January 31, 2011	In person, Capitol, Washington, DC	Staffer / Advisor to Member of Senate Banking Committee

Table 5.1
(continued)

Name	Date of Interview	Place/mode	Background of Interviewee (relevant positions at Fed or in Congress; and education)
J. Gresham Barrett	February 16, 2011	Phone	US Representative, South Carolina 3rd Congressional District (R) and Member of House Financial Services Committee, Member of the Subcommittee on Capital Markets, Insurance, and Government-Sponsored Enterprises, and Member of the Subcommittee on Financial Institutions and Consumer Credit (2003–2011) BA, The Citadel, The Military College of South Carolina
Vincent Reinhart	February 22, 24, 2011	Phone	Director, Division of Monetary Affairs, Board of Governors of the Federal Reserve, 2001–2007; Secretary and Economist FOMC, 2001–2007; Deputy Director, Division of International Finance, and Associate Economist, FOMC, 1999–2001; Deputy Associate Director, 1998–1999; Assistant Director, 1994–1998, Division of Monetary Affairs, Federal Reserve Chief, 1991–1994; Senior Economist, 1990–1991; Economist, 1988–1990, Banking and Money Market Analysis Section, Division of Monetary Affairs, Federal Reserve; Senior Economist, International Research Department, 1987–1988; Economist, Domestic Research Department, 1985–1987; Economist, International Research Department, 1983–1985, Federal Reserve Bank of New York BS, Fordham University MPhil, MA, Columbia University

we refer to all these as simply "a staffer," in order to respect confidentiality.) Notably, the sample includes six individuals, each with 30 to 40 years' experience in various positions at the Federal Reserve (Axilrod, Broaddus, Kohn, Poole, Minehan, and Reinhart), and one individual whose experience bridges the top levels at the Fed, Congress and the Executive Branch (Rivlin, as vice chair of the Fed's Board of Governors, first director of the Congressional Budget Office, and director of the Office of Management and Budget). To ensure gender diversity, our sample includes two women members of the FOMC and some women congressional staff (to respect anonymity, we do not provide the exact number).

Most of the interviews (excluding the early one with Volcker) were conducted over a period of six months—from September 2010 through February 2011, and all were done by Cheryl Schonhardt-Bailey. The average length of each interview was about an hour and with the exception of current congressional staff who requested anonymity, all the interviewees agreed to be recorded and their interviews used for purposes of this project.[2]

The chapter is organized as follows. In section 5.2 we outline our four key areas of focus for the interviews, and these constitute the next sections of the chapter: quality of deliberation (section 5.3); the effect of transparency on deliberation (section 5.4); institutional features impinging on deliberation (section 5.5); and questioning our interviewees on the findings from our textual analysis (section 5.6). Section 5.7 concludes.

5.2 Threads Left Hanging from the Textual Analysis of Transcripts

Previous chapters have provided insights into the trends, thematic content and speakers' arguments in monetary policy-making and congressional oversight committees. By employing textual analysis software, we have been able to assess a large quantity of textual data—namely (1) the transcripts of the FOMC meetings, (2) the congressional oversight hearings of the Fed's Monetary Policy Report, and (3) the Senate re-confirmation hearings for Volcker, Greenspan, and Bernanke. Textual analysis of any type does, however, have inherent limitations. Perhaps, most important, it is primarily descriptive in nature, as it captures what is said but not why it is said, and nor does it capture the interactive and cumulative effect of committee discussions on the decisions of the participants. Textual analysis software has provided a detailed and, we believe, statistically robust survey of the deliberations on monetary policy by the Federal Reserve and Congress, and to the extent that words are a representation of intentions, it has provided us some insight into the intentions of the participants.

Throughout this work we have maintained that the deliberations of committee members should reflect their distinct sets of aims and objectives; consequently, what participants say should provide an indirect measure for their motivations and intentions. We have further maintained that committee members seek to process information and arrive at judgments based on argued reasoning. Hence our analysis thus far provides us with an indirect measure of the intentions of committee members as they deliberate on monetary policy. In this chapter we strive for a more direct measure of their intentions through a series of open-ended questions to the participants themselves (and their staff).

Broadly speaking, our questions sought to illicit responses on four issue areas: (1) the quality of deliberation in committee meetings (hypotheses 1, 3, 5, 6, and 7 from chapter 2), (2) the effect that transparency has had on deliberations (hypotheses 2 and 4), (3) institutional features that enable or constrain deliberation (hypotheses 2 and 4), and (4) the extent to which key findings from our textual analysis of committee transcripts square with the experiences of participants.

With respect to the quality of deliberation, we queried the extent to which participants perceived committee discussions as consisting of argued reasoning and a reasonably frank exchange of differing views, information and judgments. For the FOMC, we asked whether the speeches were mostly pre-prepared, or whether members felt at liberty to offer impromptu statements and assessments; and more broadly, whether committee discussions altered their views in any way. For Congress, we queried whether members of Congress actually sought to understand or discuss monetary policy or whether their participation in the hearings was motivated by other interests and concerns— and in particular, whether the congressional hearings primarily offered them a venue to "speak to constituents back home." We also asked whether participants thought that decisions were made outside the official committee setting (either FOMC meetings or congressional hearings)—namely informally in bilateral discussions or in other less transparent settings. An important part of our interest lies in assessing changes over time in the form and role of deliberation.

On the topic of transparency (hypothesis 2), we asked FOMC members whether the 1993–94 decision to release the transcripts for publication had lessened deliberation within the meetings, and if so, how. More generally, we sought the views of our interviewees on the extent to which the "media circus" surrounding the oversight and reconfirmation hearings had lessened (even destroyed) the integral content of discussions on monetary policy.

We also queried our interviewees on a number of institutional features that may conceivably affect the quality and nature of deliberation—namely the role of the chairman (hypothesis 3 for the FOMC), the order of questioning (for Congress) (hypothesis 6), the numbers of members (pertaining especially to the House Financial Services Committee) (impinging on hypothesis 6), the culture of consensus decision-making (FOMC) (picked up in each of hypotheses 1 to 4 for the FOMC), and differences in the quality of deliberation between Senate and House committees, as hypothesized by (Steiner, Bächtiger, et al. 2004) (hypothesis 5).

Finally, we provided our interviewees with other empirical findings derived from our textual analysis. We prompted our interviewees to comment on whether these findings "made sense" to them, given their own personal experiences in FOMC meetings, congressional hearings, or both. In this context, we also queried our FOMC respondents on what might be called a "nonfinding" from our analysis of the FOMC transcripts. That is, we were puzzled that across all the years analyzed, we found no thematic class (or even a significant content within any class) pertaining to the formal terms in monetary policy theory (in particular, such terms as "time inconsistency" and "Phillips curve"). That members did not (apparently) discuss these terms we found puzzling, and so we asked our interviewees to comment on this, as well as on the key findings reported in chapters 3 and 4.

The specific questions are listed in tables 5.2 and 5.3. (Notably, while these questions constituted the template for our interviews, the conversational style often broadened the discussion into related topics.) As can be seen in these tables, each of our questions links to a particular area of concern, which we identify in the adjoining column.

5.3   Quality of Deliberation

5.3.1   FOMC

A strand of literature on FOMC decision-making contends that deliberation within the meetings "may have little effect on the quality of the Committee's decisions, possibly because all useful information is

Table 5.2
Questions to FOMC interviewees

Questions	Issue area
Did you tend to change your views after listening to the discussion in meetings or was your position on policy more or less fixed prior to attending each FOMC meeting? In your experience, would you say that deliberations in FOMC meetings shaped the views of members? Was there a give-and-take of ideas and a willingness to contrast opposing views?	Quality of deliberation
In your experience, what influence did the Fed chairman have on both the flow of discussion and the structure of the FOMC meetings? While we know that dissent rates were low, and that members often expressed reservations to the recommendations made by Fed staff and the chair, they tended to vote with the majority for purposes of obtaining consensus. Even if votes were constrained, to what extent did members feel at liberty to express dissenting views during the discussion?	Institutional constraints
Did it often (ever?) seem that committee members had made firm decisions on the policy prior to the actual FOMC meetings (perhaps decisions having been made by the Board, or perhaps in more informal bilateral discussions prior to the FOMC discussion)?	Transparency/quality of deliberation
As you will be aware, there was a period before 1993 when the Fed did not publish verbatim transcripts of FOMC meetings. Some would say that publication of these transcripts has adversely influenced participation and input in these meetings. Would you agree?	Transparency/quality of deliberation
In the older academic literature on politics and monetary policy, there is a strand that is often referred to as the political business cycle. According to this strand, there is a channel of political influence (driven either by Congress or the administration) that is said to shape behavior of the FOMC. In our textual analysis of FOMC transcripts, we do not observe this sort of political influence in what committee members said. Some reasons for this may be that (1) members were reluctant to give voice to political influences, and/or (2) the consensus around the idea of low inflation as the objective of monetary policy over time removed the temptation of the political business cycle to have influence. In your experience of FOMC meetings, how might you account for this absence of discussion about outside political pressure?	Key findings from our textual analysis

Table 5.2
(continued)

Questions	Issue area
Our results provide evidence that the presidents were more associated with the discussion of money and monetary aggregates than the governors. Why do you think this difference is observable quite consistently over time?	Key findings from our textual analysis
Our textual analysis of the transcripts suggests that presidents played a larger role in the deliberation of the policy decision itself than the governors in the earlier period (around the late 1970s–early 1980s). By the later 1990s the governors were relatively more associated with the deliberation on the policy decision and the presidents were more associated with commenting on the state of the economy. We would be interested in your thoughts on this result.	Key findings from our textual analysis
Our results also indicate that over time, *all* members tended to focus their discussions more on the data and the state of the economy and less on deliberating the policy decision. Do you think this might be due to greater consensus around the objectives and tools of monetary policy in the later period, as the low inflation consensus became more embedded, thus reducing uncertainty around the policy decision? Or was it more due to the well-known tendency of Alan Greenspan to focus on data and the state of the economy?	Key findings from our textual analysis
We don't observe explicit discussion of key tools of economic theory such as time inconsistency or the Phillips curve. We would be interested in your views on why this is so.	Key findings from our textual analysis
Alan Greenspan once commented (in a conference call FOMC meeting, Oct 22, 1993) that researchers would not find much of value in the FOMC transcripts [quote: "People think reading the raw transcripts is a way of learning things; I would suggest that if they spend six or eight months reading through some of this stuff, they won't like it."]. He preferred the memoranda for capturing the substance of the meeting. Our premise is that if it is worth studying the process of deliberation, the transcripts should be a good tool for understanding this process. Again, we would be interested in your thoughts on this.	Transparency/value of transcripts for research

Table 5.2
(continued)

Questions	Issue area
[Questions for FOMC members with experience of congressional hearings on monetary policy]	
Our examination of the congressional hearings on monetary policy indicates that members of Congress generally showed little interest in the detail of monetary policy. Why do you think this might be so?	Key findings from our textual analysis/merits of congressional oversight of monetary policy
More broadly, what do you think were the incentives for members of Congress to participate actively in oversight hearings?	Merits of congressional oversight of monetary policy
The scale of the challenge from members of Congress to the Fed chairman appears to have declined with the more recent success of monetary policy (at least until the recent crisis) and there is more evidence of bipartisanship. Going back to the Burns period there was more challenge and more focus on the governance of the Fed, and the challenge came more from Democrats than Republicans. Is it reasonable to think that the level of interest in monetary policy from Congress is related to the success of the policy?	Key findings from our textual analysis
The debate on fiscal policy appears to have shifted from issues on the policy mix to seeking the Fed's support for more micro tax issues. Do you think that members of Congress started to use the Fed's reputation to attach to their views on fiscal policy?	Key findings from our textual analysis

shared prior to the policy discussion" (Chappell, McGregor, et al. 2012: 840). Many of the econometric approaches to studying monetary policy committees (e.g., Havrilesky, Sapp, et al. 1975; Tootell 1991; Chappell, McGregor, et al. 2005) are dismissive of the role for argumentation, reasoned decision-making, and any frank exchange of differing views within the FOMC. Some former members of the FOMC have given further weight to this assessment—especially Larry Meyer, who as we noted in chapter 3, maintains that in his experience as Fed governor from 1996 to 2002, FOMC meetings were "not a spontaneous discussion, but a series of formal, self-contained presentations" (Meyer 2004: 39). However, he further notes that deliberation was more cumulative in nature, evolving from one meeting to the next, so that "seeds were sown at one meeting and harvested at the next . . . [and] in reality I was often positioning myself, and my peers, for the next meeting" (Meyer 2004: 53).

Using the 1999 FOMC transcripts as a case study in chapter 3, we assessed Meyer's premise and found evidence of three distinct *strategies of persuasion* that members employed in committee meetings. Here we extend our analysis of this premise by asking interviewees for their assessment of deliberation in FOMC meetings. Specifically, did deliberation in FOMC meetings shape the views of the participants, and was it, as Meyer suggests, a more "cumulative" form of deliberation? Most of our respondents concur with Meyer's general assessment, but with important variations and qualifications. Hoskins contends that his position was "fixed about 70 percent of the time prior to the meeting," while Blinder maintains that "the vote was almost 100 percent predicable at every meeting," but not for future meetings. The responses of Blinder and others (Jordan, Minehan, Lindsey, Axilrod, Broaddus, Kohn) suggest a high percentage of fixed views prior to any given meeting, but persuasion occurring over several meetings:

Blinder: You would make a point, maybe forcefully if necessary, at one meeting in the hope that it would sink in and by the next meeting . . . or the meeting after that, you are starting to persuade people.

Minehan: I viewed the FOMC as a process with discussion evolving over a series of meetings, and in that sense, views expressed in one meeting could resonate and influence the discussion and decisions of subsequent meetings.

Lindsey: I viewed the discussion at the meetings not necessarily as useful for influencing the vote of that day but as influencing the way the thinking was going to go, down the [road], in future meetings.

Axilrod: I'd say you have to think of the FOMC as a continuum. It's a discussion which is going on and on and on, so everyone is coming in knowing the

Table 5.3
Questions to congressional staff and members of Congress

Questions	Issue area
Thinking about your participation in the House Financial Services Committee (Senate Banking Committee) hearings in which the Committee hears testimony from the Fed Chairman on the Monetary Policy Report, what do you think motivates the questions and deliberations of committee members?	Quality of deliberation
Political scientists often characterize members of Congress as seeking to (1) serve the interests of their constituents back home, (2) adhere to partisan alignments, or (3) formulate "good" public policy. Realistically, all these concerns matter, but in the oversight hearings, which factor do you think appears to have greater weight?	Quality of deliberation/merits of congressional oversight of monetary policy
Our findings from our automated textual analysis of the transcripts suggest that there is a clear difference between the subject matter of questions from Democrats (real economy–labor market) and Republicans (fiscal policy). Does this accord with your experience? Do you think there is any real difference between the stance of Democrats & Republicans with respect to monetary policy?	Key findings from our textual analysis/merits of congressional oversight of monetary policy
Our examination of the committee transcripts of the hearings on monetary policy indicates that members of Congress offered relatively few questions and comments on the details of monetary policy (e.g., the Fed's forecasts on inflation and economic growth). Why do you think this might be so?	Key findings from our textual analysis/merits of congressional oversight of monetary policy
Does the ordering of speaking in the committee have an impact on the questions (e.g., in order of seniority)?	Institutional constraints
Our analysis of the hearings from the 1970s to 2008 indicates that the scale of the challenge from members of Congress to the Fed chairman appears to have declined with the apparent success of monetary policy in the 1990s, and there is more evidence of bipartisanship. Going back to the Arthur Burns period in the 1970s there was more challenge and more focus on the governance of the Fed, and the challenge came more from Democrats than Republicans. Is it reasonable to think that the level of interest in monetary policy from Congress is related to the perceived success of the policy?	Key findings from our textual analysis/merits of congressional oversight of monetary policy

Table 5.3
(continued)

Questions	Issue area
We would be interested to hear your views on another finding of our research—namely that the focus in the committee hearings on fiscal policy appears to have shifted in the 1990s from issues on the mix of monetary and fiscal policy to seeking the Fed's support for more specific tax issues (e.g., Social Security, education, energy). Do you think that members of Congress started to use the Fed's reputation under Greenspan to attach to their views on fiscal policy?	Key findings from our textual analysis/merits of congressional oversight of monetary policy
Prior to the outbreak of the current financial crisis, committee members—along with Greenspan himself—tended not to devote much attention to the stability of the financial system. Do you think that committee members were simply taking their lead from the Fed chair here or was there something else at play?	Key findings from our textual analysis/merits of congressional oversight of monetary policy
Do you think that hearings on the Monetary Policy Report are generally well-attended or do committee members tend to appear for a short time to ask questions and then leave shortly thereafter? If the latter, does this reflect more a lack of time or lack of interest?	Institutional constraints/quality of deliberation
How much does the success of the committee's proceedings depend on the quality of this committee's chairman? If this is significant, does personality or detailed knowledge of monetary policy seem to have greater bearing?	Institutional constraints/quality of deliberation
On occasion, some committee members have appeared to become quasi-celebrities with appearances on YouTube (e.g., Bernie Sanders and Alan Grayson). Do you think that the temptation to "grandstand" or "play to the gallery" during the much televised oversight hearings on the Monetary Policy Report is a strong one?	Transparency/quality of deliberation
In your experience, how much access do members of Congress have to Fed chairmen outside the hearings?	Institutional constraints

parameters within which there might be agreement and they know what they said in the past and everyone's history, so I would say basically they go in pretty much thinking what is going to happen is not predetermined but can be read from the tea-leaves of the previous meeting or meetings.

Broaddus: The reason for being pretty well prepared and fairly flexible . . . when I entered a meeting, was . . . motivated by . . . a desire to have an impact and to say something that was going to over a period of time be influential in the committee. It may sound a little bit contradictory in that I seem to be saying that I want everyone else to be flexible and listen to me whilst I wasn't willing to do that but I think the point is not that I expect statements that I made to have an immediate impact, and other guys would say "Hey, that's right. I'm going to drop my thing and go with you." It's more a matter of the long-term impact of taking a position that has consistency and coherence at several meetings over a period of time to get a given result, and it was that desire, that effort to have something that would maybe influence people over time.

Kohn: I don't recall a meeting in which I wanted interest rates to rise by 25 basis points and I was talked out of it. It's also fair to say that in many meetings I got food for thought that influenced how I was looking at the data, [and it] made me go back and rethink issues, or look at the data in a different way. It's also the case that the meetings did influence my mind-set although it was more over time, where I heard insights in the meeting. I don't remember hearing an insight that said to me "you are completely wrong" but I do remember hearing many insights which said "you need to rethink this to some degree." That was influential over the following inter-meeting period as I went about thinking about what to do next time, and I think many FOMC members think of what they say at the meetings as being important in a forward-looking way. People have kind of made up their mind coming into the meetings, not entirely, but often, and what you are doing is sort of planting seeds.

Our one exception to this view is Poole, who notes that his style contrasted with other members of the FOMC, inasmuch as he did change his views on occasion at a given meeting, after hearing the arguments of others (although he contends that Greenspan never did):

Poole: My views were certainly affected by the discussion. . . . A number of people came in with text, written out, and they might modify them during the course of the meeting. I didn't come in with any text at all. Occasionally I had some rough scribbled notes but obviously I had things in my head that I wanted to talk about, so I tried to be responsive to what else I heard in the debate around the table and I certainly did change my views from time to time. I'm pretty sure that Greenspan, in almost all cases, knew exactly the result he wanted, and his views were not affected by the meeting discussion.

There are four further qualifications to the assessment that deliberation within a given FOMC meeting did not change views. First (and following his depiction of committee types in Blinder 2004), Blinder notes that the "Greenspan Fed was the quintessential . . . autocratically collegial committee, which basically means you do what the autocrat says." With this assessment of the Greenspan Fed, Blinder then argues that for him, deliberation meant persuading the chairman of his views: "when I thought of the committee deliberating, or my role in the committee deliberating, I basically thought of my role [as] trying to persuade Alan Greenspan of my point of view. If I could succeed at that, that would move the committee, and if I couldn't succeed at that, it wouldn't move the committee." Hence, for Blinder, the key form of "deliberation" during the Greenspan years was a bilateral dialogue with the chairman.

Second, Rivlin, as vice chairman of the Board of Governors, notes that she had ample opportunities outside the FOMC to exchange views and engage in discussions with other governors, but only at FOMC meetings did she have the opportunity to hear the views of the bank presidents. With the other governors, she describes frequent and ongoing discussions:

Rivlin: The board members . . . were interacting all the time. We were talking over lunch, and we were talking at other meetings of the Board, which happened a lot, because we weren't just a monetary policy group. We had a lot of other business to do and we would have had a very good exchange of views on the Monday before the FOMC. . . . It was a weekly meeting, not just before the FOMC but we had a weekly meeting on Mondays that was a staff briefing and that was an opportunity to talk a lot among ourselves about what was happening to the economy. We weren't explicitly talking about what we should do at the next FOMC but if your views were changing in interaction with other people it happened in a lot of different ways, not just in the FOMC meeting. [For instance,] if I was being influenced by Larry [Meyer] it might be in the FOMC but it might be walking down the hall and talking to him or saying "what did you mean by that" or "how do you know that."

Her goal for the FOMC meetings, then, was to hear from the bank presidents:

Rivlin: The FOMC meeting, from my point of view, was an opportunity to hear what the bank presidents had to say about what was going on in their area, and that was the most interesting part of the meeting. I already knew what my fellow board members thought because we had been interacting a lot. . . . But what was not familiar was the president of the Reserve Bank of Dallas talking about what was going on in Texas and the immediate area and there were twelve of those.

Third, as Kohn's experience extends to the Bernanke chairmanship and the financial crisis period, his observation on the changes from 2006 onward are revealing. For him, the uncertainty and difficulties surrounding monetary policy from 2008 onward lent greater weight to the role of deliberation within FOMC meetings:

Kohn: I think it's fair to say that when we were out of interest rate room and doing unusual things, then everybody came to the meeting with a more open mind. It was harder, and I couldn't give you a specific example. But . . . [from] spring of 2008 through most recently, what was said at the meeting . . . was more influential both for the decision at the meeting—though not on interest rates per se but on how to pursue, whether to let securities run off, whether to announce, sell [etc.]. I think the meeting has been more important because it's tougher ground.

The fourth qualification pertains to the policy directive and the balance of risks policy statement (Lapp and Pearce 2000; Chappell, McGregor, et al. 2005). The policy directive is the FOMC's instructions to the manager of the Open Market Desk of the New York Fed, for conducting monetary policy.[3] From 1983 to 1998, the directive included a statement of bias toward easing or tightening, but this was not published. From February 1994, the Fed did, however, begin publishing immediately after the meeting a policy statement that explained the committee's decision. At first, it issued the statement only when the committee changed policy but eventually published the statement even when the policy decision remained unchanged.

In December 1998, the FOMC decided to begin publishing the directive's statement of bias, which has subsequently become known as the balance of risks statement. The wording of the bias is important as it communicates the FOMC's views on the probability of a change in policy both during the intermeeting period and at the next meeting, and as such it is examined carefully by market observers. For instance, the use of "would" or "might" may signal greater or lesser intent to move the policy instrument (typically the target Federal Funds Rate) in the future.

Axilrod notes that during the Volcker years, the wording of the directive was not predetermined by any means, and thus discussion on the exact phrasing and possible nuances in the wording was open to discussion and deliberation.

According to Poole, from 1983–84 until 1999, the assessment of bias was that of the chairman, not the committee. He describes a change in procedure whereby the statement came to be drafted by the committee, and this drafting-by-committee has given rise to what might be construed as "virtual deliberation":

Poole: In terms of the policy statement, as you may not know actually, that changed quite dramatically. You may not see it from reading the policy statements but the way it was put together changed quite dramatically during my term of office [1998–2008]. To begin with, it was the chairman's statement; it was not the committee's statement, and over time, what happened was that

Greenspan started to ask for more input into the statement and later started to circulate a draft of the statement to the committee so without any, as far as I know, without any formal announcement as such, the statement became the FOMC statement rather than just the chairman's statement. . . . From what I can recall, it was the chairman's statement when I came into office [1998]. . . . Greenspan would distribute a copy just before it was released or at the very end of the FOMC meeting. He would distribute a copy and say: "This is what he proposed to say and were there any comments on it?" And then, over time, it started to change and I can't tell you exactly when but Greenspan would send out a draft ahead of time, and there was some discussion of this. . . . There was actually some discussion in the FOMC about that, and that the statement would become the FOMC statement. I don't believe there was any formal announcement of that at any time. Greenspan started to distribute drafts of it and I believe that reflected the fact that there was some unhappiness in the committee that the public viewed the statement as the committee's statement rather than just the chairman's statement . . . so there was unhappiness among members of the committee that we were essentially being asked to sign on without any chance to consider it carefully. Later [by the time Bernanke came into office] the practice developed of distributing a draft statement a few days ahead of the meeting. The first draft came out probably a week before the meeting, and we would have several iterations so we would circulate comments to the entire FOMC; essentially they were posted on the secure server and would be available to everyone [to make] comments about the statement, so it really did become a committee statement.

Reinhart explains that this pre-meeting drafting of the statement by the committee members created a situation where 19 people were involved in parsing the statement "extremely closely" and "the big play was the words . . .[used] to characterize [the] decision." At the committee meeting itself, Reinhart further describes the discussion on the policy statement as sounding "like a game of Battleship or Stratego, where you have an FOMC participant say . . . 'I like the first paragraph that is in column A, row 1, but I like the second paragraph that is in column B, row 2,' and that was the discussion. So they had choices. It was not like the statement was drafted before the meeting and then they just had to sign off on it. They had . . . choices on the statement and sometimes they would suggest changes."

In sum, as the policy statement became more of a committee statement (and not simply that of the chairman), and the drafting of this statement occurred both beforehand and at the meeting itself, the form and role of "deliberation" on the wording of the statement has changed. This is consistent with the results of the textual analysis reported in chapter 3 which pointed, inter alia, to a change in the form of FOMC meetings over time and changes in the contributions of governors and reserve bank presidents.

5.3.2 Congress

As a precursor to our discussion of deliberation in the congressional setting, it is useful to remind ourselves of the purpose of hearings on monetary policy. In his book *Central Banking in Theory and Practice*, Blinder summarizes simply and succinctly the purpose of legislative oversight of monetary policy:

> Because monetary policy actions have profound effects on the lives of ordinary people, a central bank in a democracy owes these folks an explanation of what it is doing, why, and what it expects to accomplish. . . . By offering a full and coherent explanation of its actions, the bank can remove much of the mystery that surrounds monetary policy, enable interested parties to appraise its decisions contemporaneously, and then—importantly—allow outsiders to judge its success or failure after the fact. (Blinder 1998: 68–69)

A key phrase from this quote is the last three words—"after the fact." Central bankers view accountability as backward-looking, that is, judging past actions and policy decisions. For politicians, accountability is not quite as straightforward. Indeed, as we discussed in chapters 2 and 4, the motivations and incentives of members of Congress who sit on the banking committees are not easy to define or measure. Certainly, as elected representatives, they are cognizant of their electoral popularity for the next election, and this shapes their questions in a more forward looking direction when they confront the Fed chairman in committee.

What, then, motivates members of the banking committees as they conduct hearings on monetary policy? We begin first with the responses of FOMC officials familiar with the congressional oversight hearings, asking them to comment both on the motivations of members of Congress and on the effectiveness of oversight more generally. As a whole, the common view among the Fed officials is that members of Congress do not engage in actual deliberation on monetary policy–oversight as it currently operates in the congressional hearings is ineffectual.

The Views of FOMC Members

While Fed officials we interviewed were in agreement that congressional oversight of monetary policy does not "work," the underlying reasons varied. For Blinder, one problem is that members of Congress are "preening for the cameras" rather than engaging in an intellectual exchange of views:

Blinder: There is a legitimate role for oversight, a necessary role for oversight, so I'm completely on board about that. The problem is that . . . if the chairman of the Fed is in the witness seat, it is always high-profile, [and the hearings] are media circuses, and all the members are doing is preening for the cameras. You don't exercise oversight by doing that. Oversight is boring. [Having] any meeting of the minds or real intellectual interchange . . . would be nice but that's not, from the point of view of the members, that's not what they are there for. They may want their opportunity to excoriate the chairman of the Fed in public, so that they can show [to constituents that], "he is causing all this unemployment and I'm fighting him" or they may want his endorsement . . . for their pet policy but they are not really trying to do oversight of monetary policy. . . . [And] some Fed chairs go there willingly like Greenspan did, and some Fed chairs like Bernanke go there kicking and screaming, "I don't want to endorse this or that policy" but that's what they want, so they are looking for the sound-bite that says "Chairman Greenspan agreed with me that. . . ."

Both Blinder and Reinhart agree on two further reasons why oversight is ineffectual. First, central bank independence has created a "culture" where politicians perceive it as inappropriate to question the Fed chairman directly about interest rates. According to Blinder, "Congress has internalized the idea that the Congress doesn't meddle in the month-to-month monetary policy. The Fed is an independent institution." Second, "most members of Congress (there are a few exceptions) have minimal to zero understanding of what the Fed does and how it does its work and so their engaging in repartee with the chairman of the Fed on that is a losing proposition for them" (Blinder). Reinhart describes this "comparative disadvantage" as having been exacerbated by Greenspan's "long-winded" answers to questions. Indeed, Reinhart offers a humorous, but revealing, anecdote comparing questions to Greenspan and those to Bernanke:

Reinhart: My favorite was the very first testimony Chairman Bernanke gave before the semi-annual House Financial Services Committee, in which during the typical testimony Chairman Greenspan would answer about 20–25 distinct questions. In his first testimony, Chairman Bernanke answered more than 50 and what happened was that the representatives ran out of questions. Each one individually [had had staff who] . . . produced their two or three questions, because that is all they could possibly get to if Alan Greenspan were answering. But they would ask a question to Ben Bernanke and he would say "Yes, that is right" or give a one-sentence, perfectly understandable answer and move on, and so you saw this helplessness. They had their five minutes, they had asked two or three questions, and there were three minutes left.

Reinhart offers a third reason for ineffectual oversight—namely that the "multiple missions" of the Fed (including GSEs [government sponsored enterprises like Fannie Mae and Freddie Mac] or debit interchange fees) have squeezed out opportunities to ask the chairman about monetary policy.

Jordan attributes the ineffectiveness of congressional oversight more to the personalities involved and the dysfunctional mode of questioning:

Jordan: [It depended on] what kind of game was being played out in those oversight hearings, and the styles of the chairmen. . . . Arthur Burns' style was basically threaten to belittle and ridicule any congressman or senator that said something stupid so they mostly wanted to get through the hearings without being totally embarrassed whereas Greenspan played the rope-a-dope approach of just lull them into incoherent babble and they would work hard at trying to get him to utter anything coherent. He was very, very good at avoiding saying anything coherent in most of those hearings. . . . When you had Barney Frank versus Ron Paul, even when Frank was the ranking minority member, before he became chairman, you knew going in that one of them would start it off and the other one was going to come back and it was really a by-play between two flamboyant personalities on the committee attacking the central bank from a different vantage point. But it was really the two congressmen trying to out-play each other on their side and [for] the chairman of the Fed . . . [it] was simply an opportunity for these guys to go at each other . . . and neutralize each other. It was kind of fun to watch but whether it was all productive to any purpose I have no idea.

For most of the FOMC respondents, the bottom line for why oversight of monetary policy is ineffectual is that politicians do not understand monetary policy, and they have little or no electoral incentive to overcome that ignorance. The primary motivation for participating in the hearings is to score points with constituents "back home":

Broaddus: Most of these people . . . are not professional economists, they are politicians. Many of them have backgrounds in law or business, and so they are not only not conversant they are really not entirely interested in policy, except in terms of its immediate impact. They often have a political motive in the questions, you know their questions are all scripted and most of them by their staff and so they are using this as an opportunity to indirectly communicate with their constituents, their voters. . . . Playing to the cameras is a good brief. . . . I think it's mainly just there is nothing that they can benefit from in terms of talking about monetary policy per se that is going to help them get a vote in the next election.

Poole: I think everybody with a professional background who participates or just watches those, [knows that] the purpose of the hearings first and foremost, 98 percent, is for individual members of Congress to spout off and to be visible, to make the evening news, and that's why those hearings are mostly about stuff other than monetary policy. . . . The members of the congressional committees do not believe that esoteric monetary policy stuff is of any . . . interest to their constituents but it is also because they do not want to risk asking a question that will prove to be deeply embarrassing, revealing that they don't know anything of what they are talking about. So mostly the monetary policy questions that they are willing to ask are questions that come from their staff members and they will tend to be relatively minor things . . . because their knowledge of monetary economics or any economics is so weak that they understand they are in danger of asking a deeply embarrassing question that will show up in the newspapers the next day showing that Congressman X is a dolt.

Rivlin: Various members of the committee . . . may actually be trying to make points for themselves, and to say, you know, "I come from a farm district in Iowa and we think interest rates are too high here and it is bad for farmers, what do you think about that Mr. Chairman?" He doesn't care what the chairman thinks, he wants to make [his point that] he is speaking to the folks back home. . . . Most of them don't have a very keen grasp of monetary policy. They think it is something sort of mysterious and they don't want to sound stupid so they don't take it on. . . . In general if they asked questions, they were not very pointed questions. . . . I used to argue [about] this with Greenspan. Greenspan was . . . very apprehensive about the Congress. . . . He saw Congress as somewhat threatening and I thought that he was overreacting and that in fact the independence of the Fed is not going to be threatened because most congressmen don't want to run monetary policy. I mean, this is not "should we turn it over to the Chancellor of the Exchequer," when we talk about the independence of the Fed. We talk about the independence of the Fed to run monetary policy independent of the Congress, and I don't think there is any appetite in Congress for running monetary policy. It is too hard, too uncertain, it is too liable to get you in trouble, and so for that reason I've never thought that the Congress really wanted to threaten the independence of the Fed.

Blinder: It's hard for me to imagine that any voter is voting on the basis of monetary policy, except indirectly. I mean, when unemployment is high, they vote against incumbents so that has something to do with monetary policy but it has to do with lots of other things as well.

Lindsey: Well, one point to start with is a representative government is supposed to be representative of the general population which means that they probably have about as much interest as the general population in these matters and any matter that is complex. . . . [Moreover] where are the votes? Where do you get the votes back home by taking on monetary policy? . . . Now, the one guy who's come close, if you ever watch the hearings [was] Chuck Schumer: all he cares about is having his picture taken with the chairman. If you see it, if the chairman comes in, he is always escorting him because he wants the television cameras back home in New York to show how close he is to the chairman, physically close. I mean there is a joke in Washington that the most dangerous place to be is between Chuck Schumer and a television camera, and I mean it is absolutely true. . . . But that's as close as you get to caring about monetary policy. There are no votes in it.

Reinhart summarizes the nonexistent political benefits accruing from monetary policy oversight, and suggests that obtaining a preferred policy endorsement from the Fed chairman is a way of obtaining a nonpartisan official stamp of approval:

Reinhart: One reason why [the committee hearings] are not a good oversight mechanism [is] because there is not a direct benefit for being an active overseer of United States monetary policy . . . I think that when they talk about the macroeconomy they are trying to get the chairman of the Federal Reserve to opine on their view. That is why the macro questions tend to be "aren't you worried about the . . . Chinese imbalances?" or "Don't you agree with me that the tax rates need to be higher?" . . . They want to align themselves with [Alan Greenspan's view] and why? Because it meant that the next day on the floor they will be able to say "and when I directly asked Alan Greenspan, his answer would make me think he would support this legislation." . . . The chairman of the Federal Reserve has somehow become the chief economist of the United States and in not as partisan a way as the chairman of the Council of Economic Advisers or the director of the NEC. Hence both sides try to ask questions that will allow them to align their preferred policy recommendations with something the chairman says, and since Greenspan in particular would tend to answer in such obscure ways, it was usually mission accomplished for both sides.

Before turning to the views of congressional staff and members of Congress, we should add one important caveat to the negative assessment of congressional oversight given by FOMC officials—that is, in virtually all instances, our interviewees note that there were and are exceptional members of Congress who actively and earnestly engage in deliberations on monetary policy, and usually these are the committee chairmen and ranking members. Kohn notes that both Paul Sarbanes and Barney Frank "understood" monetary policy. He adds, "In the early 1990s, [I have] strong memories in the Senate of Sarbanes, Riegle, who was the Senator for Michigan, and Sasser who was from Tennessee just beating the hell out of Greenspan because interest rates were too high, the economy was growing too slowly, what was all this worry about inflation and this talk about inflation expectations." Kohn also remarks that in his view, both the mean and the median level of understanding of monetary policy is higher among senators than among representatives, inasmuch as "there is a bit of a filtering process that goes on, going from the House to the Senate." For Rivlin, the chairman and ranking member "are usually . . . trying to use the hearing to understand what the Fed is actually doing," noting that Barney Frank in particular "is very smart—he is not an economist, but a lawyer, but he understands monetary policy pretty well and he wasn't afraid to take it on," while other exceptional members "were mostly ideological like Bernie Sanders." For Lindsey, Senator Bob Corker is "the kind of person you can have a real conversation with but you are not going to do it in a hearing; you are going to do it over lunch." Broaddus adds to the list, "Congressman Neal from North Carolina, [who] was from our district and was certainly no theoretical economist but he had an innate understanding that this was an important subject and that the Federal Reserve needed to be evaluated from the perspective of received knowledge about the business of conducting monetary policy rather than just what was happening today with the unemployment vote."

Of course, for some, committee chairs also were sometimes adept at exploiting the oversight hearings for political advantage, as Jordan describes for two committee chairs, Senator Proxmire and Congressman Reuss:

Jordan: One thing about Bill Proxmire, is he was a very savvy clever manipulator of the media; he held his oversight hearings in August when . . . Congress was in recess, and the media was ready for something to fill the space. Supply creates its own demand and nobody else was generating news so Bill Proxmire would hold the hearings in August when he was the only guy in Washington. He generated a lot of tension in doing so, and often he was in competition [with] Henry Reuss over at the House side, a couple of Democrats from Wisconsin competing as to who was best at oversight hearings of monetary authorities.

The Views from Congress

Interestingly, respondents from both the Fed and Congress agree on two features of congressional oversight that diminish the quality of deliberation: (1) poor understanding of monetary policy by members of Congress, combined with minimal if any electoral incentive to overcome this ignorance; and (2) the "culture" of Central Bank Independence, which has created an unwritten rule that Congress should not interfere with, or discuss seriously, the short-term operation of monetary policy.

1. Poor Understanding of Monetary Policy

There may be many reasons why members of Congress have, broadly speaking, a poor understanding of monetary policy. Our FOMC respondents identify two straightforward reasons—namely that most politicians are not trained economists, and knowledge of monetary policy is not a clear vote-winner. From our congressional respondents, the rationale includes these reasons, but also extends into the particular institutional constraints faced by members of Congress in committee deliberations (a topic we will discuss in further detail later). From the perspective of Congress, one reason why so few members of Congress understand monetary policy is that the multitude of tasks placed upon them makes it impossible for them to become experts in more than one (or two) area(s). And, related to this, they also lament that they are unable to delve much into the intricacies of monetary policy itself within the hearing, as they have just a few minutes to ask questions of the Fed chairman.

The comments from our two members of Congress—Senator Bayh and Congressman Barratt—illustrate their contrasting views, with the former noting that he was an "atypical" committee member in that he holds a degree in economics, while the latter remarking that he, like most other committee members, possesses no particular expertise in economics. In spite of their contrasting interests and backgrounds, both agree that the time constraints are a key factor in diminishing the quality of oversight:

Bayh: In the Senate you get stretched very thin because the issues you have to deal with are many and are complex, and you don't have enough time or enough staff support to get into great detail in all of them. It is just not humanly possible, so you have to pick areas that you are more particularly interested in so you are more likely to just take questions from staff in areas that you have some responsibility for, but there is not a particular focus. Where the areas are of particular interest, then members will devote more time so there are some members on the committee who really care more about these issues more than others, and they are the ones who will really ask insightful questions, follow-up questions, and that sort of thing. I [don't] want to say that my colleagues were detached—it is just only natural that some would have a greater proclivity to really deal in depth [with these issues] on a personal level and I was one of those because I like macroeconomic issues and the economy.

Barratt: To be honest with you, congressmen [and congresswomen] . . . are extremely busy and whether it is fiscal policy, whether it is the Fed chairman coming in, it really doesn't matter what the issue is, unfortunately we have a very limited time to concentrate on one specific subject. Now, when I first got elected, one of my colleagues told me "If you don't pick an area of interest and focus on it, then you will never enjoy your time in Congress," and even though I was on the Financial Services Committee, my area of expertise and my area of passion was energy. I've got a nuclear facility, the Savannah River Site, in my district, and I love nuclear energy, I think it is a way in which we can really change the world.

Given their very different interests, these two members also convey quite different stories of their experiences in the banking committees:

Bayh: I was atypical because I've cared about economic and financial issues, well, since my days as an undergraduate where my degree from the university was in Business Economics and Public Policy. . . . What I would normally do [is] I would scan the questions but more often I'd tell my staff a week or so in advance, "Look, here are the big issues that I think are facing the country and the Fed, here is what I'm thinking of asking, can you flesh it out a little bit?" Actually then I'd also (and maybe this made me atypical as well) . . . listen to the chairman's testimony and very often there would be two or three things that he would say that would spark my interest, that I would follow up on and ask him to elaborate at greater length. . . .

[Here is] the story I want to tell . . . Greenspan [was] coming up to give . . . testimony and Summers [was] with him representing the Treasury and they were discussing their appearance beforehand. . . . The question was "What should the regulatory approach of the government be?" and Greenspan said to Summers, "Well what if anybody asks about . . . the possibility of a natural monopoly because that would be the exception to the policy that we are going to be espousing" and Summers said to him, "Don't worry, about that, none of them will ask about that." So I'm sitting up there, and I'm a junior member, [and] I'm listening to this go along and I hear [them] say . . . "Well, we need to take a more, a lighter regulatory approach and let the market function." I'm just listening and so I go back to my student days of economics and I said . . . "Mr. Chairman, what about the event of a natural monopoly, you know some markets do tend to function that way, and wouldn't that frustrate, would that not be an exception?" Ever since then, Greenspan thought I was just the smartest guy, sitting up there, and it just happened to be me sitting up there and listening to this and thinking "what can I ask to be different?" "How can I be a little bit of a devil's advocate here?" . . . He and Summers had just happened to have that very conversation before they walked in the room.

Barratt: I think it is a fair assessment to say that it seems to, for the average congressman, not all of them, Ron Paul would probably be an exception, but for the average congressman, the monetary policy seems to have been carried out very ably and [is] probably less of a focus. . . . The average congressman is not as much focused on that as probably they should be. You know, it is a case of which alligator is biting the hardest right now. I mean there are so many issues from immigration to Social Security to health care to the deficit to foreign affairs, and if that alligator is at your neck and about to bite your head off, i.e., a bail-out, i.e., an insurgency in Iraq, [it is] that issue that you are the most concentrated on and most absorbed with. If there seems to be an area that [is on], and I'm not going to say necessarily automatic pilot but [there] seems to be . . . not a lot of concern there, unfortunately you just don't have the brain power or the time . . . you just don't have the luxury of time to spend on that issue. . . .

There were times that Chairman Greenspan was very understandable, and you know, I'm certainly not an expert but I did try to do my homework and I do know a good bit about it. There were times that he lost me, and then there were times when he was very gracious, and times when he was very condescending, [as if to say] "don't tell me how to do my job because you don't know what you are talking about" and unfortunately most of the time he was right. . . . I'm probably not being very kind to some of my colleagues but a lot of my colleagues think they know a lot more than really what they do, and you know the way they present their questions and the way they have their pontifications is pretty evident in that sometimes.

These quotes make clear that (1) expertise in economics among banking committee members is "atypical" and (2) topics of the day very often prevail in committee questioning. With respect to point 1, some congressional staff respondents are more defensive in noting that members of Congress often do raise substantive issues on economics, but their phrasing and choice of words are different from what an expert might use. For instance, when asked about our empirical finding that members of Congress rarely discussed the details of monetary policy, one staff member remarked, "Baloney! Members of Congress do ask serious questions—policy questions—but they might use different language." Instead of referring to the term yield curve, committee members might simply ask about home mortgages. The staff member acknowledges that monetary policy "is like trying to pick up a cinder block with chopsticks" (i.e., hard to get a handle on it). Hence, in order to help members gain a better understanding, the committee (under Oxley and then Barney Frank) had begun holding "pre-quel" hearings prior to the formal monetary policy hearing, during which economists were invited to appear before the committee to talk about economic issues.

Other staffers concur, with one noting that "even if they phrase their questions poorly, there is often something important that they are trying to express or convey." This same respondent characterizes the dialogue between members of Congress and FOMC officials as one with an inherent communication gap, where members of Congress "tend to talk in terms of anecdotes about the economy while FOMC officials use statistics and models," adding that both parties could communicate better with one another—namely FOMC officials could use less jargon and members of Congress could acquire more expertise. Ultimately, however, committee members are not particularly incentivized to focus on monetary policy, the staffer notes (echoing Blinder's remark) since they see the Fed chairman as equivalent to the nation's "chief economic officer" and so the hearing is their opportunity to ask him anything and everything on the economy—and not just on monetary policy.

On this tendency to discuss more extraneous, though possibly topical issues (our point 2 above), a staffer estimates that issues that are "front and center" generally constitute half the questions in the committee hearing, while the other half are given to questioning the actions of the Federal Reserve. Another staff member goes a little further, noting that "broad questions of monetary policy are almost always overshadowed by events and what motivates the questioning tends to be yesterday's *Wall Street Journal* story about fraud and abuse or a visit from a constituent about his inability to get his line of credit extended or complaints more recently about mortgage fraud and the foreclosure mess." Hence this same staff member remarks, there is relatively little discussion about the Fed's monetary report or the chairman's testimony—rather, "the discussion is more impelled by much more specific and narrow concerns about economic activity."

While members of Congress may have no electoral incentive to become educated in monetary policy (according to our FOMC respondents), the view from Congress is that politicians should try to find a way to balance representing the concerns of constituents with the effort in acquiring the necessary expertise to challenge the Fed on the substance of monetary policy. One staffer remarks that "there is a balance to be struck between members of Congress being policy wonks and being populists. Straying too far in one direction probably isn't a good idea." According to this staffer, committee members would ideally listen to the concerns and anxieties of constituents, then think about these, judge their validity and merit, and finally filter these into an intelligent question which is put before the Fed chair. The Fed chair would then employ his policy expertise to tackle the question. (When it is then suggested that the member of Congress—in this ideal scenario—would translate this answer back to his constituents, the staffer thought that that might stretch the realm of what is possible.)

Regardless of whether or not this scenario is idealistic, both members of Congress were cognizant of their role as "conduits" of information on monetary policy, relaying flows of information and concerns from constituents to the Fed, and (ideally) back again. Barratt notes that because monetary policy "is a niche issue," constituents who queried it were likely to be knowledgeable about the subject, and indeed he recalls that early in his career some of his own constituents had helped him prepare questions for the Fed chairman. He remarks that,

Barratt: ... [I]t is very powerful to look at a witness whether it is the chairman of the Fed or whoever and say "you know I've got some folks in my district, here is one of their questions and let me follow up on that." I think it is very powerful for your constituents and I would hope the witnesses would think that was pretty powerful too because after all that is who I'm representing in Congress.

In a parallel vein, Bayh perceives his committee role as, in part, communicating between constituents and the Fed:

Bayh: You have to function well in multiple worlds, so it basically involves translating macroeconomic policy into terms that ordinary [people] who don't focus on that [and] have no background in that, can understand. So you talk about jobs and investment and improved wages and how that is going to make retirement more secure and college more affordable, and your home more affordable. You've got to be able to think and speak in both of those worlds and be consistent, but understand, that they are kind of distinct areas. [For instance], . . . before a group of 500 people at the Kiwanis Club in Indianapolis, you would say the same things . . . [that you would say] if you were in a one-to-one conversation with the chairman of the Federal Reserve . . . but you would say them differently.

At the same time, Bayh maintains that congressional hearings on monetary policy primarily speak to an educated few who are informed and who follow monetary policy issues; they are not a (direct) means of conveying meaningful and substantive information to the public:

Bayh: After [the Fed chairman's] testimony, there would always be an article in the *Washington Post*, the *New York Times*, the *Wall Street Journal*, the *Financial Times* or the AP . . . and that gets the message out to elites who follow these things. But in terms of the broad public . . . there was a very wise media consultant who I knew throughout my life and he had helped my father before me, and he used to tell me: "Look, it is all about staying on-message" and with all the cacophony of voices out there and the diversification in the ways that people get information, it is even more difficult today. He used to say "when you have given the same speech so many times that you are about to become physically ill, the average citizen will just be beginning to get what you are saying" because they have got so many things competing for their attention. So, the point of me saying all that is yes, it was covered [in the media] but that is not enough to get through to the American people. In order to accomplish that, you would have to have something said over and over again, and the Humphrey–Hawkins testimony and the banking committee operations don't lend themselves to that kind of public communication.

While both Barratt and Bayh saw their role as banking committee members to include acting as "conduits" for information on monetary policy, neither felt that this was a primary concern. Rather, as Bayh notes, committee members are motivated primarily by electoral concerns. Hence the main thrust of the questions in the hearings are forward-looking rather than backward looking—that is, driven by future concerns (like elections):

Bayh: "What are the challenges we face and what do we need to do about them going forward?" That tends to be the principal focus of members of Congress because we are held accountable for future events, the past as well, but what really matters is what is going to be happening next and before the next election in particular.

In the end, members of Congress know that expertise in monetary policy is not a vote-winner and so the *typical* banking committee member does not engage deeply in understanding monetary policy actions by the Fed or conveying that information to the public (even though they may acknowledge this as ideal). One staffer from the Senate side summarizes the problem in conveying monetary policy information to the public and using it for electoral advantage succinctly:

[*Anonymous staffer*]:   First, the details are not easily conveyed in simple statements. Because it takes longer to explain things, even if you were to explain the details, many people wouldn't understand them anyway. Second, even if a member of Congress tried to explain the details of monetary policy (e.g., causes and effect relationships), the media would generally ignore this technical, detailed stuff. And third, even if a member of Congress explained the details, his political opponent(s) wouldn't engage in this sort of discussion, because it is easier to go for the sound bites. The opponent wouldn't play the same game, so it doesn't pay the member of Congress to do so. It does you no good (politically) to give detailed information on monetary policy to constituents.

2. The Culture of Central Bank Independence

In previous chapters, we have discussed the evolution of the independence of the Federal Reserve—particularly vis-à-vis Congress. At the heart of the issue is the meaning of the concept of "independence." Our focus here is the extent to which the acceptance of the "independence" of the central bank has created a reticence by members of Congress to engage actively in deliberating on and challenging the monetary policy actions of the Federal Reserve.

Barney Frank's quote (from chapter 4) is once again instructive in that it conveys his dismay of this reticence by Congress to question the Fed's actions on monetary policy:

There are people who think the Fed should be above democracy. . . . We can debate the most fundamental questions in human existence, but God forbid anybody in elected office should talk about whether or not we need a 25 basis-point increase from the Fed. Representative Barney Frank, Incoming Democratic Chairman of the House Financial Services Committee (January 2007) (Guha and Kirchgaessner 2007)

In chapter 4 we also quote Blinder as writing that central bank independence and accountability go hand-in-hand—that is, part of the obligation that comes with independence is the willingness of central bank officials to explain their actions to the public. As Blinder argues, "(i)f the central bank makes good decisions, it should have no trouble explaining and defending them in public. If it cannot articulate a coherent rationale for its actions, perhaps its decisions are not as good as it thinks" (Blinder 1998: 70). Blinder then goes on to remark that the Fed is particularly poor at explaining its actions:

... the Fed still offers very scanty explanations of FOMC decisions, fearing that its announcements would be misinterpreted, that ill-chosen words might lock it into future actions, or that changing circumstances might force it to change its mind—thereby undermining the doctrine of central bank infallibility. (Blinder 1998: 75)

Blinder's more recent remarks in our interview reinforce the view that in congressional hearings on monetary policy, committee members have "internalized" the norm that questioning the Fed on short-term monetary policy is unacceptable.

One of our congressional respondents, D'Arista, who had experience as a staff economist in the 1960s and 1970s, creates a flavor for the historical progression of the culture of independence:

D'Arista: Patman of course was very active in the Depression era and he was very active on the Banking Act of 1935 which gave the [Federal Reserve] Board more control. But in going into the 1940s he was very adamantly opposed to the independence [of the Fed]. What he kept trying to remind the members of the committee was this is an agency of Congress, that Congress is in charge here, not the Treasury or the administration but under the Constitution we have the power to coin money and regulate its value. Now independence was so preached by the Fed and pushed upon other central banks around the world by the Fed, that this point got lost and in a sense I think the members of Congress just absorbed this idea: the Fed is an independent agency and we have . . . the Fed resisting any investigations by the Government Accountability Office of its monetary operations etc. [Members of] Congress bought all of that, and it is, in my view, completely contrary to their responsibility. . . . [Members of] Congress should be overseeing monetary policy—this is their agency.

Another staff member characterizes the 1990s in particular as a decade in which the prominence of the Federal Reserve in managing the economy even began to overshadow that of the Treasury:

[Anonymous staffer]:   The Bush Treasury was widely seen as marginal and useless, and the Fed, partly because of the relatively strong economy and the role that the Fed played in the second half of the 1990s, the Fed had eclipsed [the] Treasury in members' minds about who it was who was in charge of economic policy, and that, if you went back twenty years, that would be a huge shift.

Clearly, the financial crisis of 2007 to 2009 has created a new era of congressional activism vis-à-vis the Federal Reserve, and although our study does not explore this new era, it is noteworthy to include remarks from Bayh on (1) the "apolitical" nature of the Fed and how members of Congress interpret that, (2) the extent to which the macroeconomic challenges of the past few years have forced the Fed better to explain its actions, and (3) the blurring of the lines between fiscal and monetary policy, and effects of that on the Fed's independence:

1. *Bayh*:   The Fed is an apolitical body but it has to exist in a political context, and so sometimes, depending upon the agenda of the majority in Congress and the president at that time, people would try and elicit comments from the chairman whether in support of or critical of whatever agenda that member might have. And [it] was always interesting to observe [that] both chairman Greenspan and Chairman Bernanke were very artful at saying in very elegant terms as little as possible. . . .

2. [*Commenting on Bernanke's appearances on the 60 Minutes program and appearances before the Senate Banking Committee*]

Bayh: I'm a big fan of the chairman and I think he has done an excellent job but being realistic about it, I don't think most Americans eagerly anticipate tuning in and listening to a discussion on monetary policy. That is not going to get much of an audience but his efforts are to demystify the Fed, to pull back the cloak of secrecy as much as he can without impairing its functioning, [and] is very well-advised because it helps to put the lie to some of these conspiracy theories. I thought it was very effective when he was having to respond very aggressively in the depths of the financial crisis. He came before the Democratic caucus, and he . . . said "I'm handing out a copy of the balance-sheet of the Fed and you can see that it is broken down into different categories and I want to show you what we own, and I want to show you how it has changed over time to help respond to the crisis." Most of those people didn't follow those issues. . . . But the fact that he would . . . go through chapter-and-verse and say "Ask me any questions you have about this or what I'm doing" being proactive in that way is really very helpful because if you have got a good story to tell, you need to get out and tell it. The facts and the truth are your friends. [*I then asked whether this action by Bernanke was unusual.*] It had never happened before as far as I know.

3. *Bayh*:   . . . as Bernanke has been saying: "Look, monetary policy can only do so much." I mean ideally you would have fiscal and monetary policy operating in close coordination, one with the other, and you would be taking the short-term into account, and the long-term into account, and operating accordingly. But if the political process seizes up and you are only left with monetary policy then the Fed is forced to contemplate some actions that otherwise they might not have to resort to but they have got no choice because the other branch of government is not doing its part. Then [that] runs the risk of politicizing the Fed a little bit more because they are doing unusual things and some elected officials will like that and some won't.

As the comments from Bayh suggest, the recent financial crisis may have ushered in a new era of Fed transparency, but this is not the same thing as saying that members of Congress have or will ratchet up their

understanding of monetary policy in order to engage the chairman of
the Fed more substantively during the Humphrey–Hawkins hearings.
Indeed we are currently observing the Fed move toward even greater
transparency, as evidenced by Ben Bernanke's first press conference
following an FOMC meeting on April 26, 2011, and the more recent
announcement on publication of the future interest rate projections of
FOMC members. In his first press conference, while the Fed chairman
spoke eloquently and fully in responding to most of the questions, one
question he skirted entirely was raised near the end of the press conference. He was asked to compare the questions that he was currently
receiving from journalists with those he usually receives from members
of Congress during the Humphrey–Hawkins hearings, and Bernanke
carefully avoided making this comparison. Yet the informed observer
would note the vast difference between the two, as the *New York Times*
subsequently reported: the questions of the journalists "stayed focused
on the compact and complicated world of monetary policy" while
questions from members of Congress are typically on "a wide range of
issues—and sometimes issues that have little to do with economics"
(Appelbaum 2011). So, while more information and effort to explain
itself to the public may well trumpet a new era of central bank transparency, which combined with the upheavals of the financial crisis,
may lessen the reticence of members of Congress to challenge the Fed,
it does not mean that the typical congressional banking committee
member will necessarily overcome the barriers of ignorance, lack of
interest, and lack of electoral incentive to effectively challenge the Fed
chairman on monetary policy.

5.4   Transparency and Deliberation in the FOMC

It is inconceivable that extreme transparency in policy-making (e.g.,
live televised FOMC meetings) would ever allow public officials to
speak as candidly as they would in private discussions. And yet most
democratic societies have come to expect some degree of transparency
from their governing institutions—the question is, how much transparency is needed to allow the public to understand the rationale behind
and mechanisms that underpin policy-making, without undermining
the policy decision itself? There is, of course, no simple answer to this
question and indeed the degree to which monetary policy may or may
not be undermined by transparency is evolving, as the Fed's first press
conference (noted above) illustrates.

Two issues are of key import. The first relates to the publication of the verbatim transcripts of the FOMC meetings. Even with a five-year lag before publication, this level of transparency may well affect the content and mode of deliberation among the meeting participants. A second issue concerns the extent to which divisions and disagreements among committee members become known, and when. As we have noted, dissenting votes in FOMC meetings are rare, and so even when the Fed publishes the minutes of the meeting three weeks after each meeting, only those rare members who actually dissented are identified. Shades of opinion, reservations, and resistance falling short of dissent are not known until the transcripts become public many years later (although these shades of opinion can be apparent from committee members' outside speeches). We will focus on the first issue in the section below, leaving the "shades of opinion" issue for our later discussion on institutions and deliberation.

5.4.1   Publication of Transcripts

A good starting point is Larry Meyer's description of the FOMC meetings as consisting of formal, self-contained presentations, which relates to his experience as Fed governor from 1996 to 2002, and does *not* include the period during which it was not known to FOMC members that meeting transcripts were being archived (i.e., before 1993). His description thus pertains solely to a post-transparency era. In contrast, many of our interviewees have experience of participating in meetings both before and after this critical shift in transparency, so their ability to compare directly the pre- and post-transparency periods is particularly useful. Nonetheless, the views of participants from only the more recent period (like Meyer) are also relevant, as some provide contrasting perspectives from Meyer on the extent to which publication of the transcripts affects FOMC deliberation.

Our FOMC respondents divide into two distinct camps on this question: seven maintain that publication of the transcripts has *not* harmed deliberation, while four argue that it has. Within each camp there are individuals with experience in both the pre- and post-transparency periods, as well as individuals with experience in only the post-transparency period. In the first camp are Hoskins, Jordan, Poole, Minehan, Rivlin, Axilrod, and Broaddus.

Hoskins: I do not believe transcript publication has [had] much influence on members' positions. I certainly never considered publication of transcripts an issue nor do I believe others did either.

Jordan: I would attend the meeting with no scrap of paper in front of me so that I could listen to my colleagues and try and engage them eyeball to eyeball and I made damn sure that when I was speaking I didn't have anything to look down to. I could only look up at my colleagues and force them to look back at me, so that they weren't scribbling with their own notes or reading the *Wall Street Journal* or something while I was talking because I would be looking at them instead of sitting and reading something that I'd pre-prepared. So it was very different styles but I never thought that the existence of a transcript in any way inhibited the give-and-take and I don't think a fair reading of the transcripts from the previous period when they weren't being publicized to when they were [would suggest that the change] affected many people. It certainly didn't affect me.

Poole: [Publication of the transcripts mattered] to a minor degree, and I say a minor degree because I was always very careful about any off-color language for example. We all use off-color language when we're talking to friends in small, intimate gatherings and over dinner, and after a couple of glasses of wine but I never succumbed in the FOMC meetings, at least I don't think I did. That wasn't true of all of my colleagues, and you will see some off-color language on occasion in the transcript. I never thought was appropriate and so I didn't want that to be down in the transcript. [As for] my policy views, no I don't think I ever held back. My style has always been to focus on issues and to state them as clearly as I know how but not in a bombastic, confrontational way. I certainly have always steered clear both as an academic and when I was in office . . . of ad hominem attacks or comments. I try to focus entirely on issues and that was my style while I was in office and it hasn't changed.

Minehan: Now, a lot of people say it forced people to write down what they were going to say when they came in. Well, I was a person who did tend to write down what I was going to say in terms of my presentation about the district, and then the way I thought of the stance of policy but I would have done that regardless, because I think better with a pen in my hand. You know, Open Market Committee meetings are serious stuff and you want to be sure you've got all your thoughts together. Some of the people around the table may have been better on their feet than they were at writing. . . . Everybody is different. I function in a way that if I write something down I'm more logical about it at times than when I'm just talking off the top of my head so that is my way of functioning. [*CS-B: So you don't think you were conscious that your words would be published?*] I absolutely was not. I can tell you I was not. I was trying to help myself be logical in my presentations.

Rivlin: [*Comparing the contrasting views of Jordan and Meyer on publication of the transcripts*] But Jerry Jordan was there over the transition; Larry [Meyer] and I were not. . . . I don't know what Larry is basing that on but I wasn't particularly aware of the transcript in speaking. . . . [*CS-B: You don't think it dampened or shaped your comments?*] No, that was never in my mind at all. I came from a world where I did a lot of "on the record" stuff in front of Congress. I mean that was much more, partly in the Clinton administration but, much more important, when I was running the Congressional Budget Office. I was testifying two or three times a week for eight years so I was very used to being "on the record" and I was constantly careful for different reasons about what I said. But I don't remember thinking about that at the FOMC at all. . . . I mean if you said something on the record in a congressional hearing it was on the evening news. Five years [for publication of the transcripts], I mean, who cares about that? I didn't think about that at all.

Axilrod: [*He notes that in general, committee members would naturally "talk" as they would otherwise as the discussion becomes "heated." But . . .*] The discussions in my view, have been always very gentlemanly. . . . In fact, I used to joke with people at the Board: "Yeah don't worry about the public, let's televise these debates. They'll all turn it off."

Broaddus: As I think about it, there were always individual members of the committee [to a large extent under Burns and . . . a little bit less so under Volcker] who were less . . . by virtue of personality . . . scripted so to speak. They were always, in my recollection, a minority. There were always some but I think the vast majority had some sort of statement. It might not be that they actually sat there and read but there would be bullet points that they followed pretty carefully. The other point I would make here, I think this is relevant . . . is that staff members make fairly lengthy presentations, on the economy and financial markets, and those are always read verbatim. So, that kind of sets a tone and I guess the rest of us maybe you know sub-consciously fell into that type of mode. [*CS-B: Were you influenced by publication?*] . . . I wasn't motivated by fear of what the transcripts would show half a decade later.

Hence the reasons why, for these respondents, transparency did not impinge on deliberation vary. Some are quite clear that their own personality and way of working, and not transparency, dictated their degree of pre-preparedness for the meeting—whether that meant having detailed comments coming into the meeting (Minehan) or none at all (Jordan). Others feel that transparency matters only for style (e.g., omitting "off-color language"), as for Poole, or that as the discussion becomes "heated" participants naturally "talk" as they would otherwise (Axilrod). Rivlin is unique in that her previous top-level positions in government meant that transparency was second-nature to her, so transparency with a five-year lag is irrelevant. Broaddus thinks that pre-prepared statements have always been an element of the FOMC, in part because members follow the example of Fed staff who present lengthy prepared reports on the economy and markets.

A second camp of FOMC participants differ with the above assessment of transparency having a benign effect on deliberation, and these include Blinder, Lindsey, Reinhart, and Kohn. As background, Blinder outlines four levels of central bank transparency in his *Quiet Revolution* book: (1) articulating its views clearly and in "intelligible words and sentences"; (2) conveying substantive and pertinent information on monetary policy; (3) opening itself to public scrutiny by providing information about the deliberations of the FOMC, including the arguments and reasoning behind its decisions and the votes of members; and (4) allowing the proceedings of the FOMC to be televised. He argues that an "ideal central bank would meet the first three standards but not the fourth—which I believe to be unnecessarily intrusive, damaging to the deliberative process, and therefore potentially harmful to monetary policy" (Blinder 2004: 6–7). Blinder further argues that even publication of meeting transcripts well after the event is harmful to deliberation: "all the major substantive points raised in the discussion can be, and I believe should be, made public. Verbatim transcripts, however, go a step too far, in my view, as they are likely to limit frankness and everyday banter, prevent people from taking 'devil's advocate' positions, and otherwise stifle debate" (Blinder 2004: 23).

In our interview with Blinder, he recalls that during the immediate post-transparency years when he served on the FOMC (1994 to 1996), members effectively read scripts into the microphone. He adds: "I would have liked to turn off the tape [because] . . . I thought the tape just eviscerated the potential value-added of the meeting, for the reasons we have been talking about: you just get people reading scripts."

Lindsey's experience on the FOMC covers both the pre- and post-transparency periods, and as such, is particularly telling. He remarks not only on the harmful effects of transparency on deliberation, but also on having felt misled into believing (initially) that FOMC discussions were not being taped and archived.

Lindsey: When I joined the Board I was not informed that the meetings were taped, and therefore my comments at the FOMC meetings were quite candid. . . . I personally think the decision not to destroy [the] tapes has ruined the deliberative process. . . . It's terrible; they are now all set-piece speeches. [*With reference to CS-B describing a before and after period for transparency of the transcripts*] Well interestingly, it wasn't a "before" period was it? It was an unknown period when we were ignorant of the fact . . . I thought it was scandalous. I thought the people involved should have been fired. I really do. I just can't believe that they would mislead the people that they were taping. . . . Whatever the excuse is, they lied to the people that were employing them. . . . I don't care what the excuse is, if you leave the presumption that there is no taping here and you say that, and in fact you are doing the exact opposite of what you are telling your employer, I mean can you imagine doing that in any place other than the government where you wouldn't be fired? [*CS-B: What was your response at the time?*] Oh I yelled but . . . I wasn't backed up. I mean I found the whole thing really, really troubling about the institution and these people weren't even reprimanded. It was unbelievable, and it has made me very cautious ever since. They should have been fired. Every one of them should have been fired. That's the only thing you could do when you lie about something like that. [It was] lying [and] I don't overuse words, [but] that is what it was.

Lindsey goes on to say that the tangible effect of transparency has been to shift the substantive deliberation *outside* the FOMC meetings, where it is unrecorded and therefore allows frank discourse.

Lindsey: The tendency toward set-piece speeches was a habit that caught on. . . . Yes, it got worse. Now all the fun stuff happens outside the FOMC room I assume. . . . I think [having the transcripts public] is counterproductive. That was my point on the taping. I think it's a disaster. I think what they are doing is, they are subverting the deliberative process and they are actually moving the deliberative process outside of the FOMC meeting. . . . How on earth do people expect candor? You want candor in government. You've got to have candor in the deliberative process and you are not going to have candor if it is going to be exposed.

Reinhart provides further detail to the detrimental effect of transparency on the deliberative process, agreeing with Lindsey that it has shifted the substantive deliberation outside the FOMC meetings, including somewhat ironically, public speeches in which FOMC members signal their intentions to one another prior to the FOMC meeting:

Reinhart: Let me start with my strongly held view, which is a post-1994 one, and that is the FOMC meeting is a terrible way of sharing information. Basically what happened was in 1994 as a compromise with the House Banking Committee, the FOMC decided to change its information release that included releasing the transcripts with a five-year lag, increasing the amount of information in the minutes . . . and that had an important consequence. Prior to 1994, there was a transcript but members didn't even know it existed except for the chairman, and it was used only to help prepare the minutes. After 1994, since they were going to be released five years after, they were edited in real time so a participant at an FOMC meeting a couple of weeks after the meeting would get a transcript. Before 1994, a typical participant would be willing to say "I agree with what was just said" or "it works for me." After 1994, when they actually saw their names associated with comments like that, they began to prepare remarks, and so among other things you see the length of the transcripts got longer. Now there were multiple consequences about that, many of them not intended. First one: the meeting actually degrades in value. It was not uncommon . . . to become more formal because people are reading prepared remarks and they are less responsive to each other. So, for instance, it wasn't uncommon to hear three people within the space of say half an hour, say "and here is a little-noted fact" but they were noting the same fact. Some of them would actually just be reading their prepared remarks as other people were reading their own out loud. Occasionally, some of the more graceful ones would insert "as President X just said." . . . So what are the consequences?

Among those are, the meeting isn't a good way to exchange information because you don't change your prepared remarks based on what you have just heard. Second, if you do want to influence the agenda at the meetings then you either write off the current meeting and try to influence the next one or you say something before the meeting, that is, you give a public remark, and so there is also a pickup in the amount of public speaking about monetary policy in advance of [the] meeting because the sad reality was it was very much about signaling to your colleagues before the meeting.

Kohn agrees that publication of the transcripts changed the deliberative process, but not quite as disastrously as suggested by Blinder, Lindsey, and Reinhart. Kohn distinguishes between the economics and the policy discussions, with the former having been more affected by the move to transparency:

Kohn: To some extent [publication of the transcripts] . . . did shape behavior. My impression . . . is that there were many more prepared statements, [and] the statements got longer. . . . No one felt like they could just say "I agree with what Bob just said." They had to say something [more] because people would see it in five years. I remember the first meeting after the decision had been made to publish the transcripts, and one president [Melzer, from the St. Louis Fed], read his thing, and people were shocked that somebody would sit there and actually read a statement—and he read it in kind of a monotone to make a point. But everybody reads at least their economics stuff. I think there is a difference now, at least there certainly was for me, between the economics part of the meeting and the policy part of the meeting. On the economics part of the meeting, I always prepared a set of talking points and while it was in more or less in outline form it was pretty well written out. I did modify [my comments] to some extent based on what I had heard before I talked. Basically I went through the points that I had written before with small modifications. I never did that on the policy side. On the policy side, I sometimes made a list of points, usually handwritten that I thought would be important just to remind myself. But I never put my head down and read them. I was always extemporizing based on what I'd heard in the economics part; a combination of what I heard in the economics part, the points I thought should be made, [and] the points that the chairman might bring up. . . . I think others are like that too. . . . The policy part is much more spontaneous and that's good. [For] the economics part people are generally reading statements that are written out, and there is less give-and-take on that than there might otherwise be.

The contrast between the two camps is quite stark, then. Whereas for the first camp, the effects of transparency on FOMC deliberations have been minimal, the respondents in the second camp cite two specific reasons why publishing the transcripts is harmful for policymaking: (1) it encourages a less spontaneous form of discourse (e.g., members read scripts into microphones) and therefore destroys frank and candid exchanges of views; and (2) it shifts the more genuine deliberation to venues outside the FOMC meeting itself, therefore removing from the meeting the very rationale for transparency—namely to better explain to the public the FOMC's decision-making process.

Perhaps not surprisingly, no one in either camp takes the more extreme views of some of our congressional respondents, which we now present as a concluding twist for this section. For one current staffer of the House Financial Services Committee, a silver lining in the recent financial crisis has been that it has created an opportunity for more transparency in observing and understanding the "inner decision-making of the Fed"—akin to the earlier observations regarding Bernanke's press conference. D'Arista comments, however, that in her view, transparency is no longer the most important issue, since "we [Congress] have won" in forcing the FOMC to publish the transcripts. She concedes that "it inhibits the deliberations to some extent; people don't want to be on record too much, but they will get on record. When they vote they will get on record. . . ." Others argue for more extreme transparency, with one former economist of the House Financial Services Committee, Robert Auerbach, devoting much of his recent monograph to the case for a more open and "democratic" Federal Reserve. He opines that "the public should be allowed to read transcripts of FOMC meetings in a timely manner—no more than 60 days later" (Auerbach 2008: 54). As Auerbach's colleague from their years at Congress, our interviewee James Galbraith is similarly critical of the Fed's traditional resistance to transparency—and he argues that Blinder's fourth level of transparency is perfectly acceptable and desirable:

Galbraith: We've seen this time and time again, that you put something on the table that requires the Federal Reserve to give more information and whether that is monetary targets or the forecasts or the minutes of their meetings or the transcripts of their meetings, and we've all had this experience, as congressional staff do. The Federal Reserve says "the sky will fall, the world will end, Western civilization itself is at stake; we will not be able to have serious, credible, internal dialogue with our counsel of extraordinary sage and wise men and women," most of whom are not, not so extraordinary to put it mildly. The congressmen who are accustomed to operating in public don't find that very credible, and then ultimately when you reassure them that things are going to be alright and they vote it through, like clockwork the Federal Reserve comes out six weeks later and says "well, it looks like we will be able to cooperate with this no problem." [Then] they go ahead and cooperate. . . . The institution isn't in any way compromised by having important public information available to the public. . . . I have a general sense that the quality of the FOMC can only be improved by requiring people to do these exercises in full view. My impression is that these are rather ritualistic meetings at which governors come, and presidents of the regional banks come, and deliver prepared statements in very stilted conversations and that's in secret. The way to cure this is to, in my view, [follow] the whole idea of [House Committee Chairman] Henry Gonzalez. That is, put the whole thing on television and release the tape right after the decision is announced, just afterwards. And then over time you would have to say of someone who was going to be a president "is this person capable of defending their position coherently and competently in front of the camera" and if not, don't appoint him to the job.

5.4.2   Deliberation outside the FOMC

In light of Meyer's depiction of the meeting discourse as "prepared speeches," one of our questions to the FOMC respondents explored the possibility that the real deliberation on the policy decision might occur outside the FOMC meeting, perhaps in bilateral conversations or in Board of Governors meetings. Strikingly, we find roughly the same divide in opinion as we found in the two camps of FOMC respondents on the question of publication of the transcripts. In one camp we have (again) Hoskins, Jordan, Poole, Minehan, Rivlin, and Broaddus. These members are fairly dismissive of the notion that "real" deliberation (possibly leading to a policy decision) occurs prior to FOMC meetings, but they do acknowledge that the positions of most of the members were known in advance simply from experience at previous meetings. Also of note is that members of this group were mostly reserve bank presidents, not board governors.

Hoskins: I rarely discussed policy views with other members prior to meetings nor did I have the feeling that the outcome was pre-decided. I could guess the vote by knowing the position of the members from prior meetings.

Jordan: I never knew, [or] very, very rarely, when going into a meeting . . . what the chairman was going to recommend. I know that there was more of a tendency in the Volcker and Burns years for the chairman to know where the other governors were on an issue before the FOMC meeting. They would know going into a meeting whether a certain recommendation from the chairman would be supported or opposed by one or more of the governors. I'm not aware at all that Greenspan bothered to take a poll of where the other governors would be. I don't know that he even had that strongly made up his mind before a meeting what recommendation he was going to make.

Poole: I'm guessing that [Greenspan] would have been very careful in terms of his relationships with all of the members of the Board for it not to become obvious in any way that he was consulting extensively with one member or two members on a bilateral basis. . . . So it was probably a good bit more subtle than that.

Minehan: There was a meeting that the Board members had with staff, prior to each Open Market Committee meeting, and I don't think anybody said "this is the way you ought to vote" but I think you know the general information and the sort of biases. . . . I never felt that in any of the meetings for thirteen years that I was a part of, that it was a done deal going into the meeting, except for the fact that oftentimes Open Market Committee meetings are done deals. I mean the vast majority of meetings you really just stay the course. . . . And the presidents made a very, very big thing out of never talking to one another about how they were going to vote. They may talk to one another about economic issues, [since] we saw each other quite a bit. You know there were things people were concerned about, regulatory issues, and we had committees, [and] our committees had committees. But with regard to any given Open Market Committee meeting we did not discuss how we were going to vote beforehand.

Rivlin: No [decisions were not made before the FOMC] but I sometimes talked to Greenspan about "what do you think?" and "what do I think?" I remember, he was not a vote-counter, I mean he didn't have to be, I mean we weren't in territory where he could lose control. But I remember a few conversations before FOMC meetings where he would say "who have you talked to? I talked to McDonough this morning; have you talked to anyone?" Sort of trying to figure out where people are.

Broaddus: You mean there was sort of consultation ahead of time? I never participated in anything like that in my time there and I'm not aware of much of it going on. I do think there were some occasions at the staff level when a senior staff person at the Board might, I don't want to say informally, because I think it was deliberate, call someone at our board when some pretty significant issue was going to come before the committee, and give him a heads-up or maybe gently solicit their understanding, especially if they thought we would be inclined to oppose. But that was very rare. I'm talking two or three times in my career that happened. Now, we [the Richmond Fed] often had a reputation for being in opposition, the loyal opposition, a lot of the time on issues like the speed with which we were trying to bring inflation down in, intervention, those kinds of things. So it may well be the case that we naturally experienced less of this because it was anticipated that we wouldn't cooperate.

In a second camp are three of the same members who spoke disparagingly on transparency—Blinder, Reinhart, and Kohn. While none of the three maintain that a decision had been made at the Board of Governors meeting, prior to the FOMC, all three acknowledge that, at least during Greenspan's tenure, a common stance had generally been achieved at the Board meetings—and Greenspan himself engineered this stance. These three are all either former board governors or staff of the board (largely in contrast to the first group):

Blinder: [*CS-B: Were decisions made before FOMC meetings, perhaps in bilaterals?*]
Oh no, [decisions were made] by Alan Greenspan personally. . . . Taking into
account lots of things, including discussions he had with me and other members
of the Board but lots of other things. You know, he would make up his mind
and he would normally come around on Friday (our [FOMC] meetings were
Tuesdays always) and basically tell us, the governors in Washington, but then
I learnt, surprisingly, not really tell the presidents. My first vision before getting
there was that he was also making 12 phone calls, but I didn't want to say he
made zero but he certainly didn't make 12 phone calls. But he did make the
rounds of the governors and tell them in no uncertain terms what he thought
the meeting should decide on Tuesday. That was your chance, by the way, if
you wanted to object but not do it in front of the whole committee, to object
to him face to face. That was his style but I don't think that is Bernanke's style.

Reinhart: [*CS-B: Were decisions made before FOMC meetings, perhaps in bilaterals?*] Sure, under Alan Greenspan it was. Ben Bernanke decided not to. By
law the Board of Governors has to consider discount rate requests every two
weeks. It is actually a requirement. The Board has a pre-FOMC meeting on the
Monday before a meeting which is for staff presentations about the outlook
and they have an opportunity to ask questions. That is one reason why the
governors don't necessarily have to talk in public. They can signal to their colleagues by the type of questions they ask. A successful governor . . . can really
signal [his] views, by the tone or the direction of questioning. So there is that
mechanism in advance of an FOMC meeting, for the governors anyway. The
governors would have a closed session [i.e., with very few or no staff] after the
economic briefing to discuss pending discount rate requirements. . . . Chairman
Greenspan, in the latter part of his tenure . . . would use those Board meetings
to make sure all the governors were aligned with his policy recommendation
or to adjust his policy recommendation to make sure all the governors were
on board. . . . And so the Board would go in with a better understanding,
with a firm understanding of what their colleagues were going to do. . . . [By
Bernanke's tenure] the pre-meeting board discussion was a source of tension
with the bank presidents. Because the Board is the majority of the FOMC most
times, and the idea that there would be a pre-meeting meeting was what made
them uncomfortable, so board members tried not to convey that they had
already had that discussion, but I think Chairman Bernanke basically promised
everybody they wouldn't use that meeting for that purpose.

Kohn: I think the way it has evolved is the Board has had a discussion on
Monday morning before a Tuesday FOMC meeting around the discount rate
and that discussion has often involved what the decision should be at the next
FOMC meeting, but there has never been a kind of commitment made, a decision made. You just came out of that meeting with a better sense of where your
colleagues are and what their worries are and how they see things. No formal
decision is made at that meeting but it is, there is an airing of views, it's true.

On the question of the extent to which deliberation on monetary policy
occurs outside the FOMC meeting, opinion is divided, as it is on the
extent to which transparency of the transcripts has affected the meet-

ing's deliberation. Perhaps the most interesting result from the interviews is that opinion on the location of deliberation is largely divided between those associated with the Board of Governors (over time there has been more deliberation outside the FOMC) and bank presidents (the FOMC remains the focal point). This result appears to be consistent with the finding in chapter 3 that the roles of governors and presidents in the FOMC deliberation have changed over time.

5.5   Institutions and Deliberation

We outlined earlier a number of institutional features that may conceivably affect the quality and nature of deliberation. For the FOMC, these include the role of the chairman in directing the discussion and the culture of consensus decision-making. For the congressional banking committees, the role of the committee chairman is also relevant, along with the order in which members of Congress ask their questions, the size of the committee, and the institutionalized "media circus" surrounding the hearings.

5.5.1   FOMC

In our interviews with FOMC participants, we sought responses on the extent to which the Fed chairman shapes the flow of discussion within the FOMC, and in so doing, sought participants' views on both the chairman's force of personality and the broader culture of consensus decision-making within the Fed. To frame what follows, it is useful to employ Blinder's depiction of two stereotypical types of monetary policy committees—collegial and individualistic (Blinder 2004: 54–63). A collegial monetary policy committee strives for unanimity, with the chairman either "pushing and cajoling" members toward the committee's "center of gravity," or simply imposing his will on committee members. "But in either case, once a collegial committee reaches a decision, all of its members are expected to fall in line behind it. Voting is a formality . . . for it is the group that is held accountable, not each member separately" (Blinder 2004: 55). In contrast, an individualistic committee welcomes differences of opinion. Members argue the merits of different choices and reach a conclusion by majority vote. There is no expectation of consensus or unanimity; individual members vote according to their own preferences and as such, each is held individually accountable. Blinder describes the Bank of England's Monetary Policy Committee as a typical individualistic committee. The FOMC is a variant of the collegial type—namely an "autocratically collegial" committee, where "the chairman's going-in position *is* the likely consensus, and he either persuades or browbeats the others into agreement" (Blinder 2004: 58). Blinder describes Alan Greenspan as leading the FOMC "with a velvet glove, not with an iron fist" so that while he was "about as dominant a chairman as you are ever likely to see," Greenspan did occasionally modify his position ("slightly" Blinder emphasizes) to lessen dissent, perhaps by modifying the wording of the statement or by allowing other committee members to decide the bias (Blinder 2004: 59). The evidence we cite in chapter 3 on the Volcker Revolution indicates that as a chairman, Miller took the opposite approach of seeking consensus above imposing his own view.

While Blinder's general preference is for the individualistic committee, he does, however, note that it risks sacrificing clarity in allowing too many voices, thereby confusing the public and "turning transparency into noise" (Blinder 2004: 61). This brings us to what we identified earlier as a second issue surrounding transparency in monetary policymaking—namely to what extent should the divisions and disagreements among committee members become known, and when? We know that "shades of opinion" short of dissent are not made public (formally and explicitly at least) until the meeting transcripts are published some five years later. We address this issue in this section, as the "shades of opinion" within the FOMC is closely linked to its institutional norms and practices, and here Blinder's description of the FOMC as autocratically collegial is a good starting point.[4] If, as Blinder suggests, "the chairman's going-in position is the likely consensus," to what extent did other members of the committee feel pressured to adopt the chairman's position, including being dissuaded from expressing reservations or more significantly, from exercising a dissenting vote?

To begin, let us first complete Blinder's depiction of the FOMC as autocratically collegial by drawing upon our interview with him. Blinder characterizes "dissent" as equivalent to defying the chairman, and thereby an action not to be taken lightly. He also pointedly observes that as chairman, Greenspan discouraged debate, but so too did the sequential mode of speaking in the FOMC:

Blinder: A dissent was viewed as a defiance of, or a slap in the face to the chairman. . . . Think of the word "dissent." If I go vote Democratic and the Republicans win, no one says I dissented; I voted differently, but the word is dissent, and in that Greenspan period it became something you did with a great deal of thought knowing that it was defiance of the chairman. . . . You could disagree with the decision but unless your disagreement was very major, you wouldn't dissent. Now in terms of expressing [reservations], there was freedom of speech at the FOMC, but first of all Greenspan was not encouraging a healthy, robust debate. It was clear that he was not much interested in it, and didn't really like it very much, although he never tried to silence anybody. Secondly, the way it was . . . orchestrated, [was that] everybody [spoke] in their turn, so . . . it was never one person involved in a dialogue with another: "I think this, you think that, let's argue our points." It was around the table, each person in turn reading their script into the microphone. You don't get a lot of debate. You know, you may hear persons in order, person 12 saying something contradicts person 2 but person 2 and person 12 never engage each other, and the chairman of the Fed who is running the meeting, never, when person 12 speaks up, says "let's hear back from person 2 because you two just disagreed on it." It almost never happened.

One of our bank president interviewees, Hoskins, fully endorses Blinder's depiction of the FOMC as autocratically collegial under Greenspan:

Hoskins: There was a give and take on policy views but it was limited by the procedure at meetings. You could not respond directly to a statement being made. You raised your hand and got on a list kept by the secretary. I believe members' views were shaped by others but for most the chairman's view dominated.

Poole's comments also support Blinder's view, though Poole distinguishes between governors and presidents, with the latter being more likely to express "strong contrary views" than the former:

Poole: It was actually and still is rare for a member of the Board of Governors to dissent. I guess the only one I remember was actually Ned Gramlich, [who] dissented in June 2003. . . . It is quite rare for a member of the Board of Governors to dissent, and by and large, the members of the Board did not express strong contrary views whereas the bank presidents often expressed pretty strong contrary views.

Other interviewees, however, paint quite a different picture of the constraining nature of both Greenspan as chairman and the institutional environment of the FOMC. Jordan, Broaddus, and Minehan all remark that they did not feel constrained in expressing dissenting views in the FOMC.

Jordan: No [discussion in the FOMC] wasn't constrained at all. . . . [Greenspan] would listen to positions taken by governors and presidents, and voting presidents as well as nonvoting presidents, and be counting votes as he listened. His recommendation was going to be influenced by what he thought he could get [people] to vote for, and very rarely did I hear him have a tone that said "I disagree with all of you and here's really what I think we ought to be doing" and try and do that.

Related to his discussion of dissents and the willingness of members to argue their views, Jordan characterizes disagreements and conflict in the FOMC as indirect—that is, rather than challenging their counterparts on the committee, members would instead level their disagreements against the Fed staff:

Jordan: [With respect to the nature of discussions] there were relatively little, very rare, challenges across the table, of one president or governor to another president or governor. That didn't happen as a two-person debate that frequently, occasionally but not often. What happened instead . . . was that you challenged the staff. . . . They make presentations at the meetings and if you get into a free-wheeling tussle with them over economic ideas, theories, and empirical evidence, and real substance, that is considered fair game. And sometimes what you wanted to do was challenge the position that you thought was just slightly short of nutty as it came up from the staff, and make it clear that you thought it was absolutely ridiculous. So you would try to, in effect, intimidate your colleagues round the table from venturing close to that wacky idea [that] you've already exposed as something being not very legitimate. . . . If I wanted to really challenge some idea that I didn't like or didn't agree with, or thought that it was heading in the wrong direction or a conclusion that I thought was derived from faulty analysis or empirical evidence, I would go at the staff. That way I send a message to my colleagues around the table, the voters, what I really believed and I didn't have to challenge them in a confrontational way across the table if they happened to hold that same wacky view.

On this notion of indirect conflict, Lindsey concurs with Jordan, adding that as a governor, challenging Fed staff was also a way to manage staff resources:

Lindsey: I used the opportunity [of challenging the staff] as a way of directing staff resources because the staff reported to the chairman and the best way of getting them to pay attention to you was to take apart one of their numbers at the meeting because there is nothing like embarrassing the staff to get them to behave. . . . I did it nicely . . ., but believe me I got answers. . . . I remember there was one time, this was in 1996, where the Fed staff came up with this projection about the future level of corporate profits. . . . It was a sort of silly consensus view, and I just went through some math. OK, if you assume this, then you have to assume [that], and you assume the other parts of your forecast, if say you've got a fixed path and nominal GDP [and] you've got an assumed rate of corporate profits, well guess what has to happen to wages? By the way, [wages] would be down if profits are going to go up. . . . So you would say little things like that and it's like saying the emperor has no clothes, but it's not something you automatically think of, right? But if I wanted to make a point, I've always found that was an effective way of making a point.

Neither Broaddus nor Minehan allude to this type of indirect conflict, but rather remark that disagreements and dissents were not, in their views, highly constrained. Broaddus notes that he dissented six times, "but other people were less willing to use that public signal" than he was and he accounts for this in terms of individual members' personalities. On the one hand, he echoes Poole's observation that presidents are more likely to dissent than governors, adding that this tendency has increased with the Fed's move toward greater transparency:

Broaddus: My point is that the reserve bank presidents now are much more visible to the public then they were and of course their dissents are no longer kept a secret for several weeks as used to be the case. Now they are released immediately so it becomes a powerful tool for a reserve bank president to reinforce and get attention for his point of view. That's an important, very important, institutional development in the last couple of years I would say. Whether it's a good thing or not, I don't know.

Minehan, on the other hand, never dissented but still asserts that she did not feel constrained in expressing her views. Her characterization of the committee as arriving at a consensual decision echoes Blinder's argument that committees make better decisions but she describes the process more as one of deliberation (argued reasoning) rather than the aggregation of perspectives:

Minehan: I never felt constrained in giving my views, and although I never dissented I was something of an "outlier" at times. [There are] different reasons that people have for agreeing. . . . I think the strength of the committee, particularly a committee like the Open Market Committee, [is that] you've got every district represented, whether they vote or not, and political people who have been selected in a political process . . . all sitting around a table bringing [to the discussion] very different backgrounds and very different perspectives and very different thinking. . . . I think the strength of policy comes from that sort of group being able to argue that yes, for a lot of different reasons, this is the course of action to take. Coming in with a set point of view in that kind of environment, I think would just lead to people grandstanding rather than trying to find the right policy course.

She, like others (e.g., Kohn, Lindsey), believes that the decisions of the FOMC hold greater weight with the markets and with Congress when the committee speaks with a single voice (as represented by the Fed chairman). Even a relatively frequent dissenter like Lindsey (who calculates his own dissent rate at about 10 percent) comments, that, "you can express your views and you can try persuasion but ultimately, it is right for the Board or the FOMC to express a unitary point of view."

In contrast to Jordan, Broaddus, and Minehan, is a second group who ascribe to a view of the FOMC as "collegial" but not as "autocratically collegial" as Blinder depicts. For Lindsey, Rivlin, Kohn, Axilrod, and Reinhart, the driving force behind the FOMC's consensual

decision-making has more to do with institutional features of the
Federal Reserve and the FOMC procedures than with the force of the
chairman. Lindsey and Rivlin emphasize the importance of the committee arriving at a decision that is then owned by all the committee
members, with Lindsey likening the FOMC to a corporate board of
directors and Rivlin equating the FOMC to a political cabinet decision:

Lindsey: When there was [a] possibility that something less than a broad
consensus existed, then the chairman definitely smoothed the process before
the meeting. . . . [*CS-B: In bilateral conversations?*] Yes. [*CS-B: How did that work?*] . . .
If it looked like there were going to be multiple dissents, he would head them
off beforehand. . . . The FOMC is not a legislature, it is a board of directors and
it functions as such. A board of directors should, by and large, reflect a unitary
point of view. That is the only way to run a company. You can have dissents
within a board, you can have differences of opinion within a board but as far
as the voting goes, the differences should be worked out and because otherwise
you have a divided company, and you can't have a divided company and that's
why I think it's appropriate to happen that way. . . . The [Bank of England]
Monetary Policy Committee is not a board of directors. It has a responsibility
that is a subset of all of the operations of the Bank of England whereas the
Board of Governors and the FOMC are the governing body [of the Federal
Reserve]. There are other subcommittees, I mean it is obviously the FOMC
[that] is the one of most interest, but the Board of Governors and even the
System itself has a number of subcommittees that do the governance in other
areas, which also tends to operate by a consensus process. So, if you are going
to have smooth governance, and you are dealing with the same colleagues on
a variety of other issues you really have to have an extremely collegial view
toward the operations of the decision-making body.

Rivlin: Well, as to the question [about being constrained] . . . everybody was
very respectful but there was no reticence to express opinions, . . . so you might
get different versions from different people but I did not feel inhibited at all in
saying what I thought, although I didn't have a long history in monetary
policy. I came from the fiscal side, and my orientation was to real economic
data, [that is] to what was happening rather than to theory. So I was sometimes
a little reticent to take on, not with Greenspan, but to take on an argument
with say Larry [Meyer] who knew a lot more about the models than I did for
example. . . . How [the FOMC] worked was that people argued in the meeting
and with each other very politely, and very formally, but then when you got
to a decision you wanted it to be a consensus decision and when you left the
room you didn't talk about it. . . . I had come directly from the White House,
and when you are in an administration . . . you argue in a small group around
the president. But he makes the decision and you may express your views very
forcefully, and some presidents, including Clinton, occasionally set up a debate
situation to hear the opposition; he didn't do that very often but he did it on
NAFTA. . . . Once you got to a decision, then nobody went out and said "I don't
agree with [that]." It was just that you were part of the administration, you

were on the team, and you went up to Capitol Hill and defended it, and that was the way the game worked. So coming to the Fed wasn't that surprising to me. I wanted to be part of it, the group making the decision, but I certainly didn't feel I should get out there and say "well, I had a different view." That was the one place where I felt Greenspan kept pretty tight control, not so much on getting to the decision but on how you talked about it, and he took me to task a couple of times. . . . I had used the word "guess" in connection with an economic forecast, something like "best guesses," and he said he didn't think that was a good word because it made it sound too uncertain, too fuzzy, and we weren't guessing, we were taking all this information and making a decision. So I said "yes, that is right, I take your point." But that kind of thing was normal.

Rather than viewing consensus decision-making as part and parcel of committee members accepting the norm of group accountability (either akin to a corporate board of directors or a government's administrative cabinet), Kohn, Axilrod, and Reinhart adopt a more individualistic view of consensus decision-making as a way for individual members to (1) influence the decision of the current meeting's statement (at the margins) as well as the more substantive decisions of future meetings (Kohn), (2) signal to the chairman their future positions (Axilrod), or (3) tie the hands of future FOMC meetings (a form of precommitment device) (Reinhart):

Kohn: [Compared to UK's Monetary Policy Committee] in the United States there is a consensus to try and form a consensus and the hurdle for dissenting is higher. I think [that] . . . because there is that effort to form a consensus, if you're in that consensus, it is possible to help the decision or at least the wording around the decision so [that] you can influence the course of policy over time and market expectations. . . . Though you don't dissent [instead you say] "Well, I go along with you but I have these reservations, I'd really be more comfortable if the statement said something about worries about inflation" or something like [that]. The lack of dissent doesn't mean that people who are uncomfortable don't have any influence on framing the decision and its explanation to the public. . . . So it's a complicated game that happens over time. . . .

Axilrod: [Expressing reservations to the proposed policy is] a very good way of guiding the future, of making the chairman uncertain. Chairmen are always uncertain about whether they have got the committee with them or not. It's very important to them to have the committee with them because their stature, being the main spokesman, the only real spokesman for the Fed, depends on whether they can deliver the committee. So they are constantly caught inbetween leading and following. It's always the case and so some chairmen don't speak until they have a fairly good idea of the committee. . . . The chairmen constantly worry about getting a positive vote from the committee, and they constantly worry about it not being 7 to 5. . . . Arthur Burns really didn't want any dissents and Bill Martin didn't care as far as I can remember. . . .

Paul [Volcker] was more ambivalent in some ways about that. . . . The chairmen are not exactly sure [about] these nuances, [although] they are pretty sure of the parameters. . . . They might get a nuance which says yeah we're voting for you but we prefer not to tighten or not to ease any more or something like that which gets in the wording here and there, substituting "might" for "would."

Reinhart: [In the minds of committee members is] the fact that dissent is fairly rare [and] that in all their decisions they think about precedent. Part of it is I think historically the fact that the [membership of the] FOMC rotates each year. The policy decisions span multiple years, particularly when you are using statements to convey longer term intentions on interest rates and the balance sheets. That makes them want to speak with one voice so that they can in effect try to pre-commit themselves. . . . Democracy [in the FOMC] has a drawback. You can't pre-commit future governments. . . . So a more democratic FOMC has a problem, if you are trying to work on expectations. You can't pre-commit the next committee, and so unanimity or few dissents is a mechanism to convey the reassurance that the next committee will make decisions in the same manner.

Two final observations are relevant to this section, as they allow a comparison between Bernanke's FOMC, and the committee under Greenspan—and both suggest a fundamental change in the deliberation within the committee:

Kohn: Ben [Bernanke] has deliberately come in and tried to encourage more discussion on the policy side. . . . [Moreover, following the economics part of the discussion] we often have a coffee break. [Bernanke] goes into his office by himself, sometimes he will want people to come in to talk—some staff—but mostly by himself. He [returns to offer a summary of the first part of the meeting] . . . then he always says everybody has said all the good stuff, and I don't have much to add but, and then he has something interesting to add. . . . [This is] unlike Greenspan . . . who would at the end of his little interesting whatever, say "And therefore I think we need to raise the interest rate 25 basis points today." Bernanke doesn't do that. He says "Now I'd be interested in hearing your policy views." He might lay some issues on the table, particularly in this . . . quantitative easing unconventional policy period. He would say I would like to hear your views. So he doesn't lead off. . . . I think he's very good, he is a very smart guy, and he's very good at reasoning through his position, but he also listens to people and modifies things a bit around the edges to make people feel better about being in the consensus. I think he does a very good job of basically having the committee move when he thinks it should move, although he listens to people and [decides] what he thinks can be modified by what people say. . . . It's a different meeting than it was under Greenspan, particularly in the policy part.

In our interview with him, Blinder also recognizes a significant change in Bernanke's approach to balancing the "shades of opinion" with the concern for building consensus in the FOMC, when he remarks on greater acceptance of outside speeches by FOMC members, in which they express their views:

Blinder: Oh definitely [there is a change with Bernanke]. There was much, much less of that in the Greenspan period. There was some, but I stood out as an outlier. I was once negatively profiled in *Business Week* as the "leader of the open-mouth committee" because . . . you were supposed to be seen and not heard. So there was a little bit of it, and you would find it sometimes but there was very little of these outside speeches and press interviews or anything like that; not nonexistent but much, much less than today. There has been a huge change in members, and this goes both for governors and for presidents, but especially for presidents, latitude in just singing from their own hymnal book instead of the common hymnal book. There was a lot of peer-group pressure; it wasn't illegal or anything like that but there was a lot of peer-group pressure not to do that [under Greenspan].

What, then, can we conclude regarding the effects of both the chairman and the culture of consensus decision-making on deliberation in the FOMC? Two themes emerge. First, under Greenspan's tenure, not everyone felt equally constrained either in expressing reservations or in casting a dissenting vote, so Blinder's description of the committee as autocratically collegial may be said to be compromised, or less applicable, in the face of strong personalities. Second, whether we attribute it to personality, academic background, or the financial crisis, Bernanke's FOMC appears to have evolved into a forum in which deliberation is less constrained, and the differing shades of opinions among members interpreted as less of a threat to the traditional norm of consensual decision-making. As the FOMC transcripts from Bernanke's first year as chairman have only recently becoming available for analysis (i.e., in 2012) it is too early to judge with certainty. From our interviewees with first-hand experience at the Bernanke Fed (e.g., Kohn), one may, however, suggest that Bernanke's FOMC is approaching Blinder's ideal type of monetary policy committee—that is, a genuinely collegial committee but still one with a clear leader. Such a committee would be "individualistic enough to reap most of the benefits of diversity and yet collegial and disciplined enough to project a clear and transparent message"; it would allow argumentation within the bounds of committee discussion, but would be "like-minded from the outside" (Blinder 2004: 62). To this description of an ideal monetary policy committee, we would add that the ultimate decision reflects not simply an aggregation of preferences, models, and modes of thinking (as Blinder depicts) but also a fundamental respect for the deliberative process, with the legitimacy and justification to be attained from reasoned decision-making.

5.5.2 Congress

In our interviews with congressional staff and members of Congress, we asked a number of questions pertaining to the institutional environment of banking committee hearings on monetary policy. We focus here on the extent to which deliberation in these hearings is affected by (1) the quality of the chairmanship of the committee, (2) the procedures for questioning the Fed chairman, combined with the size of the committee, and (3) extreme transparency (i.e., televised hearings).

Chairmanship

Perhaps a common sense response to a query regarding the effect of the chairman's knowledge and expertise on the committee's quality of deliberation would be "it depends on the chairman." Interestingly, none of our interviewees provided us with this response. Rather, they were fairly divided on the question. Two staffers remark that the quality of the chair is not necessarily a determining factor in the success of the hearing, but they offer different reasons. One notes that while some chairmen might exceed their five minute time limit, they—like everyone else—are still allotted the same amount of time. The second staffer adds to this observation that the chairman has only limited control over the hearing, and particularly the substance of each member's questions. Hence, "if somebody wants to be a jerk, or someone wants to press an issue which had already been pressed, there is nothing at all that the chairman can do about that." In illustration, this staffer remarks that, "when Jim Bunning starts railing about socialism there is nothing Chris Dodd can do to make that a sensible discussion. It is Senator Bunning's five minutes, and he can do with it what he wants."

While Galbraith also notes that the members, rather than the chair, drive the success of the committee, in his view, the House members tend to engage the Fed chairman more than do Senate members, given the greater committee specialization that occurs in the House of Representatives:

Galbraith: I'm a members' person. I think if you have very good staff, if they are feeding questions to Roger Jepsen, it is a bit of a charade and everybody knows it. If you have a Paul Sarbanes, Henry Reuss, or Bill Proxmire, the staff are going to be good because they were demanding bosses. But it is really the member who can carry the line of questioning and follow up and see an opportunity or know when you want to pursue a matter past the hearing. . . . [To have committee members] with both perspective and independence . . . is fairly rare. . . . Sarbanes [is] an exception because he had a strong interest in this. [Members with perspective and independence] are much more likely . . . on the House side than on the Senate side and the reason is that the House members are much more specialized in their committee assignments. They don't serve on so many and they don't rotate on seniority from one committee to the next. So, you come up through the House system; your seniority is in the committee that you are in and at the end of your career, or a certain stage of your career, maybe you get to be a subcommittee chairman or ultimately the chairman of the committee. But you don't move as senators do from armed services to . . . banking, and so on. . . . . It doesn't happen.

In direct contrast to Galbraith's assessment, some staffers tend to take a different view by rating senators more highly. One staffer remarks that senators (and their staff) generally view themselves as engaged more in the broader principles of policy, whereas representatives tend to be "more in the weeds" (i.e., concerned with the lesser important details of policy).

Another set of congressional interviewees place greater weight on the importance of the banking committee chair in determining the quality of discussion. One staff advisor remarks that the chairman's decision to allow questions either by seniority (toggling back and forth between majority and minority party members), or by the order in which members of Congress arrive at the committee hearing, can allow a fair bit of control over the questioning. Another staff advisor adds to this by remarking that if the member of Congress is a junior member, the order of questioning can matter significantly, as "all the good questions are already taken," so members tend to repeat previous questions. D'Arista comments that "whoever is chair, his interests are going to dominate the discussions at the committee level—it also depends on the subcommittee chairs, and that is important." Barratt is even more definitive, adding that the partisan orientation of the committee chair can substantially shape the nature of the hearings:

Barratt: Absolutely [the chairmanship matters], and the direction too, not only the quality but the direction. For example, if your chairman is a guy like Barney Frank, you can expect the kind of emphasis that Barney Frank would bring to the table, whereas [during] my first four years, I served with Mike Oxley who was a fantastic chairman. [As chairman] you can mold the witnesses, you can mold the testimony, you can give deference to amendments, whatever, that tend to agree with the chairman's philosophy. So . . . unfortunately politics does play a huge part of that. If it is a Republican controlling the committee, yes, it is going to be mostly Republican stuff coming out of it. On the other hand, if it is Democrat, kind of the same thing there.

Questioning and Committee Size
Building on some of the comments above regarding the chair's control over the order of questioning, many of our interviewees agree that procedures for managing questions coupled with a House committee

that is too large, degrade the quality of deliberation. In particular, they comment on three factors that harm deliberation within hearings: (1) members generally come and go throughout the hearing, and therefore do not know what has been already asked and answered; (2) partly owing to (1), members are unable or unwilling to adapt their questions as the hearing progresses; and (3) House members are not even assured of any time during the hearing when they can ask their own questions, given that the committee has grown to over 70 members.

1. Committee Attendance

On the first point, Kohn (who attended all the congressional hearings during Greenspan's tenure, in addition to the last year of Volcker's tenure) and D'Arista (who recently offered expert testimony before the House Financial Services Committee) both remark on the poor attendance:

Kohn: My observation is that there are at least a handful of the representatives that tend to stay for long periods [during the hearings]. They might not stay for the entire hearing, these things go on for 3, 3½ hours sometimes. . . . Some of them drift in and drift out. I think there is a little more of that on the Senate side, the drifting in and drifting out. I think these hearings get boring after a while because they ask the same questions over and over, and they're just trying to get Greenspan, Bernanke, whomever, to buy into their particular concern.

D'Arista: Right, yes [the House Financial Services Committee hearings are not well-attended]. Part of this is technological; they can watch it in their offices. . . . That is how they know that it is their turn. They may not be watching it; their staff may be watching it, just to say "OK, you better get over now to the committee, you are now two questions up," but I think it does reflect . . . less participation, less of a sense of the deliberative [process]. I was very struck when I was testifying that day, that senior members stayed and one or two juniors but it was a very empty room.

Our two members of Congress provide an insightful contrast of experiences, with Bayh (whose interest in monetary policy is—as he describes—"atypical") opting to remain for most of the hearing, and Barratt (whose interest in the subject is more typical of the average member) describing attendance as more "hit or miss":

Bayh: The chairman is usually there for the duration. The ranking member is usually there for most of it, and there would be a few of us, I was among them, who would just like these issues and want to hear what [the Fed chairman] has to say. Also, this is going to sound kind of mundane but sometimes these things can drive the process. [In] some committees, the questions are asked in order of seniority, so no matter when you show up, if you are more senior you get to ask, you have your place in line. The Banking Committee and the Armed

Services Committee I was on as well, they operate under what is called the "early bird rule" so it is in order of when you arrive before the chairman drops the gavel. So if you arrive after that, you go to the back of the queue. . . . [I would usually arrive late and] that had the effect of me being at the back of the queue. So I had to sit there and listen to it all. But I found, notably listening to [the Fed chairman's] testimony but then [also] listening to my colleague's questions and his answers really enabled me to hone my own thinking and penetrate to the heart of the matter so that I could ask a well-informed question, because you could hear his answer, you could hear where he was trying to hedge a little bit and then follow-up. So the order in which the questions are asked sometimes determines who sticks around and if you are at the end [of the queue], you've got to stick around.

Now, with regard to people coming in and out that is true but that in some ways is a sign of the dysfunction of Congress in general, where people have so many things to do. If you are not sitting there listening to the proceedings, it is not a deliberative process. There is no give and take—you show up with a preconceived idea, you ask your questions according to your preconceived ideas, uninformed by the testimony or the previous questions and answers, then you leave, and so there is really no give and take and that is unfortunate.

Barratt: [Describing his schedule as akin to "juggling a million balls"] So when we talk about going to hearings . . . you know, we are so busy and so crammed unfortunately that [attending the hearing] . . . is a hit or miss kind of thing. There may be times, whether it is Alan Greenspan or not, that in coming to your hearing, you may have two other hearings at that same time that are as important or more important than what you are dealing with right there. So, it is sometimes a hit or a miss. If it happens to be your passion yes, you are going to be there. [For] some people, this is what really drove them and it was part of my responsibility, but it was not a passion of mine. . . .

2. Adapting Questions to the Discussion

A staffer notes that members tend to come to hearings "with something in their mind and even if it has been broached earlier, and discussed at length earlier, they nonetheless ask the question that they came prepared to ask." This staffer adds that younger committee members "are at the bottom of the food chain" and because "it is late in the day, people are tired, and the hearing has gone on for hours" and their questions have already been asked and answered, these younger members "get short shrift." Or, from a different perspective, as Barratt remarks, members often "spend their entire five minutes pontificating, and then your witness has no time to answer." He adds that, "one of the things I really tried to do is to be very short and to the point: 'Chairman Greenspan, in your testimony you said this, what about this,' and then unfortunately he would get into it a little bit and you have to cut him off and say well, 'what about this?' because it is amazing how fast five minutes goes [by]." These comments reinforce a perception of the House Financial Services Committee hearings in particular as consisting of a series of repetitive, self-contained questions, where committee members are uninterested in facilitating a cumulative exchange of views and information.

3. Size of Committee Membership

Several of our interviewees remark that the increase in size of the House Financial Services Committee (as can be seen from our details of committee memberships from 1977 to 2008, in our book appendix II) to over seventy members has severely hampered deliberation. One staffer remarks that because there is not enough time for all committee members to ask questions, many decide not to attend at all, and instead merely read the transcript after the hearing. This staffer adds that, before Greenspan, the hearing could last up to eight hours. But, from the Greenspan era onward, "the Fed chair has said that he would only come for three hours." Simple arithmetic suggests that, even if the House Financial Services Committee were to eliminate the oral presentation of the Monetary Policy Report by the Fed chairman, three hours would allow just 36 members to question the Fed chairman.

D'Arista, who served as a House staffer in the 1960s and 1970s, relays her experience when she recently returned to offer expert testimony before the House Financial Services Committee, noting (as have others, and as we describe in chapter 4) that the increased membership reflects the committee's benefit to members of Congress as a "cash cow":

D'Arista: I was very shocked when I walked in to testify in November 2009 to see what had happened to the Banking Committee's room in the House side. There were now 74 members, and someone I knew in the audience came up to me and he said "Paul Nelson would never have allowed this—you get beyond 49 and you can't have a deliberative body." That was absolutely true but all of the young members who had come in wanted to be on the Banking Committee because it was a source of funding. . . . [Expansion in membership occurred] as more Democrats came in and wanted to be, and were put, on the committee deliberately. I'm going to say something that is commonplace. I mean Rahm Emanuel sitting there in the White House, and sitting in the Congress at the time and very close to Nancy Pelosi, said "the way we keep getting these people elected is if we put them on the Banking Committee because they can get the funding." . . . [So they] really ramped up the membership of the committee.

D'Arista is correct to note that party strategies to exploit the campaign contributions accruing to House Financial Services Committee members is commonplace knowledge, as evidenced by news reports of increased contributions to these members in the midst of legislation on new banking regulations following the financial crisis—particularly for members from marginal, or swing districts. Following the 2008 election, leaders of both political parties are said to have assigned 11 of the 24 new members of the House of Representatives "who won their seats by the narrowest margins" to the House Financial Services Committee. "Now, as they consider the broadest rewrite of financial rules in decades, those members are getting money from donors such as the American Bankers Association, Citigroup Inc., and Visa Inc." (Jensen and Salant 2009, April 17).

While the ratcheting up of its membership is a more recent phenomenon, its dubious reputation as a "cash cow" for members of Congress has a longer history, and is associated with occasional corruption scandals, as Galbraith describes:

Galbraith: The Banking Committee was already developing its present reputation as a cash cow [in the 1970s], and for a great many members, and particularly this was true of liberal members, the way you financed a congressional career as a liberal, as a liberal on the side of the Vietnam war, or on social issues of various kinds, civil rights, women's rights, was to be in your Banking Committee function, was to be a faithful representative of the constituent banks, many of whom took their cues on what they wanted from the Federal Reserve. . . . So you could be a good liberal and have a very strong reputation as a liberal Democrat but still have a pretty well-funded campaign because the banks in your district felt you were a reliable ally. . . . I'm talking about the Democratic side. . . . There was openness to corruption in this too. The career of Fernand St. Germain being a classic example of that and ultimately this would lead to the bipartisan agreements on deregulation which led to disaster. . . . Just as that transition was occurring, and St. Germain became the chairman of the Banking Committee, you've got the Reaganite takeover and you've got the placing of aggressive deregulators in top regulatory positions. Then you've got the Monetary Control Act of 1980, which among other things, raised deposit insurance limits to $100,000 and in other ways opened up the floodgates for these bidding wars over bank deposits and speculative activities in the Savings and Loans debacle, and of course that was very much with a strong element of corrupt interference, notably by the majority leader who became Speaker, Jim Wright.

Transparency

Clearly, televised coverage of the congressional hearings on the Fed's Monetary Policy Report is a well-established tradition.[5] While for the FOMC, transparency of the decision-making process has been a matter of periodic controversy between the Fed and Congress, for the congressional banking committee hearings, it is an institutional norm. One ironic effect of the heavily televised oversight hearings is that it appears to have shifted at least some of the "real" deliberation outside the hearings themselves. Our interviewees comment that if one is interested in finding "real" deliberation on monetary policy in Congress, it is not found in the high profile congressional hearings, but rather elsewhere, for example, during lunches (as Lindsey describes of Senator Corker, noted earlier). A staffer remarks that important deliberation on monetary policy is likely not to happen in committee meetings but rather in "hallway conversations, staff briefings, and weekly meetings of same-party members of the Banking Committee." As this staffer also concedes, no minutes or notes are taken of these meetings and so they are in no way "transparent" or available for public scrutiny. Hence, while the hearings themselves may be entirely transparent, it is not at all evident that "real" deliberation in Congress is equally as transparent.

Indeed Poole argues that, because extreme transparency in the congressional hearings has shifted real deliberation outside the hearings, the actual record of decision-making is more transparent for the FOMC than it is for Congress, in part because the minutes of the FOMC function as a "check" for the transcript:

Poole: The FOMC deliberations . . . are obviously confidential but the transcript is released with a five-year lag. And the transcript is a very complete record of, well, it is a verbatim transcript. There are a few things which are excised as you will know, redacted, but it's a pretty complete record. One difference between the two institutions that you are talking about is that for the congressional stuff, a lot of the main decisions are taken in the offices, and are confidential, and they are never exposed unless somebody writes about them. . . . My sense was that the [FOMC] transcript was quite accurate, and I used to say any number of times when reviewing the minutes, that the minutes have got to be true to the transcript because in five years the transcript will be published and at some point somebody is going to compare the transcript to the minutes that are released with what, a three-week lag. . . . [*CS-B: So what does one do about this from a research perspective?*] One thing you do about it is you simply make note of it so that the reader understands that the key considerations from the congressional point of view are simply hidden whereas there is much more in the open for the FOMC stuff.

But, what are the effects of extreme transparency on deliberation within the hearings themselves? We prompted our interviewees with the question of whether, having the intensive media focus of the monetary policy hearings, committee members were tempted to "grandstand"—that is, take a public position with the primary intention of speaking to one's constituents—rather than to participate in any deliberative discussion. We pointed to YouTube videos of Bernie Sanders and Alan Grayson as examples. All of our congressional interviewees accepted grandstanding as a natural element of the oversight hearings, with some adding more names to our list—such as Ron Paul, Chuck Schumer, and to a lesser extent, Maxine Waters. Barratt remarks that heavily televised monetary policy hearings are both "the best and worst thing in the world":

Barratt: I mean, it is the best thing because the average person can tune in if they so choose to do so. I think I would rather watch grass grow, but you can watch what is going on in the hearing, and be very well-informed about the policy, the hearings, the issues. But unfortunately, on the down-side, it does give each and every congressperson a tremendous way to "grandstand" and that unfortunately happens all the time but I do think that is a very fair assessment.

D'Arista comments that new media outlets have increased the opportunity to exploit the media presence at the hearings:

D'Arista: Yes, I think it was always there but it was not, it could never have been, as great until the present time when we have YouTube and all of this going on. I mean it just has ramped up the situation tremendously, and given someone like Grayson who was a one-termer, after all, a sort of a huge position. It didn't mean that he would get re-elected on it, but at least he got a lot of attention and he asked some very good questions. He did his job.

By "doing his job" D'Arista sets the tone for many of the observations from congressional staffers, one of whom notes that "speaking to the cameras" is simply a reflection of the committee hearings being "closely linked to what is going on outside of Congress. What is of concern to the public is reflected by members of Congress in the hearings—it is all intertwined." Another says that committee members have real concerns which "they don't get much of an opportunity to raise, and they take advantage of the fact that these hearings are unusually well-attended by the press, to press those concerns." Even if committee members take what appear to be offensive and/or extreme views, "one should not confuse being annoyed at the persona of folks who have a hobbyhorse with the fact that hobbyhorses are a perfectly legitimate thing for someone who has a serious interest in these issues to have."

Whereas for some committee members with specific and ongoing concerns (e.g., Grayson with governance and democratic accountability), grandstanding may afford an opportunity to raise the public profile for these concerns, for other committee members, the cameras are more a means of raising one's own recognition with constituents back home. This fleeting recognition may serve a political purpose, but it does not contribute to effective oversight, as Barratt astutely notes from his own experience:

Barratt: To do correct oversight, especially on an issue that is as important as monetary policy, you have got to have members that can spend the time, that can roll up their sleeves and get more involved coming in. Getting the attention of the chairman, asking your little question, and then you are gone; because you are playing to the cameras, you want to make sure constituents back home [are saying] "There is Gresham, I saw you." You ask your one question, and you were thinking about ten other things when you did it, and then you were gone. So, having some dedicated time is extremely important.

From these responses one is left with a somewhat jaded view of the merits of heavily televised congressional hearings on monetary policy. Although for a dedicated few, the cameras may allow a higher profile to push substantive policy concerns (which, notably, may or may not pertain to monetary policy), for others, the cameras merely serve as an instrument of self-promotion. And, even more damaging, the intensive media coverage diverts at least some of the "real" deliberation to back-room venues, thereby potentially making claims to "government in the sunshine" a sham.

5.6   Textual Analysis Findings: Do They Make Sense to Participants?

5.6.1   FOMC

As can be seen from table 5.2, we queried FOMC participants on five specific findings that pertained to our textual analysis of the FOMC transcripts: (1) the lack of references to "politics" or political influence; (2) the tendency for bank presidents (not governors) to talk about money and monetary aggregates; (3) the apparent shift in discourse over time, with presidents playing a larger role in deliberation on the policy decision in the late 1970s/early 1980s, but by the later 1990s, governors taking this role, leaving presidents focusing more on the state of the economy; (4) a tendency over time for all the members to focus their discussions more on the data and state of the economy and less on deliberating the policy decision; and (5) no explicit discussion of key tools of economic theory, such as time inconsistency or the Phillips curve. We address the responses from interviewees to each of these findings, in order.

"Politics" or Political Influence in FOMC Discussions

None of our FOMC interviewees were surprised that we found no evidence in the transcripts to suggest that members were cognizant of political pressures on the Federal Reserve, but they offered different reasons for this. One group argues strongly that because the Fed really is independent of politics, FOMC members behave accordingly [Hoskins]. Part of this behavior may, however, reflect (1) norms of etiquette within the FOMC meeting (Blinder); (2) that political pressure—should it exist—would be more likely to be felt by the Fed chairman, outside the FOMC meeting itself (Broaddus); or (3) that politicians are sometimes tempted to exert pressure on the Fed but are dissuaded by their advisors (Rivlin). And Minehan notes that where monetary policy intersected with fiscal policy, political considerations may have influenced the discussion—but perhaps not to the extent that our textual analysis captured this.

Hoskins: Members believe that the Fed is independent of politics and tend to behave that way. Some members may have tempered their statements with political considerations in mind, particularly when political critics were aggressively outspoken. They did this not to help a party but to protect the independence of the Fed. . . . The lack of discussion at meetings about political pressure is because there was rarely any direct pressure put on members by political agents.

Blinder: One of the things that I found most gratifying when I went from an outsider to an insider is that what I thought might be part myth about the apolitical technocratic nature of Federal Reserve decision-making was more or less correct. It is very nonpolitical, so it is not just that it's not polite to say these things and you don't want to put them on the tape, but people for the most part really felt that way, that politics should not enter the room. . . . Talking political was like slurping your soup. It was just very impolite; you weren't supposed to do it. Even if you had political thoughts, you were not supposed to voice them.

Broaddus: [Political influence] was never very prominent in my view, and I think this one of the great strengths of the Fed. Keep in mind that I wasn't the chairman. Obviously the chairman is in contact with the political authorities. The Treasury secretary, you know, typically meets with the Fed chairman once a week so he's fairly exposed to those kinds of pressures to a far greater degree than a reserve bank president like me would have been. . . . I never experienced that and I didn't sense it.

Rivlin: No, you didn't even think about [political influence]. The culture of the Fed was "we don't do that; we do what is right for the economy." . . . I never saw this in the Fed at all, [but] I did see it in the other side because I was in the Clinton administration in 1994 when the Fed was raising rates. . . . They were worried about inflation creeping up, and so they raised rates in 1994 quite aggressively and Clinton was upset about it. He thought they are going to derail our recovery. . . . In the meetings in the White House, people like me and Alan Blinder, and others, Laura Tyson, the economists, were saying "Mr. President, don't say anything." He wanted to talk about it, he wanted to say this is bad, go out publicly and we were saying "no, no, that is not a good idea," and he didn't. . . . We certainly thought it was inappropriate for a president but also that it might even backfire and that we had better let the Fed do its thing. But that is the only time I ever encountered that issue, [and] that was from the other side.

Minehan: Frankly, we never talked about that. . . . The minutes correctly reflect the fact that we took it as a matter of obligation that we voted on the basis of our understanding of the economics, and not the political cycle, so you know I have always wondered about this extreme focus on "you can't do this because this is happening in Congress, you can't do that because that is happening, an election, and this and that." We just did not talk about that . . . unless of course it was something that had both economic and political implications, you know, the fiscal deficit issue that clearly has both economic [and political implications]. If the Congress is really going to tighten fiscal policy, well, monetary policy has to take account of it, and vice versa.

Broaddus adds a further, more nuanced, observation on measuring the influence of political pressure on the Federal Reserve, which points to the limitations of models which fail to consider the actual decision-making process (and conversely, illustrates the value in adding contextual insights from interviews to textual data analysis). He argues that FOMC members (particularly prior to the emergence of the low inflation consensus) might have behaved as though they were following the political business cycle, when in fact this was not at all their intention:

Broaddus: The individual members of the FOMC might have behaved in a way that is consistent with a political-business cycle simply because that's the way they view the proper function of monetary policy, you know, resisting weakening of the economy. Although . . . we have a consensus now [which] I think it's pretty strong, that the Fed's principal objective is price stability, despite the dual mandate, mainly because that's the way you get both of the mandates met. But that was not always the case. . . . [In the earlier period, when credibility was not a consensus.] . . . there were people who were much more interested in fine-tuning the economy, and actively, we called it "activist policy"—[i.e.,] reacting to what was happening currently and maybe in the expected near-term future and letting that be the main driver for their monetary policy preferences. I can imagine that people in that group would behave in a way that might make it look like they were responding to political pressures when they weren't actually doing that.

Others place a greater weight on the role of politics, but predominantly at the level of the Fed chairman—and only during the Burns (and possibly Martin) chairmanships. Hoskins, Blinder, and Lindsey comment that during these previous chairs, the Fed was more influenced by politics. Hoskins notes simply that "in earlier days, two Fed chairmen did react directly to the president: Martin and Burns." Blinder characterizes monetary policy in this earlier period as more partisan (though also notes its possible resurgence in the aftermath of the financial crisis). He remarks that "the old-fashioned Republican–Democrat division" in terms of emphasis on inflation versus unemployment "may be coming back now." But,

Blinder: . . . if you look historically, the Republican Party and its predecessors going back to the Federalists in America were much more anti-inflation and much less worried about "full employment." We didn't have that phrase back in the old, old days, you know, and the Democrats [were] conversely much less worried about inflation if not indeed at some periods of time favoring inflation, and much more worried about growth and employment. That ended around Reagan, and there ceased being a political difference on the short-run trade-off between inflation and unemployment around Reagan's time. As to the political-business cycle, as to trying to juice up the economy before an election, other than the Fed under Arthur Burns . . . the Fed just didn't do that.

Lindsey explains that "it was the Carter experience that really galvanized the Board and created its political independence, because Carter and his manipulation of monetary policy was such a disaster. [Hence] the Board was able to assert itself as independent of the political institutions."

Another group of interviewees (Jordan, Axilrod, Kohn, Poole) does not disagree with the first group, but their general assessment is that politics may matter in a more subtle way for the Fed, namely in terms of constraining the FOMC to "lay low" around election time:

Jordan: There certainly would have still been some amount of reluctance to talk about proximity to an election in the influence of a decision though I'm sure that all of us were aware that if we didn't move in the July or August meeting, it was unlikely we would move in the September–October meeting, immediately before an election if it was in a tightening direction.

Axilrod: It was generally accepted that . . . about three months before an election you didn't want to change policy. Now one of the chairmen, Paul [Volcker] actually, was quite proud of the fact that we raised the discount rate within a month or two of Carter's second running.

Kohn: I think what I've seen on the political-business cycle with respect to the Fed has said, they try and stay out of the limelight near elections, and I think there may have been some of that going on. So, if we can avoid being in the headlines in September and October, then let's do it. I think there was a little of that but you know that wasn't about favoring one party or another, it was about protecting the institution.

Poole: The Fed tried very, very hard, and I believe on the whole has been quite successful to be apolitical. . . . On occasion, I might have said something to the effect that "We need to be aware, let's say in the springtime, we need to be aware that it's going to become increasingly difficult as we come up to election time to make a decision, let's say, to raise rates, or whatever it was." And I was usually beaten back by others on that: "no, we'll do what we have to do." . . . The Fed does not want to rock the political boat if it can help it. . . . I think it would be quite rare for the FOMC to act in September ahead of the November election. . . . The Fed tries to lie low before an election, it doesn't want to attract any visibility at all. . . . The major exception is 1980, and Carter was so weakened and Volcker was so determined to re-establish Federal Reserve credibility, that there were very sharp interest rate increases.

Two remarks, by Kohn and Reinhart, point to one further subtlety with respect to the influence of political pressure on the FOMC— namely with the acceptance of the low inflation consensus, political influence was simply less relevant to the formulation of monetary policy:

Reinhart: [The] political aspect of monetary policy was essentially the thing that should not be said and it was understood as that. That it was just not done in that environment. [Think of] the example of the billiards player, who doesn't need to know geometry, he just needs to know how to play billiards. The fact that they haven't worked it out and explicitly said it doesn't mean that it is not done internally. So I don't have a lot of trouble rationalizing the two. The fact that they might not have talked about [politics], doesn't mean that it wasn't an influence. Part of it is clearly the great moderation. . . . For the 1983–2005 [period] they weren't really significantly tested by events, so in some sense it is just not informative, but clearly there is an ethos that you don't talk about politics. . . .

Kohn: It is certainly the case that I have hardly ever heard a political dimension. I can't recall any case where someone was overtly bringing political inclinations to bear on their monetary policy decision. . . . I can only recall a couple of occasions where someone would raise a criticism of the incumbent administration and someone else would jump to their defense. But even that kind of stuff was very, very rare, so politics didn't really enter into it . . . particularly as inflation came down and the consensus was [that] low, stable inflation was a contribution the central bank could make to stable growth There was less reason for all that [i.e., politics].

A Focus on Money and Monetary Aggregates by Bank Presidents

Our question concerning the tendency of reserve bank presidents to focus on the topic of money and monetary aggregates elicited four types of responses. First, some simply accept the finding as according with their own experience, and offer little in the way of comment (Rivlin, Kohn). A second group reason that the finding reflects a period

(1979 to 1999) during which the serving reserve bank presidents had greater expertise in economics than did board governors. This expertise was further aided by a large discrepancy in staff resources, with the former enjoying reasonably large research departments while the latter had virtually no support staff. On the first point, Hoskins remarks, that "most governors were not PhD economists and felt more comfortable with ad hoc discussions of the economy." On the second point, Lindsey, as a board governor, declares that "I was support staff for me!" Jordan and Poole go on to expand on both points:

Jordan: For the period you are studying, the presidents were for the most part economists, picked by the directors of the reserve bank because of their views on inflation principally and on growth, the factors that created growth. So the selection process was biased in favor of economists who had gained a reputation for certain kinds of approaches to macroeconomic issues and to be more in the direction of what we would call hawkish on inflation. Some of those governors that carried over the 1970s often didn't know any economics at all. The process of selecting governors [entailed selecting] somebody that was a banker, or a campaign contributor, party chairman, or somebody that needed to be rewarded. . . . That had happened occasionally with presidents but by the period you are looking, from 1979 on, that was not so much of a factor. Even those that came in say from Wall Street, or from the private sector somewhere, tended to be pretty solid in their determination, [and] ridding the country of inflation was the top priority.

Also each of the presidents had a minimum of a dozen economists, often career staffers at the reserve banks that had devoted a tremendous amount of time into studying the issues of the way the FOMC works, the way monetary policy in other countries works, and the issues of inflation. Most were well-versed in all the literature of the so-called Philips curve and the notion of a trade-off. . . . So even reserve bank presidents that came in with little academic background in economics or were staffers within the reserve bank and [were] elevated to president . . . tended to be surrounded by a staff of pretty solid people, and that influenced them going into an FOMC meeting.

The governors were, by comparison, quite handicapped. Except for the chairman, there is no effective staff for a member of the board of governors, and so if they came in as a trained economist, like a Larry Meyer or an Alan Blinder or something, they could certainly hold their own at the table with anyone. They had been doing it in their academic lives whereas the other governors were severely handicapped, as they were really on their own. [Governors had] no staff [and] maybe no background [in economics]. Even if they were trained in economics, they sometimes had not practiced as academic economists, [nor had] experience in give and take with other economists and arguing things, so it was kind of hard to know what to expect from them.

Poole agrees that the greater professional expertise of reserve bank presidents vis-à-vis that of governors helps to explain the difference, but he adds to this the longer tenures of presidents as also enhancing their expertise and experience relative to that of governors, and intriguingly, he offers a number a reasons for why governors leave their positions prematurely:

Poole: The bank presidents almost always had a much longer tenure. If you look at the average tenure of members of the Board of Governors, putting the chairman aside, you'll probably come up with four years or something like that. . . . It's pretty short. There's a lot of turnover at the Board of Governors, whereas the bank presidents would often be in office for . . . 12 or 15 years. So the reserve banks in a way provide institutional memory for the Federal Reserve. And [from them] you have people on the FOMC who can talk from firsthand experience about what happened, something that happened ten years ago, or fifteen years ago. So that's one difference that I think is pretty marked and is a source of considerable strength to the FOMC that you've got people who have that long experience.

[*CS-B: Why is the turnover higher for governors?*] Why is it higher? I think it is higher for a couple of reasons. One is that the pay is a lot lower. . . . Oh yes, the pay is dramatically lower. . . . The bank presidents are paid a good bit more, not anything close to what is paid in the private sector, but still a lot more than the Board of Governors. That's part of it; another part of it is the members of the Board of Governors often take those employments, I'm sure quite explicitly, with the idea that they will spend a few years there and then they will go out, and having had that experience and having added that to the résumé they can make a lot more money. A third thing is, I think many members of the Board of Governors come in and end up being a bit disillusioned by the experience, and how much influence they actually have. I'll give you an example. . . . Henry Wallich was a distinguished academic at Yale University, who was appointed to the Board by Nixon. I remember talking with him a few years after he was appointed, and he said "99 percent of this job is worse than grading exams." That's what he said, and the reason was that the Board of Governors [had] a tremendous load of stuff that they have to do. Back in that era, the Board had to okay every single merger application. I think they also had to approve the opening of new branches on the corner of Market and Main Street. . . . The law was subsequently changed . . . but they have an enormous load of courtesy visits. There are fifty state banking associations in the United States; every one of them sends a delegation to Washington once a year. . . . They want to go and visit the Board. . . . There is a steady stream of foreign visitors who come through. . . . So you've got a steady stream of luncheons and meetings. That's really not all that interesting but you've got to do it, it is part of the job. . . . I think a lot of people get worn down by that, and [hold the view] that "I don't want to spend any more years of my life doing that stuff."

A third type of response focuses on the institutional differences between the board governors and reserve bank presidents. Reinhart, for instance, agrees that bank presidents and governors have different backgrounds and expertise, but he argues that the contrasting selection processes for each gives rise to differences in their economic perspectives:

Reinhart: Historically, it is important [to consider] the selection process, that governors tend to be drawn, among the economists . . . from the narrower set of policy "wonks" [that is,] . . . people who believe in models and believe in a fairly traditional view of the monetary transmission mechanism. . . . It is the Council of Economic Advisors and the Treasury that draw up a list of potential candidates, so economists are asked to come up with a list of candidates. In boards [of reserve banks] . . . it could be bankers coming up with a list of candidates. . . . So, if it is a bunch of Washington economists sitting round saying "Who do you think would be a good governor?" the odds are the list is going to be filled with people who more [often] than not believe in the Phillips curve, who believe in a narrow channel of monetary policy that works through interest rates. If it is a bunch of bankers that [are seeking] . . . a different strain of economic thought, you could wind up with a different outcome.

Lindsey offers another institutional perspective, but one that focuses more on the nature of the requisite duties of each job:

Lindsey: Again, this is institutional. The balance sheet of the Federal Reserve sits on the member banks' balance sheets, meaning the 12 districts' balance sheets, so these guys really cared, because they are the chief executive officers who sign off the integrity of the balance sheet. So part of it is that is part of their job.

Presidents have small corporations that they have to manage out there in the real world . . . so they have got other obligations.

For members of the Board, we were all on other governing committees, supervisory and regulation. The one I was responsible for was Community and Consumer Affairs, and that was most of my job. . . . This is the committee that no one wants to be in charge of, because it was fair lending, and community re-investment, and anti-discrimination laws.

Broaddus offers a fourth perspective on the finding—namely that over time, the regional reserve banks tended to follow the lead of the St. Louis Fed in growing their research departments, and so the focus on money and monetary aggregates by presidents simply reflects the enhanced research staff serving them. This also had the effect of building the prominence of the relevant reserve bank, so that when its president spoke at the FOMC, he would have "more weight and credibility":

Broaddus: [In the 1950s and 1960s] the reserve banks were not very influential. . . . I think it was mainly dominated by the governors in Martin's years, and in Burns's. . . . It seemed to me that it was St. Louis that really broke that. St. Louis went out on a limb and I think Burns didn't like it. They challenged him and I think he pushed back some. . . . St. Louis was really the leader in that. Minneapolis is another bank that began to really get serious about research. They had this long-running relationship with some very good economists at the University of Minnesota, a good department. We [the Richmond Fed] got into the act fairly early on, and I think built a strong research department, so in a sense, maybe some of what you are observing there is the strengthening of the research efforts of the reserve banks. That's a good way to put it. I think it may well be the case that the governors were dominant in the sixties, and early 1970s as a group. But that balance began to change and become more equal over the years that I was there. What happened was that the reserve banks made a point to build their own credibility by getting their research staff stronger so that when the president said something at a meeting it would have more weight and credibility. . . . I would hammer that point.

The Apparent Shift in Discourse over Time: Presidents versus Governors

We asked our interviewees for their views on our finding that presidents tended to participate relatively more in the deliberation on the policy decision in the earlier period, while in the later period, it was governors who focused more on the policy decision, leaving presidents to focus more on the state of the economy. Many of our interviewees were somewhat puzzled by our finding. A first group implicitly suggests that it may simply be a spurious result, reflecting no more than a change in the nature of the identities and backgrounds of the members at the time. Hoskins, for example, thinks that the result emerges from the "mix of members with respect to training" in economics; for Broaddus, it is more from "a random impact of personalities on the Board as distinct from presidents" than from any "systematic institutional difference between the behavior of the governors and the behavior of the presidents"; and for Kohn, it is quite simply from "the people involved, the particular folks who were occupying those seats at the time."

Reinhart and Poole do, however, suggest a possible explanation for this finding, namely that it may reflect the nature of the chairmanships of the FOMC:

Reinhart: It has got to be chairman-specific. Chairmen over the years have viewed themselves as holding different roles. William Miller brought in the egg timer and thought his job was to facilitate the discussion. He viewed himself as among everybody who was at the table. Paul Volcker's policy decisions were made in his office. . . . Alan Greenspan and Ben Bernanke are economists and like talking about that stuff. I think probably part of it is also how much the governors felt that they had already talked about those things, and so the briefing documents got more complicated over time. You know, the Green Book and the Blue Book had all sorts of policy simulations and alternatives, and so governors would have discussions with staff in their office before the meeting, the pre-FOMC meetings. My bet [is they were] more involved in those sorts of things. So they had already talked about [that], they had already signaled. So the only contribution in terms of an economic discussion would be was there anything heard out there in the regions? And the bank presidents would be relied on to talk more.

Reinhart thus suggests that as more of the economics discussion occurred among the governors prior to the FOMC meeting, this left them wanting to hear more from the presidents about the state of the economy in their districts during the meeting itself—which accords with Rivlin's earlier remarks that she went to the FOMC wanting to hear what the presidents had to say.

Poole's slant is more specific to Volcker's chairmanship, and suggests at least an implicit alliance between the bank presidents and Volcker, which may have enhanced their relative contributions to the policy discussion in the earlier period.

Poole: Volcker had a tremendous amount of opposition on the Board. . . . The Board was mostly opposed to Volcker, [but] . . . Volcker had a tremendous amount of support in the FOMC because the bank presidents were with him. And yet . . . Volcker had to contend with a Board that simply was not at all sympathetic to what he wanted to do, feared the consequences of tight money, did not think that bringing inflation down was worth the cost, and so forth. So my guess is that Volcker knew of the opposition on the Board and probably . . . found [difficult] some comments of board members indicating that they were not on board but they didn't make a big deal out of it, whereas the bank presidents were probably quite clear on the whole in their support of Volcker.

Taken together, Reinhart's rationale for the increased focus on the state of the economy by the presidents in the later period, coupled with Poole's rationale for Volcker's reliance on the president in the earlier period for his policy decisions may together offer a coherent explanation for this finding.

An Overall Decline in Deliberation on the Policy Decision by the FOMC

Our interviewees had probably the most to say (and hypotheses to offer, with some interviewees offering multiple ones) on our finding that over time, members of the FOMC tended to deliberate less on the policy decision and focus more on discussing the data and state of the economy. We prompted our interviewees by offering two hypotheses of our own for this finding: (1) it may reflect Alan Greenspan's well-known tendency to focus on data and the state of the economy (thereby encouraging other members to do likewise), and/or (2) the increasing acceptance of the low inflation consensus might have led to greater consensus on the objectives and tools of monetary policy among committee members (thereby lessening discussion on uncertainty and alternatives surrounding the policy decision). Some of our interviewees reckoned that one or both of these hypotheses offered sufficient explanation, but many others developed their own variants of our hypotheses or offered entirely new ones.

1. A Data-Driven Chairman

Greenspan's attention to economic data is well-known, as he describes himself quite explicitly (Greenspan 2007), so this hypothesis resonated immediately with many of our interviewees: "Chairman Greenspan really liked talking about economic data" (Reinhart); "That is what [Greenspan] really loved and what he really liked to get into. It was astounding to me" (Axilrod); "He was, and is still, a master of data, so he did bring it to bear, and I think it maybe gave us all greater comfort to get into the data-wheeze a little bit more" (Broaddus); "He just loved those sort of off-beat macroeconomic things: 'Did you know that the relationship between this variable and that variable had changed dramatically over the last six months?' He was suddenly fascinated by something that might or might not have some relevance to macro-policy or to monetary policy" (Rivlin). She also notes that Greenspan reflected a larger economics discipline that had become more "data-oriented over that period."

Kohn adds to this explanation his own variant—namely that because Greenspan had "proved himself to have better analysis intuition over the economy" members tended to defer to him, and consequently arguments and discussion concerning the policy decision "withered away to some extent":

Kohn: Greenspan became more and more dominant over time in part because he was right on [a number of things], particularly through the 1990s, and certainly on the productivity surge issue and a lot of other people were wrong. So when you have this guy who has proved himself to have better analysis intuition over the economy over a long period of time, I think there is a tendency to defer to him. So . . . the policy discussions at those meetings withered away to some extent in the late 1990s. . . . The way [Greenspan] handled these meetings [was that] . . . he formed a bridge between the economics and the policy discussion and he would give some wild idea about what was going on in the economy. [It] would seem wild but was more often right than wrong, and then he would say "I think we should do such and such." Bill McDonough would be the next speaker always, and he would say "I agree with you, Mr. Chairman." And then there was no discussion to speak of often. At least I'm sure that is what you are seeing in the transcripts. So I think this is partly the Greenspan dominance because he was right.

2. The Influence of Ideas

Our fourth hypothesis lends weight to the role of ideas (i.e., the emerging low inflation consensus) as the explanatory factor for declining deliberation on the policy decision. Kohn and Reinhart add to this a contextual factor—namely that as the low inflation consensus evolved and as price stability became more embedded, the decisions became easier. Conversely, when inflation was high and the transmission mechanism less certain, policy decisions were more difficult and more contentious:

Kohn: In the earlier period, the situation was much more difficult. . . . You had started with this very high inflation period and getting that down, that was very painful, and [led to] a big recession. The kinds of choices that needed to be made were harder . . . so I can understand why the policy discussions in the late 1970s and early 1980s were more intense. Everything kind of settled down in part because of the actions those guys took, in large part to get inflation under control but that was a very difficult period for the nation, for the global economy, and certainly for the committee trying to figure out what to do, so [the result you find] is not surprising.

Reinhart comments that "the Great Moderation [of the 1990s] was associated with low variance of a lot of things including the discussions at the FOMC meetings. When the world is going to hell in a handbasket [in the 1970s or during the financial crisis], they have a much broader range of things to talk about."

Most of our interviewees seemed to accept the low inflation consensus as a background factor, but some tended to offer more explicit ideas that may have lessened the policy deliberation while enhancing the focus on economic data. Hoskins, Broaddus, and Poole note that the prevailing economic models had changed, thereby shaping the discussion among FOMC members:

Hoskins: I believe it had to do more with the adoption of gap models by staff economists in the early 90s. Those models and Taylor rules focused the discussion on potential GDP versus actual [GDP]. Monetary aggregates are not part of the discussion with these models.

Broaddus: When I first went into the Fed and started going to FOMC meetings in the early 1970s that was the heyday of the monetarist/Keynesian debate . . . when Milton Friedman's influence was just beginning to be felt. You had people in the Federal Reserve like Jerry Jordan. He wasn't a bank president but he was working in St. Louis and he was the leading monetarist and so [monetarism and Keynesianism] . . . were actively debated and that spilled over into FOMC meetings. Now . . . eventually that debate goes away. . . . [In the 1980s] all the interest rate deregulation made it much more difficult to measure the relationship between the various M's that we used to use to understand economic activity. . . . So there was maybe less discussion of the policy differences of opinion . . . and more focus on just the state of the economy. . . . [But] I don't want to overdo that because as we get into the 1990s there were still very meaningful debates about policy.

Poole: I'll throw out another hypothesis for you. The academic work in the 1970s clearly had a major effect on the thinking of the individual members of the FOMC before Lucas and Sargent, John Taylor, before the rational expectation analysis. There was a lot of confusion in macroeconomics. . . . So the rational expectation revolution took hold not instantaneously but over a period of years and you had people coming into the FOMC who had . . . adopted those ideas and those ideas emphasized the importance of great clarity in the policy decision and transmission of information about that. Then the logic of it is that, to make the policy decision correctly, you needed to know as much as you could about the state of the economy. The earlier view was much more from an optimal control framework and the Board of Governors staff actually [put an] extraordinary amount of resources into optimal control models. The problem with those models is that they [paid] . . . almost no attention to the role of expectations in the private sector about what the central bank was going to do. And there was also elaborate modeling, very computer-intensive, and it was driven by guys who had a very high degree of technical competence in constructing elaborate computer models, stochastic simulations, and stuff like that; whereas the later emphasis was much, much more in both the academic work and the policy discussion on the expectation in the private sector about what the Fed was going to do. So . . . I think you would find a lot more discussion about expectations, extracting private sector expectations from the data that became particularly clear when we had trading in the index bonds. Before that in terms of inflation expectations, you had various surveys, so I think you would find over time substantial increase in the attention paid to the role of expectations, and what those expectations are or what they were at any particular time.

3. Changing Institutions and Procedures

Our interviewees offered three distinct hypotheses that we had not previously considered—namely the effect of changing institutions and procedures within the FOMC on the committee's deliberations.

The first hypothesis emerges from the 1994 development of the immediate post-meeting announcement of the committee's policy stance in a press release (rather than simply signaling the decision to the trading desk). In a lengthy email following our interview, Jordan provides the contextual backdrop for this change, humorously remarking that "this very significant development was a historical accident and all the fault of the British." In Jordan's telling of the story, Greenspan's attendance in London for a special event to celebrate the Bank of

England's tercentenary—conflicting with a critical FOMC meeting—prompted the new procedure, which was not intended as a precedent but nonetheless became one.[6] Kohn points to these press releases of the policy decision as having the effect of reducing the discretion of the chairman during the intermeeting period to take action without a conference call among the FOMC members. Hence, with less scope for discretion by the chairman in the intermeeting period, the knock-on effect may have been to lessen deliberation within the FOMC meeting itself on defining what would previously have been the agreed boundaries for the chairman's discretion.

Kohn: I do recall long discussions that Volcker would have with a handful of other interested members of the committee at the end of the meeting about the wording of the [unpublished] directive to the New York Fed. . . . This really was about the instructions the committee sent to the New York Fed in a very nontransparent way to the general public. Through part of the period there was a considerable amount of leeway in those instructions to have things changed over the intervening period with regard to interest rates in particular. That was partly because we were operating on a money supply target and the money supply was supposed to dictate the interest rates. So you needed scope for interest rates to move around but there was a lot of discretion for the chairman to do intermeeting changes, and that has faded out over time. I think the last one we did that wasn't in the middle of a crisis was in 1994. So a lot of the members of the committee who were very . . . aware of what was going on and why it was important engaged in some pretty long discussions of exactly how to word that directive. It wasn't so much about what they were telling the New York Fed, it was about what they were telling the chairman—[that is,] what order should words come in. There were "woulds" and "mights" and . . . those were all signals really to the chairman from the committee, even though it was framed as signals to the Desk about intermeeting changes in the Federal Funds Rate and under what circumstances those could be made. All that's faded so there is no need for that complex discussion on intermeeting changes.

Jordan offers a second institutional hypothesis—namely that as bank presidents increasingly sought ways to challenge Fed staff forecasts and persuade other FOMC members of their arguments, they tended to employ more anecdotal evidence from their districts (evidence, which Greenspan welcomed and encouraged)—thereby giving greater weight to discussions of the state of the economy in the overall meeting transcript:

Jordan: I think it reflected Greenspan's interest [in] . . . the regional reports and anecdotal information . . . and it took up more time in the meeting just because there were twelve of us from the hinterland. . . . I certainly was very conscious and deliberate in seeking out little anecdotal stories from [meetings of boards of] directors and others as I traveled the district or brought them into meetings that would help me to build a case for something or other in an FOMC meeting. It was a slow process, it was cumulative. I didn't expect to go in and affect the decision of any one FOMC meeting by doing this but I thought that over a period of time if I built on the consistent theme, as reflected in the anecdotal reports that I made, that it might be woven into something that would be coherent and substantive from the standpoint of my colleagues. . . . The purpose in reflecting in district reports the anecdotal argumentation was more to make it fit, be consistent with, or fail to be consistent with, something larger that you were trying to develop.

Let me be clear about that. In the case of the 1990s, when we had the dot-com boom and productivity surprises . . . meeting after meeting, year after year, we saw upward revisions of Board staff estimates of what productivity both had been and what it was likely to be in the future, consistent with what the Bureau of Economic Analysis was doing, Labor Department was doing, and so on. What we could do in the anecdotal information from the district is point out the degree to which our skepticism about the official data series was reflected in the anecdotal information and try and pull the consensus of opinion in a direction and try and influence the chairman and others to be skeptical of staff estimates because we had other information coming there from the grassroots that simply didn't jive with what those data were [saying]. . . . For the 1990s for the most part it was a period of trying to drag a very grudging Board staff, a career bureaucracy in Washington, not just in the Fed but in the Commerce Department and other agencies to believe that something was going on in the economy that was not readily being reflected in the data both in the employment statistics and the productivity output numbers. They were constantly being surprised and having to revise upward very consistently throughout that period. The FOMC discussions showed that we were ahead of the real data that were coming in. Greenspan was a part of that. [He] was excellent, in trying to say, let's find out from real people about what's really going on out there, whether we even believe these numbers that are being reported, let alone the forecasts and projections at what the future is going to be like.

As a third hypothesis for declining deliberation on the policy decision, Poole and Blinder reflect on changes made by Greenspan in the organization and structure of the FOMC. Specifically, Greenspan more firmly embedded the division of discussion on (1) information and analysis on the economy, and (2) the policy decision. By dividing the meeting more clearly into two separate discussions, Greenspan could then exert greater control by allowing himself "first-mover advantage" in shaping the discussion.

Poole: When I arrived [1998] the pattern of the two separate go-rounds was thoroughly established and Greenspan encouraged that . . . division of labor, division of concentration. The idea was that you would have a more disciplined policy meeting if you could focus the first go-round on what was going on in the economy, the anecdotal information, the analysis, and the second go-round on the policy. . . . I think it was the right way to go, and some of my colleagues used to get very frustrated with that organization and would start discussing policy in the first go-round. By and large, I resisted that, but Greenspan may have encouraged it to work that way because he would lead off the policy discussion in the second go-round making his position quite clear at least most the time and that probably served his purpose in terms of retaining control over the meeting and how it was going to progress. But the two go-rounds that go back . . . in the seventies [were] not structured so clearly between the analysis go-round and the [policy go-round].

Blinder: [Greenspan] would end the economy round with a lengthy speech, on how he saw the economy. Then in that same speech without an intermission, he would go right into his policy recommendation which was not a surprise to most of us. . . . So the ground rules were that you were not supposed to poach into policy when you talked about the economy, although people did. [They did so] because, if you were going to get your two cents in about the policy, that was almost the only time to do it because once Greenspan's policy recommendation was on the table, you were either going to defy the chairman or you were not.

The effect of this sharpened division in discussions does not necessarily translate into a plausible explanation for our finding. While Greenspan probably did not intend to impinge on the deliberative content of the policy decision, it may have had that effect nonetheless. Or, it is possible that the division between the discussions simply sharpened the definition of the words and phrases, and thereby creating what appears to be a decrease in the deliberation on the policy decision that may be an artifact of the textual analysis. Reinhart seems to square the circle here by lending weight to the validity of this hypothesis, but at the same time justifying the greater weight given to deliberation on the state of the economy by pointing to the increasing length and level of specificity in the briefing documents:

Reinhart: Increasingly over time, Chairman Greenspan . . . was not big on improvising on policy, so, by the time you got into the meeting, he had pretty much laid out the key policy choices. [*CS-B: You mean laid them out in communications with members prior to the meeting?*] Yes, I would say in multiple ways. We did talk about how the board would use the discount rate decision at the Board meeting to argue in advance of the meeting so [that] board members didn't have to talk as much about monetary policy deliberations. They already did. Briefing documents also probably got more explicit, particularly as the statement became more important, so if you look at Bluebooks from the 1970s and 1980s, the mid-1980s until the early part of the 1990s, they gave generic choices: you could be easier, you could be tighter, but didn't necessarily tell you what to do explicitly. Within the Fed, what Alan Greenspan was called by about the 1990s was "quarter-point Al": from 1989 to 1993 the FOMC raised the funds rate 24 times on quarter-point increments. So, if it is all going to be quarter-point increments, you have got fewer things to talk about, since you know what you are doing. Also to the extent that you [have] embarked on a gradual path then decisions at each meeting accumulate. [*CS-B: So it all becomes a bit marginal?*] Yes, I mean you have already decided to embark on a quarter-point hike, [so] you don't let them talk about it in the real meetings.

No Explicit Discussion of Key Tools of Economic Theory

Our finding of no explicit discussion of what might be considered to be key tools of economic theory—such as time inconsistency or the Phillips curve—received very mixed views from our interviewees, ranging from somewhat skeptical to completely accepting.

Hoskins, Blinder, and Kohn all thought that the concepts surrounding these terms were discussed at meetings, but perhaps not as explicitly as we might have anticipated (and, as Kohn adds, the use of some terms may have been discouraged by Greenspan):

Hoskins: Early on members tried to exploit the Phillips curve but discussed it as a trade-off between inflation and employment. Later on no one supported it. Time inconsistency and other economic terms are not understood by many non-economist members so the terms are not used directly. You must look for inferences.

Blinder: I thought there was a great deal of discussion of the Phillips curve but maybe without using that name. It was about marginal effects of this or that policy on both unemployment and inflation, and what the trade-offs were. . . . I would not have thought that the Philips curve was a neglected subject and indeed in my period at the Fed, a crucial question that we were constantly debating tacitly or explicitly was where was the natural rate? How far could unemployment go down without there being a danger of inflation? Or . . . was the choice between "deliberate" and "opportunistic" (that was my coinage) disinflation. Deliberate means you deliberately try to ride down the Philips curve and opportunistic is [that], you just let shocks happen and you react asymmetrically to shocks. So when you have a shock that brings down inflation, you welcome it, and when you have a shock that brings up inflation, you fight it; that's the opportunistic. . . . There was some discussion of that.

Kohn: You know, maybe those words don't show up, but the concepts certainly do. . . . But the other part is that Greenspan was not a big believer in the Phillips curve. He felt that, with some justification, it was a reduced-form kind of thing, and it didn't really get at the underlying dynamics of price and wage determination. . . . So maybe one reason why the two words didn't get mentioned was, you would get a reaction from Alan Greenspan but you could still talk about it, and we did. I can remember being on the staff and talking about it so the concepts, certainly that concept, was there. On the time inconsistency, I don't recall a direct discussion of that. There were discussions however in the mid-1990s, [when] Larry Meyer was on the Board, and Gary Stern was engaging in this.

A variant of this perspective is that because many were not professional economists, they did not readily employ the technical or theoretical language of economics:

Broaddus: In the early years when I was there [*early 1970s*], the simple fact is there . . . weren't many people capable of doing that. I would argue that at the end of my years there, the last ten years or so . . . still many people on the FOMC are not professional economists, or if they are, they are not heavily theoretical. So you still had some reticence about that. . . . On average, around the table the vast majority of members were not really heavily conversant with those ideas because . . . if they were economists, myself included, [they] had not focused their career on research. It's changing a little bit. . . . Going back to my own period, there was some bias against doing that. You could be dismissed as academic. There was a real risk that if you were to come out with something about "time inconsistency," and I won't name names, but some people there would turn to you and say "what in the hell is that all about" or they might . . . say "despite President Broaddus's highfalutin language I still think he is full of baloney." . . . That's not misleading. That is an accurate point.

Others embraced the finding more readily, remarking either that as the focus of the meetings was more on the practical aspects of policy-making, such theoretical terms were not particularly relevant (Rivlin, Minehan, Axilrod), or that such terms were more appropriately discussed at longer meetings specifically set aside for this purpose (Jordan, Reinhart):

Rivlin: Well, I'm a little surprised about the Phillips curve because we did talk about that some, but I think we were more practical-oriented. We were trying to figure out what was really going on, and we talked about inflation and prices you know, and housing, and so forth, but we didn't put it in very theoretical terms probably.

Minehan: We had all kinds of economic conferences on issues to do with time inconsistency and the usefulness of the Phillips curve and NAIRU. That was the background to our discussion. We weren't at an Open Market meeting to talk about the basics of economic theory. I mean it was assumed people understood and had perspectives on all of those things, which would then feed in to the policy discussions. . . . We work in the Federal Reserve all the time and we interact with each other on a thousand subjects all the time, so we know each other's perspectives, we'd talked at each other's seminars, we'd read each other's stuff, we'd read each other's staff stuff, so we really didn't need to talk about time inconsistency necessarily.

Axilrod: [You do not find discussion of those terms] because they were talking about whether they ought to raise the funds rates a quarter or an eighth or a half. Basically what you are talking about in the end when you get down to [it is] policy. . . . So who cares whether it was rational expectations that had a big prevalence in economics. . . . There would be no reason to talk about it every day or every meeting. You are down to very practical problems. We are here to decide whether to raise the funds rate or lower it.

Jordan: The second half of the 1990s you would get more in the transcripts; in fact we had one whole debate of pretty much the bulk of a day was on what was called "longer term objectives" and a lot of that had to do with notions about the Philips curve.

Reinhart: I think part of the answer is where you are looking at the discussion at a meeting, you are looking at a discussion on monetary policy in the next six weeks [that is, not the longer term], and so these other issues might not come up. When the committee did talk about those things, it was back when they had two-day meetings, without a crisis to occupy their time, so I think from about probably the late 1990s through to the mid-2000s, a one day or half-day meeting was about topics of particular interest to the committee of a longer term nature, so there were several of those meetings on the Philips curve, one on the credit channels, one on policy gradualism.

One further explanation offered for this finding is that over time, many of the committee members simply did not find either the long-run Phillips curve or time inconsistency persuasive, and so had dismissed either or both from consideration:

Poole: By, I'll say 1980, the overwhelming consensus in the economics profession and among PhDs in the FOMC and the senior staff was that there was no long-run Phillips curve and that was taken for granted, so we didn't have to discuss that . . . but the role of expectations in terms of affecting even current inflation became a more key thing to talk about.

Jordan: I think there evolved a fairly firm understanding that . . . coming into the 1970s, we had switched as a nation from a regime in which people believed that *increases* in inflation and interest rates were temporary . . . to an environment where the dominant psychology of households and businesses was that *declines* in inflation and interest rates were temporary. . . . What was needed was to reverse the paradigm again, and so that people tended to think that increases were temporary and trust the central bank to beat it back down again. It took all of the 1980s and well into the 1990s before I felt that had been achieved. As it became more evident that there [was] success on that, then you started to see a re-surfacing of people saying that tolerance of a bit more inflation in exchange for lower unemployment or faster growth was somehow possible or something desirable to have. But that changed, I would say, in the second half of the 1990s as we got certain governors that came in, arguing for those kinds of things. Rarely did I see that come from the presidents, certainly never from the chairman, but we would get more governors that would play the trade-off game or assert that there was a trade-off to be exploited.

Blinder: The time inconsistency is an easier one. I think everyone on the committee thought it was balderdash. . . . The notion that we as a committee or even any one individual via their vote would favor a short-term goosing of the economy to play on the short-term trade-off at the expense of the long run I think was just considered poppycock. I don't think the thought of actually doing it ever crossed anybody's mind.

Minehan: Well, "time inconsistency?" . . . I read all of that with a lot of interest and really felt that it was time-constrained by a particular set of circumstances that applied in the 1970s and with the wringing out of inflation during the Volcker era.

Taken together, we may conclude from these varied perspectives that (1) perhaps because many FOMC members were not professional economists, they were not as comfortable using the more theoretical language of economics; (2) most of the time, the decisions of the committee were more oriented toward the practicalities of policy-making, not the theory; (3) where relevant, more theoretical discussions were held in other meetings; and (4) the relevance of key theoretical tools of economic theory evolved over time, so that perhaps for our time period, certain concepts held less sway over members.

We conclude this section by drawing upon our interview with Paul Volcker. Our interview with him was shorter than our other interviews, and for that reason we focused specifically on his experience and thinking surrounding the time period of the Volcker Revolution. Hence, as our findings and Volcker's responses to those are so specific to that discussion, we do not address them here—except for one fascinating exchange, which pertains here to how FOMC members think about economic theory. We sought to gain some understanding of the mechanisms through which important ideas from the academic literature percolate through to FOMC decision-making, hypothesizing that Kydland and Prescott's famous 1977 article (Kydland and Prescott 1977) could have shaped Volcker's thinking in 1979, when he launched his historic policy change. When asked whether he was aware of the Kydland and Prescott piece, Volcker replies: "I have no idea whatsoever" and "The what article?" The important part of this exchange is that Volcker later explains how he became convinced of the importance of credible commitment—namely via an academic advisory meeting:

Volcker: So I think there was also a kind of collegial spirit at that point because we had embarked upon this new policy, and it was arguably politically dangerous with extremely high interest rates and there was kind of a feeling that we were all in this together and we ought to see it through. Now there was a lot of worry about expectations and credibility. I don't remember whatsoever that article. . . . I don't pay attention to the economic literature. But I was convinced that expectations were important. And credibility was important. . . . And I can remember we had this academic advisory board meeting and there was a guy there who was a professor of mine, Willy Fellner. He was very well known and . . . he made a big point about credibility and expectations, so I lapped that up because that mattered.[7]

In respect to the extent to which theoretical literature pertains to discussions within the FOMC, part of the exchange with Volcker was relayed to Blinder, who then quite astutely comments that being a technical economist is not necessarily essential to excellence in monetary policy decision-making:

Blinder: Paul Volcker was never a technical economist; he was a business economist before he was a government official. I don't think he has a PhD in economics; he has a Masters degree from the LSE. . . . Most members or many members of the FOMC were not technical economists. Volcker was one of those that is not a technical economist. What he is, is a saint, which is better. You got your choice—take the saint.

5.6.2 Congress

In the earlier section on the quality of deliberation, we examined the key finding—that committee members tended to devote very little attention to the details of monetary policy. Here we focus on respondents' views with respect to four other findings from our textual analysis of the congressional oversight hearings (table 5.3): (1) the tendency for Democrats to question the Fed chairman more on labor market issues, and Republicans to give greater weight to fiscal policy; (2) the apparent tendency of Congress to gauge oversight of and interest in monetary policy in accordance with the perceived success of the Fed's policy; (3) the growing tendency of members of Congress to use the Fed's reputation (and Greenspan's in particular) to underpin their own fiscal policy objectives; and (4) the lack of attention to issues of financial stability, prior to the recent financial crisis.

Democrats and Jobs; Republicans and Fiscal Policy
On the one hand, none of our respondents perceive monetary policy oversight hearings as nonpartisan; on the other hand, neither do they all interpret the partisan differences as simply as "Democrats talk about jobs; Republicans talk about fiscal policy." One congressional staff member dismisses the issue of partisan influence on the hearings, except for the appointment of the Federal Reserve chairman by the Senate Banking Committee. For these hearings, and these hearings alone, the partisanship of those who decide matters. Another staffer remarks that "by and large" partisan divisions have not mattered, but for this staffer, the exception is that Republican members tend to focus

more on inflationary pressures—or, "in the case of sophisticated Republicans, inflationary expectations."

Others—including our two members of Congress—place a greater weight on partisan differences. Galbraith remarks that during the Reagan years, Democrats used the hearings to try "to limit the political reach of a very successful and powerful president [while] the Republicans . . . were trying to deflect criticism and defend him." D'Arista also comments on a clear partisan divide, which she also notes has increased as the amount of "money in the political process" has grown:

D'Arista: It was definitely the case that the Republicans were just not that interested in employment. They were also less interested in housing. . . . The Democrats were interested in housing: housing was mother and apple-pie to them. If they satisfied [their housing constituency], it was doing their duty as members of the committee. I would say that was the large proportion of the Democrats, that was their focus in the 1970s . . . [CS-B: *Do you think the area of the difference in focus between Democrats and Republicans was more a reflection of their ideological differences or of the constituents who might be coming to them with particular requests or questions?*] I think it depended on the district itself and there were many Democrats who were very beholden to and concerned about their community banking system, the smaller banks, and that led them to be concerned about interest rates as well and they were trying to protect that system. Democrats from the larger cities, including Barney Frank, during that period and later . . . were much more concerned about some of the larger banks. . . . [Even] Democrats who had sterling records in terms of social policy were nevertheless very beholden to large banks, and would hide behind various votes where they were favoring those banks, and then . . . their modus operandi of this was to . . . promote the savings and loans. So there were some real divisions there. Now some Republicans were more concerned about community banks, and very hostile to the large city banks, but in general, it was not ideological, it was more a question of the business and financial interests among the Republicans, and the constituents, the workers on the part of the Democrats.

I think [the partisan divide] has grown because there is so much more money in the process. What we talk about in this country about the lobbying and the buying of votes, and that organization of buying of votes is very strong within the Wall Street sector, and the community banks have fallen to some extent by the wayside. They can't afford to compete in terms of the amount of contributions.

Both our members of Congress—Bayh a Democrat; Barratt a Republican—agree that the parties tend to divide in the monetary policy oversight hearings. For Barratt, the divide is precisely as our findings suggest:

Barratt: I would say that is a fair assessment . . . unfortunately, because the Republicans tend to be as guilty as the Democrats. There is always [some partisanship] in the way you ask your questions or follow-up questions, you can always mold that to your particular party or your particular philosophy. [As for the Democrats talking about labor markets and the Republicans talking about fiscal policy]: that is spot-on, right there.

Bayh is more nuanced in his interpretation, noting that occasionally—as with the post-financial crisis anti–Federal Reserve grouping between Democratic Populists and Tea Party supporters—we may observe "populist strains in both parties" so that sometimes "it is not ideological, it is not Left versus Right, it is big versus small":

Bayh: You do get small government Republicans on the Right who would be suspicious of the Fed, and then you got on the Left people who are suspicious of large institutions, capitalism in general, and would feel that the Fed's mandate to restrain inflation should be subordinated to easier money and leaning on the side of more growth and that sort of thing. So yes it is true there are Populist strains in both parties, and I think that is a non-ideological phenomena.

In short, the empirical finding of a partisan divide seems to resonate with our interviewees, with the caveat that other divisions (big versus small financial institutions) can often intersect this partisan divide, thereby, in the words of one staffer, creating "strange bedfellows" for monetary policy.

Oversight as a Function of the Fed's Policy Success or Failure

From our analysis of the hearings from the mid-1970s to 2008, we found that the scale of challenge from members of Congress to the Fed chairman declined with the apparent success of monetary policy in the 1990s. Whereas in the 1970s and early 1980s, members of Congress (and particularly Democrats) tended to challenge issues concerning the core governance of the Fed, by the late 1990s, support for the Fed had become bipartisan (or cross-partisan). Perhaps not surprisingly, our staff respondents point out the obvious: "Everyone loves a hero. In the late 1990s, everyone wanted their photo taken with Greenspan"; "If it seems to be working, why change it?" One remarks: "That is sort of self-evidently correct"—although this staffer adds that Greenspan enjoyed "a fortuitous set of circumstances where you could have put the Fed on automatic pilot in the late 1990s."

The flip side to "everyone loves a hero" is, of course, that politicians (not unlike the rest of us) like to avoid blame where possible, and the Fed is a useful scapegoat, as Galbraith, D'Arista, and Bayh concede:

Galbraith: [In the 1970s] I think it is fair to say that the Congress, under a lot of electoral discontent over economic conditions, wanted to bring the Federal Reserve into the game and deflect some of the pressure on to them . . . [which in part] factored into the decision to pass House Concurrent Resolution 133 in early 1975.

D'Arista: Well, I think [the empirical finding] is right, but I would also say in a very cynical and simplistic way that the Fed is a wonderful kicking ball. In other words, is the Fed our friend or is the Fed our enemy? It is possible to generate up among constituents considerable distrust of the Fed and that has been done, and the interesting thing is, in the entire time that I have been involved in these issues, going back to the 1960s I would say it is both on the Right and the Left. . . . So it is wonderful to use the Fed. . . . It is this mysterious and powerful organization, so a member can either make it the great friend, as they did under Greenspan, or the great enemy.

Bayh: It is not uncommon for members of the elected branches of government to seek to deflect criticism or public anger on to nonelected branches of government, so the Fed is a convenient scapegoat because you can say "oh, those elitists over in the Fed, they just don't understand the need to do X, Y, or Z," so it is a way to kind of shift the blame so to speak.

Employing the Fed's Reputation for Fiscal Policy Objectives

We observed from our textual analysis of the congressional hearings that members of the House and Senate Banking Committees tended to discuss fiscal policy not in the traditional sense of analyzing the mix between monetary and fiscal policy, but rather by focusing on specific tax issues—Social Security, education, energy, and so on. We thus asked our congressional interviewees whether this merely reflected the tendency for committee members to use the Fed's reputation to bolster members' views on fiscal policy. Staffers offer some disparate interpretations, including the possible impact of Reagan's focus on tax policy or Clinton's budget surplus. But one staffer manages to pull all the threads together, explaining that the Humphrey–Hawkins hearings offered members of Congress their only opportunity within the congressional setting to discuss the budget situation:

[Anonymous staffer]:   It's important to remember that there is not a venue on either side of the Capitol in which members get to think about broad macro-policy issues except in the context of the Humphrey–Hawkins hearings. The Budget Committee doesn't think about fiscal policy; they think about deficits. But that is a very narrow piece of fiscal policy. In the second half of the 1990s, all of a sudden for the first time in anybody's memory, the Federal government ran surpluses three years in a row—not big but a dramatic change from the late seventies and early eighties when the deficit concern had been paramount. All of a sudden this raised sort of goofy conversations—Greenspan being concerned about not eliminating the deficit; eliminating the deficit would screw up the bond market, which would screw up Social Security. That became, in 1997–98, a fiscal policy question which members of Congress had seldom ever thought about, and more importantly, outside the context of talking to the Fed,

didn't have a way to talk about it. The budget debate was always much narrower than that, and the budget debate, dominated by how the budget was allocated rather than its size. . . . The concern about Social Security in the late 1990s and early part of the last decade was driven in part by this crazy privatization debate that was going on.

Similar to the institutional hypotheses suggested to us by the FOMC respondents, this is an excellent example where our textual analysis offered us little in the way of context for understanding the constraints and opportunities for deliberation on particular topics which might emerge from particular institutional settings.

Financial Stability

As the saying goes, one always has 20–20 vision in hindsight—so, of course, it is easy to question why, prior to the financial crisis, congressional banking committee members failed to devote much attention to the stability of the financial system. We therefore phrased our question more benignly by prompting our interviewees whether committee members were simply taking their lead from the Fed chairman in giving little attention to financial stability or whether there was something else at play. D'Arista offers the typical response—namely that when times are good, why question things?

D'Arista: Well, I would say that they were [taking a lead from Greenspan] and that they were looking at a situation in which everything looked so rosy and the financial sector was making so much money and everything was going [well], competition with the rest of the world, it all looked so [good], why would you want to change it? Clearly, people were getting houses and for many people the fact that housing prices were rising, was great news. So they were complacent, and they were certainly seeing the chair of the Fed as complacent, if not more so than they, and reassuring them constantly with the constant belief that the Fed had the power to stop a problem should it arise. I think some of that faith began to dissipate a little bit with the dot-com crisis but at the same time, you know, it was not as pervasive as what was to come.

To this explanation, other staffers add that "committee members were put off by Greenspan's long sentences, where you couldn't follow him from the beginning of the sentence to the end," or that on the whole, "about ten people in the country understood the exposure of American financial institutions." Another staffer remarks that "it also depends on the definition of what constitutes financial stability. If we include housing prices, then probably we would find that more members of Congress *were* talking about financial stability" (i.e., the housing bubble).

Our two members of Congress both admit that in the end, oversight is invariably reactionary. For Barratt, this is because members of Congress have too many other issues to address, and so the tendency is not to be forward-looking:

Barratt: If things seem to be on automatic pilot, and it is not a problem, at least in the immediate future, then there are too many other things that are a problem right now that you are dealing with. . . . [When] the banking system is askew is when we start really focusing on it. . . . When things are good and the economy is clicking along, you don't stop and think "are we doing what we really need to do." . . . We were not being as forward-thinking as we needed to be because the crisis had not hit, and once it did, we were more reactionary.

Bayh offers an excellent (though somewhat disheartening) rationale for the improbability of Congress ever being prescient in anticipating problems when the economy seems to be working well:

Bayh: Well, I think so much of life, particularly public life, gets into the realm of basic human psychology. I think it is only human nature when times are good to not want to rock the boat and to think that whatever the current structure is must be appropriate because times are good. And there is a certain amount of natural inertia to government. It is only when there is a crisis or times are bad that it leads to a fundamental rethinking. Now, of course, it would be better to be prescient and to see beyond the horizon and anticipate problems, and as Greenspan used to say "You can recognize bubbles in hindsight and you think you might recognize one when you are in the middle of it but you never really know." Valuations and other things can deviate from the mean for quite a period of time before they correct themselves, so it is basic human psychology when times are good to not have that kind of fundamental re-thinking about it if there are flaws in the system. So, in my time, you had the crash in 1987; certainly that focused attention on some of the problems; you had the tech bubble and collapse, [and] that was another moment of introspection. Long-Term Capital [Management] was another situation, and then . . . some of the international episodes, but . . . the political class here didn't really see that as touching upon us so much at least with regard to the systemic stability of our own system. That was something that happened in Third World countries. Well then, lo and behold, we had the crash here that emanated out and affected the rest of the world and had its roots in the housing markets. People had been talking about Fannie Mae and Freddie Mac—you can go back and look at my own testimony. I asked Greenspan very directly. I said "Mr. Chairman, how long can housing price increases outstrip real wages growth?" I mean, at some point, this was not sustainable, and his response was "well, that is right but" and he kind of gave a non-answer answer. I can't claim that I foresaw [the financial crisis], that would be totally inaccurate. But from time to time, some of us were saying "well, look, aren't there imbalances in the system here that the longer they compound, the day of reckoning will be more painful?" Yes, some of that went on, but when the party is going strong, it takes a strong individual to take away the punch bowl, and particularly in a free society. That is a difficult thing, and there are interests who like to make their voices heard. But I think the most difficult thing is, when things are going well, it is only natural to think "well, the system must be functioning because we feel good about things." It takes a pretty far-sighted individual during good times to say "Now, wait a minute, there may be some fundamental flaws here that we are just now recognizing and we need to fix them." It is difficult to get a political consensus for that because you know voters are feeling good and are reluctant to change.

5.7   Conclusion

The purpose of this chapter is to use interviews with participants from both the FOMC meetings and the congressional oversight hearings on monetary policy to provide context and understanding of the motivations of both the central bankers acting as monetary policy makers and the politicians whose role is to hold the chairman of the Federal Reserve accountable for the decisions of the FOMC. We asked the interviewees to explain the reasons for their behavior and that of their colleagues in their respective venues, focusing predominantly on their discussions within the meetings. In doing so, we have sought to obtain in their own words an assessment of the intentions and motivations of Fed officials and congressional participants as they discuss monetary policy. We focused on three key issue areas: the quality of deliberation, the effect of transparency on deliberation, and institutional features in either the FOMC or congressional committees that might impinge on deliberation.

We have found clear endorsement that the nature of deliberation has changed over time, both in the FOMC and in the congressional oversight committees, which supports the results from our use of textual analysis. This is an important conclusion not only for understanding policy-making and the exercise of accountability over time but also because it suggests that there is a reason for studying deliberation in these settings. Moreover we find supporting evidence from the interviews that the form of deliberation varies with the context of the policy-setting. Put simply, it is a different process when policy is perceived to be achieving its goals than it is when policy is clearly failing to achieve its goals. That is not surprising because the public and therefore elected representatives and appointed officials are more likely to be concerned when policy is failing to achieve its objectives and likewise more likely to be less attentive when policy is perceived as successful. Interviewees also provided confirmation that the form and therefore role of deliberation changes as the personalities involved change. There have been changes in the makeup of the FOMC and changes in chairmen. Likewise the role of congressional oversight has altered as the personalities involved have changed.

On the FOMC, the conclusion that deliberation in the committee has changed over time was linked by interviewees to the apparent success of policy at any given time, and particularly the evidence that monetary policy became more successful over the course of the period we study. This reflects the emergence of greater confidence in the framework and objectives of policy-making, and recognition that policy discussions were almost inevitably more intense in the late 1970s and early 1980s. Success over time has also insulated the FOMC more from political pressures, a point we consider below in relation to Congress. A further cause of change in the form of deliberation has been the trend toward greater transparency in policy-making, notably as the FOMC policy statement has become a matter of public record and thus a statement by the committee of its conclusion. The emphasis here is on the committee making a statement rather than a private instruction to the open market desk at the New York Fed. Our interviewees also contend that changing personalities on the FOMC, and particularly the chairmen, have influenced deliberation and thus where at any time the FOMC has stood on the spectrum of individual to autocratic collegiality, as Blinder puts it. But we disagree with Blinder that policy formation is the aggregation of preferences in a committee setting. Our interviewees tend to confirm that over time (meaning, from meeting to meeting) deliberation within the committee setting can adjust and alter the preferences of individual members. Finally, they also tend to confirm that new ideas and models that derive from economic theory take hold over years rather than at an instantaneous moment, and that the nature of deliberation in the FOMC means that such ideas and models were more likely to be used implicitly and as a backdrop to deliberation on the policy decision rather than explicitly as such, thus helping explain why FOMC transcripts do not feature references to Phillips curves or the time consistency of policy.

Turning to Congress, our interviewees were consistent in concluding that members of Congress generally have a very limited understanding of monetary policy as well as little electoral incentive to overcome this ignorance. The process of accountability of the Fed chairman to Congress depends on a very few members engaging actively and earnestly, but these people are the exception and this is a pattern that holds throughout the period we study. Typically these exceptional members are committee chairmen (though not all chairmen fall into this class), senior ranking members (who may be past or future chairmen) and a very few outliers such as Bernie Sanders. Taking advantage of the high media profile of the hearings, other less exceptional members tend to speak to the cameras in order to obtain recognition for themselves and/or for issues that are often unrelated to monetary policy. Is this necessarily a "bad" thing? Here interpretations differ. While the FOMC members speak disparagingly about the lack of focus and informed questioning by congressional committee members, the view from congressional staff is quite defensive. Several argued that questions on disparate topics unrelated to monetary policy simply reflect "what is going on outside of Congress" and are therefore perfectly legitimate. This is even more so, since the hearings enable members of Congress to probe the nation's de facto "chief economic officer" on a variety of topics that may relate to the economy.

Our interviewees also confirmed that the challenge from Congress on monetary policy itself declined over the period we study. An important reason for this trend was the apparent success of monetary policy, combined with the view that "everyone loves a hero" in the chairman, and Alan Greenspan was viewed as such, increasingly so during his tenure. This pattern of behavior reinforces our conclusion that apparently successful policy tends to lead to a less rigorous process of accountability as the oversight of monetary policy by Congress is essentially reactionary.

We now return to the hypotheses set out in chapter 2 in order to consider to what extent the interviewees have provided support or otherwise. The first hypothesis suggests that deliberation in committees plays more of a role if we can locate evidence of persuasion via reason giving in the process of discourse. We suggested that this hypothesis could apply to both the FOMC and congressional hearings. Our interviewees have provided evidence that there is consistently evidence of reason-giving and persuasion (from meeting to meeting) in the FOMC, albeit within a changing form of deliberation over time. But we do not find much evidence that congressional oversight involved both reason-giving and persuasion on monetary policy per se (i.e., that it was a meaningful two-way exchange of views). Committee members may use their time in the hearings to persuade an outside audience—their constituents—on their stands on nonmonetary policy issues. This may serve a legitimate purpose in highlighting other issue areas, but it is hard to see how this enhances the oversight of monetary policy.

Hypotheses 2 to 4 concern the FOMC, namely that deliberation in the FOMC can be influenced by changes in the procedures and rules of the committee (particularly with respect to the transparency of its proceedings), by changes in membership and particularly the chairman, and finally by changes in the operating environment, and particularly the clarity of the objective of policy and the apparent success of policy. Our interviewees have provided support for each of these hypotheses, and in doing so, they confirm our view that deliberation does make a difference as part of the policy-making process.

The last three hypotheses (5 to 7) relate specifically to congressional oversight and the process of accountability. They suggest that the Senate committee will demonstrate a higher quality of deliberative process compared to the House committee, that the congressional process will be a mixture of point-scoring on popular and high-profile issues alongside more expert exchanges on monetary policy, and that greater consensus around the objective of monetary policy (accompanied by the greater success of policy over time) will affect the process of oversight. We find no clear evidence that deliberations were of better quality in the Senate hearings, relative to those in the House (hypothesis 5): while one interviewee supported this contention (Kohn), another argued that greater committee specialization in the House facilitated better deliberation in its committee (Galbraith). Moreover, while our textual analysis does not measure quality of deliberation directly, we found no indirect evidence (e.g., measuring quality by the prevalence of vacuous discourse) of a difference between the Senate and the House, except to note differences in areas of focus and coverage.

Our interviewees recognize the evidence of point-scoring, which unfortunately outweighs that of exchanges on the details of monetary policy (hypothesis 6). However, we think that the findings from textual analysis put this into starker relief than is perhaps common from more anecdotal observation (in other words, individuals can see that it goes on but do not have a ready means to systematically assess its prevalence).

Finally, our interviewees did tend to confirm that greater success and consensus around monetary policy had shaped the evolution of congressional oversight (hypothesis 7). One interviewee (D'Arista) emphasized that central bank independence—as a core tenet of the low inflation consensus—had been so absorbed by Congress that it had, in some respects, allowed (or even encouraged) Congress to become more passive in its oversight of the Fed. Intriguingly, then, the idea of central bank independence may well have served as a brake on questions pertaining to the Fed's decisions (particularly in the short term)—although one must also add to this that the apparent success of monetary policy contributed as well (and these two factors are difficult to separate). The second part of this hypothesis contends that the convergence around the low inflation consensus outweighed the effects of partisan polarization within the oversight hearings. Although some partisanship is noted by our interviewees (which concurs with our finding that Democrats tended to be sensitive to jobs and Republicans relatively more attuned to fiscal issues), this was not interpreted as indicative of an underlying ideological conflict, resulting from polarization. Indeed, as a staffer comments, monetary policy can create "strange bedfellows"—that is, alliances that cut across party lines. Moreover, to the extent that the hearings were interpreted as deficient, this was attributed to the broader institutional constraints and incentives of holding office in the US Congress (i.e., constraints on time and expertise, and electoral disincentives to engage in committee deliberations). Or, to reiterate Barratt's assessment:

> To do correct oversight, especially on an issue that is as important as monetary policy, you have got to have members that can spend the time, that can roll up their sleeves and get more involved coming in. Getting the attention of the chairman, asking your little question, and then you are gone, because you are playing to the cameras, you want to make sure constituents back home [are saying] "There is Gresham, I saw you." You ask your one question, and you were thinking about ten other things when you did it, and then you were gone. So having some dedicated time is extremely important.

Unfortunately, "dedicated time" is a scarce commodity in Congress—and this has meaningful repercussions on the oversight of monetary policy, as we will discuss in our next chapter.

In sum, the interviews have therefore provided broad support for most but not all of the hypotheses, and in doing so cast important light on their interpretation. In the final chapter we pull together all the evidence.

6 Does Deliberation Matter for Monetary Policy-Making?

6.1 Reason-Giving and Persuasion

We began this study with the somewhat optimistic premise that *deliberation* (i.e., reason-giving argument with the intended purpose of persuading) does indeed matter for monetary policy-making in the United States. But, we also noted that, having looked at what central bankers actually said in policy-making meetings and what politicians discussed when holding the Federal Reserve chairman accountable, we might ultimately find that it does not matter much, or perhaps matters only under certain circumstances. We anticipated finding both in the FOMC and in congressional oversight hearings some evidence of reason-giving and that some members are subsequently persuaded by the arguments of their colleagues (hypothesis 1). In order further to define this hypothesis, we suggested three relevant issue areas: the quality of deliberation, the effect that transparency has had on deliberation, and institutional features of the setting that enable or constrain deliberation in the two settings. For the FOMC we suggested that the assessment of quality of deliberation should focus on whether contributions from members appeared to be pre-prepared speeches or whether there was real give and take. The latter should better facilitate persuasion than the former, although pre-prepared speeches do not entirely preclude the possibility that members may over time change their views as a consequence of the deliberative process. For Congress the test of quality of deliberation was more basic, namely whether members appeared to seek to understand and discuss monetary policy in oversight and re-confirmation hearings, and that discussion reflected a two-way exchange of views. Without this basic level of deliberation, it is difficult to conceive of meaningful persuasion.

For us, deliberation in both the Fed and Congress is a process of reason-giving that involves conveying information and arguments about a public good (monetary policy) where participants are not expected to behave to promote their private interests in a self-serving manner. As such, participants could use the deliberative process in which they engage as a means to learn from one another. We may then expect to observe participants in the process persuading each other of the quality of their arguments and case, though the act of persuasion may occur over time rather than as a "blinding flash of light." The key point here is that the preferences of individual actors in the process are not unchangeable over time and that learning is possible.

In studying deliberation in Congress where the end product is not a vote, we confront the question of what are members of Congress seeking to achieve by participating in oversight hearings. Transparency of the deliberative process is likely to encourage legislators to describe their preferences and interests as being aligned with the public good of monetary policy. Nonetheless, as we noted in chapter 2, re-election is generally taken to be the primary motive of members of Congress. Thus, they may use monetary policy oversight hearings to make a name for themselves by advertising their credentials to the public at large and/or take positions on policy matters. They may also seek to share in the credit for favorable actions undertaken by the government or by the Fed. In this sense members of Congress are presumed to be acting more like delegates to their constituents rather than as trustees of the wider public interest. We have, however, noted that monetary policy oversight is a subject which is not intrinsically likely to yield strong re-election benefits, because the benefits and costs of monetary policy are widely diffused (it does not create concentrated interests unlike some other policy areas), and the policy decisions themselves are the responsibility of an independent agency (the Fed). Thus there is a strong likelihood that members of Congress will allow time for such oversight to be crowded out by other activities that are more directly beneficial to their re-election. Promoting a "good" monetary policy, and receiving whatever credit is on offer for doing so, is likely at best to be a minority pursuit in Congress.

6.2   Who Is Persuaded?

To be sure, finding clear evidence that deliberation actually affects outcomes is a tall order. If measuring empirically the existence (or lack thereof) of reasoned argument is not enough of a challenge, linking this with evidence of others actually having been persuaded by the reasoned argument in question may seem an impossible task (not to mention any added effort to hold all else constant in order to measure the effect of persuasion). Having said all this, we do indeed find four instances in which persuasion affected monetary policy outcomes.

The first instance came to light in our interview with Paul Volcker, in which we queried his thoughts and behavior surrounding the famous Volcker Revolution of 1979. Specifically, how did Volcker himself come to be persuaded by the idea of credible commitment (i.e., the importance of the Federal Reserve acquiring a reputation for its anti-inflation commitment), which came to be the cornerstone of the Volcker Revolution? Volcker remarks that he became convinced of the importance of expectations and credibility not through FOMC policy deliberations or through reading of the academic literature on this subject, but rather from an academic advisory board meeting in which the macroeconomist William Fellner "made a big point about credibility and expectations." As Fellner's arguments appear to have set the train in motion toward the Volcker Revolution, one might tentatively conjecture that sometimes important ideas from academics are particularly persuasive when made in person.

Our second instance of persuasion emerges from our textual analysis of the critical FOMC meetings of 1979 to 1981, in which Chairman Volcker then went on to persuade FOMC members to focus on achieving credibility for tackling inflation. Our textual analysis finds a two-stage process in FOMC deliberations, starting with an emphasis on the importance of money as the means to achieve the policy shift in 1979, but then changing decisively in 1980 to an emphasis on achieving credibility. We show that both stages were led by Volcker himself, and that in 1980, as the policy change came under intense pressure, the nature of the deliberation within the FOMC changed to one with a marked focus on one subject, namely achieving credibility for tackling inflation.

A third piece of evidence refers to the broader question of whether FOMC members are persuaded to change their minds (or shift their positions) as a result of the reasoned argument of their colleagues in the FOMC. In our interviews we find that FOMC members rarely if ever were persuaded to change their minds in the space of a single meeting, but rather many noted that an argument made by a colleague in one meeting might persuade a committee member to re-think or reconsider his position or understanding of policy (regardless of whether that argument was in the form of a pre-prepared speech or during more spontaneous discussion). Hence, while reasoned argument is a regular feature of FOMC meetings (as measured by our analysis of the thematic content of the transcripts), persuasion involves a more dynamic and subtle process of planting seeds at one point in time, letting them take hold, and reaping the (persuaded) effects at a later time. We explore this proposition in chapter 3, where we use the FOMC transcripts from 1999 to examine the role of persuasion over the course of several meetings. While we do not find abrupt and conspicuous episodes of conversion (e.g., where a member explicitly announces his or her conversion), we do find evidence of three distinct *strategies of persuasion* employed by FOMC members, along with a clear ability of the deliberative process to bring these different approaches to an agreed outcome.

Finally, our textual analysis of both the oversight and re-confirmation hearings revealed the presence of Volcker's concerted efforts to convince members of Congress to accept the need for a strong policy stance against inflation. Indeed Volcker's anti-inflation thematic class constituted over a quarter of the classified content of the Senate oversight hearings between 1980 and 1981 and 19 percent of the classified content of his Senate re-confirmation hearing in 1983. Clearly, members of Congress were subjected to Volcker's anti-inflation arguments during his repeated testimonies in congressional committees, but were they persuaded by his arguments? The evidence is by no means conclusive, but we do find that inflation became a non-issue during the Greenspan years, as members of Congress appear to have accepted the low inflation consensus as the objective of monetary policy. Tentatively we might conjecture that Volcker's arguments before Congress were persuasive enough to allow the Fed a window of opportunity to pursue Volcker's anti-inflation stance. The Greenspan years then further embedded the low inflation consensus, yielding what appeared to be a highly successful monetary policy (and affording members of Congress the opportunity to exploit the perceived success of the Fed by attaching Greenspan's name to their views on other aspects of public policy, including fiscal policy, Social Security reform, education and training).

6.3   Deliberation and Monetary Policy: The Policy Objective, the Institutional Arrangements for Conducting Policy, and the Process for Holding Policy Makers Accountable

Aside from the product of persuasion, our focus on deliberation has sought to examine how the thinking of policy makers and politicians on monetary policy has evolved over the past several decades. We have focused on three important aspects which shape the activity, namely the objective of policy and how it is pursued, the institutional arrangements for conducting policy-making, and the process for holding policy makers accountable to the public. These three aspects of policy-making—the objective, the institutional arrangements, and accountability—are central to our study of the role of deliberation in US monetary policy-making over the last three and a half decades. We have focused on the contribution of deliberation because instinctively we do not side with those who think that policy made in a committee setting remains a matter of aggregating the preferences of individuals where those preferences are wholly determined outside the immediate policy-making process. Likewise we do not find compelling the view that the behavior of policy makers can be discerned using a reaction function approach which estimates responses to news based solely on the past behavior of policy makers.

A further criticism of preference aggregation or reduced form functions is that some policy makers probably matter more than others in a deliberative setting. But without studying the process and content of deliberation we cannot readily determine who matters and why. In fact our results indicate that in Congress very few members of the oversight committees really matter in terms of influencing the accountability hearings with the Fed chairman. In the FOMC we find that the pattern changes over our time period as the form of deliberation in the FOMC changes. The personality of the chairman appears to influence the form of deliberation, as does the changing perceived success of policy and possibly changes in the transparency of the policy-making process. We therefore conclude that in a setting where policy is made in a committee (the FOMC) and likewise accountability is carried out in congressional committees, personalities do matter.

Looking at the three important aspects of public policy-making, the statutory *objective* of US monetary policy under which the Fed operated did not change during the period we study. The "dual mandate"—as amended in the Federal Reserve Act of 1977—requires the Board of Governors and the FOMC to "promote effectively the goals of maximum employment, stable prices and moderate long-term interest rates." Despite repeated efforts in many sessions of Congress since the 101st to remove the maximum employment portion of this mandate and focus exclusively on price stability, the dual mandate remains unchanged to date.[1] Nor was there change in the formal *institutional structure* of policy-making in terms of the powers and organization of the Fed.

Finally, the form and process of accountability was essentially unchanged after the passing of the Humphrey–Hawkins Act in 1978. On the face of it, this was a landscape of policy-making in which not much happened over a period of thirty years or so. A casual study of the history of US monetary policy over this period indicates quite the contrary—a lot did happen. Policy-making went from being unsuccessful in the face of high inflation in the 1970s, through a difficult period conquering high inflation in the early 1980s, into the low inflation period that followed. In short, US monetary policy went from being unsuccessful to successful via a difficult transition.

Moreover during this period an international consensus emerged in which achieving and maintaining low inflation was agreed to be an essential foundation for stable economic growth. Central bank independence from political intervention in respect of the operation of monetary policy (as distinct from setting the objective of policy, which remained a political act) became the consensus model around the world. In the United States the emergence of this consensus did not require a change to the statutory position of the Fed. But, once Paul Volcker had set the course toward increasing the independence of the Fed in practice with his strong focus on reducing inflation, success in the pursuit of low inflation increasingly insulated the Fed more from direct political challenge from Congress. In turn this allowed the Fed to operate more freely from the threat of legislation by Congress to modify and shackle the form and substance of independence. In other words, successful execution of monetary policy by the Fed thus reduced the force and threat of congressional intrusion into the Fed's governance and operations (as seen from our evidence of the oversight committee discourse in chapter 4). The Fed's *accountability* to Congress had most certainly changed.

So where does deliberation fit into this picture? A description of the benefits of deliberation in monetary policy-making must take into account the absence of a single mandate in terms of the policy objective. The United States has so far not followed the United Kingdom and the euro area in adopting a policy objective that emphasizes the primacy of the single mandate of sustained low inflation as the best means to create stable growth and employment in the economy. Instead, it has maintained the dual mandate that places low inflation and high employment (and therefore economic growth) on the same footing. On the face of it, we might expect that this lack of clarity in the form of a single objective might feature prominently in the deliberation of both the FOMC and members of Congress. Our results do not support this view readily. In the early part of the period we study, when monetary policy was clearly unsuccessful in achieving the goals of the dual mandate, we observe a lack of clarity over the objective of policy that appeared to cloud the process of deliberation within the FOMC and carried over to the process of accountability to Congress.

We observe a change over time as monetary policy was perceived to become more successful, and an orthodoxy grew around the world that low inflation was the best objective for monetary policy whether the formal objective and mandate of policy said so in those terms or not. We observe that the intensity of congressional challenge to the Fed declined in the Greenspan years as policy, and thus the Fed, were seen to be successful. Everyone likes a winner, and our results indicate that the process of accountability of the Fed to Congress became less challenging and more accepting of the Fed's success as the record grew. We conclude from this observation that the accountability process for public policy is prone to be pro-cyclical in its own right, in other words, less challenging in the good times whatever seeds of future problems are being sowed at that time.

The one important caveat to this assessment of congressional passivity on accountability is that a small number of legislators *did* offer challenge to the Fed on the second part of the dual mandate—that is, jobs and the labor market. Our textual analysis from chapter 4 shows that throughout the Greenspan era and into the early years of Bernanke's tenure, a small number of legislators (and particularly Bernie Sanders) became adept at challenging the Fed chairman on economic growth. So, in the more recent period of low inflation, to the extent that Congress can be said to have held the Fed accountable to the policy objective in oversight hearings, our results indicate that it was more a matter of a few members challenging on one-half of the dual mandate (employment/economic growth), while very little challenge was made on the other half (price stability/inflation). It is then perhaps not surprising that repeated efforts to enact legislation that would strip the Federal Reserve of its mandate to ensure maximum employment have failed thus far. After all, the dual mandate is politically useful as it enables some members of Congress to challenge the Fed on at least one aspect of the policy objective (jobs/growth), and shift blame to the Fed when that aspect is not meeting expectations. In view of our depiction of legislators' goals from chapter 2, oversight hearings under the auspices of the dual mandate offer members of Congress the best of both worlds. On the details of monetary policy that underpin the price stability objective, members adhere to a passive stance, which reflects an electoral motivation that is risk adverse and thus satisfied with shifting the responsibility for implementing unpopular policy to the Fed. But, at the same time, the full employment and economic growth half of the mandate provides some opportunity for active participation that serves a distinct electoral advantage—namely demonstrating to constituents a concern for jobs.

In comparative perspective then, while other countries adopted the more modern formulation that makes low inflation the first objective of policy and other objectives such as growth and employment subordinate so that they are pursued subject to achieving low inflation, the success of the Fed and political incentives of members of Congress meant that the dual equal objective of low inflation and high employment has been able to survive largely unchallenged in a world in which both elements of the objective seemed to be going in the right direction more often than not. These circumstances therefore obscured whether the dual mandate has been a problem of practice in the way that economic theory suggested.

Setting aside the issue of jobs and economic growth, accountability of the Fed to Congress evolved from a tumultuous period in which members of Congress sought to challenge the legal status of the Fed to a more stable period in which they sought to praise the chairman and get him to lend support to their views on other areas of economic and social policy (e.g., more detailed aspects of fiscal policy). Our evidence indicates that oversight does not rank highly in the objectives of members of Congress probably because it has little direct electoral connection and incentive, and it tends to be pro-cyclical in the sense that Congress is prone to criticize failure and praise success. Previous studies of congressional oversight have noted that the "cost–benefit ratio of much of what one thinks of as oversight behavior is low relative to the alternatives" and so oversight hearings will inevitably be a low priority as members of Congress adopt a passive/reactive stance: "Most legislators respond to the incentives presented to them by their environment. No amount of wishing or pontificating about what ought to be done can significantly change this" (Aberbach 1990: 189).

So what might we add to this assessment? For monetary policy, such a stance means that accountability of the Fed to Congress is lessened, as it suggests that the process is inherently backward looking insofar as it concentrates on discussing the past record. Moreover we find that members of Congress show little grasp of the technical content of monetary policy. Over the 33-year period from which we sample hearings, at best perhaps nine individual members of Congress (six of whom were committee leaders) have shown a strong grasp of the content of monetary policy.[2] This is an important conclusion because it tends to suggest that as an oversight and accountability body, Congress is compromised by a lack of technical understanding and a strong tendency to follow a pro-cyclical bandwagon. Moreover interviewees suggested that the growth of the culture of central bank independence ("culture" is used here as a shorthand to describe the changes that insulated the Fed from political interference) has tended to create an unwritten rule that Congress should not interfere or debate seriously immediate short-term decision-making in monetary policy. This combination points to a paradox, namely that greater de facto independence should argue for more effective accountability, whereas our evidence indicates that the more successful pursuit of policy by the Fed encouraged the culture of greater de facto independence while at the same time the force of accountability from Congress appeared to weaken. The paradox that we identify was therefore most obvious during the Greenspan period, and Congress followed the theme of "everyone loves a winner."

One final aspect of the issue of Fed independence is worth noting. Our results show that over time the contribution to deliberation on monetary decisions in the FOMC made by the governors of the Federal Reserve Board increased substantially, if anything at the expense of the contribution of the presidents of the regional Federal Reserve banks. There may be several reasons for this change over time. One is that better people were chosen as governors by the administration of the day. Another is that as political appointees, the governors were able to function more effectively and independently on technical matters of policy in an environment where policy-making was more insulated from political interference—in other words, in a setting where de facto independence of the Fed was more entrenched. This underlines that when we think about the independence of agencies like the Fed, we should focus as much or more on the de facto operating environment as on the statutory position.

6.4 Hypotheses on Deliberation

In chapter 2 we sought to go beyond the statement that deliberation matters for both policy makers and politicians exercising the accountability role by setting out a number of hypotheses on how and why deliberation can be important. Our approach throughout this book has been to measure in full and thus dissect what committee members actually say in meetings or hearings. We then seek to use this understanding of the content to explain the evolution of US monetary policy-making over a critical period in which it went from failure to apparent success. Our approach is deliberately not to rely solely on automated textual analysis but rather to put it to work as a tool that should help facilitate our understanding of what was going on in the two forums in which the deliberation occurred (the FOMC and Congress).

For our overarching first hypothesis, we have already noted specific instances where we perceive evidence of persuasion—and to the extent that such persuasion is measurable, it appears that more happens in the FOMC than in congressional committees. In general, conditions that do not enhance deliberation in the oversight of monetary policy include large numbers of committee members (particularly in the House where only a fraction of the members even have time to pose questions), lack of technical expertise by members (or even an interest in gaining expertise), severe overall constraints on members' time, extreme transparency (the so-called media circus), and accountability that is mostly reactionary, or backward-looking. Though we have not measured it, a further condition might be the inherent electoral constraint upon members of Congress not to appear to change their minds (or "flip-flop") when faced with better arguments. The persuasion element of deliberation requires an independence of judgment by legislators—that is, legislators who might perceive themselves more as trustees than as delegates (Rehfeld 2009).

6.4.1 FOMC

Our basic premise is that deliberation is the process through which policy makers seek to diagnose the impact of developments in the economy and thereby form a judgment on the precise implications of those developments for monetary policy on a forward-looking basis (bearing in mind that monetary policy is inherently forward-looking because it is focused on future inflation and economic growth). This appears to be much nearer to a description of the actual process of making policy than an approach to the study of it which uses the average reaction properties of an econometric equation. Moreover our analysis of the transcripts shows that there have clearly been changes in the content of deliberation in the FOMC over time, and we believe these changes deserve more attention and should be studied on a more consistent basis than previously.

We set out three hypotheses in chapter 2 specific to deliberation in the FOMC, namely that it can be influenced by: the procedures and rules of the institution (including the rules surrounding the transparency of its proceedings—hypothesis 2); the membership of the committee, which changes over time and particularly the personality and reputation of the chairman (hypothesis 3); and the environment in which the committee is operating at any given time (notably the clarity of understanding of the objective of policy and the perceived success of the operation of policy—hypothesis 4).

In chapter 3 we point to a clear change in the substance and form of deliberation in the FOMC over the period we study. In both respects (substance and form) we conclude that an important determinant was the change from an environment of unsuccessful policy-making to one where policy was acknowledged to be successful in terms of achieving its objectives. From this, we conclude that the context of policy-making influences the deliberative process. This is in our view an important conclusion because it indicates that we should not take deliberation to be an unchanging "given." As a policy-making process comes under more or less stress because of its apparent success or failure, we should expect to see changes in the dynamics of the process as they are represented by deliberation. We therefore conclude that hypothesis 4 is important when considering monetary policy-making, and it may well have wider relevance in other areas of public policy.

We also conclude that the deliberative process of the FOMC changed with different chairmen. Our results indicate that the change of chairmen from Paul Volcker to Alan Greenspan appears to have been more fundamental in terms of altering the form and content of deliberation in the FOMC than the subsequent decision in 1993 to release the transcripts of meetings. The evidence suggests that changes were under way before that date, so at most the decision on release of the transcripts created further momentum for a process already under way. This provides strong support for hypothesis 3, namely that leadership matters and can be exercised through the deliberative process. We have also noted earlier that the relative scale and content of contributions to FOMC meetings changed over time, with the role of board governors growing and bank presidents becoming more focused on the economies of their regions. This, too, serves to underline the relevance of hypothesis 3. We do not suggest that hypothesis 2 is irrelevant (i.e., that the rules and procedures of the committee do not matter) but our evidence tends to suggest that leaders matter more than rules.

6.4.2 Congress

There is a larger literature from which to draw hypotheses on deliberation in Congress, and from that we constructed three hypotheses: the
reasoning skills of senators should outweigh those of their House colleagues (hypothesis 5); hearings on monetary policy may exhibit a
mixture of both public discourse and nonpublic discourse—that is, we
expected to find both point-scoring on popular and high-profile issues,
along with exchanges with experts on the details of monetary policy
(hypothesis 6); and on balance we anticipated a greater influence for
the new consensus surrounding monetary policy (and less of an influence for ideological or political polarization), and expected to find
some evidence for the progression toward this consensus among legislators over time (hypothesis 7).

For hypothesis 5, we find no clear evidence that deliberations were
of better quality in Senate hearings, relative to those in the House,
although we did note differences in areas of focus and coverage. For
instance, senators appear to have been more focused on institutional
issues than House members (e.g., the relationship of the Fed to government) and on aspects of foreign economic policy. More intriguingly,
senators appear to react more to the perceived success or failure of the
Fed's conduct of monetary policy than House members (i.e., senators
are more likely to either praise or censure the chairman).

The first part of hypothesis 6 expects to find evidence of point-
scoring on popular issues. On this aspect, members of Congress did
not disappoint. Broadly speaking, committee members sought to shift
discussion to fiscal policy issues—perhaps to enable them the opportunity to take positions on issues for which legislators could attract
more direct electoral benefit than possible from monetary policy. By
the late 1990s, these issues had shifted further afield to include Social
Security reform, education and training, and energy. On such issues,
committee members sought to attach the name of a successful chairman
(Greenspan) to their policy views. On the second half of this hypothesis—
the expectation of exchanges with experts on the details of monetary
policy—members of Congress fell woefully short. Few members have
demonstrated an interest in using the Humphrey–Hawkins hearings to
challenge the Fed chairman on the more technical aspects of monetary
policy-making. The exceptions have been a number of the committee
chairs in both chambers and a very small number of members who
have taken a strong stance in opposition to the Fed. For some committee chairmen, the task appears to carry an obligation to play a dominant

role in providing the challenge to the Fed chairman on the intended subject matter of the hearings.

In brief, most members appear to take advantage of the high media profile of the hearings in order to gain recognition for themselves and/ or for issues that are often unrelated to monetary policy. In our interviews we asked respondents whether they perceived this tendency as necessarily a "bad" thing. Interpretations differed. FOMC members spoke disparagingly about the lack of focus and informed questioning by congressional committee members, while congressional staff members were quite defensive. The latter argued that questions on topics unrelated to monetary policy reflected the mood outside of Congress and were therefore legitimate—even more so, since the hearings afforded members to probe the nation's de facto "chief economic officer" on a variety of topics that only indirectly relate to the economy.

We have discussed above our evidence of the progression of members of Congress toward the low inflation consensus; here we examine the possibility of ideological/partisan cleavage surrounding monetary policy (hypothesis 7). Whereas we do find that on average, Democrats offer more challenge to the Fed chairman, there is no evidence of the endemic ideological polarization that we observe elsewhere in Congress. Indeed, even in the heated and frenzied aftermath of the financial crisis, there was no clear partisan divide on either the discourse or the voting of members with respect to the re-confirmation of Ben Bernanke. Instead, the committee discourse reflected confusion as to where to pin the blame for the crisis and how to acquire political credit for a legislative remedy to prevent such events in the future.

6.5   Final Thoughts

Deliberation is an understudied area of policy-making. This is probably because it is hard to do in at least two respects. First, it is hard to reduce words into a measurable form while maintaining the integrity of the concepts and arguments. Thus assessing deliberation is not a matter of studying a random bag of words. Second, even if we can capture the content of deliberation in a more systematic fashion that preserves meaning, we face the question of how we then assess whether and how deliberation makes a difference. For us, deliberation matters because it can change the views and preferences of participants, and these changes can in turn result in both abrupt policy consequences (e.g., the Volcker Revolution) and longer term policy consequences (e.g., cementing a legislative consensus around the primacy of low inflation as a precursor to stable economic growth). Simply put, deliberation matters in a process where policy is made in a committee setting because committee members (1) seek to persuade others to alter their views and (2) are themselves persuaded to revise their own views. The views of committee members are malleable. Thus, it is not satisfactory to assess policymaking using just a crude measurement of preferences in a statistical framework. But, undoubtedly, more work is needed in measuring and understanding the consequences of deliberation, particularly in real world policy settings.

Our final remarks concern accountability. Recalling Blinder's depiction of accountability as described in chapter 4, central bank independence requires an explanation of its policy decisions, and congressional oversight hearings are the formal venue for this accountability. From our analysis, what can we say about the ability of Congress to hold the Fed accountable? With respect to jobs and economic growth, members of Congress are willing and able to engage the Fed chairman in deliberation; but with respect to the details of monetary policy, engagement falls woefully short (with the notable exception of a select group of members). In conducting oversight, Congress is constrained by its reactionary nature and by specific institutional features—particularly, the electoral incentives of members (which affect their ability and time to learn from deliberation), the lack of technical expertise in monetary policy, the extreme transparency of the oversight hearings, and the membership size of the House and Senate banking committees.

Should we conclude that effective monetary policy oversight— through a deliberative process—is a futile exercise by Congress? A cynic might reach this conclusion, but this would be both unwarranted and unnecessary. Challenging the Fed chairman on jobs and growth is core to accountability on the dual mandate, and this should not be underrated. Nor should the engagement on the technicalities of monetary policy by a small number of committee chairs and others be dismissed. In the end, however, we do conclude that the effectiveness of Congress as an institution for holding monetary policy makers to account is limited at best.

Notes

Chapter 1

1. The following draws from (Schonhardt-Bailey 2012).

2. The FOMC can meet during the "inter-meeting period" by conference call.

3. The District banks are located in Boston, New York, Philadelphia, Cleveland, Richmond, Atlanta, Chicago, St Louis, Minneapolis, Kansas City, Dallas, and San Francisco.

4. There is a staggering of terms so that one term expires on January 31st of each even-numbered year. A member of the Board may serve only one full term, though an individual originally appointed to fill the remainder of an unexpired term of a previous appointee who has left the Board may be reappointed to fill a subsequent full term. The chairman and vice chairman of the Board (who are designated by the president from among the appointed governors) are appointed for four-year terms and subject to Senate confirmation. The limit on the time in office of the chairman and vice chairman is set by the limits on their terms as governors.

5. The board of directors of each regional bank has nine members: three class A directors representing banking interests; three class B directors representing industry, agriculture, and commerce; and three class C directors representing the general public interest. Class A and B directors are elected by the member banks within the district. Class C directors are appointed by the Board of Governors.

6. The rotation of voting rights among the district presidents is prescribed as follows: the banks are divided into four groups: (1) Boston, Philadelphia, and Richmond; (2) Cleveland and Chicago; (3) Atlanta, St Louis, and Dallas; (4) Minneapolis, Kansas, and San Francisco. Voting rotates among the presidents in each group.

7. There is a very large literature in this field; for instance, see (Bean 2007; Goodfriend 2007).

8. Unfortunately, Meltzer has commented to us that he has no intention of writing a third volume for this history.

9. This short-run perspective has been attributed to the late 18th/early 19th century economist Henry Thornton, but was largely ignored until well into the 20th century.

10. As an (important) example, Meltzer notes that he found no mention of the distinction between nominal and real interest rates in Federal Reserve minutes until late into the

inflation period of the 1960s and 1970s. In contrast, the Fed used an absolute standard of nominal rates to judge whether monetary policy was tight or loose (Meltzer 2009: 1234).

11. To name but a few, Cukierman (1992), Bernhard (1998), and Blinder (1998).

12. A variant of this arrangement is the Bank of England, which does not have independent responsibility for setting the target but instead "receives" a numerical inflation target set by the government of the day.

13. This is a clear distinction from, say, the Bank of England.

14. For example, when quantitative easing is not in use.

15. Meade estimates a 30 percent rate of internal dissent, based on her reading and manual coding of the transcript data (Meade 2005).

16. The re-confirmation hearing for Bernanke in 2009 extends our time period by one year for these hearings only.

17. The text of Resolution 133 included that the Federal Reserve should:.

(1) pursue policies in the first half of 1975 so as to encourage lower long term interest rates and expansion in the money and credit aggregates appropriate to facilitating prompt economic recovery; and
(2) maintain long run growth of the money and credit aggregates commensurate with the economy's long run potential to increase production, so as to promote the goals of maximum employment, stable prices, and moderate long term interest rates. (Reproduced in Meltzer 2009: 986)

In 1977 Congress amended the Federal Reserve Act to incorporate the provisions of Resolution 133.

18. Formally, the Humphrey—-Hawkins Act is known as the Full Employment and Balanced Growth Act of 1978 (P.L. 95–523).

19. The goals set out in the Act included unemployment and inflation rates, balanced growth, productivity growth, full parity income for farmers, and so on. As Meltzer notes many of these objectives were beyond the competency of the Fed.

20. An excerpt from one of our interviewees, Jane D'Arista (see chapter 5).

21. The Fed derives its revenue from (1) interest on government securities through its open market operations and (2) interest from loans to depository institutions. Regional Federal Reserve Banks also charge fees for services provided to banks and other financial institutions. Excess revenue from the Fed is remitted to the Treasury. Notably, however, the Federal Reserve Board publishes the financial statements and budgeted expenses of the Board and the Reserve Banks in its annual report to Congress. The Board also provides a report on its performance, although clearly stating that "(a)lthough the Federal Reserve Board is not covered by the Government Performance and Results Act of 1993 (GPRA), the Board has chosen to voluntarily comply with the spirit of the act." Finally, in response to the financial crisis of 2007–2009, the Fed began to publish monthly reports on credit and liquidity programs "to ensure appropriate accountability to the Congress and the public" (2011).

22. See, for example, (Oleszek 2007: 294–306).

23. One recent exception is the work of Ainsworth et al. (Ainsworth, Harward, et al. 2010). While these authors examine congressional hearings on oversight, they (like others) do not study the arguments or deliberation within the hearings.

24. The House hearings covered were in: February 1976, July 1976, February 1977, July 1977, February 1979, July 1979, November 1979, February 1980, July 1980, February 1981, July 1981, February 1984, February 1985, July 1985, February 1986, July 1991, February 1992, July 1992, February 1993, July 1997, February 1998, July 1998, February 1999, July 2003, February 2004, July 2004, February 2005, July 2006, February 2007, July 2007, and February 2008. Unusually, the House held a third hearing on monetary policy in November 1979, immediately following the Volcker Revolution in October 1979.

25. The Senate hearings covered were in: May 1976, November 1976, May 1977, November 1977, February 1979, July 1979, February 1980, July 1980, February 1981, July 1981, July 1984, February 1985, July 1985, February 1986, February 1991, February 1992, July 1992, February 1993, July 1997, February 1998, July 1998, February 1999, July 2003, February 2004, July 2004, February 2005, July 2006, February 2007, July 2007, and February 2008. No Senate hearing was held in July 1991, so the February 1991 hearing was used instead.

26. See http://www.federalreserve.gov/fomc/minutes/19990202.htm.

Chapter 2

1. We describe the composition of the FOMC in our first chapter, where bank presidents "represent" the 12 districts of the Federal Reserve. It is not the role of the bank president to represent in any narrow sense the economic interests of the district, and so they should not be seen as a "delegate" of the district.

2. The feedback coefficients in estimated rules do not have a structural interpretation and do not identify key policy parameters, such as the implicit inflation target (Dennis 2004).

3. As Meltzer describes, the Fed has never committed to a single analytical model of US monetary policy; rather, use of judgment has co-existed with more formal theory and econometric models, with successive Fed chairmen being "appropriately skeptical" about formal models (Meltzer 2009: 1218–21). This approach, with its emphasis on the use of judgment outside a formal framework, is found in other central banks, though Meltzer suggests that the US system, with its 12 separate reserve banks each of which has an economic research department, may be an even stronger case of opposition to a single model.

4. We explain this policy shift in chapter 3.

5. Researchers are, however, increasingly employing automated content analysis software to analyze floor debates (Monroe, Colaresi, et al. 2008; Monroe and Schrodt 2008; Schonhardt-Bailey 2008). Moreover the Congressional Hearings Data Set (http://www.policyagendas.org/) provides tabulated and coded information on hearings from 1947 to 2004, but it does not include verbatim transcripts, which are essential for textual analysis. Part of the reason for the lack of attention to committee hearings may owe to the difficulties in obtaining these. For instance, our efforts to obtain the hearing transcripts for this book took many months (and years)—and the persistence of our excellent colleagues in the British Library of Political and Economic Science. As of late 2011,

however, most of these hearing transcripts are now easily available on line at ProQuest Congressional Hearings Collection.

6. Article II, section 2, clause 2, of the US Constitution stipulates that "The president shall nominate, and by and with the Advice and Consent of the Senate, shall appoint Ambassadors, other public Ministers and Consul, Judges of the supreme Court, and all other Officers of the United States"—which includes Federal Reserve Board Governors.

7. The remaining members, as presidents of the regional reserve banks, are appointed by the board of directors of each reserve bank, with the consent of the Fed's Board of Governors.

8. Indeed, to the extent that scholars have noted district-specific motivations from banking committee members, these appeared to derive from nonmonetary policy issues (e.g., housing, urban affairs) for which banking committees may hold jurisdiction (Adler and Lapinski 1997; Adler 2002).

9. While our *systematic* approach to studying the verbatim transcripts of the committee hearings is new, Havrilesky (1993) has attempted a form of content analysis on the congressional hearings records. His approach is quite simple, using a raw word count of references to the words "unemployment," "employment," "interest," "interest rates," "inflation," and "inflationary" measured separately between members of Congress and the Fed chairman of the day, from 1975 to 1992. Havrilesky assumes that mentioning inflation indicates a desire for tighter monetary policy, while mentioning unemployment or interest rates indicates a desire for easier monetary policy. He ignores references to other terms such as credit conditions, capital formation, and the budget deficit, on the grounds that they are not synonyms for the essential variables of monetary policy, and that they have appeared inconsistently throughout the period. While Havrilesky's findings are informative about the possible correlation between hearings and Fed policy, his approach reveals little about the deliberations of members of Congress in these hearings. Havrilesky's results suggest that Fed chairmen do not telegraph Fed policy intentions in their dialog with Congress. But he does achieve statistical significance for a model whereby the concerns of senators help to explain the change in the Fed funds rate in the month after the hearing. A second finding from this work is that there has been little correlation between Senate and House state-of-the-economy concerns over time. Havrilesky suggests that this difference—whereby senators but not representatives are found to have a significant impact on the Fed funds rate one month ahead—reflects the veto power of the Senate over appointments to the Fed Board. This is consistent with Grier's finding that the liberal/conservative bias of the chairman of the House Banking Committee has no influence on the ease/tightness bias of monetary policy, in contrast to the chairman of the Senate Banking Committee.

10. Ideally we might seek to address other relevant hypotheses from the empirical literature on legislative deliberation—for example, from Lascher's work (Lascher 1996: 513). It would be useful to investigate such hypotheses as (1) *Deliberation will be of a higher quality when banking committees members spend less time on constituency service*, and (2) *Deliberation will be of a higher quality when banking committee members have fewer committee assignments*. Lascher may well be correct that deliberation is time-intensive and, as such, when legislators spend too much time on casework or on constituency matters, or their attention is divided across too many issue areas, their ability to engage in serious deliberation will decline. Unfortunately, measuring systematically the direct effects of such factors on the *quality* of deliberation is beyond the scope of our present work.

Chapter 3

1. This can be thought of in an optimization framework in which the central bank seeks to minimize a quadratic loss function with the inflation and output gap as arguments for given structural parameters of the macroeconomy (Beechey and Österholm 2007).

2. Ironically, the Burns lecture was chaired by his predecessor William McChesney Martin, who famously described the role of the central banker as being to take away the punch bowl just as the party was getting going.

3. This observation on the quality of governors is consistent with Meltzer's claim that in the 1970s, reserve bank presidents were generally ahead of governors in seeing the need to slow inflation by anchoring monetary policy to a longer run objective (Meltzer 2009: 911).

4. Some authors adopt a more ad hoc approach (e.g., Abolafia 2004).

5. They also have to omit a number of meetings during the Burns period where it was not possible to identify the preference of Burns himself even after studying the transcript.

6. In doing so, Chappell et al. (2005) acknowledge that the transcripts are a rich source material, ignored by many students of the FOMC.

7. The discussions excluded from the analysis include the micro detail of Federal Reserve foreign exchange operations (e.g., the so-called warehousing arrangements); staff research studies that, while having a broad impact on policy, were not directly related to the immediate decision; discussion of leaks of information; the annual process of re-appointing the chairman and system manager; and so on.

8. Our improvements to the lemmatization process have yielded results for 1979 and 1980 that vary slightly from those reported in (Bailey and Schonhardt-Bailey 2008), but the substantive findings remain unchanged.

9. Much of the following narrative is drawn from (Goodfriend 1993).

10. Plurals and conjugation endings are reduced to a single form and nonce words are eliminated from the analysis. This leaves a smaller word count that is analyzed by the program.

11. These are deemed "passive" as they do not contribute to either the calculation of the word classes or the factors in the correspondence analysis.

12. A contextual unit is equivalent to one or more successive ECU(s). The two calculations are done with two different parameters for the selected number of words per contextual unit in order to check the reliability of the classes and the stability of the results (Reinert 1998: 14).

13. The minimum chi-squared value for selecting a word is as follows for each file: 7 (Miller 1979), 16 (Volcker 1979), 20 (1980), 16 (1981), 17 (1991), 15 (1992), 16 (1993), 19 (1997), 16 (1998), and 16 (1999). The higher thresholds for the post—Miller transcripts reflect the relatively larger word counts for these text files compared with that of the Miller file. The basic rule of thumb with Alceste is (as with any data)—the more data, the easier it is to attain statistical significance. Hence, for files with more data, the threshold for statistical significance is set higher (with 20 being the top threshold set within Alceste and 2.13 the minimum).

14. The standard report lists the top 19 or 20 ECUs for each class, ranked by chi-square association. However, a separate file is produced that lists all the ECUs for each class, where the default cutoff for selection is zero.

15. Our analysis of the text files is focused on the monetary policy-making process of the FOMC. We have therefore not included those parts of the meetings that form outside the discussion of monetary policy (e.g., discussions that happened after the committee reached its decision on monetary policy, and were thus distinct). In fact there were few such elements to the meetings, but a prime example is the discussion of the failure of the Long-Term Capital Management hedge fund in 1998. Further details of our editing of the transcripts are given in the Methodology appendix.

16. The difference in sample sizes between the voting and transcript approaches used by Chappell et al. reflect difficulties they found in estimating a score for a member who shows no disagreement with the Chairman in the transcripts (the difference here is accounted for by Governor David Mullins who falls into this category in the Greenspan period). We are grateful to Henry Chappell for confirming this result from their work.

17. Non-borrowed reserves comprise the (seasonally adjusted) monetary base of member banks of the Federal Reserve system minus holdings of currency by the member banks and the contribution of borrowing by member banks to the base (neither of which in Volcker's view the Fed could directly control). Volcker's intent was to use the target of non-borrowed reserves as a proxy means to control total reserve or monetary base growth. Thus, an increase in total reserves could be offset by the Fed lowering the path of non-borrowed reserve growth. Meltzer discusses at length two problems with the framework that were known by the FOMC at the time but not acted upon, namely the complication of lagged reserve requirements and the weakness of the variable (over time) relationship between the discount rate (the rate at which banks could borrow from the Fed at the discount window) and the market overnight rate (the Fed Funds rate) (Meltzer 2009: 1027). These two problems no doubt complicated the implementation of the change in policy, but we do not regard them as fundamental to our analysis of the causes of the shift in policy in 1979 and 1980. Meltzer also traces the history of recommendations to the FOMC to use a non-borrowed reserves target, noting that the idea was not new in 1979, and not new to Volcker (Meltzer 2009: 891, 907–908, 911, 982).

18. Meltzer adds a number of other elements to the list of problems faced by the Fed in 1980. The economic and monetary data were extremely uncertain and prone to subsequent revision. There were large errors (identified ex post) in the staff forecasts of inflation and economic growth. Beyond these problems, the Fed faced the problem that financial markets tended to interpret a decline in the Funds rate as a policy easing even though the Fed insisted that moves in rates reflected moves in the monetary aggregates. The volatility of the aggregates did not help here. And the Fed was flawed in its reasoning on the link between the behavior of bank reserves and interest rates (a flawed reliance in Meltzer's view on an old reasoning of the 1930s—the Riefler—Burgess reasoning). And, because the Fed did not move the discount rate in line with movements in the Funds rate—for the reasoning that they were seeking to avoid targeting interest rates— the behavior of borrowing by banks at the discount window was affected in ways that complicated the interpretation of movements in total reserves (Meltzer 2009: 1048–58).

19. The evidence for political support for Volcker was reinforced by our interview with former Cleveland Fed President Jerry Jordan, who was a member of the Council of Economic Advisers in the early years of the Reagan presidency (see chapter 5). Jordan

highlighted that Volcker had the support of Reagan when Treasury officials were not supportive.

"[low inflation consensus was a priority in post 1979 . . .] It wasn't a partisan thing. It was Democrat economists as well as Republican-oriented economists and the fact that in the private meetings Volcker had 100 percent support from President Reagan made it a non-issue. . . . Chairman Volcker knew that [the Treasury Department] . . . didn't reflect the president's view and he had the president's full support to persist with an anti-inflationary policy. And he had congressional support in doing whatever he wanted to do because he was their guy and [yet] he was being attacked by the Reagan Treasury. So there wasn't any effective criticism of the idea of persisting to eliminate inflation."

20. Meltzer adds that by early 1981, in the FOMC meetings some reserve bank presidents were citing evidence of industrialists supporting the anti-inflation policy at the expense of lower short-run output for their firms (Meltzer 2009: 1085).

21. To fit such models to history, it is necessary to make assumptions about the weight that policy makers place on recent information, and to what extent they employ a smoothing component that acts against big shifts in policy (Woodford 2003; Primiceri 2005).

22. It was not until 1985 that Rogoff filled in the important gap of explaining how a central bank could attain credibility in the first place (Rogoff 1985; Bernanke, Blinder, et al. 2005).

23. Meltzer describes Burns as never distinguishing "between permanent and temporary reductions in aggregate spending. He blamed unions and budget deficits for inflation and only occasionally mentioned money growth" (Meltzer 2009: 919).

24. While correspondence analysis is well-established in the French literature (see Benzecri 1973 and the journal *Cahiers de l'Analyze des Donnees*) its use has spread with the publication of English applications (Greenacre and Underhill 1982; Greenacre 1984; Weller and Romney 1990; Greenacre 1993), and is occasionally used by political scientists (Blasius and Thiessen 2001). Correspondence analysis using numerical data is available in several major statistical packages, including BMDP, SPSS, and SAS.

25. For this, correspondence analysis uses the "chi-squared distance," which resembles the Euclidean distance between points in physical space. (Here chi-squared distance—which is distinct from the chi-squared statistic used to measure the significance of the words and tags—can be observed in Euclidean space by transforming the profiles before constructing the plots.) In correspondence analysis, each squared difference between coordinates is divided by the corresponding element of the average profile (where the profile is a set of frequencies divided by their total). The justification for using the chi-squared concept is that it allows one to transform the frequencies by dividing the square roots of the expected frequencies, thereby equalizing the variances. This can be compared to factor analysis, where data on different scales are standardized. For more detailed discussion and further geometric reasons for using the chi-squared distance in correspondence analysis, see Greenacre (1993: 34–36).

26. Correspondence analysis usually refers to the "inertia" of a table, which can also be called "association" (Weller and Romney 1990). (A corresponding chi-squared value can be obtained by multiplying the association value by the total n of the table.) Conceptually, inertia represents a cloud of profile points with masses that sum to one: "These points

have a centroid (i.e., the average profile) and a distance (chi-squared distance) between profile points. Each profile point contributes to the inertia of the whole cloud" (Nagpaul 1999). For the computation of inertia, see Nagpaul (1999).

27. The association and chi-squared statistic may be interpreted geometrically as the degree of dispersion of the set of rows and columns (or, profile points) around their average, where the points are weighted.

28. However, where the correspondence space contains high dimensionality (e.g., over six factors) or the weight of the classes is highly skewed, this may not always hold. For 1979 Miller, the inertia and percentage contribution of each factor are, respectively, 0.33 (31.9 percent), 0.26 (24.9 percent), 0.20 (19.6 percent), 0.13 (12.8 percent), and 0.11 (10.9 percent). For 1979 Volcker, the corresponding statistics are 0.26 (38.7 percent), 0.18 (27.5 percent), 0.13 (19.7 percent), and 0.09 (14.1 percent). For 1980, we have just two factors, inasmuch as the third factor is not given by the program (which relates to the peculiar arch effect of the 1980 graph and the skew in the relative size of the classes, as discussed in the text). The corresponding statistics for these are 0.25 (62.1 percent) and 0.15 (37.9 percent). For 1981, the corresponding statistics are 0.23 (46.1 percent), 0.16 (32.4 percent), and 0.11 (21.5 percent).

29. That is, because the coordinates of points reflect correlation—and the more distant the points are from one another, the less likely they are to be co-occurrent—the coordinates of points and number of columns analyzed in a two-dimensional space will result in a circular appearance.

30. The solution to the arch effect is a disputed topic—see Wartenberg, Ferson, et al. (1987), Schuur and Kiers (1994), Holland (2006), and Ordination Methods (http://ordination.okstate.edu/).

31. As with problems of degrees of freedom and multicollinearity in regression analysis, the way to resolve this difficulty is to obtain more information—that is, add more discourse from the FOMC transcripts in 1980. However, as no further transcripts exist apart from our present corpus, this was not possible.

32. Meltzer cites this from p. 183 of Mehrling's interview (Meltzer 2009: 1107–1108).

33. For one member, Governor Alice Rivlin, the higher frequency of pairs of meetings meant that there was insufficient text in at least some meeting pairs to produce results from the textual analysis. Notably, Rivlin was not present for the June meeting. We have therefore not included Governor Rivlin in this part of the assessment.

34. For a good example of this technique applied to parliamentary debates see Bicquelet (2009).

Chapter 4

1. Blinder does, however, acknowledge that central bank communications may include providing forward-looking information about monetary policy to condition market expectations (Blinder 2004).

2. We stop short of seeking to analyze the impact of the current financial crisis on congressional oversight of the Fed (with the exception that we do include Bernanke's reconfirmation hearing, in part four of this chapter). It is worth noting however that in a financial crisis of the current scale, only governments can ultimately solve the problem

since only governments can spread the cost of resolving the crisis (a) across all taxpayers, and (b) over time—in the limit they can carry out inter-generational transfers, that is, tax the next generation. The underlying rationale for such governmental activism in the face of bank failures is, of course, the "Too Big to Fail" problem, where the cost is a loss of financial stability, and thus is important to the wider economy. Invariably the fiscal implications of the current financial crisis will affect relations between Congress and the Fed, but these developments lie beyond the scope of the present project, as does the important objective of ending the dependence on public money created by Too Big to Fail.

3. The inertia and percentage contribution of each factor are (respectively): 0.14 (29.8 percent), 0.10 (20.5 percent), 0.08 (16.8 percent), 0.06 (12.9 percent), 0.04 (8.1 percent), 0.03 (7.2 percent), and 0.02 (4.7 percent).

4. The inertia and percentage contribution of each factor are (respectively): 0.14 (28.9 percent), 0.10 (20.3 percent), 0.08 (16.4 percent), 0.06 (11.3 percent), 0.04 (8.9 percent), 0.04 (7.5 percent), and 0.03 (6.8 percent).

5. An example is the "discourse quality index," which measures generic features such as levels of participation, respect toward others and their arguments, the tendency to offer mediating proposals, and so on (Steiner, Bächtiger, et al. 2004; Bächtiger, Spörndli, et al. 2005). Such an index is not specific to any issue area but rather is generic to any policy domain.

6. Chapter 1 and our book appendix II for details of the hearings included.

7. See table 1.1, chapter 1.

8. The distribution is calculated as the percentage share of ECUs (representative sentences) retained by the textual analysis that is classified into each thematic groups.

9. World economy is distinguished from the monetary policy group of classes because the US does not make monetary policy for the rest of the world. We do, however, recognize that the world economy constitutes an input to US monetary policy.

10. The ECU is ranked fifth from this class.

11. Fauntroy was a delegate from the District of Columbia.

12. Indeed the approval of the Fed chairman is becoming almost a necessity, as the *New York Times* recently remarked: "The Fed's willingness to give a nod to fiscal stimulus is important. Many lawmakers will not support action without the chairman's blessing . . ." (Andrews and Herszenhorn 2008).

13. We are grateful to Scott Adler for not only sharing his data with us, but also for lending advice and assistance as needed.

14. For the various changes in titles for this committee and its relevant subcommittees, see our book appendix II.

15. As we detail in our book appendix II, the HFSC has evolved and undergone a number of title changes since it originated in 1946. As is evident from many of the previous titles for this committee, housing and urban affairs has been a core jurisdiction of the larger committee.

16. Because our data include members of the Senate Banking Committee, we aggregate Adler's district-level data to the state level for this chamber.

17. In as much as socioeconomic data are often understood in relative rather than absolute terms and as such, are analyzed in quintiles, we calculate and employ quintiles for the constituency data in our analysis.

18. Adler's data extends only to the late 1990s, so our analysis in this section of our chapter does not extend into the 2000s.

19. The automatic cutoff for significance for tags is $\chi^2 \geq 2$, with one degree of freedom. Although this does not quite reach the 0.10 level of statistical significance, our strategy is to include all contributors to the discourse who attain this minimal level of significance.

20. In the very few instances where a member's name obtains statistical significance for two classes within a single group, we take the measure for the larger level of significance only.

21. See our previous footnote on the chi square significance of tags.

22. Neal1 is Stephen Neal of North Carolina, and Chairman of the Subcommittee on Domestic Monetary Policy. In figures 4.19 and 4.29 Neal2 is Richard Neal of Massachusetts.

23. We insert Sanders in brackets in figure 4.14, for purposes of clarity. Normally a boxplot would not list a case for a category (like Independent) for which there is just one case.

24. Notably, however, these statistics do not control for other variables or for the relative numbers of types of committee members.

25. We do not present corresponding figures for the remaining economic themes, as they lend very little further to our analysis. For instance, for inflation, the familiar two senators—Riegle, and Stewart—lead the discussion; otherwise, there appears to be little difference between House and Senate committee members. For the labor market theme, the key figure is again Congressman Sanders, whose χ^2 value dwarfs all others in either chamber.

26. A number of studies of legislative and other political behavior have sought to explore the links between multidimensionality and low dimensionality. Some of these explore the question by analyzing roll call votes (Groseclose, Levitt, et al. 1999; Norton 1999; Hurwitz, Moiles, et al. 2001), others by analyzing survey or elite interview data with correlational and confirmatory factor analysis (Craig, Martinez, et al. 1999; Levine, Carmines, et al. 1999) or principal-component analysis (Selck 2004), and others by comparing and contrasting alternative methodological approaches (Brazill and Grofman 2002; Grofman and Brazill 2002). Two further studies offer insights on multidimensionality and low dimensionality by examining the legislative *process*, both before and after floor voting (Potoski and Talbert 2000; Ringe 2005).

27. While votes on the decision to reconfirm are taken both in committee and on the Senate floor, we use the latter measurement because it is the official (and more accurate) record of their preferences.

28. These included a statement of Lyndon H. La Rouche Jr, (opposing Volcker's re-appointment & his "Programmatic Policy for Recovery"); a telegram text from the president of the Union of Engineers, in context of US economic policy directives against Brazil; and statements of opposition from trade unionists of a West German white-collar workers union (*Deutsche Angestellten Gewerkschaft*) supporting La Rouche's

stance, US trade union leaders, US farmers, minorities (NAACP), and Virginia Taxpayers Association.

29. We do not quibble on the question of bipartisan versus cross-party, as either term is consistent with our interpretation of the results.

30. See, for instance, reports in the New York Times, CNNMoney, Bloomberg, and Fox News: http://www.nytimes.com/2009/12/04/business/economy/04fed.html; http://money.cnn.com/2009/12/03/news/economy/bernanke_hearing/index.htm; http://www.bloomberg.com/apps/news?pid=newsarchive&sid=aROqfIQk1zBQ; http://www.foxnews.com/politics/2009/12/03/second-term-bernanke-heads-congress/.

31. http://www.nytimes.com/2009/12/04/business/economy/04fed.html.

32. The Act was signed into law on July 21, 2010.

33. Their names and χ^2 values are Corker (67), Dodd (58), Gregg (31), Bennett (26), Menendez (15), Johanns (13), DeMint (12), Tester (12), Schumer (11), Akaha (9), Hutchison (6), and Bayh (5).

34. For class 4, Bernanke's tag obtains a χ^2 value of 31, and Senator Vitter's obtains a value of 10; and for class 5, Bernanke' χ^2 value is 15, while Senators Johnson and Bunning both have values of 4.

35. As reported Chris Isidore of CNN (http://money.cnn.com/2009/12/03/news/economy/bernanke_hearing/index.htm;)

Chapter 5

1. Kohn was a member of the Board of Governors prior to becoming vice chairman, unlike Blinder and Rivlin.

2. All the recorded interviews were transcribed by our research assistant, Dr. Gordon Bannerman. Funding for this project has been provided by The Suntory and Toyota International Centres for Economics and Related Disciplines of the LSE. We thank Gordon for his meticulous and careful transcriptions, and STICERD for its funding.

3. The target for the manager has changed over time, and has included the Fed Funds Rate, monetary aggregates or non-borrowed reserves.

4. While Blinder's label for the FOMC reflects his own familiarity with the Greenspan Fed, it is worth adding one current observation which reinforces the continued relevance of "collegial" description of the committee under Bernanke—though perhaps not as autocratically so as under Greenspan. Following Bernanke's first press conference (noted above), one of our interviewees, Vincent Reinhart, remarks in a *New York Times* editorial that Bernanke "did not characterize the range of opinion or depth of feeling expressed at the meeting. This makes it hard to determine how the balance of opinion within the confines of the Fed's marble palace will shift as events unfold" (Reinhart 2011).

5. C-SPAN began covering proceedings in the House of Representatives in 1979, and the coverage was extended to the Senate in 1986 (Koempel, Schneider, et al. 2007: 67).

6. *Jordan*: Prior to February 1994, the decisions by the FOMC to "tighten" or "ease"—raise or lower the target Fed Funds rate—were not announced but were "signaled" by the trading desk of the NY Fed on the first business day following a meeting. This cultivated an industry of Fed Watchers (often

former Fed employees) whose role was to read and interpret the timing and types of actions of the trading desk.

At least some 20 years earlier there had been Reserve Bank presidents . . . who would occasionally ask why the committee did not simply issue a press release, like the Bundesbank and others. The Washington answers were about how the US was different. When I arrived in Cleveland in early 1992 I took up the issue again, joined by a few others, but a minority of the committee, with the governors, including the chairman, and NY much opposed.

At the December 1993 meeting my recollection is that after over two years of an unchanged Fed Funds rate of 3 percent and the economy picking up steam, the majority was solidly in favor of an increase. The argument against doing so at that meeting . . . was that we were only a few days before Christmas, so the timing was bad, and besides, a few more weeks wouldn't do any harm.

So, barring some surprising negative news, there was no disagreement that we would act at the February 1994 meeting. . . .

The first meeting of 1994 was to be two days, but could not be early in the week because the chairman would be in London for the Bank of England anniversary meeting. The FOMC would have to meet on Thursday and Friday. The staff pre-meeting materials and the discussions on Thursday were all about raising the Fed Funds rate for the first time in a couple of years, and how much should this initial increase be, with everyone acknowledging that it would be only the first of several increases and that we would set off a wave of speculation about how many increases, how fast, and how much in total would we do.

Friday morning was time to vote which was an easy decision, but all the disagreement was the "signaling" by the desk which would not take place until the following Monday morning. I and others argued that the risks that the decision would leak and be in the newspapers before Monday morning were too great, the damages of a leak too harmful politically, we had no choice but to issue a press release. Finally the chairman conceded these points and agreed that we would have a press release at 11:00 am announcing the decision to raise the target intervention rate. We all adjourned for coffee and went to the offices of the governors to watch the TVs as the news came across—and the Dow Jones plunged 100 points.

The chairman had been clear to the committee that he did not view this as a precedent, that it was only done because of having to meet on Thursday and Friday, and that we would observe and assess the effects of the announcement before ever, ever, ever doing so again. The rest is now history. Thank you, Bank of England [email correspondence to authors, September 23, 2010].

7. William J. Fellner was a professor of economics at Yale, specializing in monetary theory and inflation. Between 1973 and 1975 he served on the Council of Economic Advisors during the Nixon and Ford administrations.

Chapter 6

1. In its December 2012 meeting, the FOMC chose to provide a more explicit interpretation around the mandate—in particular, setting out a threshold unemployment rate and, while repeating its long-run inflation goal of 2 percent, it set out an inflation objective in terms of a projection "no more than a half percentage point above the Committee's 2 percent longer run goal" for the period between one and two years ahead, and that "longer term inflation expectations continued to be well-anchored."

2. In chapter 4 we found that in six of our thematic classes (inflation, labor market, money growth, financial stability, fiscal policy, challenging the Fed) only nine individual members of Congress dominate the discussions (six of which are committee leaders). However, for two themes (independence of the Fed, praising the Fed) committee members in general are engaged in discussions.

Bibliography

Aberbach, J. D. 1990. *Keeping a Watchful Eye: The Politics of Congressional Oversight.* Washington, DC: Brookings Institution.

Abolafia, M. Y. 2004. Framing moves: Interpretative politics at the Federal Reserve. *Journal of Public Administration: Research and Theory* 14: 349–70.

Adler, E. S. 2000. Constituency characteristics and the "guardian" model of appropriations subcommittees, 1959–1998. *American Journal of Political Science* 44 (1): 104–14.

Adler, E. S. 2002. *Why Congressional Reforms Fail: Reelection and the House Committee System.* Chicago: University of Chicago Press.

Adler, E. S. 2011. Congressional district data. http://socsci.colorado.edu/~esadler/Congressional_District_Data.html.

Adler, E. S., and J. S. Lapinski. 1997. Demand-side theory and congressional committee composition: A constituency characteristics approach. *American Journal of Political Science* 41 (3): 895–918.

Ainsworth, S. H., B. M. Harward, and K. W. Moffett. 2010. Presidential signing statements and congressional oversight. Working paper. University of Georgia and Southern Illinois University.

Alesina, A., and J. Sachs. 1988. Political parties and the business cycle in the United States, 1948–1984. *Journal of Money, Credit and Banking* 25: 63–82.

Allen, S. D., and D. L. McCrickard. 1991. The influence of elections on Federal Reserve behavior. *Economics Letters* 37: 51–55.

Alt, J. E. 1991. Leaning into the wind or ducking out of the storm? U.S. monetary policy in the 1980s. In A. Alesina and G. Carliner, eds., *Politics and Economics in the 1980s.* Chicago: Chicago University Press, 41–82.

Andrews, E. L., and D. M. Herszenhorn. 2008. Bernanke is said to support stimulus. *New York Times,* http://www.nytimes.com/2008/01/17/business/17fiscal.html.

Appelbaum, B. 2011. Bernanke defends Fed's role in running economy. *New York Times,* http://www.nytimes.com/2011/04/28/business/economy/28fed.html?ref=business. 27 April 2011.

Auerbach, R. D. 2008. *Deception and Abuse at the Fed: Henry B. Gonzalez Battles Alan Greenspan's Bank.* Austin: University of Texas Press.

Austen-Smith, D., and T. J. Feddersen. 2006. Deliberation, preference uncertainty, and voting rules. *American Political Science Review* 100 (2): 209–18.

Bächtiger, A., M. Spörndli, M. R. Steenbergen, and J. Steiner. 2005. The deliberative dimensions of legislatures. *Acta Politica* 40: 225–38.

Bailey, A., and C. Schonhardt-Bailey. 2008. Does deliberation matter in FOMC monetary policymaking? The Volcker Revolution of 1979. *Political Analysis* 16 (4): 404–27.

Barabas, J. 2004. How deliberation affects policy opinions. *American Political Science Review* 98 (4): 687–701.

Bean, C. 2007. Is there a new consensus in monetary policy? In P. Arestis, ed., *Is There a New Consensus in Macroeconomics?* London: Palgrave Macmillan, 167–87.

Beck, N. 1987. Elections and the Fed: Is there a political monetary cycle? *American Journal of Political Science* 31: 194–216.

Beck, N. 1990. Congress and the Fed: Why the dog does not bark in the night. In T. Mayer, ed., *The Political Economy of American Monetary Policy*. Cambridge: Cambridge University Press, 131–50.

Beck, N. 1990. Political monetary cycles. In T. Mayer, ed., *The Political Economy of American Monetary Policy*. Cambridge: Cambrige University Press, 115–30.

Beechey, M., and P. Österholm. 2007. The rise and fall of U.S. inflation persistence. Board of Governors of the Federal Reserve System and Uppsala University.

Beldon, S. 1989. Policy preferences of FOMC members as revealed by dissenting votes. *Journal of Money, Credit and Banking* 21 (Nov): 432–41.

Bendor, J. 1988. Review article: Formal models of bureaucracy. *British Journal of Political Science* 18: 353–95.

Benzecri, J.-P. 1973. *L'analyse des données. Tome 1: La Taxinomie. Tome 2: L'Analyse des Correspondances (Data analysis. Volume 1: Taxonomy. Volume 2: Correspondance Analysis)*. Paris: Dunod.

Bernanke, B. S., A. S. Blinder, and B. T. McCallum. 2005. Panel discussion I: What have we learned since October 1979? *Federal Reserve Bank of St. Louis Review—Special Issue: Reflections on Monetary Policy 25 Years after October 1979* 87 (2): 277–92.

Bernhard, W. T. 1998. A political explanation of variations in central bank independence. *American Political Science Review* 92 (2): 311–28.

Bessette, J. M. 1994. *The Mild Voice of Reason: Deliberative Democracy and American National Government*. Chicago: University of Chicago Press.

Bicquelet, A. 2009. On referendums: A comparison of French and English Parliamentary debates using Computer-assisted textual analysis. PhD dissertation. Government Department, University of Essex, Wivenhoe.

Binder, S., and M. Spindel. 2011. De-central bank: The politics of selecting the Federal Reserve Banks in 1914. Congress and History Conference. Brown University, Providence.

Blasius, J., and V. Thiessen. 2001. Methodological artifacts in measures of political efficacy and trust: A multiple correspondence analysis. *Political Analysis* 9 (1): 1–20.

Blinder, A. 1998. *Central Banking in Theory and Practice*. Cambridge, MA: MIT Press.

Blinder, A., and C. Goodhart, P. Hildenbrand, D. Lipton, and C. Wyplosz. 2001. *How Do Central Banks Talk?* London: Centre for Economic Policy Research.

Blinder, A. S. 2004. *The Quiet Revolution: Central Banking Goes Modern*. New Haven: Yale University.

Blinder, A. S., and J. Morgan. 2005. Are two heads better than one? Monetary policy by committee. *Journal of Money, Credit and Banking* 34 (5): 798–811.

Blinder, A. S., and R. Reis. 2005. Understanding the Greenspan standard. Federal Reserve Bank of Kansas City Symposium, The Greenspan Era: Lessons for the Future. Jackson Hole, WY.

Brainard, W. 1967. Uncertainty and the effectiveness of monetary policy. *American Economic Review* 57: 411–25.

Brazill, T. J., and B. Grofman. 2002. Factor analysis versus multidimensional scaling: Binary choice roll-call voting and the U.S. Supreme Court. *Social Networks* 24: 201–29.

Burns, A. F. 1987 [1979]. The anguish of central banking. *Federal Reserve Bulletin* 73 (9): 689–98 [reprint].

Canterbery, E. R. 1967. A new look at federal open market voting. *Western Economic Journal* 6: 25–38.

Chambers, S. 2005. Measuring publicity's effect: Reconciling empirical research and normative theory. *Acta Politica* 40: 255–66.

Chang, K. H. 2003. *Appointing Central Bankers: The Politics of Monetary Policy in the United States and the European Monetary Union*. Cambridge: Cambridge University Press.

Chappell, H. W., T. M. Havrilesky, and R. R. McGregor. 1993. Partisan monetary policies: Presidential influence through the power of appointment. *Quarterly Journal of Economics* 108: 185–218.

Chappell, H. W., and W. Keech. 1986. Party differences in macroeconomic policies and outcomes. *American Economic Association Papers and Proceedings* 76 (2): 71–74.

Chappell, H. W., and W. Keech. 1988. The unemployment consequences of partisan monetary policies. *Southern Economic Journal* 55: 107–22.

Chappell, H. W., R. R. McGregor, and T. Vermilyea. 2005. *Committee Decisions on Monetary Policy: Evidence from Historical Records of the Federal Open Market Committee*. Cambridge, MA: MIT Press.

Chappell, H. W., R. R. McGregor and T. Vermilyea. 2012. Deliberation and learning in monetary policy committees. *Economic Inquiry* 50: 839–47.

Chari, V. V., L. J. Christiano, and M. Eichenbaum. 1998. *Expectations Trap and Discretion: Economics*. Evanston: Northwestern.

Cho, I.-K., N. Williams, and T. J. Sargent. 2002. Escaping Nash inflation. *Review of Economic Studies* 69: 1–40.

Chopin, M. C., C. S. Cole, and M. A. Ellis. 1996. Congressional influence on U.S. monetary policy: A reconsideration of the evidence. *Journal of Monetary Economics* 38: 561–70.

Chortareas, G., D. Stasavage, and G. Sterne. 2003. Does monetary policy transparency reduce disinflation costs? *Manchester School* 71 (5): 521–40.

Christiano, L. J., and T. J. Fitzgerald. 2003. Inflation and monetary policy in the 20th century. *Federal Reserve Bank of Chicago Economic Perspectives* 27: 22–45.

Christiano, L. J., and C. J. Gust. 2000. The expectations trap hypothesis. *Federal Reserve Bank of Chicago Economic Perspectives* 24: 21–39.

Clarida, R., J. Gali, and M. Gertler. 2000. Monetary policy rules and macroeconomic stability: Evidence and some theory. *Quarterly Journal of Economics* 115 (1): 147–80.

Clarida, R. H., J. Gali, and M. Gertler. 1999. The science of monetary policy: A New Keynsian perspective. *Journal of Economic Literature* 37 (4): 1661–1707.

Cobb, M. D., and J. H. Kuklinski. 1997. Changing minds: Political arguments and political persuasion. *American Journal of Political Science* 41 (1): 88–121.

Cogley, T., and T. J. Sargent. 2001. Evolving post–World War II U.S. inflation dynamics. *NBER Macroeconomic Annual* 16: 331–73.

Cox, G., and M. McCubbins. 1993. *Legislative Leviathan: Party Government in the House.* Berkeley: University of California Press.

Craig, S. C., M. D. Martinez, and J. G. Kane. 1999. The structure of political competition: Dimensions of candidate and group evaluation revisited. *Political Behavior* 21 (4): 283–304.

Crowley, J. E., M. Watson, and M. R. Waller. 2008. Understanding "power talk": Language, public policy, and democracy. *Perspectives on Politics* 6 (1): 71–88.

Cukierman, A. 1992. *Central Bank Strategy, Credibility, and Independence.* Cambridge, MA: MIT Press.

Cusack, T. R. 2001. Partisanship in the setting and coordination of fiscal and monetary policies. *European Journal of Political Research* 40: 93–115.

Dennis, R. 2004. The policy preferences of the U.S. Federal Reserve. Working paper. Federal Reserve Bank of San Francisco.

Dietrich, F., and C. List. 2012. Where do preferences come from? *International Journal of Game Theory,* (http://link.springer.com/article/10.1007%2Fs00182-012-0333-y).

Dietrich, F., and C. List. 2011. A model of non-informational preference change. *Journal of Theoretical Politics* 23 (2): 145–64.

Dietrich, F., and C. List. 2013. A reason-based theory of rational choice. *Noûs* 47 (1): 104–34.

Economist, The. 2008. While Wall Street burns: Lawmakers fiddle, then reach for the fire-hose. *The Economist* (Oct 2), http://www.economist.com/node/12342432.

Elster, J. 1998. *Deliberative Democracy.* Cambridge: Cambridge University Press.

Esterling, K. M. 2007. Buying expertise: Campaign contributions and attention to policy analysis in congressional committees. *American Political Science Review* 101 (1): 93–109.

Falaschetti, D. 2002. Does partisan heritage matter? The case of the Federal Reserve. *Journal of Law Economics and Organization* 18 (2): 488–510.

Faust, J., and L. Svensson. 2001. Transparency and credibility: Monetary policy with unobservable goals. *International Economic Review* 42 (2): 369–97.

Federal Reserve Board, Reports to Congress. 2011. Washington, DC, http://www .federalreserve.gov/boarddocs/rptcongress/.

Fenno, R. 1973. *Congressmen in Committees*. Boston: Little, Brown.

Finlayson, A. 2007. From beliefs to arguments: Interpretive methodology and rhetorical political analysis. *British Journal of Politics and International Relations* 9: 545–63.

Fiorina, M. 1982. Legislative choice of regulatory process: Legal process or administrative process. *Public Choice* 39: 33–66.

Fiorina, M. P., S. J. Abrams, and J. C. Pope. 2005. *Culture War? The Myth of a Polarized America*. New York: Pearson Longman.

Fishkin, J. S., and P. Laslett, eds. 2003. *Debating Deliberative Democracy*. Oxford: Blackwell.

Franzese, R. J. 2002. Electoral and partisan cycles in economic policies and outcomes. *American Review of Political Science* 5: 369–421.

Fuhrer, J., and G. Moore. 1995. Monetary policy trade-offs and the correlation between nominal interest rates and real output. *American Economic Review* 85: 219–39.

Gaskell, G. 2000. Individual and group interviewing. In M. W. Bauer and G. Gaskell, eds., *Qualitative Researching with Text, Image and Sound*. London: Sage, 38–56.

Gaskell, G., and M. W. Bauer. 2000. Towards public accountability: Beyond sampling, reliability and validity. In M. W. Bauer and G. Gaskell, eds., *Qualitative Researching with Text, Image, and Sound* London: Sage, 336–50.

Geraats, P. 2002. Central bank transparency. *Economic Journal* 112: 532–65.

Goldstein, J. 1993. *Ideas, Interests, and American Trade Policy*. Ithaca: Cornell University Press.

Goldstein, J., and R. O. Keohane, eds. 1993. *Ideas and Foreign Policy: Beliefs, Institutions, and Political Change*. Ithaca: Cornell University Press.

Goodfriend, M. 1986. Monetary mystique: Secrecy and central banking. *Journal of Monetary Economics* 17: 63–92.

Goodfriend, M. 1993. Interest rate policy and the inflation scare Problem: 1979–1992. *Federal Reserve Bank of Richmond Economic Quarterly* 79 (1): 1–24.

Goodfriend, M. 2007. How the world achieved consensus on monetary policy. Working paper 13580. NBER, Cambridge, MA.

Greenacre, M., and T. Hastie. 1987. The geometric interpretation of correspondence analysis. *Journal of the American Statistical Association* 82 (398): 437–47.

Greenacre, M. J. 1984. *Theory and Applications of Correspondence Analysis*. London: Academic Press.

Greenacre, M. J. 1993. *Correspondence Analysis in Practice*. London: Academic Press.

Greenacre, M. J., and L. G. Underhill. 1982. Scaling a data matrix in low-dimensional Euclidean space. In D. M. Hawkins, ed., *Topics in Applied Multivariate Analysis*. Cambridge: Cambridge University Press, 183–266.

Greenspan, A. 1993. FOMC Transcript, October 22. Washington, DC.

Greenspan, A. 2003. Monetary policy under uncertainty. Federal Reserve Bank of Kansas City Symposium. Jackson Hole, WY.

Greenspan, A. 2005. Chairman's remarks. *Federal Reserve Bank of St. Louis Review—Special Issue: Reflections on Monetary Policy 25 Years after October 1979* 87(2): 137–38.

Greenspan, A. 2007. *The Age of Turbulence: Adventures in a New World.* London: Allen Lane.

Greider, W. 1987. *Secrets of the Temple: How the Federal Reserve Runs the Country.* New York: Simon and Schuster.

Grier, K. 1989. On the existence of a political monetary cycle. *American Journal of Political Science* 33: 376–89.

Grier, K. 1991. Congressional influence on U.S. monetary policy: An empirical test. *Journal of Monetary Economics* 28: 201–20.

Grier, K. B. 1996. Congressional oversight committee influence on U.S. monetary policy revisited. *Journal of Monetary Economics* 38: 571–79.

Grofman, B., and T. J. Brazill. 2002. Identifying the median justice on the Supreme Court through multidimensional scaling: Analysis of "natural courts" 1953–1991. *Public Choice* 112:55–79.

Groseclose, T., S. D. Levitt, and J. M. Snyder. 1999. Comparing interest group scores across time and chambers: Adjusted ADA scores for the U.S. Congress. *American Political Science Review* 93 (1): 33–50.

Guha, K., and S. Kirchgaessner. 2007. Democrats signal tough stance on Fed. *Financial Times* (London), 8.

Gutmann, A., and D. Thompson. 2004. *Why Deliberative Democracy?* Princeton: Princeton University Press.

Havrilesky, T. 1993. *The Pressures on American Monetary Policy.* Boston: Kluwer.

Havrilesky, T., and J. Gildea. 1991. The policy preferences of FOMC members as revealed by dissenting votes. *Journal of Money, Credit and Banking* 23: 130–38.

Havrilesky, T., R. Sapp, and R. Schweitzer. 1975. A test of the Federal Reserve's reaction to the state of the economy. *Social Science Quarterly* 55 (March): 835–52.

Havrilesky, T., and R. Schweitzer. 1990. A theory of FOMC dissent voting with evidence from the time series. In T. Mayer, ed., *The Political Economy of American Monetary Policy.* New York: Cambridge University Press, 197–210.

Hetzel, R. L. and R. F. Leach. 2001. The Treasury–Fed accord: A new narrative account. *Economic Quarterly—Federal Reserve Bank of Richmond* 87 (Winter): 33–55.

Hibbs, D. A. 1977. Political parties and macroeconomic policy. *American Political Science Review* 71: 1467–87.

Hibbs, D. A. 1986. Political parties and macroeconomic policies and outcomes in the United States. *American Economic Association Papers and Proceedings* 76 (2): 66–70.

Holland, S. M. 2006. Reevaluating the utility of detrended correspondence analysis and non-metric multidimensional scaling for ecological ordination. Geological Society of America Annual Meeting, Philadelphia.

Hurwitz, M. S., R. J. Moiles, and D. W. Rohde. 2001. Distributive and partisan issues in agriculture policy in the 104th House. *American Political Science Review* 95 (4): 911–22.

Issing, O. 2003. Monetary policy in unchartered territory. Stone Lecture. London (Nov 3).

Janis, I. L. 1972. *Victims of Groupthink: A Psychological Study of Foreign-Policy Decisions and Fiascoes*. Boston: Houghton, Mifflin.

Janis, I. L. 1982. *Groupthink: Psychological Studies of Policy Decisions and Fiascoes*. Boston: Houghton Mifflin.

Jensen, K., and J. D. Salant. 2009. Wall Street regulators find easy access to donations (Update 1, Apr 17). *Bloomberg*, http://www.bloomberg.com/apps/news?pid=newsarch ive&sid=a0QoxZDsHWuE&refer=home.

Kane, E. 1980. Politics and Fed policy-making: The more things change, the more they remain the same. *Journal of Monetary Economics* 6: 199–212.

Kettl, D. F. 1986. *Leadership at the Fed*. New Haven: Yale University Press.

King, M. 2004. What fates impose: Facing up to uncertainty. Eighth British Academy Annual Lecture. London.

Knight, F. 1921. *Risk, Uncertainty, and Profit*. Boston: Houghton.

Knight, J., and J. Johnson. 1994. Aggregation and deliberation: On the possibility of democratic legitimacy. *Political Theory* 22 (2): 277–96.

Koempel, M. L., J. Schneider, and P. Garvin. 2007. *Deskbook: The Practical and Comprehensive Guide to Congress*, 5th ed. Alexandria, VA: TheCapitol.Net.

Kohn, D., and B. Sack. 2003. Central bank talk: Does it matter and why. Working paper. Board of Governors of the Federal Reserve System.

Kozicki, S., and P. A. Tinsley. 2005. Permanent and transitory policy shocks in an empirical macro model with asymmetric information. *Journal of Economic Dynamics and Control* 29 (Nov): 1985–2015.

Krehbiel, K. 1991. *Information and Legislative Organization*. Ann Arbor: University of Michigan.

Kuttner, K. 2004. A Snapshot of Inflation Targeting in its Adolescence. In C. Kent and S. Guttman, eds., *The Future of Inflation Targeting*. Sydney: Reserve Bank of Australia, 6–42.

Kydland, F. E., and E. C. Prescott. 1977. Rules rather than discretion: The inconsistency of optimal plans. *Journal of Political Economy* 85 (3): 473–92.

Lapp, J. S., and D. K. Pearce. 2000. Does a bias in FOMC policy directives help predict intermeeting policy changes? *Journal of Money, Credit and Banking* 32 (3): 435–41.

Lascher, E. L. 1996. Assessing legislative deliberation: A preface to empirical analysis. *Legislative Studies Quarterly* 21 (4): 501–19.

Levin, A., V. Wieland, and J. Williams. 1999. Robustness of simple monetary policy rules under model uncertainty. In J. Taylor, ed., *Monetary Policy Rules*. Chicago: University of Chicago Press: 263–318.

Levine, J., E. G. Carmines, and P. M. Sniderman. 1999. The empirical dimensionality of racial stereotypes. *Public Opinion Quarterly* 63 (3): 371–84.

Lindsey, D. E., A. Orphanides, and R. H. Rasche. 2005. The reform of October 1979: How it happened and why. *Federal Reserve Bank of St. Louis Review—Special Issue: Reflections on Monetary Policy 25 Years after October 1979* 87 (2): 187–236.

Londregan, J., and J. M. Snyder. 1994. Comparing committee and floor preferences. *Legislative Studies Quarterly* 19: 233–66.

Lupia, A., and M. D. McCubbins. 1994. Learning from oversight: Fire alarms and police patrols reconsidered. *Journal of Law Economics and Organization* 10 (1): 96–125.

Maltzman, F. 1998. *Competing Principals: Committees, Parties, and the Organization of Congress*. Ann Arbor: University of Michigan.

Mankiw, N. G. 2001. U.S. monetary policy during the 1990s. Working paper 8471. NBER, Cambridge, MA.

Mayhew, D. R. 1974. *Congress: The Electoral Connection*. New Haven: Yale University Press.

Mayhew, D. R. 2000. *America's Congress: Actions in the Public Sphere, Lames Madison through Newt Gingrich*. New Haven: Yale University Press.

McCarty, N., K. T. Poole, and H. Rosenthal. 2006. *Polarized America: The Dance of Ideology and Unequal Riches*. Cambridge, MA: MIT Press.

McGregor, R. R. 1996. FOMC voting behavior and electoral cycles: Partisan ideology and partisan loyalty. *Economics and Politics* 8: 17–32.

Meade, E. E. 2005. The FOMC: Preferences, voting, and consensus. *Federal Reserve Bank of St. Louis Review* 87 (2): 93–101.

Meade, E. E., and D. N. Sheets. 2005. Regional influences on FOMC voting patterns. *Journal of Money, Credit and Banking* 37 (4): 661–77.

Meade, E. E., and D. Stasavage. 2008. Publicity of debate and the incentive to dissent: Evidence from the US Federal Reserve. *Economic Journal* 118 (528): 695–717.

Meade, E. E., and D. L. Thornton. 2012. The Phillips curve and US monetary policy: What the FOMC transcripts tell us. *Oxford Economic Papers* 64 (2): 197–216.

Mehrling, P. 2007. An interview with Paul A. Volcker. In P. Samuelson and W. Barnett, eds., *Inside the Economist's Mind*. Malden, MA: Blackwell, 165–91.

Meltzer, A. H. 2003. *A History of the Federal Reserve. Book 1: 1913–1951*. Chicago: University of Chicago Press.

Meltzer, A. H. 2005. Origins of the Great Inflation. *Federal Reserve Bank of St. Louis Review—Special Issue: Reflections on Monetary Policy 25 Years after October 1979* 87 (2): 145–76.

Meltzer, A. H. 2009. *A History of the Federal Reserve. Book 2: 1970–1986*. Chicago: University of Chicago.

Meyer, L. H. 2004. *A Term at the Fed: An Insider's View*. New York: Harper Business.

Monroe, B. L., M. P. Colaresi, and K. M. Quinn. 2008. Fightin' words: Lexical feature selection and evaluation for identifying the content of political conflict. *Political Analysis* 16 (4): 372–403.

Monroe, B. L., and P. A. Schrodt. 2008. Introduction to the special issue: The statistical analysis of political text. *Political Analysis* 16 (4): 351–55.

Morris, I. L. 2000. *Congress, the President, and the Federal Reserve: The Politics of American Monetary Policy-Making*. Ann Arbor: University of Michigan Press.

Mucciaroni, G., and P. J. Quirk. 2006. *Deliberative Choices: Debating Public Policy in Congress*. Chicago: University of Chicago Press.

Mutz, D. C. 2008. Is deliberative democracy a falsifiable theory? *Annual Review of Political Science* 11: 521–38.

Mutz, D. C., P. M. Sniderman, and R. A. Brody, eds. 1996. *Political Persuasion and Attitude Change*. Ann Arbor: University of Michigan.

Nagpaul, P. S. 1999. Correspondence analysis. In P. S. Nagpaul, ed., *Guide to Advanced Data Analysis Using IDAMS Software*. New Delhi: UNESCO (Division of Information and Informatics).

Nordhaus, W. 1989. Alternative approaches to the political business cycle. *Brookings Papers on Economic Activity* 2: 1–68.

Nordhaus, W. D. 1975. The political business cycle. *Review of Economic Studies* 42: 169–90.

Norton, N. H. 1999. Uncovering the dimensionality of gender voting in Congress. *Legislative Studies Quarterly* 24 (1): 65–86.

Oleszek, W. J. 2007. *Congressional Procedures and the Policy Process*, 7th ed. Washington, DC: CQ Press.

Orphanides, A. 1998. *Monetary Policy Evaluation with Noisy Data*. Washington, DC: Federal Reserve Board.

Orphanides, A. 2001. Monetary policy rules based on real-time data. *American Economic Review* 91 (4): 964–85.

Orphanides, A., and S. V. Norden. 1999. The reliability of output gap estimates in real time. Finance and Economics discussion series. Federal Reserve Board, Washington DC.

Page, B. I. 1996. *Who Deliberates? Mass Media in Modern Democracy*. Chicago: Chicago University Press.

Peltzman, S. 1984. Constituent interest and congressional voting. *Journal of Law and Economics* 27: 181–210.

Pettit, P. 2003. Deliberative democracy, the discursive dilemma, and Republican theory. In J. S. Fishkin and P. Laslett, eds., *Debating Deliberative Democracy*. Oxford: Blackwell, 138–59.

Pivetta, F., and R. Reis. 2006. The persistence of inflation in the United States. *Journal of Economic Dynamics and Control* 31 (4): 1326–58.

Poole, K. T. 2005. *Spatial Models of Parliamentary Voting*. Cambridge: Cambridge University Press.

Poole, K. T., and H. Rosenthal. 1997. *Congress: A Political-Economic History of Roll Call Voting*. Oxford: Oxford University Press.

Potoski, M., and J. Talbert. 2000. The dimensional structure of policy outputs: Distributive policy and roll call voting. *Political Research Quarterly* 53 (4): 695–710.

Primiceri, G. E. 2005. Why inflation rose and fell: Policymakers' beliefs and US postwar stabilization policy. Working paper W11147. NBER, Cambridge, MA, http://papers .ssrn.com/sol3/papers.cfm?abstract_id=669446.

Puckett, R. 1984. Federal Open Market Committee structure and decisions. *Journal of Monetary Economics* 14: 97–104.

Quirk, P. J. 2005. Deliberation and decision making. In P. J. Quirk and S. A. Binder, eds., *The Legislative Branch*. Oxford, New York: Oxford University Press, 314–48.

Rehfeld, A. 2009. Representation rethought: On trustees, delegates, and gyroscopes in the study of political representation and democracy. *American Political Science Review* 103 (2): 214–30.

Reinert, M. 1998. *ALCESTE Users' Manual* (English version). Toulouse: Image.

Reinhart, V. R. 2011. Opacity has its uses. *New York Times*, http://www.nytimes.com/roomfordebate/2011/04/27/jobs-inflation-and-what-bernanke-said/opacity-has-its-uses.

Ringe, N. 2005. Policy preference formation in legislative politics: Structures, actors, and focal points. *American Journal of Political Science* 49 (4): 731–45.

Ritter, J. A. 1993. The FOMC in 1992: A monetary conundrum. *Federal Reserve Bank of St. Louis Review* 75 (3): 31–49.

Rogoff, K. 1985. The optimal degree of commitment to an intermediate target. *Quarterly Journal of Economics* 100 (Nov): 1169–90.

Romer, C. D. 2005. Commentary on Meltzer's "Origins of the Great Inflation." *Federal Reserve Bank of St. Louis Review—Special Issue: Reflections on Monetary Policy 25 Years after October 1979* 87(2): 177–86.

Romer, C. D., and D. H. Romer. 2002. The evolution of economic understanding and postwar stabilization policy perspective. In Federal Reserve Bank of Kansas City, ed., *Rethinking Stabilization Policy*. Kansas City: Federal Reserve Bank of Kansas City, 11–78.

Romer, C. D., and D. H. Romer. 2003. Choosing the Federal Reserve chair: Lessons from history. Working paper. University of California, Berkeley.

Rudebusch, G., and L. Svensson. 1999. Policy rules for inflation targeting. In J. Taylor, ed., *Monetary Policy Rules*. Chicago: University of Chicago Press: 203–62.

Sargent, T., and N. Williams, et al. 2004. Shocks and government beliefs: The rise and fall of American inflation. Working paper 10764. NBER, Cambridge, MA.

Sargent, T. J. 1999. *The Conquest of American Inflation*. Princeton: Princeton University Press.

Schonhardt-Bailey, C. 2001. The strategic use of ideas: Nationalizing the interest in the nineteenth century. In F. McGillivray, I. McLean, R. Pahre, and C. Schonhardt-Bailey, eds., *International Trade and Political Institutions: Instituting Trade in the Long Nineteenth Century*. Cheltenham, UK: Edward Elgar, 146–97.

Schonhardt-Bailey, C. 2006. *From the Corn Laws to Free Trade: Interests, Ideas, and Institutions in Historical Perspective*. Cambridge, MA: MIT Press.

Schonhardt-Bailey, C. 2008. The congressional debate on partial-birth abortion: Constitutional gravitas and moral passion. *British Journal of Political Science* 38: 383–410.

Schonhardt-Bailey, C. 2012. Is there a single "right" way to study political text? *Methods-News: Newsletter from the ESRC National Centre for Research Methods*, Summer: 2.

Schuur, W. H. v., and H. A. L. Kiers. 1994. Why factor analysis often is the incorrect model for analyzing bipolar concepts, and what model to use instead. *Applied Psychological Measurement* 18 (2): 97–110.

Selck, T. J. 2004. On the dimensionality of European Union legislative decision-making. *Journal of Theoretical Politics* 16 (2): 203–22.

Shepsle, K. A. 1978. *The Giant Jigsaw Puzzle*. Chicago: University of Chicago Press.

Shepsle, K. A., and B. R. Weingast. 1995. Positive theories of congressional institutions. In K. A. Shepsle and B. R. Weingast, eds., *Positive Theories of Congressional Institutions*. Ann Arbor: University of Michigan, 5–38.

Sims, C. A. 1988. Projecting policy effects with statistical models. *Revista de Analisis Economico* 3: 3–20.

Snyder, J. M., and T. Groseclose. 2000. Estimating party influence in congressional roll-call voting. *American Journal of Political Science* 44 (2): 193–211.

Steiner, J., A. Bächtiger, M. Spörndli, and M. R. Steenbergen. 2004. *Deliberative Politics in Action: Analysing Parliamentary Discourse*. Cambridge: Cambridge University Press.

Stratmann, T. 2002. Can special interests buy congressional votes? Evidence from financial services legislation. *Journal of Law and Economics* 45 (2): 345–73.

Sunstein, C. R. 2003. The law of group polarization. In J. S. Fishkin and P. Laslett, eds., *Debating Deliberative Democracy*. Oxford: Blackwell, 80–101.

Sunstein, C. R. 2009. *Going to Extremes: How Like Minds Unite and Divide*. Oxford: Oxford University Press.

Svensson, L. E. O. 2002. Comments on Nancy Stokey, "Rules versus Discretion" after twenty-five years. *NBER Macroeconomics Annual* 17: 54–62.

t'Hart, P. 1990. *Groupthink in Government: A Study of Small Groups and Policy Failure*. Amsterdam: Swets Zeitlinger.

Taylor, J. B. 1993. Discretion vs. policy rules in practice. *Carnegie-Rochester Conference Series on Public Policy* 39: 195–214.

Taylor, J. B. 1999. *Monetary Policy Rules*. Chicago: University of Chicago Press.

Thompson, D. F. 2008. Deliberative democratic theory and empirical political science. *Annual Review of Political Science* 11: 497–520.

Thornton, D. 2003. Monetary policy transparency: Transparent about what? *Manchester School* 71 (5): 478–97.

Toma, M. 1991. The demise of the public-interest model of the Federal Reserve system. *Journal of Monetary Economics* 27: 157–63.

Tootell, G. M. B. 1991. Are districts presidents more conservative than board governors? *New England Economic Review* (Sep–Oct): 3–12.

Tufte, E. R. 1983. *The Visual Display of Quantitative Information*. Cheshire, CT: Graphics Press.

Tukey, J. W. 1977. *Exploratory Data Analysis*. Reading, MA: Addison-Wesley.

Volcker, P., and T. Gyohten. 1992. *Changing Fortunes: The World's Money and the Threat to American Leadership*. New York: Times Books.

Wallgren, A., B. Wallgren, R. Persson, U. Jorner, and J.-A. Haaland. 1996. *Graphing Statistics and Data: Creating Better Charts*. London: Sage.

Wartenberg, D., S. Ferson, and F. J. Rohlf. 1987. Putting things in order: A critique of detrended correspondence analysis. *American Naturalist* 129 (3): 434–48.

Weingast, B. R., and W. Marshall. 1988. The industrial organization of Congress. *Journal of Political Economy* 96: 132–63.

Weller, S. C., and A. K. Romney. 1990. *Metric Scaling: Correspondence Analysis*. London: Sage.

Williams, J. T. 1990. The political manipulation of macroeconomic policy. *American Political Science Review* 84 (3): 767–95.

Woodford, M. 2003. Optimal interest-rate smoothing. *Review of Economic Studies* 70 (4): 861–86.

Woodward, B. 2000. *Maestro: Greenspan's Fed and the American Boom*. New York: Simon and Schuster.

Woolley, J. T. 1984. *The Federal Reserve and the Politics of Monetary Policy*. Cambridge: Cambridge University Press.

Woolley, J. T. 1994. The politics of monetary policy: A critical review. *Journal of Public Policy* 14: 57–85.

Woolley, J. T., and J. Gardner. 2009. Does sunshine reduce the quality of deliberation? The case of the Federal Open Market Committee. Annual Meeting of the American Political Science Association. Toronto, Canada.

Yohe, W. 1966. A study of Federal Open Market Committee voting. *Southern Economic Journal* 12: 396–405.

Young, G., and V. Heitshusen. 2003. Party and the dynamics of congressional committee composition in the US House, 1947–96. *British Journal of Political Science* 33: 659–79.

Index

Page numbers followed by "t" or "f" refer to pages with relevant tables or figures.